D0709597

Madame Benoit

THE NEW REVISED ILLUSTRATED ENCYCLOPEDIA OF
MICROWAVE
COOKING

WITH WINE SUGGESTIONS
FROM TONY ASPLER

ÉDITIONS HÉRITAGE
MONTRÉAL

Canadian Cataloguing in Publication Data

Benoît, Jehane, 1904-1987
    The new revised illustrated encyclopedia of microwave cooking.

Issued also in French under titles : Encyclopédie illustrée de la cuisine
au four à micro-ondes.
Includes index.
Bibliography : p.

ISBN : 2-7625-5975-8

1. Microwave cookery. I. Title

TX832.B4613 1988   641.5'882   C88-096373-5

PRODUCTION
Director :
René Bonenfant
Assistant :
Ginette Guétat
Consultant :
Hélène Bélanger
Editorial consultant
Michelle Robertson

ART AND DESIGN
Director :
Christiane Litalien
Assistant :
Marc Chapdelaine

PHOTOGRAPHY
Director :
Paul Casavant
Food Stylists :
Lucie Casavant
Marie-Christine Payette
Consumer Testers :
André Joubert
Gaston Sylvain

WINE SUGGESTIONS
Tony Aspler

Dishes graciously provided by
Eaton's, downtown, Montreal,
Birks', downtown, Montreal,
Le Cache-Pot, 5047, St-Denis St, Montreal
and Le Curio, Montenach Mall, Beloeil.

Legal deposit : 4th quarter 1988
National Library of Canada

ISBN-2-7625-5975-8   Printed in Canada

Les Éditions Héritage Inc.
300, Arran
Saint-Lambert, Québec J4R 1R5
Tel. : (514) 875-0327

Table of contents

Our specialist suggests two kinds of wine for each recipe, an ordinary table wine and one of superior quality. They are identified as:

 everyday selection

 special occasion

IMPORTANT	650-700W	500-600W	400-500W
	15 seconds	18 seconds	21 seconds
	30 seconds	36 seconds	42 seconds
• The recipes in general will serve 6 average portions or 4 large portions.	45 seconds	54 seconds	1 minute
	1 minute	1 m 10 s	1 m 25 s
	2 minutes	2 m 30 s	2 m 45 s
	3 minutes	3 m 30 s	4 minutes
• The preparation, cooking and standing times given are approximate. Many factors affect cooking and standing times, including the food's temperature when placed in the microwave, its density and quality and even the shape of the cooking dish.	4 minutes	4 m 45 s	5 m 30 s
	5 minutes	6 minutes	7 minutes
	6 minutes	7 m 15 s	8 m 25 s
	7 minutes	8 m 25 s	9 m 45 s
	8 minutes	9 m 30 s	11 minutes
	9 minutes	10 m 45 s	12 m 30 s
• The recipes were tested in 650-700 watts microwave ovens. Lower-wattage ovens may require some adjustment in timing. Here is a comparative chart which will permit you to adjust the cooking time.	10 minutes	12 minutes	14 minutes
	15 minutes	18 minutes	20 minutes
	20 minutes	24 minutes	27 minutes
	25 minutes	30 minutes	34 minutes
	30 minutes	36 minutes	41 minutes

Introduction to Metric Measures

Millilitre (mL) : replaces the fluid ounce
Litre (L) : replaces the quart
Gram (g) : replaces the ounce
Kilogram (kg) : replaces the pound
Degrees Celsius (°C) : replaces
    degrees Fahrenheit
Centimetre (cm) : replaces the inch

5 cm about 2 inches
250 mL replaces an 8-ounce cup
15 mL replaces 1 tablespoon
5 mL replaces 1 teaspoon
1 kg a little more than 2 pounds
500 g a little more than 1 pound
100°C water boils

Metric Equivalents of Most Used Measures in Cooking

Teaspoon :
1/4 teaspoon . . . . .1 mL
1/2 teaspoon . . . . .2 mL
1 teaspoon . . . . .5 mL
2 teaspoons . . . . .10 mL

Tablespoon :
1 tablespoon . . . . .15 mL
2 tablespoons . . . . .30 mL
3 tablespoons . . . . .50 mL
4 tablespoons . . . . .60 mL
2 to 3 tablespoons . . . . .30 to 50 mL
4 to 6 tablespoons . . . . .60 to 90 mL

Cups :
1/4 cup . . . . .60 mL
1/3 cup . . . . .80 mL
1/2 cup . . . . .125 mL
3/4 cup . . . . .190 mL
1 cup . . . . .250 mL
1¼ cups . . . . .315 mL
1⅓ cups . . . . .330 mL
1½ cups . . . . .375 mL
2 cups . . . . .500 mL
3 cups . . . . .750 mL
4 cups . . . . .1 L
5 cups . . . . .1.25 L
6 cups . . . . .1.5 L

Temperatures
150°F . . . . .65° C
200°F . . . . .95° C
250°F . . . . .120° C
300°F . . . . .150° C
350°F . . . . .180° C
400°F . . . . .200° C
425°F . . . . .225° C
450°F . . . . .230° C
500°F . . . . .260° C

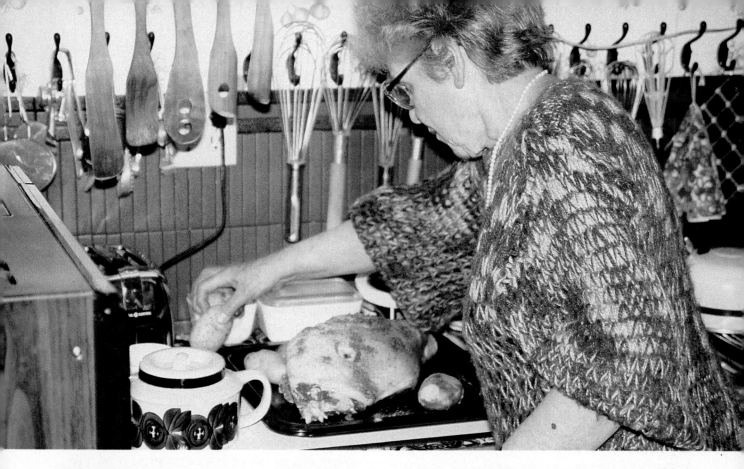

Many changes have taken place in the way we prepare and cook food and the amount of time we spend at those tasks. What a journey it has been! The wood stove was still a part of our daily life in 1920. Then, suddenly, gas and electricity were introduced for cooking, bringing with them time-saving, cleaner cooking methods — and white, elegant new stoves.

And now, a further gigantic step is changing our kitchens — the microwave oven.

You buy a microwave oven, put it in the car, drive it home, put it on the kitchen counter, plug it in and it's ready to use! And it's so easy to cook your favorite dishes in it.

I grew up with a wood stove, and the memory still lingers of large slices of homemade bread toasted on top of the stove and savored with fresh-churned butter, homemade jam and café au lait with whole milk. What a delight!

Then came the gas stove, with its coin-operated metre. If you forgot to feed in those 25-cent pieces, the gas was turned off! Still, it was an improvement over the wood stove. And then one day, the electric stove made its appearance. Another miracle! But we had seen nothing yet.

With the invention of the microwave oven, modern technology brought comfort, ease of work, perfection in cooking, the possibility of retaining the full flavor of food, an incredible reduction in the amount of time we spend in the kitchen and the feasibility of each member of the family cooking his or her own hot meal, which gives the working mother a freedom never before possible.

After thirteen years of cooking with microwave ovens, I couldn't live without one. I find that I cook more than ever before, yet I spend less time than ever in the kitchen. I have come to realize that you cannot know the true flavor of a vegetable or fish until you cook it in a microwave oven. And I can assure you that you need not learn a whole new cooking method. All you have to learn is how to adapt your cooking to the microwave oven.

Many people have said to me, "I would not have the patience to change all my recipes." I decided to write this Encyclopedia of Microwave Cooking to prove to you how successfully I converted my recipes and how easy this cooking method is once it's understood.

Microwave cooking is as convenient for working couples as it is for large families that need large servings. All that's needed is knowing how to proceed.

The importance of knowing your oven

• There are many kinds of microwave ovens, even several models of the same brand. It's of utmost importance that you become well acquainted with your own oven and know and understand all of its features. Be sure to read the manual that comes with it very carefully.

What to do

• Once the oven is plugged in, read the operation manual. Then place a microwave-safe bowl of water in it, close the door and start the oven, following every step exactly as suggested in the manual.
Example: Heat oven at HIGH for 2 minutes.

• Find out how to select a power setting of HIGH, how to set it for 2 minutes of operation and how to START it.

• Practice with various operations until you understand how your oven works — and appreciate how easy it is to use.

• The following are some features that you need to acquaint yourself with in order to take advantage of your microwave oven.

Turntable

• Some ovens are equipped with automatic turntables, small fans at the top of the ovens or invisible rotating systems. Check your oven manual to see whether your oven has one of these features. If it does, you wont't have to rotate food while it's cooking.

• If you don't have one of these features, you will have to rotate food for even cooking because the microwaves may tend to focus on one particular spot in the food — especially fat in the meat. And remember that these spots aren't always visible.

Auto Sensor cooking

• The Auto Sensor is another wonder of microwave cooking.

• If you want to cook vegetables, a roast, poultry, stew, etc., and are wondering what cooking time to allow, relax. Your microwave oven will determine the cooking time with Auto Sensor.

• If your microwave features Auto Sensor cooking, it will be indicated on the panel with a COOK or INSTA-MATIC, etc., section. Your oven manual will instruct you on its use.

• Numbers 1 to 7 or 8 may also be shown on the panel, each one indicating the type of food appropriate. Number 7, for instance, may be for cooking soft vegetables (Brussels sprouts, zucchini, etc.). Always refer to your oven manual for precise instructions.

• These are two important points to remember when cooking by Auto Sensor:

• Whatever the food, a little water must be added. Use from 1/4 cup to 1/3 cup (60 mL to 80 mL), depending on the quantity.

• The dish must be well covered with either plastic wrap or a tightfitting lid that will hold securely in place throughout the cooking period.

• Plastic dishes come in various shapes and sizes, have a lid that is perfect for Auto Sensor cooking.

• IT IS IMPORTANT THAT THE OVEN DOOR NOT BE OPENED DURING THE COOKING OPERATION, WHICH TAKES PLACE IN TWO STAGES: The selected number appears in the display window until the steam is detected by a humidity sensor inside the oven. Then a BEEP is sounded and the cooking time appears in the display window.

HIGH or full power

• This means a continuous cycle with maximum (100 %) output, whatever your brand of oven.

Let stand

• Many recipes tell you to let food stand for a certain time after cooking it in a microwave oven. Since microwave cooking actually involves intense molecular vibration, food continues to cook even after the microwave energy is turned off.

• The standing time lets the molecules come to rest — just like a bouncing ball that dribbles down to a gradual stop. In microwave cooking, the standing period is often referred to as " aftercook. "

• When a recipe says, " Let stand x minutes, stir and serve, " that is exactly what is meant.

Microwave-proof dishes and utensils

• Dishes and utensils suitable for cooking in the microwave include Pyrex, Corning, plastic and earthenware.

Elevate

• This term is most often used for meats. It means placing the meat on a rack or an inverted saucer to allow the cooking juices to drain off from under it during cooking.

• The term is also used to describe the way certain foods should be set up to cool after cooking or baking so that air can circulate around them to ensure that they cool evenly. After microwaving a roast, for instance, allow the meat to cool slightly, still on a rack.

• This is also true for muffins or cupcakes, which should be allowed to cool for at least 10 minutes on a rack.

Variable power

• This describes the choice of power levels that allow you to prepare food in the microwave that is too sensitive for continuous microwave activity. The process is actually an "on and off" cycle timed for varying amounts of microwave energy. The pulsating action effectively creates slower cooking activity, without your having to worry about it.

• If your recipe calls for half power, this equals MEDIUM, which is like constant simmering. The first microwave ovens had only COOK and DEFROST cycles. If you have such an oven, remember that you use DEFROST when you are asked to simmer or to cook on half power or MEDIUM. For all other cooking, use the COOK cycle and add a few minutes to the cooking time called for in the recipe.

Temperature probe

• The microwave oven's temperature probe is a thermometer-like, heat sensing device to measure the internal temperature of food during microwave cooking.

• Using the probe produces a perfect roast. First, prepare the roast according to the recipe you are following, then insert the probe in the meat and connect it to the oven. Then select the number that corresponds to the way you want the roast cooked; refer to your oven manual for details. The oven will start to cook and at one point will indicate the temperature needed to cook the meat according to your specifications. You never have to worry about how long it should take, since your oven will do it for you — and to perfection.

• Use only the probe designed for your oven. Never use a conventional thermometer in the microwave oven.

How it works

• Microwaves are a form of high-frequency radio wave similar to those used by radio. Electricity is converted into microwave energy by a magnetron tube. From the magnetron tube, microwave energy is transmitted to the oven cavity, where it is **reflected, transmitted and absorbed.**

Reflection

• Microwaves are reflected by metal, just as a ball is bounced off a wall. That's why the metal inside your microwave oven is covered with epoxy. A combination of stationary (interior walls) and rotating (turntable or stirrer fan) metal helps assure that the microwaves are well distributed within the oven cavity to produce even cooking.

Transmission

• Microwaves pass through some materials — such as paper, glass and plastic — much like sunlight shining through a window. Because these substances do not absorb or reflect microwave energy, they are ideal utensils for microwave oven cooking.

Absorption

• Microwaves are absorbed by food to a depth of about 3/4 to 1½ inches (2 to 4 cm). Microwave energy excites the molecules in the food — especially water, fat and sugar molecules — and causes them to vibrate at a rate of 2,450,000,000 times per second. This vibration causes friction, which produces heat. (If you vigorously rub your hands together, you will feel heat produced by friction.) The internal cooking is then done by conduction. The heat produced by friction is conducted to the centre of the food.

• Foods also continue to cook by conduction during standing time, which keeps the cooked food warm for 4 to 10 minutes after it comes out of the oven — making it possible to cook three of four dishes with only one oven and to serve everything warm.

For example, if your menu calls for a roast, potatoes and green peas, cook the roast first[1]. During its standing time, first cook the potatoes[2], which will remain warm for 20 to 30 minutes covered with a cloth. Then cook the peas[3], which have the shortest cooking time.

• If your dessert is to be served hot, cook it during the meal and let it stand in the oven until you are ready to take it to the table.

Cooking equipment

• Microwave cooking opens new possibilities in convenience and flexibility in terms of cooking containers. New microwave accessories are constantly being introduced, but don't feel you have to buy a whole set of new cooking equipment. You will be surprised at how many of the items you already have in your kitchen are suitable for microwave cooking.

Glass, ceramic and china

• Most utensils made from these materials are excellent for use in the microwave oven. Heat-resistant glassware, unless it has metallic trim or decoration, can almost always be used. However, be careful about using delicate glassware, since it can crack — not from microwave energy but from the heat of the food.

• Here are a few heat-resistant glass cookware items I find invaluable in microwave cookery. You probably already have many of these items on your shelves.

1. glass measuring cups
2. custard cups
3. mixing bowls
4. loaf dish
5. covered casserole dishes
6. oblong baking dish (non-metallic)
7. cake dishes (round, long or square ; glass, Pyrex, plastic)
8. plastic, glass or ceramic pie plate
9. large bowls, 8 to 10 cups (2 to 2.5 L), with covers

Browning dish and grill (Corning)

• There are two browning dish sizes: $8 \times 8 \times 2$ inches ($21 \times 21 \times 5$ cm) — 6 cups (1.5 L), and $9.5 \times 9.5 \times 2$ inches ($24 \times 24 \times 5$ cm) 10 cups (2.5 L). The browning grill is: 8×8 inches (21×21 cm)

• Browning dishes have a special dielectric coating on the underside that is activated by preheating them, empty and uncovered, in the microwave oven. Heat the smaller browning dish for no more than 5 minutes and the larger one and the browning grill for no more than 7 minutes.

• DO NOT REMOVE THE DISH FROM THE OVEN AFTER PREHEATING. SIMPLY PLACE IN THE PREHEATED DISH THE STEAK OR WHATEVER ELSE YOU WISH TO BROWN, pressing down on the food with a fork to obtain perfect contact with the bottom of the dish. If the recipe calls for oil or butter or other fat, it must be added after the dish is preheated. Brown 5 to 7 minutes, or according to recipe. You will be surprised by how well-browned the food will be. Turn the food and let it stand in the dish in the microwave for however long it took to brown the bottom half. Do not use heat; ad-

ding more cooking time will only dry the food. When the time is up, the food is ready to serve.

• A browning dish can be an extremely handy accessory. Don't limit it to being only a browner. Besides using it to brown steaks and chops, you can use it to stir-fry vegetables, cook omelets, reheat pizza, grill sandwiches and much more. It can also, of course, be used as regular microwave cookware. If you don't preheat it, the base won't get hot so you can use it to microwave vegetables, casseroles, desserts, fish, etc.

The browning dish cover can be used for this type of cooking.

• BROWNING DISHES ARE DESIGNED FOR USE ONLY IN MICROWAVE OVENS. THEIR COATING COULD BE SCRATCHED BY OVEN RACKS OR RANGE TOPS ON CONVENTIONAL OVENS. Do not use your oven's temperature probe with a browning dish.

Metal

• Metal containers or utensils and those with metallic trim should NOT be used in the microwave oven. Since microwave energy is reflected by metal, foods in metal containers will not cook evenly. There is also the possibility of "arcing." This is a static discharge or blue spark between gaps in the metal or between the metal and the interior of the oven. Arcing may cause damage to the oven walls.

• IF ARCING OCCURS, TURN THE UNIT OFF AND TRANSFER FOOD TO A NON-METALLIC CONTAINER.

• Although metal utensils must be avoided in microwave cooking, some metal can be helpful when used correctly.

Cooking bags

• Cooking bags designed to withstand boiling, freezing or conventional heating are safe to use in a microwave oven.

• Make six small slits in the top of the bag to allow steam to escape.

• IT IS BEST TO USE A PIECE OF COTTON STRING, A NYLON TIE OR A STRIP CUT FROM THE OPEN END OF THE BAG TO CLOSE THE BAG. If you use a twist-tie, make sure the ends are completely rolled around the bag and aren't hanging loose. Otherwise, they could act as antennae and cause arcing (blue sparks).

• DO NOT COOK FOOD IN BROWN OR WHITE PAPER BAGS.

Plastic wrap

• Plastic wrap such as Saran Wrap℠ can be used to cover dishes in most recipes.

• Over an extended cooking time, some disfiguration of the wrap may occur.

• When using plastic wrap as a casserole dish cover, fold back a small section of it from the edge of the dish to allow some steam to escape.

• When removing a plastic wrap "cover" or a glass lid, be careful to remove it away from you to avoid steam burns.

7

• After cooking, loosen the plastic wrap but let the dish stand covered. Please note that it is not necessary to cover all foods.

Food covering for Sensor cooking

• When cooking by the Sensor method, ¼ inch (1 cm) of water is needed in the bottom of the dish and the dish must be covered with plastic wrap.

• The microwave-safe plastic dish does not need plastic wrap since its cover keeps the steam inside the dish.

Paper

• **Paper napkins, waxed paper, paper towels, plates, cups and freezer wrap.** All are handy utensils for microwave cooking. Use them for foods with short cooking times and low fat content. Avoid wax coated paper goods, since the wax may melt onto the food when the food reaches high temperatures. Waxed paper is suitable to use to prevent spatter. Disposable polyester coated paperboard pans are sturdy, come in a variety of sizes, and are ideal for microwaving.

Caution: Do not use recycled paper products, such as brown paper bags, since they contain impurities which may cause arcing (blue sparks) and damage the oven.

Aluminum foil

• Aluminum foil can be used safely when certain guidelines are followed. Because it reflects microwave energy, foil can be used to advantage in some cases.

• Small pieces of foil are used to cover areas such as the tips of chicken wings, chicken legs or roasts that cook more quickly than the rest.

• FOIL IS USED IN THESE CASES TO SLOW OR STOP THE COOKING PROCESS AND PREVENT OVERCOOKING. The strips of foil placed on the edges of a roast or the ends of chicken legs can be removed halfway through the cooking period.

Straw, wicker and wooden bowls

• **Straw and wicker baskets** may be used in the microwave oven for short periods of time to warm rolls or bread. Large wooden utensils should NOT be used for prolonged heating as the microwave energy may cause the wood to become dry and brittle.

Jars and bottles

• Jars and bottles can be used to warm food to serving temperature, if the lid is removed first. Cooking should not be done in these containers since most are not heat resistant and during extended heating times, heat from food would cause cracking or breaking.

Note: Do not use bottles with narrow necks to reheat liquids, they could break.

How to test a container for safe microwave oven use

• Fill a 1-cup (250 mL) glass measure with water and place it in the microwave oven beside the container to be tested.

• Heat one minute at HIGH.

• If the container is microwave oven safe, it should remain comfortably cool and the water should be hot.

• If the container is hot, it has absorbed some microwave energy and should not be used.

• This test cannot be used for plastic containers.

Plastic dishes

• Plastic dishes that are safe for microwave cooking are readily available in the marketplace. Look for statements such as "For microwave cooking only" or "Suitable for conventional or microwave cooking" in manufacturers' brochures.

• Most microwave-safe plastic dishes are suitable for cooking vegetables, meat, poultry, fish and baked goods.

• Some plastic dishes should not be used for cooking foods with a high fat or sugar content. Check manufacturers' care instructions for recommended cooking uses.

• Plastic food storage containers can become soft, pitted or distorted from microwave cooking and should not be used.

• Melamine plastic dishes are not microwave safe.

Foil lined containers

• Either cardboard or plastic, they should NOT be used in the microwave oven.

• Foil lined milk cartons, frozen orange juice concentrate containers, or baking containers included in some cake mixes are examples of things to be avoided.

Metal twist-ties

• Metal twist-ties either paper or plastic coated, should NOT be used in the microwave oven. See pictures and information under COOKING BAGS.

Thermometers

• Special thermometers are available for use in microwave ovens. DO NOT USE CONVENTIONAL MERCURY TYPE CANDY OR MEAT THERMOMETERS in food while heating in the microwave oven.

Frozen dinner trays

• Frozen dinner trays can be used in the microwave oven, but results are only satisfactory if the container is no higher than 3/4 inch (2 cm).

• In metal containers, all the heating takes place from the top; the metal container reflects the energy directed to the sides and bottom.

Metal skewers

• Metal skewers can be used if there is a large amount of food in proportion to the amount of metal.

• Take care in the placement of the skewers to avoid arcing between the skewers or between the skewers and the sides of the oven.

• Wooden skewers are the best and can be easily purchased at your local market, grocery store, or in the housewares section of many department stores.

DO NOT USE:

• Dishes with metallic trim or containers with metal parts. Arcing may occur and/or the dish may break.

• Ceramic mugs or cups with glued-on handles. The handles may fall off with continued heating.

• Delicate glassware. Although the glassware may be transparent to microwave energy, the heat from the food may cause the glassware to crack.

Food characteristics

• Food characteristics that affect conventional cooking are more pronounced with microwave cooking.

Keys to successful cooking in the microwave

1. The degree of moisture in food:
   HIGH = fast and short cooking time
   (*e.g.*, *spinach*)
   LOW = slow and long cooking time
   (*e.g.*, *carrots*)

2. The quantity of liquid added to food:
   The greater the quantity, the longer the cooking time will be.

3. The density of food:
   Porous = fast cooking
   (*e.g.*, *tomatoes, spinach, mushrooms*)
   Denser = slow cooking
   (*e.g.*, *peas, lentils*)

4. Room temperature is the ideal temperature to start cooking:
   Food at room temperature = fast cooking
   Food taken from refrigerator or just after thawing = slow cooking

5. The structure of food:
   Small pieces = fast cooking
   (*e.g.*, *a small potato*)
   Large pieces = slow cooking
   (*e.g.*, *a large potato*)

6. Often, foods are covered during cooking to prevent their natural moisture from evaporating.

7. The degree of sugar content determines the degree of heat produced:
   The more sugar, the more intense the heat and the shorter the cooking time
   (*e.g.*, *syrup, caramel*)

8. The more fat in food, the quicker it will cook.

9. The arrangement of food is important:
   4 or 5 potatoes placed in a circle will cook faster than if they were placed indiscriminately in the oven.
   Degree of moisture, adding of water, density, thickness, structure, covers, amount of sugar, degree of fat, arrangement of food, appropriate accessories, are all key words relating your cooking to the factors of heat, weight and temperature.

Size and quantity

• The size and quantity of food play an important role in cooking time in microwave cooking because it is faster than cooking with gas or electricity.

Shape

• Pieces of uniform size cook more evenly. To compensate for irregular shapes, place thinner pieces toward the centre of the dish and thicker pieces toward the edge of the dish.

Bone and fat

• Both bones and fat affect cooking. Bone conducts heat and causes the meat next to it to be heated more quickly*. Large amounts of fat absorb microwave energy and meat next to these areas may overcook.

See: Aluminum foil.

Spacing

• When cooking more than one item of food, such as whole potatoes or hors d'oeuvres, they will cook more evenly if placed in the oven equal distances apart. When possible, arrange foods in a circular pattern.

• Similarly, when you place items of food in a baking dish, arrange them around the outside of the dish, not lined up next to one another.

• Foods should NOT be stacked on top of each other.

Turning and rearranging

• It is not possible to stir some foods to redistribute the heat. At times, microwave energy will concentrate in one area of a food. To help insure even cooking, some foods need to be turned or rearranged. Turn

11

over large foods such as roasts or turkeys. Generally, they are turned over once halfway through cooking.

Starting temperature

• Food at room temperature takes less time to cook than refrigerated, just-thawed or frozen food.

Stirring

• It often is necessary to stir food during microwave cooking. Each recipe will tell you how often and when to stir.

• For example, you should always bring the cooked outside edges of food toward the centre and the less cooked centre portions toward the outside during cooking. And some foods need to be turned in their container during cooking.

Piercing

• The skin or membranes on some foods will cause steam to build up during microwave cooking and the food may burst. Foods must be pierced, scored or have a strip of skin peeled off before cooking to allow steam to escape.

Eggs — Pierce egg yolk twice and egg white several times with a toothpick.

Whole clams and oysters — Pierce several times with a toothpick.

Whole potatoes and vegetables — Pierce several times with a fork.

Wieners and sausages — Score smoked polish sausage and wieners. Pierce fresh sausage or brown and serve sausage with a fork.

Whole apples and new potatoes — Peel off 1-inch (2.5 cm) strip of skin before cooking.

Testing for doneness

• The same test for doneness used in conventional cooking may be used for microwave cooking.

• Cakes are done when toothpick comes out clean and cake pulls away from side of the pan.

• Meat is done when fork-tender or splits at fibers.

• Chicken is done when juices are clear yellow and drumstick moves freely.

• Fish is done when it flakes and is opake.

Standing time

• Most foods will continue to cook by conduction after the microwave oven has been turned off.

• In meat, the internal temperature will rise 5°F to 15°F (3°C to 6°C) if allowed to stand, covered, for 10 to 20 minutes.

• Casseroles and vegetables need a shorter standing time, but this standing time is necessary to allow them to complete cooking in the centre without overcooking on the edges.

Power Select settings

• Some microwave ovens are equipped with multiple Power Select settings: HIGH, MEDIUM-HIGH, MEDIUM, MEDIUM-LOW, DEFROST, LOW, WARM and DELAY/STAND.

• While most foods can be heated on HIGH (full power), certain types of foods — milk, for example — will benefit from heating with a reduced amount of energy over a slightly longer time.

• This variety of settings offers you complete flexibility in microwave cooking.

Power level chart

Power	Output	Use
HIGH	100 % (700 watts)	Boil water Brown ground meat Cook fresh fruit and vegetables Cook fish Cook poultry (up to 3 lb [1.5 kg]) Heat beverages (not containing milk) Make candy Preheat browning dish (accessory)
MEDIUM-HIGH	90 % (650 watts)	Heat frozen foods (not containing eggs or cheese) Heat canned foods Reheat leftovers Warm baby food
MEDIUM	70 % (490 watts)	Bake cakes Cook meats Cook shellfish Prepare eggs and delicate food
MEDIUM-LOW	50 % (360 watts)	Bake muffins Cook custards Melt butter and chocolate Prepare rice
LOW	27 % (200 watts)	Cook less tender cuts of meat Simmer stews and soups Soften butter and cheese
WARM	10 % (70 watts)	Keep foods at serving temperature Rise yeast breads Soften ice cream
DEFROST	35 % (245 watts)	All thawing (see Defrosting charts)
DELAY-STAND	0 % (0 watt)	Start heating at later time Program standing time after cooking

WEIGHT DEFROST

• Some ovens offer a choice between defrosting by weight or defrosting by time. Defrosting by weight is very accurate, so I encourage you to use it — but be sure to read the instructions in your oven manual before you start.

• AUTO-WEIGHT DEFROST is based on the following automatic cycle: the defrost cycle for meat or poultry extends from 0.1 pound (approximately 1½ ounces - 42 g) to 5.9 pounds (3 kg). If you touch the weight and defrost pads the AUTO-WEIGHT DEFROST will show in the display window the weight from 1 to 6 pounds (0.5 kg to 3 kg), of cuts of meat or poultry that are usually thawed.

• There is less meat in a bone-in roast of beef, pork, etc., than in a boneless roast of equal weight. To defrost a bone-in roast weighing more than 4 pounds (2 kg), calculate 1 pound (500 g) less and 1/2 pound (250 g) for a similar roast weighing less than 4 pounds (2 kg).

A few hints about defrosting meat

• Defrost meat without its original wrapper by placing it in a dish to prevent its liquid from running.

• Place roast fat-side down and whole poultry breast-side down on a microwave roasting rack in an oblong dish. The rack helps prevent the food from sitting in its own juice. The juice will get hot during defrosting and if the food is sitting in the juice, the bottom will begin to cook.

• Set the oven at DEFROST and heat for the time recommended in the following chart

• Turn food over two or three times during the defrosting cycle

• Before cooking the defrosted food, let it stand for a time equal to the defrost time

• Rinse the defrosted food under cold water to remove all remaining ice particles.

Defrost chart			
Beef part	**Type of beef**	**Approx. defrosting time (minutes per pound - 500 g) at Power Select DEFROST**	**Standing time (minutes per pound)**
Roast	Tenderloin Chuck or rump Sirloin, rolled	5 to 6 5 to 6 5 to 6	5 to 6 5 to 6 5 to 6
Steak	Boneless sirloin Flank	6 to 7 4 to 5	6 to 7 4 to 5
Miscellaneous	Ground beef* Liver	5 to 6 5 to 6	5 to 6 5 to 6

Note: When defrosting ground beef, halfway through heating remove outer portions of beef (thawed) to prevent cooking of edges before center is completely thawed.

A few hints for reheating food

• The wide variety of food that can be reheated in the microwave oven will make you appreciate your oven even more. It not only saves money, time and energy, but most foods reheat so well that there is little loss of taste. Leftovers have that "just cooked" flavor that has never been possible in food reheated in a conventional oven. Many foods actually taste better after they've been reheated in a microwave oven because the flavors have been given a chance to blend.

To reheat by time

• Arrange the food on a microwave-safe plate with the thicker or denser portions toward the rim of the plate. Add gravy or butter if desired. Cover the plate with waxed paper, then reheat at MEDIUM-HIGH for 2 to 3 minutes, checking after 2 minutes.

To reheat by Sensor

• If your oven has a Sensor pad, prepare the plate of food as above, then cover completely with plastic wrap. Touch pad 1 of the Sensor, or follow the instructions in your oven manual.

• The oven will do all the work. You don't have to determine the time.

Casseroles

• Stir the casserole well, then add a small amount of liquid (water, milk, consommé, gravy, etc.) Usually 1/4 cup (60 mL) is sufficient. Cover with a glass lid or plastic wrap. If your oven has a Sensor or Instamatic setting, touch pad 1 or as directed in your manual.

• If your oven doesn't have a Sensor pad, cover the casserole with waxed paper after you've added the liquid. Heat at MEDIUM-HIGH for 2 to 6 minutes, stirring halfway through.

• For quick heating, spread out individual servings in a single serving casserole. Cover with lid or plastic wrap.

• Casseroles with crumb toppings should be covered with waxed paper. This will help prevent the crumb topping from becoming soggy.

• Stir casseroles several times during heating.

Meats

• Sliced meat will heat more evenly and quickly than a roast, and thin slices more quickly than thick slices.

Pastries

• Place pastry on a paper plate. Heat 10 to 40 seconds.

• Place slice of pie on plate. Heat 1 to 1½ minutes.

> **A personal note:** the filling and glazes will be hotter than the pastry. Be careful when eating.

Sandwiches

• Wrap closed sandwiches in a paper towel and place on glass tray. Place open-faced sandwiches on plate and cover with waxed paper. Heat just until sandwiches are warm.

Plates of food

• Arrange food on the plate with the thicker, denser food along the edge of the plate.

• Cover with waxed paper or plastic wrap.

> **A personal note:** Mashed potatoes, which are dense, should be spread out along the edge for quicker heating.

Rolls

• Wrap individual rolls in paper towel. Heat 5 to 10 seconds. Arrange 4 to 6 rolls in a serving container. Cover with a paper towel or napkin. Heat 30 seconds. Test baked goods before adding more time; when overheated they become tough and hard.

Beef

Learn to know beef cuts

• To cook a perfectly browned, tender and juicy roast, whatever cooking method you select, you must first buy the perfect cut for the cooking method you have chosen. Beef, as other meats, has more tender and less tender cuts. The diagram below shows which are the more tender and which are the less tender cuts.

• For example, a loin roast, either porterhouse or rib roast, a fine and very tender cut but also more expensive, will give a first-class roast beef.

• The eye of round, sirloin point, which is the tender cut in the hip, as well as the cross rib, the tender cut in the shoulder, are very good roasts and their cost is not high. However, a cross rib must be 4 to 5 inches — (10 to 12.5 cm) thick for a perfect roast. It is best to braise or boil a thinner cut.

Beef cuts

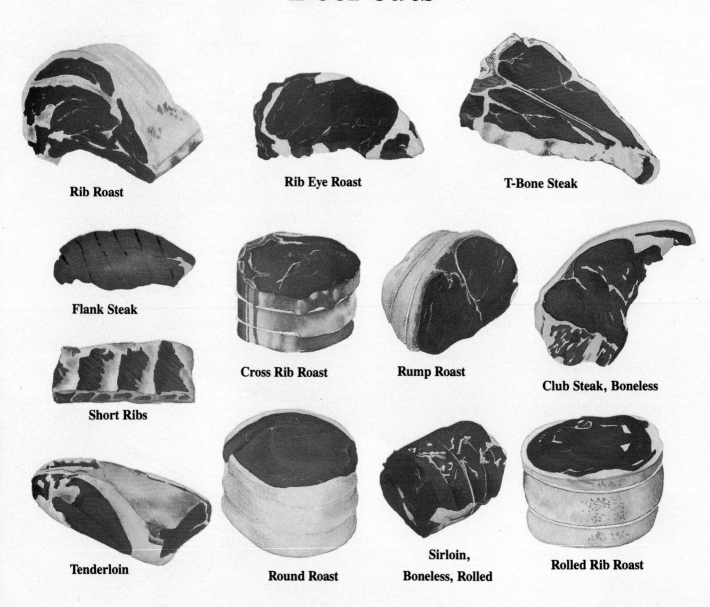

Rib Roast

Rib Eye Roast

T-Bone Steak

Flank Steak

Cross Rib Roast

Rump Roast

Club Steak, Boneless

Short Ribs

Tenderloin

Round Roast

Sirloin, Boneless, Rolled

Rolled Rib Roast

American cuts of beef

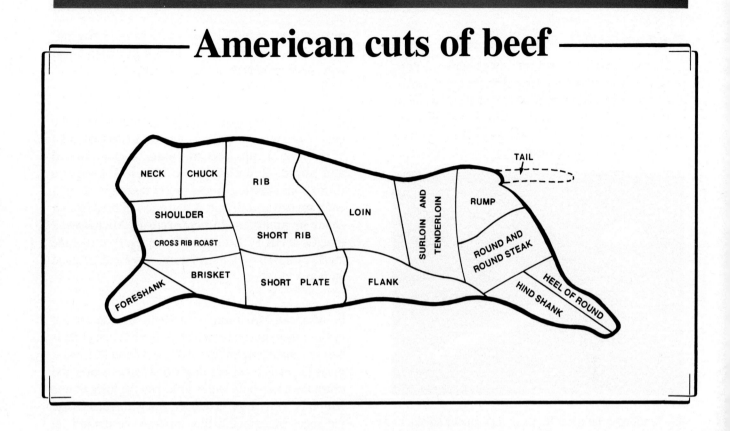

Tender cuts of beef

CANADIAN CUTS

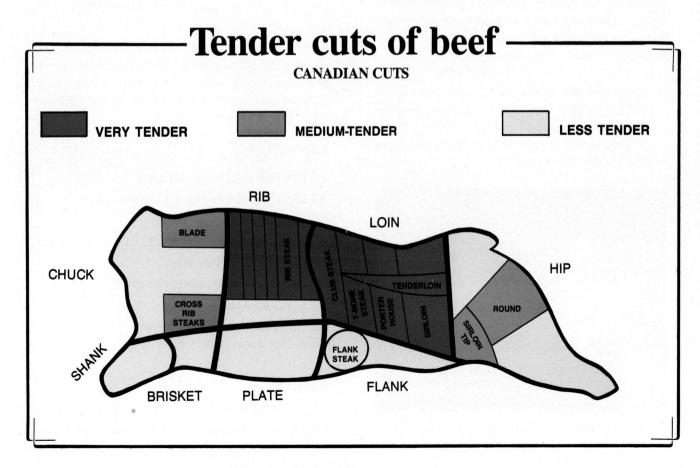

VERY TENDER MEDIUM-TENDER LESS TENDER

Tenderizing less tender meat

• There are good cuts of meat — whether beef, pork or veal — that are less tender and so are inexpensive. They can be treated in many ways to make them more tender, including marinating — which gives them an interesting flavor, too. Here are some of my favorite methods of tenderizing meat:

1. Tenderize the meat fibers in less tender steaks or in meat cubes by beating them with a wooden or metal mallet. That's what the butcher does, but it costs less to do it yourself. Very good mallets with metal tips can be found in kitchen specialty shops.

2. Baste a thin slice of meat with a mixture of vegetable oil and fresh lemon juice. For a steak, **1 tablespoon (15 mL) each of oil and lemon juice** will do. Cover and marinate from a minimum of 30 minutes to 12 hours in the refrigerator.

3. My favorite method of tenderizing cubes of meat for stew is to cover them with **buttermilk or yogurt,** mix well, cover and let stand for 12 hours, refrigerated. Before using the meat, drain it thoroughly and wipe each cube with absorbent paper.

4. For a braised roast, the French marinade is the best. Place in a 4-cup (1 L) measure **1 cup (250 mL) of red wine, 2 cups (500 mL) water, 1 onion, peeled and sliced, 2 peeled garlic cloves, 1 teaspoon (5 mL) marinating spices** or **1/2 teaspoon (2 mL) each savory and thyme, 1 teaspoon (5 mL) brown sugar or molasses, 10 peppercorns.** Microwave 2 minutes at HIGH. Let stand 20 minutes. Pour over the meat, coat well with the mixture, cover and let stand 24 hours.

5. Mexican Marinade — In Mexico, meats are not tender; they must be marinated. Here is one of their best marinating mixtures: it is not economical, but it gives the meat a perfect flavor. Peel an **avocado** and crush the green pulp with a fork, add the **juice of one lemon or lime, 2 garlic cloves, finely minced.** Baste the meat pieces with this mixture, cover and let marinate in the refrigerator for 12 to 24 hours.

6. This French marinade will keep 6 to 8 weeks in a well-covered glass jar in the refrigerator. In the French provinces, they use fresh grape juice, which I have replaced successfully with commercial unsweetened grape juice (Welch's).

Ingredients:

2/3 cup (160 mL) onion, minced

3/4 cup (190 mL) celery with leaves, diced

1/3 cup (80 mL) cider vinegar

1/2 cup (125 mL) vegetable oil

1 cup (250 mL) grape juice

1 tbsp (15 mL) Worcestershire sauce

1/2 tsp (2 mL) salt

1/2 tsp (2 mL) garlic powder *or*
   3 garlic cloves, finely minced

Method:

• Mix all the ingredients together, and refrigerate in a glass jar. To use as a marinade, pour it over meat and let it stand for 12 hours, covered and refrigerated.

Roasting methods in the microwave oven

- There are many roasting methods for meats. Depending on the model of your microwave oven, there may be one or several.
- Your oven operation manual will advise you as to what roasting methods are available.

Cooking meat in the microwave

- The microwave allows for quick and easy preparation of meat, which can be roasted, braised or boiled. Your microwave oven manual will tell you what roasting methods it offers.

1. Meat should be at room temperature. If it's just out of the refrigerator, extend the cooking time.

2. Shape and size of piece.

3. Tenderness of cut and desired degree of doneness.

- To cook a roast, place it, fat side down, in a microwave-safe baking dish. Place a microwave rack or inverted saucer or glass cover under the roast to prevent it from steeping in its juice. Give the roast — and the dish — a half turn during the cooking period. If juice accumulates in the dish, remove it. (Reserve it for making gravy.) It's important to remove the juice because it will absorb energy and prevent the meat from cooking to perfection.
- If the roast falls over, prop it up with an inverted dessert cup.
- Meat can be shielded with aluminum foil for all or part of the cooking time. Tips of bones in a roast beef should be shielded with a 2-inch (5 cm) wide strip of foil.
- Tips of rolled roasts should be shielded, too.

Note: Meat continues to cook after it is removed from the oven. Cover it and let it stand 10 to 20 minutes before carving.

Convection cooking

- Some ovens offer both convection and microwave cooking.
- Convection cooking with a microwave oven gives excellent results, just like an electric convection stove, with the constant circulation of hot and dry air blown around the food being cooked. Temperature is set as required by the recipe.
- If your oven has an automatic turntable, you will have the added advantage of food being cooked and browned absolutely evenly.
- And convection cooking, of course, allows you to use all your favorite recipes without making any changes.

Cooking by temperature probe

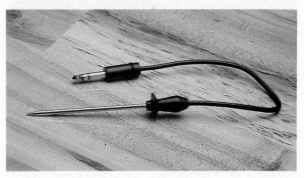

- If your microwave has a temperature probe, insert it into food during cooking to control the internal temperature.
- As soon as the selected temperature is reached, the unit will be turned off automatically.
- In some microwave ovens, the probe will also help to hold the cooked food at the final cooking temperature until serving.
- I use the temperature probe often because it gives perfect results; the probe measures the food temperature precisely and food is cooked to your specifications.

Temperature probe

- How to use it:

1. Insert the probe at least 1 inch (2.5 cm) into the food.

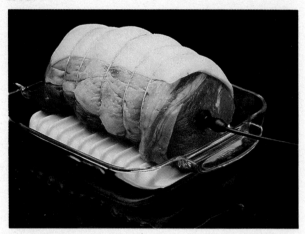

2. Always insert the probe into meat in a horizontal position.

3. If the food is being cooked covered, poke the probe through the plastic wrap into the centre of the food in a horizontal position.

4. Do NOT use the probe with frozen or with a Corning browning dish.

5. Remove the probe from the oven with oven mitts to avoid burns.

6. Clean the probe with mild detergent and a soft cloth, if necessary. DO NOT immerse it in water or wash it in an automatic dishwasher.

- DO NOT USE A CONVENTIONAL THERMO-METER WHILE HEATING FOOD IN A MICRO-WAVE OVEN. However, you can use a conventional thermometer to check the internal temperature of food after it's been removed from the oven.

Special hints for roasting meat

- Place a roast, cleaned and wiped dry, on a microwave-safe roasting rack or on an inverted plate or glass cover in a microwave-safe baking dish.

- Season to taste, but DO NOT SALT except for braised or boiled meats.

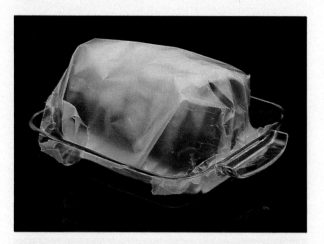

- Loosely cover the baking dish with waxed paper to prevent splattering.

- Set Power Select at HIGH or as required.

- Cover the less meaty portions with aluminum foil halfway through cooking to prevent overcooking of these areas. Use wooden toothpicks to hold the foil in place.

- Check the internal temperature of meat with a ther-mometer. Do not use a conventional thermometer in meat while it is in the oven. Allow meat to stand, co-vered, 10 to 20 minutes after cooking. This allows the temperature to equalize throughout. The internal meat temperature will rise 5°F to 10°F (3°C to 6°C) during the standing time.

Roast beef in the microwave oven

• No matter what kind of microwave oven you have, you will never fail to have a lovely browned and tender roast, cooked to your specifications, if you follow the instructions below.

• Before you start, carefully study the chart for cooking beef in a microwave, keeping in mind that the times apply to meat at room temperature. If the meat is just out of the refrigerator, or has just been defrosted and hasn't yet reached room temperature, you must add 2 minutes per pound (500 g).

• Meat at room temperature — take it out of the refrigerator 1 or 2 hours before cooking — will be juicier and more tender and will brown better.

• To defrost a frozen piece of meat you want to roast, follow the instructions in your operation manual. Once the roast is thawed, it's important to let it stand 1 hour at room temperature before roasting it.

Beef roasting chart for microwave oven		
	Cooking time	
Cooking degree	**1st pound (500 g)**	**Each additional pound (500 g)**
Rare 120°F (55°C)	5 minutes at HIGH *Example: A 3-lb (1.5 kg) roast should microwave 5 minutes at HIGH and then 16 minutes at MEDIUM.*	8 minutes per pound (500 g) at MEDIUM
Medium 140°F (60°C)	5 minutes at HIGH	9 minutes per pound (500 g) at MEDIUM
Well done 160°F (70°C)	5 minutes at HIGH	11 to 12 minutes per pound (500 g) at MEDIUM

Bone-in
Rib Roast

Preparation : . . . . 7 m
Cooking : . . . . from 37 to 53 m
Standing : . . . . 10 m

A personal note : To successfully cook a bone-in rib roast in the microwave oven, a browning dish (Corning) is a must. The tips of the flat bones under the roast must be shielded with a strip of foil.

Ingredients :

1   4-to-6-lb (2 to 3 kg) loin or wing roast with bone

2 tsp (10 mL) paprika

1 tsp (5 mL) dry mustard

2 tbsp (30 mL) soft butter or margarine

1 medium-sized onion, cut in four

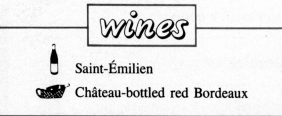

Saint-Émilien

Château-bottled red Bordeaux

Method :

• Cream the butter together with the paprika and mustard, Shield the tips of the bones with a 2-inch (5 cm) strip of foil.

• Preheat browning dish 7 minutes at HIGH. Place the roast in the oven without removing the dish from the oven, fat side down. Microwave at HIGH 5 minutes.

• Baste the meat with the butter mixture.

• Place the roast, fat side up, on a microwave rack or inverted saucer set in a baking dish. Sprinkle with paprika. DO NOT SALT.

• Place the onion pieces in the bottom of the dish. Microwave at MEDIUM 8 minutes per pound (500 g). Remove foil after the first 8 minutes, then cook to your taste following the Beef roasting chart.

• When the roast is cooked, place it on a serving dish and let stand 10 minutes, covered, in a warm place.

• Prepare the gravy to your taste, as for Rolled Rib Roast or any sauce of your choice.

Roast Beef

Convection cooking

Preparation : .20 m
　　　　　　rare : . . . . .25 m
Cooking : medium : . . . . .37 m
　　　　　　well done : . . . . .50 m
Standing : . . . . .5 to 7 m

Method :

• Cream together the fat and mustard. Pat the roast dry with absorbent paper. Spread the mustard butter over the meat. Sprinkle paprika generously over the top fat. If you have a combination microwave-convection oven, place a rack in the oven ceramic tray.

• Preheat oven to 350°F (180°C) for 15 minutes. Set a plate under the rack.

• Place the roast on the rack and cook at 350°F (180°C) for 10 minutes per pound (500 g) for rare, 15 minutes per pound (500 g) for medium or 20 minutes per pound (500 g) for well done.

• When the roast is cooked, make your gravy as for any other roast.

• This is a recipe for cooking a roast by convection in a microwave oven or electric stove.

A personal note : I recommend a Spencer, rib eye, rib or, for a more economical cut, a cross rib roast at least 4 to 5 inch - (10 to 13 cm) thick.

Ingredients :

1   3-to-5-lb (1.5 to 2.5 kg) roast beef

3 tbsp (50 mL) fat of your choice

1 tbsp (15 mL) dry mustard

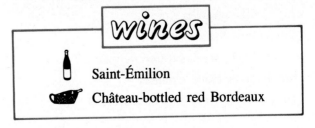

Saint-Émilion

Château-bottled red Bordeaux

25

Rolled Rib Roast

Preparation : . . . . .5 m
Cooking : . . . . .from 40 to 50 m
Standing : . . . . .from 10 to 15 m

A personal note: Make sure there are no large pieces of fat inside the meat. However, a coat of fat on top will give the roast a better flavor. THIS ROAST IS COOKED WITHOUT ANY SALT.

Ingredients :

1 4-to-5-lb (2 to 2.5 kg) loin or wing roast, boned and rolled

2 tbsp (30 mL) vegetable oil or melted butter

1 tsp (5 mL) paprika

1/2 tsp (2 mL) thyme

1/2 tsp (2 mL) fresh ground pepper

1 small garlic clove, crushed

2 tbsp (30 mL) very fine breadcrumbs

Method :

• Mix together in a bowl the vegetable oil or melted butter, paprika, thyme, pepper, garlic and bread-crumbs.

• Place the roast on a microwave rack or an inverted saucer set in an 8 × 12-inch (20 × 30 cm) micro-wave-safe baking dish.

• Baste the top fat and the sides of the roast with the spice mixture.

• Microwave according to time given in the Beef Roasting Chart.

To make gravy

• Remove the roast and rack from the baking dish. Add to the juice in the bottom of the dish **1/4 cup (60 mL) of a liquid of your choice — cold tea, Madeira, sherry or red wine — and 1 teaspoon (5 mL) Dijon mustard.**

• Mix well, crushing the tiny bits of caramel from the meat that give flavor and color to the meat juices. Microwave 1 minute at HIGH when ready to serve.

To make a creamy gravy

• Add to the fat **1 tablespoon (15 mL) flour.** Mix well, microwave 2 minutes at HIGH, stirring once.

• Add **1/2 cup (125 mL) of a liquid of your choice,** as given previously. Should you choose Madeira or sherry, add only **1/4 cup (60 mL) plus 1/4 cup (60 mL) cold water.**

• Stir well and microwave 3 minutes at HIGH, stir-ring once.

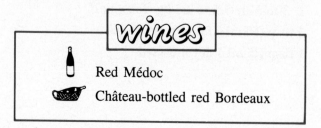

Red Médoc

Château-bottled red Bordeaux

Roast Beef

With temperature probe

Preparation: .5 m
Cooking: . . . . from 40 to 50 m
Standing: . . . . .none

A personal note: If your oven has a temperature probe, using it is the easiest way to cook a roast to perfection, whatever the cut: cross rib, eye of round or rib roast, with bone or boneless. See Cooking by temperature probe paragraph for directions. This method gives perfect results every time. The temperature probe will sense the internal temperature of food and turn off the unit automatically when the programmed temperature is reached.

wines

Red Bordeaux

Château-bottled red Bordeaux

Ingredients:

1 **4-to-6-lb (2 to 3 kg) roast of your choice**

1/2 **tsp (2 mL) ground pepper**

1/2 **tsp (2 mL) paprika**

1 **tsp (5 mL) dry mustard**

1 **garlic clove, chopped fine**

1 **bay leaf, broken up into small pieces**

1 **tbsp (15 mL) vegetable oil**

Method:

• Mix together the pepper, paprika, mustard, garlic, bay leaf and vegetable oil. Spread over the meat.

• If you have a combination microwave-convection oven, put a ceramic or Pyrex plate under the rack and place the meat on the rack.

• Insert the temperature probe in the meat and plug it in.

• Select the cooking setting for the way you want your roast cooked — rare, medium or well done.

• The temperature probe will turn off automatically when the selected temperature is reached.

• Remove the roast from the oven, remove the temperature probe and make gravy with the juice accumulated in the bottom of the plate.

Three-Star Roast Beef

Convection cooking

Ingredients:

1   4-to-5-lb (2 to 2.5 kg) beef sirloin, boned and rolled

3 tbsp (50 mL) soft butter

2 tbsp (30 mL) Dijon mustard

1 tbsp (15 mL) dry mustard

2 tbsp (30 mL) chili sauce

1/2 cup (125 mL) dry Madeira or sherry

1/2 cup (125 mL) beef consommé

Preparation:	.....................5 m
Cooking:	.......from 1 h to 1 h 40 m
Standing:	.............from 8 to 10 m

Method:

• If you have a combination microwave-convection oven, prepare the oven by placing a rack in the oven ceramic tray. Preheat oven at 375°F (190°C).

• Mix together the butter, Dijon mustard, dry mustard and chili sauce. Spread this mixture over the meat. Place a pie plate under the rack.

• Roast at 375°F (190°C) 15 to 20 minutes per pound (500 g), whether you wish your roast to be rare or medium.

• When cooked, place the roast on a warm plate and keep in a warm place.

• With a spoon, remove the fat floating on top of the gravy. To the remaining brown juice add the Madeira, sherry and consommé, scraping the plate to crush the brown particles. Microwave 5 minutes at HIGH in the microwave, stirring twice during cooking.

wines

Red Rhône

Châteauneuf-du-Pape

28

Eye of Round
À la Bordelaise

Advance preparation : . . . . .24 h
Cooking : . . . . .1 h 20 m
Standing : . . . . .10 m

A personal note : The eye of round or the sirloin are more economical beef cuts than the rib roast. This recipe results in deliciously tender meat. Serve with mashed potatoes or fine noodles topped with the meat gravy.

Ingredients :

3 to 4 lb (1.5 to 2 kg) beef eye of round
  or sirloin

1/3 cup (80 mL) olive or vegetable oil

1/2 cup (125 mL) red wine

1/2 cup (125 mL) beef broth

1 cup (250 mL) onions, thinly sliced

1/4 cup (60 mL) fresh parsley, minced

2 bay leaves

1 tsp (5 mL) thyme

1 tsp (5 mL) sugar

1 tsp (5 mL) salt

1/2 tsp (2 mL) peppercorns, coarsely ground

3 slices bacon

1 tbsp (15 mL) wine or cider vinegar

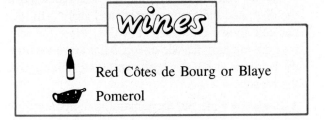

wines

Red Côtes de Bourg or Blaye
Pomerol

Method :

• Mix together in a large bowl the oil, wine, beef broth, onions, parsley, bay leaves, thyme, sugar, salt and pepper. Roll the piece of meat in the mixture, cover and marinate 24 hours, refrigerated. Turn the piece of meat 2 or 3 times while it's marinating.

• To cook, place the bacon slices on a sheet of white paper. Microwave 2 minutes at HIGH. Place in the bottom of a deep dish large enough to hold the piece of meat.

• Remove meat from marinade. Drain, reserving the juice. Place over the bacon the remaining onions and herbs in the strainer. Set the meat on top and add 1 cup (250 mL) of the marinade juice. Cover and microwave 10 minutes at HIGH, reduce power to MEDIUM and microwave 40 to 70 minutes, or until the meat is tender.

• When cooked, place the meat on a warm platter. Add to the sauce 1/4 cup (60 mL) of the remaining marinade juice and the spoonful of vinegar. Microwave 5 minutes at HIGH. Serve in a sauceboat.

Red Wine Rib Roast

Preparation:	.........from 15 to 20 m
Cooking:	........from 1 h to 1 h 15 m
Standing:	....................none

Ingredients:

1   3½-to-4-lb (1.5 to 2 kg) rib roast,
    boned and rolled

1/4 cup (60 mL) flour

1 tsp (5 mL) paprika

> **A personal note:** This is an ideal recipe when you want thinly sliced cold rib roast to serve at a buffet.

4 tbsp (60 mL) butter

1 cup (250 mL) onion, sliced

1/2 cup (125 mL) carrots, grated

1 garlic clove, minced

2 tbsp (30 mL) hot brandy

1 cup (250 mL) dry red wine

1 tsp (5 mL) salt

1/2 tsp (2 mL) fresh ground pepper

1 bay leaf

1/2 tsp (2 mL) thyme

Method:

• Pat the roast dry with absorbent paper. Mix the flour and paprika and spread on waxed paper. Roll the meat in the flour mixture to cover completely.

• Preheat a browning dish (Corning) or a "caquelon" (Panasonic) 7 minutes at HIGH. Place the butter in the hot dish without removing the dish from the oven.

• When the butter has melted, which occurs very quickly, place the roast in the dish fat side down. Microwave 2 minutes at HIGH. Turn the roast and microwave 2 minutes at HIGH. Repeat this operation for the other two sides.

• Remove roast from the dish. To the fat remaining in the dish, add the onion, carrots and garlic, stir well and microwave 2 minutes at HIGH. Place the roast over the mixture, fat side on top. Microwave the brandy 1 minute at HIGH. Ignite and pour flaming over the roast.

• Place the wine and the remaining ingredients in a microwave-safe measuring cup and microwave 40 seconds at HIGH. Pour around the roast. Cover. Microwave 15 minutes per pound (500 g) at MEDIUM. Check doneness and, if necessary, add 15 minutes cooking time.

• Remove roast from dish. Stir the juice, crushing the vegetables, and serve as is or cream in a food processor.

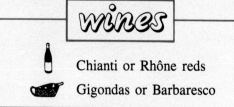

Chianti or Rhône reds

Gigondas or Barbaresco

Braised Cross Rib Roast, Bavarian Style

Preparation: . . . . .from 5 to 7 m
Cooking: . . . . .1 h 30 m
Standing: . . . . .20 m

- Add the salt, pepper and sugar; mix together.

- Add the tomatoes; stir well around the meat. Cover with a Pyrex lid or plastic wrap tightly fitted on the dish. Microwave 15 minutes per pound (500 g) at MEDIUM.

- Turn the roast, stir the sauce in the bottom of the dish and let stand, covered, 20 minutes. Place the meat on a warm platter. Add the flour to the sauce, mix well. Add the wine or vermouth and the sour cream. Mix well together and microwave 1 to 2 minutes at MEDIUM, or until the sauce boils lightly. Stir well and pour over the meat.

A personal note: Onions browned in butter and fresh tomatoes result in a smooth, pink gravy. As for any braised meat, the cooking period is slower and longer than for roasting. Serve with parsleyed noodles and green peas.

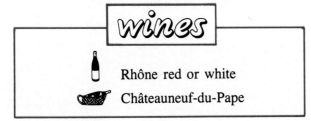

Rhône red or white

Châteauneuf-du-Pape

Ingredients:

3 tbsp (50 mL) butter or margarine

2 medium-sized onions, thinly sliced

1 3-to-4-lb (1.5 to 2 kg) cross rib roast

1½ tsp (7 mL) salt

1/2 tsp (2 mL) pepper

1/2 tsp (2 mL) sugar

1/2 cup (125 mL) fresh tomatoes, chopped

2 tbsp (30 mL) flour

1/2 cup (125 mL) wine or white vermouth

1/2 cup (125 mL) sour cream

Method:

- Place the butter in an 8 × 12-inch (20 × 30 cm) glass or ceramic baking dish and melt 3 minutes at HIGH or until browned.

- Add the onions, stir and microwave 2 to 3 minutes at HIGH or until the onions brown here and there.

- Place the meat over the onions, microwave 1 minute at HIGH.

- Turn the meat and microwave 4 minutes at HIGH.

Cross Rib Roast Maison

Preparation: . . . . .from 10 to 15 m
Cooking: . . . . . .from 1 h 10 to 1 h 20 m
Standing: .20 m

A personal note: Instead of buying ground beef, minute steaks, short ribs and a cross rib roast separately, it is more economical to buy a cross rib with bones attached. It may vary in weight from 4 to 5 pounds (2 to 2.5 kg).

I braise the remaining piece using the following recipe. Serve with noodles or rice or mashed potatoes and a bowl of grated cheese.

 Californian Zinfandel
Portuguese garrafeira

To make the most of such a cut, remove the strings to free up the bones. I cook them as short beef ribs, barbecued.

From the meat, I cut a thick slice of approximately 1 pound (500 g), which I put through the meat grinder to make meatballs, or I cut 4 thin slices, which I tenderize using a meat mallet, for minute steaks.

Ingredients:

1 3-to-4-lb (1.5 to 2 kg) cross rib roast

2 tbsp (30 mL) margarine

1 tsp (5 mL) salt

1/2 tsp (2 mL) pepper

2 tsp (10 mL) sugar

1 small unpeeled lemon, thinly sliced

2 onions, thinly sliced

2 garlic cloves, minced

1/4 cup (60 mL) chili sauce

1 cup (250 mL) hot tea

1/2 tsp (2 mL) basil

1 tsp (5 mL) savory

Method:

• Place the meat in an 8-cup (2 L) ceramic or glass baking dish. Mix together the margarine, salt, pepper and sugar. Spread the meat with the mixture. Cover with lemon slices.

• Mix the remaining ingredients together and pour over the meat. Cover tightly with the dish lid or plastic wrap. Microwave 20 minutes at HIGH.

• Turn the meat, cover and microwave 30 minutes at MEDIUM.

• Turn and baste meat with the juice accumulated in the dish. Cover and microwave 20 minutes at MEDIUM.

• Check doneness with a fork. If the roast is tender, cover and let stand 20 minutes before serving. It will remain warm.

Oxtail Stew Fermière

Preparation: . . . .**from 10 to 15 m**
Cooking: the meal: . . . .**from 40 to 60 m**
       the sauce: . . . .**10 m**
Standing: . . . .**none**

wines

Rhône red or (white) Vouvray

Barolo or (white) Californian Chenin

• This is an economical family dish. At my table, it is an unfailing success.

A personal note: I even serve this dish to friends, with boiled, parsleyed potatoes. In summer, I replace the parsley with fresh chives. The stew is easily prepared a day ahead and re-heats well, usually 20 minutes at MEDIUM, covered.

Ingredients:

1 oxtail, cut in small pieces

1 small yellow turnip, peeled and cut in four

4 medium-sized onions, whole and peeled

2 medium-sized carrots, whole and peeled

1 tsp (5 mL) thyme

1/2 tsp (2 mL) dry mustard

1 tsp (5 mL) coarse or fine salt

1/2 tsp (2 mL) black peppercorns

2 cups (500 mL) hot water or tomato juice

3 tbsp (50 mL) flour

1/2 cup (125 mL) cold water

Method:

• Place all the ingredients, except the flour and cold water, in a 6-cup (1.5 L) ceramic, glass or plastic dish with a good lid. Cover and microwave 2 minutes at HIGH. Stir well, then microwave 40 to 60 minutes at MEDIUM, stirring 3 times and checking the meat for doneness. When the meat is tender, stop cooking.

• Mix together the flour and cold water.

• Remove meat from bones. Cut the carrots in 3 pieces. Add the flour mixture. Stir well, cover and microwave at HIGH 2 to 3 minutes, or until the sauce is creamy; stir once during cooking.

• Place the meat in the sauce and heat 1 minute, if necessary.

Greek Stefatho

Preparation: .25 m
Cooking: . . . . . . from 1 h 20 to 1 h 25 m
Standing: . . . . .none

A personal note: This is a meal in a dish, made with beef or lamb, eggplant and rice. In Greece, this is family fare. It may be cooked a day in advance, refrigerated, and reheated the following day, covered, either by Sensor "Cycle A-1" or 10 to 15 minutes at MEDIUM.

Ingredients:

2-lb (1 kg) beef round, in 1-inch (2.5 cm) cubes

1/2 tsp (2 mL) pepper

1 tsp (5 mL) salt

1 tsp (5 mL) sugar

1 tsp (5 mL) cinnamon

1/3 cup (80 mL) vegetable oil

12 small white onions

2 cups (500 mL) beef broth

A 7½-oz (213 mL) can tomato sauce

1/4 cup (60 mL) vegetable oil

1 medium-sized eggplant, peeled and diced

1 green pepper, cut in strips

1/2 cup (125 mL) long grain rice

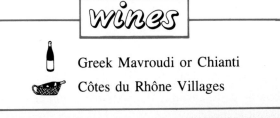

Greek Mavroudi or Chianti
Côtes du Rhône Villages

Method:

• Mix together in a plate the pepper, salt, sugar and cinnamon. Roll the beef cubes in the mixture.

• Place the oil in a browning dish (Corning) and microwave 4 minutes at HIGH.

• Add the meat cubes to the hot oil. Stir a few seconds and microwave at MEDIUM-HIGH 4 minutes. Stir and microwave another 4 minutes at MEDIUM-HIGH.

• Remove meat to an 8-cup (2 L) microwave-safe dish.

• Add the remaining fat (there is very little), microwave 1 minute at HIGH. Add the onions, microwave 2 minutes at HIGH.

• Add 1/2 cup (125 mL) beef broth and tomato sauce. Mix well. Cover with casserole lid or plastic wrap. Microwave 1 hour at MEDIUM, stirring after 30 minutes.

• Microwave the 1/4 cup (60 mL) oil 5 minutes at HIGH in the browning dish. Add the eggplant, stir well. Microwave 5 minutes at HIGH.

• Add the green pepper. Microwave 1 minute at HIGH.

• Add to the casserole at the end of its cooking period, together with the rice and the remaining beef broth. Stir well. Cover and microwave 20 to 25 minutes at MEDIUM-HIGH, stirring after 15 minutes of cooking.

Grandmother's Pot en Pot

Preparation :	. . . . .8 m
Cooking :	. . . . .1 h 30 m
Standing :	. . . . .none

• Every once in a while, most of us get an urge to cook something the way we used to or the way our mothers or grandmothers did. For me, that feeling always makes me nostalgic for my grandmother's Pot en Pot, my favorite braised roast.

Ingredients :

3 to 4 lb (1.5 to 2 kg) beef round from sirloin tip round bone

2 tbsp (30 mL) soft butter

1/4 tsp (1 mL) fresh ground pepper

1 large unpeeled lemon, diced

2 large onions, thinly sliced

1 cup (250 mL) chili sauce

1 tsp (5 mL) basil or savory

1/4 cup (60 mL) red wine or water

Method :

• Set the meat in the baking dish. Spread the soft butter on top. Salt and pepper. Mix together the lemon and onions and place on top of the meat. Mix the remaining ingredients together and pour over all.

• Cover and microwave at MEDIUM 1 hour 30 minutes, or until the meat is tender.

• To serve, slice thinly and cover with the well-stirred or strained gravy.

• Accompany with potatoes and carrots mashed together.

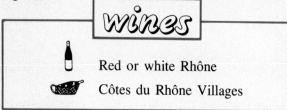

Red or white Rhône
Côtes du Rhône Villages

Genoese Beef Casserole

Preparation :	. . . . .from 5 to 10 m
Cooking :	. . . . .20 m
Standing :	. . . . .10 m

A personal note : I often make this casserole when I remove 1 pound (500 g) of beef for grinding from a piece of meat. It is important to use fine noodles.

Ingredients :

1 lb (500 g) ground beef

1½ cups (375 mL) fine noodles, in 1-inch (2.5 cm) pieces

1 onion, chopped fine

1 cup (250 mL) celery, diced

2 cups (500 mL) tomato juice

1 tsp (5 mL) sugar

1 tsp (5 mL) savory or thyme

1/2 tsp (2 mL) each of salt and pepper

Method :

• Set the ground beef in a 4-cup (1 L) microwave-safe baking dish, sprinkle the noodles, onion and celery over the meat.

• Mix together the tomato juice and remaining ingredients and pour over the meat.

• Cover and microwave 10 minutes at HIGH.

• Mix well and microwave 10 minutes more at MEDIUM. Stir, cover and let stand 10 minutes.

• Serve with a bowl of grated cheese.

Barbaresco
Amarone

Boiled Beef

Preparation: . . . . 10 m
Cooking: . . . . . . from 1 h 30 to 1 h 40 m
Standing: . . . . none

Ingredients:

8 cups (2 L) hot water

4 to 6 medium-sized carrots, peeled and cut in two

2 to 3 parsnips, peeled and cut in two

1 large onion, cut in four

1/2 tsp (2 mL) thyme

4 cloves

2 bay leaves

1 tsp (5 mL) coarse salt

1/4 tsp (1 mL) fresh ground pepper

4 lb (2 kg) stewing beef of your choice

1 lb (500 g) fresh beans or green peas

6 to 8 potatoes, peeled

Method:

• Place all the ingredients in a 18 to 20-cup (4.5 to 5 L) microwave-safe dish with a good cover. Cover and microwave 20 minutes at HIGH. Stir, then turn the meat. Cover and microwave 20 minutes at HIGH.

• Turn the meat and simmer 30 minutes at MEDIUM. Turn the meat once again and microwave 20 to 30 minutes at MEDIUM, or until the meat is tender.

Parsleyed French Dressing

• Place in a bowl **1/2 tsp (2 mL) salt, 1/4 tsp (1 mL) each of pepper and sugar, 1 tsp (5 mL) Dijon mustard, 3 tbsp (50 mL) wine or cider vinegar.** Stir well together and add **1/3 cup (80 mL) peanut oil.** Stir and add **1/4 cup (60 mL) each parsley and chives or finely chopped green onions.**

• Mix well together; this will give a rather thick dressing.

• Serve in an attractive sauceboat, with each person pouring the dressing to his taste over the meat and vegetables.

A personal note: This is an old Quebec recipe for a spring dish par excellence that is light and colorful. The parsleyed French dressing adds color. Delicious hot, the beef loses none of its flavor served cold, thinly sliced. One thing to remember: the meat must cool, refrigerated, in its stock, but it should stand at room temperature one hour before serving. Dice the remaining vegetables, add them to leftover stock along with rice, if you wish, and you will have a delicious vegetable soup.

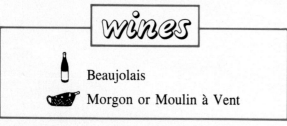

wines

Beaujolais

Morgon or Moulin à Vent

Boiled Beef with Plum Sauce

Preparation: . . . .**from 15 to 20 m**
Cooking: . . . . . .**from 1 h 53 to 2 h 05 m**
Standing: . . . .**none**

• At the end of the summer, when small blue Damson plums are sold at market, I hurry to make this dish, which I serve with fine parsleyed noodles. It's equally good hot or cold.

Ingredients:

3 lb (1.5 kg) stewing beef

1   1-lb (500 g) marrow bone

2 cups (500 mL) hot water

6 carrots, peeled and cut in four

4 small white turnips, peeled and sliced

3 medium-sized onions, each studded with 2 cloves

3 leeks, cut in 1-inch (2.5 cm) pieces

12 peppercorns

1 tbsp (15 mL) coarse salt

1 tsp (5 mL) thyme

3 bay leaves

8 to 10 sprigs of parsley (optional)

1 large white onion, chopped

2 tbsp (30 mL) butter

1 lb (500 g) blue plums, pitted

1 cup (250 mL) red wine

1 tbsp (15 mL) sugar

1/4 tsp (1 mL) pepper

Method:

• Place the meat and the marrow bone in a 12-cup (3 L) microwave-safe baking dish.

• Add the carrots, turnips, onions, leeks, peppercorns, coarse salt, thyme, bay leaves and parsley. Stir well around the meat.

• Cover and microwave at MEDIUM-HIGH 1 hour. Stir, then microwave 45 minutes at MEDIUM.

• Depending on the meat cut, cooking may require more or less than 20 minutes. It is good to check with a fork after 25 minutes of cooking at MEDIUM.

• Place the butter in a 4-cup (1 L) microwave-safe dish and melt 2 minutes at HIGH.

• Add chopped onion and 1/3 cup (80 mL) red wine; cook 3 minutes at HIGH, stirring twice.

• Sprinkle with sugar and pepper, mix well.

• Add the plums and the remaining wine, stir well, cover and cook 8 to 10 minutes at MEDIUM-HIGH, or until the plums are tender. Stir well.

• Serve in thin slices with the plum sauce in a sauceboat.

• Add the hot water. Cover, bring to a boil 15 minutes at HIGH.

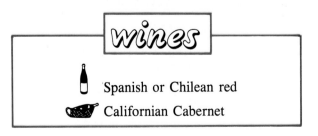

wines

Spanish or Chilean red
Californian Cabernet

Hamburgers

Hamburgers are delicious and tender when cooked in the microwave oven if you have a browning dish (Corning). If you do not have a browning dish, use the method below.

Preparation :	15 m
Cooking :	5 m
Standing :	4 m

A personal note : To improve the appearance of meat or poultry, baste with a Worcestershire or soy sauce base mixture or preparation before cooking.

Ingredients :

1 lb (500 g) ground beef

1 tsp (5 mL) salt

1/4 tsp (1 mL) pepper

1/2 tsp (2 mL) thyme

3 green onions, chopped fine

3 tbsp (50 mL) instant potato flakes or soft breadcrumbs

3 tbsp (50 mL) water, wine, apple juice or beer

Paprika

Method :

• Mix all the ingredients except the paprika, together in a bowl with your finger tips.

• Divide into 4 or 5 equal-size patties. Sprinkle with paprika on one side.

• Preheat an 8 × 8 inch (20 × 20 cm) browning dish 7 minutes at HIGH. Without removing dish from the oven, place the patties in it paprika side down.

• Microwave 4 minutes at HIGH.

• Turn the patties and let stand 4 minutes in the dish covered with waxed paper. Serve.

To cook hamburgers without a browning dish

• Mix all the ingredients in the same manner. Replace paprika with Kitchen Bouquet sauce.

• Place the hamburgers in an 8 × 8-inch (20 × 20 cm) microwave-safe dish, on a microwave rack, if possible.

• Microwave 4 minutes at HIGH. Turn the patties and complete cooking 4 minutes at MEDIUM-HIGH.

To vary the flavor of hamburgers

Add to the basic meat mixture or vary the kind of meat you use:

Meat variations

1. Mix **1/2 lb (250 g) veal** and **1/2 lb (250 g) pork.**

2. Mix **1/2 lb (250 g) ground beef** and **1/2 lb (250 g) ground pork.**

3. Mix **1/3 lb (160 g) each of ground beef, veal and pork.**

To the meat mixture of your choice, or simply to ground beef, prepared according to the Hamburger recipe, add one of the following ingredients to give the patties a distinct flavor:

1. **1 tbsp (15 mL) A-1 sauce**

2. **1 tbsp (15 mL) Worcestershire sauce**

3. **1 tbsp (15 mL) dried onion**

4. **4 fresh green onions, both green and white parts, chopped**

5. **1/2 tsp (2 mL) garlic powder or 1 clove, crushed**

6. **1 tbsp (15 mL) ketchup or chili sauce**

7. **2 tsp (10 mL) Dijon mustard**

8. **1 tsp (5 mL) curry powder**

9. **1 tsp (5 mL) ground cumin and the juice of 1 lemon**

10. **2 tbsp (30 mL) lemon juice and 1/4 tsp (1 mL) thyme**

11. **2 tbsp (30 mL) red wine and 1 tsp (5 mL) oregano**

12. **1 tsp (5 mL) basil, 1 tsp (5 mL) coriander, powder or grains, and 1 garlic clove,** chopped fine.

A few toppings for cooked hamburgers

1. Place a slice of cheese of your choice over each. Microwave 40 seconds at HIGH.

2. Sprinkle **1/2 tsp (2 mL) grated Parmesan cheese** over each patty, then microwave at MEDIUM-HIGH 20 seconds.

3. Put **1 tsp (5 mL) of sour cream** on top of each patty, sprinkle with paprika and serve.

4. Sprinkle each patty with **1 tsp (5 mL)** or **1 tbsp (15 mL) dry onion soup mixture**. Microwave 20 seconds at HIGH.

5. Place over each hamburger **1/2 tsp (2 mL) butter** mixed with **1/2 tsp (2 mL) fresh chives.**

41

Chinese Green Pepper Steak

Preparation : . . . .**10 m**
Cooking : . . . . **from 12 to 13 m**
Standing : . . . .**none**

Method :

- Slice the steak diagonally as thinly as possible.

- Microwave the oil in a browning dish (Corning) 2 minutes at HIGH. Add the garlic and microwave 40 seconds at HIGH.

- Add the meat, stir well in the hot oil. Microwave 2 minutes at HIGH.

- Place the meat around the dish. Set the onion, green pepper, salt, pepper and the ginger in the centre. Stir the whole without disturbing the meat. Cover with a waxed paper and microwave 5 minutes at MEDIUM-HIGH.

- Mix together the cornstarch, consommé, soy sauce and sugar. Pour over all after the 5-minute cooking period. Mix together the meat and vegetables. Microwave 2 to 3 minutes at MEDIUM-HIGH, stirring after 2 minutes.

- The dish is ready when the sauce is transparent. Stir and serve.

A personal note : This recipe allows you to serve 4 to 5 people with one pound (500 g) of steak. I use a 1-pound (500 g) round steak or a steak cut in one piece from a cross rib, as described for minute steaks in the recipe for Cross Rib Roast Maison. Serve with boiled rice.

Ingredients :

1 lb (500 g) steak in one piece or thinly sliced

3 tbsp (50 mL) salad oil

1 garlic clove, chopped fine

1 onion, chopped

2 green peppers, slivered

1/2 tsp (2 mL) salt

1/4 tsp (1 mL) pepper

1 tbsp (15 mL) fresh ginger, grated

1 tbsp (15 mL) cornstarch

1 cup (250 mL) consommé of your choice

1 tbsp (15 mL) soy sauce

1 tsp (5 mL) sugar

wines

White Anjou

Rheingau Spätlese

Broiled Steak, Madeira Sauce

Preparation:	...........from 7 to 10 m
Cooking: rare:	..............from 3 to 4 m
medium:	..........from 6 to 8 m
Standing:	.................3 to 4 m

Method:

• Remove a few pieces of fat from the steak. Sprinkle one side with paprika.

• Preheat an 8 × 8-inch (20 × 20 cm) browning dish (Corning) 7 minutes at HIGH. Place steak in dish, without removing from oven, paprika side down. Press top of steak with finger tips for perfect contact with the dish.

• Put the little pieces of fat around the steak. Microwave at HIGH 3 to 4 minutes, depending on how you wish to have it cooked.

• Turn the steak, cover with waxed paper, and let it stand same time as cooking time. Steak cooks on one side only. Set on warm plate.

• Prepare sauce of your choice. Pour hot sauce over the steak. Salt and pepper to taste.

A personal note: To get a grilled flavor when you cook a good steak in the microwave oven, it is important to have a ceramic browning dish (Corning).

A boneless 1 or 2-inch (2.5 - 5 cm) steak is always perfect.

The best cuts are the rib, spencer, club, tenderloin, strip loin or sirloin for a large steak. Have the meat at room temperature when possible

Ingredients:

1 steak of your choice
A few pieces of fat
Paprika
Salt and pepper

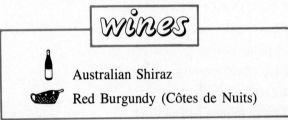

Australian Shiraz
Red Burgundy (Côtes de Nuits)

Short Beef Ribs, Barbecued

Advance preparation :	. . . . **24 h**
Cooking :	. . . . **from 50 to 60 m**
Standing :	. . . . **none**

Helpful hint : Here is a way to cook beef ribs removed from a cross rib roast. They can also be bought separately. Spareribs may be prepared in the same manner.
Serve with plain rice, or for a more elaborate meal, garnish with broiled mushrooms.

Ingredients :

2 to 3 lb (1 to 1.5 kg) short beef ribs

1/2 cup (125 mL) ketchup or chili sauce

1 cup (250 mL) water

1 tbsp (15 mL) sugar

1 tbsp (15 mL) prepared mustard

1 tsp (5 mL) salt

20 peppercorns

1 tsp (5 mL) savory

4 garlic cloves, cut in two

2 large onions, sliced thick

Juice and grated rind of 1 orange

3 tbsp (50 mL) soy sauce

Method :

• Place the beef ribs in a bowl.

• Mix the remaining ingredients.

• Pour over the beef ribs and mix thoroughly. Cover and refrigerate 24 hours, stirring 2 to 3 times during the marinating period.

• To cook, place the meat and marinade in a 16 to 20-cup (4 to 5 L) microwave-safe baking dish.

• Cover, microwave at HIGH 20 minutes. Stir well and microwave at MEDIUM 30 to 40 minutes, or until the meat is tender.

• Stir twice during the cooking period at MEDIUM.

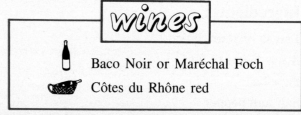

Baco Noir or Maréchal Foch

Côtes du Rhône red

Broiled Steak with Mushrooms

Preparation :	. . . .	8 m
Cooking :	. . . .	5 m
Standing :	. . . .	3 m

Ingredients :

1 steak of your choice

1 tsp (5 mL) butter

1/2 tsp (2 mL) tarragon

1 garlic clove, cut in two

1 to 2 cups (250 - 500 mL) mushrooms, thinly sliced

Salt and pepper to taste

Method :

• Broil the steak of your choice in the microwave, following the recipe for Broiled Steak, Madeira Sauce.

• When the steak has stood for 3 minutes, place it on a warm plate.

• To the cooking juice add the butter, tarragon and garlic and cook 1 minute at HIGH. Stir well.

• Add the mushrooms. Mix well. Salt and pepper, then finish cooking at HIGH 3 minutes. Pour around steak.

A personal note: Grill: partly cook chicken, chops, etc. Season and finish cooking on Broil or barbecue.

wines

🍾 Chianti

🥘 Brunello di Montalcino

Small Ground Beef Timbales

Preparation :	. . . .	from 8 to 10 m
Cooking :	. . . .	5 m
Standing :	. . . .	5 m

A personal note : A timbale is a small glass, earthenware or ceramic bowl. Ground beef patties cooked in this manner are easy to prepare and elegant.

Ingredients :

1 lb (500 g) ground beef, quite lean

1/2 cup (125 mL) light cream

1 egg, lightly beaten

1/2 cup (125 mL) quick-cooking rolled oats

2 tbsp (30 mL) celery, chopped fine

4 green onions, chopped fine

4 soda crackers, crushed

1/2 tsp (2 mL) salt

1/4 tsp (1 mL) pepper

1/2 tsp (2 mL) thyme or tarragon

Method :

• Mix all the ingredients together in a glass bowl (Pyrex) with your finger tips. Divide evenly into 6 to 8 buttered 6-oz (170 g) molds. Set in a circular pattern in the oven.

• Cover all with waxed paper or individually with plastic wrap. Microwave 5 minutes at HIGH.

• Let stand 5 minutes. Unmold in a hot dish or individually on warm plates and cover with a Timbale Mushroom Sauce.

wines

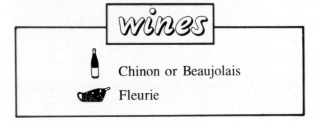

🍾 Chinon or Beaujolais

🥘 Fleurie

Bacon Meat Roll

```
Preparation : . . . . . . . . . . . . . . . . . . 15 m
Cooking : . . . . . . . . . . . from 12 to 15 m
Standing : . . . . . . . . . . . . . . . . . . . . . none
```

• This delicious meat loaf is, to my knowledge, the best. It is equally good hot or cold and it cooks to perfection in the microwave oven.

Ingredients :

1 lb (500 g) ground beef of your choice

1 cup (250 mL) soda crackers, crushed

1 medium-sized onion, minced

2 eggs, beaten

1/4 cup (60 mL) light or rich cream

1 tsp (5 mL) salt

1/4 tsp (1 mL) each pepper and nutmeg

1/2 tsp (2 mL) each thyme and allspice

6 to 8 slices bacon

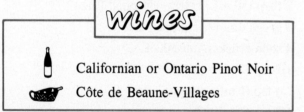

Californian or Ontario Pinot Noir
Côte de Beaune-Villages

Method :

• Place all the ingredients, except the bacon, in a bowl. Mix well and form into a roll.

• Set the slices of bacon side by side on a sheet of waxed paper.

• Place the roll of meat in the middle of the bacon. Using the waxed paper, bring the ends of the bacon slices on to the meat. Repeat the process on the other side. Form into one large roll, which is easy if you roll it slightly on a table, tightening it with the waxed paper.

• Place the roll in an 8 × 8-inch (20 × 20 cm) microwave-safe dish. Microwave at HIGH 11 to 12 minutes, until the bacon on top is well browned. Remove from dish with a wide spatula. Serve hot or cold.

Cottage Cheese Meat Patties

Preparation:	5 m
Cooking:	6 m
Standing:	5 m

• Melted butter added to the ground beef places this recipe in the gourmet roster.

Ingredients:

1 lb (500 g) ground beef, lean

1/2 cup (125 mL) cottage cheese

1 egg, lightly beaten

3 tbsp (50 mL) melted butter

1 tsp (5 mL) salt

3 green onions, chopped fine

1/2 tsp (2 mL) thyme

Method:

• Mix all the ingredients together without crushing the meat too much. Form into 4 large or 6 medium patties.

• Preheat a browning dish (Corning) 4 minutes at HIGH.

• Sprinkle paprika over the patties.

• Set them in the hot dish without removing it from the oven.

• Press each patty down for good contact.

• Microwave 6 minutes at HIGH. Turn the patties and let stand (without cooking) 5 minutes in the oven. The internal heat in the patties will finish cooking. Serve.

Bardolino

Julienas

Homemade Meat Loaf

Preparation:	15 m
Cooking:	20 m
Standing:	none

A personal note: This meat loaf, prepared in a jiffy, is well flavored, good hot or cold, and can be kept one week, well covered, in the refrigerator. It also makes delicious sandwiches with a few leaves of lettuce and a bit of celery.

Ingredients:

1/3 cup (80 mL) fine breadcrumbs

1 cup (250 mL) milk

1½ lb (750 g) ground beef

2 eggs, well beaten

1 tsp (5 mL) salt

1/4 tsp (1 mL) pepper

1 tsp (5 mL) sage or savory

Topping:

1 tbsp (15 mL) brown sugar

1/4 cup (60 mL) ketchup

1/4 tsp (1 mL) nutmeg

1 tsp (5 mL) dry mustard

Method:

• Mix together in a Pyrex or ceramic loaf pan the first 7 ingredients.

• Mix the topping ingredients, then spread on top of the meat. Cover with waxed paper.

• Microwave 20 minutes at MEDIUM-HIGH. Serve hot or cold.

Beaujolais

Tavel rose

Monique's Meat Loaf

Preparation:	**15 m**
Cooking:	**20 m**
Standing:	**none**

This quickly prepared meat loaf was one of my daughter Monique's favorite recipes. She served it surrounded with elbow macaroni mixed with butter, fresh parsley and chives.

Ingredients:

2 lb (1 kg) ground beef or a mixture or pork, veal and beef

1   10-oz (284 mL) can vegetable soup

1 egg

1/2 tsp (2 mL) salt

1/4 tsp (1 mL) pepper

1/2 tsp (2 mL) garlic powder

2 tbsp (30 mL) Cheddar cheese, grated

Method:

• Place all the ingredients in a bowl and mix.

• Pour into a 9 × 5-inch (23 × 13 cm) microwave-safe loaf pan.

• Cover with plastic wrap.

• Microwave 20 minutes at MEDIUM-HIGH.

• Serve hot or cold. I prefer to eat it cold.

wines

Valpolicella

Bourgueil

Florentine Meat Loaf

Preparation:	**20 m**
Cooking:	**20 m**
Standing:	**10 m**

A personal note: Veal often replaces beef, in Florence, where it is easier to buy than beef. Both meats give excellent results.

Ingredients:

1½ lb (750 g) ground beef or veal

1 egg

1/2 cup (125 mL) fine breadcrumbs

1/2 cup (125 mL) fresh mushrooms, thinly sliced

1 tbsp (15 mL) rolled oats

1 onion, chopped fine

1/2 cup (125 mL) fresh tomatoes, unpeeled, diced

1 tbsp (15 mL) brown sugar

2 tbsp (30 mL) cream or milk

Grated rind of 1 lemon

1 tsp (5 mL) basil

1/2 tsp (2 mL) each salt and pepper

Method:

• Mix all the ingredients together in a bowl. Place in a glass loaf pan. Sprinkle generously with paprika. Microwave 20 minutes at MEDIUM-HIGH.

• Let stand 10 minutes before serving.

wines

Chianti

Vino Nobile di Montepulciano

• Chefs often refer to veal as the chameleon of cooking because it works well with all flavors — thyme, tarragon, rosemary, sage, orange and lemon, and tomato and white wine, to name only a few.

• There are two kinds of veal, milk-fed and grass-fed. The milk-fed — from a calf that was fed only its mother's milk — is the very best. The meat is pinkish-white, the fat is ivory-white. Such veal is becoming more and more difficult to come by and its cost is high.

• The grass-fed calf is fed powdered milk and let out to pasture. Its meat is redder and firmer and it costs less.

What you should know about veal

• Avoid freezing veal, especially milk-fed veal, as it loses much of its flavor and moisture when frozen.

• Ground veal and veal scallops should be cooked no more than two days after you buy them.

• Like other meats, veal should be at room temperature before roasting in a microwave oven.

• For a perfect veal roast in the microwave oven, the meat must not be overcooked. It should be lightly browned and basted two or three times during the cooking period. If you roast it as brown as beef or lamb, it will dry up.

• Before pounding veal scallops with a meat mallet,

place them between two sheets of waxed paper to prevent moisture from escaping from the meat.

• For tender and well browned veal chops, coat them with a mixture of flour, paprika and the aromatic herb of your choice, then brown them in very hot oil, preferably olive oil. You need a browning dish to do this in the microwave.

• Veal is well done when it registers 170°F (96°C) on the meat thermometer.

• For perfect results, a 3-pound (1.5 kg) veal roast is the best size to buy for roasting in the microwave oven.

• Garlic, tarragon and thyme are the perfect flavorings for a roast of veal. Madeira sauce and all mushroom and tomato sauces are very good with veal.

Veal cuts

• **Loin roast** is divided into two parts — the rib roast and the loin roast.

• **The loin roast** is the meaty end of the whole loin, which contains the T-shaped bones and the tenderloin. Its price is quite high, as it usually is sold sliced into chops. The tenderloin is a very good piece of meat when roasted in the microwave oven, but it must be boned and rolled.

• **The rib roast,** the less meaty part of the whole loin, contains rib bones and no tenderloin. It is a little less expensive. My favorite cut for braising, it is best when it is deboned and rolled.

• **Shoulder roast** is sold boned and rolled or cut into shoulder chops. It is used for simmered steaks or cubed for stewing. Rolled and tied, it can be braised or roasted by convection.

• Usually, veal is not indicated even though it does cook very well in the microwave oven, no matter what method is used.

• **Rib chops,** which contain the rib bones, are cut in a triangular shape.

• **Veal shank** is one of my favorite cuts for braising. It can be used for stewing, or simmered at MEDIUM or cooked with the SENSOR.

• **The breast** is the cut next to the shoulder. I consider it to be the best for ground veal.

Veal cuts

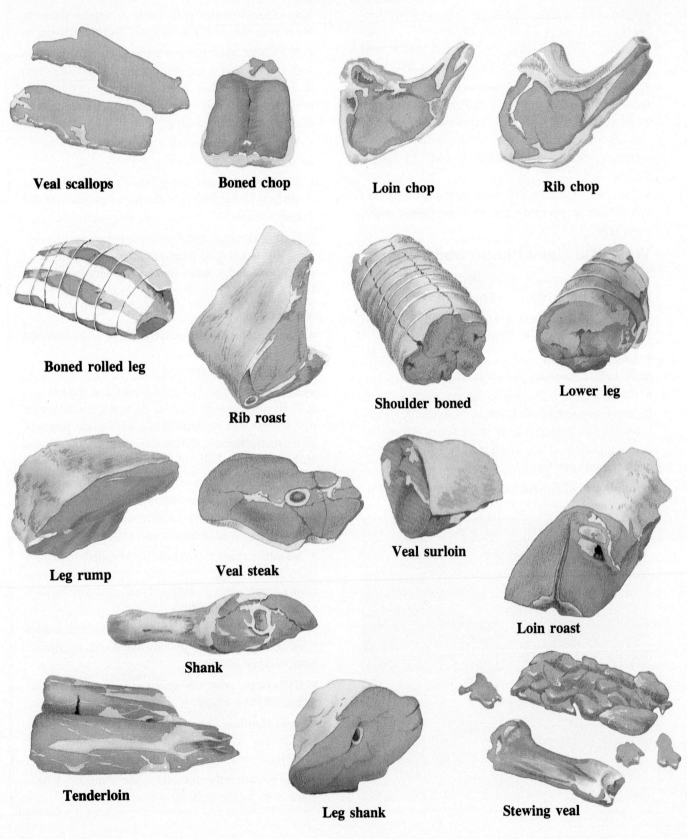

Veal scallops

Boned chop

Loin chop

Rib chop

Boned rolled leg

Rib roast

Shoulder boned

Lower leg

Leg rump

Veal steak

Veal surloin

Loin roast

Shank

Tenderloin

Leg shank

Stewing veal

Diagram of veal cuts

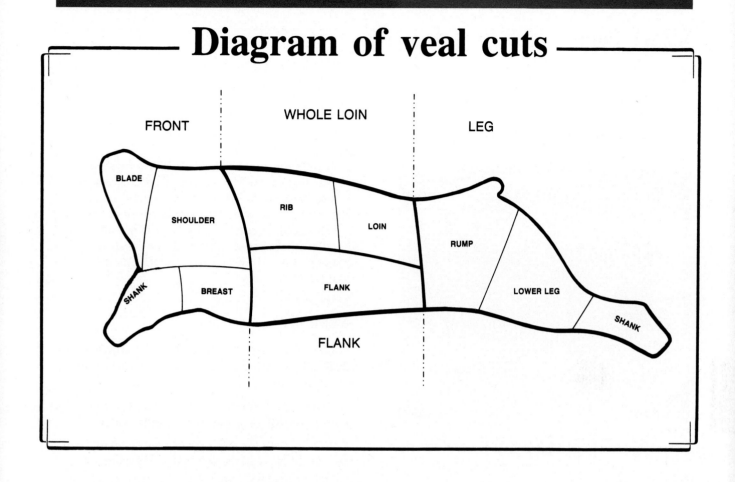

American cuts of veal

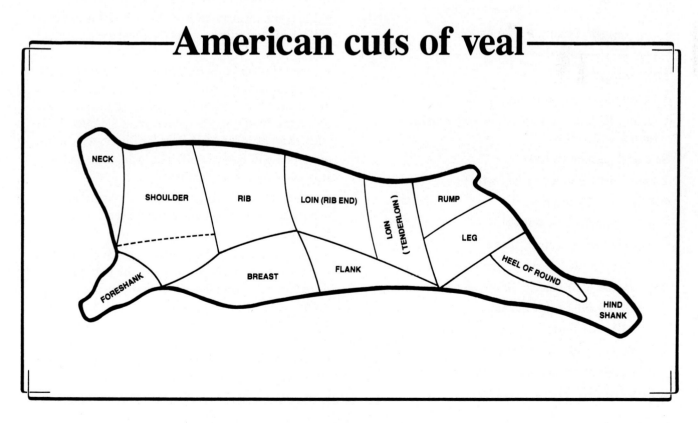

Slovina
Veal Roast

With temperature probe or comb

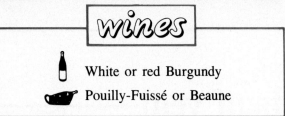

White or red Burgundy
Pouilly-Fuissé or Beaune

Ingredients:

4 bacon slices, cut into sticks

1   3-to-4-lb (1.5 - 2 kg) loin or leg roast, boned and rolled

Salt and pepper to taste

1 tsp (5 mL) marjoram or savory

1/4 tsp (1 mL) thyme

3 tbsp (50 mL) soft butter

1 cup (250 mL) onions, diced

1/2 cup (125 mL) carrots, grated

1/4 cup (60 mL) celery, thinly sliced

1/4 cup (60 mL) table cream

2 tsp (10 mL) flour

1/2 cup (125 mL) beef broth or white wine

1/2 lb (250 g) mushrooms, thinly sliced

3 tbsp (50 mL) parsley, minced

Preparation: . . . . **30 m**	
Cooking: the meal:. . . . . . . **from 27 to 36 m**	
the sauce: . . . . **7 m**	
Standing:. . . . .**none**	

A personal note: This is a Polish method of cooking a roast of veal in which the vegetables and meat juices make a creamy gravy. I cook this roast following the oven instructions given for medium beef. Usually, veal is not indicated even though it does cook very well in the microwave oven, no matter what method is used.

Method:

• Place the bacon pieces in a small microwave-safe dish, cover with hot water. Microwave 3 minutes at HIGH. Drain.

• Make 6 to 8 slits in the meat with the point of a knife, and fill each one with a little bacon.

• Mix together the salt, pepper, marjoram or savory and the thyme with the soft butter. Put a little in each slit and spread the remaining mixture over the roast.

• Place the meat in an 8 × 13-inch (20 × 33 cm) glass dish, and stir the vegetables and cream around it.

• Insert the temperature probe into the side of the meat, plug into the oven if you have a combination microwave-convection oven, place the meat on the low rack in the oven, program at "COMB" or "PROBE" at BEEF MEDIUM RARE. Start the oven; the probe will decide on the cooking time and will stop cooking automatically.

• When the roast is cooked, remove the probe with oven mitts, as it is hot, and place the roast on a plate. Keep warm.

• Pour the juice and vegetables from the baking dish in a food processor. Blend. Add the beef broth or the white wine; mix together. Add the sliced mushrooms and the minced parsley. Stir well and microwave 4 minutes at HIGH, stirring halfway through cooking.

• Add the puréed vegetables, mix together and microwave 3 minutes at HIGH.

• Serve separately in a sauceboat or pour around the meat.

Leg of Veal
À la Française

Convection cooking

A personal note: The upper part of the leg is more tender than the lower but is more difficult to carve. In roasting veal, there are two important factors to remember: Its fat content is lower and it has a higher proportion of muscular tissue than beef. Therefore, slow cooking is recommended for a veal roast. Well done, it will be brownish-red outside and greyish-white inside, and the internal juice will flow easily into the serving plate.

Ingredients:

1 4-to-5-lb (2 - 2.5 kg) leg of veal
2 - 3 garlic cloves, peeled and cut in two
1 tsp (5 mL) salt
1/2 tsp (2 mL) pepper
1 tsp (5 mL) thyme or tarragon
2 tbsp (30 mL) butter
3 tbsp (50 mL) margarine
Grated rind of half a lemon
2 tsp (10 mL) dry mustard
1 - 2 onions, peeled and thinly sliced

Preparation: . . . . **10 m**
Cooking: . . . . **from 1 h 40 to 2 h 05**
Standing: . . . . **none**

Method:

• Make slits in the meat and fill with garlic halves.

• Mix the remaining ingredients except the onions and spread over the meat.

• Preheat oven at 350°F (180°C). If you have a combination microwave — convection oven, place the meat on a rack with a pie plate underneath (See your oven operational manual on Convection Cooking.

• Microwave 25 minutes per pound (500 g). Baste twice during cooking with the juices accumulated in the plate, or with **1/4 cup (60 mL) brandy.**

Variation: Peel **6 medium potatoes** and **6 medium onions.** Spread **Kitchen Bouquet** over each, and place around the roast on the rack as you set the roast on it.

• The whole meal cooks to perfection all at once.

White Burgundy or Spanish Rioja red

Saint-Véran or château-bottled Saint-Émilion

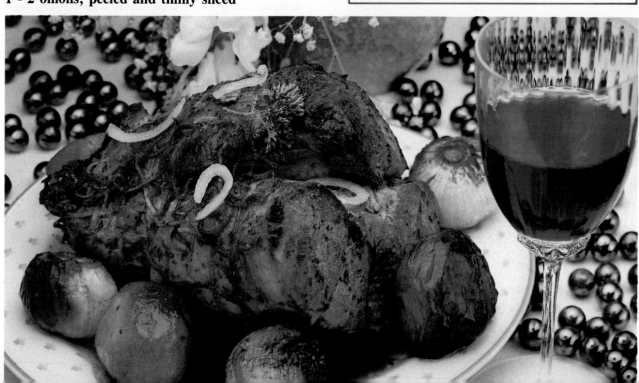

Rosemary Veal Roast

A personal note: This recipe produces a tender and juicy roast, light pink in the centre, as it should be. A mushroom sauce may be added to the meat juices just before serving.

Ingredients:

1 3-to-4-lb (1.5 - 2 kg) rib or shoulder roast, boned and rolled

1 tbsp (15 mL) olive oil or melted butter

1 tsp (5 mL) paprika

1 tsp (5 mL) Kitchen Bouquet sauce

1/2 tsp (2 mL) brown sugar

1/4 tsp (1 mL) pepper

1/2 tsp (2 mL) salt

1 garlic clove, chopped fine

1 tsp (5 mL) rosemary

Method:

• Mix the olive oil or melted butter with the paprika, Kitchen Bouquet and brown sugar.

• Crush together in a plate the salt, pepper, garlic and rosemary.

• Make incisions in the meat here and there with the point of a knife. Stuff each one with the mixture.

• Baste the roast with the oil mixture.

• Place the roast in an 8 × 8-inch (20 × 20 cm) ceramic or Pyrex baking dish. Cover with waxed paper.

• Microwave 5 minutes at HIGH. Turn the roast and baste with the pan juices.

• Then microwave 10 minutes per pound (500 g) at MEDIUM-HIGH.

• Turn the roast once again halfway through the cooking at MEDIUM-HIGH; baste all over and continue cooking.

• When cooked, place the roast on a warm platter, cover with aluminum foil and let stand in a warm place for 20 minutes. If you have a meat thermometer, insert it through the foil. It should register between 160°F and 170°F (82°C and 87°C) after a few minutes.

• To make gravy with the cooking juices, simply add **1/2 cup (125 mL) of a liquid of your choice — port, Madeira, chicken broth, cold tea or red wine.** Stir and microwave 2 minutes at HIGH.

wines

Saint-Émilion or (white) Vouvray

Californian Merlot or Australian Chardonnay

Lemon Braised Veal

Preparation: . . . . **20 m**
Cooking: . . . .**55 m**
Standing: . . . . **20 m**

A personal note: For me, this braised veal is "Paris in the spring." Easy to prepare, it is a recipe I adapted to the microwave oven a long time ago. In Paris, the dish is served with cubed potatoes browned in butter, then mixed with lots of parsley and chives, chopped fine, and a plain watercress salad.

Ingredients:

2 tbsp (30 mL) olive or vegetable oil

1 3-lb (1.5 kg) veal shoulder, rolled

Paprika

Salt and fresh ground pepper to taste

1/4 tsp (1 mL) mace

1/2 tsp (2 mL) tarragon

1 unpeeled lemon, thinly sliced

1 large tomato, diced small

1/2 tsp (2 mL) sugar

Method:

• Heat a browning dish 7 minutes at HIGH, pour oil into it and heat 2 minutes at HIGH.

• Pat the meat dry with absorbent paper. Place it in the hot oil, fat side down, without removing dish from oven. Brown 5 minutes at HIGH.

• Remove roast from dish, place in an 8 × 13-inch (20 × 33 cm) glass dish, the browned fat side on top. Sprinkle with paprika, salt, pepper, mace and tarragon. Top with lemon slices. Place the diced tomato around the meat, sprinkle with the sugar. Cover with plastic wrap. Microwave 20 minutes at HIGH.

• Stir the dish to move the juices in the bottom, but do not uncover the meat. Return to the oven and microwave 35 minutes at MEDIUM. Let stand 20 minutes in a warm place before serving.

• Remove the lemon slices. Place the juice in a bowl, add **2 tbsp (30 mL) cream or Madeira.** Mix well and heat 2 minutes at HIGH.

White Rhône
Condrieu

Veau dans le Chaudron

• This is an old Québec recipe, which I like very much. One day I tried it in the microwave oven, wondering what it would be like. To my surprise, it was superb.

Ingredients:

3 tbsp (50 mL) vegetable oil or bacon fat

2 garlic cloves, cut in two

1 3-to-4-lb (1.5 - 2 kg) veal leg or shoulder, boned and rolled

1 tbsp (15 mL) Kitchen Bouquet sauce

1 tsp (5 mL) salt

1/4 tsp (1 mL) pepper

1/2 tsp (2 mL) thyme

Preparation:	**20 m**
Cooking:	**from 40 to 50 m**
Standing:	**none**

1/4 tsp (1 mL) savory

1 bay leaf

6 medium potatoes, peeled

6 medium onions, peeled, whole

Method:

• Microwave the oil or the bacon fat 5 minutes at HIGH in an 8-cup (2 L) ceramic baking dish.

• Make incisions in the meat and stuff with the garlic.

• Baste the meat with the Kitchen Bouquet.

• Place it in the hot fat. Microwave 8 minutes at HIGH.

• Turn the meat, sprinkle top with salt, pepper, thyme, savory and bay leaf.

• Place the potatoes and onions around it. Cover and microwave 40 to 50 minutes at MEDIUM, or until the meat is tender.

• The shoulder will take a little longer to cook than the leg.

A personal note: There is no liquid to add to this recipe.

Cooked in this way, the meat has enough juice to make its own gravy. Some veal cuts release more moisture than others.

Should there be too much juice after cooking, simply remove roast to a warm plate, surround with the potatoes and onions. Keep in a warm place. Return the baking dish to the microwave oven, uncovered. Boil the juice 3 to 6 minutes at HIGH or until the desired consistency is reached. Serve in a sauceboat.

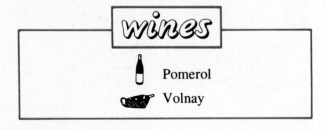

wines

🍾 Pomerol

🥢 Volnay

Veal Hash with Dumplings

Preparation: . . . . **30 m**
Cooking: . . . . **40 m**
Standing: . . . . **none**

• Dumplings cooked in the microwave oven are light and cook very fast. This dish is a complete meal — veal, vegetables, sauce, and the dumplings replacing potatoes.

Ingredients:

1/3 cup (80 mL) flour

1 tsp (5 mL) salt

1/4 tsp (1 mL) pepper

2 lb (1 kg) veal shoulder, cubed

3 tbsp (50 mL) vegetable oil or butter

1 cup (250 mL) celery, diced

6 small whole carrots *or*
   1 cup (250 mL) carrots, thinly sliced

2½ cups (625 mL) hot water or chicken broth

Dumplings:

1½ cups (375 mL) flour

1 tsp (5 mL) parsley, minced

1/2 tsp (2 mL) savory

2 tsp (10 mL) baking powder

1/2 tsp (2 mL) salt

2/3 cup (160 mL) milk

1 egg

2 tbsp (30 mL) vegetable oil

Method:

• Mix together the flour, salt and pepper. Roll the veal cubes in the mixture. Microwave 3 minutes at HIGH in an 8-cup (2 L) dish.

• Microwave the vegetable oil or the butter. Place the veal cubes in the hot oil, microwave 2 minutes at HIGH, stir, microwave again 2 minutes at HIGH.

• Add celery and carrots, stir. Add water or chicken broth. Cover and microwave 40 minutes at MEDI-UM, or until the meat is tender. Stir twice during cooking.

Prepare the dumplings as follows:

• Mix together in a bowl the flour, parsley, savory, baking powder and salt.

• Place in another bowl the milk, egg and oil. Mix the two together only when ready to add to the veal cooking juices.

• Remove the meat from the juices. Keep in a warm place.

• Mix together the ingredients in the two bowls just enough to blend. If stirred too much, the dumplings will not be as light. Drop into the broth with a tablespoon, all around the dish and in the centre. Cover and microwave 6 minutes at HIGH. They are cooked when the dumplings are no longer shiny.

• Place around the veal and pour the sauce over all.

wines

Chilled Beaujolais
Côte de Beaune-Villages

Veal Scallops, Tomato Sauce

Preparation: . . . . 10 m
Cooking: . . . . 15 m
Standing: . . . . none

A personal note: In this recipe, I use veal scallops cut from the mid-section of the leg (See Veal cuts), or 1-inch (2.5 cm) thick veal chops. Serve with noodles mixed with fried onions or parsley, or serve with mashed potatoes.

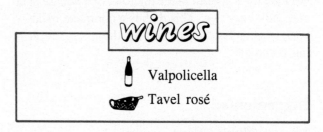

Valpolicella

Tavel rosé

Ingredients:

1/4 cup (60 mL) vegetable oil

1 garlic clove, chopped fine

4 to 6 small veal scallops or chops

1/2 tsp (2 mL) paprika

2 medium onions, thinly sliced

2 tbsp (30 mL) flour

1/2 tsp (2 mL) salt

1/4 tsp (1 mL) pepper

1/2 tsp (2 mL) basil

1 7½-oz (213 mL) can tomato sauce

1/2 cup (125 mL) water or white vermouth

Method:

• Preheat a browning dish (Corning) 7 minutes at HIGH. Add the oil; heat 2 minutes at HIGH.

• Brush one side of the scallops or chops with the paprika. Without removing the dish from the oven, place the meat in the hot oil, paprika side down. Press each piece of meat down with the fingers for good contact with the bottom of the dish. Microwave 3 minutes at HIGH.

• Turn the meat, add the garlic and onions, microwave 1 minute at HIGH. Remove the scallops or chops from the dish, and add the flour, salt, pepper and basil to the fat; stir. Add tomato sauce, water or vermouth, mix well. Microwave 4 minutes at HIGH, stir. Add the veal, browned side on top, and make sure the bottom part is in the sauce. Microwave 3 minutes at MEDIUM and serve.

Breaded Veal Chops

Advance preparation: . . . . 30 m
Cooking:. .6 m
Standing: . . . . 10 m

A personal note: Veal chops prepared in this manner are golden and crisp. I remove them from the refrigerator one hour before cooking.

I coat them with breadcrumbs and let them stand on absorbent paper for 30 minutes. I prefer to bone the chops but they also cook very well with the bone.

Method:

• Mix in a plate the flour and paprika. Roll each chop in the mixture to coat well.

• Beat the egg with the milk in a large plate.

• Mix the rosemary or tarragon and breadcrumbs in another plate.

• Dip each chop in the milk mixture, then roll it in the breadcrumbs and herbs. Let stand 30 minutes.

• Preheat a browning dish (Corning) 7 minutes at HIGH.

• Add the butter, which will brown very fast.

• Without removing the dish from the oven, place one chop at a time in the dish, pressing each chop down for perfect contact with the hot butter. Microwave at HIGH 3 minutes, plus 3 minutes at MEDIUM.

• Turn the chops and let stand 10 minutes at room temperature, without cooking.

• Serve with a sauce of your choice.

Ingredients:

4 to 6 veal loin chops, 1/2-inch (1.5 cm) thick

3 tbsp (50 mL) flour

1 tsp (5 mL) paprika

1 egg, beaten

2 tbsp (30 mL) milk

2/3 cup (160 mL) fine breadcrumbs

1/2 tsp (2 mL) rosemary or tarragon

2 tbsp (30 mL) butter

wines

🍾 Dolcetto

Alsatian Pinot Noir

Veal Printanier

• In this recipe — one of the roster of old Québec recipes — a piece of veal shoulder is simmered in a light white sauce until it's perfectly cooked.

Preparation: . . . . **30 m**
Cooking: . . . . **from 45 to 50 m**
Standing: . . . .**none**

Ingredients:

2 tbsp (30 mL) veal fat or butter

2-lb (1 kg) veal shoulder, cut in small pieces

1 tsp (5 mL) paprika

3 tbsp (50 mL) butter

3 tbsp (50 mL) flour

3 cups (750 mL) milk

1/2 tsp (2 mL) thyme and 1 bay leaf

1/4 tsp (1 mL) marjoram

1/2 lb (250 g) mushrooms, thinly sliced

10 to 12 small white onions, peeled, whole

2 carrots, thinly sliced

1 cup (250 mL) fresh or frozen green peas

Method:

• Microwave the 2 tbsp (30 mL) fat or butter 3 minutes at HIGH in a 6-cup (1.5 L) ceramic baking dish. The butter should brown lightly; microwave one minute more if necessary.

• Sprinkle meat with paprika, place in the browned butter, stir and microwave 5 minutes at HIGH.

• To make a white sauce, place the butter in a 4-cup (1 L) glass measuring cup and microwave 2 minutes at HIGH. Add the flour and mix together.

• Add the milk, mix, then microwave 2 minutes at HIGH. Stir, microwave 2 minutes more at HIGH. Stir, and continue in this manner until you have a light white sauce.

• Salt and pepper to taste and add the thyme, bay leaf and marjoram. Mix together. Pour over the meat. Stir, cover and microwave 8 minutes at HIGH.

• Add the mushrooms, onions, carrots and green peas*. Mix well together. Cover and microwave 35 to 40 minutes at MEDIUM.

• Serve with parsleyed rice or fine noodles and a bowl of grated cheese, allowing each person to help himself.

Frozen green peas are just as good as fresh peas in this recipe.

Helpful Hint: To soften cream cheese or butter, microwave a 3-ounce (90 g) package of cream cheese or 1/4 pound (125 g) of butter 30 seconds to 1 minute at LOW.

 White Burgundy or Beaujolais

 Californian Chardonnay or Fleurie

Veal Shank Osso Bucco

Preparation: . . . . 20 m
Cooking: . . . . 1 h 10 m
Standing: . . . . 10 m

• Full of flavor, easy and economical, this is the Italian method for cooking veal shanks.

A personal note: It is perfect served with a dish of parsleyed long grain rice.

Ingredients:

5 to 6 pieces of veal shank, 2 in. (5 cm) each

1/2 cup (125 mL) browned flour

1/3 cup (80 mL) vegetable or olive oil

2 medium onions, chopped fine

1/2 cup (125 mL) celery, diced

1/2 cup (125 mL) sliced mushrooms

3 tbsp (50 mL) parsley, minced

1 large carrot, grated

2 garlic cloves, chopped fine

1 tsp (5 mL) oregano or basil

1/2 cup (125 mL) white wine or vermouth

1 19-oz (540 mL) can of tomatoes

Grated rind of one lemon

1 cup (250 mL) chicken broth

1/2 tsp (2 mL) sugar

wines

Chianti
Barolo

Method:

• Roll each piece of shank in the browned flour.

• Microwave the oil in an 8-cup (2 L) ceramic dish 5 minutes at HIGH.

• Place the meat pieces in it side by side and micro-wave, uncovered, 5 minutes at HIGH. Turn the meat.

• Add the remaining ingredients. Cover and micro- wave 1 hour at MEDIUM, turning the meat twice during the cooking.

• When cooked, remove meat from dish and keep in a warm place.

• Continue cooking the sauce 8 to 10 minutes at HIGH or until it becomes very smooth.

• Coat the meat with the sauce.

Calves' Brains in Browned Butter

Advance preparation: . . . . .1 h
Cooking: the meal: . . . . .4 m
          the butter: . . . . .5 m
Standing: . . . . 2 m

• Known as a great favorite among amateur gourmets, this is a very easy dish to cook in the microwave oven. The only garnish required is a few pickled capers.

Ingredients:

3 to 4 calves' brains

3 cups (750 mL) cold water

3 tbsp (50 mL) vinegar of your choice

2 bay leaves and 2 whole garlic cloves

1 tsp (5 mL) salt

10 peppercorns

2 cups (500 mL) hot water

3 tbsp (50 mL) butter

1 tbsp (15 mL) parsley, minced

1 tsp (5 mL) pickled capers

Method:

• Soak the calves' brains one hour in the cold water and vinegar.

• Drain and remove the red veins and small black spots on top of the brains (this is easy to do).

• Place them in a clean dish with the bay leaves, garlic, salt, peppercorns and hot water.

• Cover and microwave 4 minutes at HIGH. Let stand in cooking water 2 minutes, drain and place on a warm dish.

• Put the butter in a ceramic dish and microwave at HIGH 3 to 5 minutes, or until the butter is dark brown. It is important to watch closely, as browning time may vary with different brands of butter.

• Add the parsley and capers.

• Pour very hot over the brains and serve.

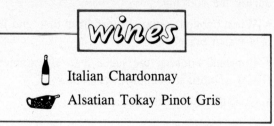
Italian Chardonnay
Alsatian Tokay Pinot Gris

Veal Meat Loaf

Preparation:	**20 m**
Cooking:	**from 20 to 22 m**
Standing:	**10 m**

A personal note: If your oven has an Auto Sensor system or Insta-matic, program it as indicated in your operational manual. The oven will decide on the cooking time. If you use this method, it is important to cover the mold with plastic wrap.

Ingredients:

1½ lb (750 g) veal, ground

1 egg, lightly beaten

1/2 cup (125 mL) stale bread, crushed

1/3 cup (80 mL) chili sauce

1/2 cup (125 mL) onion, chopped fine

2 garlic cloves, chopped fine

1 tsp (5 mL) thyme or tarragon

Grated rind of one lemon

Salt and pepper to taste

1/4 tsp (1 mL) nutmeg or mace

Method:

• In a bowl, mix together all the ingredients, except the nutmeg or mace. When thoroughly mixed, pack into an 8 x 4-inch (20 x 10 cm) mold. Sprinkle top with nutmeg or mace. Cover with waxed paper. Microwave 20 to 22 minutes at MEDIUM-HIGH.

• When serving hot, let stand 10 minutes before serving. To serve cold, cover well and refrigerate 12 hours before serving.

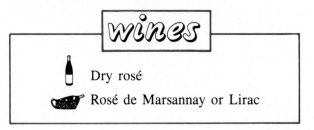

Dry rosé

Rosé de Marsannay or Lirac

Venitian Calf Liver

Preparation:	**10 m**
Cooking:	**7 m**
Standing:	**none**

• I have not yet met the person who does not like calf liver who tried this dish and didn't love it. It is perfect with mashed potatoes and an endive or crisp Boston lettuce salad.

Ingredients:

1 lb (500 g) calf liver

3 tbsp (50 mL) butter

2 cups (500 mL) onions, thinly sliced

1 tsp (5 mL) salt

1/4 tsp (1 mL) pepper

2 tbsp (30 mL) white wine or Madeira or lemon juice

1 tbsp (15 mL) parsley, minced

Method:

• Slice the liver as thinly as possible, then cut it into strips.

• Preheat a browning dish (Corning) 7 minutes at HIGH, and melt the butter in it without removing it from the oven. Add the onions, mix and microwave 3 minutes at HIGH. Add the salt and pepper.

• Add the liver strips, stir. Microwave 2 minutes at HIGH, stir and microwave another 2 minutes at HIGH.

• Add the white or Madeira wine or the lemon juice, together with the parsley and microwave 1 minute at HIGH. Stir and serve.

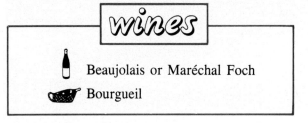

Beaujolais or Maréchal Foch

Bourgueil

Homemade Foie Gras

Convection cooking

> **A personal note:** This "pâté" is at its best when made with calf liver. When that is too expensive, use half calf liver and half lamb or beef liver. The foie gras keeps 8 to 15 days in the refrigerator, tightly covered.

Advance preparation: . . . . **24 h**	
Cooking: . . . . **1 h 20 m**	
Standing: . . . . **none**	

Ingredients:

1 lb (500 g) calf, beef or lamb liver or a mixture of two

1/2 lb (250 g) ground pork

1 envelope dehydrated onion soup mix

2 eggs

1½ cups (375 mL) table cream

1 tsp (5 mL) pepper

2 tsp (10 mL) salt

1 cup (250 mL) flour

4 to 5 bay leaves

4 slices of bacon (optional)

Method:

• Chop the liver and the pork very fine, using a meat grinder or processing it for 40 seconds in a food processor.

• Add the remaining ingredients, except the bacon slices.

• Mix well until creamy. Line the bottom of a Pyrex bread pan with 2 slices of bacon.

• Fill with the liver mixture. Top with 2 more slices of bacon.

• If you have a combination microwave-convection oven, preheat the convection oven at 350°F (180°C).

• Place the pan on the low rack. Cook 1 hour and 20 minutes or until the top is well browned.

• Cool, cover and refrigerate 24 hours before serving.

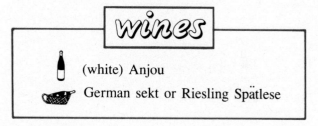

wines

(white) Anjou

German sekt or Riesling Spätlese

• When you're cooking lamb, as with all kinds of meat, it is important to be familiar with the different cuts and to know what type of cooking applies to each for perfect results.

• Color and texture are very important when you're buying lamb. Young, quality lamb will have firm, smooth, tender, whitish pink fat. The flesh will be firm to the touch, never flabby or tough, and the bones will be moist and pinkish.

• The weight of a leg is a good indication of its quality. To be "perfect," it should weigh from 4 to 5 pounds (2 to 2.5 kg). If it's much heavier than that, the leg will have too much fat and the meat won't be as delicately flavored or as tender.

The cuts

• A lamb carcass is split into two equal portions through the back to create a fore quarter, which is the neck end, and a hind quarter, or leg.

The fore quarter

• **The neck** is cut just in front of the shoulder and usually is 1-inch (2.5 cm) thick. This is a tender and tasty meat for making delicious casseroles and soups.

• **The shoulder** is the front leg of the lamb. (It is the back leg that is the true "leg of lamb.") From the shoulder are cut steaks, ones with round bones and ones with long bones. The shoulder is boned and

rolled to make a roast. Boned and unrolled, it can be marinated for a delicious roast, cubed for tasty stews or put through the meat grinder for ground lamb.

• **The fore shanks** are the two front legs of the lamb, which can be simmered or made into delicious casserole dishes.

The hind quarter

• **The rack and loin chops** are the two cuts most in demand.

• **The whole loin** contains the loin chops and the rib section, which consists of 12 ribs. It is a deluxe cut.

• **The leg** can be cut in two, providing the top of the leg and a hind shank roast, which usually is smaller than the top end and therefore less expensive. Both are very tender.

Cooking a leg of lamb

• Since lamb is a red meat like beef, it can be roasted and is at its best rare or medium. Well done lamb is neither as good nor as tender.

• To check for doneness, check the roasted lamb with a thermometer after you take it out of the microwave oven. (DO NOT USE AN ORDINARY MEAT THERMOMETER WHILE COOKING IN YOUR MICROWAVE OVEN.)

• 145°F (63°C) on the thermometer indicates rare.

• 155°F (68°C) on the thermometer indicates medium.

Lamb can be roasted by microwave

• By convection

• With a temperature probe.

• By Auto Sensor or by weight.

• Some microwaves offer all of these methods, others only one or two.

• Here again, it's very important to read your oven manual so you will be aware of all of its features.

Lamb cuts

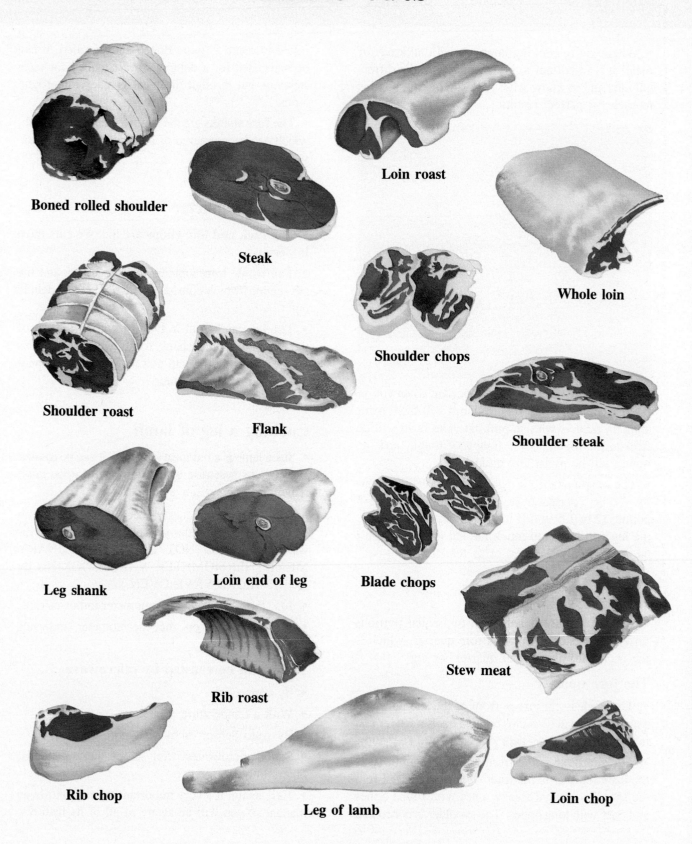

Boned rolled shoulder

Loin roast

Steak

Whole loin

Shoulder chops

Shoulder roast

Flank

Shoulder steak

Leg shank

Loin end of leg

Blade chops

Stew meat

Rib roast

Rib chop

Leg of lamb

Loin chop

Diagram of lamb cuts

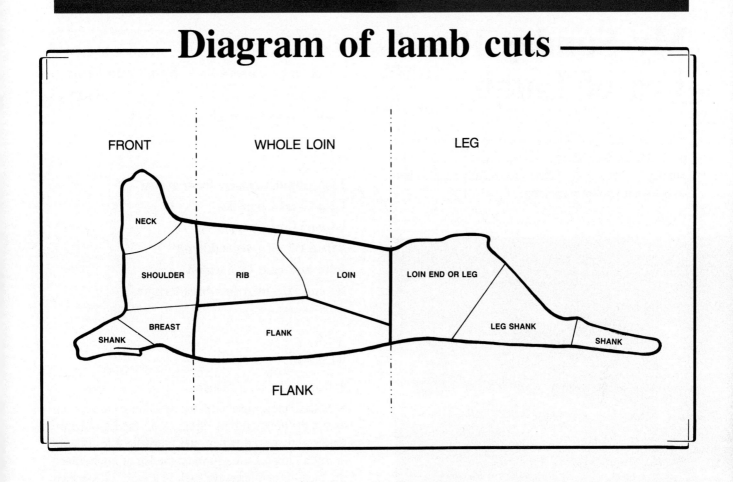

FRONT | WHOLE LOIN | LEG

NECK

SHOULDER | RIB | LOIN | LOIN END OR LEG

BREAST | FLANK | LEG SHANK

SHANK | | SHANK

FLANK

American cuts of lamb

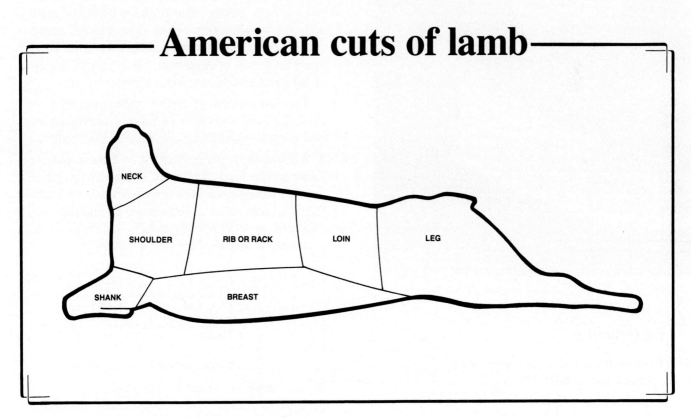

NECK

SHOULDER | RIB OR RACK | LOIN | LEG

SHANK | BREAST

My Sunday Roast Leg of Lamb

Advance preparation: . . . . . **from 4 to 5 h**
Cooking: . . . . **from 42 to 60 m**
Standing: . . . . **15 m**

• My mother often served a roast of lamb, to everyone's delight. Our favorite was the one she called "My Sunday Leg of Lamb." I have successfully adapted her recipe to microwave cooking.

2 tsp (10 mL) ginger, fresh grated
1 tsp (5 mL) paprika
1/4 tsp (1 mL) pepper
1 tbsp (15 mL) vegetable oil
Juice and rind of 1 lemon
1/2 cup (125 mL) fine breadcrumbs

Method:

• Place meat on a platter.

• Make a clear paste with the remaining ingredients, except the breadcrumbs. Spread over the leg of lamb. Cover with waxed paper, and marinate 4 to 5 hours at room temperature. To roast the leg of lamb, place the meat on a microwave rack in a glass 12 x 8-inch (30 x 20 cm) baking dish. Sprinkle fat top of roast with the breadcrumbs. Then pour the remaining marinating mixture into the baking dish. Cover bone tips with a strip of aluminum foil to prevent drying of the meat around the bones during cooking.

• Roast 10 minutes at HIGH, then lower heat to MEDIUM and roast 8 to 10 minutes, depending on whether you wish to have your roast rare or medium.

• When cooked, place the roast on a warm platter. Cover and let stand 15 minutes. In the interval, make gravy by adding to the juice in the baking dish **1/2 cup (125 mL) cold coffee or red wine** or **1/4 cup (60 mL) Madeira or "White Brandy."** Stir well. Heat 3 minutes at HIGH. Pour into a sauceboat.

Ingredients:

1 4-to-5-lb (2 - 2.5 kg) leg of lamb, boned and rolled
1 garlic clove, crushed

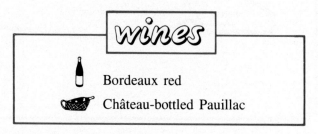

wines

Bordeaux red
Château-bottled Pauillac

Rosemary Roast of Lamb

Convection cooking

Preparation: . . . . **10 m**
Cooking: . . . . **from 20 to 60 m**
Standing: . . . . **15 m**

A personal note: Rosemary and basil are without doubt the best flavoring herbs for roasted lamb. In Italy, the combination of rosemary and garlic is used.

Ingredients:

1 4-to-5-lb (2 - 2.5 kg) leg of lamb

1 tsp (5 mL) pepper, freshly ground

1 tsp (5 mL) ginger, freshly grated

2 tsp (10 mL) rosemary

1 tsp (5 mL) basil

1 tbsp (15 mL) vegetable oil

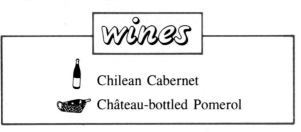

wines

🍷 Chilean Cabernet

🥘 Château-bottled Pomerol

1/4 cup (60 mL) fine breadcrumbs

Method:

• Preheat the convection section of your microwave oven at 375°F (190°C) (check for procedure in your oven operational manual).

• Place a rack in the oven ceramic tray with a pie plate underneath.

• Mix all the ingredients together and spread on top of the roast, then set it on the rack.

• Microwave 15 minutes per pound (500 g) at 375°F (190°C) for medium and 5 minutes per pound (500 g) for medium-rare.

• Let stand 15 minutes in a warm place before serving.

To make gravy

• Add to the juice in the plate **1/3 cup (80 mL) red wine or chicken broth.**

• Scrape the bottom of the plate and crush all the browned bits. Microwave 1 minute at HIGH.

• Pour into a sauceboat.

English Glazed Roast of Lamb

With temperature probe

> **A personal note:** A boned and rolled lamb shoulder can be prepared and cooked the same way as a leg of lamb. When using a temperature probe, all you have to do is prepare the meat, insert the probe in the meat and plug it into the oven, select the desired degree of cooking, e.g. MEDIUM-RARE for the leg, and MEDIUM for the shoulder. The oven decides on the cooking time and will automatically stop cooking when the roast is done.

Preparation:	. . . . **15 m**
Cooking:	. . . . **from 45 to 60 m**
Standing:	. . . . **none**

Ingredients:

1 leg or half a leg of lamb *or*
  1 boned and rolled lamb shoulder
Grated rind of 1 orange
Juice of 2 oranges
Juice of 1 lemon
1/4 cup (60 mL) soft butter
1/4 cup (60 mL) fresh mint, chopped fine
1 tsp (5 mL) paprika
1/4 tsp (1 mL) pepper

Method:

• Place the meat in a 9 × 12-inch (23 × 30 cm) glass dish. Mix the remaining ingredients. Spread over the meat. Wrap the tip of the leg with a strip of aluminum foil.

• Insert the temperature probe into the side of the roast (read instructions given in your oven operation manual), plug opposite end into the oven. Select desired cooking.

• Baste meat twice during cooking.

Note: If you have a combination microwave-convection oven, place the ready-to-cook roast on the low rack included with your oven accessories.

To make gravy

• Remove cooked roast to a warm platter.

• Add to the juice in the baking dish **1/3 cup (80 mL) cold tea.** Stir well to crush the brown caramelized bits in the bottom of the dish, which give color and flavor to the gravy. Microwave 2 minutes at HIGH.

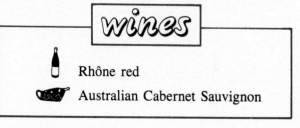

Rhône red
Australian Cabernet Sauvignon

Portuguese Leg of Lamb

Preparation: . . . . **10 m**
Cooking: . . . . **from 38 to 48 m**
Standing: . . . . **15 m**

A personal note: The combination of Madeira, garlic and lemon rind gives this roast a very distinct flavor. Serve with long grain rice boiled with grated carrots, green peas and diced green onions.

wines

Dao red

Portuguese garrafeira

Ingredients:

1/4 cup (60 mL) Madeira or dry sherry

1 tbsp (15 mL) paprika

2 tbsp (30 mL) Kitchen Bouquet sauce

2 tbsp (30 mL) vegetable oil

2 garlic cloves, minced

Rind of 1 lemon

1 3-to-4-lb (1.5 - 2 kg) leg of lamb or shoulder boned and rolled

Method:

• Mix together the first 6 ingredients in a microwave-safe measuring cup. Microwave 2 minutes at MEDIUM-HIGH.

• Place the roast on a microwave rack, place in a 12 × 8-inch (30 × 20 cm) glass dish.

• Baste the roast all over with the hot mixture. Microwave 8 minutes at HIGH, then baste the meat thoroughly with the juice in the bottom of the dish.

• Microwave 10 minutes per pound (500 g) at MEDIUM-HIGH.

• When cooked, place on a hot platter, cover and let stand 15 minutes.

To make gravy

• Add to the cooking juices **1/3 cup (80 mL) consommé or cream or coffee.** Mix well. Microwave 1 minute at HIGH when ready to serve.

Curried Poached Leg of Lamb

Preparation: . . . . 30 m

Cooking: . . . . from 60 to 70 m

Standing: . . . . 15 m

A personal note: This dish is wonderful at any temperature. Served hot, it's golden and well-flavored. I also like to slice it thinly and serve at room temperature. And it makes an excellent cold meat for a buffet, with fruit chutney and a curried rice salad.

Ingredients:

1 whole or half a leg of lamb, boned and rolled

1 garlic clove, quartered

1 tbsp (15 mL) rosemary

1 tsp (5 mL) salt

1/2 tsp (2 mL) pepper

1 tbsp (15 mL) curry powder

6 medium carrots, whole

6 celery stalks, diced

8 to 10 medium potatoes

10 small white onions

1/2 cup (125 mL) water

1/2 cup (125 mL) cider or apple juice

Method:

- Make 4 to 5 slits in the meat. Stuff each one with a piece of garlic and a pinch of rosemary.

- Mix together the salt, pepper and curry powder. Sprinkle on top of the roast.

- Place the meat in the centre of a glass or ceramic dish, with a lid if possible. Place the vegetables around the meat.

- Pour the water and the cider or apple juice over the vegetables. Cover with waxed paper or plastic wrap or the lid from the dish. Microwave 20 minutes at HIGH, then turn the meat. Cover and microwave 10 minutes per pound (500 g) at MEDIUM.

- Let stand 15 minutes before removing lid.

- To serve, place the vegetables around the roast and the gravy in a sauceboat.

Zinfandel or white Rhône

Châteauneuf-du-Pape or white Hermitage

Poached, Glazed Lamb Shoulder

Advance preparation: . . . . **5 to 6 h**
Cooking: . . . . **65 m**
Standing: . . . . **20 m**

A personal note: The mint or currant jelly glaze gives a special flavor to the meat. The shoulder can also be served without the glaze.

Ingredients:

1 2-to-3-lb (1 - 1.5 kg) lamb shoulder, rolled
1/4 cup (60 mL) butter or margarine
2 garlic cloves, finely chopped
1 tsp (5 mL) thyme
1 tbsp (15 mL) flour
1 tsp (5 mL) salt
1/4 tsp (1 mL) pepper
Rind of 1 lemon
1 tbsp (15 mL) lemon juice
1/2 cup (125 mL) mint or currant jelly

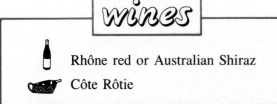

Rhône red or Australian Shiraz
Côte Rôtie

Method:

• Cream together the butter or margarine, garlic, thyme, flour, salt, pepper and lemon rind. Spread over the meat. Place in an 8 × 12-inch (20 × 30 cm) glass dish. Cover with waxed paper and refrigerate 4 to 5 hours.

• Remove from refrigerator and let stand one hour on kitchen counter. Do not remove liquid that may have accumulated in the bottom of the dish.

• Cover with plastic wrap. Microwave 15 minutes at HIGH, then reduce to MEDIUM and microwave 50 minutes. Turn the meat and let stand 20 minutes in the juice.

To glaze

• Remove meat from baking dish.

• To the liquid in the dish add the lemon juice and the mint or currant jelly. Stir well. Do not cover, microwave at HIGH 2 to 4 minutes, or until the juice thickens, stirring twice during the cooking.

• Pour over the meat and baste it 7 or 8 times.

• If necessary, heat roast 3 minutes at MEDIUM.

• Serve hot with boiled rice garnished with green peas.

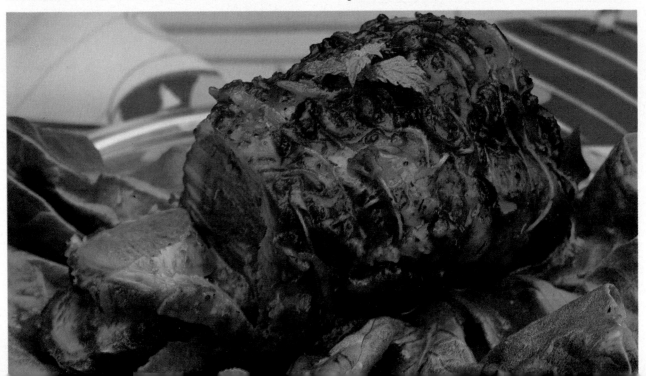

West Indian Lamb Shoulder

Microwave or convection cooking

Advance preparation: . . . . **24 h**
Cooking: convection: . . . . **1 h 15**
         microwave: . . . .**1 h**
Standing: . . . . **15 m**

A personal note: This is one of my family's favorite meals, which I serve with curried fried rice and parsleyed cauliflower.

Ingredients:

1 3-lb (1.5 kg) lamb shoulder, boned and rolled

4 garlic cloves, finely chopped

1/2 cup (125 mL) boiling water

1/3 cup (80 mL) honey

1/2 cup (125 mL) soy sauce*

Juice of 1 orange

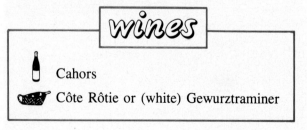

wines

Cahors

Côte Rôtie or (white) Gewurztraminer

Method:

• Mix together in a large bowl the garlic, boiling water, honey and soy sauce.

• Roll the meat in the mixture, cover and refrigerate 24 hours before cooking.

• Remove meat from marinade. Place in an 8 × 13-inch (20 × 33 cm) glass dish.

• Add 1/2 cup (125 mL) of the marinade. Cook according to one of the two following methods:

Convection:

• Preheat the oven at 350°F (180°C) and roast 25 minutes per pound (500 g).

OR

Microwave:

• Cover the meat with plastic wrap.

• Microwave 15 minutes at HIGH. Turn the roast and baste with the juices.

• Cover and microwave 15 minutes per pound (500 g) at MEDIUM.

• Let stand 15 minutes before serving.

To make gravy

• Whether the shoulder of lamb is cooked by convection or microwave, gravy is prepared the same way.

• Remove the roast from the dish, then add the orange juice to the liquid in the dish. As much as **1/3 cup (80 mL) Sake (Japanese wine)** may be added. Stir well.

• Microwave 2 minutes at HIGH when ready to serve.

• Pour into a sauceboat.

* Japanese soy sauce is more delicate in flavor than Chinese soy sauce, but either one can be used.

Lamb Chops Maison

Preparation: . . . . **7 m**
Cooking: . . . . **6 m**
Standing: . . . . **10 m**

• With a browning dish, you can cook lovely, golden chops in the microwave oven. To my taste, they are perfect.

Ingredients:

4 lamb chops
1/2 tsp (2 mL) sugar
1/2 tsp (2 mL) paprika
1/2 tsp (2 mL) rosemary or basil
1 tbsp (15 mL) of fat removed from chops

wines

Spanish red
Californian Merlot

Method:

• Preheat browning dish (Corning) 7 minutes at HIGH.

• Mix together the sugar, paprika, rosemary or basil. Rub each chop with the mixture.

• Without removing the browning dish from the oven, place the pieces of fat in it. Spread in the dish with a fork and place in the center.

• Set each chop in the dish, pressing it down with the finger tips.

• Brown 6 minutes at HIGH.

• Turn the chops and let stand 10 minutes in the dish without cooking (internal heat will finish the cooking).

• Serve.

Lamb Meat Balls

Lamb Meat Loaf

Preparation: . . . .**5 m**
Cooking: . . . . **8 m**
Standing: . . . . **none**

Preparation: . . . .**15 m**
Cooking: . . . .**20 m**
Standing: . . . .**20 m**

A personal note: Make small meat balls to serve hot as appetizers or divide the ground lamb into four portions and serve as lamb patties.

A personal note: This meat loaf can be served hot, but it is especially good cold. When cooked, cover it with waxed paper and place a weight over the paper. I have a brick that I keep for this purpose. Place a brick or a heavy object over the waxed paper, and cool. Refrigerate until ready to serve.

Ingredients:

1 lb (500 g) ground lamb

1/4 cup (60 mL) soy sauce*

1 garlic clove, chopped fine

1 tbsp (15 mL) vegetable oil

1/3 cup (80 mL) plum sauce, Oriental

Ingredients:

1½ lb (750 g) ground lamb

1½ cups (375 mL) rice, cooked

1/2 cup (125 mL) tomato juice

2 eggs, lightly beaten

2 garlic cloves, minced

1 tsp (5 mL) salt

1/2 tsp (2 mL) sugar

1 small onion, chopped fine

2 tbsp (30 mL) chili sauce

4 slices of bacon

Method:

• Mix together in a bowl the ground lamb, soy sauce and garlic. Make into small meat balls or four patties, depending on how you wish to serve them.

• Microwave the vegetable oil 3 minutes at HIGH in a ceramic dish. Sprinkle the meat balls or the patties with paprika. Pour them into or place them in the hot oil. Microwave the meat balls 5 minutes at HIGH, stirring twice. Microwave the patties 3 minutes at HIGH. Turn, then microwave 2 minutes at HIGH.

• Add the plum sauce to the meat balls, shaking the dish to coat them with the sauce. Heat 2 minutes at HIGH. Stir and serve.

• For the patties, baste the top of each with the plum sauce, then baste with some of the juice accumulated in the bottom of the dish. Cover with waxed paper and microwave 3 minutes at HIGH. Serve.

Japanese soy sauce is more delicate in flavor than Chinese soy sauce, but either one can be used.

Method:

• Mix all the ingredients together except the bacon. Place in an 8 × 4 × 2½-inch (20 × 10 × 6.25 cm) microwave-safe loaf pan. Pack down.

• Place the bacon slices on top. Microwave 10 minutes at HIGH. Microwave another 10 minutes at MEDIUM. Let stand 20 minutes.

• Cover with waxed paper and place a weight on top. Refrigerate when cooled.

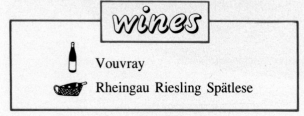

Vouvray

Rheingau Riesling Spätlese

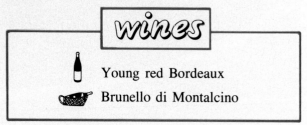

Young red Bordeaux

Brunello di Montalcino

Baked Lamb Liver

Convection cooking

Preparation: . . . . **10 m**
Cooking: . . . . **from 30 to 40 m**
Standing: . . . . **10 m**

A personal note: A whole 1 - 2-lb (500 g - 1 kg) lamb liver roasted in one piece is excellent served hot or cold. Slice it thinly and serve it hot with its sauce; cold, with a cranberry sauce, or hot with chutney to taste.

Hot service

Cold service

Ingredients:

3 tbsp (50 mL) butter

1 large onion, thinly sliced

1 small green pepper, slivered

2 tbsp (30 mL) chili sauce

1 tbsp (15 mL) A-1 sauce

1/4 tsp (1 mL) thyme

1 1½-to 2-lb (500 g - 1 kg) whole lamb liver

1/3 cup (80 mL) Port or cold coffee

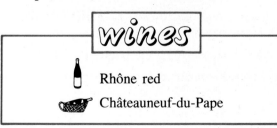

wines

🍾 Rhône red

🥘 Châteauneuf-du-Pape

Method:

• If you have a combined microwave-convection oven, preheat the convection section at 350°F (180°C).

• Melt the butter 3 minutes in an 8 × 8-inch (20 × 20 cm) ceramic dish or 2 minutes in a small metal saucepan of the same size. Or melt the butter 2 minutes at HIGH in a ceramic dish.

• Add the onion, stir well and microwave 4 minutes at HIGH. The onion will brown lightly here and there. Stir, add the green pepper, stir and microwave 1 minute at HIGH.

• Place the low rack in the preheated 350°F (180°C) oven. Add the remaining ingredients to the onion and green pepper. Set the lamb liver in the centre and baste with the vegetables and juice in the bottom of the dish. Roast 30 to 40 minutes in the preheated oven.

• Let stand 10 minutes. Baste 7 or 8 times during that time.

• Slice thinly and serve with its sauce.

Scottish Lamb Casserole

Preparation: . . . . **15 m**
Cooking: . . . . **from 40 to 50 m**
Standing: . . . . **10 m**

A personal note: This dish can be prepared with pieces of lamb neck, leg or shoulder steak, cubed or thinly sliced.

Ingredients:

2 tbsp (30 mL) butter or bacon fat

2 onions, peeled and thinly sliced

2 lb (1 kg) lamb of your choice, cubed

1 tsp (5 mL) salt

1/4 tsp (1 mL) pepper

1/4 tsp (1 mL) allspice

1 19-oz (540 mL) can tomatoes

2 tsp (10 mL) sugar

2 cups (500 mL) bread cubes

1/4 tsp (1 mL) aniseed

1/2 tsp (2 mL) salt

1 tbsp (15 mL) butter

Method:

• Heat the butter or the bacon fat 4 minutes at HIGH.

• Add the onions, stir well and microwave 3 minutes at HIGH.

• Stir and add the cubed lamb. Stir together. Microwave 3 minutes at HIGH.

• Mix together the salt, pepper and allspice. Sprinkle over meat. Stir.

• Mix together the sugar and tomatoes. Pour over the meat.

• Stir the bread cubes with the 1/2 tsp (2 mL) salt and the aniseed. Sprinkle over the whole.

• Dot with butter. Cover with lid or plastic wrap. Microwave 10 minutes at HIGH.

• Uncover and microwave at MEDIUM 20 to 25 minutes or until the meat is tender.

• Check doneness with the point of a knife.

• Let stand 10 minutes in a warm place before serving.

Barbaresco

Amarone

Country Casserole

Preparation: . . . . 20 m
Cooking: . . . . 15 m
Standing: . . . . none

- A meal-in-a-dish

Ingredients:

1 lb (500 g) ground lamb
1/2 tsp (2 mL) basil
1/4 tsp (1 mL) pepper
1/2 tsp (2 mL) salt
4 slices of bacon
4 small potatoes
4 small fresh tomatoes
1 cup (250 mL) corn kernels
2 tbsp (30 mL) cheese, grated

Method:

- Mix together the lamb, basil, salt and pepper. Make into four patties. Wrap a slice of bacon around each patty, holding it with a wooden pick. Sprinkle with paprika.

- Microwave the potatoes 6 minutes at HIGH. Remove from oven and place on absorbent paper.

- Remove pulp from tomatoes and sprinkle inside with salt, pepper and a pinch of sugar.

- Divide the corn equally among the tomatoes.

- Preheat a browning dish (Corning) 7 minutes at HIGH. Without removing it from the oven, place the meat patties in the dish, paprika side down. Press each patty down with the finger tips for perfect contact between meat and dish. Microwave 4 minutes at HIGH.

- Turn the patties, place the cooked potatoes and stuffed tomatoes all around. Cover the dish with waxed paper, microwave 4 to 5 minutes at MEDIUM-HIGH. Serve.

A personal note: You can use canned well-drained corn kernels or you can use frozen corn cooked before cooking the patties. Microwave approximately 1 cup (250 mL) of corn, covered, without water, 4 minutes at HIGH. Drain and use.

 Red Bordeaux or red Rioja
Saint-Estèphe

Fore Shanks with Beer

Preparation: . . . . **10 m**
Cooking: . . . . **from 45 to 65 m**
Standing: . . . . **none**

A personal note: It is not easy to find small 1-to-2-lb (500 g — 1 kg) lamb shoulder shanks. Order them ahead of time from your butcher. They are economical, tender and easy to cook.

wines

Bordeaux
Médoc

Ingredients:

2 garlic cloves, cut in three

2 to 3 shoulder shanks

3 tbsp (50 mL) bacon fat

3 tbsp (50 mL) flour

Salt and pepper to taste

1 tsp (5 mL) savory

1/4 cup (60 mL) beer of your choice

1 tsp (5 mL) sugar

2 bay leaves

Juice and rind of one lemon

Method:

• Make slits in the meat and place a sliver of garlic into each.

• Mix together the flour, salt, pepper, savory. Coat the shanks thoroughly with the mixture.

• Heat a browning dish (Corning) 7 minutes at HIGH. Without removing the dish from the oven, add the bacon fat, then place the floured shanks one next to the other in it. Brown 5 minutes at HIGH.

• Turn each piece of meat.

• Add the beer, sugar, bay leaves, lemon juice and rind. Cover and microwave 10 minutes at HIGH.

• Remove the shanks to another dish, pour the gravy all around. Cover and microwave 30 to 40 minutes at MEDIUM. Halfway through the cooking, baste the meat with the cooking juices.

• It is sometimes necessary to allow an extra 10 to 12 minutes of cooking if the meat is less tender.

To make gravy

• Add **1/4 cup (60 mL) water or cold tea** to the juices in the dish. Stir well and heat 2 minutes at HIGH when ready to serve.

Helpful hint: To make garlic butter, peel and split 3 garlic cloves in two, then microwave them with 1 cup (250 mL) butter or margarine 3 minutes at MEDIUM-HIGH. Let stand 18 minutes. Remove garlic. Pour butter into glass jar. Cover, refrigerate. The garlic butter will keep for months. When needed for buttering bread, seasoning steak or flavoring chicken, simply take out the amount you need.

• Pork is the most inexpensive meat, and it has many possibilities to offer. Pork can be fresh or smoked and there are a great variety of cuts. Its mild flavor blends well with sage, aniseed, fennel, Juniper berries, thyme, marjoram, garlic, onion and apples. The choice is wide and varied.

Pork cuts

• **The loin roast** can be divided into two parts — the tenderloin end and the mid-section. The tenderloin end is the meaty part of the loin and contains most of the tenderloin and some bones. But it is also the least meaty part when the tenderloin is removed and is sold separately.

• The mid-section is less meaty than the tenderloin end and contains rib bones, T-shaped bone and little or no tenderloin. It is sold as roast or chops.

• **The loin roast rib end** contains the ribs, a portion of the blade bone but no tenderloin. It is cut into roast or chops.

• **The tenderloin** is a choice cut, sometimes difficult to find, which is long, lean, tapered and very tender. It can be roasted whole or cut into 1-inch (2.5 cm) slices and flattened with a meat mallet for delicious, tender grilled meat.

• **The shoulder roast** is an economical cut. Sold fresh, it is cut as roasts or into cubes for stewing; smoked, it is sold as picnic ham.

• **Butt shoulder chops**, which contain part of the long bone and rib bones, are good for braising.

• **Picnic shoulder chops** are the arm chops — they're cut from the shoulder — and are easy to recognize by the round bone at the top. They are very tender and make good steaks.

Pork chop cuts

• Pork chops have always been a family favorite, and their price is usually reasonable.

• When you're buying pork chops, look for the meat to be firm, tender, pink in color and to have a good rim of fat. The bones should be porous and pink.

• There are various kinds of pork chops. It's important to be able to recognize them, as both price and cooking method vary.

• Pork chops, like beef, are cut from both the loin and the rib end of the loin.

Make the most out of a loin of pork

1 4-lb (2 kg) bone-in pork loin roast

• To get the most out of it, cut it up in the following manner:

a) Bone the roast and use the bones for Bavarian Sauerkraut Dumplings.

b) Remove 2 chops and mince them for use in a spaghetti sauce.

c) Roll and tie the remaining roast and cook it by convection at 165°F (78°C), with baked potatoes.

• If you wish to have 4 to 6 servings, add 1-lb (500 g) pork loin, stir-frying it.

Pork cuts

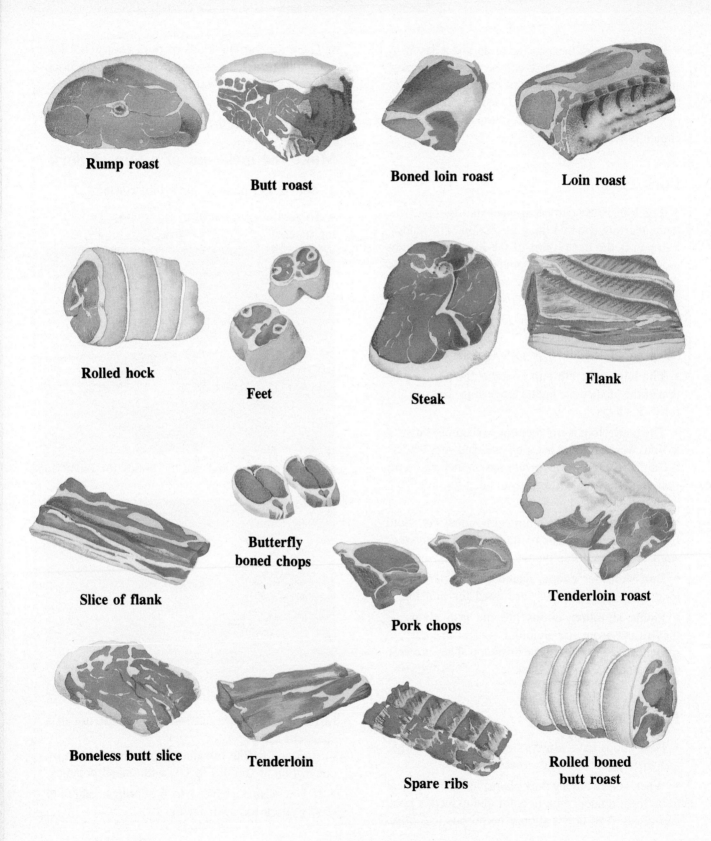

Rump roast

Butt roast

Boned loin roast

Loin roast

Rolled hock

Feet

Steak

Flank

Slice of flank

Butterfly
boned chops

Pork chops

Tenderloin roast

Boneless butt slice

Tenderloin

Spare ribs

Rolled boned
butt roast

Diagram of pork cuts

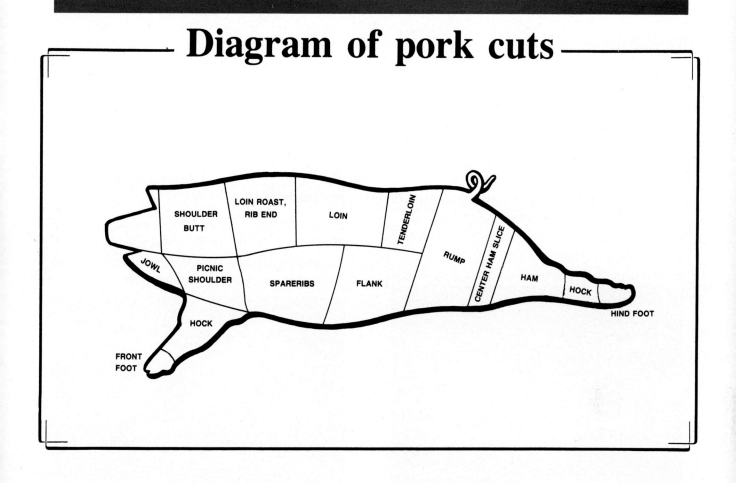

American cuts of pork

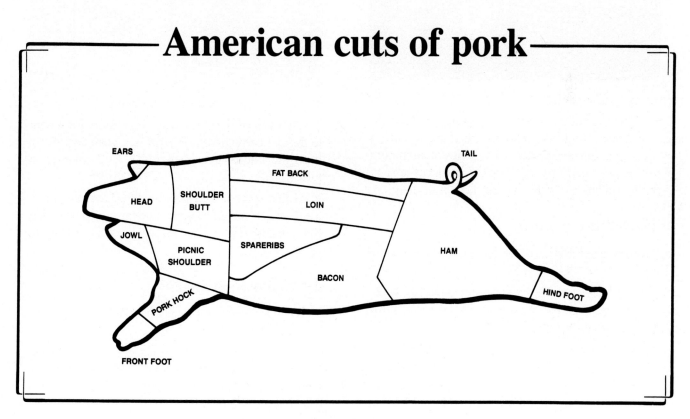

To defrost pork

• I may be of the old school, but I still prefer to defrost roasts by placing them, wrapped, in a cool place for 10 to 12 hours, or in the refrigerator for 24 hours. Then I let the meat stand for 1 or 2 hours on the kitchen counter. Defrosted this way, the meat relaxes, the fibres become tender, excess moisture evaporates — and it cooks perfectly.

• Remember that boneless, rolled roasts take longer to defrost than bone-in roasts.

• It's important to turn rolled roasts twice during the defrosting process.

• Well thawed pork will feel cold to the touch and

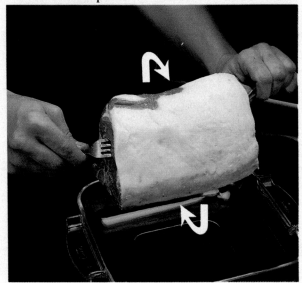

the fat will be shiny.

• If the piece of the meat is irregularly shaped, with visible bone tips, the tips must be shielded during cooking in the microwave oven. Strips of aluminum foil on the bone tips will prevent the meat next to the bones from drying out and becoming tough.

To defrost a roast

• Place the wrapped frozen roast in the microwave oven.

• Calculate 10 to 12 minutes per pound (20 to 25 minutes per kg) and microwave on DEFROST for half the required time.

• Unwrap the meat and check whether some spots are warmer than others. Cover the warm spots with pieces of foil.

• Turn the roast, place it on a microwave rack and

DEFROST for the other half of the required time.

• I like to insert a wire tester in the middle of the roast to ensure that it is completely defrosted.

• Cover with a cloth and let stand 20 to 30 minutes before serving.

To defrost chops, meat cubes and ground pork

• Calculate 4 to 8 minutes per pound (10 to 20 minutes per kg) on the DEFROST cycle.

• Place the frozen meat in the microwave oven and DEFROST for half the required time.

• Unwrap and break the meat apart.

• Let the meat stand at room temperature for 1 hour to defrost completely, or set it in a plate and return it to the microwave oven for 1 or 2 minutes at DEFROST.

• At this stage it's easy to break up the remaining meat, which should be pink. The fat should be white; if it's transparent, it means the meat is starting to cook.

To defrost sausages

• Calculate 3 to 4 minutes per pound (6 to 10 minutes per kg).

• Place the wrapped frozen sausages in the oven and DEFROST for 1 minute. Turn the package, then continue to DEFROST. The sausages are defrosted when they can be separated.

Hints on roasting pork in a microwave oven

- As with the other kinds of meat, it's important that you know the cuts of pork and the best way to cook each one to ensure flavor and tenderness.

- In microwave cooking — as in any other type of cooking — the weight, shape of the meat and tenderness of the cut all play an important role. Pork roasts and chops will be more tender and will brown better if they've been allowed to reach room temperature before they're cooked.

Microwave pork roasting chart

Piece of meat	Weight	Cooking time	Cooking temperature
Loin **Bone-in loin**	3 to 5 lb (1.5 to 2.5 kg)	13 to 15 m/lb (27 to 30 m/kg)	MEDIUM
Boneless loin	3 to 5 lb (1.5 to 2.5 kg)	13 to 15 m/lb (27 to 30 m/kg)	MEDIUM
Shoulder **Butt**	3 to 5 lb (1.5 to 2.5 kg)	16 to 18 m/lb (40 m/kg)	MEDIUM
Boneless shoulder		16 to 18 m/lb (40 m/kg)	MEDIUM
Fresh leg *Roast only one half at a time (shank or upper end of the leg)*	2.5 to 3 lb (1 to 1.5 kg)	16 to 18 m/lb 40 m/kg)	MEDIUM

* It is best to have pork roast rolled and boned for perfect cooking in the microwave oven although bone-in roasts do cook well.

Loin of Pork, Kentish

With temperature probe

> **A personal note:** This is an old English recipe that I cook in the microwave oven using a temperature probe. (If your oven has a probe, see your oven operation manual for how to use it.) In my oven, I use the C.5 setting indicated for pork. The oven then takes over as to cooking time.

Ingredients:

1/2 cup (125 mL) sherry
1/4 cup (60 mL) brown sugar
Grated rind of one orange
1/3 cup (80 mL) orange juice
1 tsp (5 mL) prepared horseradish
1 tsp (5 mL) prepared mustard
1 4-lb (2 kg) loin of pork

Preparation: . . . . **7 m**
Cooking: the meal: . . . . **1 h 30 m**
          the sauce: . . . . **1 m 30 s**
Standing: . . . . **none**

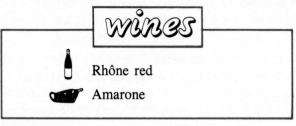

Rhône red
Amarone

Method:

• Place the first 6 ingredients in a 4-cup (1 L) microwave-safe bowl. Microwave 3 minutes at HIGH.

• Place the roast in a 9 × 12-inch (23 × 30 cm) glass or ceramic dish, with bones in the bottom.

• Pour the hot mixture over all.

• Place a rack in the oven ceramic tray with a plate underneath.

• Insert the temperature probe into the roast and plug it in the oven.

• Touch the PORK setting and start the oven. The oven will decide as to the time.

• When the meat is cooked, remove from dish. Add **1/3 cup (80 mL) cold water** to the cooking juice, stir well. Heat at HIGH 1 minute 30 seconds.

Boned and Rolled Loin of Pork with Mustard

Preparation: . . . . 15 m
Cooking: . . 14 m + 13 m per pound (500 g)
Standing: . . . . 10 m

wines

Red Bordeaux or Spanish white
Saint-Estèphe or Californian Chardonnay

A personal note: 1 3-to-4-lb (1.5 – 2 kg) boned and rolled roast is the perfect cut for microwave roasting. The roast will be well browned and cooked to perfection. When possible, let the meat stand one hour at room temperature before cooking.

Ingredients:

1 3-to-4-lb (1.5 - 2 kg) loin roast, boned and rolled

2 tbsp (30 mL) vegetable oil

1/2 cup (125 mL) fine breadcrumbs

2 tbsp (30 mL) French mustard

1/4 tsp (1 mL) pepper

1 tsp (5 mL) paprika

2 garlic cloves, chopped fine

9 cloves

Method:

• Pat the roast dry with absorbent paper.

• Microwave vegetable oil 4 minutes at HIGH in an 8 × 8-inch (20 × 20 cm) glass dish.

• Mix together the remaining ingredients, except the whole cloves. Spread part of the mixture over the meat. Do not spread any on the fat. Place the fat part of the roast in the hot fat. Microwave 10 minutes at HIGH.

• Turn the roast and place it on a microwave rack, fat on top. Push the cloves into the fat. Cover the fat with the remaining breadcrumbs. Microwave at MEDIUM 13 minutes per pound (27 minutes per kg).

• Set the roast on a platter. Cover with waxed paper and let stand 10 minutes before serving.

• Salt and carve.

Pork Loin Maison

Convection cooking

> **A personal note:** This recipe produces a loin of pork that is well browned and delicious. It is equally good hot or cold. The loin of pork can be roasted with the bone, too.

Ingredients:

1 3-lb (1.5 kg) loin of pork, boned and rolled
1 cup (250 mL) fine breadcrumbs
2 tsp (10 mL) paprika
1 tsp (5 mL) savory

Preparation:	**10 m**
Cooking:	**18 m per pound (500 g)**
Standing:	**15 m**

1 tsp (5 mL) salt
1/4 tsp (1 mL) pepper
1/2 tsp (2 mL) garlic powder
2 tbsp (30 mL) melted margarine
1 egg white, lightly beaten
1 tbsp (15 mL) cold water

Method:

• Mix together the breadcrumbs, paprika, savory, salt, garlic powder and pepper. Add the melted margarine. Mix the egg white and the cold water in another bowl.

• If you have a combination microwave-convection oven, place a rack in the oven ceramic tray with a pie plate under the rack. Or follow directions given in your oven operation manual for setting the rack.

• Preheat oven at 375°F (190°C).

• Roll the roast in the egg white and then in the breadcrumbs mixture.

• When the oven is hot, set the roast on the rack and roast at 375°F (190°C) 18 minutes per pound (36 minutes per kg).

• When cooked, place the roast on a hot dish, cover and let stand 15 minutes.

To make gravy

• Add the juice accumulated in the plate, **1/2 cup (125 mL) of either apple juice, cider, cold tea or white wine.**

• Stir well while scraping the bottom of the plate. Add **1 tsp (5 mL) cornstarch or flour.**

• Mix well and microwave 2 minutes at HIGH. Stir and serve.

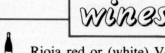

 Rioja red or (white) Verdicchio

Château-bottled Saint-Julien or (white) Saint-Véran

Normandy Loin of Pork

Preparation:	. . . .	**20 m**
Cooking: the meal:	. . . .	**1 h**
the sauce:	. . . .	**3 m**
Standing:	. . . .	**none**

A personal note: A mixture of vegetables cooked with the roast, then put through a food processor, serves to thicken the gravy for this roast. The mixture of the fat and the orange juice gives a delicate flavor.

Ingredients:

1   **3-lb (1.5 kg) loin of pork, boned**

2 **tbsp (30 mL) butter**

2 **medium onions, diced**

3 **medium carrots, peeled and diced**

1 **leek, cleaned and sliced**

1 **garlic clove, minced**

1 **small parsnip, peeled and thinly sliced**

1 **tsp (5 mL) thyme**

2 **tsp (10 mL) salt**

1/2 **tsp (2 mL) pepper**

1/4 **cup (60 mL) Port wine**

Juice and grated rind of 2 oranges

1 **orange, peeled and thinly sliced**

Method:

• Place the butter in a 6-cup (3 L) microwave-safe dish and melt 3 minutes at HIGH. Place the roast in it, fat side down. Microwave 5 minutes at HIGH. Remove roast from dish. Place the minced vegetables in the baking dish, stir. Microwave 5 minutes at HIGH, stirring once during the cooking.

• Add the thyme, salt and pepper; stir. Set the meat over the mixture, the bones touching the bottom of the dish.

• Add the Port wine, orange juice and rind. Cover and microwave 30 minutes at MEDIUM. Check for doneness; if necessary, microwave 10 minutes more at MEDIUM.

• When cooked, place the roast on a warm service dish. Purée the vegetable mixture in a food processor or blender.

• Add **1/4 cup (60 mL) tea or water** and the **thin orange slices.** Cover and microwave 3 minutes at HIGH, stirring once halfway through the cooking.

• Pour a few spoonfuls over the roast. Serve remaining gravy in a sauceboat.

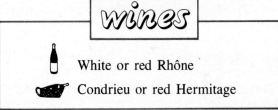

wines

White or red Rhône

Condrieu or red Hermitage

Roasted Boneless Loin of Pork

Convection cooking
with temperature probe

Preparation: . . . . **5 m**
Cooking: . . . . **with temperature probe**
Standing: . . . . **15 m**

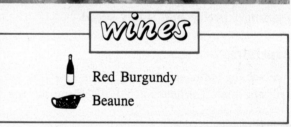

Red Burgundy

Beaune

Ingredients:

1   3-to-4-lb (1.5 - 2 kg) boned and rolled loin roast

3 tbsp (50 mL) bacon fat or margarine

1 tsp (5 mL) dry mustard

1 garlic clove, minced

1/4 tsp (1 mL) black pepper

1 tsp (5 mL) savory or sage

6 potatoes

1 tsp (5 mL) coarse salt

A personal note: Study the instructions in your oven manual for cooking by convection with probe, which could differ slightly from ordinary convection cooking. It is easy to adapt as the preparation does not change.

Method:

• Cream together the bacon fat or margarine, mustard, garlic, black pepper, savory or sage. Spread on top of roast.

• If you have a combination microwave-convection oven, place a rack in the oven ceramic tray with a pie plate under the rack. Set roast on rack, insert probe in top of oven and in meat. Select the appropriate cooking cycle by reading your oven manual. The oven decides the cooking period. Let stand 15 minutes, covered.

• Rub potatoes with a little fat, then roll in coarse salt. Place around the roast.

Roast of Pork with Sauerkraut

Preparation: . . . . 10 m
Cooking: . . . . 1 h 15 m
Standing: . . . . 20 m

A personal note: This is a favorite Alsatian dish for which you can use the cut of your choice. Personally, I prefer a bone-in pork rib. This dish reheats very well. I often cook it a day ahead, then need only warm it up. Use the REHEAT cycle, if your oven has one, or 10 to 20 minutes at MEDIUM.

wines

Gewurztraminer

Rheingau Riesling Spätlese

Ingredients:

1   3-to-4-lb (1.5 - 2 kg) pork roast

1   32-oz (909 mL) jar of sauerkraut with wine

2 onions, cut in four

1 garlic clove, finely chopped

1 tsp (5 mL) salt

10 juniper berries (optional)

12 peppercorns

6 medium potatoes, peeled

1/2 cup (125 mL) white wine or water

Method:

• Place the pork roast in a ceramic dish with cover.

• Mix the sauerkraut with the remaining ingredients, except the potatoes. Place all around the roast.

• Add the white wine or water. Bury the potatoes in the sauerkraut.

• Cover tightly and microwave 1 hour and 15 minutes at MEDIUM.

• Let stand 20 minutes before serving.

Pork Roast Fines Herbes

Convection cooking

A personal note: Your oven may offer convection cooking under a different name, for instance, Insta-matic. This is why I emphasize the importance of clearly understanding your oven's operation manual.

Ingredients:

1 **3-to-4-lb (1.5 - 2 kg) pork loin roast, boned**

2 tbsp (30 mL) flour

3 tbsp (50 mL) vegetable oil

1 tsp (5 mL) paprika

1/4 tsp (1 mL) each thyme and oregano

1/2 tsp (2 mL) fennel seeds or aniseed

1/4 tsp (1 mL) black pepper

1/2 tsp (2 mL) salt

Method:

- Mix the flour with the next 6 ingredients, which will give you a light batter.
- Baste the top and sides of the roast with it.
- Place a rack in your oven.

Preparation:	. . . .	**10 m**
Cooking:	. . . .	**1 h 30 m**
Standing:	. . . .	**20 m**

- Place a plate under the rack (or follow directions in your operation manual).

- Roast at 350°F (180°C) 1 hour and 30 minutes.
- Remove roast from the oven, set on a hot dish. Cover and let stand 20 minutes.

- Remove rack.
- To the juice accumulated in the plate — add **1/3 cup (80 mL) cold coffee or tea or red wine.**
- Stir well, crushing the small brown particles that add color and flavor to the gravy.
- Heat 2 minutes at HIGH and serve with the roast.

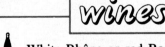

 White Rhône or red Bordeaux

White Châteauneuf-du-Pape or Château-bottled Saint-Émilion

Roast of Pork Boulangère

Preparation: . . . . **10 m**
Cooking: . . . . **1 h**
Standing: . . . . **15 m**

• A meal-in-one, the roast cooks surrounded with potatoes and onions, all deliciously flavored with sage and marjoram. Of course, you can cook the pork without the potatoes and onions. Serve with a gravy of your choice. (See chapter on sauces.)

Ingredients:

1   3-to-4-lb (1.5 - 2 kg) roast of pork, boned and rolled

1 tsp (5 mL) paprika

1 tbsp (15 mL) vegetable oil

3 tbsp (50 mL) fine breadcrumbs

1 tsp (5 mL) sage

2 tbsp (30 mL) butter

4 medium potatoes, peeled and thinly sliced

4 medium onions, peeled and thinly sliced

1 bay leaf

1/2 tsp (2 mL) marjoram

1 tsp (5 mL) salt

1/2 tsp (2 mL) fresh ground pepper

Method:

• Mix together the paprika, vegetable oil, breadcrumbs and sage. Roll the roast in this mixture.

• Preheat a browning dish (Corning) 7 minutes at HIGH. Without removing the dish from the oven, set the roast in it, fat side down. Brown 6 minutes at HIGH.

• Turn the roast and cook 25 minutes at MEDIUM. Remove the roast from the dish.

• Melt the butter in the dish, 1 minute at HIGH. Add the potatoes and onions.

• Add the bay leaf, marjoram, salt and pepper. Mix well and place in a circular pattern around the dish.

• Place the roast in the middle. Roast, uncovered, 20 minutes at MEDIUM-HIGH.

• Let stand 15 minutes before serving.

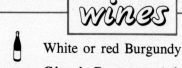

 White or red Burgundy

Côte de Beaune or (white) Rhine Riesling Kabinett

Pork Shoulder Roasted in a Bag

Preparation:	**15 m**
Cooking:	**1 h 15 m**
Standing:	**20 m**

A personal note: This is actually a braised roast. If you don't have a cooking bag, place the meat in a deep baking dish and cover it with plastic wrap. Serve the roast with frozen or canned corn kernels and mashed potatoes.

3 sprigs of fresh parsley

1 leek, cut in three

1/2 cup (125 mL) white vermouth or chicken consommé

1 tbsp (15 mL) cornstarch

1/2 cup (125 mL) cold water

Method:

- Mix together the rosemary or sage, salt and pepper. Brush over the meat.

- Place it in a plastic cooking bag.

- Add onions, carrot, parsley, leek and the white vermouth or consommé.

- Tie the bag with a string, not too tightly.

- With the point of a knife, make 2 or 3 cuts in the top of the bag.

- Put in a 9 × 13-inch (23 × 33 cm) glass dish. Microwave 15 minutes at HIGH.

- Move the bag while holding it with a cloth, so as to stir the juice inside. Microwave 15 minutes per pound (500 g) at MEDIUM.

- Let the roast stand in the bag for 20 minutes.

- Cut a corner of the bag with scissors to let the juice run into the baking dish. Place the roast on a platter without removing it from the bag. Keep in a warm place.

- Dilute the cornstarch in the water and add it to the juice in the baking dish. Stir well, then cook 1 minute at HIGH. Stir and cook 1 minute more, if necessary, for a light, transparent gravy.

- Place the roast and vegetables on a serving dish and serve hot with the hot gravy.

Ingredients:

1 tsp (5 mL) rosemary or sage

1/2 tsp (2 mL) salt

1/4 tsp (1 mL) pepper

1 4-lb (2 kg) boned pork shoulder

2 medium onions, cut in four

1 carrot, peeled and cut in four

Red Bordeaux

Château-bottled Médoc

Spanish Roast of Pork

Preparation: . . . . **15 m**
Cooking: . . . . **1 h 05 m**
Standing: . . . . **20 m**

A personal note: A pork roast orange glazed half-way through cooking. I like to use this recipe for half a leg of fresh ham, butt end. Superb cold, it is like a glazed smoked ham, a fine piece for a buffet.

Ingredients:

1   3-to-4-lb (1.5 - 2 kg) half leg of fresh ham
1/2 tsp (2 mL) ground ginger *or*
   1 tbsp (15 mL) fresh ginger, grated
1 tsp (5 mL) paprika

The glaze:

1/2 cup (125 mL) marmalade
3/4 cup (200 mL) orange juice
Grated rind of one orange
2 tbsp (30 mL) cornstarch
1/2 tsp (2 mL) salt
1/2 tsp (2 mL) powdered ginger
1 cup (250 mL) fresh grapes, cut in half
1/3 cup (80 mL) orange liqueur or brandy

Method:

• Mix together the ginger and the paprika.
• Brush the top of the roast with the mixture.

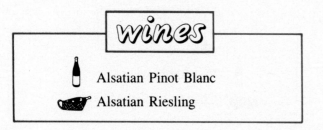

wines

Alsatian Pinot Blanc
Alsatian Riesling

• Set the roast on a microwve rack in a glass baking dish. Microwave 30 minutes at MEDIUM, then remove from oven.

• Mix the glaze ingredients in a 4-cup (1 L) measuring cup.

• Remove roast and rack from baking dish.

• Pour the glaze mixture into the dish. Microwave 5 minutes at HIGH, stirring twice during the cooking.

• Return the roast to the dish and spoon the glaze over it for 1 or 2 minutes.

• Cover with plastic wrap. Microwave another 30 minutes at MEDIUM, or until a thermometer put into the roast to test it when it's outside of the oven registers 165°F (75°C). After 15 to 20 minutes standing time, covered with waxed paper, the temperature will rise to 170°F (80°C).

• Baste the roast 4 to 5 times with the glaze. Serve with parsleyed rice or a barley casserole.

Pork Chops or Steak

Preparation:	**5 m**
Cooking:	**15 m**
Standing:	**3 m**

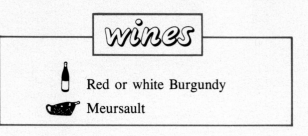

Red or white Burgundy
Meursault

A personal note: For chops more than 1-inch (2.5 cm) thick, add 3 minutes more at MEDIUM-HIGH.

This recipe will work for steaks or chops; only the cooking time varies.

Ingredients:

4 loin or rib pork chops, 1-inch (2.5 cm) thick
1 tbsp (15 mL) vegetable oil
1 tsp (5 mL) paprika
1 tsp (5 mL) savory or sage
1/2 tsp (2 mL) salt
1/4 tsp (1 mL) pepper
1/2 tsp (2 mL) sugar

Method:

• Preheat an 8 × 8-inch (20 × 20 cm) browning dish (Corning) 7 minutes at HIGH.

• Mix the remaining ingredients together.

• Dip one side of the chops into the mixture, using your fingers to make it stick to the meat. Without removing the hot browning dish from the oven, place the chops in, flavored side in the bottom. Brown 4 minutes at HIGH. Turn the chops and finish cooking 3 minutes at MEDIUM-HIGH.

• Let stand 3 minutes and serve.

Chinese Pork Chops

Preparation: . . . . 15 m
Cooking: .25 m
Standing: .none

A personal note: This dish, inspired by Chinese cooking, is delicious when prepared with thinly sliced pork chops, which are often offered as supermarket specials. Remove bones and cut in strips.

Ingredients:

1 lb (500 g) thin chops or pork shoulder

2 tbsp (30 mL) vegetable oil

1 garlic clove, minced

1 tsp (5 mL) salt

1/4 tsp (1 mL) pepper

1 10-oz (284 mL) can pineapple chunks

1/2 cup (125 mL) barbecue or plum sauce

1 tbsp (15 mL) cornstarch

2 tbsp (30 mL) soy sauce

1 green pepper, slivered

Method:

• Cut the meat diagonally into thin slices.

• Heat the vegetable oil 3 minutes at HIGH in an 8 × 8-inch (20 × 20 cm) ceramic dish.

• Place the meat in the hot oil. Mix well and microwave 2 minutes at HIGH. Salt and pepper.

• Add the juice drained from the pineapple, the garlic and barbecue or Chinese plum sauce. Mix well.

• Cover and microwave 15 minutes at MEDIUM.

• Mix the cornstarch with the soy sauce. Add to the meat together with the green pepper.

• Stir well and microwave 5 minutes at MEDIUM.

• Stir halfway through the cooking.

• Serve with boiled rice.

 Liebfraumilch

 Tokay Pinot Gris Vendange Tardive

Normandy Pork Chops

A personal note: In Normandy, this recipe is made with a cider with a very high alcohol content. I have replaced it with brandy. Serve the chops with wild rice or mashed potatoes.

Preparation: . . . . **15 m**	
Cooking: the meal: . . . . **from 35 to 40 m**	
the sauce: . . . . **7 m**	
Standing: . . . . **none**	

Ingredients:

6   1-inch (2.5 cm) thick pork chops

1/4 cup (60 mL) flour

Salt and pepper to taste

1/2 tsp (2 mL) thyme

1/2 tsp (2 mL) paprika

2 tbsp (30 mL) butter

8 to 12 prunes, pitted

1 cup (250 mL) Port wine

2 tbsp (30 mL) each brandy and
   whipping cream

Method:

• Soak the pitted prunes 15 minutes in hot water. Drain thoroughly.

• Mix together the flour, salt, pepper and thyme in a large plate. Roll the chops in the mixture to coat well, then sprinkle each with paprika.

• Place the butter in an 8 × 8-inch (20 × 20 cm) ceramic dish and melt 3 minutes at HIGH. Add the chops. Microwave 4 minutes at MEDIUM-HIGH, turn. Cover the dish with plastic wrap and microwave the chops 20 minutes at MEDIUM. Check for doneness; if necessary, microwave another 5 minutes.

• Add the Port wine to the prunes and heat together 4 minutes at HIGH. Remove the chops from the dish, keep in a warm place, and add the brandy to the meat juice. Microwave 1 minute at HIGH.

• Add the Port from the prunes and the cream. Mix together, microwave 3 minutes at HIGH. Add the prunes. Microwave 2 minutes at HIGH.

• Serve in a sauceboat or set the prunes around the chops and serve the juice in a sauceboat.

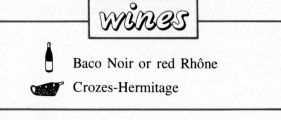

Baco Noir or red Rhône

Crozes-Hermitage

Shoulder Chops with Sauerkraut

Preparation: . . . . 10 m
Cooking: . . . . 40 m
Standing: . . . . 10 m

• Once in a while I love a good dish of sauerkraut. I learned to appreciate it during a stay in Strasbourg, where excellent sauerkraut is served. This dish is family fare, easy to prepare. The first time I cooked it in the microwave oven, it was simply to see how it would turn out. To my surprise, it had never tasted so good.

wines

Gewurztraminer

Alsatian Muscat or
Rheinhessen Riesling Spätlese

Ingredients:

4 slices bacon *and*
  4 arm pork chops *or*
  8 arm pork chops
1½ lb (750 g) sauerkraut *or*
  1 32-oz (909 mL) jar sauerkraut with wine
1 large onion, diced
1 tsp (5 mL) pepper
1/2 tsp (2 mL) juniper berries
1/2 tsp (2 mL) aniseed
1/2 tsp (2 mL) coarse salt
1/3 cup (80 mL) water or beer or white wine
4 to 6 medium potatoes

Method:

• Place half the sauerkraut in an 8-cup (2 L) ceramic baking dish. Place on top the bacon and 4 chops or the 8 chops. Sprinkle the meat with the onion.

• Mix together the pepper, juniper berries, aniseed and salt. Sprinkle half over the meat, then cover it with the remaining sauerkraut.

• Place the potatoes on top, half burying them in the sauerkraut. Sprinkle the remaining seasoning on top.

• Add the chosen liquid. Cover. Microwave 40 minutes at MEDIUM-HIGH.

• Let stand 10 minutes in the oven or in a warm place and serve.

Cooked Pork Risotto

Preparation: . . . . **5 m**
Cooking: . . . . **20 m**
Standing: . . . . **none**

• A few minutes of cooking with no effort using one or two cups (250 or 500 mL) of already-cooked leftover pork gives you a meal for four people.

Ingredients:

1 to 2 cups (250 to 500 mL) cooked pork, thinly sliced or diced

1/3 cup (80 mL) chili sauce

1/4 tsp (1 mL) salt

1 tsp (5 mL) celery seeds

1/4 tsp (1 mL) nutmeg

3 tbsp (50 mL) cider or wine vinegar

1 bay leaf

1 cup (250 mL) water

1/2 cup (125 mL) long grain rice

Method:

• Place the pork in a glass baking dish.

• Mix the remaining ingredients, then pour over the meat.

• Cover and microwave 20 minutes at MEDIUM-HIGH, stirring once during the cooking.

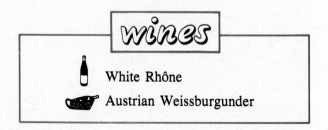

wines

White Rhône

Austrian Weissburgunder

Stir-fried Pork Tenderloin

Preparation: . . . . **10 m**
Cooking: . . . . **from 11 to 16 m**
Standing: . . . . **none**

Ingredients:

1/4 cup (60 mL) toasted sesame seeds
1 small pork tenderloin
1 tbsp (15 mL) water
1/4 cup (60 mL) soy sauce (Kikkoman)
4 - 6 green onions, chopped
1 tbsp (15 mL) vegetable oil
1 or 2 garlic cloves, minced
2 tbsp (30 mL) ginger root, minced

• Toast at HIGH 3 to 5 minutes, stirring often and taking out as soon as seeds are golden brown.

• Set aside in a small dish and reserve.

• Place whole tenderloin in dish.

• Combine remaining ingredients and pour over tenderloin.

• Cover, microwave at HIGH 5 to 8 minutes. Baste pork.

• Cover and microwave 3 minutes at HIGH.

• Stir and serve, thinly sliced.

Method:

• Spread sesame seeds in an 8 × 8-inch (20 × 20 cm) ceramic or glass dish.

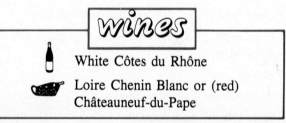

wines

White Côtes du Rhône

Loire Chenin Blanc or (red) Châteauneuf-du-Pape

Alsatian Poached Ham

Preparation: . . . . 15 m
Cooking: . . . . .43 m
Standing: . . . . 20 m

• This ham can be served hot or cold. There are very few ways of poaching a ham that can equal this Alsatian method for flavor and tenderness.

Ingredients:

1/4 cup (60 mL) butter or margarine

2 medium carrots, peeled and thinly sliced

2 leeks, washed and thinly sliced

1 large onion, thinly sliced

2 branches of celery, diced

1 3-to-5-lb (1.5 – 2.5 kg) pre-cooked ham

2 cups (500 mL) white wine or dry cider or light beer

4 cloves

4 tbsp (60 mL) brown sugar

3 tbsp (50 mL) cornstarch

2 tbsp (30 mL) rum or brandy

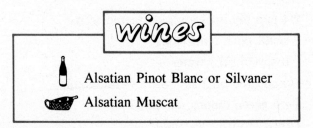

Alsatian Pinot Blanc or Silvaner

Alsatian Muscat

Method:

• Place the butter in an 8-cup (2 L) ceramic baking dish and melt 3 minutes at HIGH.

• Add the carrots, leeks, onion and celery. Mix well. Microwave 5 minutes at HIGH.

• Stir together and set the ham on this bed of vegetables.

• Add the remaining ingredients, except the cornstarch, rum or brandy.

• Roll the ham in the mixture, cover and microwave 30 minutes at MEDIUM, turning the ham halfway through the cooking.

• Let stand 20 minutes, covered.

• Remove the ham from the dish. Strain the juice and pour it into the baking dish.

• Mix together the cornstarch and rum or brandy. Stir into the juice.

• Microwave 4 to 5 minutes at MEDIUM-HIGH, stirring twice during cooking. When cooked, the gravy will be creamy, light and transparent.

• Pour into a sauceboat and warm up as needed before serving.

A personal note: To serve the ham cold, place it in a large dish, pour the cooked gravy on top and baste the ham many times with the gravy during the next 15 to 20 minutes. This will form a glaze on top of the ham.

Boiled Ham

• This is an old recipe from the repertoire of Québec cuisine. One day, out of curiosity, I tried to adapt it to microwave cooking. It was such a success that my family and I vowed that we would always boil ham this way.

Ingredients:

4-lb (2 kg) shoulder of ham *or*
4-to-6-lb (2 - 3 kg) half-ham

1 bay leaf

10 peppercorns

6 whole allspice cloves

2 large onions, quartered

2 carrots, sliced

1 bunch of celery leaves

1 tbsp (15 mL) dry mustard

1/2 cup (125 mL) molasses

Boiling water

  Beaujolais or off-dry white Bordeaux

  Tavel rosé

Preparation:	15 m
Cooking:	from 40 to 60 m
Standing: served hot:	30 m
served cold:	from 9 to 11 h

A personal note: Be sure to choose a baking dish that will hold enough water to completely or almost completely cover the ham. Remove the plastic casing and the net around the ham, if necessary.

Method:

• Place the ham in the dish with all the ingredients.

• Pour boiling water over all to cover the ham, if possible.

• If your dish has a cover, use it, or cover with plastic wrap.

• As to cooking time, you must know the exact weight of the meat cut. Microwave 10 minutes per pound (500 g) at HIGH.

• When the ham is cooked, remove the rind and turn the ham so the top part will be submerged.

• Cool 4 to 5 hours in the cooking water.

• To serve cold, remove from the water, cover with a bowl or a plastic sheet and refrigerate 5 to 6 hours.

• To serve hot, let stand 30 minutes in its cooking water, set on a serving platter and serve.

Orange-glazed Ham Steak

Preparation: . . . . 8 m
Cooking: . . . . 20 m
Standing: . . . . 5 m

A personal note: This is one of my favorite ham dishes. It is quickly prepared and very attractive with a 2-inch (5 cm) thick ham slice. Excellent as a hot or cold buffet dish.

Ingredients:

1/2 cup (125 mL) brown sugar

1 tbsp (15 mL) cornstarch

1/4 tsp (1 mL) curry powder

1/2 cup (125 mL) fresh orange juice

Grated rind of 2 oranges

1 ham slice, 1 to 2-inch (2.5 to 5 cm) thick

6 cloves

Method:

• In a 12 × 9-inch (30 × 23 cm) glass baking dish, combine brown sugar, cornstarch and curry powder.

• Stir in the orange juice and rind. Mix well.

• Place the ham slice in the mixture, then turn it two or three times to coat it well on both sides.

• Stud the fat here and there with the cloves. Microwave 10 minutes at MEDIUM, uncovered, moving the ham slice and spooning the sauce halfway through the cooking.

• Then cover and microwave 10 minutes at MEDIUM. Let stand 5 minutes, covered.

• Set the ham on a platter, stir the sauce and use to glaze the top of the ham slice.

• It's very interesting surrounded with cranberry sauce.

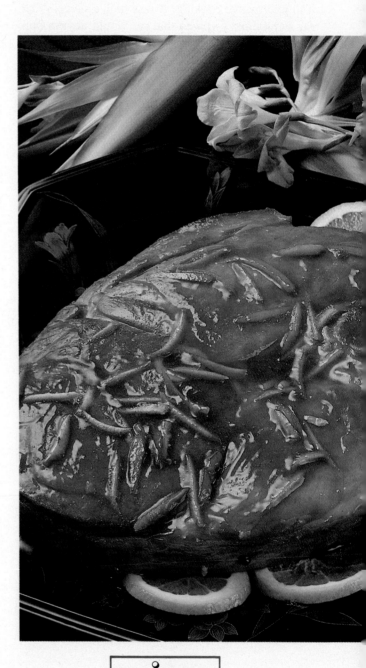

Liebfraumilch

Coteau du Layon

Honey-glazed Half Ham

Preparation: . . . . **15 m**
Cooking: . . . . **52 m**
Standing: . . . . **none**

A personal note: This dish is perfect when prepared with a ham that is not pre-cooked. Read the label carefully for instructions. You can use the recipe with half a leg of ham or with a small whole shoulder.

Ingredients:

1   4-to-5-lb (2 - 2.5 kg) shoulder or
    leg of ham

1/2 cup (125 mL) brown sugar

1 cinnamon stick

6 cloves

10 peppercorns

6 whole allspice

1 small onion, peeled and cut in four

Method:

• Remove casing from ham. Place it in a plastic cooking bag and add all the ingredients.

• Tie with a wet string or a strip cut off the top of the bag. Do not tighten the bag too much around the ham.

• Make a slit with the tip of a knife on the top of the bag.

• Set in a 12 × 7-inch (30 × 18 cm) glass dish. Microwave 10 minutes at HIGH, then microwave for 35 minutes at MEDIUM, turning the bag halfway through cooking.

• When cooked, remove ham from the bag and place it in the baking dish.

• Remove the rind, if need be.

• Spoon the following glaze over the ham.

The glaze:

Ingredients:

1/2 cup (125 mL) honey

1 tbsp (15 mL) cider vinegar

1 tsp (5 mL) cornstarch

Grated rind of one orange

Juice of half an orange

Method:

• Place all the ingredients in a 4-cup (1 L) microwave-safe measuring cup. Microwave 2 minutes at HIGH.

• Stir and spread over the ham. Baste 5 or 6 times. Microwave 4 to 5 minutes at MEDIUM, basting the ham with the sauce 3 times during the cooking.

• Remove from oven and continue basting 5 or 6 times. Serve hot or cold.

wines

Liebfraumilch

Semi-sweet Jurançon

Ham Loaf

Convection cooking

Preparation: . . . . **10 m**
Cooking: . . . . **from 30 to 40 m**
Standing: . . . . **none**

A personal note: I serve it cold, very thinly sliced, with a salad of cucumbers and white onions, marinated two hours in a French dressing.

Ingredients:

1½ lb (750 g) ground ham, raw or cooked

1/4 lb (125 g) ground pork

3 eggs, lightly beaten

1/2 cup (125 mL) cream of celery soup, undiluted

1/2 tsp (2 mL) marjoram or curry

1/2 tsp (2 mL) dry mustard

1 cup (250 mL) fine breadcrumbs

Method:

• Mix all the ingredients together in the order given.

• Pack well into a 9 × 5-inch (23 × 13 cm) bread pan.

• If you have a combined microwave-convection oven, place the rack over the ceramic tray.

• Preheat oven to 350°F (180°C).

• Place the meat loaf on the rack. Bake 30 to 40 minutes or until the meat loaf is golden brown.

wines

Beaujolais or Rhine Mueller-Thurgau

Rheingau Riesling Spätlese

Bavarian Sauerkraut Dumplings

Preparation:	15 m
Cooking:	40 m
Standing:	none

🍷 Gewurztraminer

🥘 Franconian Riesling Spätlese

Ingredients:

1 large can sauerkraut

2 medium onions, chopped

Bones from roast*

2 garlic cloves, minced

1 tsp (5 mL) salt

1 tsp (5 mL) dill seeds

1½ cups (375 mL) water or white wine

Method:

• In a microwave-safe dish, make layers of sauerkraut, onions, garlic and bones, spraying each layer with some of the salt and dill seeds mixed together.

• Pour water on top. Cover. Microwave 30 to 35 minutes at HIGH.

To make the dumplings:

• Mix in a bowl:

1½ cups (375 mL) all-purpose flour

1 tsp (5 mL) dried parsley

1 tsp (5 mL) savory

2 tsp (10 mL) baking powder

1/2 tsp (2 mL) salt

• Mix in a second bowl:

2/3 cup (160 mL) milk

1 egg

2 tbsp (30 mL) vegetable oil

• Mix the two together only when you're ready to cook the dumplings.

To cook

• Remove meat from dish. Mix dumplings. Place on top of sauerkraut by spoonfuls. Cover and cook 5 to 6 minutes at HIGH.

Ask your butcher to give you the bones removed from a 4-lb (2 kg) loin of pork, or use 2 lb (1 kg) pork spareribs.

Sausage and Corn Pancake

Preparation:	. . . . **8 m**
Cooking:	. . . . **1 h**
Standing:	. . . . **none**

Convection cooking

A personal note: This pancake can be made with half a pound or 1 pound (250 or 500 g) of sausages. If you serve it with a green salad, you will have a complete meal, easily prepared.

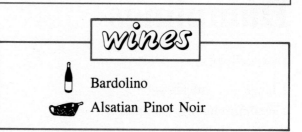

wines

Bardolino

Alsatian Pinot Noir

Ingredients:

1 lb (500 g) sausages of your choice

1 12-oz (341 mL) can of whole kernel corn

2 eggs, lightly beaten

4 green onions *or* 1 small onion, chopped

2/3 cup (160 mL) soda crackers, crushed

3 tbsp (50 mL) parsley, minced

1 tsp (5 mL) marjoram

1/4 tsp (1 mL) pepper

1 tsp (5 mL) salt

Method:

• Place the sausages in a microwave-safe dish and cover with hot water. Microwave 10 minutes at HIGH. Drain thoroughly and place the sausages in a deep 9-inch (23 cm) microwave-safe pie plate.

• Drain the corn, reserving the liquid, and pour the corn over the sausages.

• Add enough **milk to the reserved liquid to make 1½ cups (375 mL)**. Add the remaining ingredients, mix well. Pour over the sausages. Microwave in the convection oven preheated at 350°F (180°C), 35 to 45 minutes or until the pancake is puffed and golden.

Sausages, Fried Eggs and Browned Potatoes

Preparation: . . . . **10 m**
Cooking: . . . .**20 m**
Standing: . . . .**none**

A personal note: This is an excellent lunch — nutritious, quick and easy. This recipe can also be prepared with scrambled eggs.

Ingredients:

2 medium potatoes*

1/2 lb (250 g) sausages

4 eggs

Salt and pepper

1 tbsp (15 mL) butter

Green onions or minced parsley

* *Potatoes already cooked can also be used.*

Beaujolais
Fleurie

Method:

• Scrub the potatoes. Make one or two incisions in each one with the point of a knife. Place on a microwave rack. Microwave 5 to 6 minutes at HIGH. Cool.

• Sprinkle the sausages with paprika. Place in an 8 × 8-inch (20 × 20 cm) baking dish and microwave 5 to 6 minutes at HIGH, turning the sausages halfway through the cooking. Sausages will be browned here and there.

• Place on a warm serving platter. Keep in a warm place.

• Peel the potatoes, dice, sprinkle with paprika and green onions. Mix and pour into the sausage cooking fat. Mix together and place in the shape of a crown around the dish. Microwave 5 minutes at HIGH. Stir well and add the sausages.

• Melt the butter 1 minute at HIGH in the middle of the dish.

• Break the eggs into it. Prick each yolk and each white with the point of a knife. Cover the dish with plastic wrap or waxed paper. Microwave at MEDIUM 1 minute for each egg or a little more if you wish.

• Serve with the sausages and potatoes.

Broiled Sausages

Preparation: . . . . **5 m**
Cooking: . . . . **11 m**
Standing: . . . . **none**

• Once you have tasted pork sausages cooked in the microwave oven, you will never again cook them in a frying pan.

Ingredients:

1/2 lb (250 g) pork sausages
Paprika and garlic salt
A pinch of savory, to taste

Method:

• Preheat an 8 × 8-inch (20 × 20 cm) browning dish (Corning) 7 minutes at HIGH.

• Sprinkle the sausages with paprika and garlic salt. Without removing the hot dish from the oven, place the sausages in it. Broil 2 minutes at HIGH. Holding the dish by the two handles, shake it back and forth to turn the sausages. Microwave 2 minutes at HIGH. Serve.

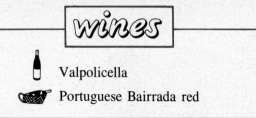

Valpolicella
Portuguese Bairrada red

Yorkshire Sausages

Convection cooking

Preparation: . . . . **10 m**
Cooking: . . . . **30 m**
Standing: . . . . **none**

A personal note: Nice golden sausages cooked in a pancake is the perfect dish for a brunch or light meal.

Ingredients:

6 to 8 pork sausages
3 eggs, lightly beaten
1 cup (250 mL) milk
1/2 cup (125 mL) flour
1/2 tsp (2 mL) salt
1/4 tsp (1 mL) savory or curry
Paprika

Method:

• Place the sausages in a dish. Cover with hot water (tap water will do). Microwave 5 minutes at HIGH. Drain thoroughly.

• Mix the eggs, milk, flour, salt and savory or curry into a nice smooth batter.

• Set the sausages in a 9-inch (23 cm) microwave-safe pie plate. Cover with the batter. Sprinkle lightly with paprika. If you have a combination microwave-convection oven, place the pie plate on a rack.

• Microwave at 425°F (220°C) for 20 to 25 minutes or until the pancake is all puffy and the sausages are well browned.

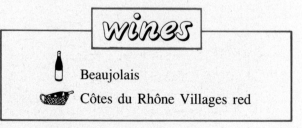

Beaujolais
Côtes du Rhône Villages red

112

Sauces and their Magic

- There is almost no limit to the number of ingredients, both cooked and uncooked, that can be mixed together to create delicious sauces. Once you have mastered the classic sauces, some methods of preparing them and their basic ingredients, you will be able to use your imagination to develop other variations.

- The perfect sauce enhances both the appearance and the flavor of the food with which it is served.

- If you've never bothered much with sauces because you think they're time consuming, you will marvel at how easily and quickly they are prepared in a microwave oven. Lumps, burning, constant stirring — all are eliminated. You can even prepare some sauces ahead of time, then refrigerate them or keep them at room temperature for quick reheating when needed.

- You will quickly learn how to adapt your favorite sauce recipes to microwave cooking.

- **The important thing is to stir a sauce thoroughly, sometimes two or even three times during the cooking, and to use your own common sense as to the time required.**

- For example, if your white sauce recipe calls for a 5-minute cooking period at HIGH but the milk and butter are very cold, or the butter is soft and the milk at room temperature, there may be a 1 or 2-minute variation in cooking time. Of course, if you want to proceed more slowly and cook the sauce at MEDIUM, then 2 to 4 minutes more will be required than at HIGH.

- **Don't be afraid to open the oven door to check the cooking, as residual heat remains in the ingredients while you are stirring.**

- You won't change the texture of a sauce by adding more herbs, extracts or spices than a recipe calls for. And you can make a sauce thinner or thicker without changing its taste.

- Sauces are an important element of good cuisine. They garnish, extend or bind together the food you are serving and, of course, they enhance the flavor.

The finishing touches to a perfect roast

There are three kinds of gravy:

3. The perfect gravy, made by adding a can of cold, undiluted consommé to the hot fat for more flavor and color.

• Good flour gravy has an appetizing color. The perfect proportions for a flour gravy are equal parts of flour and fat — for instance, **2 tablespoons (30 mL) of flour to 2 tablespoons (30 mL) of fat.** If you use a higher proportion of fat, the gravy separates and becomes greasy. For a thick sauce, use **1 tablespoon (15 mL) of flour** for each **1/2 cup (125 mL) of liquid.** Add flour to the fat in the pan, stir well, cook 2 minutes at HIGH, then stir again.

• What cold liquid you use makes a big difference. Don't think you can use only cold water. Leftover tea or coffee, tomato juice, milk, cream and wine can all be used — and each gives a completely different color and flavor.

1. A creamy sauce, made by adding flour.

2. A clear sauce, made by adding a cold liquid to the hot fat.

A few notes on sauces and variations

You can use any flour for the starch — wheat or potato flour, cornstarch or fine tapioca. Each will give a lightly different texture to the finished sauce.

• Whichever ingredients you use — and remember that the liquid must be cold — **the method is the same:**

• Add the starch to the cold liquid, stir to a smooth cream or thin paste, then add to boiling stock or gravy or water.

• Beat with a wire whisk until thoroughly blended.

• To obtain a smooth, creamy texture free from any starchy flavor, microwave the mixture 1 to 3 minutes at MEDIUM-HIGH, stirring to mix after each minute of cooking, until you have the desired consistency.

• The usual proportion of flour to liquid for a flour-thickened sauce is **2 teaspoons (10 mL) flour to 1/2 cup (125 mL) liquid,** although some recipes call for different amounts. To substitute another starch for the **2 teaspoons (10 mL) wheat flour,** use any one of the following: **1 teaspoon (5 mL) cornstarch, 1⅔ teaspoons (8 mL) rice flour, 2/3 teaspoon (3 mL) potato flour or arrowroot.**

Sauce Velouté

• The liquid that accumulates under the roast is called a fumet and there usually is from 3/4 to 1 cup (200 to 250 mL).

To make the sauce Velouté

• Remove to a dish **3 tablespoons (50 mL) of fat,** add **2 tablespoons (30 mL) flour** and stir. Cook 1 minute at MEDIUM-HIGH, stirring twice during cooking.

• Put the remaining fumet in a measuring cup and add enough **chicken, beef consommé, cream or light white wine** to make up **1 to 1½ cups (250 to 375 mL) of liquid.** (Flavor will vary with the liquid used.) Stir thoroughly, then add the **starch mixed with the 3 tablespoons of fat.**

• Mix well and microwave 2 to 3 minutes at HIGH. Stir once or twice, preferably with a whisk, to obtain a smooth, creamy texture. Salt and pepper to taste.

Basic Brown Sauce

Preparation: . . . . **15 m**
Cooking: . . . . **12 m**
Standing: . . . . **none**

Ingredients:

1/2 cup (125 mL) celery, chopped

1/2 cup (125 mL) carrots, chopped

1/2 cup (125 mL) onion, chopped

1/4 tsp (1 mL) dried thyme

1 bay leaf

1/4 tsp (1 mL) dried marjoram, savory or tarragon

3 tbsp (50 mL) roast fat

4 tbsp (60 mL) flour

2 cups (500 mL) beef stock *or*
Fumet accumulated under the roast
PLUS water, *or* red wine (white with
white meat and red with red meat) to make up
2 cups (500mL) of liquid

Method:

• Prepare the vegetables, put them in a microwave-safe bowl, then add the herbs and mix.

• Remove the 3 tablespoons (50 mL) fat from the fumet, stir in the vegetables and the herbs with a wooden spoon, add **2 tablespoons (30 mL) water.** Microwave 3 minutes at HIGH, stirring once during cooking.

• Sprinkle the softened vegetables with the flour and stir until well mixed. Microwave 3 to 4 minutes at HIGH or until small brown spots appear here and there.

• Add **1 tsp (5 mL) the Kitchen Bouquet** or **1/2 tsp (2 mL) molasses.**

• Add the chosen liquid, stir to blend well, season to taste, then microwave 5 minutes at MEDIUM-HIGH, stirring once or twice during cooking.

Basic Brown Sauce Variations

Sauce Robert

- For roasted pork, or to warm up beef and root vegetables:
- Instead of the 3 vegetables and herbs, use only **4 chopped onions.**
- Flavor with **1/4 teaspoon (1 mL) dried thyme** and the **grated rind of 1 lemon.**
- Use **1/2 cup (125 mL) white wine** to replace 1/2 cup (125 mL) of the liquid.
- When the sauce is finished, flavor it with **1 teaspoon (5 mL) of Dijon mustard.**

Sauce Piquante

- For roasted veal, all pork dishes and all chops:
- Instead of the vegetables, use only **onions, as in Sauce Robert.**
- Flavor with **1 bay leaf** and **1/4 teaspoon (1 mL) salt.**
- Replace 1/4 cup (60 mL) of the liquid with **1/4 cup (60 mL) cider vinegar.** Add **1 teaspoon (5 mL) sugar.**
- When the sauce is finished, add **4 tablespoons (60 mL) thinly sliced baby gherkins.**

Sauce Espagnole

- Add **2 minced garlic cloves** and a generous amount of **freshly ground pepper** to the vegetables of the Basic Brown Sauce.
- When the vegetables are soft and translucent, add **2 tablespoons (30 mL) tomato paste.**
- Finish the sauce in the usual way.

Sauce Madère or Madeira Sauce

- For all roasted meats and for boiled ham:
- Add **1/4 cup (60 mL) dry Madeira** to the 2 cups (500 mL) liquid of the Basic Brown Sauce, or substitute **1/2 cup (125 mL) Madeira** for 1/2 cup (125 mL) of the liquid.

Devilled Sauce

Preparation: . . . . **8 m**
Cooking: . . . . **10 m**
Standing: . . . . **none**

Ingredients:

4 green onions, chopped

1 tbsp (15 mL) butter

1 cup (250 mL) white wine *or*
   2/3 cup (160 mL) French vermouth

Fresh ground pepper

2 cups (500 mL) Basic Brown Sauce

Method:

• Place the green onions and the butter in a baking dish, microwave 2 minutes at HIGH.

• Mix well, add the wine or vermouth, microwave 3 minutes at HIGH.

• Stir and microwave 2 more minutes at HIGH, or until the wine is almost totally reduced.

• Add the Basic Brown Sauce and microwave 2 minutes at MEDIUM, stir well and serve.

Sauce Chasseur

Preparation: . . . . **12 m**
Cooking: . . . . **17 m**
Standing: . . . . **none**

A **personal note:** Serve with veal, ground meat, meat loaf, etc.

Ingredients:

4 green onions, chopped

2 tbsp (30 mL) butter

1 cup (250 mL) fresh or well drained canned tomatoes

1 small garlic clove

1/4 tsp (1 mL) salt

1/2 tsp (2 mL) basil

1/2 tsp (2 mL) sugar

1/2 cup (125 mL) white whine

1 cup (250 mL) Basic Brown Sauce

1/4 lb (125 g) mushrooms, thinly sliced

2 tbsp (30 mL) butter

Method:

• Place the green onions in a dish and microwave 3 minutes at HIGH, stirring once.

• Peel or drain and dice the tomatoes, add to the onions together with the garlic, salt, basil and sugar. Cover and microwave 5 minutes at MEDIUM.

• Add the wine and the Basic Brown Sauce. Stir well and microwave 5 minutes at MEDIUM.

• In a separate dish, melt the 2 tablespoons (30 mL) butter 1 minute at HIGH.

• Add the mushrooms, mix well and microwave 2 minutes at HIGH. Stir well. Add to the brown sauce.

• Taste for seasoning. If necessary, heat 1 minute at HIGH.

Chef's Brown Sauce

Preparation: . . . . **10 m**
Cooking: . . . . **7 m**
Standing: . . . . **none**

Ingredients:

1/2 tsp (2 mL) sugar

1 small onion, chopped

3 tbsp (50 mL) butter

2 tbsp (30 mL) flour

1   10-oz (284 mL) can beef broth, undiluted

1/8 tsp (0.5 mL) thyme

1 bay leaf

1/4 cup (60 mL) milk

1/2 cup (125 mL) dry skim milk

1/4 cup (60 mL) water

2 tsp (10 mL) tomato paste

Method:

• Place the sugar in a 4-cup (1 L) microwave-safe bowl. Microwave, uncovered, 2 minutes at HIGH, or until sugar is partially browned.

• Add butter. Microwave, uncovered, 1 minute at HIGH. Mix well.

• Stir in flour, blend well. Add beef broth, thyme, bay leaf and the 1/4 cup (60 mL) milk. Mix well, then microwave, uncovered, 1 minute at HIGH. Stir well.

• Add dry milk, water and tomato paste. Blend well. Microwave, uncovered, 2 to 3 minutes at HIGH, or until sauce is creamy, stirring once during cooking.

Simplified Brown Sauce

Preparation: . . . . **8 m**
Cooking: . . . . **13 m**
Standing: . . . . **none**

A personal note: If you like gravy, make this sauce, which is easy to prepare. It will keep 8 to 10 days refrigerated.

Ingredients:

1/4 cup (60 mL) onion, minced

1/2 tsp (2 mL) sugar

2 tbsp (30 mL) butter

2 tbsp (30 mL) flour

2 cups (500 mL) canned beef consommé*

1/8 tsp (0.5 mL) pepper

1/4 tsp (1 mL) thyme

1 bay leaf

2 tsp (10 mL) tomato paste

Method:

• Place in a microwave-safe dish the onion, sugar and butter and microwave 2 minutes at HIGH.

• Stir well and microwave 1 minute more, if necessary, for the onions to brown slightly here and there.

• Add the flour. Stir well.

• Add the consommé, pepper, thyme, bay leaf and tomato paste.

• Microwave 10 minutes at MEDIUM-HIGH, stirring three times during the cooking.

* Add enough water to the consommé to have 2 cups (500 mL) of liquid.

Sauce Robert with Simplified Brown Sauce

Preparation:	**7 m**
Cooking:	**10 m**
Standing:	**none**

Ingredients:

1 tbsp (15 mL) each butter and vegetable oil

1 onion, minced

1 cup (250 mL) white wine

1 recipe simplified brown sauce

3 to 4 tsp (15 - 20 mL) Dijon mustard

3 tbsp (50 mL) soft butter

3 tbsp (50 mL) parsley, minced

Method:

• Place the butter, vegetable oil and onion in a microwave-safe dish. Mix well. Add the wine, stir and microwave 5 to 8 minutes at HIGH, stirring three times during the cooking. The wine must reduce without the onion drying up.

• Place the brown sauce in a microwave-safe dish and microwave 1 minute at HIGH. Add the reduced wine.

• Mix together in a bowl the mustard, soft butter and minced parsley. Add to the sauce. Stir to mix well. Microwave 1 minute at HIGH, stir well. Serve.

Quick Madeira or Port Sauce

Preparation:	**3 m**
Cooking:	**5 m**
Standing:	**none**

• A classic of the English cuisine

Ingredients:

1/4 cup 60 mL) Madeira or Port wine

1 recipe of Simplified Brown Sauce

2 tbsp (30 mL) butter

Method:

• Add the Madeira or Port wine to the Simplified Brown Sauce in a microwave-safe dish. Microwave 5 minutes at MEDIUM-HIGH, stirring three times during the cooking. Remove from oven.

• Add the butter. Stir to melt the butter.

Ready basting for beef

Preparation: . . . . 1 m
Cooking: . . . . 30 s
Standing: . . . . none

Ingredients:

2 tbsp (30 mL) Madeira or whisky or cold tea
or

1 tsp (5 mL) tomato paste *and*
3 tsp (15 mL) water
or

4 tbsp (60 mL) canned consommé, undiluted

Method:

• Microwave the ingredient of your choice 30 seconds at HIGH.

• Use to baste meat before and during cooking.

Ready basting for pork

Preparation: . . . . 1 m
Cooking: . . . . 30 s
Standing: . . . . none

Ingredients:

Rind and juice of half an orange
or

1/4 cup (60 mL) cranberry juice mixed *with*
1 tsp (5 mL) cornstarch
or

3 tbsp (50 mL) water *and*
2 tsp (10 mL) instant coffee

Method:

• Microwave the ingredient of your choice 30 seconds at HIGH.

• Use to baste meat before and during cooking.

122

Preparation:	1 m
Cooking:	30 s
Standing:	none

Ready basting for veal

Ingredients:

3 tbsp (50 mL) white wine or dry sherry

or

**1 tbsp (15 mL) soy sauce
(preferably Japanese)**

or

2 tbsp (30 mL) Teriyaki sauce (bottled)

or

2 tsp (10 mL) Worcestershire sauce

or

2 tbsp (30 mL) sour cream

Method:

• Add **1 tsp (5 mL) paprika** to the ingredient of your choice.

• Microwave 30 seconds at HIGH.

• Mix well and baste meat with it before and during cooking.

Preparation:	1 m
Cooking:	30 s
Standing:	none

Ready basting for lamb

Ingredients:

2 to 3 tbsp (30 to 50 mL) Madeira

or

1 tbsp (15 mL) mint sauce (not jelly)

or

**2 tsp (10 mL) instant coffee *and*
3 tbsp (50 mL) water**

or

**Juice and rind of half a lemon *and*
1/2 tsp (2 mL) fresh grated ginger**

Method:

• Microwave the ingredient of your choice 30 seconds at HIGH.

• Use to baste meat before and during cooking.

Basting Sauce for Meats

Preparation: . . . . **5 m**
Cooking: . . . . **none**
Standing: . . . . **none**

A personal note: Basting meats with this sauce gives them more flavor and makes them brown when roasted in the microwave oven. This basting sauce can be used with all meats and poultry.

Ingredients:

1 tbsp (15 mL) vegetable oil or unsalted margarine or butter (melted 1 minute at HIGH)

1 tsp (5 mL) paprika

1 tsp (5 mL) Kitchen Bouquet

1/4 tsp (1 mL) thyme, tarragon, basil, marjoram, cumin or curry

Method:

• Stir all ingredients together and brush mixture all over meat before cooking.

Basting Sauce for Roasts

Preparation: . . . . **5 m**
Cooking: . . . . **none**
Standing: . . . . **none**

A personal note: Use this sauce to baste any roast, on microwave broiled steak, or over chicken, duck or lamb. One or two bastings during the cooking should be sufficient to give a very interesting flavor to the meat.

Ingredients:

1 garlic clove, halved

1/2 cup (125 mL) each of lemon juice and vegetable oil

2 tsp (10 mL) marjoram or basil

1/2 tsp (2 mL) fresh ground pepper

2 tsp (10 mL) salt

1/3 cup (80 mL) Worcestershire sauce

Method:

• Place the ingredients in a glass jar.

• Close the jar, shake vigorously and refrigerate. The sauce will keep for one month.

• Shake well before using.

Meat Tenderizer Marinating Sauce

Advance preparation: .. **from 12 to 24 h**
Cooking: . . . . **none**
Standing: . . . . **none**

A personal note: Less tender meat cuts such as shoulder, brisket, heel of round and stewing beef will become tender after marinating in this mixture.

Ingredients:

2/3 cup (160 mL) onion, chopped fine

3/4 cup (200 mL) celery leaves, minced

1/3 cup (80 mL) cider vinegar

1/2 cup (125 mL) vegetable oil

1 cup (250 mL) grape juice

1 tbsp (15 mL) hot sauce

1/2 tsp (2 mL) salt

1/8 tsp (0.5 mL) powdered garlic

Method:

• Combine all the ingredients together and mix well. Pour over the meat to be marinated, covering it.

• Refrigerate 12 to 24 hours.

• To roast the meat, remove it from the marinade. Roast following your recipe.

• Baste the roast 2 to 3 times with the marinating sauce during the cooking.

Helpful hint: Add honey to lemon or orange juice to make a drink or to glaze ham or chicken. Delicious!

True Hollandaise

- A sheer delight to make, this recipe never fails.

Ingredients:

1/3 to 1/2 cup (80 – 125 mL) salted or unsalted butter

2 egg yolks

Juice of one small lemon

Method:

- Place the butter in a small casserole or a 2-cup (500 mL) microwave-safe measuring cup. Microwave, uncovered, 1 minute at MEDIUM-HIGH.

- Add egg yolks and lemon juice. Beat well with a small whisk. Microwave 20 seconds at MEDIUM-HIGH. Beat well and, if necessary, microwave 20 seconds more at MEDIUM-HIGH to achieve a creamy texture.

- Whisk, salt to taste and serve.

Hollandaise in the Food Processor

Preparation: . . . . **5 m**
Cooking: . . . . **3 m**
Standing: . . . . **none**

A personal note: Hollandaise prepared this way will keep refrigerated for 2 to 3 days. Use it cold over steaks garnished with avocado or over thin slices of veal. This sauce is easily reheated, 30 seconds to 1 minute at MEDIUM; stir well after 30 seconds and heat another 20 to 30 seconds, if necessary.

Ingredients:

1/2 cup (125 mL) cold butter
2 tbsp (30 mL) lemon or lime juice
1/2 tsp (2 mL) Dijon mustard
1/8 tsp (0.5 mL) pepper
2 egg yolks at room temperature

Method:

• Dice the butter and place in the food processor bowl without the metal blade. Place the bowl in the microwave oven and microwave at HIGH 30 seconds to 1 minute. The butter must not melt but only soften.

• Return the bowl to the food processor, insert the blade, add the lemon or lime juice, mustard and pepper. Cover and operate 2 seconds or until the mixture is creamy. Without stopping the motor, add the egg yolks through the tube, 1 at a time, blending 30 seconds after each addition.

• Uncover, remove the blade and microwave at MEDIUM approximately 1 minute. Stir, and microwave another 20 seconds if necessary.

• Serve, or refrigerate in a well-covered container.

• The explanation is rather lengthy, but the process is easy.

Hollandaise Variations

Sauce Mousseline

- Add to Hollandaise **2 egg whites** beaten stiff.
- For a light and fluffy sauce, add the egg whites immediately before serving.

De Luxe
Mustard Sauce

- Replace the lemon juice in your Hollandaise recipe with **2 tablespoons (30 mL) of cold water** and **1 tablespoon (15 mL) of Dijon mustard.** Mix well.

Sauce Maltaise

- Replace the lemon juice in your Hollandaise recipe with **4 tablespoons (60 mL) of the juice** and **grated rind of one orange.**

Chantilly Hollandaise

Ingredients:

1 recipe of Hollandaise Sauce
1/2 cup (125 mL) whipping cream

Method:

- Prepare the Hollandaise of your choice.
- Immediately before serving, whip the cream and beat it into the sauce.
- This sauce is served warm. Don't reheat it; it won't remain fluffy and it might curdle.

My Favorite Tomato Sauce

Preparation: . . . . **8 m**
Cooking: . . . . **11 m**
Standing: . . . . **none**

A personal note: Serve the sauce with veal or pork, or over thin slices of leftover meat, cover with the sauce, heat and serve.

Ingredients:

3 slices bacon, diced

1 large onion, minced

1 tbsp (15 mL) flour

4 large fresh tomatoes

1/8 tsp (0.5 mL) nutmeg

1/2 tsp (2 mL) thyme

1/2 tsp (2 mL) salt

1/2 cup (125 mL) tomato paste

1 tsp (5 mL) sugar

Method:

• Place the bacon in a 4-cup (1 L) microwave-safe bowl, cover with waxed paper. Microwave 2 minutes at HIGH.

• Remove diced bacon from fat and drain. Cool.

• To the remaining fat, add the onion, stir. Microwave 4 minutes at HIGH, stirring halfway through the cooking.

• Add the flour and mix well. Add the remaining ingredients. Stir to blend. Cover and microwave 5 minutes at HIGH, stirring twice.

• Taste for seasoning. Add the bacon and stir well.

• This sauce will keep one week refrigerated in a glass jar.

• To reheat, pour into a bowl and microwave 2 to 3 minutes at HIGH.

Applesauce

Preparation: . . . . **12 m**
Cooking: . . . . **6 m**
Standing: . . . . **none**

A personal note: It is delicious with pork or ham.

Ingredients:

4-5 apples, quartered
4 tbsp (60 mL) water
2 tbsp (30 mL) butter

Method:

• Peel and quarter the apples, place them in a baking dish and add water. Cover and microwave 5 minutes at HIGH.

• Remove from oven, pass through a sieve or use a food processor.

• Place in the oven and microwave 1 minute at HIGH.

• Add the butter, stir well until the butter has melted. Do not sweeten.

How to thicken a sauce

• To the fat in the pan or the plate, add **2 tbsp (30 mL) flour** before adding the liquid.

• Blend well.

• Add **cold water or tea, or port wine or vodka or white vermouth or red wine.**

• Stir scratching the bottom of the pan.

• Microwave 2 minutes at HIGH.

• Stir until the sauce is creamy.

Raisin Sauce for Ham

Preparation: . . . . **5 m**
Cooking: . . . . **5 m**
Standing: . . . . **none**

A personal note: Delicious served with boiled or braised ham, this sauce will keep 3 to 4 days in the refrigerator.

Ingredients:

1/2 cup (125 mL) brown sugar

2 tbsp (30 mL) cornstarch

1 tsp (5 mL) dry mustard

2 tbsp (30 mL) cider vinegar

2 tbsp (30 mL) lemon juice

Grated rind of half a lemon

1½ cups (375 mL) water

1/3 cup (80 mL) seedless raisins

1 tbsp (15 mL) butter

Method:

• Combine all the ingredients together in a 4-cup (1 L) microwave-safe bowl. Microwave, uncovered, 4 minutes at HIGH, stirring twice during the cooking. If necessary, continue to cook 1 minute at a time until the sauce is light and creamy.

Sauce Aurore

| Preparation: . . . . **10 m** |
| Cooking: . . . . **10 m** |
| Standing: . . . . **none** |

A personal note: Serve with veal.

Ingredients:

3 tbsp (50 mL) butter

3 tbsp (50 mL) flour

2 cups (500 mL) milk or chicken broth

1/2 cup (125 mL) whipping cream

Salt and pepper to taste

3 tbsp (50 mL) tomato paste

1 tsp (5 mL) basil

3 tbsp (50 mL) parsley, minced

1 tbsp (15 mL) soft butter

Method:

• Place the butter in a microwave-safe bowl and melt 1 minute at HIGH. Add the flour and stir well. Add the milk or chicken broth, stir well. Microwave 4 minutes at HIGH. Stir well.

• When the sauce is smooth and creamy, gradually add the cream, stirring constantly. Salt and pepper to taste.

• Add the tomato paste, basil and parsley. Mix thoroughly. Microwave 2 minutes at HIGH. Stir well. If necessary, microwave another 2 minutes at HIGH, or until the sauce is creamy.

• Add the soft butter, stir to melt the butter.

• Do not reheat the sauce after adding the tablespoon (15 mL) of butter.

Herb Butter

Preparation: . . . . 10 m
Cooking: . . . . none
Standing: . . . . none

Ingredients:

1 cup (250 mL) unsalted butter

1 tsp (5 mL) dill

1/2 tsp (2 mL) tarragon

1/2 tsp (2 mL) savory

1/4 cup (60 mL) parsley, chopped

4 green onions, chopped fine, the white and the green

1 tsp (5 mL) powdered coriander (optional)

1 tsp (5 mL) salt

1/4 tsp (1 mL) fresh ground pepper

Grated rind of half a lemon

A personal note: If you use salted butter, reduce the salt called for in the recipe to **1/4 tsp (1 mL).**

A personal note: This butter may be kept 1 month in the refrigerator and 12 months in the freezer. Shape the butter into small balls. Place them in a box with a tight lid to refrigerate them. To freeze, refrigerate the butter balls 1 hour, then spread them on a cookie sheet and freeze; this may take 3 to 4 hours. Then place the balls in a freezer bag. To serve, just drop a butter ball over each serving.

Method:

• Cream all the ingredients together, cool one hour in the refrigerator.

• Shape into small balls and refrigerate or freeze.

Onion Butter
for Steak

Preparation: . . . . **10 m**
Cooking: . . . . **none**
Standing: . . . . **none**

A personnal note: I always keep some of this butter in my refrigerator, to put on microwave broiled steaks, hamburgers, sausages or chicken. The heat of the meat melts the butter.

Ingredients:

4 tbsp (60 mL) onion, grated
4 tbsp (60 mL) parsley, minced
4 tbsp (60 mL) soft butter
1 tsp (5 mL) A-1 Sauce or chutney
1/2 tsp (2 mL) salt
1/4 tsp (1 mL) dry mustard
1/2 tsp (2 mL) fresh ground pepper

Method:

• Mix all the ingredients together.

• Place in a container or form into small balls. Place the butter balls on a baking sheet and freeze, uncovered, for about 1 hour.

• When they are frozen, place the butter balls in a plastic box with a sheet of waxed paper between the rows.

• Keep in the refrigerator or in the freezer.

• Even when frozen, the butter melts when placed on hot meat.

Green Sauce

Preparation: . . . . 12 m
Cooking: . . . . none
Standing: . . . . none

A personal note: This is a delicious, classic sauce to serve with all boiled meats. Served cold on hot meat, it is in a sense a French dressing. It may be kept from 4 to 6 weeks refrigerated in a glass jar. To serve, let it warm 3 to 4 hours at room temperature.

Ingredients:

1 onion, peeled and grated *or*
  6 green onions minced

3 tbsp (50 mL) parsley, finely minced

1 tbsp (15 mL) marinated capers

1 garlic clove, crushed

1 tbsp (15 mL) fine breadcrumbs

4 to 5 tbsp (60 to 75 mL) vegetable oil

Juice and rind of 1 lemon

Salt and pepper to taste

Method:

• Place in a bowl the grated onion or the green onions, parsley, capers, garlic and breadcrumbs.

• Mix well.

• Add the oil and lemon juice and rind, stirring constantly.

• Salt and pepper to taste.

Reducing a sauce with no starch

• A sauce is reduced to give it a more concentrated flavor, as well as to thicken it.

• Boil the sauce at HIGH one minute at a time, stirring well each time, until you reach the desired consistency.

Sauce Béarnaise

Preparation: . . . . **8 m**
Cooking: . . . . **4 m**
Standing: . . . . **none**

A personal note: A Béarnaise is a Hollandaise seasoned with tarragon and white wine vinegar. It is the ideal sauce to serve with broiled steak.

Ingredients:

3 tbsp (50 mL) white wine or cider vinegar

1 green onion, chopped

1 tsp (5 mL) tarragon

4 peppercorns, ground

1/3 cup (80 mL) butter

2 egg yolks, beaten

Method:

• Place the vinegar, onion and tarragon in a 2-cup (500 mL) microwave-safe bowl. Microwave, uncovered, 2 minutes at HIGH.

• Put through a sieve into an attractive microwave ovenware dish, pressing the onions. Add the ground peppercorns and butter.

• Melt 1 minute at HIGH. Add the beaten egg yolks.

• Microwave, uncovered, 30 seconds at HIGH, beat well and microwave 20 seconds more, or until the sauce is creamy.

Sour Cream Sauce

Preparation: . . . . .5 m
Cooking: . . . . .3 m
Standing: .none

A personal note: Flavorful, creamy and easy to prepare, this sauce is the perfect accompaniment to veal, poultry and vegetables.

Ingredients:

1 cup (250 mL) sour cream
1/2 tsp (2 mL) salt
1/2 tsp (2 mL) curry
1/8 tsp (0.5 mL) pepper
1 tbsp (15 mL) lemon juice
Grated rind of 1 lemon

Method:

• Combine all the ingredients together in a 2-cup (500 mL) microwave-safe bowl.

• Microwave, uncovered, 2 minutes at MEDIUM, stirring twice during the cooking.

• If necessary, microwave one minute more.

Gravy without starch

• Add to the fumet from your roast **1/4 cup (60 mL) cold tea, water, port wine, vodka, white vermouth, red wine or dry Madeira**

• Stir with a wooden spoon, scratching the bottom of the roasting pan or plate.

• Microwave 1 minute at HIGH and serve.

Sauce Ravigote

A personal note: This sauce is good with roasted or boiled beef, spare-ribs or reheated leftover meat.

Ingredients:

4 green onions, chopped, the green and the white

3 tbsp (50 mL) wine vinegar

1/3 cup (80 mL) parsley, chopped fine

1 tbsp (15 mL) tarragon

1¼ cups (300 mL) broth of your choice

1 tbsp (15 mL) butter

1 tbsp (15 mL) flour

1 egg yolk

Salt and pepper to taste

Method:

• Place in a microwave-safe measuring cup the onions and the wine vinegar.

• Microwave 2 to 3 minutes at HIGH, or until there is only 1 spoonful of vinegar left.

• Pass through a sieve and pour the juice into the broth. Add the parsley and tarragon.

• Place the butter and flour in a microwave-safe bowl. Microwave 1 minute at HIGH.

• Stir well, then keep on cooking 1 minute at a time, stirring after each minute, until the sauce browns lightly.

• Pour into the broth, add the beaten egg yolk, mix well and microwave 2 minutes at HIGH, stirring after 1 minute.

• Taste for seasoning. This sauce is slightly thick.

• This sauce can also be prepared by replacing the ground pepper with **4 black peppercorns** coarsely ground and **1 tablespoon (15 mL) of cognac or white whine.**

White Vermouth Sauce

Preparation: . . . . 12 m
Cooking: . . . . 9 m
Standing: . . . . none

A personal note: This is one of my favorites. It is quickly prepared, it enhances the flavor of kidneys and calves' brains, and is perfect for reheating thin slices of leftover beef or veal.

Ingredients:

2 tbsp (30 mL) vegetable oil

1 medium onion, chopped fine

1 French shallot, chopped fine

1 tbsp (15 mL) flour

2 tsp (10 mL) tomato paste

1/3 cup (80 mL) dry white vermouth

1 cup (250 mL) beef broth

1 tbsp (15 mL) lemon juice

1/4 tsp (1 mL) sugar

Salt and pepper to taste

Method:

• Heat the oil in a 4-cup (1 L) microwave-safe bowl, 1 minute at HIGH.

• Add the onion and shallot, mix well and microwave 2 minutes at HIGH. Stir in the flour and tomato paste, mix well.

• Add the vermouth and beef broth. Beat with a wire whisk.

• Microwave 4 minutes at MEDIUM-HIGH, stirring halfway through the cooking.

• Add the lemon juice and the sugar, beat well and microwave 2 minutes at HIGH.

• Salt and pepper to taste. Serve.

• This sauce reheats very well at MEDIUM-HIGH.

White Wine Mushroom Sauce

Preparation: . . . . 11 m
Cooking: . . . . 5 m
Standing: . . . . none

A personal note: Serve this sauce with veal or pork. It's excellent with leftover meat that has been diced or thinly sliced. It needs to be heated only 2 minutes at HIGH when ready to serve. Serve with Rice Pilaff.

1 tbsp (15 mL) cream
Salt and pepper to taste

Method:

• Place the butter in a 4-cup (1 L) microwave-safe bowl and melt 1 minute at HIGH.

• Add the washed mushrooms, thinly sliced.

• Finely chop the shallots or green onions. Add to the mushrooms together with the cornstarch, mix well.

• Microwave 2 minutes at HIGH. Stir.

• Add the white wine or the lemon juice, cream, salt and pepper to taste, and microwave 2 minutes more at HIGH, stirring halfway through the cooking.

• This sauce reheats well, 2 minutes at MEDIUM.

Ingredients:

1 tbsp (15 mL) butter

1 cup (250 mL), very full, thinly sliced mushrooms

2 French shallots *or* 4 green onions

1 tbsp (15 mL) cornstarch

1/2 cup (125 mL) white wine or juice of half a lemon

Timbale Mushroom Sauce

Preparation: . . . . **10 m**
Cooking: . . . . **7 m**
Standing: . . . . **none**

A personal note: This is the recipe to use whenever you wish to serve a mushroom sauce. Depending on whether you use dry Madeira or soy sauce, the flavor will vary and so will the color, from light beige to golden brown. Both are good.

Ingredients:

3 tbsp (50 mL) butter or margarine

2 tbsp (30 mL) flour

1 tsp (5 mL) soy sauce *or*
  1 tbsp (15 mL) dry Madeira

3/4 cup (200 mL) light cream or milk

1/4 tsp (1 mL) salt

1 4-oz (112 g) can chopped mushrooms,
  undrained

1/4 tsp (1 mL) tarragon or curry powder

Method:

• Place butter in a 4-cup (1 L) glass bowl. Microwave 1 minute at HIGH.

• To the melted butter add the flour and soy sauce or dry Madeira. Blend to a smooth paste.

• Add cream or milk, stir until smooth. Add salt, mushrooms, tarragon or curry powder.

• Microwave, uncovered, 2 minutes at HIGH. Stir well.

• Microwave another 4 minutes. Stir well.

• By this time sauce should be thick and creamy.

• If it gets cold before you are ready to serve, stir well, then heat 1 minute at HIGH, uncovered.

Sauce Vaucluse

Preparation: . . . . **10 m**
Cooking: . . . . **6 m**
Standing: . . . . **none**

Ingredients:

2 tbsp (30 mL) butter

2 tbsp (30 mL) flour

1½ cups (375 mL) cream

Salt and pepper to taste

2 egg yolks, beaten

1 recipe of Hollandaise Sauce

Method:

• Melt the butter 1 minute at HIGH. Add the flour and mix well.

• Add the cream and stir. Microwave 3 to 4 minutes at HIGH, stirring a few times, until sauce is creamy.

• Add the beaten egg yolks, stirring constantly, then add the Hollandaise while stirring, until sauce is smooth and creamy.

• To reheat, place the sauce in the oven and microwave 1 minute at HIGH, stir well and, if necessary, microwave 30 seconds more at MEDIUM-HIGH. Stir and serve.

Barbecue Sauce

Preparation: . . . . 10 m
Cooking: . . . . 5 m
Standing: . . . . none

A personal note: This sauce will keep 10 days refrigerated or two months frozen.

Ingredients:

3 tbsp (50 mL) vegetable oil or olive oil

1 envelope onion soup mix

1/2 cup (125 mL) celery, diced

3/4 cup (190 mL) chili sauce or ketchup

1/4 cup (60 mL) tomato juice, red wine or water

1/4 tsp (1 mL) celery seeds

1/4 cup (60 mL) cider vinegar

1/4 cup (60 mL) well-packed brown sugar

1 tbsp (15 mL) Dijon mustard

Grated rind of 1 orange or 1 lemon

Method:

• Place oil and onion soup mix in a 6-cup (1.5 L) microwave-safe casserole. Stir well and microwave 1 minute at HIGH.

• Add all the remaining ingredients, stir well. Microwave 4 minutes at HIGH, or until sauce bubbles. Stir well. If you wish to refrigerate or freeze sauce, cool first.

The Finishing Touch: Buttering a sauce

• The French chef's method of finishing a sauce is to add butter to the sauce as soon as it is cooked and to stir until the butter is melted.

• The heat of the completed sauce melts the butter; it is not necessary to return it to the oven.

• This is called "buttering a sauce."

My Barbecue Sauce

Preparation: . . . . **10 m**
Cooking: . . . . **13 m**
Standing: . . . . **none**

A personal note: Through the years, I have made many barbecue sauces. This one has remained my favorite. It can be used with pork, beef, lamb or poultry. When cooled, place in glass jar, cover and refrigerate. It will keep 2 to 3 weeks.

1/2 cup (125 mL) corn syrup

1/2 cup (125 mL) cold water

1/4 cup (60 mL) rum or orange liqueur

Ingredients:

1/2 cup (125 mL) dark brown sugar

1 tbsp (15 mL) cornstarch

1 tsp (5 mL) curry or chili powder

1   8-oz (250 mL) can tomato sauce

1/2 cup (125 mL) cider or wine vinegar

1/2 cup (125 mL) chili sauce or ketchup

Method:

• In a large microwave-safe measuring cup place the brown sugar, cornstarch, curry or chili powder. Stir to mix.

• Add the tomato sauce, vinegar, chili sauce or ketchup, corn syrup and cold water. Stir to mix. Microwave, uncovered, at HIGH for 10 minutes.

• Stir well, add the rum or orange liqueur. Microwave 3 minutes at MEDIUM. Stir.

• Pour into a glass jar. Cover, use, or refrigerate.

Fish

ish occupies a most important place among the foods essential to a properly balanced diet, so we should cook it and eat it as often as we can. In fact, nutritionists recommend that we eat fish as often as four times a week.

In the first place, fish is very low in that universal problem "cholesterol fat." Instead of saturated fat, it has polyunsaturated fat. Saturated fat is the kind that clogs arteries and is linked to heart disease; the polyunsaturated kind can actually protect against artery disease by lowering the fat that clogs arteries. Fish is also one of the most digestible of high-protein foods and compared with red meat, fish contains only about one-third the number of calories per serving. What's more, fish is relatively low in sodium but high in iron and iodine and it's an excellent source of vitamins A and D.

Because fish lacks fibre, I always serve it with vegetables and grains such as rice and barley.

I have always enjoyed fish because my mother, who did not particularly like to cook, amazingly enough could always cook fish to perfection. I have adapted many of her recipes to microwave techniques. Not only were they successful, but the flavor and texture of the fish actually was enhanced by cooking it in the microwave.

Why was that? The primary reason is that 60 to 80 per cent of fish is moisture, juices that must be retained through the cooking period if the fish is to be tender and flavorful. No other cooking method does this as well as microwave cooking.

The advent of the microwave oven cut the time and effort involved in cooking. Suddenly, all family members — even the very young — can cook their own meals, giving working mothers a freedom they never knew before. And the biggest plus, of course, is that the quality, texture, color and flavor of food is protected by microwave cooking.

People often tell me they would never have the patience to change all their recipes to microwave cooking. But microwave cooking doesn't involve learning a whole new method of cooking; it's simply a matter of adapting. And it is so easy with fish.

Remember when you're cooking fish that although it contains the same amount of protein as meat, it contains a much lower proportion of fat. Fat is a poor conductor of heat and the lack of it in fish means that heat penetrates much faster in fish than it does in meat.

The most important point is to be careful of how long you cook fish. Always check the fish for doneness two or three minutes before the recommended cooking time. Why? Because the thickness and the moisture of each type of fish varies, which can alter the cooking time by a minute or so, more or less.

It's easy to know when fish is cooked, because the proteins become firm. They set in the same way as the white of an egg.

Another good rule is to cook a fish fillet or steak 5 minutes per inch (2.5 cm) of thickness. If the fish is frozen, double the cooking time.

Don't salt fish before cooking because salt draws out the juices and makes it taste flat rather than enhancing its flavor. Except in those recipes that call for salt because of a sauce or vegetables that are part of the recipe, salt when the fish is cooked.

Fish cuts

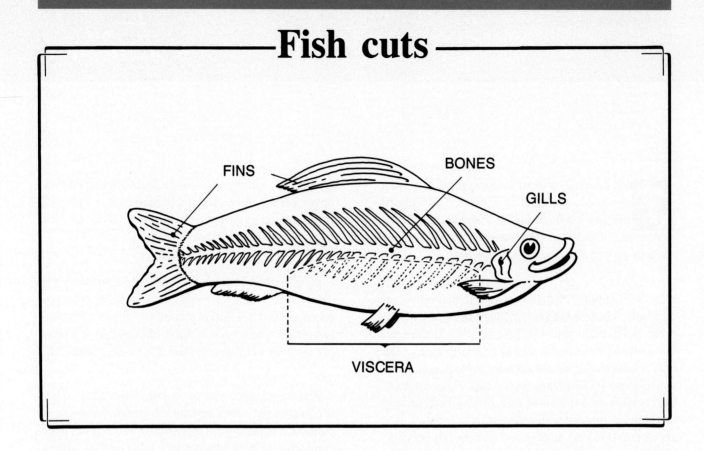

FINS

BONES

GILLS

VISCERA

Before cooking you can remove fins, scales
and head.

Steaks

Fillets

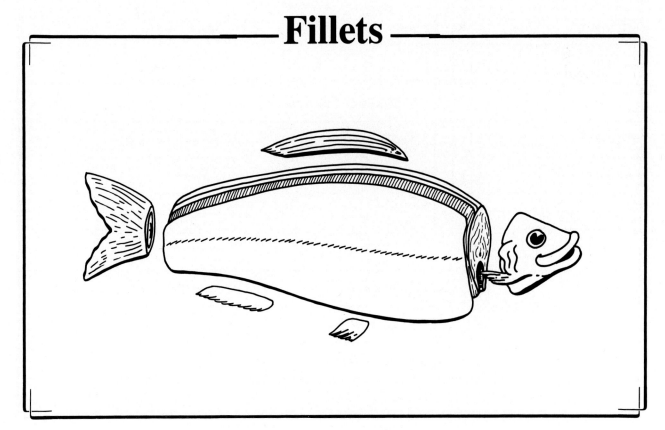

Common varieties of fish and shellfish

Lean Species

Boston Bluefish	A		Ocean Perch/Redfish	A	P		Smelt	A		F
Capelin	A		Pike			F	Sole	A	P	
Cod	A	P	Plaice	A			Tuna (light meat)	A	P	
Cusk	A		Red Snapper		P		Walleye Pickerel			F
Flounder	A	P	Rockfish		P		Walleye Pollock		P	
Haddock	A		Sauger			F	Yellow Perch			F
Hake	A	P								

Shellfish

Abalone		P	Mussel	A		Scallop	A	
Clam	A	P	Oyster	A	P	Shrimp	A	P
Crab	A	P	Prawn		P	Squid	A	
Lobster	A							

Medium Fat Species

Catfish	A		Lake Whitefish			F	Tuna (dark meat)	A	P
Halibut	A	P	Skate	A			Turbot	A	
Lake Herring			F						

Fat Species

Artic Charr			F	Lake Trout			F	Swordfish	A	
Eel	A		F	Mackerel	A			Tuna (dark meat)	A	P
Herring	A	P	Salmon	A	P	F			

A – Atlantic Ocean   P – Pacific Ocean   F – Freshwater

Tips for buying

The chart "Common varieties" and the Tips for buying are reproduced with the permission of Fisheries and Oceans Canada.

Fresh whole fish

• Full, clear, bright eyes. Bright red or pink, clean gills. Fresh, mild odour.

• Shiny, brightly coloured skin with tightly adhering scales.

• Firm flesh, elastic to the touch, clinging tightly to the bones.

• Proper display: on ice tables or in refrigerated units at 1°C to 2°C (34°F to 36°F).

Fresh fillets, steak and shucked shellfish

• Glossy and freshly-cut appearance, firm texture.

• No signs of browning or drying around cut edges.

• No discolouration.

• Proper display: in perforated plastic containers or metal trays to drain liquid; placed in closed refrigerated units at 1°C to 2°C (34°F to 36°F) or surrounded by crushed ice.

Fresh whole, shellfish

• Whole, tightly closed shells. Fresh, mild odour.

• Proper display: in baskets, trays or original commercial containers placed in refrigerated units at 1°C to 2°C (34°F to 36°F) or on crushed ice.

Frozen fish and shellfish

• Look for solidly frozen products.

• If surface is visible through clear plastic packaging, make sure there are no dried cottony patches or discoloured spots on the surface of the fish or shellfish, and there are no ice crystals or frost inside the wrapping.

• When buying frozen whole fish, choose fish with an ice coating or glaze, which prevents discolouration and drying. When buying frozen brand-name packages or store-wrapped packages, look for undamaged sealed wrapping, with little or no empty space inside the wrapping.

General directions

• Clean fish before starting a recipe.

• Arrange fish in a single layer; do not overlap edges.

• You can also roll each fillet into a little bundle — especially good for thin fillets.

• Test for doneness at end of cooking time. Fish should be opaque and flake when tested with a fork.

• If undercooked, return to oven and cook for 30 to 60 seconds more.

• Let fish dishes stand, covered, for 5 minutes after cooking.

To cook by Time:

• Cover dish with plastic wrap or a lid.

• Cook on the power level and for the minimum time recommended in the chart.

To cook by Auto Sensor or "COMB" (Combination)

• Cover dish completely with plastic wrap.

• Cook on Auto Sensor cycle COOK A8, or as directed in your oven manual.*

• FOR FISH DISHES, LET STAND, COVERED, 5 MINUTES AFTER COOKING.

• Check for doneness before cooking further

* Study your oven manual instructions carefully to clearly understand instructions given in the chart next on page 152.

> **Helpful hint:** Before cooking a whole fish or a thick piece of fish, wash it in very cold salted water. Use **1/4 cup (60 mL) coarse salt** to **6 to 8 cups (1.5 to 2L) cold water.** Let stand a few minutes and remove from water. Wipe excess water with paper towel.

Method for defrosting fish in the microwave oven at DEFROST cycle

- Make a slit in top of a package with the tip of a knife.

- Open package at both ends.

- Place the package on an inverted plate covered with a paper towel, which allows hot air to circulate around fish and helps defrosting. Program the oven at DEFROST cycle and proceed as follows:

- DEFROST for 2 minutes 15 seconds, let stand 3 minutes (there is no need to remove it from the oven).
- Turn, then DEFROST another minute and let stand 2 minutes.
- Turn and DEFROST for 2 minutes.
- Remove fish from package. It may still be slightly frozen in the center, which will not prevent you from cutting the fish in four equal parts or dividing it into fillets, to cook it as you wish.

WEIGHT DEFROST

- Certain ovens have a choice of defrosting by weight or defrosting by time-defrost method.
- You can use your WEIGHT DEFROST method which is very accurate by first reading the directions given in your operation manual. WEIGHT DEFROST is based on the following automated cycle.
- DEFROST cycle for meat, poultry and fish goes between 1½ oz and 5.9 lb (42 g and 3 kg). By touching the weight and defrost pads of your oven control panel, the automatic count-up system will indicate in the display window the weight from 1 to 6 lb (0.5 to 3 kg) of such common meat, poultry and fish items that are usually defrosted.
- Again I would like to repeat, if your oven has this automatic WEIGHT DEFROST make sure you read the instructions given in your oven manual so it will be fully understood.

Another method for defrosting fish

- If your oven does not have a special Defrost button or a DEFROST BY WEIGHT, here is the way to proceed:
- Place the frozen package (unless wrapped in foil, then it must be opened) on a double thickness of paper towel laid on the oven tray.
- Set oven at DEFROST or MEDIUM, turn package once during thawing time.
- It usually takes a 1-pound (500g) fish fillet 3 minutes to defrost sufficiently to allow you to separate fillets under cold water.
- Always cook defrosted frozen fish shortly after defrosting.

To defrost fish sticks

• If your oven has a DEFROST-COOK cycle, follow the instructions given in your oven manual.

• If you don't have such a cycle, here's how to proceed.

Ingredients:

1 lb (500 g) frozen fish sticks
Grated rind of half a lemon
1 tbsp (15 mL) fresh dill, minced (optional)

Method:

• Place a rack in the botton of a 12 × 8-inch (30 × 20 cm) microwave-safe dish.

• Place the fish sticks on the rack, one next to the other, leaving a slight space between them. Do not cover. Microwave 2 minutes at HIGH.

• Give the dish a quarter turn if your microwave oven does not have a turntable. Microwave again 2 minutes at HIGH.

• Remove from oven and let stand 5 minutes. Microwave 1 minute more at HIGH.

• The fish sticks will be completely thawed and very tasty.

• Serve with a sauce of your choice or sprinkle the fish sticks with lemon rind and dill — which is my favorite way to serve them.

Basting fish

> **A personal note:** Unlike meat, fish is more tasty and moist if you baste it at least once during its cooking period.

• If there is a sauce surrounding the fish, use it to baste the fish, or use one of the following:

2 tablespoons (30 mL) hot water *and*
2 tablespoons (30 mL) butter
or
2 tablespoons (30 mL) hot water *and*
4 tablespoons (60 mL) white wine
or
1/4 cup (60 mL) hot water *and*
Juice of half a lemon
or
1/3 cup (80 mL) hot tomato juice
or
3 tablespoons (50 mL) sour cream or whipping cream

• Obviously, each of these combinations will produce a different flavor, as well as give a different texture to the fish. But all enhance its flavor.

Cooking fish chart

	Amount	Power	Approx. cooking time (in minutes)
All fish fillets	1 lb (500 g)	HIGH	4 to 6
Fish steaks	4 (6 oz - 185 g each)	HIGH	6 to 8
Whole fish stuffed or unstuffed	1½ to 1¾ lb (750 g to 875 g)	HIGH	9 to 11

Preparing and cooking frozen fish
FREEZE-COOK cycle

	Auto Sensor cycle **FREEZE-COOK**	Approx. cooking time (in minutes)	Special instructions
Fish steaks 1 lb (500 g)	FROZ-COOK A8	20 to 21	Individually frozen Add 1/4 cup (60 mL) water per pound (500 g)
Fish fillets 1 lb (500 g)	FROZ-COOK A8	18 to 19	Individually frozen Arrange in single layer
Whole fish 1 lb (500 g)	FROZ-COOK A6	20 to 21	Arrange in single layer Add 1/4 cup (60 mL) water per pound (500 g)

Water
Poached Fish

Preparation: . . . . **1 m**
Cooking: . . . . **from 13 to 19 m**
Standing: . . . . **5 m**

A personal note: Use this method to cook small whole fish or slices of larger fish.

Method:

• Season each slice of fish with a few drops of lemon juice and a dash of pepper.

• Place fish slices or steaks one next to the other, as they were before being cut. Wrap whole fish in a cloth (any white cloth will do).

• Pour

2 cups (500 mL) of warm or cold water

into a 4-cup (1 L) plastic or glass dish with cover.

• Microwave 10 minutes at HIGH.

• Uncover, place the wrapped fish in the hot water. Microwave 3 minutes per pound (500 g) at HIGH.

• DO NOT COOK MORE THAN 3 POUNDS (1.5 KG) AT A TIME.

• Let stand 5 minutes in water.

• Remove and refrigerate or serve with the sauce of your choice.

Fish
Boiled in Milk

Preparation: . . . . **8 m**
Cooking: . . . . **from 6 to 15 m**
Standing: . . . . **none**

Method:

• Cut the fish of your choice into individual portions.

• Place in cold water to cover and add

1 tablespoon (15 mL) of coarse salt.

• Soak 5 minutes. Drain.

• Pour into a 6-cup (1.5 L) microwave-safe dish

2 cups (500 mL) of milk

• Cover and microwave 2 minutes at HIGH.
• Place the fish in the boiling milk, cover and microwave at HIGH 4 minutes per pound (500g).
• DO NOT COOK MORE THAN 3 POUNDS (1.5 KG) AT A TIME.

A personal note: To make a sauce with the milk, remove fish from dish with a perforated spoon. Cream together **2 tablespoons (30 mL) flour** with **2 tablespoons (30 mL) butter.** Add to hot milk. Stir well. Microwave 2 minutes uncovered. Stir well; if not sufficiently thickened, microwave one more minute or as needed.

wines
White Côtes de Duras
Muscadet

wines
Alsatian Riesling
Alsatian Pinot Blanc

Fish Poached in Court-bouillon

Preparation:	7 m
Cooking:	15 m
Standing:	15 m

Ingredients:

6 cups (1.5 L) water
1 tbsp (15 mL) coarse salt
1/2 cup (125 mL) of cider vinegar
1 large carrot, sliced
A few sprigs of parsley, fresh or dry
1 bay leaf
1/4 tbsp (3.75 mL) thyme
1/2 tbsp (7.5 mL) whole peppercorns
2 onions cut in four

Method:

• Place all the ingredients in an 8-cup (2 L) microwave-safe baking dish. Microwave at HIGH 15 minutes.

• Let stand 15 minutes.

• Pass through a sieve, reserving liquid. Put back liquid in the baking dish.

• Add the fish and microwave at HIGH. Time according to weight and type of fish.

> **A personal note:** The vinegar can be replaced by an equal amount of fresh lemon juice or a small unpeeled lemon, thinly sliced.

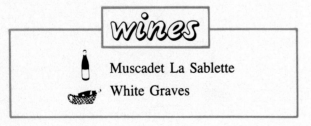

Muscadet La Sablette
White Graves

For poaching thin fish fillets

Preparation:	2 m
Cooking:	3 m
Standing:	5 m

Method:

• Use this method when poaching thin fillets such as sole or other fish of similar type.

• Place fillets one next to the other in a buttered glass dish. Pour on top

1/4 cup (60 mL) of cream or water or white wine

• Each liquid will give a different flavor.

• Sprinkle **pepper and nutmeg** on top of fillets.

• Cover dish with plastic wrap.

• Microwave 3 minutes at HIGH.

• Let stand 5 minutes, salt fish and serve with your favorite sauce.

How to poach fish to serve it cold

Advance preparation: .... **from 6 to 12 h**
Cooking: ...... **2 m per pound (500 g)**
Standing: .... **none**

A personal note: There are many ways to poach fish. The following is a basic recipe that comes in handy when time is short. It can also be used as an aromatic bouillon in which the fish can be refrigerated when it is to be served cold.

- Flavor as for poaching fresh fish.

Ingredients:

1/2 cup (125 mL) of water per pound (500 g) of fish

4 to 5 whole peppercorns

1 tsp (5 mL) coarse salt

1 bay leaf

1/4 tsp (1 mL) thyme

2 unpeeled slices of lemon (optional)

Method:

- Bring the water to boil.

- Pour over the fish. Cover the dish with plastic wrap and poach 2 minutes per pound (500 g) at HIGH.

- Make one or two slits in the plastic wrap and let fish cool in its cooking water.

- Then, without removing the cover, place in the refrigerator for 6 to 12 hours.

- To serve, remove the skin when necessary, place the fish on an attractive platter and coat with a gelatine mayonnaise.

Fish Fumet

Preparation: .... **10 m**
Cooking: .... **20 m**
Standing: .... **15 m**

A personal note: A fumet is used to poach fish and as the liquid used to make an aspic or gelatine coating on top of a poached fish. It is also used to make a Velouté or Sabayon sauce to serve with fish. I always keep some in my freezer in 2-cup (500 mL) quantities.

Ingredients:

2 lb (1 kg) fish heads, bones and trimmings*

1 large onion, sliced

1 leek, sliced (optional)

1 celery stalk, diced

2 tbsp (30 mL) celery leaves

1 bay leaf

1/2 tsp (2 mL) thyme

10 peppercorns

6 cups (1.5 L) water

1 tsp (5 mL) coarse salt

2 cups (500 mL) white wine

Method:

- Place in a 12-cup (3 L) microwave-safe pan the fish heads, bones and trimmings, the onion, leek, celery, celery leaves, bay leaf, thyme, peppercorns, water and salt. Cover.

- Microwave 10 minutes at MEDIUM-HIGH. Remove the scum that rises to the surface with a perforated spoon.

- Add the wine, cover. Microwave at MEDIUM-HIGH 10 minutes.

- Let stand 15 minutes.

- Strain through a sieve lined with a cloth. You will have a clear liquid.

* It is easy to obtain fish trimmings from a fish shop.

Baked Small Fish in the microwave oven

Advance preparation : . . . **from 2 to 3 h**
Cooking: . . . . . . **4 m per pound (500 g)**
Standing: . . . . **none**

A personal note: This method will give you a crusty fish on top and a poached fish inside.

Ingredients:

2 cups (500 mL) of milk
1/2 tsp (2 mL) each salt and dry mustard
1 bay leaf
1/2 tsp (2 mL) thyme

Method:

• Mix all the ingredients in an 8-inch (20 cm) microwave-safe cake pan.

• Cut the chosen fish in individual portions.

• Roll in this mixture and marinate 2 to 3 hours at room temperature.

• Remove fish from milk and roll into fine bread-crumbs until well coated.

• Butter a microwave-safe dish large enough in which to place your pieces of fish, one next to the other.

• Pour the following mixture on top: **3 to 4 tablespoons (50 to 60 mL) each of melted butter and lemon juice,** using a large spoon to pour some of the mixture onto each piece of coated fish.

• Microwave at HIGH 4 minutes per pound (500 g).

• Serve as soon as cooked.

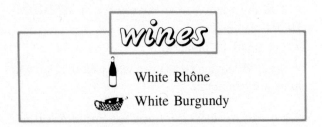

wines

White Rhône
White Burgundy

Stuffed Fillets of Fish

Preparation: . . . . **10 m**
Cooking: . . . . **12 m**
Standing: . . . . **none**

• Butter generously an 8 × 8-inch (20 × 20 cm) ceramic or glass dish.

• Cover bottom with fish fillets placed one next to the other. Cover with the following stuffing:

Stuffing

• This is a basic recipe that can be varied to taste.

• Butter **2 slices of bread** on both sides. Crust can be removed. Dice the bread.

• Add

1 egg lightly beaten

2 small pickles, diced

1/2 tsp (2 mL) paprika

1/4 tsp (1 mL) thyme

4 tbsp (60 mL) milk

Salt and pepper to taste

• Mix thoroughly and use to cover fillets.

• Cover stuffing with another layer of fillets.

• Melt 1 minute at HIGH, **3 tablespoons (50 mL) of margarine or butter per pound (500 g) of fish.**

• Add

1 tsp (5 mL) Dijon mustard

1/4 tsp (1 mL) curry powder

Grated rind of 1/2 lemon

• Stir well and pour evenly over the top of the stuffing and fillets.

• Microwave 12 minutes at MEDIUM-HIGH.

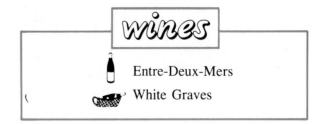

Entre-Deux-Mers

White Graves

Oriental Steamed Fish

Preparation: . . . . **3 m**
Cooking: . . . . **3 m or more**
Standing: . . . . **10 m**

A personal note: Any kind of fish can be steamed. It is equally good served hot or cold. This method is especially recommended for a low fat or reducing diet.

Method:

- Use an 8 or 10-inch (20 or 25 cm) square ceramic or glass dish with a good cover.

- Choose a rack on which at least 2 pieces of fish can be placed, although 1 to 6 individual pieces can be steamed at one time.

- Pour 1½ to 2 inches (4 to 5 cm) of hot water in bottom of dish — or just what is needed to come to the level of the rack.

- Place the pieces of fish on a plate or small platter, dot each piece with **butter**

- Add **a few drops of fresh lemon or lime juice.**

- Set the plate on the rack.

- Cover the dish. Steam at HIGH 3 minutes per fillet or steak.

- Add 1 minute for each additional piece of fish. When cooked, remove from oven. Leave cover on, let stand 10 minutes, then serve.

Muscadet La Sablette

Menetou-Salon

Japanese Steamed Fish

Preparation: . . . . **12 m**
Cooking: . . . . **from 12 to 14 m**
Standing: . . . . **none**

• Roasted sesame seeds mixed with fresh ginger give a delicate and interesting flavor to fish fillets or smelts poached this way.

Ingredients:

2 to 3 tbsp (30 to 50 mL) sesame seeds
1 tsp (5 mL) vegetable oil
1/4 cup (60 mL) Sake, water or white wine
1 tsp (5 mL) fresh ginger root, grated
1/2 tsp (2 mL) salt
2 lb (1 kg) fish of your choice

Sauce:

3 tsp (15 mL) vegetable oil
1/4 cup (60 mL) soy sauce
   (Kikkoman if available)
1/4 tsp (1 mL) fresh ground pepper
Roasted sesame seeds
1/2 cup (125 mL) green onions, minced

Method:

• Place the sesame seeds and the 1 teaspoon (5 mL) vegetable oil in a small glass bowl.

• Brown 1 or 2 minutes at HIGH, stirring 3 times.

• When the sesame seeds are golden brown, set aside.

• Choose a microwave-safe dish large enough to contain all the ingredients. Pour into it the Sake, water or white wine, ginger root and salt.

• Cover and microwave 5 minutes at MEDIUM to bring out the delicate ginger flavor.

• Add the fish to the hot liquid, basting it 3 or 4 times.

• Cover and microwave 5 to 7 minutes at MEDIUM-HIGH, depending on type of fish used.

• Check doneness with a fork. The fish is cooked when it flakes.

• Let stand, covered, while you prepare the sauce.

To make the sauce

• Mix together in a microwave-safe bowl the vegetable oil, soy sauce, pepper and sesame seeds.

• Microwave 40 seconds at HIGH.

• Pour over the cooked fish and sprinkle with minced green onions. Serve.

Alsatian Silvaner
Alsatian Muscat

Fish Fillets Baked by Convection in microwave oven

Entre-Deux-Mers
Menetou-Salon

Preparation:	**5 m**
Cooking:	**3 m**
Standing:	**none**

A personal note: Fish cooked by this method will have a nice brown color and will be moist and tender. It's an excellent method to cook salmon steaks, fresh thick fillets of cod, halibut or turbot.

• Brush each piece of the chosen fish with butter or oil or soft bacon fat, then roll in fine breadcrumbs.

• Place pieces of fish one next to the other on a low heat-proof glass or ceramic dish.

• Do not overlap.

• Place low rack on turntable in your oven, if your model has one. Preheat the convection part of the microwave oven at 450°F (230°C).

• Place fish dish in preheated oven. Bake 3 minutes per 3 pieces of fish.

• Time will vary slightly, depending on the type of fish. Check doneness before removing from oven.

• Serve with a sauce of your choice.

Fish Fillets Bonne Femme

• Fresh or frozen fillets of a fish of your choice can be prepared with this classic of the French cuisine. You need a browning dish to make this recipe.

Ingredients:

1 to 2 lb (500 g to 1 kg) fish fillets
   of your choice

1 tsp (5 mL) salt

1/4 tsp (1 mL) pepper

3 tbsp (50 mL) butter

2 garlic cloves, chopped fine

1 medium-sized onion, cut in slivers

3 green onions, chopped

1/2 lb (250 g) fresh mushrooms, cut in four

1/2 cup (125 mL) dry cider or white wine

1/4 cup (60 mL) whipping cream

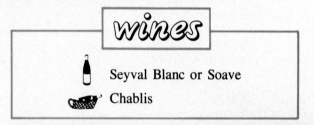

Seyval Blanc or Soave

Chablis

Preparation:	15 m
Cooking:	17 m
Standing:	3 m

Method:

• Roll the fillets in absorbent paper to remove excess moisture. Sprinkle with pepper and only 1/4 teaspoon (1 mL) of the salt.

• Preheat a browning dish 5 minutes. Without removing the dish from the oven, add the following into the hot dish: butter, garlic, onion, green onions and half the mushrooms. Stir well. Add the remaining salt; stir. Microwave at HIGH 2 minutes. Stir well.

• Place the fillets, rolled or left whole, over the vegetables. Sprinkle remaining mushrooms on top. Pour the cider or wine over all. Cover pan with waxed paper and microwave 4 to 5 minutes at HIGH. Let stand 3 minutes.

• Gently remove the fish to a hot platter with a perforated spoon. Also with the spoon, drain out most of the mushrooms and sprinkle on top and around the fish. Microwave the sauce 5 to 7 minutes at HIGH, or until reduced by half.

• Whip the cream and fold into the hot gravy while beating with a whisk. Pour over fish and serve.

Butter Poached Fish Fillets

Advance preparation: **from 30 m to 2 h**
Cooking:..................**9 m**
Standing:.....................**none**

A personal note: This recipe is super with fresh fillets of sole. Haddock or cod are equally good, but the cooking time can vary slightly, depending on type of fish and thickness of fillets. The simplicity of the sauce makes it even better. The fresh dill and parsley each gives a different flavor. You need a browing dish for this recipe.

Ingredients:

1 to 1½ lb (500 to 750 g) fish fillets.

2 tbsp (30 mL) coarse salt

1/3 cup (80 mL) butter

Salt and pepper to taste

Grated rind of 1 lemon

1 tbsp (15 mL) fresh dill, chopped *or*
  1/4 cup (60 mL) fresh parsley, minced

Method:

• Place fish in a dish, cover with very cold water and the coarse salt. Let stand 30 minutes to 2 hours. This prevents the fish from drying during the cooking period and accentuates its flavor.

• Remove the fish from water and dry thoroughly with paper towel. Dispose of the water and salt.

• Preheat a browning dish 6 minutes at HIGH. Butter each fillet on one side. Without removing dish from the oven, place fish in it, buttered-side down. Microwave 2 to 3 minutes at MEDIUM-HIGH. Check for doneness with a fork. Microwave 1 or 2 minutes more, if necessary.

• Turn fillets, taking care not to break them. Microwave 1 minute at HIGH.

• Remove fish to a hot dish, sprinkle with salt and pepper, lemon juice, dill or parsley, and to taste, some melted butter.

wines

Canadian Chardonnay
Mâcon Villages

Fish Fillets or Slices Browned in Butter

Preparation: . . . . **8 m**
Cooking: . . . .**12 m**
Standing: . . . . **10 m**

A personal note: You can make nice brown fish fillets or slices in the microwave oven using a browning dish.

Ingredients:

1 lb (500 g) fish fillets or slices

1 egg white

2 tbsp (30 mL) cold water or lemon juice

1 cup (250 mL) fine breadcrumbs

1 tsp (5 mL) paprika

2 tbsp (30 mL) butter, margarine or vegetable oil

Method:

• Cut fillets into individual portions.

• Slightly beat the egg white with cold water or lemon juice in a small bowl.

• Place breadcrumbs and paprika on a piece of waxed paper.

• Melt butter or margarine or heat vegetable oil 1 minute at HIGH.

• Roll each fish piece in the egg white mixture, then in the breadcrumbs.

• Place the fish pieces on waxed paper and pour some of the chosen fat over each piece.

• Preheat a browning dish 5 minutes at HIGH. Without taking the dish out of the oven, put the fish pieces in it, buttered-side down. Press each piece with a fork.

• Microwave 5 to 6 minutes at MEDIUM. Turn each piece with a spatula.

• Let stand 10 minutes in the oven or outside, covering dish with a cloth.

• The top of the fish will be brown and crusty and they will be well cooked.

wines

Italian Chardonnay
Californian Chardonnay

Chinese Fish Fillets

Preparation: . . . . 7 m
Cooking: . . . . from 5 to 6 m
Standing: . . . . 5 m

Liebfraumilch

Entre-Deux-Mers

Helpful hint: To remove cooking odor from a microwave oven, mix in a bowl the juice and peel of half a lemon with a little water. Microwave 5 minutes at HIGH. Then wipe the interior with a damp cloth.

Ingredients:

2 tbsp (30 mL) soy sauce

Grated rind of 1 lemon

1 tbsp (15 mL) lemon juice

1 tbsp (15 mL) ketchup

1 garlic clove, minced

1 tbsp (15 mL) fresh ginger root, grated

1 lb (500 g) fish fillets of your choice, fresh or frozen

Method:

• Mix together in an 8 × 8-inch (20 × 20 cm) glass dish the soy sauce, lemon juice and rind, ketchup, garlic and ginger.

• Cut the fish into individual pieces and set in the dish, rolling them around in the sauce. Cover with waxed paper. Microwave 5 to 6 minutes at HIGH, until the fish flakes easily. Let stand 5 minutes, covered.

• To serve, baste with the sauce in the dish.

Fillets
À l'Anglaise

Preparation: . . . . **5 m**
Cooking: . . . . **from 4 to 6 m**
Standing: . . . . **5 m**

A personal note: This is the easiest way to cook fish, but it's so tasty. Use fresh fish or thaw frozen fillets.

Ingredients:

1 lb (500 g) fillets of your choice

Juice and rind of 1 lemon

3 tbsp (50 mL) melted butter or margarine

1/2 tsp (2 mL) paprika

Salt and pepper to taste

Dry Orvieto

Alsatian Riesling

Method:

• Cut fillets into individual pieces.

• Roll each piece in the lemon juice and rind mixed together.

• Place in a single layer in an 8 × 8-inch (20 × 20 cm) glass dish or a 9-inch (23 cm) microwave-safe pie plate.

• Brush each fillet with melted butter or margarine. Sprinkle with paprika.

• Cover dish with waxed paper and microwave 4 to 6 minutes at HIGH, depending on type of fish. Do not turn.

• Let stand 5 minutes. Salt and pepper. Serve with butter remaining in baking dish.

Fish Fillets Meunière

Preparation: . . . . **8 m**
Cooking: . . . . **13 m**
Standing: . . . . **6 m**

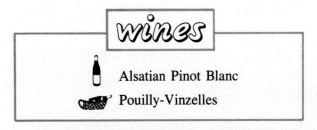

Alsatian Pinot Blanc
Pouilly-Vinzelles

• This is the classic method of French cuisine for browning fish fillets. A well-browned fish steak or fillet can be cooked with success in the microwave oven.

A personal note: It is important to note that fish, with its 60 to 80 per cent moisture content and approximately 18 per cent albuminoid, must cook in a minimum amount of time to retain its natural juices. Use olive or vegetable oil in preference to butter, which burns easily and gives the fish a milky taste. This recipe requires a browning dish.

Ingredients:

1 egg white
2 tbsp (30 mL) cold water
2 tbsp (30 mL) flour
1 tbsp (15 mL) cornstarch
Salt and pepper to taste
1 lb (500 g) thin fish steaks or fillets
2 tbsp (30 mL) vegetable oil
2 tbsp (30 mL) butter
1 tsp (5 mL) capers or small gherkins, diced

Method:

• Mix together the egg white and the water in a deep plate.

• Mix together the flour, cornstarch, salt and pepper on a piece of waxed paper.

• Roll each piece of fish in the egg white mixture, then in the flour.

• Preheat a browning dish (Corning) 6 minutes at HIGH.

• Without removing the dish from the oven, add the oil.

• Place the fish pieces in it one next to the other and press them down with a fork for perfect contact with the dish.

• Brown 6 minutes at HIGH. Turn carefully and let stand 6 more minutes in the oven, without heat.

• Place on a hot plate, browned-side up.

• Place butter and capers or gherkins in a microwave-safe dish. Microwave 1 minute at HIGH. Pour over fish. Serve.

Sauce Velouté

Preparation:	**2 m**
Cooking:	**from 8 to 9 m**
Standing:	**none**

• A basic white sauce, made with fish stock or canned clam juice or milk or light cream, this sauce has many delicious variations.

Ingredients:

2 tbsp (30 mL) butter
2 tbsp (30 mL) flour
1 cup (250 mL) fish stock or milk
Salt and pepper to taste

Method:

• Place the butter and flour in a 4-cup (1 L) measuring cup, stir well. Microwave 4 minutes at HIGH, stirring after 2 minutes. The mixture will have little spots of brown here and there. This is as it should be.

• Add the fish stock, the juices from a poached fish or the milk. Salt and pepper. Microwave 4 to 5 minutes at HIGH, stirring once.

• The Velouté has the consistency of a light white sauce.

Sauce Aurore

Preparation:	**5 m**
Cooking:	**from 4 to 5 m**
Standing:	**none**

Variation of Sauce Velouté

A personal note: This sauce is excellent with salmon, cod and halibut.

Ingredients:

1 cup (250 mL) Velouté Sauce
1/2 cup (125 mL) tomato sauce
1/2 cup (125 mL) light cream
2 egg yolks, lightly beaten

Method:

• In a 4-cup (1 L) microwave-safe measuring cup combine the ingredients.

• Stir until well mixed.

• Microwave at MEDIUM 4 to 5 minutes or until creamy, stirring once.

• The sauce should be light and creamy.

Fish Marinade

Advance preparation: .. **from 6 to 12 h**
Cooking: . . . . **none**
Standing: . . . . **none**

A personal note: The flavor of fish — of whatever kind, and whether fresh or frozen — can be enhanced by marinating the fish before cooking. I particularly advise marinating fish that is to be served cold.

1/4 cup (60 mL) olive or vegetable oil

1/2 tsp (2 mL) each dill, tarragon and sugar

Method:

• Mix all the ingredients together, pour over a piece of fish of 2 to 3 pounds (1 to 1.5 kg).

• Cover and refrigerate from 6 to 12 hours.

• To cook the fish, remove from marinade, wipe dry with paper towel, and cook according to the recipe you've chosen.

Ingredients:

1/4 cup (60 mL) fresh lemon juice

1/4 cup (60 mL) fresh lime juice (optional)

Hollandaise in food processor or blender

Preparation:	**5 m**
Cooking:	**3 m**
Standing:	**none**

- Hollandaise is amazingly easy to prepare in the microwave oven and a food processor or blender.

Ingredients:

3/4 cup (190 mL) butter, cut up in squares
2 egg yolks
1 tbsp (15 mL) fresh lemon juice
Salt and pepper to taste

Method:

- Place the butter in a 2-cup (500 mL) microwave-safe measuring cup.
- Microwave 3 minutes at HIGH.
- Place the egg yolks and the lemon juice in the blender or food processor, cover and start the machine. Slowly pour in the hot butter. When all is added, turn off the motor.
- Season to taste.

Dijon Hollandaise

- Especially good with hot or cold salmon or poached cod, this sauce can be served hot or cold.
- Replace the lemon juice in the Hollandaise sauce with **2 tablespoons (30 mL) cold water** mixed with **a heaping tablespoon (15 mL) of Dijon mustard.**

Watercress Mayonnaise

Preparation:	**10 m**
Cooking:	**none**
Standing:	**none**

- An uncooked sauce prepared in the food processor. Its deep green color is most appetizing.

Ingredients:

1 bunch watercress, stems and leaves*
1/4 cup (60 mL) dill weed, fresh if available
4 green onions, coarsely chopped
1 tbsp (15 mL) fresh lemon juice
1 cup (250 mL) mayonnaise (unsweetened)

Method:

- Place all the ingredients in the food processor, cover and process until the whole is creamy, with a beautiful green color.
- Refrigerate until ready to serve.
- Taste for seasoning.

* About 2 to 3 full cups (500 to 750 mL).

Blender Mustard Hollandaise

Preparation:	**7 m**
Cooking:	**2 m**
Standing:	**none**

• One minute in a blender to mix the ingredients and you have a super Hollandaise to serve with fish.

Ingredients:

4 egg yolks

2 tbsp (30 mL) fresh lemon juice

1 cup (250 mL) butter

4 tsp (20 mL) hot water

1/2 tsp (2 mL) salt

1 tbsp (15 mL) Dijon mustard

Method:

• Combine the egg yolks and the lemon juice in the blender. Cover, blend 10 seconds.

• Melt butter 2 minutes at HIGH.

• Gradually add hot water to egg yolks, while blending at medium speed, then add the hot butter, in a slow steady stream. Stop blender.

• Add the salt and mustard. Beat 20 seconds.

• Pour into warm dish and serve.

A personal note: To turn leftover ketchup into a sauce, remove metal cap from bottle, add a spoonful or two of leftover red wine or cream or orange juice or Madeira, and a square of butter. Microwave 2 to 3 minutes at MEDIUM, depending on quantity. Add to brown sauce or spaghetti sauce or serve over rice.

Mock Hollandaise

A personal note: Not as rich as the true Hollandaise, this sauce is excellent with cod, halibut and other types of white fish. I like to roll the cooked fish in minced parsley or chives, then top it with the Mock Hollandaise.

Preparation: . . . . **6 m**
Cooking: . . . .**5 m**
Standing: . . . .**none**

Ingredients:

2 tbsp (30 mL) butter

2 tbsp (30 mL) flour

1/2 tsp (2 mL) salt

1 cup (250 mL) milk

2 egg yolks, lightly beaten

2 tbsp (30 mL) fresh lemon juice

Grated rind of 1/2 a lemon

2 tbsp (30 mL) margarine or butter

Method:

• Place the butter in a 4-cup (1 L) microwave-safe measuring cup, and melt 1 minute at HIGH.

• Add the flour, mix well. Add the salt and the milk.

• Stir and microwave 3 minutes at HIGH, stirring once after 2 minutes of cooking.

• When sauce is creamy, stir in the egg yolks. Beat until well blended.

• Add the lemon juice and rind. Mix well. Microwave 1 minute at HIGH. Beat and cook another 30 seconds.

• Add the margarine or butter.

• Taste for seasoning. Stir until the butter is melted. Serve.

Sauce Bercy

Preparation: .7 m
Cooking: . . . . .5 m
Standing: . . . . .none

A personal note: Here's an elegant sauce to make with the liquid remaining in the pan after you've cooked a fish.

Ingredients:

2 tbsp (30 mL) butter

4 green onions, chopped fine

2 tbsp (30 mL) margarine or butter

2 tbsp (30 mL) flour

1/2 tsp (2 mL) salt

1 cup (250 mL) fish cooking liquid

2 tbsp (30 mL) fresh parsley, minced

Method:

- Place in a dish the first 2 tablespoons (30 mL) butter and the green onions.

- Microwave 2 minutes at HIGH.

- In a 4-cup (1 L) microwave-safe measuring cup, stir together the margarine or butter and the flour, then add the salt and the fish cooking liquid.

- Microwave 1 minute at HIGH. Stir well and microwave 2 minutes at MEDIUM-HIGH. Stir thoroughly.

- The sauce should be smooth and creamy.

- Add the parsley, stir well. Pour over the fish or serve separately.

Onion-Sage Fish Sauce

Preparation: .8 m
Cooking: . . . . .8 m
Standing: .none

A personal note: I make this sauce in the summer when fresh sage is plentiful in my garden and at the market. This sauce is good with all fish except sole.

Ingredients:

1 tbsp (15 mL) butter

1 large onion, minced

Salt and pepper to taste

1/2 tsp (2 mL) dried sage *or*
  1 tsp (5 mL) fresh sage, minced

1/2 cup (125 mL) light cream

1/4 cup (60 mL) water

2 tbsp (30 mL) breadcrumbs

Method:

• Place the butter in a microwave-safe bowl and melt 1 minute at HIGH.

• Add the onion, stir well and microwave 3 minutes at MEDIUM-HIGH, stirring once. Salt and pepper to taste.

• Add the sage. Mix well and add the cream, water and breadcrumbs. Stir well.

• Microwave 5 minutes at MEDIUM, stirring once during the cooking.

• The sauce should be thick and creamy.

• Season to taste.

Sea Island Curry Sauce

Preparation: . . . . 12 m
Cooking: . . . . 18 m
Standing: . . . . 30 m

A personal note: This intriguing sauce is flavored with curry and textured with coconut. When possible, use fresh coconut, grated, and use 1/2 cup (125 mL) of the coconut milk to replace 1/2 cup (125 mL) of the milk. This sauce is good on all poached or grilled fish.

Ingredients:

1/2 cup (125 mL) coconut, grated

1 cup (250 mL) milk

4 tbsp (60 mL) butter

2 onions, chopped fine

1 unpeeled apple, cored

2 small tomatoes, peeled and seeded

1 tbsp (15 mL) curry powder

1 cup (250 mL) white wine

Method:

• Place the coconut and milk in a bowl. Soak 30 minutes.

• Place the butter in a microwave-safe bowl and melt 3 minutes at HIGH.

• Add the onions, stir and microwave 4 minutes at HIGH.

• Stir, add the apple, tomatoes, curry powder and salt to taste. Stir thoroughly.

• Microwave 5 minutes at MEDIUM-HIGH.

• Stir, add the coconut and milk and the white wine.

• Mix and microwave 3 minutes at HIGH.

• Purée in a food mill or food processor.

• Adjust seasoning.

• Warm 3 minutes at HIGH. Serve.

Oriental Sauce

Preparation: . . . . **7 m**
Cooking: . . . . **9 m**
Standing: . . . . **none**

A personal note: Interesting and different, this sauce is easy to make. Serve it on any poached or steamed fish. Whenever possible, use the Japanese wine called Sake. If it isn't available, use white dry vermouth instead.

Ingredients:

2 tbsp (30 mL) cornstarch

1 cup (250 mL) pineapple juice or apple juice

1/4 cup (60 mL) Sake or white vermouth

2 tbsp (30 mL) soy sauce

1 tbsp (15 mL) dark brown sugar

1/4 cup (60 mL) cider vinegar

1 tbsp (15 mL) fresh ginger root, grated

Method:

• Mix the cornstarch with 1/4 cup (60 mL) of the pineapple or apple juice.

• Place in a large microwave-safe cup the Sake or white vermouth, the rest of the pineapple or apple juice, soy sauce, brown sugar and cider vinegar. Microwave 5 minutes at HIGH, stir well.

• Add the well-stirred cornstarch mixture and the fresh grated ginger. Microwave 4 minutes at HIGH.

• Stir well until creamy and transparent.

• Taste, add salt if necessary. Pour over cooked fish.

Sauce Verte

Preparation: . . . . **10 m**
Cooking: . . . . **none**
Standing: . . . . **none**

A personal note: If you have a food processor or a blender, this sauce will be ready in minutes. If not, the ingredients will have to be chopped very finely. It is an uncooked sauce, equally good with hot or cold fish.

Ingredients:

1/2 cup (125 mL) green onion tops or chives

1/2 cup (125 mL) parsley

1/2 cup (125 mL) spinach leaves, uncooked

2 tbsp (30 mL) fresh lemon juice

1 cup (250 mL) mayonnaise

Method:

• Coarsely chop the green onions or chives, the parsley and spinach.

• Place in food processor or blender, add the lemon juice and process until everything is in small bits.

• Add to mayonnaise. Stir well.

• Keep refrigerated, well covered.

Italian Baked Sole Fillets

Preparation:	**8 m**
Cooking: fresh fillets:	**6 m**
frozen fillets:	**from 12 to 14 m**
Standing:	**5 m**

A personal note: Fresh or frozen sole can be used for this dish. Defrost fish before cooking. Serve with creamed spinach mixed with small noodle shells.

Ingredients:

1 lb (500 g) frozen or fresh sole fillets

1 cup (250 mL) sour cream

1/2 cup (125 mL) green onions, chopped

1/2 tsp (2 mL) salt

1/4 tsp (1 mL) pepper

1 tsp (5 mL) basil, chopped

1/2 cup (125 mL) Parmesan or strong Cheddar cheese, grated

Paprika

Method:

• Place either fresh or thawed frozen sole in a heavily buttered 8 × 12-inches (20 × 30 cm) microwave-safe dish.

• Combine remaining ingredients and spread evenly over the fish. Sprinkle the whole with paprika.

• Cover with plastic wrap, microwave at MEDIUM 12 to 14 minutes for frozen fillets, 6 minutes for fresh fillets.

• Let stand 5 minutes before serving.

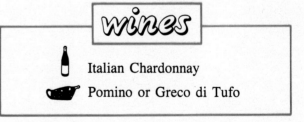

Italian Chardonnay

Pomino or Greco di Tufo

Sole Embassy

Preparation: . . . . .12 m
Cooking: . . . . .11 m
Standing: . . . . 3 m

A personal note: In England, this dish is a super spring specialty, when asparagus and Dover sole are at their best. It's one of my favorite light lunches. Any type of sole can replace the Dover. Serve with fine noodles mixed with parsley and butter.

Ingredients:

1 lb (500 g) fresh asparagus

Salt and pepper to taste

Grated rind of half a lemon

1 lb (500 g) sole fillets

3 tbsp (50 mL) butter

2 green onions, minced

2 tbsp (30 mL) lemon juice

1 tsp (5 mL) Dijon mustard

Method:

• Clean asparagus and cut into 3-inch (7.5 cm) lengths. Place in a microwave-safe dish, add 1/4 cup (60 mL) water, a pinch of sugar. Cover and microwave 5 minutes at HIGH. Drain.

• Stir with salt, pepper to taste and lemon rind. Divide equally over fillets. Roll up and secure with wooden picks, or tie with soft string.

• Place the fish rolls side by side in a thickly buttered baking dish.

• Melt the 3 tablespoons (50 mL) butter 1 minute at HIGH.

• Add the green onions, lemon juice and the Dijon mustard. Heat 40 seconds at HIGH.

• Pour mixture over fish. Cover with waxed paper or a cover. Microwave 6 minutes at MEDIUM-HIGH. Let stand 3 minutes and serve.

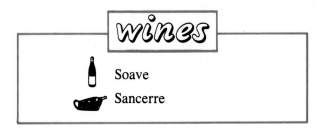

Soave

Sancerre

Sole Dugléré

• This is another great dish of the French cuisine. When the first fresh tomatoes appear in my garden, it's time for that yearly delight — a Dugléré.

Ingredients:

1 lb (500 g) sole fillets

2 tomatoes, peeled and diced

1 tsp (5 mL) sugar

1 medium-sized onion, diced

1 garlic clove, chopped fine

1 tbsp (15 mL) parsley, chopped

1 tbsp (15 mL) butter

2 tbsp (30 mL) flour

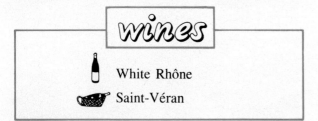

🍾 White Rhône

🥘 Saint-Véran

Preparation: . . . . 15 m
Cooking: . . . . 12 m
Standing: . . . . **none**

1/2 cup (125 mL) white wine or white vermouth

Salt and pepper to taste

Method:

• Place in a glass or ceramic dish the tomatoes, sugar, onion and garlic. Mix well. Microwave 2 minutes at HIGH. Stir well, add the parsley.

• Place the fillets of sole on top of this mixture. Salt and pepper. Cover with waxed paper or plastic wrap. Microwave 6 minutes at HIGH. Let stand 4 minutes. Remove the fillets to a hot platter.

• Mix the butter and flour together and stir into the tomato mixture. Mix well.

• Add the white wine or vermouth. Microwave 4 minutes at HIGH, stirring well after 2 minutes.

• When sauce is creamy and piping hot, pour over the fish and serve.

Sole Amandine

• One of the most popular of all fish dishes, this is from the classic French cuisine. It's quick and easy to prepare in a microwave.

Preparation: . . . . **10 m**
Cooking: . . . . **10 m**
Standing: . . . . **none**

Ingredients:

1 to 1½ lb (500 - 750 g) sole fillets
2 tbsp (30 mL) butter
1 tbsp (15 mL) cornstarch
Juice and rind of 1 lemon
Pepper and paprika

Topping:

2 tbsp (30 mL) butter
3 tbsp (50 mL) almonds, thinly sliced

A personal note: Fish is done when it flakes and is opaque.

Muscadet-sur-lie
Pouilly Fumé

Method:

• Place the first 2 tablespoons (30 mL) butter in a 12 × 8-inch (30 × 20 cm) glass or ceramic dish and melt 1 minute at HIGH.

• Add the cornstarch, mix thoroughly.

• Add the lemon juice and rind. Stir to mix. Dip each fillet in this mixture.

• Roll each fillet. Place one next to the other in the baking dish.

• Sprinkle with the pepper and paprika. Cover dish with a piece of waxed paper or a cover.

• Microwave 6 minutes at HIGH. Let stand 3 minutes. Salt to taste.

• Place the butter and almonds in a small bowl. Brown 2 minutes at HIGH. Stir well; if the almonds are not sufficiently browned, microwave another 30 seconds, stir. This operation can be repeated a third time. However, be sure to stir often, as the almonds can brown quite fast. They should be golden brown.

• Pour over hot fish and serve.

Sole Bercy

• This dish tops my list of favorites for its simplicity. The combinations of ingredients give each variation of this dish a special finish.

Muscadet

Sancerre

Preparation:	10 m
Cooking:	15 m
Standing:	none

A personal note: The fillets of sole can be replaced by haddock or halibut steak. Both will take 3 minutes longer to cook than fillets of sole.

Ingredients:

6 green onions *or* **4 French shallots***

1/4 cup (60 mL) fresh parsley or dill, chopped

1/4 cup (60 mL) white wine or dry white vermouth

1/4 cup (60 mL) fish fumet or clam juice

1½ to 2 lb (750 g to 1 kg) sole fillets

Juice of 1/2 a lemon

3 tbsp (50 mL) unsalted or salted butter, melted

1 tsp (5 mL) cornstarch

Salt and pepper to taste

* French shallots have more flavor than green onions, but are sometimes hard to find and definitely are more expensive.

Method:

• Sprinkle the finely chopped green onions or French shallots, and the parsley or dill, over a generously buttered 8 × 12-inch (20 × 30 cm) glass or ceramic dish. Pour in the white wine or dry white vermouth the fish fumet or clam juice. Lightly pepper the inside of each fillet, roll and set over ingredients in baking dish. Sprinkle with the lemon juice and the melted butter.

• Cover dish with waxed paper. Microwave at HIGH 6 minutes per pound (500 g) of fish, basting once during cooking period. Remove fish to a platter, keep warm.

• Add the cornstarch to liquid in the pan. Stir until thoroughly mixed. Salt and pepper to taste. Microwave at HIGH 2 to 3 minutes or until creamy. Pour over the fish.

• To taste, surround with small boiled potatoes drained and rolled in finely chopped parsley.

Sole Vin Blanc

Preparation: . . . . **7 m**
Cooking: . . . . **15 m**
Standing: . . . . **10 m**

A personal note: In France, dry white Chablis is used to prepare this dish, which is usually referred to as Sole Chablis. However, any white wine can be used.

Ingredients:

1 lb (500 g) fresh sole fillets
3 tbsp (50 mL) butter
4 green onions, minced
1 cup (250 mL) dry white wine
4 tbsp (60 mL) flour
3/4 cup (180 mL) cream
Juice of half a lemon
Salt and pepper to taste

Method:

• Stretch out each fillet on paper towelling and pat dry.

• In an oblong baking dish melt 1 tablespoon (15 mL) of the butter 1 minute at HIGH.

• Add the green onions; stir well. Microwave 1 minute at HIGH. Remove from baking dish and place rolled fillets in dish.

• Spread softened green onions on top.

• Pour wine over the fillets, cover dish with waxed paper or lid. Microwave 5 minutes at MEDIUM-HIGH.

• Let stand 10 minutes, then remove fillets with a perforated spoon to a hot platter.

• Place baking dish in microwave, cook uncovered 5 minutes at HIGH.

• Blend remaining butter with the flour.

• Add the cream and the lemon juice. Do not mix; simply pour the whole in the wine remaining from the fish.

• Stir well and microwave 3 minutes at HIGH. Stir once during the cooking period.

• When smooth and creamy, salt and pepper to taste. Microwave another 30 seconds, pour over the fish.

 (same wine as used in the recipe) or Vinho Verde

Coteaux Champenois or champagne.

Sole Fillets En Cocotte

Preparation: . . . . **10 m**
Cooking: . . . . **from 6 to 8 m**
Standing: . . . . **none**

A personal note: This is a very elegant luncheon dish or dinner entrée. Easy to prepare and cook, it can be prepared in lovely English egg cups, with their covers, or in earthenware ramequins.

Ingredients:

6 small fresh sole fillets

3 tbsp (50 mL) butter

Juice of 1 lemon

1/4 tsp (1 mL) curry powder

1 tsp (5 mL) brandy or scotch

1/4 cup (60 mL) fresh mushrooms, finely minced

Salt and pepper to taste

Minced parsley or chives to garnish

Helpful hint: When using plastic wrap as a casserole dish cover, fold back a small section of plastic wrap from the edge of the dish to allow some steam to escape

Method:

• Roll fillets into individual portions. Place each portion in an English egg cup or ramequin.

• Place the butter in a microwave-safe bowl and melt 1 minute at HIGH. Add the lemon juice, curry, scotch or brandy and mushrooms. Stir well. Divide equally over the fish. Cover with plastic wrap.

• Place in a circle in the microwave and cook 6 to 8 minutes at HIGH, or until fish is tender.

• Very nice garnished with watercress, or with minced parsley or chives.

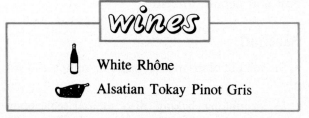

White Rhône

Alsatian Tokay Pinot Gris

Sole Fillets Stuffed with Shrimp

Preparation: . . . . **15 m**
Cooking: . . . . **13 m**
Standing: . . . . **none**

A personal note: The sole in this recipe can be replaced with a white fish steak of your choice or with haddock fillets. Sole cooks faster than any other fish, so when using another type, remember to check for doneness every 2 minutes.

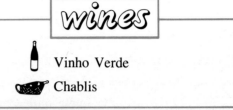

wines

🍾 Vinho Verde

🥘 Chablis

Ingredients:

6 sole fillets

1/4 cup (60 mL) butter, melted

1/2 cup (125 mL) fresh white breadcrumbs

1/2 tsp (2 mL) paprika (optional)

Filling:

1 tbsp (15 mL) butter

2 tbsp (30 mL) flour

1/2 cup (125 mL) milk or cream

1 cup (250 mL) shrimp, peeled and diced

1/2 cup (125 mL) mushrooms, sliced

Method:

• Prepare filling by melting the butter 1 minute at HIGH, stir in the flour; add the milk or cream, salt and pepper to taste. Stir well.

• Microwave 2 minutes at HIGH. Stir until creamy.

• Add the mushrooms and the shrimp. Adjust seasoning.

• Microwave 1 minute at HIGH. Stir well.

• Cover the bottom of a dish with half the fillets, pour the shrimp mixture on top.

• Cover mixture with the rest of the fillets.

• Mix the breadcrumbs with the melted butter and the paprika, scatter over the fillets.

• Microwave 10 minutes at HIGH.

• Garnish with little bunches of watercress before serving.

Sole in Sauce Rosée

Preparation: . . . . **14 m**
Cooking: . . . . **12 m**
Standing: . . . . **none**

• The white wine, mushrooms and tomatoes combine in a creamy sauce that cooks with the fish.

Ingredients:

1 lb (500 g) sole fillets
Freshly ground pepper and salt to taste
1/4 cup (60 mL) parsley, finely minced
1 cup (250 mL) peeled tomatoes, finely chopped
1/2 tsp (2 mL) sugar
1 cup (250 mL) mushrooms, sliced
1/4 cup (60 mL) dry white wine or white Vermouth
1/2 cup (125 mL) light or heavy cream
3 tbsp (50 mL) cornstarch or flour

Spanish white or Seyval Blanc
Rheingau Riesling Kabinett

Method:

• Salt and pepper each fillet, then sprinkle each with some fresh parsley.

• Roll and place in an 8 × 12-inch (20 × 30 cm) glass or ceramic dish.

• Peel, seed and chop tomatoes and sprinkle evenly over the fish. Sprinkle sugar on top.

• Spread mushrooms evenly over the tomatoes.

• Mix together the wine, cream and cornstarch or flour. Pour over the fish.

• Cover with plastic wrap or a cover. Microwave at MEDIUM-HIGH 9 minutes, or longer depending on thickness of fillets.

• Remove fish to a hot platter.

• Stir sauce thoroughly, microwave at HIGH, 2 minutes. Stir well. The sauce should be creamy. It is sometimes necessary to microwave it another 30 seconds to 1 minute, depending on the moisture in the fish.

• When creamy and hot, pour over the fish. Serve.

Poached Salmon

Preparation: . . . . **10 m**
Cooking: . . . . **from 30 to 35 m**
Standing: . . . . **10 m**

• I like to serve poached salmon hot with an egg sauce or cold with a sour cream cucumber sauce.

Ingredients:

8 cups (2 L) water

Juice of 1 lemon

2 carrots, peeled and sliced

12 peppercorns

1 tbsp (15 mL) coarse salt

6 to 10 parsley sprigs *or*
1 tbsp (15 mL) dried parsley

1 bay leaf

3 to 4 lb (1.5 to 2 kg) fresh salmon,
in one piece

Italian Pinot Bianco

Puligny-Montrachet

Method:

• Choose a dish large enough to hold the salmon.

• Place all the ingredients in the dish except the salmon.

• Cover and microwave at HIGH 15 minutes.

• Wrap the salmon in a wet J-cloth, sew up in a neat bundle and place in the boiling water. Cover fish with water.

• Cover dish and microwave at MEDIUM-HIGH, 5 minutes per pound (500 g). Let stand 10 minutes.

• Remove fish from water with two forks. Set on a plate.

• To serve hot, unwrap and set on a dish.

• Top with finely chopped fresh parsley or dill and melted butter or use a sauce of your choice.

• To serve cold, do not unwrap; refrigerate 6 to 12 hours.

• Remove cloth and garnish to taste. Serve with a bowl of cold sauce of your choice.

Poached Salmon À la Française

Advance preparation: . . . . **from 6 to 8 h**
Cooking: . . . . **from 8 to 12 m**
Standing: . . . . **10 m**

A personal note: In France, they prefer to use salmon steak for this dish. When I cannot get salmon, I replace it with halibut or fresh cod. It is served cold with the classic Sauce Verte.

wines

White Rhône
Condrieu

Ingredients:

1 tbsp (15 mL) olive or vegetable oil
4 to 6 salmon steaks of your choice
Juice of 1 lemon
Grated rind of 1/2 a lemon
6 peppercorns, crushed
1 medium-sized onion, peeled and cut in four
1 tbsp (15 mL) coarse salt

Method:

• Spread the oil in the bottom of a 12-inch (30 cm) square dish. Place the fish steaks one next to the other, not overlapping. Add the lemon juice and rind.

• Sprinkle the peppercorns and onion on top and add enough hot water to come just to the top of the fish. Sprinkle the coarse salt in the water around the fish.

• Cover and poach fish at HIGH 2 minutes per piece of fish. Let stand 10 minutes.

• Uncover and let the fish cool in its water. Then remove each piece with a perforated spoon and remove the skin if necessary. Arrange on a serving plate.

• Completely cover top of fish with French Sauce Verte.

• Can be refrigerated 6 to 8 hours.

English Poached Salmon

• This is perfect cold buffet dish.

Advance preparation: . . **from 10 to 12 h**
Cooking: . . . . **from 30 to 35 m**
Standing: . . . . **10 m**

Ingredients:

A 3-to-4-lb (1.5 to 2 kg) piece of salmon, cut from the center

2 cups (500 mL) milk

2 cups (500 mL) water

1 tbsp (15 mL) coarse salt

2 bay leaves

1/4 cup (60 mL) parsley, coarsely chopped

1/2 tsp (2 mL) basil

1/4 tsp (1 mL) dill seeds

1 cup (250 mL) mayonnaise

1 peeled lemon cut into thin slices

2 hard-cooked eggs

2 carrots, finely shredded

Method:

• Wrap and sew the piece of salmon in a J-cloth, as for Poached Salmon.

• Place in an 8-cup (2 L) microwave-safe bowl the milk, water, salt, bay leaves, chopped parsley, basil and dill.

• Cover and microwave at HIGH 15 minutes.

• Add the salmon, pour some of the hot liquid on top.

• Cover and microwave at MEDIUM-HIGH 5 minutes per pound (500 g). Let stand 10 minutes.

• Cool 1 hour at room temperature.

• DO NOT UNWRAP; refrigerate overnight.

• To serve, unwrap, remove the skin, set on a serving plate.

• Spread the mayonnaise all over the fish. On top, make a long line of overlapping slices of lemon.

• Grate the hard-cooked eggs and sprinkle over the whole fish.

• Place the shredded carrots all around the fish, to form a sort of crown.

• Set on a bed of crisp lettuce leaves.

wines

🍾 Italian Chardonnay

🥄 Californian Chardonnay or Condrieu

Poached Salmon Hollandaise

Convection cooking

> **A personal note:** This is an excellent recipe to cook a thick piece of fresh salmon to serve cold with a French mustard Hollandaise. It's perfect for a buffet or an intimate garden party. Cook this dish in the convection section of your microwave oven.

Advance preparation: . . . . **12 h**
Cooking: . . . . **30 m**
Standing: . . . . **none**

> **Helpful hint: Lemon Honey** is an interesting topping for hot rolls or toasts that you should make the evening before you want to serve it at breakfast. To make it, add the juice and grated rind of 1 lemon to 1 cup (250 mL) honey in a small bowl. Microwave 1 minute at HIGH. Stir for a few seconds. Let stand at room temperature overnight. Lemon Honey will keep 4 to 6 weeks in the refrigerator.

Ingredients:

2 lb (1 kg) centre piece of salmon

1/3 cup (80 mL) butter

1/3 cup (80 mL) dry vermouth or fresh lemon juice

Salt and pepper to taste

3 sprigs of fresh basil *or*
  1 tsp (5 mL) dry basil

Method:

• Place the piece of salmon on a rack and set in a 9-inch (23 cm) microwave-safe pie plate. Melt the butter 1 minute at HIGH and pour over the fish. Then pour the vermouth or lemon juice around it. Salt and pepper to taste. Sprinkle with the basil.

• Preheat the convection part of a microwave oven at 350°F (180°C).

• Bake 30 minutes or 10 minutes per inch (2.5 cm) of thickness.

• When cooked, remove from oven, cover dish with plastic wrap. Cool, then refrigerate for 12 hours.

• The juice turns into a delicious jelly to serve with the fish, along with the Dijon Hollandaise.

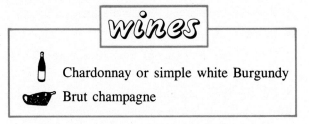

Chardonnay or simple white Burgundy

Brut champagne

Nova Scotia Spicy Salmon

Advance preparation: . . . . **2 days**	
Cooking: . . . . **from 32 to 44 m**	
Standing: . . . . **30 m**	

A personal note: At the beginning of spring, I prefer fresh salmon, especially when it comes from Gaspé. My next choice is salmon from Nova Scotia. If you cook it in court-bouillon, it will keep refrigerated for 2 or 3 days. Serve it cold with hot boiled potatoes (cooked in the microwave, of course) rolled in fresh parsley, and a small bowl of mayonnaise stirred with an equal amount of Dijon mustard or horseradish.

Ingredients:

1/2 cup (125 mL) cider vinegar

2 cups (500 mL) water

3 tbsp (50 mL) coarse salt

2 tbsp (30 mL) honey

2 tbsp (30 mL) peppercorns

2 cinnamon sticks

1 handful of fresh dill (if possible) *or*
   2 tbsp (30 mL) dried dill

2-to-4-lb (1 - 2 kg) piece of fresh salmon

Method:

• In a plastic or ceramic dish large enough to hold the fish place all the ingredients except the salmon.

• Bring to boil 10 minutes at HIGH. Then microwave, covered, 10 minutes at MEDIUM.

• Put the salmon piece into the court-bouillon while it is still hot.

• Cover and microwave 6 minutes per pound (500 g) at MEDIUM, turning the fish over after 6 minutes.

• Remove from oven. Baste the fish.

• Remove the cinnamon sticks.

• Cover and let it cool for 30 minutes before refrigerating it.

• Let the fish marinate in its juice for 2 days before serving it. Serve as indicated above.

wines

🍾 Vidal or Seyval Blanc

🥄 Canadian Chardonnay

My Mother's Curried Salmon

Preparation: . . . . **30 m**
Cooking: . . . . **40 m**
Standing: . . . . **none**

Rhine Riesling (dry)

Italian Traminer or Alsatian Muscat

• In the spring, whenever my mother was able to buy a nice piece of fresh salmon, she cooked it this way.

Ingredients:

2½ cups (625 mL) white wine,
  or water or half and half

2 tsp (10 mL) salt

2 bay leaves

1 cup (250 mL) long grain rice

2 tbsp (30 mL) butter

1 tsp (5 mL) curry powder

2 lb (1 kg) fresh salmon

3 tbsp (50 mL) butter

3 tbsp (50 mL) flour

1 cup (250 mL) milk

1/2 cup (125 mL) light cream

3 egg yolks, lightly beaten

Salt and pepper to taste

Method:

• Pour into a 12-cup (3 L) microwave-safe dish the white wine or the water or half and half.

• Cover and bring to boil 4 minutes at HIGH.

• Add the salt, bay leaves and rice. Stir well.

• Cover and microwave at MEDIUM-HIGH 15 to 18 minutes.

• Remove from microwave, stir and let stand covered 10 minutes.

• Melt the 2 tablespoons (30 mL) butter 2 minutes at HIGH.

• Add the curry and stir to mix thoroughly.

• Leave the fish in one piece or cut into 4 thick steaks. Roll each steak or the whole piece of fish in the hot curried butter.

• Cover and microwave at MEDIUM-HIGH 6 to 8 minutes, or until the fish flakes. Set aside and keep warm.

• Place the 3 tablespoons (50 mL) butter in a microwave-safe bowl or measuring cup and melt 1 minute at HIGH.

• Add the flour; stir.

• Add the milk and cream and microwave 4 to 5 minutes at HIGH, stirring twice.

• Beat the egg yolks, mix in 1/2 cup (125 mL) of the hot sauce, then add the remaining hot sauce. Beat with a whisk.

• Microwave 2 minutes at MEDIUM, stirring once. Salt and pepper to taste.

• Make a rice nest on a hot plate.

• Remove fish from cooking dish with a perforated spoon and place it in the middle of the cooked rice. Pour the hot sauce over it.

• If necessary, reheat 2 minutes at MEDIUM and serve.

Scottish Molded Salmon

Advance preparation: . . . . . **a few hours**
Cooking: . . . . **1 m**
Standing: . . . . **none**

• This is an attractive and tasty way to use fresh or leftover poached salmon.

Ingredients:

2 to 3 cups (500 to 750 mL) **poached salmon**
1 envelope **unflavored gelatin**
1/4 cup (60 mL) **scotch or white wine or water**
2 tsp (10 mL) **prepared mayonnaise**
1 tsp (5 mL) **curry powder**
Capers and Lemon wedges
Shredded lettuce or watercress

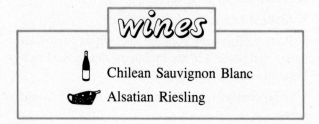

Chilean Sauvignon Blanc
Alsatian Riesling

Method:

• Remove skin and bones from the fish. Measure the 2 to 3 cups (500 to 750 mL). Oil a nicely shaped mold of your choice and pack in the salmon. Cover and refrigerate for a few hours.

• Sprinkle gelatin over the cold liquid of your choice. Microwave 1 minute at MEDIUM.

• Meanwhile, pour into a bowl the mayonnaise and curry powder. Add the gelatin to this mixture while beating constantly. Refrigerate 10 minutes, or until it is partly set.

• Unmold the fish on a serving platter, spread generously with the jellied mayonnaise.

• Decorate the top with capers. Place lemon wedges around, standing them against the fish. Surround with a thick layer of shredded lettuce or watercress.

• Refrigerate until ready to serve.

Scandinavian Marinated Salmon

Advance preparation: . . . . . **a few hours**
Cooking: . . . . **from 20 to 25 m**
Standing: . . . . **none**

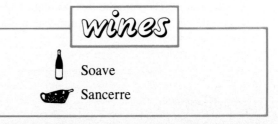

Soave

Sancerre

A personal note: In the Scandinavian countries, where salmon abounds in season, raw fish is cooked in a marinade mixture and can be kept, refrigerated and covered, in excellent condition for 2 to 3 weeks. Turn fish over in the marinating mixture once a week.

Ingredients:

1/3 cup (80 mL) cider or white wine vinegar

2 cups (500 mL) of any type of white wine

1 large onion, thinly sliced

2 tbsp (30 mL) coarse salt

1 carrot, peeled and thinly sliced

3 whole cloves

1 tbsp (15 mL) dried dill or dill seeds *or* 6 to 10 sprigs of fresh dill

1 tsp (5 mL) whole peppercorns

1 3-to-4-lb (1.5 to 2 kg) fresh salmon, whole or sliced

Method:

• Place all the ingredients, except the salmon, in a dish large enough to hold the whole fish.

• Cover and microwave at HIGH 6 minutes.

• Add the fish. Roll around in the liquid.

• Cover and microwave at MEDIUM 5 minutes per pound (500 g). The fish is cooked at MEDIUM because it must not boil.

• Cool for 20 minutes, then refrigerate in its *court-bouillon*, well covered.

• In Norway, where I learned to cook salmon in this manner, it is served cold in a glass dish with some of the strained marinade poured on top.

• A dish of hot boiled new potatoes, a small bowl of minced dill and a bottle of Scandinavian mustard (Dijon type can replace it) are served with the salmon.

• It's super delicious with a glass of aquavit.

Vancouver Salmon Loaf

Preparation: . . . . **12 m**
Cooking: . . . . **from 6 to 9 m**
Standing: . . . . **5 m**

A personal note: Serve the loaf hot with a herb or green pea white sauce, or cold with mayonnaise garnished with diced gherkins, finely chopped parsley and green onions.

Ingredients:

1 15.5-oz (439 g) can salmon, undrained

1 lightly beaten egg

1 cup (250 mL) fresh breadcrumbs

1/4 cup (60 mL) whipping or sour cream

2 tbsp (30 mL) celery leaves, minced

1/2 tsp (2 mL) curry powder

1 small onion, grated

1 tsp (5 mL) salt

1/4 tsp (1 mL) pepper

Juice and grated rind of half a lemon

Method:

• Empty the can of salmon into a bowl, crush the bones with a fork, flake the undrained fish, and mix together with a fork.

• Add the remaining ingredients. Mix thoroughly and place in a 9 × 5-inch (23 × 13 cm) loaf pan. Cover with waxed paper.

• Microwave 6 to 9 minutes at HIGH. Let stand 5 minutes.

• Unmold and serve.

Auxerrois or Vidal

Canadian Chardonnay

Boiled Salmon at its Best

Preparation: . . . . **9 m**
Cooking: . . . . **from 30 to 35 m**
Standing: . . . . **20 m**

• To my taste, the best way to cook fresh salmon in order to retain its delicate flavor is to boil or steam it. This recipe has remained one of my favorites for years. I have now adapted it to microwave cooking and I believe I could no longer return to the old method.

Ingredients:

4 cups (1 L) hot water

2 bay leaves

1 tbsp (15 mL) coarse salt

1 tsp (5 mL) paprika

1 tbsp (15 mL) marinating spices*

1/2 a large lemon, chopped

A 3-to-4-lb (1.5 - 2 kg) piece of fresh salmon

* Commercial marinating spices are sold at the herb and spice counter in food stores.

 Simple white Burgundy

 Autralian or Californian Chardonnay

Method:

• Place all the ingredients except the salmon in a 12-cup (3 L) microwave-safe dish. Cover and microwave 15 minutes at HIGH.

• In the meantime, wrap the salmon in cheese-cloth or a piece of cotton. Sew it up to wrap tightly.

• When the bouillon is hot, place the fish in it. Cover and microwave at HIGH 5 minutes per pound (500 g). Remove from microwave and let stand covered 20 minutes.

• Unwrap the fish when ready to serve and place it on a serving dish. Remove the skin and backbone.

• To serve it cold, let salmon cool in cooking water for 1 hour at room temperature, then refrigerate. It will keep perfectly for 3 days. To serve, unwrap, remove skin and bones.

• Serve the salmon hot with a Hollandaise, Bercy or Egg Sauce. Serve it cold with watercress mayonnaise or any mayonnaise of your choice.

A personal note: Remember, salmon is at its best in the spring.

Cold Salmon Superbe

White Graves
Pouilly-Fuissé

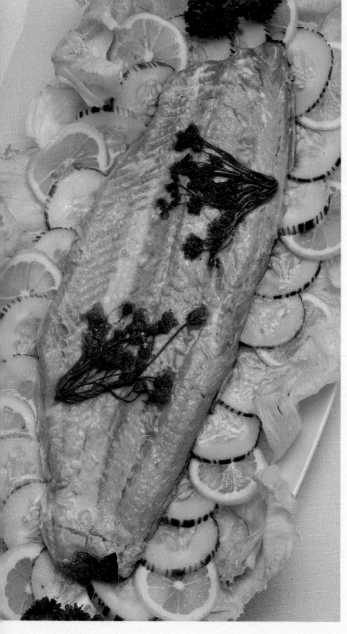

Advance preparation: . . . . **12 h**
Cooking: . . . .**20 m**
Standing: . . . . **20 m**

A personal note: A speciality of Norwegian cuisine, this dish is cooked in parchment paper. It is traditional to serve it with a cucumber salad and steamed potatoes.

Ingredients:

A 2-lb (1 kg) piece of salmon
1/3 cup (80 mL) melted butter
Juice of 1/2 a lemon
1/3 cup (80 mL) vodka or white vermouth
Salt and pepper to taste
A few branches of fresh dill

Method:

- Take a square of parchment paper large enough to wrap around the fish.
- Place the paper in an 8 × 8-inch (20 × 20 cm) glass dish. Set the fish on it.
- Rub all over with the melted butter.
- Pull up the paper to form a sort of open bag.
- Add the lemon juice, the vodka or vermouth, salt and pepper to taste.
- Place 2 to 3 flowering tops of dill on the fish. Close the bag by folding the paper together.
- Microwave 20 minutes at MEDIUM-HIGH. Let stand 20 minutes. Do not open the package.
- When cool, refrigerate 12 hours. The juice will form a sort of jelly.
- Serve on a bed of lettuce.
- Surround with parsley, alternating with thin slices of lemon and cucumber.

A personal note: Parchment is not easily available. If you cannot find any, use a double layer of waxed paper.

Darvish Salmon

Preparation: . . . .**8 m**
Cooking: . . . .**15 m**
Standing: . . . .**none**

• I have often wondered where the name of this simple family dish came from. Wherever, the dish is economical, as you can serve 4 to 6 people with a can of salmon.

Ingredients:

1 15.5-oz (439 g) can salmon, undrained

3 tbsp (50 mL) butter

3 tbsp (50 mL) cornstarch

2 cups (500 mL) milk

3 green onions, finely minced

Salt and pepper to taste

**1 full cup (250 mL) soda crackers,
    crushed fine**

3 tbsp (50 mL) butter

Method:

• Empty a can of salmon into bowl and flake with a fork. Divide into 2 portions.

• Place the 3 tablespoons (50 mL) of butter in a microwave-safe dish, melt 2 minutes at HIGH. Remove from oven, stir in cornstarch. Mix well.

• Add milk and green onions, salt and pepper, stir well. Microwave at HIGH 4 minutes; stir well. The sauce should be creamy. If necessary, microwave 1 or 2 minutes more.

• Butter an 8 or 9-inch (20 or 23 cm) glass casserole, place in it one portion of the salmon and top with 1 cup (250 mL) of the sauce.

• Sprinkle with half the crackers. Dot with 1 tablespoon (15 mL) butter. Repeat layers.

• Dot with remaining butter. Sprinkle generously with paprika.

• Cover with waxed paper or a cover.

• Microwave 8 or 10 minutes at MEDIUM-HIGH.

wines

White Rhône
Mâcon Villages

199

Salmon Mousse

Advance preparation: . . **from 12 to 14 h**
Cooking: . . . . **none**
Standing: . . . . **none**

A personal note: You can use canned salmon for this mousse if you are unable to buy fresh salmon. This light and delicate mousse is the ideal dish on a warm day or for a buffet.

Ingredients:

1 envelope unflavored gelatin

2 tbsp (30 mL) fresh lemon juice

Grated rind of half a lemon

2 French shallots *or* 4 green onions

1/2 cup (125 mL) boiling water or
   white wine or Sake

1/2 cup (125 mL) mayonnaise

1 tsp (5 mL) tarragon *or*
   1 tbsp (15 mL) fresh minced dill

2 cups (500 mL) cooked, fresh salmon *or*
   1 15.5 oz (439 mL) can pink or
   red salmon, with juice

1 cup (250 mL) whipping cream
Salt and pepper to taste

Method:

• In a food processor or blender place the gelatin, lemon juice, lemon rind, French shallots or green onions and the water, wine or Sake.

• Mix together at high speed until the onions are minced.

• Add the mayonnaise, tarragon or fresh dill and the salmon undrained (if using canned salmon).

• Cover and mix again 1 minute.

• Whip cream, and add it, one third at a time, beating 20 seconds after each addition. Season to taste with salt and pepper.

• Rinse a 4-cup (1 L) mold in cold water, pour in the mousse, cover and refrigerate 12 to 14 hours.

• To unmold, dip mold 2 seconds in hot water and invert on a serving dish.

• Devilled eggs can be placed around the mousse as a garnish.

Helpful hint: If you want to boil the water in the microwave, heat it 1 to 2 minutes at HIGH.

wines

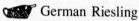
Seyval Blanc or Italian Chardonnay
German Riesling

Fisherman's Delight

Preparation: . . . . **10 m**
Cooking: . . . . . . **3 m per pound (500 g)**
Standing: . . . . **none**

• If someone at your house has the good fortune to catch some fine small brook trout for you to cook, why not try the following recipe? This is my favorite way to cook them.

Ingredients:

Fresh trout

Green onions

Melted butter

Fresh ground pepper

Paprika

Method:

• Clean and wash the trout under cold water. Pat them dry with a paper towel.

• Place a green onion cut in half inside each fish, close the opening with a wooden pick.

• Place the trout in a large microwave-safe dish, one next to the other, alternating heads and tails. Wrap the heads and tails separately in narrow strips of aluminum foil to prevent drying.

• Melt a little butter to which you add pepper and paprika. DO NOT SALT.

• Brush each fish on both sides with this butter.

• Cover (for best results, fresh trout must be poached, not fried).

• It is important to choose fish of almost equal weight, from 1½ to 2 pounds (750 g to 2 kg). If they vary too much in size, some fish will overcook while others do not cook enough.

• Allow 3 minutes per pound (500 g) at MEDIUM.

• Check if done after 10 minutes and unwrap heads and tails.

• Place the fish in a serving dish. Add melted butter to the juice in the serving dish.

Alsatian Pinot Blanc

White Burgundy

Helpful hint: To reheat food, place thick, dense pieces toward the outside of the dish. Place vegetables and other foods that cook quickly in the centre.

Potted Trout

Advance preparation: . . . . **6 h**
Cooking: . . . . **8 m**
Standing: . . . . **none**

A personal note: It is impossible to be in England in the spring and not eat their famous potted trout. It can be prepared with fresh or frozen trout. It's very nice to serve as an *amuse-gueule*, or around the swimming pool.

Ingredients:

2 to 3 small trout, fresh or frozen
1/4 cup (60 mL) all-purpose flour
1 tbsp (15 mL) butter
2 tbsp (30 mL) vegetable oil
1/2 tsp (2 mL) curry powder
Salt and pepper to taste
1 or 2 tbsp (15 or 30 mL) butter
Grated rind of 1 lemon

Canadian Riesling (dry)
Gewurztraminer

Method:

• Roll each trout in the flour.

• Place butter in a 9-inch (23 cm) ceramic or glass pie plate and melt 1 minute at HIGH. Add the oil, stir in the curry powder and microwave 1 minute at HIGH.

• Roll the trout in this mixture. Microwave 5 minutes at HIGH. Turn fish and let stand 5 minutes.

• Cool until it can be handled, then carefully lift flesh from bones and place in a dish.

• Break up into small pieces with a fork.

• Divide into small ramequins, add to remaining butter in the plate 1 or 2 tablespoons (15 or 30 mL) of butter and the grated rind. Microwave 40 seconds at HIGH.

• Divide the butter equally over each ramequin of fish.

• Cover and refrigerate at least 6 hours before serving.

• The potted trout is very nice served with hot French bread.

Venetian Trout

Preparation: . . . . **15 m**
Cooking: . . . . **16 m**
Standing: . . . . **none**

Method:

- Clean the trout.

- Place them one next to the other in an 8 × 12-inch (20 × 30 cm) glass dish.

- Add the wine or fish fumet, the lemon juice and water; salt and pepper to taste.

- Cover dish with waxed paper or a cover. Microwave at MEDIUM-HIGH 10 to 12 minutes. When fish is cooked whole, turn with two forks after 3 minutes of cooking.

- In the meantime, peel and dice the cucumber.

- Wash and chop the spinach.

- When using fresh herbs, chop them and measure them.

- Place the tablespoon (15 mL) of butter in a microwave-safe dish and melt 1 minute at HIGH.

- Remove from heat, add the flour, mix well. Set aside.

- Remove fish to a platter with a perforated spoon. Keep warm.

- Pour the juice from the fish into the flour mixture. Beat in the egg yolks, add the cucumber and spinach. Stir well.

- Add shallots or green onions and microwave 2 minutes at HIGH, stirring once.

- Remove from oven, add the remaining butter, a small piece at a time, beating well at each addition.

- Microwave another minute at MEDIUM-HIGH, and pour over the fish.

A personal note: The combination of cucumber, fresh spinach and tarragon gives Venetian trout a very special and interesting flavor. In the summer, I replace the tarragon by an equal amount of chervil.

Ingredients:

4 medium or 6 small trout

1/2 cup (125 mL) white wine or fish fumet

1 tbsp (15 mL) fresh lemon juice

1/4 cup (60 mL) water

1 small cucumber, peeled and diced

1 cup (250 mL) well-packed fresh spinach, chopped

1 tsp (5 mL) tarragon or chervil

1 tbsp (15 mL) butter

1½ tbsp (23 mL) flour

2 egg yolks

2 French shallots *or*
    6 green onions, peeled and chopped

1/4 cup (60 mL) butter

Soave

Pinot Grigio

Broiled Trout

Preparation: . . . . **10 m**
Cooking: . . . . **21 m**
Standing: . . . . **none**

A personal note: Any small whole fish can be cooked in this manner. In Belgium, where the recipe was created, they use small whiting. This recipe requires a browning dish.

wines

Lacrima Christi

Pouilly Fumé

Ingredients:

4 to 6 small trout or whiting

3 tbsp (50 mL) milk

1/4 cup (60 mL) flour

1 cup (250 mL) fine dry breadcrumbs

3 tbsp (50 mL) butter

1 small onion, chopped fine

1 French shallot *or*
  3 green onions, peeled and chopped

1/4 cup (60 mL) white wine

1 tbsp (15 mL) cider vinegar

Method:

• Wash fish under cold running water. Wipe with paper towel.

• Place milk in plate and roll fish in it, then in flour and breadcrumbs.

• Preheat a browning dish 7 minutes at HIGH.

• Without removing the dish from the oven, add the butter. It will brown very quickly.

• Without delay, place fish, one next to the other. Press lightly on each one to create perfect contact with the dish. Microwave 4 minutes at HIGH.

• Turn fish over with a spatula. Let stand 5 minutes without any heat.

• Then microwave 2 minutes at MEDIUM. Remove fish to a hot platter.

• To the butter remaining in the dish add the onion and shallot or green onions. Stir well.

• Microwave 2 minutes at HIGH.

• Add the white wine and the vinegar. Stir well. Microwave 1 minute at HIGH.

• Pour over the fish and serve with steamed potatoes.

Stuffed Brook Trout

Preparation:	**20 m**
Cooking:	**20 m**
Standing:	**none**

• Fresh trout caught in cold brook water in the early spring is a delight! Should you not have trout, any small fish may be prepared in this manner.

Ingredients:

1/4 cup (60 mL) butter

4 to 6 green onions, minced

1 to 2 cups (250 - 500 mL) fresh mushrooms, minced

1 tbsp (15 mL) dill, dried or fresh

1 tbsp (15 mL) Dijon mustard

1/4 tsp (1 mL) pepper

1 tsp (5 mL) salt

2 tbsp (30 mL) dry sherry

2 tbsp (30 mL) butter

3 tbsp (50 mL) flour

1/2 cup (125 mL) cream

6 fresh trout, 1/2 lb (250 g) each

1/2 cup (125 mL) white wine or white vermouth

2 tbsp (30 mL) butter

1/4 tsp (1 mL) sugar

Method:

• Mix together in a dish the 1/4 cup (60 mL) butter, green onions, mushrooms, dill, mustard, pepper, salt and sherry. Cover and microwave 5 minutes at MEDIUM-HIGH, stirring once.

• In another dish, melt the 2 tablespoons (30 mL) butter 1 minute at HIGH.

• Add the flour and cream, stir and microwave 3 to 4 minutes at HIGH, stirring after 2 minutes of cooking. When the mixture is thick and creamy, add it to the mushroom mixture.

• Clean the fish and stuff them with the mushrooms. Secure the openings with wooden picks, place the fish in a dish, one next to the other.

• Heat the white wine or white vermouth, butter and sugar 2 minutes at HIGH. Pour over the fish, cover and microwave 8 to 9 minutes at MEDIUM-HIGH, or until the fish flakes.

• Serve with lemon slices.

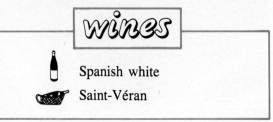

wines

Spanish white
Saint-Véran

Preparation of a trout for stuffing

1. Remove the scales, holding the knife at an angle.

2. Gut the trout and remove fins.

3. To bone, slit the blade of a knife between the flesh and the back bone.

4. How to tie a stuffed trout for baking.

Poached Trout with Clam Dressing

A personal note: If someone brings you a prize catch of trout or any other small fish, this is a good way to prepare them. They will keep refrigerated for 3 to 5 days.

Advance preparation: . . . . . **a few hours**
Cooking: . . . . **from 6 to 12 m**
Standing: . . . .**none**

wines

Aligoté
Chablis

Ingredients:

2 tbsp (30 mL) vegetable oil

1 to 3 lb (500 g to 1.5 kg) fresh trout, whole or filleted

1 tsp (5 mL) salt

1 tbsp (15 mL) each, parsley and sage

Juice of 1 lemon

1 5-oz (142 g) can baby clams

1/4 tsp (1 mL) thyme

12 stuffed olives, sliced, to garnish

Method:

• Pour the oil into an 8 × 12-inch (20 × 30 cm) glass or ceramic dish and, without overlapping the pieces, place the whole or filleted fish in the dish.

• Sprinkle with salt, parsley and sage. Sprinkle lemon juice over all.

• Drain the clams and pour the juice over the fish. Sprinkle with the thyme. Cover dish with cover or waxed paper and microwave at MEDIUM-HIGH 6 to 12 minutes, depending on whether you have thin fillets or whole fish.

• Cool, then drain the juice carefully without disturbing the fish. Refrigerate the fish and the broth separately.

• When ready to serve, mix together the reserved clams and sliced olives. Add just enough broth to make a light sauce and pour over the fish.

A personal note: This dish is excellent served with long grain rice cooked in the leftover fish stock.

Haddock

Icelandic Poached Haddock

Preparation: . . . . **8 m**
Cooking: . . . . **20 m**
Standing: . . . . **none**

A personal note: What makes this special is the coating of fresh parsley and dill. In the winter, when fresh dill is difficult to find, replace it with 1/2 teaspoon (2 mL) of dill seeds.

Italian Chardonnay
Mâcon Villages

Ingredients:

1½ to 2 lb (750 g to 1 kg) **haddock fillets or any other fish, fresh or frozen**

4 cups (1 L) **boiling water**

3 **medium-sized onions**

1 **bay leaf**

1 tbsp (15 mL) **fresh dill** *or* 1/2 tsp (2 mL) **dill seeds**

1/4 tsp (1 mL) **each of thyme and whole peppercorns**

2 tbsp (30 mL) **butter**

1 tbsp (15 mL) **flour**

2 tbsp (30 mL) **fine dry breadcrumbs**

1/4 cup (60 mL) **parsley, finely chopped**

Method:

- If fish is frozen, defrost.
- Cut thawed or fresh fish into individual portions.
- Place in a microwave-safe dish large enough to hold the fish pieces one next to the other.
- Place in a microwave-safe bowl the boiling water, onions, bay leaf, dill, thyme, peppercorns and 1 tablespoon (15 mL) of the butter.
- Microwave 10 minutes at HIGH. Pour over the fish. Cover with waxed paper.
- Microwave at HIGH 6 minutes per pound (500 g), more or less, depending on type of fish used. Test with the point of a knife after 4 minutes of cooking, and cook 1, 2 or 3 minutes more. This is necessary because some types of fish take slightly longer to cook than others.
- When fish is cooked, set aside in a warm place.
- Melt the remaining butter in another dish 1 minute at HIGH. Mix in the flour, breadcrums and 1 cup (250 mL) of strained fish stock.
- Stir and microwave 3 minutes at HIGH.
- Stir; if necessary, microwave another minute or 2 until sauce is lightly creamy.
- Pour on top of fish and sprinkle with parsley.

A personal note: The leftover fish stock can be strained, frozen and used as liquid in any fish sauce, or to cook fish.

Butter Poached Haddock

Advance preparation: . . . . **from 1 to 2 h**
Cooking: . . . . **from 10 to 13 m**
Standing: . . . . **none**

A personal note: This is easy and quick to make. Fresh cod can replace the haddock. Do not let the simplicity of the sauce deceive you; it is colorful and very tasty.

Ingredients:

1 ½ to 2 lb (750 g to 1 kg) haddock fillets

1/3 cup (80 mL) butter

Salt and pepper to taste

Grated rind of 1 lemon

Juice of 1/2 a lemon

2 tbsp (30 mL) dill, fresh or dried

1 tbsp (15 mL) fresh parsley, minced

Method:

• Place the fish in a bowl.

• Cover with cold water and add 3 tablespoons (50 mL) coarse salt.

• Let soak for 1 to 2 hours. This is done to prevent the fish from drying while cooking.

• Then remove from the water, dry with paper towel.

• Place the butter in an 8 × 8-inch (20 × 20 cm) baking dish and melt 1 minute at HIGH.

• Place the fillets, either cut in individual portions, rolled or left whole, in the dish.

• Cover with plastic wrap or lid.

• Microwave 6 minutes per pound (500 g) at HIGH. Let stand 3 minutes, covered.

• Then remove fish from dish with a spatula or a perforated spoon.

• Place on a warm platter. Salt and pepper to taste.

• To juice in the baking dish add the lemon rind and juice, the dill and parsley.

• Microwave 1 minute at HIGH.

• Pour over the fish and serve with boiled potatoes.

 Portuguese white

 Ontario or BC Chardonnay

Haddock À la Royale

Preparation: . . . . 7 m
Cooking: . . . . 15 m
Standing: . . . . none

• **À la Royale** is the name given to fish cooked in a piece of parchment or in a cooking bag.

Ingredients:

4 medium haddock fillets

2 tbsp (30 mL) butter, melted

4 tbsp (60 mL) flour

1 tsp (5 mL) salt

1/2 tsp (2 mL) pepper

1/2 tsp (2 mL) paprika

1/2 cup (125 mL) mild cheese, grated

1/2 cup (125 mL) milk or cream

wines

Verdicchio

Australian Chardonnay

Method:

• Cut the fillets into individual portions.

• Brush each piece with melted butter.

• Mix together the flour, salt, pepper and paprika.

• Roll each piece of fish in this mixture, then in the grated cheese.

• Place a cooking bag on a plate or in a 12 × 8-inch (30 × 20 cm) microwave-safe dish, and put the fish fillets into the bag one next to the other. Add the milk gradually.

• Close the bag loosely and make two small incisions on top with the point of a knife. Microwave 15 minutes at HIGH.

• When the fish is cooked, remove the fillets from the bag and place them on a serving dish. Sprinkle with minced parsley.

• In the summer, I sprinkle the fish with fresh minced chives and I pour the sauce remaining in the bag over the fish.

American Haddock Casserole

Preparation: . . . . 7 m
Cooking: . . . . from 8 to 10 m
Standing: . . . . none

A personal note: You can use fresh or frozen cod instead of the haddock in this recipe.

Ingredients:

1 lb (500 g) haddock fillets

1/4 tsp (1 mL) each salt and pepper

A pinch of nutmeg

1 small can cream of mushroom soup

1/4 cup (60 mL) cream

1/4 cup (60 mL) milk or white wine

1/2 tsp (2 mL) tarragon or thyme

1 cup (250 mL) Swiss or Cheddar cheese, grated

Method:

• Cut the fillets into individual portions. Place in an 8 × 8-inch (20 × 20 cm) microwave-safe dish, one next to the other, whole or rolled, with thicker pieces toward the edges of the dish.

• Mix together the salt, pepper and nutmeg. Sprinkle over the fish.

• Mix together the cream of mushroom soup, cream, wine or milk and tarragon or thyme. Spread over fish. Sprinkle grated cheese over all. Microwave 8 to 10 minutes at MEDIUM.

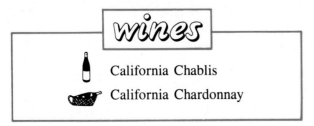

wines

California Chablis

California Chardonnay

Finnan Haddock

Preparation: . . . . 5 m
Cooking: . . . . 8 m
Standing: . . . . none

• Smoked or finnan haddock is one of the world famous specialties of Scotland. It is possible all over Canada to find good smoked haddock. The following recipe is an authentic Scottish way of preparing it and, I would like to add, the very best way.

Ingredients:

1 lb (500 g) haddock, smoked

2 tbsp (30 mL) butter

1/4 tsp (1 mL) pepper

1 cup (250 mL) milk or light cream

1 tbsp (15 mL) cornstarch

Method:

• Remove all skin from the fish, if necessary, and cut into serving-size or bite-size pieces.

• Pour butter in a 9-inch (23 cm) microwave-safe pie plate and melt 2 minutes at HIGH.

• Add the fish, sprinkle with the pepper, cover.

• Microwave at MEDIUM-HIGH 3 minutes.

• Mix the milk or cream with the cornstarch. Pour over the fish.

• Simmer at MEDIUM-LOW 5 minutes.

• Stir and serve as soon as ready.

• The traditional garnish is boiled peeled potatoes and finely chopped parsley.

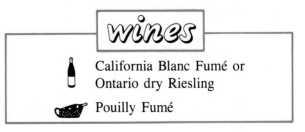

wines

California Blanc Fumé or Ontario dry Riesling

Pouilly Fumé

Fish Custard

Haddock À la Grecque

Preparation:	**10 m**
Cooking:	**from 4 to 7 m**
Standing:	**none**

• This is the Scandinavian way to serve fillets of haddock or flounder.

Ingredients:

4 haddock or flounder fillets

1 tsp (5 mL) lemon juice

Salt and pepper to taste

2 tbsp (30 mL) fresh dill, chopped

1 egg

1/2 cup (125 mL) milk

Method:

• Brush each fillet lightly with lemon juice. Salt and pepper to taste. Roll up the fillets, hold with pick if necessary, sprinkle with the dill. Place in a 9-inch (23 cm) microwave-safe pie plate or a small quiche dish.

• Beat egg and milk together and pour over the fish. Cover and microwave at MEDIUM 4 to 7 minutes, or until custard is set.

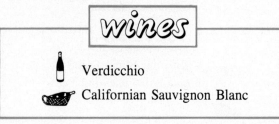

Verdicchio

Californian Sauvignon Blanc

Preparation:	**8 m**
Cooking:	**10 m**
Standing:	**5 m**

Ingredients:

1 19-oz (540 mL) can tomatoes, undrained

1/2 cup (125 mL) soda crackers, crumbled

1 tsp (5 mL) sugar

1/4 tsp (1 mL) basil

1/2 tsp (2 mL) salt

1 lb (500 g) haddock, frozen

3 green onions, chopped fine

1/4 cup (60 mL) parsley, chopped

1/4 cup (60 mL) vegetable oil

2 tbsp (30 mL) flour

1 tbsp (15 mL) paprika

Method:

• Place the tomatoes and soda crackers in the bottom of an 8 × 8-inch (20 × 20 cm) glass dish.

• Sprinkle with sugar, basil and salt. Mix together with a fork.

• Set the frozen block of fish over the tomatoes.

• Mix together the remaining ingredients and pour over the fish.

• Cover with waxed paper. Microwave at HIGH 8 to 10 minutes, until the fish is well cooked in the center.

• Let stand 5 minutes. Serve.

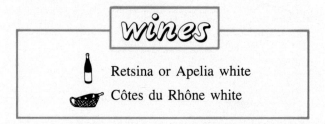

Retsina or Apelia white

Côtes du Rhône white

English Farmhouse Finnan Spaghetti

Preparation:	15 m
Cooking:	from 41 to 44 m
Standing:	2 m

• This is a true English family recipe and a pleasant change from the usual spaghetti sauce. The smoky taste of the haddock gives it an intriguing flavor.

Ingredients:

1 lb (500 g) finnan haddock

1/4 tsp (1 mL) savory

1 tbsp (15 mL) vegetable oil

1 tsp (5 mL) salt

8 oz (225 g) fine spaghetti

4 slices of bacon

1 large onion, thinly sliced

3 tbsp (50 mL) butter

3 tbsp (50 mL) flour

2 cups (500 mL) milk

Salt and pepper to taste

1/4 tsp (1 mL) nutmeg

3/4 cup (190 mL) grated cheese

1 cup (250 mL) bread, toasted and diced

1 tsp (5 mL) paprika

Method:

• Bring 2 cups (500 mL) of water to a boil by heating 5 minutes at HIGH.

• Place the fish in a microwave-safe dish, just large enough to hold it. Pour water over the fish, add the savory. Cover and microwave 10 minutes at MEDIUM.

• Remove fish from water, let cool, then flake.

• Place 2 cups (500 mL) of water in a 6-cup (1.5 L) bowl, bring to boil by heating 5 minutes at HIGH.

• Add the vegetable oil, salt and spaghetti. Stir well and microwave 13 to 15 minutes at MEDIUM. Stir after half the cooking period. Spaghetti cooked in the microwave is drained but not rinsed.

• Dice the bacon, place in a dish, microwave 2 minutes at HIGH. Stir well.

• Add the onion, stir and microwave 2 minutes at HIGH. Add to the spaghetti with the flaked fish. Stir with a fork, blending gently.

• In a 4-cup (1 L) microwave-safe measuring cup, make a white sauce by melting the butter 1 minute at HIGH. Add the flour. When well mixed, add the milk, stir and microwave 2 minutes at HIGH. Stir well and microwave another 2 to 3 minutes, or until creamy.

• Salt and pepper to taste. Stir in the nutmeg and grated cheese.

• Place the fish and spaghetti mixture in a microwave-safe bowl. Pour the cheese sauce over all.

• Cover with the diced toasted bread mixed with the paprika.

• When ready to serve, cover and reheat at MEDIUM 3 to 5 minutes or warm "SENSOR I" or "COMB. I" if your oven has these features. The oven determines the time needed.

• Let stand 2 minutes.

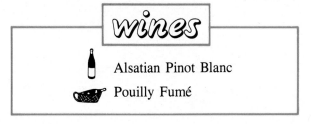

wines

Alsatian Pinot Blanc

Pouilly Fumé

Finnan Haddock Pudding

Preparation: . . . . **12 m**
Cooking: . . . . **25 m**
Standing: . . . . **none**

A personal note: A smoked or finnan haddock pudding is a light, fluffy pudding. Serve it with a green salad prepared with oil and wine vinegar.

Ingredients:

1 lb (500 g) finnan haddock

2 slices of bacon, diced

1 tbsp (15 mL) butter

2 cups (500 mL) mashed potatoes

Pepper to taste

Juice and grated rind of 1/2 a lemon

1 small onion, minced

1/2 tsp (2 mL) celery salt

1/4 cup (60 mL) parsley, minced

1/2 tsp (2 mL) savory

3 tbsp (50 mL) butter

3 eggs

Paprika

Spanish white

Sancerre

Method:

• Place the fish in a 9-inch (23 cm) microwave-safe pie plate.

• Sprinkle bacon on top and add just enough water to cover bottom of dish. Cover and microwave 10 minutes at MEDIUM.

• Remove fish to a hot plate and rub top of fish with the 1 tablespoon (15 mL) butter. Cool.

• When fish is cool, flake and add to the mashed potatoes.

• Add pepper, lemon juice and rind, onion, celery salt, parsley and savory. Beat together until thoroughly mixed.

• Melt the 3 tablespoons (50 mL) butter 1 minute at HIGH. Add the fish mixture.

• Separate the eggs, beat the yolks until light. Stir into fish and potato mixture.

• Beat the egg whites and fold gently into the mixture.

• Butter a 4-cup (1 L) microwave-safe casserole and pour in the mixture.

• Sprinkle top generously with paprika.

• Bake 12 to 14 minutes at MEDIUM. Serve as soon as ready.

Haddock Printanier

• Haddock cooked this way is often served in Scotland as a late Sunday breakfast with a basket of hot scones or biscuits, and a pot of very hot, very strong tea.

Ingredients:

1 ½ lb (750 g) haddock steaks or fillets

4 tbsp (60 mL) oil of your choice

3 garlic cloves

1 bay leaf

1 tbsp (15 mL) flour

1/4 cup (60 mL) parsley, minced

1/2 cup (125 mL) fish fumet or water

1 to 2 cups (250 to 500 mL) green peas, frozen

Salt and pepper to taste

3 to 4 eggs

Method:

• Wipe the steaks or fillets with absorbent paper.

• In an 8 × 8-inch (20 × 20 cm) ceramic dish, heat the oil 3 minutes at HIGH.

• Add the garlic, bay leaf, flour and parsley.

• Stir thoroughly, add the fish fumet or water, stir well.

• Add the fish and the green peas. Cover with waxed paper. Microwave 5 minutes at HIGH. Stir peas and juice. Let stand 4 to 5 minutes.

• Remove fish to a hot dish with a perforated spoon.

• Break the eggs into the juice. Pierce each yolk with the point of a paring knife.

• Cover with waxed paper and cook at MEDIUM, allowing 1 to 2 minutes per egg.

• As soon as the eggs are cooked, serve a portion of fish, an egg, and some gravy.

Helpful hint: To reheat 4 to 6 dinner rolls, place them in a microwave-safe dish and cover with a paper towel. Heat 20 to 30 seconds at HIGH.

Preparation:	10 m
Cooking:	10 m
Standing:	from 4 to 5 m

🍾 Entre-Deux-Mers

🥄 White Burgundy

Baked Haddock Casserole

Preparation: . . . . **10 m**
Cooking: . . . .**15 m**
Standing: . . . .**none**

A personal note: This recipe produces an easily baked fish topped with a creamy tomato sauce. Serve it with rice or mashed potatoes.

Ingredients:

1 lb (500 g) fresh haddock fillets *or*
   1 16-oz (450 g) box haddock fillets, frozen
Salt and pepper to taste
1 tsp (5 mL) basil *or*
   1/4 tsp (1 mL) curry powder
1 19-oz (540 mL) can tomatoes
2 tbsp (30 mL) flour
1 onion, minced
2 celery stalks, chopped fine
1 tbsp (15 mL) butter
1 egg, lightly beaten
1/4 cup (60 mL) cream
1 tsp (5 mL) Worcestershire sauce

Method:

• Season the fillets with salt and pepper to taste. Place them one next to the other in a 9 × 12-inch (23 × 30 cm) glass or ceramic dish.

• Blend together the basil or curry powder, tomatoes, flour, onion, celery.

• Melt the butter 1 minute at HIGH. Add to mixture.

• Pour tomato mixture over fish. Cover dish with lid or waxed paper and microwave 10 minutes at MEDIUM-HIGH.

• Baste fish and, if necessary, microwave 1 or 2 minutes more at MEDIUM-HIGH.

• Remove fish from sauce to a hot platter.

• Beat the egg and cream together.

• Add the Worcestershire sauce and beat mixture into the fish tomato sauce. Microwave 2 minutes at MEDIUM, stirring once after 1 minute.

• Pour over fish. Serve.

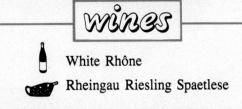

wines

White Rhône
Rheingau Riesling Spaetlese

Poached Cod Fines-Herbes

Preparation: . . . . 10 m
Cooking: . . . . .10 m
Standing: . . . . 3 m

A personal note: Despite its bad reputation, fresh cod is delicious - and doubly so when poached in the microwave. Frozen cod can be used, but it must be thawed before cooking.

Ingredients:

2 lb (1 kg) fresh cod steaks or fillets

1 ¼ cups (310 mL) water or milk

1 medium onion, minced

3 slices of lemon, unpeeled

1 bay leaf

1 tsp (5 mL) salt

4 peppercorns

2 tbsp (30 mL) butter

2 tbsp (30 mL) flour

1 tbsp (15 mL) lemon juice

1/4 cup (60 mL) fresh parsley *or*
   2 tbsp (30 mL) fresh dill

Method:

• Set the steaks or fillets in one layer in an 8 × 12-inch (20 × 30 cm) glass dish.

• Pour the liquid over the fish.

• Cover with the onion and lemon slices, the bay leaf, salt and peppercorns. Microwave, uncovered, 3 minutes at HIGH.

• Tilt the dish and pour the cooking juice over the fish with a spoon. Microwave 4 minutes more at HIGH. Cover and let stand 3 minutes.

• Remove fish to a warm platter with a perforated spoon.

• Mix together the butter and flour, add to the fish juices, mix thoroughly.

• Add the lemon juice, parsley or dill. Mix well. Microwave 2 minutes at HIGH. Stir. The sauce should be light and creamy; microwave 1 minute more, if necessary. Pour over the fish.

Soave

Alsatian Riesling

Poached Cod with Egg Sauce

A personal note: This makes a very interesting lunch that's very New England in the spring. The cod is delicious served with small boiled new potatoes and fresh June green peas, both easy to do in the microwave.

Ingredients:

2 lb (1 kg) cod steaks or fillets, fresh or frozen

1½ cups (375 mL) boiling salted water

1 tsp (5 mL) thyme

1 medium-sized onion, thinly sliced

1 bay leaf

4 sprigs of parsley

1 celery stalk, quartered

Sauce:

1/4 cup (60 mL) butter or margarine

3 tbsp (50 mL) flour

Cooking liquid from fish, drained

1/4 tsp (1 mL) salt

1/4 cup (60 mL) cream, light or heavy

1/4 cup (60 mL) parsley, minced

2 to 3 hard cooked eggs, sliced

Salt and pepper to taste

Method:

• If frozen fish is used, thaw 1 hour before cooking.

• Place the steaks or fillets of cod in a glass or ceramic dish.

• Add enough boiling water to just come to edge of fish without covering it, then add thyme, onion, bay leaf, parsley and celery. Cover and microwave 10 minutes at HIGH. Let stand 10 minutes.

• To make sauce, place the butter or margarine in a 4-cup (1 L) microwave-safe measuring cup and melt 1 minute at HIGH. Add the flour, mix well, add 1 cup (250 mL) cooking liquid and the salt. Stir well. Microwave 4 minutes at MEDIUM-HIGH.

Preparation:		20 m
Cooking:	the meal	10 m
	the sauce	8 m
Standing:		10 m

Dry Orvieto

White Burgundy

• Stir well, add the cream and the parsley and microwave another 3 minutes at MEDIUM. Stir well, add the eggs. Salt and pepper to taste.

• Drain the remaining water from the fish. Place on a warm dish and pour the sauce over all.

Scandinavian Poached Cod

Preparation: . . . . **10 m**
Cooking: . . . . **9 m**
Standing: . . . . **from 5 to 8 m**

A personal note: You can use this recipe to poach salmon instead of cod. Small, 6-ounce (175 g) fillets or steaks are the easiest to poach.

Ingredients:

1 cup (250 mL) hot water

Juice of 1 lemon

1 small onion, thinly sliced

1 celery stalk, diced

2 garlic cloves, crushed

1 bay leaf

1/4 tsp (1 mL) thyme

4 whole cloves

1 tsp (5 mL) salt

1/4 tsp (1 mL) peppercorns

4 to 6 6-oz (175 g) each cod steaks or fillets

Method:

• Place all the ingredients, except the cod, in a glass dish. Cover, microwave 6 minutes at HIGH to bring to boil.

• Stir thoroughly, and place the fish pieces side by side. Cover and poach 2 minutes at HIGH.

• Turn each piece carefully, cover and poach 1 minute at HIGH.

• Let stand 5 to 8 minutes before serving.

• Serve with butter melted with a little lemon juice and chopped parsley, or with a parsleyed white sauce.

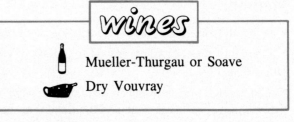

Mueller-Thurgau or Soave

Dry Vouvray

Helpful hint: To melt butter or other fat, place the butter or fat in a glass dish. Microwave, uncovered, from 30 seconds to 2 minutes at HIGH, depending on the amount and temperature of the fat.

Acadian Baked Cod with Vegetables

Preparation: . . . . 35 m
Cooking: . . . . 10 m
Standing: . . . . 3 m

• This is a summer meal in one dish – fish, tomatoes, green pepper and potatoes. It's tasty, colorful and economical.

Ingredients:

About 2 lb (1 kg) fresh cod steak
Grated rind of 1 lemon
1 tsp (5 mL) salt
1/4 tsp (1 mL) pepper
1/4 tsp (1 mL) thyme
Juice of 1/2 a lemon
1 onion, thinly sliced
2 tomatoes, peeled and sliced
3 potatoes, peeled and sliced paper-thin
1 green pepper, cut in slivers
2 tbsp (30 mL) butter or margarine
3 tbsp (50 mL) parsley, minced

Method:

• Mix the lemon rind, salt, pepper and thyme, rub all over the fish.

• Place in a 7 × 11-inch (18 × 28 cm) microwave-safe dish.

• Sprinkle with the lemon juice. Let stand 20 minutes. Remove fish from dish.

• Arrange half the onion, tomatoes, potatoes and green pepper in the dish.

• Top with fish and add the remaining vegetables.

• Melt the butter or margarine 1 minute at HIGH. Add the parsley.

• Pour over the vegetable topping. Cover with waxed paper.

• Bake 8 to 10 minutes at HIGH, basting once with juice in the dish after 3 minutes.

• Let stand 3 minutes and serve.

 White Rhône or Seyval Blanc

Chardonnay

223

Gratin of Cod and Celery

Advance preparation: . . . . **1 h**
Cooking: . . . . **13 m**
Standing: . . . . **5 m**

• Red snapper is also very interesting prepared in this manner. The flavoring of dill and celery seeds and the topping of braised celery give it color and flavor.

Ingredients:

1/2 tsp (2 mL) dill seeds

1/4 tsp (1 mL) celery seeds

1/2 tsp (2 mL) salt

1/4 tsp (1 mL) pepper

1½ lb (750 g) cod or red snapper fillets

2 tbsp (30 mL) butter

Paprika to taste

Braised celery:

1 tbsp (15 mL) butter

4 celery stalks, sliced

1 tbsp (15 mL) water

1 thick slice of lemon, unpeeled

3 tbsp (50 mL) parsley, chopped

Salt and pepper to taste

Method:

• Combine dill and celery seeds with salt and pepper. Sprinkle over the fish.

• Refrigerate, covered, for 1 hour.

• Place fish fillets in an 8 × 12-inch (20 × 30 cm) buttered microwave-safe dish one next to the other, seasoned side up.

• Melt the butter 1 minute at HIGH, pour over fish. Sprinkle the whole with paprika.

• To prepare the celery, melt the butter in a microwave-safe dish 1 minute at HIGH.

• Add the celery, water and lemon slice.

• Cover and microwave 3 minutes at HIGH. Stir well. Let stand 5 minutes.

• Stir in the parsley, salt and pepper to taste. Place around the fish.

• Cover and microwave 6 to 8 minutes at HIGH, according to thickness of fillets.

• Serve with parsleyed noodles or rice.

wines

Cortese di Gavi

White Graves

Hungarian Cod Casserole

Preparation: . . . . **10 m**
Cooking: . . . .**25 m**
Standing: . . . .**none**

• This is an unusual and interesting combination of fish, sour cream and potatoes.

Ingredients:

3 medium potatoes

1 lb (500 g) cod or halibut steaks

Salt and pepper to taste

1½ cup (375 mL) onions, thinly sliced

4 to 6 bacon slices

Juice and rind of a small lemon

2/3 cup (160 mL) sour cream

Salt and pepper to taste

1/4 cup (60 mL) sour cream

1/2 tsp (2 mL) paprika

Method:

• Wash and scrub the potatoes, make 2 or 3 incisions in the peel with the point of a knife. Place the potatoes in a circle on a microwave rack.

• Microwave 8 to 9 minutes at HIGH. Check doneness with the point of a knife. If necessary, microwave 1 or 2 minutes more.

• When cooled, peel the potatoes, slice them and place them in an 8 × 8-inch (20 × 20 cm) well-buttered microwave-safe dish. Salt and pepper to taste.

• Place the onions in another dish, without fat. Microwave 3 minutes at HIGH, stirring after 2 minutes of cooking. Remove from microwave.

• Place the bacon on two layers of paper towel, cook 3 or 4 minutes at HIGH or until crisp. Some bacon may require only 2 minutes of cooking. Crumble the bacon.

• Place the fish steaks over the potatoes. Sprinkle with the lemon juice and the rind, then with the onions, and finally with the crumble bacon.

• Cover it all with the 2/3 cup (160 mL) sour cream. Salt and pepper to taste.

• Cover the dish and microwave at HIGH approximately 8 minutes or until the fish flakes.

• Mix the remaining sour cream with the paprika.

• Spread over the cooked fish, cover and microwave 1 more minute at HIGH.

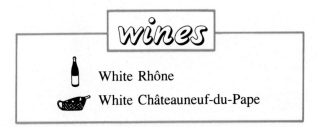

wines

White Rhône
White Châteauneuf-du-Pape

Spring Breeze Cod

Preparation: . . . . **10 m**
Cooking: . . . . **from 19 to 21 m**
Standing: . . . . **none**

Method:

- Snap off the tough lower portion of each asparagus stalk; it will break where the tender part begins.
- Wash the asparagus and place in a dish.
- Add the cold water and a pinch of sugar.
- Cover and microwave 5 to 7 minutes at HIGH, or until the asparagus is tender. Check doneness with the point of a knife.
- Remove the asparagus from its juice, setting it aside. Keep the asparagus warm.
- Place the butter or oil, garlic, parsley and tarragon in a baking dish.
- Microwave 3 minutes at HIGH, stirring once.
- Top with the fish, add the lemon rind and juice and the asparagus cooking juice. Salt and pepper to taste.
- Cover. Microwave 6 minutes at MEDIUM-HIGH.
- Place the asparagus over the fish, cover and microwave 2 minutes at MEDIUM.
- Place the fish and asparagus in a warm serving dish.
- Add the cream to the juice in the cooking dish, microwave 3 minutes at HIGH, stir well and pour over the fish.

- Asparagus and cod are an amazing combination. Their flavors blend very well.

Ingredients:

1 lb (500 g) fresh asparagus

1/4 cup (60 mL) cold water

3 tbsp (50 mL) unsalted butter or olive oil

2 medium garlic cloves, minced

1/4 cup (60 mL) fresh parsley, minced

1/2 tsp (2 mL) tarragon

2 lb (1 kg) fresh cod, cut into 6 fillets

Rind and juice of half a lemon

Salt and pepper to taste

3 tbsp (50 mL) heavy cream

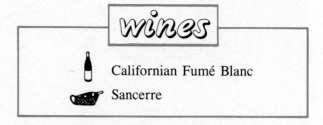

Californian Fumé Blanc

Sancerre

A personal note: You can also cook asparagus by Sensor, if your oven has that feature. The oven determines the cooking time.

Kedgeree

Preparation: . . . . 20 m
Cooking: . . . . from 25 to 30 m
Standing: . . . . 15 m

• An old English breakfast or light lunch, this dish is still very much in favor. It's an interesting way to use leftover poached salmon or canned salmon.

Ingredients:

1/4 cup (60 mL) butter or magarine

1/2 cup (125 mL) onions, chopped fine

1 garlic clove, chopped fine

2 celery stalks, diced

1/4 cup (60 mL) celery leaves, minced

1 tart apple, peeled, cored and chopped

1 to 2 tbsp (15 to 30 mL) curry powder

1 cup (250 mL) long grain rice, cooked

2 cups (500 mL) chicken stock or water

1 tsp (5 mL) salt

2/3 cup (160 mL) milk or cream

1 lb (500 g) cod, haddock or salmon, cooked

Method:

• Place the butter or margarine in an 8-cup (2 L) microwave-safe dish. Microwave 2 minutes at HIGH.

• Add the onions, garlic, celery, celery leaves and apple. Stir well. Microwave 5 minutes at HIGH. Add the curry powder, stir thoroughly.

• Then add the cooked rice, chicken stock or water, salt and milk or cream. Stir well. Cover. Microwave 20 minutes at MEDIUM-HIGH, stirring after 10 minutes. Let stand 15 minutes and stir in the fish of your choice. Serve.

• When prepared ahead of time, do not refrigerate, reheat 5 minutes at MEDIUM, covered, or use "COMB. I" to indicate reheating; the oven determines how long it will take.

wines

Gewurztraminer

Mosel Riesling Spaetlese

Helpful hint: The dish must be well covered with plastic wrap if you use the "COMB." setting.

Halibut

Halibut Orange

Preparation: . . . . **8 m**
Cooking: . . . . from **10 to 12 m**
Standing: . . . . **5 m**

A personal note: Delicious served hot, this dish is equally good served cold. As halibut is available almost all year round and is easily found frozen, I recommend this dish for guests when time is at a premium. I always keep a few boxes of frozen halibut in my freezer for emergencies

Ingredients:

2 lb (1 kg) halibut, fresh or frozen

Grated rind of 1 orange

Juice of 1 orange

4 tbsp (60 mL) butter

1 tsp (5 mL) lemon juice

Salt and pepper to taste

1/8 tsp (0.5 mL) nutmeg

1/4 cup (60 mL) parsley, minced

Method:

• If frozen halibut is used, thaw fish 1 hour before cooking. When thawed, wrap it in paper towel to remove excess moisture.

• For fresh fillets, simply wrap in paper towel for a few minutes.

• Place fish in a single layer in a large, thickly buttered microwave-safe dish.

• Combine remaining ingredients, except the minced parsley, and pour over the fish.

• Microwave 10 to 12 minutes at HIGH, or until fish flakes when tested with a fork.

• Let stand 5 minutes, then remove to a hot dish.

• Pour on top any sauce remaining in the dish. Sprinkle with the minced parsley and serve.

wines

Verdicchio

Dry Vouvray

Halibut
À la Grecque

Preparation: . . . . **15 m**
Cooking: . . . . **15 m**
Standing: . . . . **5 m**

A personal note: In Greece, each portion of fish is wrapped in vine leaves. When I have the bottled type that can be purchased in Greek shops, I use them. But the recipe has been adapted to the use of Boston lettuce instead.

Ingredients:

2 lb (1 kg) halibut fillets or steaks

1 head of Boston lettuce

1/4 cup (60 mL) parsley, minced

1 bay leaf, broken up

1 small onion, diced

1/4 cup (60 mL) olive or vegetable oil

1/2 cup (125 mL) white wine or white vermouth

1 tsp (5 mL) salt

1/4 tsp (1 mL) cumin seeds

1 chicken broth cube

1 cup (250 mL) caper sauce

Method:

• Arrange a layer of lettuce leaves on the bottom of an 8 × 12-inch (20 × 30 cm) glass dish.

• Top with half the parsley, the bay leaf and onion slices.

• Place the halibut on top of this herb layer.

• Combine the oil, wine or vermouth, salt and cumin seeds. Pour over the fish.

• Break up the broth cube and scatter over the fish.

• Sprinkle the remaining parsley on top.

• Top with more lettuce leaves, enough to completely cover the fish.

• Bake 10 minutes at HIGH, and 5 minutes at LOW. Let stand 5 minutes.

• Set on a hot platter. Pour caper sauce on top and serve with rice, stirred with butter and minced parsley.

Entre-Deux-Mers
Australian Chardonnay

Halibut
À la Russe

Preparation: . . . . **6 m**
Cooking: . . . . **from 6 to 9 m**
Standing: . . . . **2 m**

A personal note: You can use either fresh or frozen fish for this recipe. If you use frozen fish, it must be thawed before being prepared for cooking. You can prepare this dish a few hours ahead of time. Keep it refrigerated until you're ready to cook.

Chilean Sauvignon Blanc

Californian Fumé Blanc

Ingredients:

4 to 6 individual portions of halibut

1/2 tsp (2 mL) each of salt and sugar

1/2 tsp (2 mL) paprika

1 medium onion

6 thin slices of lemon, unpeeled

1 tbsp (15 mL) butter

2 tbsp (30 mL) chili sauce

Method:

- Put the individual portions of fish in a round 8-inch (20 cm) microwave-safe dish.

- Mix together the salt, sugar and paprika. Sprinkle over the fish.

- Peel the onion and slice thinly. Spread over the fish. Top with the lemon slices.

- Heat the butter and chili sauce 40 seconds at HIGH. Pour over the fish.

- Cover the dish with waxed paper. Microwave 5 minutes at HIGH or 8 minutes at MEDIUM.

- Let stand 2 minutes before serving.

Helpful hint: Individual foods like potatoes and hors d'oeuvres will cook evenly if you space them evenly in the microwave. If possible, arrange them in a circle.

Halibut Stew

Preparation: . . . . **12 m**
Cooking: . . . . **13 m**
Standing: . . . . **3 m**

• Most of us seldom think of making a fish stew. But if it is well prepared, a fish stew is a very economical and flavorful dish.

Ingredients:

2 tbsp (30 mL) butter

1 large onion, chopped fine

2 garlic cloves, chopped fine

1 small green pepper, diced

1 tomato, peeled and chopped

1 cup (250 mL) potatoes, peeled and chopped

1/2 cup (125 mL) water or clam juice

1 tsp (5 mL) salt

1/2 tsp (2 mL) pepper

1 tsp (5 mL) dill or marjoram

4 to 6 halibut or cod fillets

Method:

• Place the butter in a microwave-safe bowl and melt 1 minute at HIGH. Add the onion, garlic, green pepper and stir together. Microwave 2 minutes at HIGH.

• Stir and add the remaining ingredients except the fish. Stir well, microwave 5 minutes at MEDIUM-HIGH.

• Cut the fillets into individual portions and place them in the hot mixture. Salt and pepper lightly. Cover and microwave 5 minutes at HIGH.

• Let stand 3 minutes, then serve with hot French bread.

wines

Italian Chardonnay

Tavel Rosé

Poached Halibut Rolls

Preparation:	10 m
Cooking:	18 m
Standing:	none

A personal note: Served in a nest of lemon rice, Poached Halibut Rolls make a delicious light meal. Add a green salad, a fruit, and your meal is complete.

Ingredients:

1 ½ lb (750 g) halibut or sole fillets

3 tbsp (50 mL) butter

1/2 cup (125 mL) chicken broth or white wine

1 small garlic clove, minced

1/2 tsp (2 mL) tarragon or basil

1 tsp (5 mL) Dijon mustard

1 cup (250 mL) fresh tomatoes, minced

1/2 tsp (2 mL) sugar

1/2 cup (125 mL) heavy cream

1/2 tsp (2 mL) paprika

Method:

• Wipe each fillet with a paper towel, cut in half length-wise and roll up each piece.

• Melt the butter in a 9-inch (23 cm) round microwave-safe dish and melt 1 minute at HIGH.

• Add the chicken broth or white wine, garlic, tarragon or basil, Dijon mustard, tomatoes and sugar.

• Cover and microwave 5 minutes at HIGH. Stir well.

• Place the fish rolls side by side in the dish and baste with the sauce.

• Microwave 8 minutes at MEDIUM-HIGH, basting with the juice halfway through the cooking.

• Remove the fish with a perforated spoon and place it in a warm dish. Cover.

• Add the cream and paprika to the sauce remaining in the cooking dish.

• Stir and microwave 4 minutes at HIGH, stirring once.

• Pour over the fish and serve.

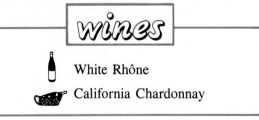

wines

White Rhône

California Chardonnay

Other Delicious Fish

Baked Pike with Sour Cream

Preparation: .... 10 m
Cooking: .... .8 m
Standing: .... 5 m

A personal note: Whenever I can buy a 2-to-3-pound (1 to 1.5 kg) pike and I have fresh dill in my garden, plus a good piece of Cheddar, I make this recipe to best enjoy my pike. A small sea bass can replace the pike.

Ingredients:

1/2-lb (1 kg) pike, cleaned but not split

1 tsp (5 mL) salt

1/2 tsp (2 mL) pepper, freshly ground

1 cup (250 mL) sour cream

1/2 cup (125 mL) Cheddar cheese, freshly grated

1/4 cup (60 mL) fresh dill, minced

Paprika

Method:

• Make 4 to 5 shallow gashes on both sides of the fish and season inside with salt and pepper.

• Make a paste with the sour cream, grated Cheddar and dill, and spread on top and sides of the fish.

• Sprinkle generously with paprika.

• Place in a thickly buttered microwave-safe dish, long enough to hold the fish. Do not cover.

• Bake 6 to 8 minutes at MEDIUM-HIGH. The time will vary slightly, depending on the size of the fish.

• A good test is to lift a bit with a fork; if it flakes, it is cooked.

• When done, let stand 5 minutes, covered.

• To taste, sprinkle top with more minced dill.

wines

Muscadet or Frascati

Alsatian Riesling

Flounder Fillets Louisiana

Preparation: . . . . **9 m**
Cooking: . . . . **9 m**
Standing: . . . . **none**

A personal note: When I have small fresh trout, I substitute them for the flounder in this recipe. The flounder can also be replaced by fillets of sole, and canned salmon can replace the snow crabmeat.

Ingredients:

1 ½ lb (750 g) flounder fillets

1 tbsp (15 mL) butter or margarine

3 tbsp (50 mL) green onions, minced

3 tbsp (50 mL) parsley, minced

1 medium-sized onion, minced

1/2 lb (250 g) fresh crabmeat *or*
   1 8-oz (250 g) can snow crabmeat,
   with its juice

1/4 cup (60 mL) fine cracker crumbs

1/4 tsp (1 mL) curry powder

1/2 tsp (2 mL) pepper and salt

1 egg white, lightly beaten

2 tbsp (30 mL) cream or milk

Method:

• Cut fish into 6 serving pieces, pat dry with paper towels. Place in a 7 × 11-inch (18 × 28 cm) glass baking dish.

• Place butter or margarine in a microwave-safe dish, add the green onions, parsley and minced onion.

• Microwave 2 minutes at HIGH. Stir well and microwave at MEDIUM-HIGH another 2 minutes.

• Stir in the crabmeat (use juice, when canned crab is used) and add the remaining ingredients. Stir the whole together.

• Spread mixture over fillets in baking dish. Cover with waxed paper. Microwave at HIGH 5 minutes or until fish flakes easily with a fork.

• Garnish with parsley and lime or lemon slices.

wines

Sicilian Regaleali (white) or
German Riesling

Gewurztraminer

Flounder Fillets Vin Blanc

Sauvignon Blanc

Château-bottled white Graves

Preparation: . . . . **10 m**
Cooking: . . . . **9 m**
Standing: . . . . **none**

• The flavor combination of thyme and white wine is perfect with all white fish.

Ingredients:

1½ to 2 lb (750 g to 1 kg) flounder fillets

2 tbsp (30 mL) butter

1 10-oz (284 mL) can sliced mushrooms, drained

4 green onions, minced

Salt and pepper to taste

1 bay leaf

1/4 tsp (1 mL) thyme

1/2 cup (125 mL) breadcrumbs

1/2 tsp (2 mL) paprika

2 tbsp (30 mL) butter, melted 1 minute at HIGH

1 cup (250 mL) white wine

Method:

• Place fish in baking dish, either rolled fillets or spread out, one next to the other.

• Melt the first 2 tablespoons (30 mL) of butter 1 minute at HIGH. Pour over fish.

• Mix the mushrooms, green onions, salt, pepper, bay leaf and thyme. Sprinkle over the fish.

• Mix the breadcrumbs, melted butter and paprika, sprinkle over the fish.

• Pour the white wine around the fish, not on top.

• Bake at HIGH 5 minutes, baste with juice in dish, then cook for 1 to 3 minutes more at HIGH.

Red Snapper Guadeloupe

Preparation: . . . . 12 m
Cooking: . . . . from 8 to 9 m
Standing: . . . . none

• This was the very first dish I ate on my arrival on Guadeloupe. I have made it often since. The lime, fresh mushrooms and parsley are very important. It's also nice prepared with fillets of flounder.

Ingredients:

2 lb (1 kg) red snapper fillets

1/4 cup (60 mL) butter or margarine

1/2 lb (500 g) fresh mushrooms, sliced

4 green onions, chopped

1/4 cup (60 mL) fresh parsley, minced

Juice of lime *or*
  2 tbsp (30 mL) lemon juice

1 garlic clove, crushed or chopped fine

1/2 tsp (2 mL) salt

1/4 tsp (1 mL) pepper, freshly ground

Method:

• Wipe fish with paper towel and place in an 8 × 8-inch (20 × 20 cm) glass or ceramic baking dish.

• Place the butter or margarine in a microwave-safe bowl and melt 1 minute at HIGH.

• Add mushrooms, green onions, parsley, lime or lemon juice, garlic, salt and pepper. Mix well.

• Microwave 2 minutes at HIGH.

• Mix well, pour over fish, spreading evenly. Cover with waxed paper.

• Microwave at MEDIUM 6 to 7 minutes or until fish flakes easily.

• Serve with lime or lemon wedges.

wines

Muscadet

Chablis

Tuna and Macaroni Casserole

Preparation:	8 m
Cooking:	18 m
Standing:	5 m

Californian French Colombard

German Riesling or
Mueller-Thurgau Spaetlese

Ingredients:

2 cups (500 mL) elbow macaroni

1 tsp (5 mL) salt

4 cups (1 L) boiling water

1 6½-oz (181 g) can flaked tuna

1 small onion, chopped fine

2 tbsp (30 mL) parsley, chopped

1/2 tsp (2 mL) curry powder

1 10-oz (284 mL) can cream of chicken soup

1/2 cup (125 mL) buttered breadcrumbs

Method:

• Place macaroni in an 8-cup (2 L) baking dish. Add salt and pour boiling water on top. Microwave 6 to 8 minutes at HIGH. Stir thoroughly.

• Let stand 5 minutes, then drain.

• Place all the ingredients except the buttered breadcrumbs in the baking dish and stir until well mixed.

• Add the macaroni. Mix well, top with buttered crumbs and dot with butter. Microwave, uncovered, 6 to 8 minutes at MEDIUM-HIGH.

• Let stand 5 minutes, then serve.

• Using different kinds of creamed soup in this casserole produces different flavors.

Helpful hint: Food well spaced in a shallow dish will reheat more quickly than in a narrow, deep dish.

Fish Casserole Creole

Preparation: . . . . **12 m**
Cooking: . . . . **17 m**
Standing: . . . . **none**

A personal note: Use leftover fish or a poached frozen or fresh fish to make this tasty "meal-in-a-dish."

 Liebfraumilch

 Rhine Riesling Kabinett

A personal note: This casserole can be prepared early in the day and refrigerated. Microwave it 10 minutes at MEDIUM-HIGH when ready to serve.

Ingredients:

1 to 1 ½ lb (500 to 750 g) fish, cooked broken into pieces

3 tbsp (50 mL) butter

3 tbsp (50 mL) flour

2 cups (500 mL) milk

1/4 tsp (1 mL) dry mustard

Salt and pepper to taste

1 tsp (5 mL) sage or savory

1 10-oz (284 mL) can whole corn

2 eggs, separated

1/2 cup (125 mL) Cheddar cheese, grated

3 tbsp (50 mL) soft breadcrumbs

1/2 tsp (2 mL) paprika

Method:

• Place the butter in a large measuring microwave-safe cup and melt 1 minute at HIGH.

• Add the flour, mix and add milk. Microwave 3 minutes at HIGH.

• Stir well and microwave another 2 minutes at HIGH or until creamy.

• Add mustard, salt, pepper to taste, sage or savory and corn.

• Stir, then microwave another minute at HIGH.

• Add the egg yolks and 1/4 cup (60 mL) of the grated Cheddar cheese. Mix thoroughly.

• Beat the egg whites until they hold a stiff peak, then fold into the sauce.

• Butter an 8 × 8-inch (20 × 20 cm) glass or ceramic baking dish or a deep microwave-safe pie plate.

• Fill with alternate layers of fish and sauce, ending with sauce.

• Mix the remaining cheese with the breadcrumbs.

• Sprinkle on top of the sauce, then sprinkle paprika over all. Cover with waxed paper.

• Microwave 10 minutes at MEDIUM-HIGH.

General Directions

• Clean seafood,

• and shellfish before preparing for cooking.

• Trim mussels.

• Shrimp and scallops should always be placed in a single layer for cooking.

> **A personal note:** Pierce oysters and clams several times with a tooth-pick before cooking.

To cook by time

• Cover dish with plastic wrap or a lid.

• Microwave on the power level and for the minimum time recommended in the chart.

• Make sure to stir or re-arrange them halfway through the cooking period.

To cook by auto sensor or "COMB"
(Combination)

• Cover dish completely with plastic wrap.

• Cook on Auto Sensor Cycle COOK A8, or as indicated in your oven Manual.*

• With shrimp or scallops, stir when cooking time appears in the display window of your oven.

• ALL SEAFOOD AND SHELLFISH SHOULD STAND 5 MINUTES AFTER COOKING.

• Test for doneness before adding extra heating time.

• When cooked, seafood should be opaque in color. If undercooked, return to oven and continue cooking 30 to 60 seconds more.

Study your own oven manual instructions carefully to clearly understand instructions given in the chart on next page.

Cooking seafood and shellfish

Seafood and shellfish	Amount	Power	Approx. cooking time (in minutes)
Scallops	1 lb (500 g)	MEDIUM	6½ to 8½
Shrimp, medium size *(shelled and cleaned)*	1 lb (500 g)	MEDIUM	4½ to 6½
Lobster *	3/4 to 1¼ lb (340 to 570 g)	HIGH	5 to 8 **
Lobster tails *	1 lb (500 g)	HIGH	8 to 10 **

* *Barely cover with hot water. Add 1/2 teaspoon (2 mL) salt.*
** *Check doneness. Cooked when shell is bright red.*

Preparing and Cooking frozen seafood FREEZE-COOK CYCLE

Seafood and shellfish	Auto Sensor cycle FREEZE-COOK	Approx. cooking time (in minutes)	Special instructions
Frozen lobster tails *8 oz ea. (250 g)*	FROZ-COOK A8	15 to 19	
Scallops *1 lb (500 g)*	FROZ-COOK A8	21 to 22	Arrange in single layer
Shrimp (peeled or in shell) *1 lb (500 g)*	FROZ-COOK A6	22	Arrange in single layer

Boiled Lobster

• Steamed lobster, hot melted butter, crusty bread and a fine well chilled white wine — what more could one wish?

Ingredients:

2 live lobsters, approximately 1½ lb (750 g) each

3 cups (750 mL) boiling water

2 bay leaves

3 slices of unpeeled lemon

Method:

• The lobsters are cooked one after the other.

• Place the first one in a 12 × 8-inch (30 × 20 cm) microwave-safe dish and pour boiling water over it.

• Add bay leaves and lemon. Cover and microwave 5 minutes at HIGH, turning the lobster twice.

• Remove from water.

• Microwave the second lobster in the same manner. There is no need to change the water.

• To serve, split the lobsters lengthwise.

• Remove the sac and vein, crack the claws. Serve on a warm platter with a small bowl of hot, melted butter.

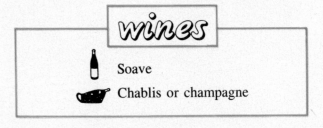

wines

Soave

Chablis or champagne

Lobster Newburg

Preparation: .5 m
Cooking: . . . . .8 m
Standing: .5 m

A personal note: This recipe may be used to garnish *vol-au-vent* shells, over toasted, buttered French bread or simply served on a bed of parsleyed rice. Frozen tails must be thawed, and left to stand during preparation of the sauce.

White Burgundy

Pouilly Fumé

Ingredients:

1/4 cup (60 mL) butter

3 tbsp (50 mL) flour

2 cups (500 mL) light cream

1 egg, well beaten

1 tsp (5 mL) salt

2 tbsp (30 mL) dry sherry

2 5-oz (142 g) cans each *or*
   1 10-oz (280 g) package frozen lobster *or*
   lobster tails, of your choice

Method:

• Place the butter in a 6-cup (1.5 L) microwave-safe baking dish and melt 1 minute at HIGH.

• Add the flour and mix thoroughly.

• Add the cream and microwave 3 to 4 minutes at HIGH, until thick and creamy, stirring twice.

• Add the egg gradually, beating with a whisk for perfect blending.

• Add salt and sherry, then the well-drained lobster, broken up into pieces, or the thawed lobster tail meat.

• Microwave the sauce, uncovered, 3 minutes at HIGH. Adjust seasoning and serve.

How to cook lobster tails

Preparation: . . . . 7 m
Cooking: . . . . 6 m
Standing: . . . . 5 m

A personal note: Lobster tails are more economical to buy than whole lobsters, as proportionately there is more meat in the tails. Lobster tails are very easily cooked in the microwave oven.

Ingredients:

2 lobster tails approximately 8 oz (250 g) each

1/4 cup (60 mL) salted or unsalted butter

2 tbsp (30 mL) brandy, orange liqueur or lemon juice

Method:

• Cut each tail lengthwise with kitchen shears.

• Brush the meat with melted butter.

• Place the lobster tails in a shallow microwave-safe dish, side by side.

• A good pinch of curry or tarragon may be added to the brandy or lemon juice, but not to the orange liqueur. Brush evenly over each lobster tail.

• Cover and microwave 4 to 6 minutes at HIGH, according to size. When cooked, they will turn red.

Clarified butter:

• Place **1/2 cup (125 mL) salted or unsalted butter** in a microwave-safe cup, do not cover. Microwave 2 minutes at HIGH. Cool.

• Then, with a small spoon remove the fat that has risen to the top.

• The milky residue remains in the bottom of the cup.

• Keep the clarified butter in the refrigerator until ready to use.

• Only 20 to 40 seconds at HIGH will be needed to reheat the butter. **One teaspoon (5 mL) of orange liqueur, or scotch, or lime or lemon juice** can be added to the butter before reheating.

A personal note: Do not discard the butter sediment. I use it in preparing soup, sauces and mincemeat.

Buttered Lobster Tails

A **personal note:** The easiest recipe is often the most flavorful. To give the tails some style, serve them with imported chutney to which you add a few spoonfuls of brandy.

Ingredients:

3 tbsp (50 mL) butter

2 tsp (10 mL) lemon or lime juice

1 10-oz (280 g) package frozen lobster tails

Method:

- Remove the tails from the package and place them in an 8-inch (20 cm) microwave-safe cake pan or in a 9-inch (23 cm) microwave-safe pie plate.
- Microwave 2 minutes 30 seconds at HIGH without covering.
- Let stand approximately 5 to 10 minutes, covered, to thaw thoroughly.

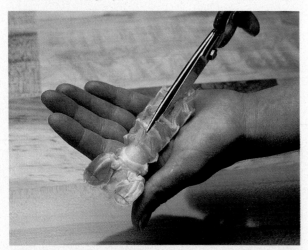

- Split the shells with kitchen shears by cutting the underpart lengthwise.

wines

Dry Vouvray

Australian or Californian Chardonnay

Preparation:	10 m
Cooking:	3 m
Standing:	5 m

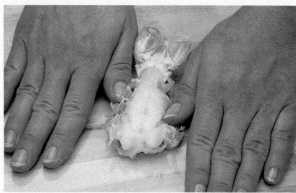

- Press down to keep flat.

- Set the tails side by side in a microwave-safe dish, meaty side up.
- Melt the butter 1 minute at HIGH in a small bowl or a measuring cup, add the lemon juice. Stir to mix then brush on the lobster tails generously.

- Cover and microwave 2 minutes at HIGH, or just enough for the flesh to lose its transparency and turn pink.

Shrimp

Shrimp Vollarta

A personal note: This simple, elegant dish calls for raw shrimp. Choose medium-sized shrimp to cut costs. The dish is most attractive served in shells.

wines

🍾 Aligoté

🥄 Chablis

Ingredients:

1½ lb (750 g) fresh shrimp, medium-sized
Juice of 1 or 2 fresh limes
2 tsp (10 mL) coarse salt
2 to 3 tbsp (30 to 50 mL) vegetable oil

Method:

• Split the shrimp in half lengthwise through the shell and tail.

• Rinse out dark vein.

Advance preparation: . . . . . **a few hours**
Cooking: . . . . **8 m**
Standing: . . . . **5 m**

• Dry shrimp on a paper towel, set on a pie plate and sprinkle the cut side of the shrimp generously with the lime juice. Salt and let stand a few hours in the refrigerator.

• When ready to serve, heat the vegetable oil 2 minutes at HIGH in a ceramic pie plate.

• Place about half the shrimp in the hot oil and microwave until they turn pink, 3 minutes at HIGH.

• Microwave the remaining shrimp in the same manner.

• Serve piping hot, surrounded with quartered limes.

Shrimp Marinière

Preparation: . . . . **8 m**
Cooking: . . . . **9 m**
Standing: . . . . **5 m**

• Parisians are fond of this dish in the spring time. Fresh or frozen shrimp can be used.

wines

Spanish or Portuguese white

Saint-Peray or white Châteauneuf-du-Pape

Ingredients:

1 10-oz (280 g) package uncooked, shelled frozen shrimp

1/4 cup (60 mL) very hot water

2 tsp (10 mL) lemon juice

1/4 tsp (1 mL) salt

1/4 tsp (1 mL) thyme or basil

1/3 cup (80 mL) dry white wine or vermouth

1/2 tsp (2 mL) sugar

2 tbsp (30 mL) oil

1 garlic clove, minced

1 medium tomato, peeled and chopped

2 green onions, finely chopped

Method:

• Thaw shrimp, separate and place them in a 4-cup (1 L) microwave-safe baking dish.

• Combine hot water, lemon juice, salt, basil or thyme, wine or vermouth and sugar. Pour over shrimp.

• Microwave, uncovered, 4 minutes at HIGH. Let stand 1 minute. Drain and set aside.

• Pour oil into the 4-cup (1 L) baking dish, heat 1 minute at HIGH.

• Add garlic, tomato and green onions. Microwave, covered with waxed paper, for 2 minutes at HIGH.

• Add shrimp, heat 2 minutes at HIGH.

• Serve with parsleyed rice.

Shrimp Provençale

Preparation: . . . . **15 m**
Cooking: . . . . **13 m**
Standing: . . . . **5 m**

- This is one of the great recipes of Provence!

Ingredients:

1 lb (500 g) uncooked shrimp

1/2 cup (125 mL) water

1/2 cup (125 mL) button mushrooms, cut in four

2 medium-sized tomatoes, diced

6 peppercorns

Sauce:

2 French shallots *or* 6 green onions, chopped

1/2 cup (125 mL) white wine or white vermouth

1 bay leaf

1/4 tsp (1 mL) thyme

1 tsp (5 mL) basil

2 tbsp (30 mL) butter

2 tbsp (30 mL) flour

1 garlic clove, crushed or finely chopped

1 tsp (5 mL) tomato paste

1/2 cup (125 mL) water or fish fumet or clam juice

Method:

- First, prepare the sauce.
- Place the shallots or green onions, white wine or vermouth, bay leaf, thyme and basil in a microwave-safe dish.
- Microwave, uncovered, 3 minutes at HIGH.
- Mix together the butter and flour. Add to the wine sauce, stir well.
- Microwave 2 to 3 minutes at HIGH, stirring once.
- Add the garlic, tomato paste and the liquid of your choice.
- Stir well and microwave 4 minutes at MEDIUM-HIGH, stirring once.
- Place the cleaned shrimp in a dish, add the water,

wines

Portuguese or Spanish white

White Rhône or Bandol

mushrooms, tomatoes and peppercorns.

- Microwave 3 minutes at MEDIUM-HIGH, stirring once. Remove peppercorns.
- Pour the sauce over the shrimp or serve sauce separately.

A personal note: A nice way to serve these is to place the shrimp in a chafing dish and pass the sauce separately.

Shrimp in Hot Lime Butter

Preparation: . . . . **7 m**
Cooking: . . . . **6 m**
Standing: . . . . **5 m**

A personal note: You can use lemon instead of lime in this recipe, which is a quick and easy way to serve shrimp. They are at their best served hot.

wines

Soave

Alsatian Riesling

Ingredients:

1 6-oz (170 mL) bottle light beer

1/4 tsp (1 mL) curry powder

1/2 tsp (2 mL) paprika

1/2 tsp (2 mL) dill seeds

1 onion, minced

1 lb (500 g) medium-sized shrimp

Melted or clarified butter to taste

Rind and juice of 1 lime or lemon

Helpful hint: To dry orange or lemon rind, spread it on a microwave-safe pie plate and microwave 1/2 to 1 minute at HIGH. Stir once during drying time.

Method:

• Pour the light beer into a large microwave-safe bowl, add the curry, paprika, dill and onion.

• Bring to boil 4 minutes at HIGH. Stir well.

• Add the shrimp. Stir. Cover and microwave 2 minutes at HIGH. Let stand covered 5 minutes.

• Remove the shrimp to a warm dish with a perforated spoon.

• Add the lime or lemon juice and the rind to the melted or clarified butter and serve with the shrimp.

• Peel off the shell and dip each shrimp in the hot lime butter.

• Serve with lemon rice and hot crusty bread.

Shrimp Victoria

Preparation: . . . . **45 m**
Cooking: . . . . **12 m**
Standing: . . . . **5 m**

• This dish was created for Queen Victoria to celebrate her fiftieth birthday. It is easy and quick to prepare and delicious to eat.

Ingredients:

1 lb (500 g) medium-sized green shrimp *or*
 1 lb (500 g) fresh scallops
1/4 cup (60 mL) butter
6 green onions, chopped fine
1 tsp (5 mL) curry powder
1/2 lb (250 g) fresh mushrooms, thinly sliced
2 tbsp (30 mL) flour
1/4 cup (60 mL) dry sherry
1¼ cups (310 mL) sour cream
Salt and pepper to taste

Method:

• Peel and butterfly the green shrimp by cutting inside the curve but without detaching.

• If you are using scallops, split in half on the thickness.

• Place in an 8-inch (20 cm) round microwave-safe dish the butter and green onions. Microwave 1 minute at HIGH.

• Add the curry powder, stir until well mixed, add the shrimp or scallops and the mushrooms. Microwave 3 minutes at HIGH. Stir well.

• Stir in the flour until well blended.

• Add the sherry and stir. Microwave 2 minutes at MEDIUM-HIGH.

• Stir thoroughly and set aside until ready to serve, as this portion of the recipe can be prepared 1 to 2 hours ahead of time. Do not refrigerate.

• To reheat, microwave 2 minutes at MEDIUM-HIGH, stir well, add the sour cream, salt and pepper to taste, stir to mix and heat at MEDIUM 3 to 4 minutes, or until hot.

• Serve in a nest of long grain rice stirred with lots of chopped parsley.

A personal note: Scallops or fresh oysters can replace the shrimp.

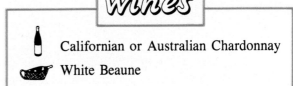

Californian or Australian Chardonnay
White Beaune

Oriental Shrimp

Preparation: . . . . 40 m

Cooking: . . . . from 8 to 10 m

Standing: . . . . 5 m

A personal note: Shrimp have become a great luxury because of their cost, so I recommend that you use the green shrimp (raw), which are more tender and tastier. Serve this dish with Rice Pilaf.

wines

Vouvray or Vidal

Italian Traminer or Alsatian Muscat

Ingredients:

1 lb (500 g) shrimp, large or medium

3 tbsp (50 mL) chili sauce

1 tsp (5 mL) sugar

2 tsp (10 mL) cornstarch

1/2 tsp (2 mL) salt

1 tbsp (15 mL) vegetable oil

2 tbsp (30 mL) fresh ginger root, grated

1 garlic clove, crushed

1 small green pepper, slivered (optional)

1 tbsp (15 mL) each soy sauce and sherry

Method:

• Butterfly the shrimp:

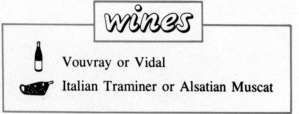

1. Remove the shell by cutting with scissors all along the stomach and pull.

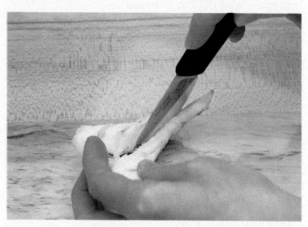

2. Then, slit the stomach the length of the shrimp but without separating it in two.

3. Flatten it with your hands to shape it like a butterfly.

• Mix together the chili sauce, sugar, cornstarch and salt.

• Place in an 8-inch (20 cm) microwave-safe round bowl the oil, grated ginger and garlic. Cover with waxed paper and heat 2 minutes at HIGH.

• Remove garlic, add the green pepper and the chili sauce mixture, stir thoroughly, cover and microwave 2 minutes at HIGH, stirring halfway through cooking.

• Add the shrimp, mix well, cover and microwave 4 to 6 minutes at HIGH, stirring once halfway through cooking.

• Add soy sauce and sherry. Stir well and serve.

Seafood Casserole

Preparation: . . . . **10 m**
Cooking: . . . .**10 m**
Standing: . . . . **5 m**

A personal note: A culinary delight from Nice, France, this dish is ready to serve in 8 minutes. It's excellent fare for a friendly dinner, preceded by chicken consommé or cream of mushroom soup, with buttered rice and green peas as accompaniment.

Ingredients:

2 tbsp (30 mL) butter

1 tbsp (15 mL) olive oil

A pinch of saffron *or*
   1/2 tsp (2 mL) curry powder

1 tsp (5 mL) paprika

1 medium onion, chopped fine

2 garlic cloves, chopped fine

2 tomatoes, peeled and quartered

1/2 tsp (2 mL) sugar

1 green pepper, slivered

1/2 lb (250 g) medium shrimp, raw

1/2 to 3/4 lb (250 to 350 g) scallops

1/4 cup (60 mL) white wine or vermouth or
   fish fumet

Method:

• Place the butter and olive oil in an 8 × 8-inch (20 × 20 cm) microwave-safe dish. Microwave 3 minutes at HIGH.

• Add the saffron or curry powder, paprika, onion and garlic. Stir. Microwave 1 minute at HIGH.

• Add the tomatoes, sugar and green pepper. Microwave 1 minute at HIGH. Mix thoroughly.

• Shell the shrimp and cut each scallop into 2 or 3 thin slices.

• Add to the tomatoes and stir well.

• Add the wine or vermouth or fish fumet. Cover the dish with waxed paper and microwave 5 minutes at HIGH.

• Stir well and serve.

wines

White Rhône

Tavel rosé

Hockey Night Seafood

Preparation: . . . . 12 m
Cooking: . . . . 24 m
Standing: . . . . 5 m

A personal note: Here is another fine fish stew to serve with a basket of large, hot, buttered biscuits.

wines

🍾 Muscadet

🥢 Tavel rosé

Ingredients:

1/4 cup (60 mL) butter or margarine

2 medium potatoes, diced

1/2 cup (125 mL) carrots, diced or minced

1 large onion, diced

1/4 cup (60 mL) water

1 lb (500 g) haddock, fresh or frozen

2 5-oz (142 g) cans clams, with juice

1 lb (500 g) scallops, cut in half

1 lb (500 g) small shrimp (optional)

1 cup (250 mL) light cream

1/2 tsp (2 mL) curry powder (optional)

Salt and pepper to taste

Method:

• Place the butter or margarine in an 8-cup (2 L) microwave-safe bowl and melt 1 minute at HIGH.

• Add the potatoes, carrots and onion.

• Stir, add the water, cover and microwave 10 minutes at MEDIUM-HIGH, stirring once after 5 minutes of cooking.

• Cut the haddock into small individual portions, then add to the vegetables together with the clams and their juice.

• Microwave 6 minutes at MEDIUM.

• Add the remaining ingredients. Stir well.

• When ready to serve, cover and microwave 8 minutes at MEDIUM.

259

Scallops

Scallops Saint-Jacques

Preparation: . . . . **10 m**
Cooking: . . . . **from 10 to 12 m**
Standing: . . . . **5 m**

A personal note: This delectable scallops dish can be served either in a shell or in a nest of rice and topped with fresh minced parsley.

Ingredients:

1 lb (500 g) fresh scallops

2 tbsp (30 mL) butter

1/4 cup (60 mL) green onions, chopped

2 tbsp (30 mL) flour

3/4 cup (190 mL) white or red wine

1/4 cup (60 mL) rich cream

1 small tomato, peeled, seeded and chopped

1/4 tsp (1 mL) sugar

Salt and pepper to taste

2 tbsp (30 mL) parsley, finely chopped

Method:

• When using big scallops, cut them in half to make two round slices. Leave the small ones whole.

• Place the butter in an 8 × 8-inch (20 × 20 cm) glass or microwave-safe plastic dish and melt 2 minutes at HIGH.

• Roll the scallops in absorbent paper. Add to the butter.

• Microwave 2 minutes at HIGH. Stir well.

• Remove scallops from butter with a perforated spoon, cover and let stand.

• To the butter remaining in the pan add the green onions. Stir well, microwave 2 minutes at HIGH.

• Add the flour, stir until well mixed, add the wine and the cream. Stir to mix.

• Add the chopped tomato and the sugar. Salt and pepper to taste.

• Stir the whole, microwave 3 to 4 minutes at HIGH, stirring twice and cooking until creamy. Adjust seasoning.

• Add the scallops. Let stand, covered, until ready to use.

• To serve, either fill each shell, sprinkle with parsley, place shells in the oven on a sheet of absorbent paper, warm, counting 1/2 minute per shell, or place in a ring of rice, sprinkle parsley over the whole, cover and warm up 3 minutes at MEDIUM-HIGH.

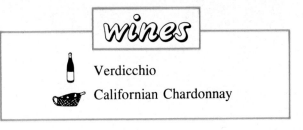

Verdicchio

Californian Chardonnay

London Delight

• Strolling along in London one day, I caught sight of a superb fish display. When I stopped to admire it, the owner came out, we talked, and he invited me to see how he cooked his scallops. Super!

Ingredients:

1 lb (500 g) fresh scallops
6 to 10 slices of bacon
Chutney
Fresh lime, quartered (optional)

Method:

• Pat the scallops dry in paper towels, then place them side by side in the bottom of a shallow pan. Fit a microwave-safe open low rack on top of scallops.

Preparation:	. . . .	**5 m**
Cooking:	. . . .	**from 9 to 12 m**
Standing:	. . . .	**5 m**

• Place slices of bacon on rack, one next to the other.

• Microwave at MEDIUM-HIGH 6 to 8 minutes or until bacon is crisp.

• Remove bacon and keep warm.

• Remove grill. Stir scallops.

• Microwave 3 to 4 minutes at MEDIUM-HIGH.

• Drain fat. Add bacon, crumbled.

• Sprinkle with chopped parsley.

• Serve with toast or fine cooked noodles tossed with parsley or buttered rice, chutney and lime.

wines

Muscadet

Pouilly Fumé

Scallop Soup

• A kind of milk soup, this soup is a speciality of Cape Cod. It has a fine and subtle taste.

Preparation: . . . . **28 m**
Cooking: . . . . **15 m**
Standing: . . . . **none**

Ingredients:

2 cups (500 mL) scallops, uncooked

Juice of 1/2 a lemon

1 cup (250 mL) boiling water

2 tbsp (30 mL) butter

2 tsp (10 mL) salt

1 tsp (5 mL) paprika

4 cups (1 L) milk

Method:

• Thinly slice the scallops and place them in a 4-cup (1 L) microwave-safe bowl.

• Add the lemon juice.

• Mix well and let stand 20 minutes.

• Add the boiling water. Microwave at HIGH 5 minutes.

• Add the remaining ingredients and microwave at HIGH 10 minutes.

• Serve with a thin slice of lime in each bowl.

Oysters and Clams

How to open oysters and clams

- Many people find it difficult to open oysters and clams.
- Your microwave oven will make it easy for you.

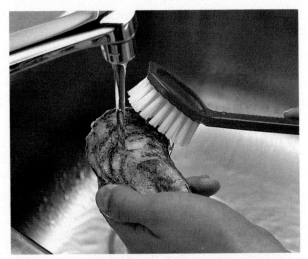

- Rinse the shells quickly under cold water, one at a time, as they should not soak.

- When rinsed, place the oysters or clams on a piece of newspaper (newspaper absorbs excess water) and cover them with paper towels.

- To open: place four or six oysters or clams in a circle on a double layer of paper towels in the microwave oven. Microwave 10 to 15 seconds at HIGH.

- If the oysters are very large or very cold, it may take 16 to 17 seconds.

- Remove from oven as soon as you notice a fine split between the shells.

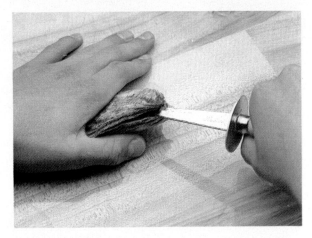

- It is then easy to open them with an oyster knife.

Nova Scotia Clam Chowder

Preparation: . . . . **10 m**
Cooking: . . . . **from 22 to 24 m**
Standing: . . . . **none**

A personal note: A real treat from Eastern Canada, this is an interesting dish. Serve with hot biscuits or oatmeal bread. The clam chowder is served in a soup bowl although, strictly speaking, it is not a soup.

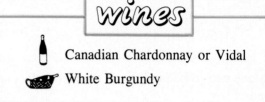

Canadian Chardonnay or Vidal

White Burgundy

Ingredients:

4 slices bacon, cut into small pieces

1 tbsp (15 mL) butter or margarine

1 large onion, minced

1 cup (250 mL) potatoes, peeled and minced

2 cups (500 mL) hot water

20 oz (570 mL) fresh clams or canned clams, undrained

2 cups (500 mL) light cream

Salt and pepper to taste

Method:

• Place the bacon slices between two sheets of white paper towelling and microwave 2 minutes at HIGH. Set aside.

• Melt the butter or margarine in an 8-cup (2 L) microwave-safe bowl, add the onion and microwave 10 minutes at HIGH, stirring twice.

• Add the potatoes and water. Cover and microwave at HIGH 4 to 6 minutes, or until the potatoes are cooked.

• Add the clams and their liquid together with the cream. Salt and pepper to taste. Stir thoroughly. Microwave at HIGH 6 to 8 minutes, or until the chowder is hot.

• Garnish each bowl with bacon pieces.

Clam Chowder

Preparation: . . . . **12 m**
Cooking: . . . . **25 m**
Standing: . . . . **none**

• Two small cans of clams, a few potatoes, one onion and — thanks to microwave cooking — you will have a nourishing and elegant soup.

Ingredients:

6 bacon slices, diced

1 medium-sized onion, minced

3 cups (750 mL) potatoes, diced

2 5-oz (142 g) cans small clams

1 cup (250 mL) water

2 to 3 cups (500 to 750 mL) milk

Method:

• Drain the clams, reserving the juice.

• Place the diced bacon and the minced onion in a 12-cup (3 L) microwave-safe dish. Microwave 3 or 4 minutes at HIGH. Stir well. Add the potatoes, the juice from the clams and the water. Microwave 15 minutes at HIGH. Stir well every 5 minutes.

• Add the clams, milk, salt and pepper to taste. Microwave 5 minutes at HIGH.

• Serve with soda crackers, buttered, placed on absorbent paper and heated 1 minute at HIGH.

Tomato Clam Chowder

Preparation: . . . . **10 m**
Cooking: . . . . **18 m**
Standing: . . . . **none**

• Each country has its special fish and shellfish soup. In Italy, it is zuppa; in France, it's bouillabaisse. Chowder is the North American version.

Ingredients:

2 bacon slices, diced

1 large onion, finely chopped

2 celery stalks, diced

1 medium-sized potato, peeled and diced

3 tbsp (50 mL) flour

1 19-oz (540 mL) can of tomato juice

1 8-oz (250 mL) bottle clam juice

1 5-oz (142 g) can clams, minced

1 cup (250 mL) boiling water

1/4 tsp (1 mL) thyme

Salt and pepper to taste

Method:

• Drain the clams, reserving the juice, and mince them.

• Place the bacon in a 6-cup (1.5 L) microwave-safe bowl. Microwave 2 minutes at HIGH. Remove the pieces of bacon with a perforated spoon.

• To the fat add the onion, celery and potato. Microwave 2 minutes at HIGH; stir well.

• Add the flour, mix well. Add the tomato juice, clam juice and juice from the well-drained clams (do not include the clams), and the boiling water. Microwave 10 minutes at HIGH stirring well after half the cooking time.

• When cooked, add the clams, thyme, salt and pepper. Microwave 4 minutes at HIGH.

Oyster Soup

Preparation: . . . . **7 m**
Cooking: . . . . **16 m**
Standing: . . . . **none**

• This perfect oyster soup is my grandmother's recipe, which I adapted for the microwave.

Ingredients:

1/4 cup (60 mL) butter

1 medium-sized carrot, grated

1/2 cup (125 mL) celery, finely diced

The white part of a leek, thinly sliced

3 cups (750 mL) milk *or* half milk, half cream

Salt and pepper to taste

2 cups (500 mL) fresh oysters with their juice

Method:

• Place the butter in a 4-cup (1 L) microwave-safe bowl and melt 1 minute at HIGH.

• Add the carrot, celery and leek; stir well.

• Microwave 3 minutes at HIGH; stir well.

• Add the milk or milk and cream, salt and pepper. Microwave at MEDIUM-HIGH 10 minutes, stir.

• Add the oysters. Salt and pepper to taste.

• Microwave 3 minutes at HIGH.

Crab Quiche

Preparation: .... **10 m**
Cooking: .... **10 m**
Standing: .... **5 m**

• I first ate this beautiful crustless quiche in Covey Cove, Nova Scotia. It can be made with canned, fresh crab or lobster. It was served with a fine-shredded cole slaw mixed with slivers of green and red peppers, lots of parsley and French dressing.

 Dry Rosé or German Riesling

Tavel rosé or Alsatian Tokay Pinot Gris

Ingredients:

1 cup (250 mL) fresh mushrooms, thinly sliced

1 cup (250 mL) canned crab or lobster

2 tbsp (30 mL) brandy or fresh lemon juice

**1 cup (250 mL) Cheddar or
Gruyere cheese, grated**

2 eggs

1 tsp (5 mL) curry powder or tarragon

1 tbsp (15 mL) flour

1/2 tsp (2 mL) salt

1 cup (250 mL) light cream

Method:

• Generously butter an 8-inch (20 cm) microwave-safe pie plate. Spread the mushrooms in the bottom.

• Shred the lobster or crabmeat, remove the bones, stir with the brandy or fresh lemon juice. Spread over the mushrooms. Top with the grated cheese.

• Stir together until well mixed, the eggs, curry powder or tarragon, flour, salt and cream. Beat until well blended. Pour over the crab and mushrooms.

• When ready to serve, microwave 10 minutes at MEDIUM-HIGH. Let stand 5 minutes.

• If the custard is not sufficiently set, heat another 2 to 3 minutes at MEDIUM.

• Serve hot or cold.

270

Crab Bisque

Preparation: . . . . **5 m**
Cooking: . . . . **10 m**
Standing: . . . . **none**

Ingredients:

2 10-oz (284 mL) cans cream of mushroom
1 cup (250 mL) light cream
1/2 cup (125 mL) milk
1/2 small onion, finely chopped
1 7½-oz (220 mL) can crab with its juice
Juice and rind of 1 small lemon
2 tbsp (30 mL) walnuts, chopped

Method:

• Place all the ingredients in a glass casserole. Cover.

• Microwave 5 minutes at HIGH, stirring twice during the cooking.

Lemon Rice

Preparation: . . . . 7 m
Cooking: . . . . .17 m
Standing: . . . . 15 m

A personal note: Rice and fish always go very well together. You can, if you wish, prepare Lemon Rice ahead of time in a microwave-safe dish and reheat it, covered, 5 minutes at MEDIUM-HIGH, just before serving.

A personal note: Pierce oysters and clams several times with a toothpick before cooking.

Ingredients:

1 cup (250 mL) short grain rice

1½ cups (375 mL) water

1/2 tsp (2 mL) salt

1/2 cup (125 mL) lemon juice

Rind of 1 lemon

3 tbsp (50 mL) butter

2 to 3 tbsp (30 to 50 mL) parsley, minced

Method:

• Place the water, salt and lemon juice in an 8-cup (2 L) microwave-safe dish.

• Bring to boil 5 minutes at HIGH.

• Add the rice, stir well, cover and microwave 10 minutes at MEDIUM-HIGH.

• Stir well, let stand 15 minutes, covered.

• Cut the lemon rind into slivers.

• Place the butter in a dish, add the lemon slivers and juice, and the parsley. Microwave 2 minutes at HIGH.

• Add this mixture to the cooked rice, stirring with a fork.

• Reheat 1 minute at HIGH, if necessary.

• Season to taste.

Helpful hint: Dry herbs quickly in your microwave oven. Place a few sprigs or 1/2 cup leaves between paper towels and heat at HIGH 2 to 3 minutes or until dry and crumbly. Timings may vary with different herbs.

Vegetables

"You will love vegetables if you give them what they need most, attention and loving care." I was 8 years old when my "grand-mère" told me that one day, just after I had refused to eat my turnips. After lunch she made me peel a turnip and showed me how to cook it to perfection. Then she mashed it into a "golden" cream. She sprinkled fresh chopped parsley and chives on top and presented it to me. Tasting it, I knew that the flavor and creamy texture justified the care my grandmother had given it.

So all my life I have tried to cook all vegetables as perfectly as possible and I soon discovered that they respond beautifully to tender care and fresh herbs, spices and even fresh fruit or juice.

Then the microwave oven came into my life — the super short-order way to cook vegetables to perfection, whether I want them crisp or tender, with perfect color and flavor.

Microwave and vegetables

• Vegetables can be cooked by microwave or by Sensor, if your microwave has that feature, which determines the cooking period and stops automatically when it is completed.

• There are microwave ovens that also have Defrost-Cook and Defrost by Weight programs in which the oven does all the work to perfection.

• If long cooking by conventional methods destroys a lot of nutrients in vegetables, just think what re-warming does!

• When cooked or reheated in a microwave oven, vegetables remain bright and appetizing and their texture is not altered.

The composition of vegetables

• Vegetables include all sorts of plants, and we eat different parts of them, including:

• **tubers,** which are swellings on the roots, such as Jerusalem artichokes and potatoes

• **roots,** such as carrots and turnips

• **bulbs,** such as onions

• **stalks,** which are whole plants with leafy tops, such as celery

• **leaves,** such as spinach

• **flowers,** such as cauliflower

• **fruits,** such as eggplant and tomatoes

• **pods,** such as green and wax beans and green peas.

• For general purposes, vegetables can be divided into two main categories: root vegetables and green vegetables.

Root vegetables

• Include the tubers and roots, which contain a large percentage of water and store nourishment in the form of starch.

• They are also, in most cases, high in mineral salts.

• There is practically no protein or fat present.

• Their fibres are formed by a woody substance known as cellulose, which in some cases must be softened before the digestible content can be extracted. The older they are, the coarser the cellulose becomes.

• This explains why winter turnips, beets and carrots take longer to cook than younger, spring ones.

• Of course, some roots can be eaten raw — carrots and radishes, for example.

• Bulbs, such as onions, are sometimes grouped with root vegetables. Like the roots and tubers, they can be kept for winter use.

• On the other hand, green onions, such as scallions and leeks, are perishable like other green vegetables.

Green vegetables

• Include the other groups.

• Even white, red or purple vegetables like cauliflower, tomatoes and eggplant have green leaves at their stem or base.

• As with root vegetables, the cellulose toughens with age.

• Young, fresh green vegetables naturally have a much sweeter flavor than older ones. Young or old, they contain practically no starch, and absolutely no fat or protein. But mineral salts are well represented and these form the chief value of greens in the diet.

• Unlike roots, green vegetables are quite perishable and should be eaten within 3 or 4 days of purchase.

General rule for storing vegetables

• The general rule for all vegetables is "the fresher the better."

• Use them as soon as possible after purchase, but in the meantime some need to be refrigerated to protect them from moisture evaporation, while others should be kept in a cool storage bin outside the refrigerator.

• Still others need room temperature and a maximum of air circulation.

• Learn which is which for best care before cooking.

Keeping qualities

Perishables:

• Asparagus, corn, cucumbers, green onions, green and red peppers, radishes, tomatoes and all salad greens.

• Keep them in plastic bags in the crisper bin of your refrigerator, with paper towelling in the bottom of the bag to absorb moisture.

Semi-perishables:

• Green and wax beans, broccoli, Brussels sprouts, cabbage, cauliflower, celery and peas in the pod.

• Remove excess dirt without washing, put into plastic bags or covered containers and store on a shelf in the refrigerator.

• It is important to store peas in their pods; otherwise, they will dry up.

Long-keeping vegetables:

• Eggplant, pumpkin, squash, beets, carrots, onions, parsnips, potatoes and turnips.

• Onions do well at room temperature, providing air can circulate around them.

• Keep them in a net bag or a wire basket and keep them away from humidity.

• Squash, pumpkin, turnips and winter beets can be kept where it is cool and dry.

Microwave vegetable terms

• To achieve perfection when cooking fresh vegetables in the microwave, it is important to be aware of the following.

The shape of the vegetables

• Uniform shape is important to ensure uniform cooking.

• For example, do not microwave a large potato and two or three small potatoes at the same time and make sure that sliced vegetables are cut in even thicknesses.

Elevating

• Placing such vegetables as squash and artichokes on a rack (there are many types available on the market) will assure you of more even cooking.

Piercing

• When cooked in their own skins, certain vegetables — such as potatoes, squash and whole tomatoes — must be pierced with the point of a knife to prevent them from bursting when steam builds up during cooking.

Placing

• Small pieces should be placed in the middle of the dish, larger pieces around the edges, since cooking is faster on the edges than in the middle of the dish.

• Potatoes, wrapped, ears of corn, wrapped, and artichokes should be placed around the tray and should be of even size.

• Asparagus spears should be placed one next to the other, alternating heads and stems.

Covering

• Pyrex covers, plastic dishes with covers that hold the hot moisture inside the container and plastic wrap will hold the heat and moisture needed to cook fresh vegetables that are not in nature's own skin.

• For example, a squash or potato will cook in its own skin, but if it is peeled and sliced, it must be covered.

Basic preparation of fresh, frozen and canned vegetables

Fresh vegetables

• When a recipe gives weights for vegetables, it is the weight before peeling, trimming, etc.

• Always pierce with the point of a knife the skins of vegetables to be cooked whole or unpeeled, such as potatoes, squash and eggplant. This allows steam to escape and prevents vegetables from popping or bursting.

• Arrange vegetables in a circle on a white paper towel (do not use colored), or on oven rack.

• As a rule of thumb, add 2 to 3 tablespoons (30 to 50 mL) of water per pound (500 g) of vegetables.

• Salt or sugar, when used together or separately, should be placed under the vegetables. Otherwise, they discolour the vegetables and can even retard the cooking period.

Frozen vegetables

• If vegetables are frozen in pouches, set on a pie plate and pierce top of pouch.

• If packages are foil wrapped, remove foil.

• When using frozen vegetables from a large commercial bag, heat them in a covered casserole dish, stirring once halfway through cooking period.

• No added liquid is necessary.

• If vegetables are frozen in one piece, empty container in dish, *ice side up*; if separate (such as green peas), spread on plate.

• Cover. Microwave 3 to 5 minutes at HIGH or DEFROST-COOK*, depending on vegetables.

• When done, remove from oven, let stand covered 5 minutes. Season and serve.

* If your oven has a DEFROST-COOK, it will defrost and cook the frozen vegetables according to the setting.

Canned vegetables

• Simply empty vegetables with liquid into a dish and heat, covered.

• The contents of a 10-oz (284 mL) can will heat in 1½ to 2 minutes, a 19-ounce (540 mL) can in 2½ to 3 minutes.

• In both cases, use MEDIUM-HIGH power.

Residual heat

• With all cooked vegetables, you must allow time for residual cooking.

• In microwave cooking, the intense heat accumulated in the vegetables while cooking does not stop when they are taken from the oven but keeps on tenderizing them.

• That is why they should not be overcooked.

Cooking vegetables by the Auto Sensor method

Most of the recipes in this book can be cooked by the Sensor method.

1. For proper Sensor cooking results, foods must be microwaved in containers covered with either plastic wrap or properly fitting lids. If a loose fitting lid is used, the plastic wrap is not tightly secured around the utensil or the plastic wrap has been punctured, the steam will be released prematurely, causing undercooking. It is not necessary to use both plastic wrap and a lid.

2. Most oven glass, such as Pyrex, glass ceramic (Corning) and other heat-resistant glass utensils, and plastic dishes with cover are excellent.

3. Cover dishes without lids with plastic wrap. When using plastic for large dishes, use two pieces of plastic overlapped down the centre. Firmly press down the overlapped portion. The wrap should extend about two to three inches (5 to 7.5 cm) past the edges of the dish and be tightly secured to its sides.

4. Plastic storage bags and "cooking" bags are not suitable for Auto Sensor cooking.

5. If the plastic wrap or cover is removed when the Auto Sensor program goes into time cooking, undercooking will result. This remaining cooking time relies on the steam being retained to assist the cooking. Do not remove the plastic until the oven shuts off. At this point, release the corner of the plastic wrap, then recover and let stand for a few minutes or until ready to serve.

Blanching vegetables for freezing

- It is essential to blanch vegetables before freezing, otherwise the natural enzymes in the vegetables will change the plant sugars to starch during the freezing time.

- The vegetables will then taste less sweet and more starchy.

- Blanching in a microwave oven is not only time saving, but quick and easy, resulting in a perfectly finished product.

- For uniform blanching and freezing, make sure vegetables are cut into uniform pieces.

- Place just enough vegetables to fill one container in a microwave-safe dish.

- When adding flavoring, such as herbs, salt or sugar, place it in the bottom of the dish. Seasoning and flavoring set on top tend to dehydrate or discolor the vegetables.

- Pour 1/2 cup (125 mL) *boiling* water on top of 2 cups (500 mL) of prepared vegetables. Cover with waxed paper or saucer.

- Microwave 2 or 3 minutes, stirring once, depending on type of vegetable, e.g.: broccoli stems (hard) 3 minutes, fresh green peas (soft) 2 minutes.

- When blanching is done, pour vegetables into a colander, rinse under cold running water for 2 seconds. Drain well, package, label and freeze.

- Use a 6 to 8-cup (1.5 to 2 L) microwave-safe dish, covered, to cook.

- Add no water.

- Microwave at HIGH.

- Times given are for standard frozen packages from the supermarket.

- Allow a 2 - 3 minute standing time after cooking. Stir before serving.

Cooking chart for frozen vegetables		
Vegetable	**Quantity***	**Time (min)**
Artichoke hearts	300 g	6
Asparagus	300 g	5-6
Beans, green cut	300 g	7
Beans, wax	300 g	6-7
Broccoli, chopped	300 g	5
Broccoli, spears	300 g	8
Brussels sprouts	300 g	9-10
Carrots	300 g	6
Cauliflower	300 g	5-6
Corn niblets	300 g	4
Mixed vegetables	300 g	5-6
Peas	350 g	5-6
Spinach	300 g	5
Squash	300 g	5-6

* Some frozen vegetables are sold in 500 g or 1 kg bags. In that case, remove the quantity you need and microwave following the timings above.

How to dry herbs in the microwave

For many years I have successfully dried herbs from my garden. They retain their flavor and color.

For all fresh herbs

• Tarragon, basil, marjoram, savory, sage, thyme, mint, etc., all come out with flying colors. Separate the leaves from the stem. Spread the leaves on a sheet of paper towelling. Cover the leaves with another sheet of paper and microwave about 1 minute at HIGH. Turn over, if bottom sheet is damp, microwave 40 to 50 seconds at HIGH. When dried, pour into a bowl and let them cool. Bottle and cover. They will keep in perfect condition for a full year.

• Herbs all have different texture, thickness and moistness, which explains why no absolutely exact time applies to them all. After drying a few, you will understand the easy process.

Artichokes

- Artichokes are often referred to as ''Globe Artichokes.'' They should be bright green and have plump leaves. If the top leaves have a sort of black stain, it means frost has touched them. However, they can still be eaten, as the frost usually affects only the top leaves, which can be removed.

- Look for plump, firm, tightly closed buds. When buds are opening, are light in weight or turning brown at the tip of each petal, they have passed their prime.

Artichokes "Nature"

To prepare for cooking

- First, cut the stem off the artichoke. Cut the dark end of the stem and peel. Set aside to be cooked.
- Then cut the point of each leaf to remove the sharp, prickly tip.
- If the small leaves at the base of the artichoke are tough, black or woody, cut with scissors.
- Place prepared artichoke in a bowl, cover with cold water, let soak 10 minutes. Drain, shaking to remove excess water.

To cook

- Wrap each prepared artichoke in plastic wrap (this way it cooks in its own steam).
- Place the artichokes in a circle on the oven tray.
- Then count 5 minutes at HIGH for the first one and add 2 minutes for each additional artichoke.
- Microwave one at a time or five at the most.

To eat artichoke

1. Pull off the leaf.

2. Dip the leaf in the dressing.

3. Pull the inside of the leaf between your teeth.

4. Remove the fibres from the heart before dipping it in the dressing.

Artichokes À la Grecque

Preparation: . . . . **16 m**
Cooking: . . . . **from 23 to 25 m**
Standing: . . . . **5 m**

• Artichokes were first grown in the lands of the Central and Western Mediterranean, then they spread around the world.

• In Greece, they have a special and very tasty way of cooking them.

Ingredients:

4 medium-sized artichokes

1 cup (250 mL) water

10 cardamom seeds

2 garlic cloves, peeled

Grated rind of 1 lemon

Juice of 1 lemon

1/4 tsp (1 mL) thyme

1/4 tsp (1 mL) salt

1/4 cup (60 mL) parsley, minced

A good pinch of pepper

1/3 cup (80 mL) olive oil

Method:

• Prepare the artichokes as for Artichokes "Nature."

• Set them stem-side down in a microwave-safe dish one next to the other.

• They can also be cut in half and placed in the dish with the pointed part toward the middle, the larger part toward the edges.

• Mix all the remaining ingredients. Stir until well blended. If the artichokes are cut in half, pour the mixture over them.

• If they are left whole, spoon mixture over the top so that some of it runs down between the leaves. Cover dish with lid or plastic wrap. Microwave 10 minutes at HIGH.

• Lift a corner of the lid, move the artichokes around. Microwave another 10 minutes at MEDIUM-HIGH. Remove from microwave.

• Let stand 5 minutes. Uncover and baste with juice in the dish.

• Remove the artichokes to a serving platter.

• Microwave the sauce, uncovered, 3 to 5 minutes at HIGH or until slightly thickened.

• Pour over the artichokes.

• Serve hot, preferably.

• They are also tasty served at room temperature.

• Do not refrigerate.

Artichokes Barigoule

Preparation:	48 m
Cooking:	from 24 to 25 m
Standing:	15 m

A personal note: Covered and refrigerated, these artichokes will keep three to four days. They're equally good hot or cold.

Ingredients:

4 medium-sized artichokes

5 cups (1.25 L) cold water

3 tbsp (50 mL) white vinegar

3 tbsp (50 mL) butter

1 tbsp (15 mL) vegetable oil

2 onions, chopped fine

1/2 tsp (2 mL) thyme

1 bay leaf

3 tbsp (50 mL) cider vinegar

1/4 cup (60 mL) dry vermouth

Salt and pepper to taste

Method:

• Prepare artichokes as for Artichokes "Nature."

• Place in a microwave-safe dish, cover with the cold water. Add the first 3 tablespoons (50 mL) vinegar and let stand at least 30 minutes. When ready to cook, drain well and cut each in half.

• Place butter and oil in a 10 × 6-inch (25 × 15 cm) microwave-safe baking dish.

• Add the onions.

• Microwave, uncovered, 4 to 5 minutes at MEDIUM, stirring once during the cooking period.

• Remove from microwave. Stir in the thyme, bay leaf, vinegar and vermouth.

• Place the well-drained artichoke halves around the dish; leave centre free. Cover with waxed paper.

• Microwave, uncovered, 4 to 5 minutes at MEDIUM, stirring once during the cooking period.

• Remove from microwave. Let stand covered 15 minutes.

• Place artichokes attractively in a dish and pour sauce over. Cover and let cool to room temperature.

• They should be served tepid or cooled.

• When refrigerated, take out one hour before serving.

Asparagus

- A plant of the lily-of-the-valley family, the highly esteemed asparagus has an elegance, a style, a "je ne sais quoi" that never seems to be equalled. It comes to us with the first breath of spring and early-season asparagus is considered a delicacy.

- Allow 1½ to 2 pounds (750 g to 1 kg) for 4 servings.

To keep

- Wrap cut ends in wet paper towels, put in plastic bag and refrigerate.

- Use within a day or two at the most.

Asparagus "Nature"

Preparation: . . . . 3 m
Cooking: . . . . from 6 to 7 m
Standing: . . . . 2 m

- To me, asparagus, rhubarb and the red robin are the sure signs of spring.
- The asparagus season begins slowly in April and finishes in early July.
- Enjoy it at its peak.

Ingredients:

1 lb (500 g) fresh asparagus
2 tbsp (30 mL) butter
1/4 tsp (1 mL) salt
Grated rind of 1/4 lemon

Method:

- Snap off the tough lower portion of the stalk; hold the vegetable with both hands and bend gently to find the place where the tough portion ends.
- Even if you wish to have them all the same length for the sake of appearance, snap them first, then place tips evenly together and cut the ends level with each other.
- Rinse the trimmed asparagus under cold running water; rinse very thoroughly because sand often accumulates in the small scales.
- Do not let them soak in water, however.
- Do not dry them after washing.

To cook

- Arrange them in a long plastic or glass dish, alternating heads and stems, or in a glass pie plate with asparagus tips to the centre and stems to the outer edge.
- Do not add salt or water.
- Cover with lid or waxed paper.
- Microwave 6 to 7 minutes at HIGH depending on their size.
- Let stand covered 2 minutes.
- Place butter, salt and lemon rind in a small microwave-safe dish.
- Melt 1 minute at HIGH. Pour over the asparagus and serve.
- To serve asparagus as an entrée or a luncheon dish, prepare and microwave according to rule for Asparagus "Nature," then cool to room temperature.
- Pour French dressing on top and sprinkle with grated hard-cooked eggs, capers and a dash of grated nutmeg.

A personal note: Should you wish to cook 2 pounds (1 kg) of asparagus, use a larger dish and microwave at HIGH 10 to 12 minutes.

Asparagus Teriyaki

Preparation: . . . . 7 m
Cooking: . . . . from 9 to 11 m
Standing: . . . . 10 m

 Australian Chardonnay

 Californian Sauvignon Blanc

• Fresh or frozen asparagus, crunchy celery, almonds and water chestnuts are combined in this unusual dish.

Ingredients:

2 tbsp (30 mL) butter

2 tbsp (30 mL) almonds, sliced and blanched

1 lb (500 g) fresh asparagus *or*
  1 10-oz (300 g) package frozen cut asparagus

1/2 cup (125 mL) celery, sliced diagonally

1 5-oz (142 g) can water chestnuts, drained and sliced (optional)

1 tbsp (15 mL) soy sauce*

* If available, I recommend the use of Kikkoman Japanese soy sauce.

Method:

• Place the butter and almonds in a 4-cup (1 L) microwave-safe casserole.

• Microwave at HIGH, uncovered, 2 to 3 minutes or until almonds are golden brown, stirring a few times during the cooking period.

• Remove almonds with a perforated spoon, set aside.

• To butter remaining in dish, add fresh or frozen asparagus, iced side up, if frozen, celery and well-drained and sliced water chestnuts.

• Microwave, covered, at HIGH 7 to 8 minutes, stirring twice during last half of cooking.

• Stir in soy sauce and almonds.

• Cover, let stand 10 minutes.

Asparagus Italiano

Preparation: . . . . 25 m
Cooking: . . . . 8 m
Standing: . . . . none

• This recipe, a favorite of the classic Italian cuisine, is served as a luncheon dish. When I adapted this recipe to the microwave oven, I realized that the bright green color and the flavor of the cooked dish were more delectable and brighter than after conventional cooking.

Ingredients:

2 lb (1 kg) fresh asparagus

1/4 cup (60 mL) water

1/4 cup (60 mL) butter

1 7½-oz (213 mL) can tomato sauce

1/4 tsp (1 mL) sugar

1/2 tsp (2 mL) basil

1 cup (250 mL) Swiss cheese, grated

wines

Italian Riesling

Alsatian Gewurztraminer

Method:

• Prepare the asparagus as for Asparagus "Nature."

• Place the trimmings in a dish with the water and butter.

• Cover and microwave 4 minutes at HIGH. Let stand 15 minutes. Drain, reserving the water.

• Place the asparagus in a 10 × 6-inch (25 × 15 cm) microwave-safe casserole, keeping the tender heads in the middle of the dish and the hard stems on the edges.

• Sprinkle with the sugar and basil.

• Pour the reserved water from the trimmings over the asparagus. Add the tomato sauce.

• Sprinkle the whole with the grated cheese.

• Cover dish with lid or waxed paper. Microwave 4 minutes at HIGH.

• This dish is very attractive served with cooked shell pasta, buttered and sprinkled with finely chopped parsley.

Asparagus Amandine

Preparation: . . . . **5 m**
Cooking: . . . . **from 8 to 10 m**
Standing: . . . . **2 m**

A personal note: Perfect to serve with roast chicken or veal, or as an entrée.

Ingredients:

1 lb (500 g) fresh asparagus

Salt and pepper to taste

1/4 cup (60 mL) slivered blanched almonds

3 tbsp (50 mL) butter

Method:

• Prepare and microwave asparagus as for Asparagus ''Nature.''

• When cooked, salt and pepper to taste.

• Place the almonds and butter in a small dish.

• Microwave at HIGH 2 to 3 minutes, stirring twice.

• When golden brown, pour over the cooked asparagus.

Asparagus À la Dutch

Preparation: . . . . **10 m**
Cooking: . . . . **from 6 to 7 m**
Standing: . . . . **2 m**

A personal note: This makes a very nice spring lunch served with a piece of Swiss cheese and hot French bread.

Ingredients:

1 lb (500 g) fresh asparagus

3 to 4 eggs, hard cooked

Salt and pepper to taste

A pinch of nutmeg

A bowl of melted butter

Method:

• Prepare and microwave asparagus as for Asparagus ''Nature.''

• To serve, place individual servings on hot plates.

• Quarter each egg and place attractively around the asparagus.

• Mix salt, pepper and nutmeg.

• Sprinkle to taste over asparagus.

• Pass around the bowl of hot butter for everyone to help themselves.

Crustless Asparagus Quiche

A personal note: Serve this quiche hot or cooled to room temperature. It makes a very nice lunch accompanied by an endive or lettuce salad.

Ingredients:

1 tbsp (15 mL) butter

1 large onion, peeled and thinly sliced

1 lb (500 g) asparagus, cut into 1 inch (2.5 cm) pieces

1/2 cup (125 mL) Cheddar cheese, grated

4 eggs

1/2 tsp (2 mL) dried tarragon

1 tbsp (15 mL) butter, melted

1/2 cup (125 mL) wholewheat breadcrumbs

Method:

• Melt the butter in a 9-inch (23 cm) ceramic pie plate 1 minute at HIGH.

• Add the onion, stir well. Microwave 2 minutes at HIGH.

• Scatter the cut asparagus over the onion.

• Stir together. Cover dish with a lid or waxed paper, microwave at HIGH 4 minutes.

• Sprinkle the whole with the grated cheese.

• Beat the eggs. Add the tarragon and pour over the asparagus.

• Melt the butter 1 minute at HIGH, add the bread-crumbs. Sprinkle over the eggs.

• Place the dish on a rack. Microwave at MEDIUM-HIGH 12 to 15 minutes or until puffed and cooked.

A personal note: There could be a slight variation of cooking time, depending on how cold the eggs are.

wines

Entre-Deux-Mers

Condrieu

Eggplant

- The eggplant is as beautiful as it is delicious. A member of the tomato and potato families, it is believed to be native to China and India. It is grown in many colors and shapes. In Japan there is a long cylindrical one, very tasty and delicate. We are more familiar with the long, egg-shaped purple type. It is easy to cook and perfect in flavor when done in the microwave oven.

- Select a firm eggplant, heavy for its size, with smooth, shiny purple skin free of rust spots.

- It will keep in perfect condition for five to six days in an open plastic bag in the vegetable bin of your refrigerator.

- 1 pound (500 g) is equivalent to 1 large eggplant or 3 cups (750 mL) cooked, which yields 4 servings.

- Although available almost all year round, it is at its best and in abundance from July to the end of September.

Eggplant "Nature"

To prepare for cooking

• Young and very fresh eggplant does not need to be peeled.

• If your recipe calls for peeled eggplant, however, this can be done.

• As eggplant discolors very quickly, peel and slice or dice it only when ready to cook, or rub it with fresh lemon juice.

• Place the eggplant in a microwave-safe dish.

• Add one tablespoon (15 mL) water.

• Cover and microwave 4 minutes at HIGH.

Salting eggplant

• Some eggplant recipes require a short period of salting before cooking to prevent the vegetable from becoming watery.

Here's how to proceed:

• Slice or dice the unpeeled or peeled eggplant, according to the recipe you are following.

• Place eggplant slices on a plate in a single layer and sprinkle with salt. When diced, salt and toss in a bowl. One tablespoon (15 mL) of salt per eggplant is sufficient.

• Let stand at room temperature for 20 to 30 minutes.

• Quickly rinse under cold running water and wipe as dry as possible with paper towelling.

• Then proceed as called for in your chosen recipe.

Creamy Eggplant

Preparation:	10 m
Cooking:	8 m
Standing:	none

• This recipe is simple, quick, attractive and so tasty.

Ingredients:

1 large eggplant

3 tbsp (50 mL) butter

1 cup (250 mL) sour cream

4 to 6 green onions, chopped fine

Salt and pepper to taste

Grated rind of 1/2 a lemon

Method:

• Peel, dice and salt eggplant as for Eggplant "Nature."

• When ready, rinse under cold water, dry with paper towelling.

• Melt the butter in a 6-cup (1.5 L) microwave-safe dish 1 minute at HIGH. Add the diced eggplant to the melted butter, stir until well mixed.

• Cover and microwave at HIGH 5 minutes.

• Stir and add the sour cream, green onions, salt and pepper to taste and the grated lemon rind.

• Stir until well mixed.

• Microwave at MEDIUM-HIGH 3 minutes.

• Serve hot or cold.

Cheese and Cracker Eggplant

Preparation: . . . . **15 m**
Cooking: . . . . **from 12 to 13 m**
Standing: . . . . **from 3 to 4 m**

• A friend who lives in Ontario gave me this recipe, which she adapted from a recipe from the South of Italy. She uses a strong Canadian Cheddar, at its best when from Ontario.

Ingredients:

2½ cups (625 mL) eggplant, peeled and cubed

1 tbsp (15 mL) water or white wine

15 to 18 soda crackers, crushed

1/2 cup (125 mL) strong Cheddar cheese, grated

1/4 cup (60 mL) finely chopped celery

1 tsp (5 mL) basil

1 tbsp (15 mL) melted butter

1/2 tsp (2 mL) each sugar and salt

1/4 tsp (1 mL) pepper

1/2 cup (125 mL) cream

1 tbsp (15 mL) cornstarch

Method:

• Place the eggplant cubes in a 4-cup (1 L) microwave-safe dish.

• Add the water or white wine.

• Cover and microwave at HIGH 4 minutes.

• Drain thoroughly and set aside.

• Mix all the remaining ingredients.

• Add to the eggplant. Stir until well mixed.

• Cover and microwave at HIGH 8 to 9 minutes.

• Let stand 3 to 4 minutes. Stir and serve.

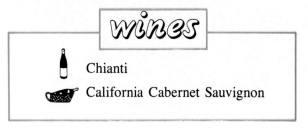

wines

Chianti

California Cabernet Sauvignon

Eggplant Italiano

Preparation: . . . . **12 m**
Cooking: . . . . **from 22 to 25 m**
Standing: . . . . **5 m**

- Eggplant is one of the most widely used vegetables in Italy. Each part of the country has a different way to cook it.
- This recipe is a favorite in Northern Italy.

Ingredients:

2 tbsp (30 mL) olive oil

1 cup (250 mL) onions, chopped fine

1-28 oz (796 mL) can tomatoes

1/2 tsp (2 mL) each thyme and basil

1 large garlic clove, chopped fine

1 tbsp (15 mL) sugar

1/4 tsp (1 mL) salt

1 large or 2 medium-sized eggplants

6 to 7 slices of mild Canadian or Gruyere cheese

Method:

- Place the oil and onions in a 4-cup (1 L) microwave-safe dish. Stir until onions are well coated with the oil. Cover and microwave at HIGH 4 minutes.
- Drain the tomatoes, reserving the liquid.
- Chop the tomatoes, if necessary. Add to the onions and stir until well mixed.
- Add the thyme, basil, garlic, sugar and salt.
- Stir well and microwave at HIGH 8 to 9 minutes or until creamy soft.
- Peel and slice the eggplant. Cut each slice in half.
- Sprinkle lightly with salt and place on paper towelling for 20 minutes. Rinse under cold water, pat dry. Brush each slice on both sides with olive oil.
- Then place a layer of eggplant in a 12 × 9-inch (30 × 23 cm) dish.
- Spread with half the tomato sauce, then half the slices of cheese.
- Add the remaining eggplant. Top with the remaining tomato sauce and cheese.
- Measure 1/4 cup (60 mL) of the juice removed from the tomatoes and pour on top.
- Do not cover.
- Microwave at HIGH 10 to 12 minutes. Let stand 5 minutes and serve.
- I like to serve this the Italian way, with a dish of small pasta tossed with olive oil or butter and chopped chives or parsley.

Valpolicella

Barbaresco

Helpful hint: For fresh coffee any time, refrigerate leftover coffee and microwave in a large cup 1½ to 2 minutes at HIGH.

Eggplant Casserole

Preparation: . . . . 10 m
Cooking: . . . . 6 m
Standing: . . . . 1 m

A personal note: To make a meatless meal of this casserole, serve it with parsleyed rice or noodles cooked in chicken consommé. It's also very good served with roast chicken instead of potatoes.

Ingredients:

1 medium or 2 small eggplants

2 tbsp (30 mL) flour

1/2 cup (125 mL) fine breadcrumbs

1 tsp (5 mL) sugar

1/2 tsp (2 mL) basil

1 tsp (5 mL) salt

1/4 tsp (1 mL) pepper

3 tbsp (50 mL) butter or margarine, melted

1 cup (250 mL) tomato-mushroom sauce

Method:

- Peel eggplant and cut into thin slices.
- Blend together the flour, breadcrumbs, sugar, basil, salt and pepper.
- Dip each slice of eggplant in a little milk, then roll in the breadcrumb mixture.
- Place in layers in bottom of an oblong microwave-safe dish or a 10-inch (25 cm) Corning dish.
- Sprinkle each slice with some of the melted butter or margarine.
- Pour the tomato sauce around the edges, leaving the middle free of sauce. Cover.
- Microwave 6 minutes at HIGH.
- Let stand 1 minute and serve.

Valpolicella

Vino Nobile di Montepulciano

Baked Eggplant Slices

Preparation: . . . . **28 m**
Cooking: . . . . **20 m**
Standing: . . . . **none**

Convection cooking

• This is an excellent, quick and easy recipe, providing you have a convection system in your oven.

Ingredients:

1 medium eggplant, peeled and sliced in 1/2 inch (1.25 cm) thick slices

1/2 cup (125 mL) mayonnaise (unsweetened)

2 green onions, chopped fine

1/2 tsp (2 mL) basil or thyme

1/2 cup (125 mL) Cheddar cheese, grated

1 cup (250 mL) fine soda cracker crumbs

Method:

• Place the eggplant slices on a large plate.

• Sprinkle each slice generously with salt.

• Let stand 20 minutes, then pat dry to remove the accumulated moisture.

• Blend together the mayonnaise and the green onions, basil or thyme.

• Butter both sides of each eggplant slice with this mixture.

• Blend in a large plate the Cheddar and cracker crumbs. Dip each eggplant slice in it.

• Place on a cookie sheet or in 2 pie plates.

• Place on microwave oven rack.

• Bake 20 minutes in convection part of microwave oven at 375°F (190°C). Serve as soon as ready.

Ratatouille

Preparation: . . . . **20 m**
Cooking: . . . . **16 m**
Standing: . . . . **10 m**

A personal note: This is the perfect relish to serve with all types of meat, hot or cold. If you're in the south of France, you absolutely must eat it.

Ingredients:

1/4 cup (60 mL) olive or vegetable oil

2 garlic cloves, chopped fine

2 medium-sized onions, thinly sliced

2 medium-sized eggplants, cut into fingers

6 medium-sized zucchini, unpeeled, thinly sliced

2 green peppers, diced

2 tsp (10 mL) salt

1 tsp (5 mL) thyme

1 tsp (5 mL) sugar

1/2 tsp (2 mL) basil

Method:

• Pour the oil into an 8-cup (2 L) microwave-safe dish. Microwave at HIGH 2 minutes.

• Add the garlic and onions, stir well. Microwave 3 minutes at HIGH. Stir.

• Add the eggplants, zucchini and green peppers, stir well.

• Microwave 3 minutes at HIGH.

• Add the remaining ingredients, stir until well mixed.

• Cover and microwave at MEDIUM 8 to 9 minutes. Let stand 10 minutes. Stir.

• Serve hot or pour into a ceramic dish, cover when cooled and refrigerate.

A personal note: It can be kept 8 to 10 days and served as a cold relish. I like to take mine out of the refrigerator one hour or so before serving.

Added attraction:

• If you like pizza and make your own crust (microwave 3 to 4 minutes at HIGH) or buy it ready cooked but not garnished, here is how to make a "Ratatouille Pizza", very popular in the south of France.

Method:

• Prepare the ratatouille as outlined before. Cool.

• Then spread a thick layer on the cooked pizza dough.

• Top with **1 cup (250 mL) grated Gruyere cheese** or sprinkle generously with **Parmesan cheese.**

• To serve hot, place in your microwave oven tray.

• Microwave 3 minutes at MEDIUM, just as you are ready to serve.

Eggplant Caviar

Preparation: . . . . **10 m**
Cooking: . . . . **from 26 to 33 m**
Standing: . . . . **15 m**

A personal note: An almost world famous dip, Eggplant Caviar is easy to prepare the microwave way and always popular at parties. I like to serve mine with large hot potatoes or corn chips.

Ingredients:

1 large eggplant, unpeeled

1/2 cup (125 mL) olive or other oil of your choice

1 medium-sized onion, chopped fine

1 green pepper, chopped fine

1 large garlic clove, chopped fine

1/2 tsp (2 mL) salt

1/4 tsp (1 mL) pepper

2 tbsp (30 mL) white vermouth or wine *or* 1 tbsp (15 mL) wine vinegar

Method:

• Wash the whole eggplant, wipe dry. Place on a microwave-safe rack.

• Microwave at MEDIUM-HIGH between 15 and 20 minutes. Let stand 15 minutes, then peel and chop into small dice.

• Place the oil in a microwave-safe dish. Add the onion, green pepper and garlic. Stir until well mixed.

• Microwave at HIGH 6 to 7 minutes, stirring after 4 minutes of cooking. Add the remaining ingredients and the eggplant. Stir until well mixed.

• Microwave at HIGH 5 to 6 minutes or until mixture starts to thicken. Stir thoroughly.

• Pour into a nice bowl, cool, cover and refrigerate until ready to serve. Serve as a dip with any vegetables or mild cheese sticks.

légume ou des bâtonnets de fromage doux, à votre choix.

Beets

- Beets are a generous vegetable; not only do they give us the deep red root but also the beet greens, so tasty yet so often discarded.

- Choose beets that are even-sized, with fresh leaves. Even size is important, as "quite large" beets mixed with "quite small" means two cooking batches if you wish to eat them just cooked and buttered.

Beets "Nature"

To prepare for cooking

- In conventional cooking, it is necessary to leave the beet root on and about 2 inches (5 cm) of stem.

- In microwave cooking, stems and roots may be cut off flush with the beet.

- Scrub the beets, wash under running water and they are ready to be cooked.

- Place 6 to 8 even-sized beets in an 8-cup (2 L) microwave-safe bowl. Cover with cold water enough to have at least 2 inches (5 cm) of water over the beets.

- Cover, microwave 20 minutes at HIGH. Stir. Test for doneness with the tip of a pointed knife. Small beets or fresh from the garden beets should be done, but winter beets usually take another 20 minutes at HIGH. Test again.

- As soon as the beets are cooked, drain the water, place them in a bowl of cold water and pull skin off by rolling the beets in your hands, using a little pressure when necessary.

Harvard Beets

Preparation:	**5 m**
Cooking:	**from 24 to 44 m**
Standing:	**none**

A personal note: This is a North American favorite, prepared with freshly cooked beets. The beets can be microwaved in the morning and reheated, covered, 3 minutes at MEDIUM-HIGH, when ready to be served.

Ingredients:

3 to 4 cups (750 mL to 1 L) beets, cooked and sliced

4 tsp (20 mL) cornstarch

1/3 cup (80 mL) sugar

1/3 cup (80 mL) cider vinegar

1/3 cup (80 mL) water

3 tbsp (50 mL) butter

Salt and pepper to taste

Method:

- Microwave 6 to 8 medium-sized beets, as for Beets "Nature."

- When cooked and sliced, place them in a microwave-safe casserole dish.

- Place the cornstarch and sugar in a microwave-safe bowl, mix well.

- Add the remaining ingredients, mix well. Microwave 3 minutes at MEDIUM-HIGH or until creamy and transparent.

- Pour over the beets. Stir until well mixed.

- Microwave 1 minute at HIGH when ready to serve.

Harvard Beets ➞

Young Beets in Sour Cream

Preparation: . . . . **8 m**
Cooking: . . . . **from 25 to 45 m**
Standing: . . . .**none**

• A Polish friend taught me how to make this dish, which has become a must whenever I roast a large chicken.

Ingredients:

6 to 9 medium-sized beets, cooked

3 tbsp (50 mL) butter

2 tbsp (30 mL) lemon juice

Salt and pepper to taste

1/4 tsp (1 mL) nutmeg

1 tbsp (15 mL) honey

4 green onions, chopped fine

1/2 to 3/4 cup (125 to 190 mL) sour cream

Method:

• Microwave the beets as for Beets "Nature." Peel and grate the cooked beets.

• Place them in a 4-cup (1 L) microwave-safe dish, add the remaining ingredients.

• Stir until well mixed.

• When ready to serve, cover and microwave 5 minutes at MEDIUM, stirring after 3 minutes of cooking.

Beets Orange

Preparation: . . . . 6 m
Cooking: . . . . 4 m
Standing: . . . . 5 m

A personal note: Peeling and grating raw beets is somewhat messy, but this recipe is fast and the result is well worth the trouble. To clean your hands, wash them with lemon.

Ingredients:

4 medium-sized beets

1/4 cup (60 mL) fresh orange juice

Grated rind of half an orange

1 tbsp (15 mL) butter

Salt and pepper to taste

Method:

• Peel and grate the raw beets.

• Place them in a 4-cup (1 L) microwave-safe dish.

• Add the remaining ingredients. Mix well. Cover and microwave 4 minutes at HIGH. Stir well. Let stand 5 minutes, then serve.

Variation:

• Add to the grated beets **1 cup (250 mL) whole green seedless grapes.**

• Microwave the same time as above.

• Perfect to serve with roast pork and duck.

Helpful hint: To soften or pit prunes, place them in glass bowl or jar, barely cover with leftover tea or coffee or part water, part orange juice. If you so wish, add 1 star anise or 1 stick cinnamon or 2 cloves or the grated rind of an orange or lemon. Microwave, uncovered, 8 minutes at MEDIUM. Let stand 10 minutes. Warm pitted prunes to serve over your hot cereal. They will keep 4 to 5 weeks refrigerated, covered, in their liquid.

Grandmother's Beets

Preparation: . . . . **9 m**
Cooking: . . . . **7 m**
Standing: . . . . **5 m**

A personal note: Here's another way to cook grated raw beets. This dish is perfect to serve with game, sausage or liver. If you have a food processor, the grating of the beets, apple and onions is very quick and easy.

Ingredients:

4 medium-sized raw beets, peeled

1 large apple, unpeeled

2 medium-sized onions, peeled and sliced

3 tbsp (50 mL) butter

3 tbsp (50 mL) water

1/4 tsp (1 mL) allspice

Method:

• Peel and grate the raw beets and onions. Grate the apple.

• Add the butter, water and allspice.

• Place in a 4-cup (1 L) microwave-safe dish, cover.

• Microwave 5 minutes at HIGH.

• Stir well, salt and pepper to taste. Microwave at HIGH another 2 minutes.

• Let stand, covered, 5 minutes. Stir and serve.

Pickled Beets

Preparation: . . . . **5 m**
Cooking: . . . . **from 20 to 40 m**
Standing: . . . . **none**

• Most people appreciate a jar or two of pickled beets in their pantry. Nothing is easier to prepare.

Method:

• Microwave beets as for Beets "Nature."

• Place small beets together in a jar.

• Slice the larger ones and also place in a jar.

• Pour good quality cold **white vinegar** on top to completely cover the beets.

• Sprinkle into each jar **1 teaspoon (5 mL)** or **1 tablespoon (15 mL) of white sugar**, depending on how sweet you like your beets.

Variations:

• Place **1 head of fresh dill** or **1 large garlic clove**, peeled and cut in half, or **4 round cloves of allspice** on the side of the jar, after adding the **vinegar**.

• Cover jars and keep in a cool place.

• They need not be refrigerated until they are opened.

• Make sure the beets are completely covered with vinegar.

Helpful hint: To prepare croutons or bread-crumbs, place 2 cups (500 mL) of bread cubes in a pie plate and microwave 3 to 4 minutes at HIGH, stirring a few times.

Leafy Beet Greens

Preparation: . . . .**3 m**
Cooking: . . . .**3 m**
Standing: . . . .**none**

A personal note: When buying beets, choose them with bright, fresh green leaves. They are delicious cooked or used raw in a salad.

Ingredients:

The leaves from 5 to 8 beets
1 tbsp (15 mL) butter
Grated rind of 1 lime or 1 lemon
1/2 tsp (2 mL) sugar
Salt and pepper to taste

Method:

- Cut the hard stems from the beet leaves.
- Wash the leaves under cold running water.
- Place the butter in a microwave-safe bowl and microwave 30 seconds at HIGH.
- Add the grated lemon or lime rind and the sugar. Stir to mix.
- Add the beet leaves, stir well. Cover and microwave 3 minutes at HIGH.
- Stir well, salt and pepper to taste.

Variation:

- Sprinkle top with a pinch of nutmeg.

Creamy Beet Leaves

- Proceed as above for cooking, adding **1 teaspoon (5 mL) of cornstarch** when you add the beet leaves. Stir until well mixed.
- Add **1 tablespoon (15 mL) cream**. Stir again.
- Cover and microwave 3 minutes at HIGH. Salt and pepper to taste. Stir until well mixed and creamy.

Idea:

- I love to add my beet leaves to **1 pound (500 g) of spinach** and microwave as for Creamy Beet Leaves.
- Microwave 4 minutes at HIGH.

Broccoli

• Broccoli is a plant of the cabbage family. When buying, look for broccoli with heavy heads of *tightly-closed* buds. Avoid broccoli whose flower buds are opening or turning yellow.

Broccoli "Nature"

- In preparing broccoli, first remove the top leaves. Then separate the heads from the stems.

To prepare for cooking

- It is easy to cook broccoli to perfection by the microwave method.
- The success is in the placing of the vegetable. Cut the flowered heads near the stalks, place in the middle of a long microwave-safe dish. Peel the stalks, slice diagonally and place at each end of the dish.
- If your microwave oven has a Sensor method, it will cook broccoli to perfection.
- See your oven manual for directions.

Or keep the heads in the middle of the dish and place the cut stems around the dish.

Or serve the heads for one meal and the tail ends whole or sliced for another meal.

Or if you wish to cook the whole tail ends, wash, peel them, then split them here and there with the point of a knife.

- They will cook to a deep green color and be very tender.

To cook

- If the broccoli heads and stems are chopped to be cooked together, mix well, add **1/4 cup (60 mL) water and 1/2 tsp (2 mL) sugar**, cover and microwave at HIGH 7 to 9 minutes, depending on the quantity cooked.
- Stir twice during the cooking period and check doneness with the point of a knife.

Helpful hint: To toast almonds, spread 1 cup (250 mL) of blanched whole, slivered or halved almonds — or any other kinds of nuts — on a plate. Microwave 2 or 3 minutes at MEDIUM-HIGH, stirring every minute so they will brown evenly. Let stand 2 minutes as they continue to brown. Stir again. These are handy to have on hand to sprinkle on fish, vegetables or desserts.

Broccoli California

Preparation: . . . . **4 m**
Cooking: . . . . **from 9 to 13 m**
Standing: . . . . **none**

• Fresh broccoli and fresh orange juice have great affinity and yet are rarely prepared this way.

Ingredients:

1 lb (500 g) broccoli

2 tbsp (30 mL) butter or margarine

2 tbsp (30 mL) flour

1 cup (250 mL) *fresh* orange juice

A pinch of salt

Method:

• Prepare broccoli according to your taste as for Broccoli "Nature."

• Place in a microwave-safe dish. Sprinkle on top 3 tablespoons (50 mL) of the orange juice.

• Cover and microwave 6 to 9 minutes at HIGH. The time depends on how the broccoli has been cut.

• Place the butter or margarine in a microwave-safe bowl and melt 1 minute at HIGH.

• Stir in the flour, mix well. Add the orange juice, stir well.

• Microwave at HIGH 3 to 4 minutes, stirring once, until creamy and transparent.

• Stir in the salt.

• Drain the broccoli and top with the orange sauce.

Broccoli Italiano

Preparation: . . . . 6 m
Cooking: . . . . from 8 to 11 m
Standing: . . . . 3 m

A personal note: I first tasted this dish in Florence. It is colorful, tasty and very easy if you prepare the ingredients for the sauce while the broccoli is being cooked and microwave the sauce as it is standing. The Florentine way to serve broccoli is with fine boiled noodles and a bowl of grated cheese.

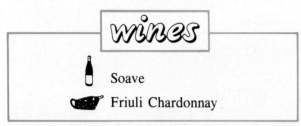

wines

🍾 Soave

🥄 Friuli Chardonnay

Ingredients:

1 lb (500 g) fresh broccoli

1/4 cup (60 mL) water

2 tbsp (30 mL) butter

4 green onions, minced

1 green pepper, diced

Grated rind of 1 lemon

2 tbsp (30 mL) lemon juice

1/2 tsp (2 mL) basil

Salt and pepper to taste

Method:

• Prepare broccoli according to your needs, as for Broccoli "Nature."

• Place it in a microwave-safe dish. Add water.

• Microwave covered 6 to 8 minutes at HIGH or until crisp yet tender. Test for doneness.

• Remove from microwave, keep covered and let stand 3 minutes.

To make the sauce

• Place the butter in a microwave-safe measuring cup and melt for 30 seconds at HIGH.

• Add green onions. Stir until well coated with butter.

• Microwave 1 minute at HIGH. Add remaining ingredients. Stir to mix.

• Pour over cooked broccoli. Adjust seasoning.

• Heat 1 to 2 minutes at HIGH. Serve.

Chinese Broccoli

Preparation: . . . . **8 m**
Cooking: . . . . **10 m**
Standing: . . . . **none**

A personal note: More and more people are enjoying the Oriental way of cooking vegetables. The broccoli in this recipe can easily be replaced by another type of green vegetable. This is another perfect example of how vegetables cooked in the microwave retain their fresh green color and delicate flavor.

Ingredients:

1 lb (500 g) broccoli

3 tbsp (50 mL) vegetable oil

1 small onion, diced

2 tbsp (30 mL) soy sauce or teriyaki sauce

1/2 tsp (2 mL) sugar

1/2 cup (125 mL) chicken consommé

2 tsp (10 mL) cornstarch

Method:

• Cut the broccoli stems diagonally, making long, slender cuts, and break the heads into small flowerets.

• In an 8 × 12-inch (20 × 30 cm) microwave-safe dish heat the vegetable oil 30 seconds at HIGH. Add the onion and microwave, covered, 3 to 4 minutes at HIGH.

• Add the broccoli. Stir until well coated with the oil and onion.

• Microwave 4 minutes at HIGH, stirring twice.

• Blend the remaining ingredients together. Add to the broccoli, stir.

• Microwave 2 minutes at MEDIUM-HIGH.

• Stir until well blended; the sauce should be creamy and somewhat transparent.

• If not, microwave 1 more minute at HIGH. Adjust seasoning. Serve.

Carrots

- Another very old root vegetable, carrots were grown in China by the 1200s. The carrot is well known for its Vitamin A content.

- Look for carrots that are smooth, since they will have less waste when they are pared or scraped. Avoid carrots that are limp. When bought packed in a bag, make sure they are of equal length and size.

Carrots "Nature"

A **personal note:** An average 1-pound (500 g) bag of 7-to-8-inch (18 to 20 cm) carrots will give 2 cups (500 mL) peeled and sliced carrots and will average 4 to 5 servings.

To prepare for cooking

• Small carrots left whole, either from the garden or bought in plastic bags, should be scrubbed with a stiff brush under cold running water. They need not be peeled.

• Garden fresh carrots will cook faster than bought ones.

• Older or larger or winter carrots should be peeled with a vegetable peeler and soaked 10 minutes in cold water before cooking, because winter carrots are more fibrous and have a tendency to dry up or stay hard when they are cooked.

To cook

• Peel with a vegetable peeler if necessary and place them in a dish of cold water. Let stand 10 minutes. Drain.

• Use a long microwave-safe cooking dish, if possible. Lay half the carrots with their thick top ends to one end of the dish. Lay the other half with their thick top ends to the other side of the dish.

• Add **1/4 cup (60 mL) liquid — water, consommé, white wine, milk, cream or cranberry or tomato, apple or fresh orange juice.**

• Sprinkle **1/2 teaspoon (2 mL) sugar** over all. Cover with the container lid or with plastic wrap.

• Microwave 1 pound (500 g) at HIGH 7 to 9 minutes, depending on the size of the carrots and the season. Test doneness after 5 minutes with the point of a knife, passing it through the plastic wrap if it has been used to cover. Stir.

• When available, I sprinkle a chopped fresh herb on top of the prepared carrots, either **4 or 5 leaves of fresh basil,** chopped fine, or **dill seeds to taste,** or **a head of dill** placed on top of the carrots, or **chopped fresh mint** with a good pinch of **fresh grated lemon rind,** or 1/2 teaspoon (2 mL) of **honey** instead of the sugar, or **1/4 cup (60 mL) fresh minced parsley.**

• I sometimes like to replace the water by apple juice or fresh orange juice or cranberry juice.

C.C.O.

• My family has nicknamed this favorite way of eating carrots C.C.O., for "carrots, celery, onion." We used to cook them on the stove. Since doing them in the microwave, they have become doubly popular.

Ingredients:

5 medium-sized carrots, thinly sliced

1 tbsp (15 mL) butter

1 cup (250 mL) diced celery

1 large onion, chopped

1/2 tsp (2 mL) sugar

Grated rind of 1/2 a lemon

Preparation: . . . . **24 m**
Cooking: . . . . **from 6 to 8 m**
Standing: . . . . **none**

Method:

• Prepare the carrots as for Carrots "Nature."

• Cover with cold water. Let stand 15 minutes. Drain.

• Place the butter in a 6-cup (1.5 L) microwave-safe dish. Melt 1 minute at HIGH.

• Add the carrots, stir well. Add the remaining ingredients. Stir together.

• Cover and microwave 6 to 8 minutes at HIGH, stirring after 4 minutes of cooking.

• There is no liquid in this recipe, which explains the importance of soaking the carrots before adding them to the other ingredients.

Devonshire Carrots

Preparation: . . . . **8 m**
Cooking: . . . . **from 10 to 12 m**
Standing: . . . . **none**

A personal note: An English favorite to serve with roast lamb or duck.

Ingredients:

6 to 8 long carrots, peeled and thinly sliced

1 tsp (5 mL) sugar

1/2 cup (125 mL) water or chicken consommé

2 tbsp (30 mL) butter

1 tsp (5 mL) cornstarch

Salt and pepper to taste

Juice and grated rind of 1/2 a lemon

2 tbsp (30 mL) fresh mint leaves, chopped fine

Method:

• Place in a microwave-safe dish the carrots, sugar and water or chicken consommé.

• Cover with lid or waxed paper. Microwave at HIGH 6 to 8 minutes, stirring twice during the cooking period, after 3 and after 5 minutes of cooking.

• Drain the carrots, reserving the liquid. Set aside.

• Melt the butter in a microwave-safe bowl 1 minute at HIGH.

• Stir in the cornstarch, salt and pepper to taste. Add the water or chicken consommé drained from the carrots.

• Stir until well mixed.

• Add the juice, the grated lemon rind and the chopped mint, stir to mix.

• Microwave 2 minutes at HIGH, stir well. Add the cooked carrots, stir. Microwave 2 minutes at MEDIUM-HIGH. Serve.

313

Carrots Glacées

Preparation: . . . . **9 m**
Cooking: . . . . **from 12 to 14 m**
Standing: . . . . **none**

A personal note: This is the French way to glaze carrots. They are elegant served with a bowl of buttered green noodles and sautéed chicken livers. Large winter carrots may be used.

Method:

• Peel the carrots and cut into thin slices.

• Place the butter in a 4-cup (1 L) microwave-safe dish. Melt 1 minute at HIGH.

• Add the carrots and the water, stir well. Cover.

• Microwave 7 minutes at HIGH. Stir and add the remaining ingredients. Stir until well mixed.

• Microwave uncovered 5 to 7 minutes at MEDIUM, stirring 2 or 3 times during the cooking period. Serve.

Ingredients:

1 lb (500 g) large carrots

3 tbsp (50 mL) butter

1/3 cup (80 mL) water

1/4 cup (60 mL) light brown sugar

2 tbsp (30 mL) French Dijon mustard

2 tbsp (30 mL) minced parsley

3 green onions, chopped fine

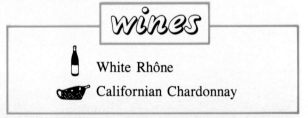

White Rhône

Californian Chardonnay

Glazed Carrot Sticks

Preparation:	. . . . **7 m**
Cooking:	. . . . **from 11 to 12 m**
Standing:	. . . . **none**

A personal note: This recipe produces slightly sweet carrots, shiny and tender, to serve with steak or roasted veal or beef.

Ingredients:

6 to 8 young carrots, cut into sticks

1/4 cup (60 mL) water

1/2 tsp (2 mL) brown sugar

3 tbsp (50 mL) butter

1 tsp (5 mL) brown sugar

1/2 tsp (2 mL) salt

Method:

• Peel the carrots and cut into small sticks.

• Place in a 4-cup (1 L) microwave-safe dish.

• Add the water and the 1/2 teaspoon (2 mL) brown sugar.

• Stir. Cover and microwave 7 to 8 minutes at HIGH. Stir well after 5 minutes of cooking.

• Add the remaining ingredients. Stir well and microwave at HIGH 4 minutes. Stir and serve.

Maple Glazed Carrots

Preparation:	. . . . **10 m**
Cooking:	. . . . **from 12 to 13 m**
Standing:	. . . . **none**

A personal note: When, in spring, the maple syrup is boiling and new carrots are still rare on the market, these glazed carrots are the perfect choice.

Ingredients:

6 to 8 medium-sized carrots

1/2 cup (125 mL) fresh orange juice

Grated rind of 1 orange

3 tbsp (50 mL) maple syrup

A pinch of mace or nutmeg

3 tbsp (50 mL) butter

Method:

• Peel the carrots. Cut into sticks.

• Pour the orange juice into a 4-cup (1 L) microwave-safe dish. Heat 1 minute at HIGH.

• Add the carrots and the orange rind, stir to coat the carrots with the orange juice.

• Cover and microwave 8 to 9 minutes at HIGH. Stir again.

• Add the remaining ingredients. Microwave, uncovered, for 3 minutes at HIGH, stirring after the first 2 minutes.

• Check doneness, as some carrots may be glazed and soft after 2 minutes.

Helpful hint: To heat liquid honey, corn syrup or maple syrup, remove metal cap from the container, then microwave, uncovered, 30 to 45 seconds at HIGH for a 13-ounce bottle or until bubbles appear. If the container isn't microwave-safe, pour the honey or syrup into a glass container before heating.

315

Carrots Oriental

Preparation: . . . . 12 m
Cooking: . . . . **from 13 to 14 m**
Standing: . . . . **none**

A personal note: Fresh ginger root and browned almonds give carrots an elegant touch. Serve with roast chicken or barbecued spare-ribs.

Ingredients:

1/4 cup (60 mL) butter

9 to 10 medium-sized carrots, thinly sliced

1/4 cup (60 mL) slivered almonds

1 tbsp (15 mL) butter

1/4 cup (60 mL) light cream

1 tsp (5 mL) brown sugar

1 heaping tbsp (15 mL) fresh ginger root, grated

1/4 tsp (1 mL) salt

Method:

• Melt the 1/4 cup (60 mL) butter in a 6-cup (1.5 L) microwave-safe dish 2 minutes at HIGH.

• Add the carrots. Stir until well buttered.

• Cover with dish lid or waxed paper.

• Microwave 8 minutes at HIGH. Stir well. Set aside, covered.

• Place in a microwave-safe bowl the almonds and the 1 tablespoon (15 mL) butter.

• Microwave at HIGH 1 minute, stir. Microwave again at HIGH 1 or 2 minutes or until the almonds are a golden color.

• Add to the cooked carrots. Stir and add the remaining ingredients.

• Stir again until everything is well mixed together.

• This can be done ahead of time, but do not refrigerate.

• When ready to serve, stir and reheat 3 minutes at HIGH. Serve.

Celery

• We usually think of celery as a vegetable to be eaten raw, so the many delicious ways it can be cooked may come as a surprise. Cooked or raw, all of it can be used. The leaves should be used finely chopped and added to soup, stew or a lettuce or meat salad. They give a lot of flavor. Try some of the following recipes to learn how to cook celery.

Celery "Nature"

To keep

• Fresh celery is almost all usable and its cooking time is brief. Here is the way I like to prepare mine so that all of it can be used. Prepared in the following manner, it will keep fresh from 2 to 3 weeks refrigerated in a plastic bag.

• Choose an even green color celery as it has more flavor and is usually of a better keeping quality than white celery.

• Place the whole celery in a plastic bag after removing an inch (2.5 cm) of the top leaves and any of the top stalks that are discolored.

• Do not cut the bottom part of the root, as it helps to keep it fresh.

• I sometimes place the whole celery on a wooden board and chop off the top leaves, then I place them in a plastic container. Well covered and refrigerated, they will keep for as long as two weeks.

• Use them as you would fresh herbs, tossed with a salad, added to a soup or a stew or to mashed potatoes or stuffing, etc.

• Then, when I need some diced celery, I take the whole head and pass one inch (2.5 cm) or more, as needed, under cold running water. Shake it hard and chop as needed, then place the remainning clery head in the plastic bag and refrigerate. This way you will use all of it at its best.

• To eat raw, simply cut and wash as many celery stalks as you need, then cut them into small lenghts or sticks.

To cook

• Remove from a head of celery as many stalks as you need. Cut them into 1-or-2-inch (2.5 or 5 cm) pieces or into small sticks or dice.

• Remember that the large stalks are better than the heart for cooking, while the heart has more flavor eaten raw.

• Place the prepared celery in a microwave-safe dish with **1 teaspoon (5 mL) water for 2 to 4 cups (500 mL to 1 L) of celery sticks or dice**.

• Sprinkle with **1/2 teaspoon (2 mL) sugar**.

• Cover and microwave 4 to 8 minutes at HIGH. Drain and prepare according to recipe.

• If your microwave oven has a Sensor method to cook vegetables, do use it. It is like magic.

• You press the Sensor button as indicated on the microwave oven for Hard Vegetables.

• The microwave oven then does all the work, cooking the celery to perfection.

> **A personal note:** Any liquid remaining after cooking celery can be added to a soup or white sauce since it is very flavorful.

Simmered Celery
à la Française

Preparation: . . . .**46 m**
Cooking: . . . .**15 m**
Standing: . . . .**none**

A personal note: A delicious way to serve cooked celery with roast chicken, this recipe is easy to make and reheats without losing any of its quality.

Ingredients:

5 to 6 celery stalks, diced

Milk as needed

1/2 cup (125 mL) potato water*

2 tbsp (30 mL) butter

Salt and pepper to taste

1/4 cup (60 mL) grated cheese (optional)

* *Potato water gives a special flavor to the celery. If not available, use plain water.*

Method:

• Place the prepared celery in a bowl, cover with milk. Let stand 40 minutes.

• This step can be omitted, but some of the texture and flavor will not be as delicate.

• After 40 minutes, drain the milk from the celery.

• Use it to make white sauce or add to soup. It will keep 3 to 4 days refrigerated, covered.

• Pour the potato water over the celery, add the butter.

• Cover and microwave 15 minutes at HIGH. Salt and pepper to taste. Serve.

Crisp Hot Celery

Preparation: . . . . **8 m**
Cooking: . . . . **4 m**
Standing: . . . . **none**

A personal note: This is a very old English way to serve celery. Beware of overcooking, as its secret is its crunchiness.

Ingredients:

6 to 8 celery stalks

1/4 cup (60 mL) consommé of your choice

2 tbsp (30 mL) vegetable oil

1 tsp (5 mL) capers, well drained

1/4 tsp (1 mL) tarragon

Salt and pepper to taste

1 tsp (5 mL) wine or malt vinegar

Method:

• Cut the celery diagonally, in small slices.

• Place in a microwave-safe dish. Add the consommé, stir well.

• Cover and microwave at HIGH 3 minutes. The celery must remain crunchy. Drain.

• Put celery back into the dish and add the oil, capers and tarragon. Salt and pepper to taste.

• Cover. Microwave 1 minute at HIGH. Pour into a serving dish, add the wine or malt vinegar. Toss.

• Serve warm or cool, but not refrigerated.

Devilled Celery

Preparation: . . . . **10 m**
Cooking: . . . . **from 5 to 7 m**
Standing: . . . .**none**

A personal note: This is one of my favorite ways to cook celery. It is important to use a strong mustard, such as Keen's or Dijon.

Ingredients:

4 cups (1 L) celery, diced

1/2 tsp (2 mL) sugar

3 tbsp (50 mL) cold water

2 tbsp (30 mL) butter

1 tsp (5 mL) French or English strong mustard

Salt to taste

A pinch of nutmeg

Method:

• Prepare the diced celery as for Celery "Nature." Place it in a microwave-safe dish. Add the sugar and the cold water.

• Microwave at HIGH 4 to 6 minutes, depending on the size of the dice, or microwave by Sensor for hard vegetables. When cooked, drain thoroughly.

• Melt the butter 1 minute at HIGH. Add the remaining ingredients to the melted butter, stir until well mixed.

• Add the cooked celery. Stir well. Microwave 1 minute at HIGH. Serve.

Green on Green

Preparation: . . . . **7 m**
Cooking: . . . .**5 m**
Standing: . . . .**none**

A personal note: A Southern American way to prepare celery to serve with roast chicken, this recipe is quick and easy to prepare. I often make it to pour over boiled noodles and serve it with grated cheese.

Ingredients:

1 beef bouillon cube

1/4 cup (60 mL) water

4 celery stalks, sliced diagonally

A pinch each of thyme and sugar

2 tbsp (30 mL) butter

2 cups (500 mL) frozen green peas

1/4 tsp (1 mL) salt

Method:

• Place in a 4-cup (1 L) microwave-safe dish the beef bouillon cube and the water.

• Microwave at HIGH 1 minute and 10 seconds. Stir well.

• Add the celery, thyme, sugar, butter and the green peas. Stir well and cover. Microwave 3 minutes at HIGH.

• Stir and microwave another minute. Salt to taste and serve.

Celery root

• Celeriac or celery root or celery knob is so named because of its celery flavor. It is a root vegetable like carrots or turnip and it is round, cream colored and has a rugged peel. It can be cooked or eaten raw in salads, shredded like cabbage. It is at its best from October to December.

Celery Root "Nature"

To buy

• Choose firm, crisp, round roots, the size of a medium turnip.

• The 1-pound (500 g) to 1½-pound (750 g) size is best. This weight gives 4 good servings or 5 medium servings.

To keep

• Being a root, celeriac is a good keeper. It will keep for as long as 3 to 4 weeks, simply placed in the vegetable drawer of your refrigerator.

• No need to wrap it or place it in a plastic bag.

To prepare for cooking

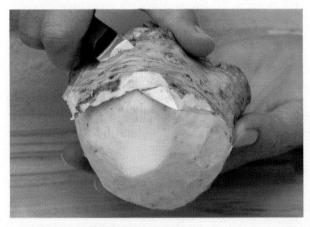

• When ready to cook, peel the root somewhat thicker than you would a carrot.

• Then slice it or make small or large sticks.

• It can also be cut in four or cooked whole.

• It has a tendency to brown slightly after being peeled, so do this only when you are ready to cook it.

• If you wish to use only half, cut it before slicing, then rub the cut part with a slice of lemon, place it in a plastic bag and keep it refrigerated; use it within 6 to 10 days.

• As you will see in the following recipes, there are many ways to cook celery root.

• It also gives a lovely flavor when added diced to any soup.

Whole Baked Celery Root

Preparation: . . . . **2 m**
Cooking: . . . . **from 8 to 10 m**
Standing: . . . . **10 m**

A personal note: This is a splendid way to microwave a whole celery root to be mashed or diced and topped with Hollandaise Sauce or simply topped with melted butter and the juice of half a lemon.

Ingredients:

1 medium-sized celery root
1/2 tsp (2 mL) each salt and sugar

Method:

• Peel celery root. Mix the salt and sugar in a plate. Roll the celery root in it, then wrap in plastic wrap*.

• Set on a rack. Microwave at HIGH 8 to 10 minutes, depending on the size of the root.

• Check doneness with the point of a knife passed through the paper.

• Let stand 10 minutes before unwrapping.

• **To serve:** Unwrap and roll in soft or melted butter and minced parsley or chives, or mash with butter until creamy, or dice and add to a stew.

* Do not wrap too tightly.

Celery Root Fines-Herbes

Preparation: . . . . 7 m
Cooking: . . . . **from 15 to 20 m**
Standing: . . . . **10 m**

A personal note: Only in the microwave oven have I ever succeeded in cooking a celery root, half or whole, and sealed. Nothing is better to serve with lamb or beef roast.

Ingredients:

1 medium-sized celery root*

2 tbsp (30 mL) butter

1 tbsp (15 mL) fresh parsley

1 tbsp (15 mL) fresh or dried basil

1 tsp (5 mL) sugar

Grated rind of 1/2 a lemon

Any size celery root can be prepared and cooked this way. Microwave time may be increased or reduced.

Method:

- Peel the celery root. Cream the butter with the remaining ingredients. Spread the herb butter all over the celery root.

- Wrap it in plastic wrap**. Place on a microwave-safe rack. Set it on the oven turntable, if there is one. If not, place the rack in a microwave-safe pie plate or dish and turn the pie plate or dish 3 times during the cooking period.

- Microwave at HIGH 15 to 20 minutes. Check doneness with the point of a knife after 15 minutes of cooking. Time can vary by a few minutes, depending on the size of the celery root.

- Let stand 10 minutes before unwrapping.

- To serve, unwrap, set on a platter and sprinkle with salt to taste.

** *Do not wrap too tightly.*

Celery Root Purée

Preparation: . . . . **10 m**
Cooking: . . . . **10 m**
Standing: . . . . **none**

A personal note: In France, they often serve small roasted chicken on a bed of this celery root purée. It's also delicious with roast Cornish hen or partridge.

Ingredients:

2 medium-sized celery roots

1/2 cup (125 mL) milk

1/2 tsp (2 mL) each salt and sugar

1/2 cup (125 mL) parsley, minced

2 tbsp (30 mL) butter

Salt and pepper to taste

Method:

• Peel and slice the celery roots as for Celery Root "Nature."

• Place in a microwave-safe dish with the milk, salt and sugar.

• Microwave at HIGH 8 minutes. Drain, reserving the milk.

• Purée in a food processor, a blender, or mash by hand.

• Add the parsley, butter, salt and pepper to taste, and a little milk if necessary.

• Place in a vegetable dish, cover. Reheat 2 minutes at HIGH.

Mashed Celery Root

Preparation: . . . . 8 m
Cooking: . . . . 10 m
Standing: . . . . 5 m

A **personal note:** It is light, with a delicate flavor. Serve as you would mashed potatoes.

Ingredients:

1 celery root, peeled and sliced

2 medium-sized potatoes, peeled and sliced

1/4 cup (60 mL) consommé of your choice

2 tbsp (30 mL) butter

1/2 tsp (2 mL) salt

1/2 tsp (2 mL) savory

Pepper to taste

Method:

• Peel celery root as given in basic preparation for cooking. Cut in half and slice.

• Place in a microwave-safe dish. Add the potatoes and the consommé. Stir. Cover and microwave at HIGH 10 minutes. Test doneness with the point of a knife.

• Let stand 5 minutes after cooking period. Drain, reserving the consommé. Mash.

• Add remaining ingredients. Beat until creamy, adding a bit of consommé if needed.

• Place in serving dish, cover and, if necessary, reheat at MEDIUM 2 minutes before serving.

Celery Root Bolognese

Preparation: . . . . 8 m
Cooking: . . . . from 10 to 12 m
Standing: . . . . none

A personal note: In Bologna, Italy, they layer cooked sliced celery root with grated Swiss cheese, then bake it. I find it one of the most interesting ways to serve celery root with poultry.

Ingredients:

1 celery root

2 to 3 slices of lemon

2 tbsp (30 mL) water

1/2 cup (125 mL) grated Swiss cheese

2 tbsp (30 mL) soft butter

Salt and pepper to taste

Method:

• Peel and slice the celery root as for Celery Root ''Nature.''

• Rub each slice with lemon, place in a microwave-safe dish. Add water.

• Cover and microwave at HIGH 6 to 8 minutes or until just tender. Drain.

• Make a layer of the cooked celery root in a serving dish.

• Dot here and there with half the soft butter. Salt and pepper to taste. Sprinkle with half the grated Swiss cheese.

• Top with remaining celery root and the rest of the cheese. Salt and pepper.

• Set aside if you are not ready to serve, keeping it covered at room temperature.

• To reheat, place dish in microwave 4 minutes at MEDIUM-HIGH when ready to serve.

Helpful hint: To produce a browned look on meat, brush it with a browning agent such as Worcestershire or soy sauce before cooking.

Celery Root Dijonnaise

Preparation: . . . . **5 m**	
Cooking: . . . . **from 5 to 7 m**	
Standing: . . . .**none**	

A personal note: This celery root salad can be served with broiled steak or with cold, thinly sliced roast beef or veal. Quite delicious.

Ingredients:

1 celery root

3 tbsp (50 mL) olive or vegetable oil

2 tbsp (30 mL) Dijon mustard

1 tbsp (15 mL) wine or cider vinegar

1/4 tsp (1 mL) salt

Pepper to taste

Method:

• Peel and slice the celery root, as for Celery Root ''Nature.''

• Place in a microwave-safe dish with 2 tablespoons (30 mL) of water.

• Cover and microwave at HIGH 5 to 7 minutes. Since this is to be served cold as a salad, the celery root should be a little crisp. Drain and leave uncovered while preparing the dressing.

• Mix the remaining ingredients together. Pour over the cooled celery root. Toss gently.

• Serve in a bowl or surround with thinly sliced cold roast beef or veal.

A personal note: In late summer, I add chives to the oil and vinegar mixture.

328

Mushrooms

• Cultivated mushrooms have become part of our cooking, whether added to a sauce or sautéed to serve with steaks and chops, or simply fried and served on toast.

Mushrooms "Nature"

To buy

- When buying fresh mushrooms, select those with tightly closed caps, an indication of young mushrooms that will keep longer, as the earth from the growing soil has not had a chance to work inside the mushroom.

- I realize it is not easy to look for all that when mushrooms are packed in little boxes that you can't open, but look carefully through the plastic wrap.

- Look for mushrooms with short stems, since stems weigh more than caps and little of them are used since the beautiful white round caps are the delicious part of a mushroom.

To keep

- They will keep about 4 to 6 days, refrigerated. Make 4 to 5 incisions in the plastic wrap with the point of a knife.

- When the box is opened to take only a few mushrooms, place the box with the remaining mushrooms in a plastic bag.

- Keep refrigerated, but not in the vegetable bin, simply on a shelf.

To prepare for cooking

- Mushrooms can be washed, but very quickly. Place them on a sheet of paper, roll to dry.

- The best way to clean them is by using a little mushroom brush or any soft small brush.

- Clean before removing the tail end.

- It is important to clean them this way as they are very porous and can absorb lots of water.

- When your recipe calls for fried mushrooms, do not wash them; use a brush or a cloth to clean them.

- When the recipe calls for sliced or chopped mushrooms, clean them but cut only when ready to cook.

To cook:

- Always melt or heat the fat called for in the recipe, then add the mushrooms whole, sliced or cut in half as the recipe demands.

- Microwave, uncovered, at HIGH for the time required by the recipe. Serve as soon as ready.

> **Helpful hint:** Remember, you can always prolong cooking time. But once foods are over-cooked, nothing can be done to change them.

The Best of Creamed Mushrooms

Preparation: . . . . 7 m
Cooking: . . . . from 8 to 9 m
Standing: . . . . none

• My Polish friend Irene taught me how to make these most unusual and so very good creamed mushrooms.

Ingredients:

1 medium-sized onion, chopped fine

1/2 lb (250 g) fresh mushrooms, sliced

1/4 cup (60 mL) cold water

2 tbsp (30 mL) butter

2 tbsp (30 mL) flour

1/2 cup (125 mL) sour cream

Salt and pepper to taste

Method:

• If you have a Corning Browning dish*, heat it at HIGH 6 minutes.

• Without removing the hot dish from the oven, add the chopped onion. Microwave 1 minute at HIGH.

• Remove dish from the oven, scrape the onion, add the mushrooms.

• Stir well, while scraping the bottom of the dish.

• Add the water, mix again and microwave at HIGH 3 minutes.

• Drain the mushrooms, reserving the water.

• In another microwave-safe dish place the butter. Microwave 2 minutes at HIGH.

• Add the flour to the butter, mix well. Add the water drained from the cooked mushrooms, stir thoroughly.

• Add the sour cream. Salt and pepper to taste.

• When ready to serve, microwave at HIGH 2 to 3 minutes, stirring once.

If you do not have a Browning Dish, use a Corning 8-inch (20 cm) dish, heated 3 minutes at HIGH. The onion will not be as brown but will have the flavor.

Leyden Mushrooms

Preparation: . . . . **12 m**
Cooking: . . . . **15 m**
Standing: . . . . **none**

A personal note: Leyden in Holland is Rembrandt's birth place. Smothered mushrooms are a speciality of this interesting town. The addition of a couple of wild mushrooms gives this dish a distinctive flavor, although they can be omitted.

Ingredients:

1 lb (500 g) fresh mushrooms

2 dried mushrooms (optional)*

1 cup (250 mL) sour cream

1 tbsp (15 mL) parsley, chopped

6 green onions, chopped fine

1 tbsp (15 mL) butter

1/4 tsp (1 mL) each of salt and pepper

1 tbsp (15 mL) fresh lemon juice

2 tbsp (30 mL) Gouda or Gruyere cheese, grated

Paprika to taste

Method:

• Generously butter an 8 × 8-inch (20 × 20 cm) microwave-safe dish.

• Cut off the mushroom stems. Wipe the tops with a paper towel.

• Place one next to the other in the buttered dish.

• It does not matter if they overlap here and there.

• When using the dried mushrooms, break them up and sprinkle over the fresh ones.

• Mix the remaining ingredients, except the grated cheese, thoroughly.

• Spread over the mushrooms. Top with the cheese. Sprinkle with paprika.

• Microwave at MEDIUM-HIGH 15 minutes. Cook only when ready to serve.

* Many types can be found in speciality shops. They can be bought in small quantities, broken up or whole.

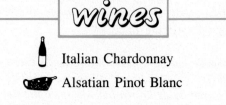

wines

Italian Chardonnay

Alsatian Pinot Blanc

Finnish Baked Mushrooms

Preparation: . . . . **10 m**
Cooking: . . . . **from 13 to 17 m**
Standing: . . . . **3 m**

A personal note: This recipe is another creation of my Finnish friend Marta. It can be served as a vegetable or poured as a sauce over a poached fish.

Ingredients:

1 tbsp (15 mL) butter

1/4 cup (60 mL) fine dry breadcrumbs

1/2 lb (250 g) fresh mushrooms, thinly sliced

1 tbsp (15 mL) fresh lemon juice

1/4 tsp (1 mL) dry dill *or*
  2 tsp (10 mL) fresh dill, chopped fine

4 green onions, chopped fine

2 tbsp (30 mL) butter

3 tbsp (50 mL) flour

1 cup (250 mL) whipping cream

2 egg yolks, lightly beaten

Salt and pepper to taste

Method:

• Melt the butter in a microwave-safe dish 1 minute at HIGH. Add the breadcrumbs.

• Toast at HIGH 3 to 5 minutes, stirring every minute until golden brown. Set aside.

• Stir together the fresh, thinly sliced mushrooms, lemon juice, dill, green onions and the 2 tablespoons (30 mL) of butter. Cover, microwave at HIGH 4 minutes.

• Stir the flour into the cooked mushrooms. Add the cream gradually, stirring until all lumps disappear.

• Add 1 egg yolk at a time, beating until well blended.

• Microwave at MEDIUM-HIGH 6 to 8 minutes, stirring every 2 minutes until sauce is creamy and thickened. Salt and pepper.

• Pour into a warm dish and top with the buttered breadcrumbs.

• Let stand 3 minutes in a warm place before serving.

Mushrooms and Peas

Preparation:	**8 m**
Cooking:	**8 m**
Standing:	**none**

• In winter I use frozen peas. They are tasty and surprisingly good cooked in the microwave.

Ingredients:

2 tbsp (30 mL) butter
3 green onions, chopped fine
2 cups (500 mL) fresh mushrooms, thinly sliced
2 cups (500 mL) frozen green peas
1 tsp (5 mL) sugar
1/4 tsp (1 mL) basil
Salt and pepper to taste

Method:

• Place in a 4-cup (1 L) microwave-safe dish the butter and green onions.

• Microwave at HIGH 2 minutes.

• Add the remaining ingredients, except salt and pepper.

• Stir and microwave at HIGH 6 minutes.

• Stir well. Salt and pepper to taste.

To cook by Sensor

• If your microwave oven has a Sensor, set at VEGETABLES SOFT.

• The oven will stop when they are cooked.

• When done by Sensor: Melt the butter 1 minute at HIGH.

• Add all the ingredients and cook covered with plastic wrap.

Mushrooms on Toast

Preparation: . . . . **10 m**
Cooking: . . . . **from 11 to 13 m**
Standing: . . . . **none**

A personal note: Quick and easy to make. Serve as an entrée or as a canapé with a glass of good Port wine or as a light meal with a tossed salad.

Ingredients:

6 bacon slices

1 medium-sized onion, chopped fine

1/2 lb (250 g) fresh mushrooms, thinly sliced

1/4 tsp (1 mL) dried tarragon

Salt and pepper to taste

Toasted buttered bread

Method:

• Place the bacon in an 8 × 8-inch (20 × 20 cm) microwave-safe dish.

• Microwave at HIGH 4 to 5 minutes.

• Remove bacon to paper towelling, let it cool, then crumble.

• Add the chopped onion to 2 tablespoons (30 mL) of the bacon fat. Discard the remaining fat.

• Microwave at HIGH 4 to 5 minutes, stirring once.

• When the onion is soft, add the sliced mushrooms, stir well. Add the tarragon, stir again.

• Microwave at HIGH 2 minutes. Add the bacon, stir.

• Microwave at MEDIUM-HIGH 1 minute.

• Cut the toasted buttered bread in halves or quarters, top with the mushrooms and serve.

A personal note: These can be prepared 3 to 4 hours ahead of time, kept at room temperature and reheated when needed, 1 minute at MEDIUM.

wines

Chilled Beaujolais

Moulin-à-vent

Dried Mushrooms

- Place 6 to 8 dried mushrooms in a bowl.
- Pour 1 cup (250 mL) boiling water on top.
- Place a weight over the mushrooms to keep them under water.
- Soak them 40 minutes. Drain from water, squeeze dry in a paper towel.

- If you wish to use dried mushrooms instead of fresh mushrooms in any recipe, prepare them first this way:
- When using them to replace fresh mushrooms, use only half the quantity required because dried mushrooms are more pungent than fresh.
- If the recipe calls for 1 cup (250 mL) fresh mushrooms, use only 1/2 cup (125 mL) dried mushrooms.

- Remove tough stems and slice mushrooms into 1/4-inch (.65 cm) sticks.
- you can reserve the soaking water to use in any sauce.

Cabbage

• Cabbage, one of the oldest vegetables, is eaten in every country of the world. Its big plus is that it is an excellent source of Vitamin C.

• I have often asked myself: "Is it part of our melting pot heritage that when we say beets, we mean pickled, turnips seem to be forever mashed and cabbage instantly turns into coleslaw?" There are so many other ways to serve cabbage. And its low cost and its availability as a fresh vegetable throughout the long winter months are not to be overlooked.

• If you wish to get acquainted with the true flavor and color of cabbage, which it loses when it is overcooked or boiled, microwave it. You will be delighted.

Cabbage "Nature"

To buy

• Choose a firm, heavy head.

• If the top leaves are wilted or yellowed, or have been trimmed back to make it look fresh, the head has been around a long time.

To microwave a whole head of cabbage

• Choose a medium-sized head. Remove the top few leaves.

• Soak the head 20 minutes in a bowl of cold water, stem down. Drain well. Wrap in plastic wrap. Place in a microwave-safe dish.

• A medium-sized head will take 15 to 18 minutes at HIGH. Test with the point of a knife for doneness after 12 minutes of cooking.

To microwave wedges of cabbage

• Cut the cabbage into wedges of equal size.

• Place in a microwave-safe dish.

• Add **2 tablespoons (30 mL) of water, 1/4 teaspoon (1 mL) of sugar**. Cover.

• A 1½-to-2-pound (1 kg) head cut into wedges takes 8 to 9 minutes at HIGH.

• For even cooking, the wedges should be rearranged at the end of each 3 minutes of the cooking period. Simply move them with a spoon.

To microwave cabbage thinly sliced or cut into thin wedges

• Cut the cabbage into small wedges or slice it thinly. Add only 2 tablespoons (30 mL) of water; the cut cabbage will give off enough water during the cooking process. Make sure the dish is well covered.

• Four cups (1 L) of chopped cabbage should cook in 5 to 7 minutes at HIGH, covered.

Cabbage 1900

Preparation: . . . . **10 m**
Cooking: . . . . **from 12 to 14 m**
Standing: . . . . **none**

A personal note: I have failed to find out why this dish is referred to as Cabbage 1900. A favorite of Old Québec, and a favorite of mine. I often replace the salt pork with bacon, as it is easier to buy.

Ingredients:

1/2 cup (125 mL) diced salt pork or bacon

A medium or small cabbage, cut into thin wedges

4 apples, peeled and sliced

1 tbsp (15 mL) fresh lemon juice or cider vinegar

2 tbsp (30 mL) brown sugar

2 to 4 whole cloves

Method:

• Dice the salt pork or the bacon. Place it in a microwave-safe dish.

• Microwave 3 minutes at HIGH, stirring once.

• Add the remaining ingredients. Stir until well mixed.

• Cover, microwave 4 minutes at HIGH.

• Stir again until the whole is well mixed.

• Microwave at MEDIUM 5 to 7 minutes. Stir well and serve.

Marta's Cabbage

Preparation: . . . . **15 m**
Cooking: . . . . **from 6 to 8 m**
Standing: . . . . **none**

• My friend Marta is Finnish and a wonderful cook. I successfully adapted her cabbage recipe to the microwave.

Ingredients:

3 tbsp (50 mL) butter

6 to 8 cups (1.5 to 2 L) cabbage, shredded

1 onion, thinly sliced

3 tbsp (50 mL) cider or wine vinegar

1 tsp (5 mL) caraway or dill seeds

Salt and pepper to taste

3 fresh tomatoes, diced

2 tbsp (30 mL) sugar

Method:

• Place the butter in a 12-cup (3 L) microwave-safe casserole and melt 2 minutes at HIGH.

• Add the cabbage, onion and vinegar, stir until the whole is well mixed.

• Add the caraway or dill seeds. Salt and pepper to taste. Stir again to mix.

• Top with the tomatoes, unpeeled and diced.

• Sprinkle the tomatoes with the sugar.

• Cover and microwave at HIGH 6 to 8 minutes. Mix well and serve.

Belgian Creamed Cabbage

Preparation: . . . . **15 m**
Cooking: . . . . **10 m**
Standing: . . . . **none**

A personal note: Chopped cabbage is cooked in cream without any thickening in this recipe. To serve it as a meal, as they do in Belgium, place the cabbage in the middle of a warm platter and surround it with microwaved small potatoes. Serve with thin slices of ham and mustard.

Ingredients:

1/2 cup (125 mL) cream of your choice

1 tbsp (15 mL) butter

1 tbsp (15 mL) minced parsley

1 medium-sized onion, chopped fine

2 whole cloves

5 cups (1.25 L) cabbage, chopped fine

Salt and pepper to taste

Method:

• Place in a 6-cup (1.5 L) microwave-safe dish the cream, butter, parsley, onion and whole cloves.

• Microwave 4 minutes at HIGH.

• Add the cabbage, salt and pepper.

• Stir until well mixed. Cover and microwave 5 to 6 minutes at HIGH. Stir well.

• Taste for doneness, since the way the cabbage has been chopped may make a difference of one or two minutes.

• Stir well before serving.

Tyrolean Cabbage

Preparation: . . . . **15 m**
Cooking: . . . .**20 m**
Standing: . . . .**none**

A personal note: A small to medium-sized cabbage cooked whole and topped with a creamy white sauce makes a vegetarian lunch when served with baked potatoes.

Ingredients:

1 medium-sized cabbage

2 tbsp (30 mL) butter

1/2 tsp (2 mL) salt

1/2 tsp (2 mL) sugar

1 tbsp (15 mL) fresh dill, chopped, *or*
   1 tsp (5 mL) dried dill *or*
   rind of 1 lemon or lime

Method:

* Remove top leaves from cabbage.

* Remove hard core under the cabbage, which is easily done with a pointed knife.

* Cream together the remaining ingredients. Open the top 6 to 9 leaves and spread some of the butter mixture on the inside of the leaves.

* Push the buttered leaves back by pressing with your hands.

* Wrap the cabbage in a piece of plastic wrap large enough to cover it completely.

* Place on a rack. Microwave 20 minutes at HIGH.

* Do not unwrap until ready to serve. It will stay piping hot for 15 to 20 minutes.

To serve

* Place the unwrapped cabbage in the middle of a platter. Surround with baked potatoes. Top cabbage with 1 cup (250 mL) white sauce or Sauce Mornay, which may be microwaved while cabbage is standing.

White Rhône

Alsatian Riesling

Bavarian Cabbage

Preparation: . . . . **15 m**
Cooking: . . . . **from 8 to 10 m**
Standing: . . . .**none**

• The Juniper berry used in this recipe is the small fruit of the Juniper tree. It is round and black, with a deep purple tint throughout. It is used commercially to make gin, which gives you an idea of its flavor. It is mild, pleasant and easy to remove from the cooked cabbage, as it is quite visible.

Ingredients:

2 tbsp (30 mL) butter

5 to 6 cups (1.25 to 1.5 L) cabbage, shredded

2 apples, peeled, cored and sliced

6 Juniper berries (optional)

1/2 cup (125 mL) white wine or consommé

3 tbsp (50 mL) cornstarch

Salt and pepper to taste

Method:

• Use a large microwave-safe dish. I use a 12-cup

(3 L) plastic dish or a large Pyrex dish with a cover.

• Melt the butter in the dish 2 minutes at HIGH.

• Stir in the cabbage and the apples until both are well coated with the butter.

• Add the Juniper berries. Mix the cornstarch with the white wine or consommé. Add to the cabbage, stir well.

• Cover. Microwave at HIGH 8 minutes, stir well.

• If needed, microwave another 1 or 2 minutes. Salt and pepper to taste. Serve.

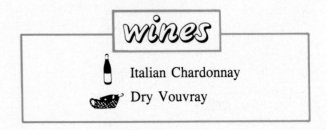

wines

Italian Chardonnay

Dry Vouvray

Sweet and Sour Red Cabbage

Preparation: . . . . **10 m**
Cooking: . . . . **from 4 to 6 m**
Standing: . . . .**none**

A personal note: In Holland and Germany, this dish is served with roast pork or baked ham.

Ingredients:

4 to 5 cups (1 to 1.25 L) red cabbage, chopped fine

2 cups (500 mL) apples, unpeeled, thinly sliced

3 tbsp (50 mL) cider or wine vinegar

1/4 cup (60 mL) water

1/3 cup (80 mL) brown sugar

6 whole cloves

1 tsp (5 mL) salt

3 tbsp (50 mL) butter

Method:

- In a 6-cup (1.5 L) microwave-safe dish place all the ingredients except the butter. Stir until well mixed.
- Cover and microwave at HIGH 4 to 5 minutes.
- Stir well. Taste for doneness.
- If necessary, add another minute of cooking.
- Add the butter, stir until well mixed in the cabbage.
- Microwave 1 minute at HIGH. Stir and serve.

Helpful hint: To soften hardened brown sugar, place 1 cup (250 mL) sugar in a dish with a slice of fresh bread or a quarter of an apple, cover and microwave ½ to 1 minute at HIGH.

Cauliflower

- The cauliflower is a plant of the cabbage family. The word cauliflower is derived from the Latin caulis floris, which I learned as a student way back. The two words were used to teach us how to pronounce the ''is'' ending — with a soft (L) and with a hard (R) letter before it. For years I did not want to eat cauliflower because of that and also because it was always served overcooked and slightly brown in color. But now that it can be cooked to super perfection in a microwave oven — white and tender, with a delicate flavor and no strong smell — it has become one of my favorite vegetables.

- In Spain, they often referred to it as Syrian Cabbage, a very old name.

Cauliflower "Nature"

The best time to buy

• The productive season is from September to the end of November. It is sometimes available later, but the quality and flavor are past their prime and the price is higher.

To buy

• Look for firm, compact, white heads.

• Check the leaves near the white head. They should be deep green, fresh and crisp.

• Do not buy cauliflower with yellowed leaves, a sure sign that it is past its prime.

To keep

• Do not wash a cauliflower before placing it in the refrigerator.

• Remove the heavy green leaves, if it is too large, and place it in a plastic bag, tied loosely.

• It will keep in perfect condition without losing its freshness up to one week.

To prepare for cooking whole

• Cut off the green leaves and make a hole in the hard core under the cauliflower.

• Place it in a bowl, cover with cold water. Add 1 tablespoon (15 mL) coarse salt and 2 slices of lemon (optional).

• Let stand 10 minutes. I do this just before I am ready to cook it.

• If there isn't enough time, just rinse under cold running water for 2 minutes.

To prepare for cooking cut in flowerets

• To cook it in flowerets, divide the head into flowerets, keeping them as even in size as possible, which sometimes means that large flowerets will have to be cut in two.

• Soak in salted water and drain, then proceed as for whole cauliflower.

To cook a whole head of cauliflower

• Whenever I serve beautiful white cauliflower, cooked whole, everyone is surprised and delighted with its perfect flavor. It is very easy to prepare, and leftovers reheat without losing any of their quality.

Ingredients:

1 medium-sized cauliflower
3 tbsp (50 mL) butter
1 tbsp (15 mL) parsley, finely minced
Salt and pepper to taste

Method:

• Clean and prepare the whole caulifrower as for Cauliflower "Nature." Sprinkle top with a pinch of sugar. Wrap in plastic wrap, pulling the ends under the cauliflower.

• Place on a microwave oven rack, head up. Microwave 15 minutes at HIGH. Let stand 10 minutes.

• Check doneness with the point of a knife. If necessary, cook it another 3 minutes at HIGH.

• Unwrap: set on serving platter. Salt and pepper to taste.

• Melt the butter 1 minute at HIGH. Add the parsley and pour over the cauliflower.

New England Cauliflower

Preparation: . . . .**15 m**
Cooking:. . . . .**17 m**
Standing: . . . .**none**

A personal note: This is an interesting casserole of cauliflower and eggs, perfect for a light meal. Serve it with toasted English muffins.

Ingredients:

1 medium cauliflower

1/4 cup (60 mL) water

3 tbsp (50 mL) butter

2 tbsp (30 mL) flour

1 cup (250 mL) milk

1/2 cup (125 mL) light cream or plain yogurt

Salt and pepper to taste

3 green onions, chopped fine

1/2 tsp (2 mL) basil or oregano

3 to 4 hard cooked eggs, thinly sliced

1/2 cup (125 mL) cracker crumbs

1/4 cup (60 mL) fresh parsley, minced

Method:

• Separate cauliflower into flowerets as for Cauliflower ''Nature'' and microwave at HIGH 8 or 9 minutes with the 1/4 cup (60 mL) water.

• To make the sauce, melt the butter in a microwave-safe bowl 1 minute at HIGH. Add the flour, mix well. Add the milk and the cream or yogurt. Salt and pepper. Stir until well mixed.

• Add the green onions, basil or oregano. Stir well.

• Microwave at HIGH 3 minutes, stir again. Microwave at HIGH 2 minutes more or until the sauce is creamy.

• Hard cook the eggs on the stove. Slice them, add to the sauce.

• Add the undrained cooked cauliflower to the sauce. Stir gently.

• Place in a microwave-safe dish. Mix together cracker crumbs and minced parsley and sprinkle over all. Cover. Warm 3 minutes at MEDIUM and serve.

wines

Australian Chardonnay
White Côte-de-Beaune

Cauliflower Italiano

Preparation: . . . . **10 m**
Cooking: . . . .**12 m**
Standing: . . . . **from 10 to 15 m**

A personal note: One of my favorite cauliflower recipes, this is equally good served hot, tepid or cold. The fresh tomatoes cannot be replaced by canned tomatoes; the flavor and texture will not be the same.

Ingredients:

1 medium head of cauliflower

3 tbsp (50 mL) olive or vegetable oil

1 medium onion, chopped fine

1 garlic clove, chopped fine

3 tbsp (50 mL) fresh parsley, minced

1 tsp (5 mL) basil or oregano, chopped

Salt and pepper to taste

2 to 3 medium-sized tomatoes, diced

2 tbsp (30 mL) butter or margarine

1 slice of bread, cubed

Method:

• Prepare the cauliflower as for Cauliflower "Nature" cut into flowerets.

• Heat the oil in a 4-cup (1 L) microwave-safe dish 2 minutes at HIGH. Add the onion and garlic, stir well. Microwave 2 minutes at HIGH, stirring after 1 minute.

• Add the cauliflower and all the other ingredients. Stir well.

• Place the butter or margarine in a microwave-safe pie plate. Melt 1 minute at HIGH.

• Add the bread cubes, stir. Microwave 2 minutes at HIGH. Stir well, microwave another minute at HIGH. Sprinkle on top of cauliflower. Microwave at HIGH 10 minutes. Stir well.

• Let stand covered 10 to 15 minutes. Serve, tepid or cold, but not refrigerated.

Cauliflower Pie

Preparation: . . . . **10 m**
Cooking: . . . . **from 13 to 14 m**
Standing: . . . . **none**

A personal note: An English country light dinner, Cauliflower Pie can also be served with roast beef or roast duck. It is a pie without dough.

Ingredients:

1 medium-sized cauliflower

2 tbsp (30 mL) milk or water

1/2 cup (125 mL) cheese, grated

1/4 cup (60 mL) parsley, chopped fine

3 tbsp (50 mL) butter

2 tbsp (30 mL) milk

Salt and pepper to taste

1 medium-sized onion, peeled and thinly sliced

3 tomatoes, peeled and sliced

1 tsp (5 mL) savory or tarragon

4 to 5 potatoes, cooked and mashed

White Bordeaux
Pouilly-Fumé

Method:

• Divide the cauliflower into flowerets as for Cauliflower "Nature."

• Place in a dish with the milk or water. Cover and microwave 8 to 9 minutes at HIGH.

• Let stand 5 to 10 minutes; do not drain the milk or water.

• Add the grated cheese, parsley, butter and the 2 tablespoons (30 mL) milk.

• Beat the whole until creamy, quickly done in a blender or a food processor.

• Season to taste and place in a nice casserole dish or a 9-inch (23 cm) pie plate.

• Top with the sliced tomatoes and onions. Salt and pepper lightly.

• Sprinkle with the savory or tarragon.

• Cook and mash the potatoes.

• Place on top of the casserole, sprinkle with paprika.

• When ready to serve, cover dish with lid or plastic wrap, microwave 5 minutes at MEDIUM-HIGH and serve.

Indonesian Cauliflower

Preparation: . . . . 10 m
Cooking: . . . . 4 m
Standing: . . . . 5 m

A personal note: This is a sort of curried cauliflower dish in which the fresh ginger root flavor seems to permeate the whole dish. It makes an elegant light lunch served in a nest of cooked rice mixed with a handful of nuts.

Ingredients:

4 tbsp (60 mL) vegetable oil

2 tsp (10 mL) fresh ginger root, grated

1/2 tsp (2 mL) turmeric

2 tsp (10 mL) ground coriander

1 or 2 garlic cloves, chopped fine

1 medium-sized cauliflower

1/4 cup (60 mL) water

1/4 tsp (1 mL) sugar

Method:

• Blend together the vegetable oil, grated ginger root, turmeric, coriander and garlic. Set aside.

• Cut the cauliflower into flowerets, as for Cauliflower ''Nature.''

• Place it in a ceramic dish (Corning) or any nice microwave-safe dish.

• Add the water, sugar and the spice mixture. Cover.

• Microwave at HIGH 2 minutes.

• Test for doneness; if necessary, add 2 minutes of cooking.

• Let stand 5 minutes and serve.

Vouvray

Rhine Riesling Spätlese

Cauliflower Vinaigrette

Preparation: . . . . **10 m**
Cooking: . . . . **from 6 to 8 m**
Standing: . . . . **none**

A personal note: Tepid or cold, this perfect cauliflower salad makes an interesting lunch served with a platter of thinly sliced, hot or cold poached chicken.

Ingredients:

1 medium-sized cauliflower

3 green onions, green and white, chopped fine

3 tbsp (50 mL) vegetable or olive oil, to taste

1 tbsp (15 mL) fresh lemon juice

1/2 tsp (2 mL) prepared mustard

1/4 tsp (1 mL) salt

A pinch of pepper

Method:

• Clean cauliflower and cut into flowerets as for Cauliflower "Nature."

• Place in microwave-safe dish. Add 3 tablespoons (50 mL) water, cover and microwave 6 to 8 minutes at HIGH.

• Check with the point of a knife after 6 minutes; do not overcook. Drain the water. Place the cauliflower in an attractive salad bowl. Top with the chopped green onions.

• Mix the remaining ingredients and pour over the cauliflower. Toss only when ready to serve.

• Serve warm or at room temperature. Do not refrigerate.

Brussels Sprouts

• Brussels sprouts belong to the cabbage family —
instead of one large head, they are miniature heads
of cabbage formed along a heavy stem. Like all plants
of the cabbage family, they are a cool-weather crop,
which for us means that September and October
produce the best, although they are available most
of the year as imports from different countries.

Brussels Sprouts "Nature"

How to buy

• They are sold mostly off their stems.

• Occasionally, in the autumn, they can be purchased on their stems; they are elegant and I love to use them as a centerpiece for a special occasion.

• Look for firm-head Brussels sprouts of an even size, since having them all the same size, small or large, simplifies cooking them in the microwave.

• The size is a personal preference.

To prepare for cooking

• Wash thoroughly in a bowl of cold water.

• Drain in a colander for 10 to 15 minutes.

• Trim off top leaves or any that are blemished.

To cook

• These instructions are for 1 pound (500 g) of Brussels sprouts*.

• First, if there are small heads, put them aside; cooking the large ones will take more time and the small ones will be overcooked. They should be cooked in a separate dish.

• Place the Brussels sprouts in a microwave-safe dish with 1/4 cup (60 mL) water and 1/4 teaspoon (1 mL) sugar.

• Cover and microwave 6 to 8 minutes at HIGH. The time will vary, depending on the size of the heads. Test them with a fork for doneness after 6 minutes.

• Let stand covered for 3 to 5 minutes.

• To cook 1 pound (500 g) by the Sensor method*, place them in a microwave-safe dish, cover with plastic wrap unless you have plastic dishes with a lid. In that case, use the lid instead of plastic wrap.

See your oven manuel for Sensor instructions.

Brussels Sprouts Beurre Doré

Preparation: . . . . **10 m**
Cooking: . . . . **from 6 to 8 m**
Standing: . . . . **from 3 to 5 m**

A personal note: A golden butter with lemon rind poured over cooked Brussels sprouts is a favorite of the French cuisine.

Ingredients:

1/2 tsp (2 mL) sugar

1 lb (500 g) Brussels sprouts

2 tbsp (30 mL) butter

Grated rind of 1 lemon

Salt and pepper to taste

Method:

• To microwave the Brussels sprouts, place the sugar in the bottom of the dish, then follow instructions for Brussels Sprouts ''Nature.''

• Drain. Place the butter and the lemon rind in a microwave-safe dish.

• Microwave at HIGH 2 minutes. Stir.

• When the butter is golden brown, pour it over the Brussels sprouts. Stir. Salt and pepper to taste. Serve.

Finnish Brussels Sprouts

Preparation: . . . . **5 m**
Cooking: . . . . **from 5 to 7 m**
Standing: . . . . **5 m**

• Easy and quick to prepare, this dish has a touch of lemon flavor.

Ingredients:

1 lb (500 g) Brussels sprouts
4 tbsp (60 mL) water
1 tsp (5 mL) butter
Juice and grated rind of 1/2 lemon
1/4 tsp (1 mL) sugar
Salt and pepper to taste

Method:

• Prepare the Brussels sprouts as for Brussels Sprouts "Nature."

• Place in a microwave-safe dish the water, butter, lemon juice and grated rind and sugar. Stir to mix.

• Microwave at HIGH 1 minute.

• Add the Brussels sprouts. Stir well. Cover and microwave at HIGH 4 to 6 minutes, depending on the size of sprouts.

• Stir well. Salt and pepper. Cover and let stand 5 minutes before serving.

Curried Brussels Sprouts

Preparation: . . . . **10 m**
Cooking: . . . . **from 11 to 13 m**
Standing: . . . . **none**

• Brussels sprouts respond very pleasantly to the spicy flavor of curry.

Ingredients:

2 tbsp (30 mL) butter

1/2 to 1 tsp (2 to 5 mL) curry powder

2 tbsp (30 mL) flour

1 cup (250 mL) milk or chicken consommé

1 apple, peeled and grated

1 lb (500 g) Brussels sprouts

Method:

• Place the butter in a microwave-safe bowl and melt 1 minute at HIGH.

• Add the curry powder and the flour, stir until well mixed.

• Add the milk or chicken consommé, stir. Microwave 3 minutes at HIGH, stir.

• Add the grated apple and microwave another minute at HIGH or until sauce is creamy.

• Microwave the Brussels sprouts as for Brussels Sprouts ''Nature.'' Drain the water.

• Add the curried sauce, stir. Microwave 1 minute at HIGH. When ready to serve, salt to taste.

Brussels Sprouts Oriental

A personal note: When served with baked potatoes and a piece of cheese, this dish makes an excellent light meal.

Ingredients:

1 tbsp (15 mL) butter
6 green onions, chopped fine
1 lb (500 g) Brussels sprouts
3 tbsp (50 mL) water
2 tsp (10 mL) wine or cider vinegar
1 tsp (5 mL) sugar
Salt and pepper to taste

Method:

• Place the butter in the microwave-safe dish to be used for cooking the Brussels sprouts and melt 1 minute at HIGH.

• Add the green onions, stir well. Microwave 1 minute at HIGH, stir well.

• Add the Brussels sprouts, prepared as for Brussels Sprouts "Nature." Add the water. Stir. Cover and microwave 6 minutes at HIGH.

• When done, remove the Brussels sprouts from the water. Add to the water the wine or cider vinegar and the sugar. Stir well.

• Microwave 4 minutes at HIGH or until most of the liquid has boiled away.

• Salt and pepper the Brussels sprouts to taste.

• Add to the vinegar mixture, stir gently. Microwave 1 minute at HIGH. Serve.

• For a light meal, I sometimes microwave 1/2 pound (250 g) bacon 5 minutes at HIGH and place it around the Brussels sprouts.

• Served with hot French bread or toasted English muffins, it makes a pleasant light meal.

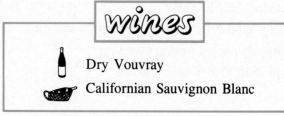

wines

Dry Vouvray
Californian Sauvignon Blanc

Squash

- There are summer squash and winter squash, the pattypan, yellow crookneck, yellow straightneck, zucchini, acorn, butternut, turban and many more. When at the market, ask for squash by name to learn what each type is like. They are economical to buy and most are excellent keepers.

- Cooked by microwave, they are excellent. As a matter of fact, you will know the true taste of squash only after eating it cooked by microwave. Remember that almost all squash are cooked in the microwave in the same manner.

Squash "Nature"

To keep

• Keep summer squash refrigerated, about 10 days at the most.

• Winter squash has the great quality of not losing its flavor and texture after being picked. For example, Hubbard squash and a few others will stay perfect for as long as four months, providing they are kept in a cool dark room, even if a wedge has been cut from the whole.

• Wrap what is left in plastic wrap and keep in a cool place.

• The 2½-to-3-pound (1.25 to 1.5 kg) squash are the best for flavor and texture. Over that weight, they are quite watery and have less flavor.

To prepare and cook

• The preparation and cooking of all types of squash in the microwave oven is so easy, with such perfect results in flavor, texture and color, that you truly can appreciate them at their best with hardly any work.

• Wash whole squash, any type you choose.

• Make 4 to 5 incisions through the peel with the point of a paring knife.

• Place it in the microwave oven on a rack or an inverted saucer.

• Microwave at HIGH 6 to 10 minutes, depending on the size of the squash.

• Remove from microwave with a cloth, as the squash will be very hot.

• Let it stand for 10 to 15 minutes.

• Then, split it in half and remove seeds and membranes, which is easily done with a spoon.

• Add brown sugar or maple syrup or molasses and butter to taste, mash with the pulp right in the shells.

• Either cover each half with a piece of waxed paper, or place the mashed squash in a long dish and cover.

• When ready to serve, microwave at HIGH 5 to 6 minutes.

Squash Maison

Convection or microwave cooking

Preparation: . . . . **10 m**
Cooking: microwave: . . . . **22 m**
            convection: . . . . . . **from 35 to 40 m**
Standing: . . . .**none**

A personal note: I like to serve this with thinly sliced hot ham or with Orange-glazed Ham Steak. Use any type of squash you prefer.

Ingredients:

1 3-to-4-cup (750 mL to 1 L) squash of your choice, mashed

1/4 cup (60 mL) butter or margarine

1 tsp (5 mL) salt

1/4 tsp (1 mL) pepper

6 green onions, chopped fine

1 tsp (5 mL) savory

1/2 tsp (2 mL) dill weed or seeds

1/4 cup (60 mL) cream or milk

3 eggs, well beaten

1/4 cup (60 mL) buttered crushed cracker crumbs

Method:

• Cook and mash squash of your choice according to the recipe for Squash ''Nature.''

• When mashed, add butter or margarine, beat until melted. Add salt, pepper and onion. Mix well.

• Add the remaining ingredients, except the cracker crumbs. Stir until well mixed. Place in a dish. Top with the buttered cracker crumbs.

To cook by convection

• Place casserole on rack. Set convection section of microwave oven at 400°F (200°C).

• Bake 35 to 40 minutes or until a knife inserted in centre comes out clean.

To cook by microwave

• Place casserole on a rack. Microwave, covered, at HIGH 10 minutes.

• Lower heat to MEDIUM and microwave 12 minutes.

• When cooking by microwave, top of casserole can be sprinkled with paprika to taste.

Zucchini

To buy

• Choose the young tender type, about 4 to 8 inches (10 to 20 cm) long, with smooth skin and a pale green color.

To keep

• Zucchini are very good keepers. It is best to keep them refrigerated in the vegetable bin.

• When you have too many from your garden, or even the market, freeze them. Nothing to it.

• Wash the zucchini, cut a slice off each end, cut in pieces and pass through your food grinder or food processor, skin and all.

• Then place in plastic bags by the cupful or more, as you prefer, label and freeze.

• When you wish to use, pour the contents of the bag into a colander.

• Set in a bowl and let it thaw. Then use for pie, cake, vegetable, soup or as you desire.

360

Zucchini St-Raphaël

Preparation: . . . . **10 m**
Cooking: . . . . **from 6 to 9 m**
Standing: . . . . **none**

• Zucchini are very popular in the south of France. I ate this dish in St-Raphaël, served with luscious chicken roasted on a spit in a fireplace. The chef very graciously gave me his recipe, which I adapted to microwave cooking. The color and flavor are even better.

Ingredients:

4 medium-sized zucchini*
4 tbsp (60 mL) butter
6 green onions, diced
1 tsp (5 mL) tarragon
1/4 cup (60 mL) cream
Salt and pepper to taste

* *About 7 to 8 inches (l8 to 20 cm) each and almost 3 pounds (1.5 kg) in all.*

Method:

• Wash the zucchini under running cold water.

• Remove top and bottom.

• Slice the zucchini.

• Place the butter in an 8-cup (2 L) microwave-safe casserole and melt 2 minutes at HIGH.

• Add the green onions, tarragon and zucchini. Stir until zucchini are buttered.

• Microwave, uncovered, at HIGH, 4 to 6 minutes, stirring once.

• When done, drain the water. Add the cream, salt and pepper to taste, stir well.

• When ready to serve, microwave at HIGH 2 to 3 minutes.

• The sauce is clear. If you find there is too much liquid (that depends on the zucchini), strain the whole.

A personal note: In the south of France, they serve this zucchini over buttered toast, which absorbs the liquid and is delicious to eat after the zucchini.

361

Orange Zucchini

Ingredients:

3 or 4 medium-sized zucchini
1/2 cup (125 mL) water
1½ tsp (7 mL) salt
1/3 cup (80 mL) brown sugar
2 tbsp (30 mL) cornstarch
Grated rind and juice of 1 orange
2 tsp (10 mL) butter

Preparation:	. . . . **10 m**
Cooking:	. . . . **from 11 to 14 m**
Standing:	. . . .**none**

Method:

• Wash zucchini. Cut one inch (2.5 cm) off each end, then split in half lengthwise.

• Place zucchini pieces in a microwave-safe pie plate one next to the other, slightly overlapping. Add the water. Microwave at HIGH 5 to 6 minutes. Drain thoroughly.

• Place remaining ingredients in a microwave-safe bowl, stir well.

• Microwave at HIGH 2 minutes, stir until smooth and creamy. It may require another minute of cooking at HIGH.

• When ready to serve, reheat at MEDIUM 3 to 5 minutes or until bubbly hot.

Zucchini Casserole

Preparation: . . . . **10 m**
Cooking: . . . . **from 14 to 18 m**
Standing: . . . . **none**

A personal note: Economical, easy to make and quick to prepare, this dish is an interesting way to mix vegetables and minced beef or pork or lamb, or even minced leftover roast, whatever you like.

Ingredients:

2 tbsp (30 mL) vegetable oil or margarine

1 large onion, chopped fine

1/2 to 1 lb (250 to 500 g) ground meat

1 small green or red pepper, diced

1 tsp (5 mL) savory or sage

2 cups (500 g) tomatoes, peeled and diced *or* 2 cups (500 g) canned whole tomatoes, drained

1 tsp (5 mL) sugar

4 to 5 cups (1 to 1.25 L) sliced zucchini

Method:

• Place in a 6-cup (1.5 L) microwave-safe dish vegetable oil or margarine. Microwave at HIGH 1 minute.

• Add the onion, stir well. Microwave 2 minutes at HIGH, stir well. Add the meat, mix thoroughly.

• Microwave *raw ground meat,* 4 minutes at HIGH; *cooked ground meat,* 2 minutes at HIGH. Stir well.

• Add the remaining ingredients. Stir until well mixed. Cover and microwave at HIGH, 10 to 12 minutes, stirring once. Serve with **a bowl of grated cheese.**

Variation

• Replace meat with **2 cups (500 mL) of cottage cheese.** Microwave in same manner as *raw ground meat.*

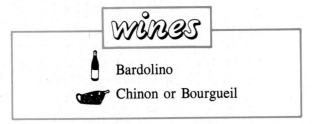

Bardolino

Chinon or Bourgueil

Winter Casserole

Preparation:	. . . .	**15 m**
Cooking:	. . . .	**25 m**
Standing:	. . . .	**none**

A personal note: An Italian speciality, this dish is nice to serve as a light meal, with a bowl of boiled rice or noodles.

Ingredients:

1/4 cup (60 mL) vegetable oil or butter

1 19-oz (540 mL) can tomatoes

4 to 5 cups (1 to 1.25 L) zucchini, unpeeled and diced

1 green pepper, diced

1 cup (250 mL) frozen green peas

1 cup (250 mL) frozen corn kernels (optional)

1 cup (250 mL) potatoes, cut in small dice

2 medium-sized onions, thinly sliced

1 tsp (5 mL) each savory and dill

1½ tsp (7 mL) salt

1/4 tsp (1 mL) pepper

Method:

• Place the oil in a 12-cup (3 L) microwave-safe bowl. Microwave at HIGH 3 minutes.

• Place all the ingredients in the hot oil.

• Stir until well mixed. Do not cover.

• Microwave at HIGH 15 minutes.

• Stir well and microwave at MEDIUM-HIGH 10 minutes.

• When served with rice or noodles, remove vegetables with a perforated spoon.

• Serve juice separately in a jug.

• Each one can use it to taste.

Valpolicella

Chianti Classico

Helpful hint: To refresh potato chips or crackers, place soggy chips or crackers on a plate and microwave 45 seconds to 1 minute at MEDIUM-HIGH. Let stand 1 minute to crisp. They are delicious with a bowl of soup.

Zucchini Casserole

Preparation:	. . . .	**10 m**
Cooking:	. . . .	**from 14 to 18 m**
Standing:	. . . .	**none**

A personal note: Economical, easy to make and quick to prepare, this dish is an interesting way to mix vegetables and minced beef or pork or lamb, or even minced leftover roast, whatever you like.

Ingredients:

2 tbsp (30 mL) vegetable oil or margarine

1 large onion, chopped fine

1/2 to 1 lb (250 to 500 g) ground meat

1 small green or red pepper, diced

1 tsp (5 mL) savory or sage

2 cups (500 g) tomatoes, peeled and diced *or* **2 cups (500 g) canned whole tomatoes, drained**

1 tsp (5 mL) sugar

4 to 5 cups (1 to 1.25 L) sliced zucchini

Method:

• Place in a 6-cup (1.5 L) microwave-safe dish vegetable oil or margarine. Microwave at HIGH 1 minute.

• Add the onion, stir well. Microwave 2 minutes at HIGH, stir well. Add the meat, mix thoroughly.

• Microwave *raw ground meat,* 4 minutes at HIGH; *cooked ground meat,* 2 minutes at HIGH. Stir well.

• Add the remaining ingredients. Stir until well mixed. Cover and microwave at HIGH, 10 to 12 minutes, stirring once. Serve with **a bowl of grated cheese.**

Variation

• Replace meat with **2 cups (500 mL) of cottage cheese.** Microwave in same manner as *raw ground meat.*

Bardolino

Chinon or Bourgueil

Endives

• Endives often are referred to as Belgian endives, simply because the Belgian type is recognized the world over as the best.

• Endives are somewhat expensive because growing them requires a lot of work and attention. In the spring, we can buy local endives; in winter, they are mostly imported from Europe and the U.S.A. They are worth every penny we pay for them.

Braised Endives

Preparation: . . . .**5 m**
Cooking: . . . .**6 m**
Standing: . . . .**none**

A personal note: Although endives are eaten mostly in salads, they are a delicious delicacy when braised.

Ingredients:

4 heads of endives

2 tbsp (30 mL) butter

1/2 tsp (2 mL) sugar

2 slices unpeeled lemon

Salt and pepper to taste

Method:

• Remove a thin slice from the root part of the endives.

• If some of the top leaves are bruised, simply remove them.

• Wash each head of endive under cold running water, without opening the inner leaves.

• Wrap in a sheet of towelling, to remove excess moisture on the top leaves.

• In a long microwave-safe dish, melt the butter 3 minutes at HIGH.

• Place the whole heads in the dish, rolling each one in the melted golden butter.

• Place the endives one next to the other, alternating thick ends and pointed ends.

• Sprinkle the whole with the sugar and top with the lemon slices.

• Do not cover. Microwave 3 minutes at HIGH.

• Turn each endive over.

• Microwave another 3 minutes at HIGH. Salt and pepper to taste.

• Remove to a serving dish. Pour the juice left in the dish over the endives and serve.

Helpful hint: Always keep your microwave oven clean. To remove any sticky spots or spills, heat 1 cup (250 mL) water for 5 minutes at HIGH. Then wipe the interior of your microwave with a soft, clean cloth. Spots should disappear.

Creamed Endives

A personal note: These are prepared the same way as braised endives, but the juice is finished as a cream sauce. Perfect to serve with roast quail or young chicken.

Preparation: . . . . 5 m
Cooking: . . . . from 10 to 11 m
Standing: . . . . none

Ingredients:

4 to 6 heads of endives

2 tbsp (30 mL) butter

1/2 tsp (2 mL) sugar

1 tsp (5 mL) fresh lemon juice

2 tsp (10 mL) flour

1 tbsp (15 mL) butter

A pinch of nutmeg

1/2 cup (125 mL) cream of your choice

Salt and pepper to taste

Method:

• Cook the endives as for Braised Endives, using fresh lemon juice instead of lemon slices. Cooking time remains the same.

• Remove the cooked endives to a warm dish.

• Blend together the flour, butter and nutmeg. Add to the cooking juice remaining in the dish, stir well.

• Add the cream, salt and pepper to taste. Microwave 3 minutes at MEDIUM-HIGH, stir well. Microwave another minute or two, or until sauce is creamy.

• Salt and pepper to taste and pour cream sauce over the endives.

• When necessary, the creamed endives may be warmed 2 to 4 minutes at MEDIUM.

Spinach

- Spinach is so versatile, with a delicate and subtle flavor and such a beautiful color, which explains why it is so popular. In the summer, when fresh herbs are easily available, flavor spinach with fresh basil, dill or tarragon. Each one is a joy!

Spinach "Nature"

To buy

• In the summer, I prefer to buy fresh spinach by the pound (500 g). In the winter, I use the fresh spinach sold in 10-oz (284 g) bags.

To keep

• Fresh spinach is a poor keeper, but the winter type, tightly packed in plastic bags, is easier to store.

• **The fresh summer type** should be refrigerated, loosely packed in a bag.

• It will keep 3 to 4 days at most in good condition.

• **The fresh winter type** is tightly packed in plastic bags.

• Make sure when buying that the spinach is fresh.

• It will keep 8 to 9 days refrigerated, preferably on a shelf rather than in the vegetable bin.

• Make sure no weight of any kind is placed on the bag.

• Fresh spinach, either summer or winter type, should always be washed in cold water.

To cook

• The leaves with or without the stems attached can be microwaved whole.

• Whether to cook the spinach whole or cut up is a matter of choice.

• What is important is to wash the spinach thoroughly in *cold* water.

• Place it in the dish you're going to cook it in without squeezing it dry, just letting the cold water pass through your fingers. Microwave according to recipe, or just for 2 to 3 minutes at HIGH, covered.

• Then pass the spinach leaves through a sieve, pressing on them with the back of a spoon.

• Keep the green water, which can be used in gravy, soup or to make a cream sauce, using half milk, half spinach water.

Cottage Cheese Spinach

Preparation: . . . . **12 m**
Cooking: . . . . **from 7 to 9 m**
Standing: . . . .**none**

A personal note: Cottage cheese, added to vegetables or pasta, always makes an interesting meal. This one is very colorful and very tasty.

Ingredients:

1 10-oz (284 g) bag fresh spinach, chopped

1 cup (250 mL) cottage cheese

2 eggs, lightly beaten

3 tbsp (50 mL) Cheddar cheese, grated

3 green onions, chopped fine

1/2 tsp (2 mL) dill weed or savory

2 tbsp (30 mL) butter

1/4 cup (60 mL) breadcrumbs

1/2 tsp (2 mL) salt

1/4 tsp (1 mL) pepper

Paprika

Method:

• Mix in a bowl the spinach, cottage cheese, eggs, 2 tablespoons of the grated cheese, green onions, dill or savory. Stir until well mixed.

• Pour into a 9-inch (23 cm) microwave-safe pie plate, cover with plastic wrap or a lid.

• Microwave 4 to 5 minutes at MEDIUM. Remove wrap or lid.

• Place butter in a microwave-safe bowl and melt 1 minute at HIGH.

• Add breadcrumbs, remaining grated cheese, salt and pepper.

• Mix together and sprinkle on top of spinach.

• Sprinkle with paprika.

• Microwave at MEDIUM-HIGH 3 to 4 minutes. Serve.

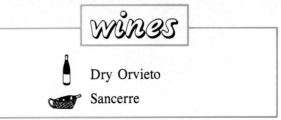

wines

Dry Orvieto

Sancerre

Spinach aux Croûtons

Preparation: . . . . **10 m**

Cooking: the meal . . . . **from 8 to 9 m**

            the sauce . . . . **from 8 to 11 m**

Standing: . . . . **none**

A personal note: This very quickly prepared spinach dish can be put together an hour or so before cooking, but should not be refrigerated.

Ingredients:

2 10-oz (284 g) bags fresh spinach

1 cup (250 mL) bread cubes

3 tbsp (50 mL) butter

2 tbsp (30 mL) flour

1 cup (250 mL) milk

1/2 tsp (2 mL) dry mustard

1/4 cup (60 mL) grated cheese

3 tbsp (50 mL) spinach water

Salt and pepper to taste

Italian Riesling

Alsatian Riesling

Method:

• Clean and microwave the spinach, covered, as for Spinach ''Nature,'' 3 minutes at HIGH.

• Drain well, reserving 3 tablespoons (50 mL) of the spinach water.

• Place the bread cubes and 1 tablespoon (15 mL) of the butter in a microwave-safe plate, stir well. Microwave 5 to 6 minutes at HIGH, or until the bread cubes have browned, stirring twice during the cooking period. Set aside.

To make the sauce

• Place remaining butter in a microwave-safe bowl and melt 2 minutes at HIGH.

• Add remaining ingredients, mix well.

• Microwave, uncovered, 3 to 4 minutes at HIGH, stirring once. Microwave at HIGH 2 to 3 minutes more or until sauce is creamy.

• Place spinach in a serving dish, pour creamy sauce over, top with the browned diced bread.

• When ready to serve, microwave 3 to 4 minutes at MEDIUM-HIGH.

Creamed Spinach
À la Française

Preparation: . . . . **8 m**
Cooking: . . . . **7 m**
Standing: . . . . **none**

A personal note: You can turn this creamed spinach dish into a very tasty soup by adding **2 cups (500 mL) of light white sauce** made with milk, or preferably with **chicken consommé.** In France, they often add **one cup of small shrimps (Matane type),** or **one cup of small fresh oysters;** stir well and microwave the whole 5 minutes at HIGH. It is amusing that with one recipe you can produce a very tasty vegetable dish or an elegant soup.

Ingredients:

1   10-oz (284 g) bag of fresh spinach
1 tbsp (15 mL) flour
2 tbsp (30 mL) butter
2 tbsp (30 mL) milk or light cream
Salt and pepper to taste
1/4 tsp (1 mL) nutmeg
A pinch of garlic powder (optional)

Method:

• Clean and microwave the spinach as for Spinach "Nature."

• Do not drain. Chop the spinach with 2 knives and add remaining ingredients, stir well to mix thoroughly. Microwave 4 minutes at HIGH, stirring twice during the cooking period.

• The mixture should be a beautiful deep green and very creamy.

• To taste, just before serving, add **1 teaspoon (5 mL) of grated lemon rind** or **1/2 teaspoon (2 mL) fresh lemon juice.**

373

Spinach Oriental

Preparation: . . . . **5 m**
Cooking: . . . . **6 m**
Standing: . . . . **none**

A personal note: I serve this dish with hot hard-cooked eggs. All of it is quickly prepared when time is at a premium and you want a well-balanced meal.

Ingredients:

1 10-oz (284 g) bag fresh spinach

2 tbsp (30 mL) vegetable oil

1 garlic clove, chopped fine

1/4 tsp (1 mL) salt

1 tsp (5 mL) sugar

1/2 tsp (2 mL) soy sauce

1 square of Tofu, broken into 4 pieces

Method:

• Clean and microwave spinach as for Spinach "Nature."

• Place all the remaining ingredients in a microwave-safe bowl or in an 8 × 8-inch (20 × 20 cm) dish.

• Mix the whole gently. Microwave 2 minutes at MEDIUM-HIGH.

• Stir again gently. Microwave 1 minute at MEDIUM. Serve.

wines

Liebfraumilch

Alsatian Gewurztraminer

Finnish Spinach Crêpe

Convection and microwave cooking

Preparation: . . . . **10 m**
Cooking: . . . . **45 m**
Standing: . . . . **none**

A personal note: It is essential to have a convetion section in your microwave oven to prepare this dish. It can be served instead of potatoes or noodles, or topped with creamed eggs, or leftover diced meat or chicken and made into a cream sauce. It can be served on either the browned side or on the white and green side.

Ingredients:

1 10-oz (284 g) bag of spinach *or*
   1 lb (500 g) of fresh summer spinach

2 tbsp (30 mL) butter

1½ cups (375 mL) milk

2 eggs

1 tsp (5 mL) salt

1/4 tsp (1 mL) nutmeg

3/4 cup (190 mL) flour

1 tsp (5 mL) baking powder

1/2 tsp (2 mL) sugar

Method:

• Wash spinach in cold water. Remove very coarse part of the stems and place spinach in a microwave-safe dish.

• Cover and microwave at HIGH 3 minutes. Pour into a colander to drain excess water. Set aside.

• Place the butter in a microwave-safe 4-cup (1 L) dish and melt 2 minutes at HIGH.

• Add the milk, beaten eggs.

• Mix together in another bowl the salt, nutmeg, flour, baking powder and sugar.

• When ready to bake, preheat convection section of the microwave oven to 400°F (200°C).

• Mix together the flour and the liquid, add the spinach, mix well.

• Butter an 8-inch (20 cm) pizza or quiche pan or a 9-inch (23 cm) glass or ceramic round plate. Pour the spinach mixture in. Place in the oven on a rack that is 4 to 5 inches (10 to 13 cm) high.

• Reset preheated oven at 375°F (190°C) and bake crêpe 40 minutes or until golden brown.

• Serve in wedges, or as you please.

Green and Wax Beans

- Fresh beans come in many shades — green, yellow, purple — and their size varies, too. When you can gather them from your own garden, the size of half a little finger, and cook them in the microwave, they are sheer delight.

- When they are picked too young, they are delectable to eat, but have very poor keeping quality. If they are picked too mature, they are tough and tasteless. So this is a vegetable that should be bought with care.

Green and Wax Beans "Nature"

To prepare for cooking

• Remove both ends of the beans, pulling out the small strings, usually along the inside curve.

• Wash and drain. Do not let them soak in water.

• They can be cooked whole, cut into lengthwise strips or cut into 1-inch (2.5 cm) pieces, cut straight or diagonally.

• As with other fresh vegetables, the maturity and size of the beans affect the cooking period.

• It is advisable to have beans of even size to cook in the microwave.

To cook

• Whole beans, depending on their size, microwave in 8 to 12 minutes per pound (500 g) at HIGH.

• Juliennes or French-cut should take 5 to 7 minutes per pound (500 g) at HIGH.

• In both cases, add 1/4 cup (60 mL) water for each pound (500 g) of beans. Microwave covered.

• Let cooked beans stand 5 minutes before draining. Then drain and add salt and butter to taste or as directed in the recipe.

• If your microwave has a Sensor function (see your oven manual), prepare the beans as above. Make sure the dish has a tight-fitting cover so the steam will not escape or use plastic wrap. Using the Sensor method, the oven does the cooking automatically and when it stops, the vegetables are ready to be drained, buttered and served.

Bean Sprouts "Nature"

Preparation: . . . . **5 m**
Cooking: . . . . **3 m**
Standing: . . . . **none**

A personal note: This is a very popular crunchy vegetable dish that can be served with all pork dishes, chops or roats, or added to any other type of green light vegetable. It's light and non-fattening.

Ingredients:

4 cups (1 L) bean sprouts
2 tbsp (30 mL) vegetable oil
1/2 tsp (2 mL) salt
1 tsp (5 mL) Kikkoman soy sauce
3 green onions, chopped fine

Method:

• Rinse bean sprouts in cold water. Drain and place in a dish. Let stand 2 minutes, then drain again, simply by placing your hand over the sprouts and tilting the dish.

• Place in a 6-to-8-cup (1.5 to 2 L) microwave-safe bowl. Microwave at HIGH 2 minutes.

• Add the remaining ingredients, stir thoroughly.

• Taste for salt. Adjust if necessary. Serve.

• If it has cooled, microwave 1 minute at HIGH.

Creamed Green or Wax Beans

Preparation:	**10 m**
Cooking:	**7 m**
Standing:	**none**

A personal note: This is a very good companion to serve with chicken or roast pork.

Ingredients:

1 lb (500 g) green or wax beans

2 tbsp (30 mL) butter

3 tbsp (50 mL) water

1/2 tsp (2 mL) basil

1/4 tsp (1 mL) sugar

1/4 cup (60 mL) light cream

Salt and pepper to taste

Method:

• Clean the beans as for Green or Wax Beans ''Nature.'' Cut into 1-inch (2.5 cm) pieces.

• Place butter in a ceramic (Corning) dish and melt 1 minute at HIGH.

• Add the cut green beans, water, basil and sugar. Stir. Cover and microwave 6 minutes at HIGH, or cook by the Sensor method.

• When cooked, drain well and add the cream, salt and pepper to taste. Microwave, covered, 1 minute at HIGH. Serve.

Green Beans À la Française

Preparation:	**10 m**
Cooking:	**10 m**
Standing:	**none**

• Cooked green beans are garnished with mushrooms and almonds in this classic of French cuisine.

Ingredients:

4 cups (1 L) green beans, cut diagonally

2 tbsp (30 mL) butter

1/4 cup (60 mL) almonds, thinly sliced

1/2 cup (125 mL) canned mushrooms, sliced and drained

1/4 tsp (1 mL) savory

1 tsp (5 mL) lemon juice

* 4 cups (1 L) is approximately 1 pound (500 g).

Method:

• Microwave green beans as for Green or Wax Beans ''Nature.''

• Place the butter in a microwave-safe serving dish and melt 40 seconds at HIGH. Add the almonds. Microwave 2 minutes at HIGH, stir well.

• Add the mushrooms, stir. Microwave 2 minutes at HIGH.

• Add the cooked beans, salt and pepper to taste, the savory and lemon juice. Stir to mix.

• Warm 30 seconds at HIGH.

Green Beans Lyonnaise

Preparation:	**10 m**
Cooking:	**11 m**
Standing:	**none**

• The combination of melted onions and crusty croûtons has made the reputation of vegetables Lyonnaise.

Ingredients:

1 lb (500 g) green or wax beans

1/4 cup (60 mL) chicken consommé or water

1/4 tsp (1 mL) thyme

1/2 tsp (2 mL) salt

1/4 tsp (1 mL) pepper

2 tbsp (30 mL) butter

1 cup (250 mL) onions, thinly sliced

1 tbsp (15 mL) butter

1 cup (250 mL) fresh bread cubes

Method:

• Cut green beans into slivers. Place in a 4-cup (1 L) microwave-safe casserole dish with the chicken consommé or water and the thyme, cover.

• Microwave at HIGH 8 minutes. Drain liquid. Keep beans covered.

• Place the 2 tablespoons (30 mL) butter in a microwave-safe dish and melt 1 minute at HIGH.

• Add the onions, stir. Microwave 2 minutes at HIGH, stir well. Salt and pepper to taste, stir. Pour over the green beans.

• Place 1 tablespoon (15 mL) butter in a microwave-safe pie plate and melt 1 minute at HIGH.

• Add the bread cubes. Stir until well coated with the butter. Microwave, uncovered, 1 minute at HIGH. Stir well.

• Microwave 30 to 40 seconds or until browned inside (break one to check as they remain pale on the outside). They should be crisp, buttery and flavorful. Pour over the onions.

• If needed, warm up the whole dish, covered with waxed paper, 1 minute at HIGH. Serve.

Wax Beans
À la Russe

Preparation: .... **10 m**
Cooking: .... **from 13 to 14 m**
Standing: .... **none**

A personal note: I serve this dish cold in the summer and warm on cold days. It's perfect to serve with thinly sliced cold roast.

Ingredients:

1 lb (500 g) wax or green beans

1/4 cup (60 mL) water or consommé

1/2 cup (125 mL) chicken stock or consommé

1/4 cup (60 mL) green onions, minced

1 small garlic clove, chopped fine

1/2 tsp (2 mL) paprika

1/2 tsp (2 mL) salt

1/2 tsp (2 mL) sugar

2 tbsp (30 mL) cider or red wine vinegar

1/2 cup (125 mL) walnuts, chopped fine

2 tbsp (30 mL) fresh parsley, chopped fine

Method:

• Remove the ends of the beans as for Green and Wax Beans "Nature."

• Leave beans whole. Place in a microwave-safe dish, add the water or consommé.

• Cover, microwave at HIGH 8 to 9 minutes.

• Check beans for tenderness. If necessary, microwave them 1 to 2 minutes more.

• When ready, let stand covered.

• Make the sauce by placing the chicken stock or consommé in a large microwave-safe measuring cup or bowl, add the green onions, garlic, paprika, salt, sugar, cider or red wine vinegar.

• Stir well. Microwave 3 minutes at MEDIUM-HIGH.

• Add the walnuts and parsley, stir.

• Pour over the cooked beans and serve hot or let them cool, but do not refrigerate.

Vegetarian Luncheon Plate

Preparation:	. . . .	**10 m**
Cooking:	. . . .	**from 19 to 21 m**
Standing:	. . . .	**none**

 Mâcon Blanc

 Rheingau Riesling Kabinett

A personal note: This is a true late summer dish, when green or wax beans and the little red potatoes are on the market. The flavor is very interesting. This dish can also be cooked ahead of time, as it reheats very well.

Ingredients:

1 lb (500 g) green or wax beans, cut into 1/2-inch (1.5 cm) pieces

1/2 cup (125 mL) chicken consommé or water

1 lb (500 g) small red potatoes, peeled and finely diced

The sauce:

2 tbsp (30 mL) butter

2 tbsp (30 mL) flour

1 cup (250 mL) liquid (cooking liquid plus milk or cream)

Salt and pepper to taste

Method:

• Cut the green or wax beans. Place them in a microwave-safe dish, add the chicken consommé or water, cover and microwave at HIGH 8 to 9 minutes or until they are tender. Set aside.

• Peel, wash and dice the potatoes, place in a dish.

• When the beans are cooked, drain their water over the potatoes. Stir well, cover and microwave at HIGH 6 to 8 minutes or until tender. Stir and test for doneness with a fork. Do not cook them too soft.

• Drain the potatoes' liquid into a 1-cup (250 mL) measuring cup. Fill cup with milk or light cream.

• Place the butter in a microwave-safe bowl and melt 1 minute at HIGH.

• Add the flour, mix well. Add the liquid, mix and microwave 2 minutes at HIGH. Stir well. Microwave another 2 minutes at MEDIUM. Salt and pepper to taste.

• Mix the cooked beans and potatoes together, pour the sauce over. Adjust seasoning. Serve.

Corn

• Corn on the cob is the only way we can buy fresh corn. You will not know how good corn can be until you've eaten it cooked in the microwave oven, but that is a late summer pleasure; the rest of the year we can enjoy frozen corn prepared in many interesting ways. There is also canned creamed corn that can be used in soups, in Shepherd's Pie and many other ways.

Corn on the Cob "Nature"

To buy

- When buying corn, choose ears of the same size when possible.

- Generally, corn with big, deep yellow kernels is mature corn and has a high starch content.

- The best ears of corn are those with a pale yellow color and smaller kernels.

- Fresh corn with husk will keep 4 to 5 days refrigerated, but it is sweeter and tastier when eaten as soon as possible after being picked.

- I have a favorite, fairly new on the market, named Peaches and Cream. It has an odd name for corn but it is superb to eat.

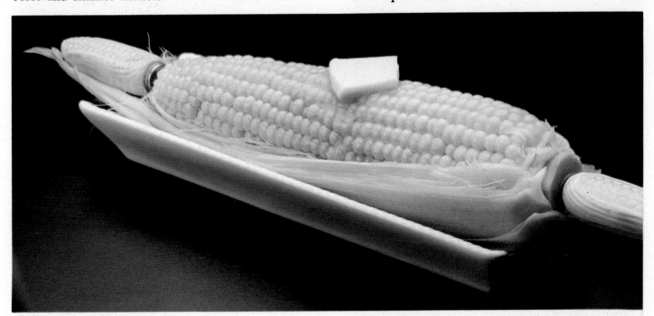

To prepare for cooking

- There are two methods to prepare to microwave corn on the cob.

The first method

- To cook corn in the husk, pull the husk back carefully and remove all the silk, then replace the husk.

- Remove the first 5 or 6 top leaves and cut the hard knob at the bottom of the ear.

The second method

- Remove all the husks and silk, then wrap each ear of corn in plastic wrap.

To cook by either method

- Place 6 to 8 ears of corn, prepared as above, in a circle with the small point of the cob toward the middle of the turntable.

- To cook them, count 2 minutes at HIGH for the first ear of corn and 1 minute each for the others.

- So, if you have 6 ears of corn, the cooking period will be 7 minutes at HIGH.

- If your microwave has no turntable, move corn around after the first 3 minutes of cooking.

- If you have a large quantity or corn to cook, proceed in the following manner: start with 8 ears of corn wrapped in plastic wrap.

- When cooked, remove to a basket lined with a folded napkin. Cover basket with a terry cloth.

- Cook remaining corn.

- Place the next batch of corn on top of the first, cover, and so on.

- The cooked ears of corn will stay piping hot for 25 to 35 minutes — and how delicious!

Swiss Cheese Corn Casserole

Convection or microwave cooking

• Many years ago, while travelling in Switzerland, I was served this casserole. I enjoyed it so much I asked for the recipe. Now that I can microwave the fresh ears of corn, the dish is twice as good.

Preparation:	....	12 m
Cooking:	microwave:	15 m
	convection:	from 30 to 35 m
Standing:	....	8 m

A personal note: It is a meal in itself, or serve it with meatballs or chicken legs.

Ingredients:

6 ears of corn

1/2 cup (125 mL) light cream or milk

1 egg, beaten

4 green onions, chopped fine

1/2 tsp (2 mL) salt

1/4 tsp (1 mL) pepper

1 cup (250 mL) Swiss cheese, grated

1/2 cup (125 mL) cracker crumbs

1 tbsp (15 mL) butter

Method:

• Microwave ears of corn as for Corn on the Cob "Nature."

• Unwrap or remove husks, let cool 10 minutes, then cut corn from the cobs.

• Add the cream or milk, beaten egg, green onions, salt and pepper and the grated Swiss cheese. Stir until well mixed.

• Butter an 8 × 7-inch (20 × 18 cm) casserole dish and pour in the corn mixture.

• Stir the cracker crumbs with the butter and sprinkle over the corn. Microwave at MEDIUM-HIGH 6 to 8 minutes. Let stand 8 minutes before serving.

• If your microwave oven has a convection cooking cycle, you can bake this casserole at 350°F (180°C) 30 to 35 minutes.

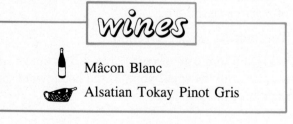

wines

Mâcon Blanc

Alsatian Tokay Pinot Gris

Quick and Easy Fresh Corn Relish

Preparation: . . . . **10 m**
Cooking: . . . . **7 m**
Standing: . . . . **none**

A personal note: This relish is nice to serve with any type or roasted meat. I also like to add one tablespoon or two (15 or 30 mL) to a green salad. This relish will keep 3 to 4 months refrigerated.

Ingredients:

1 green pepper, diced

4 to 5 celery stalks, diced

3 tbsp (50 mL) water

2 large onions, chopped fine

3 to 4 cups (750 mL to 1 L) corn cut from cooked or uncooked ears of corn

1/4 cup (60 mL) sugar

1 tbsp (15 mL) salt

1 tbsp (15 mL) mustard seeds

1/2 cup (125 mL) white or cider vinegar

1/2 cup (125 mL) water

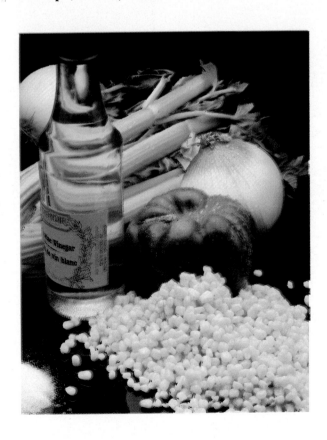

Method:

• Place in an 8-cup (2 L) microwave-safe dish the green pepper, celery and the 3 tablespoons (50 mL) of water. Stir.

• Cover and microwave at HIGH 2 minutes.

• Add the onions and corn. Microwave at MEDIUM 2 minutes.

• Add the remaining ingredients, stir until well mixed. Microwave at MEDIUM 3 minutes. Stir well. Pour into a jar.

• Keep refrigerated. Serve cold.

Corn and Cabbage

Preparation: . . . . 7 m
Cooking: . . . . 11 m
Standing: . . . . , 5 m

A personal note: A traditional Québec autumn speciality, serve this dish with sausages or cold roast pork.

Ingredients:

5 to 6 slices of bacon

2 tbsp (30 mL) margarine

1/4 cup (60 mL) water

2½ cups (625 mL) corn cut from the cob or frozen corn

2 cups (500 mL) cabbage, shredded

1/2 tsp (2 mL) savory

1/2 tsp (2 mL) salt

1/4 tsp (1 mL) pepper

1 tbsp (15 mL) sugar

Method:

- Place bacon on a microwave-safe rack or on 2 sheets of white paper towelling.

- Microwave at HIGH 3 to 4 minutes or until crisp. Crumble and set aside.

- Place the margarine in a 4-cup (1 L) microwave-safe dish and melt 2 minutes at HIGH.

- Add the water, corn, cabbage, savory, salt, pepper and sugar.

- Stir until thoroughly mixed.

- Cover. Microwave at HIGH 4 minutes.

- Stir and let stand 5 minutes.

- The cabbage and corn must remain a little crunchy.

- Top with bacon.

- Microwave 1 minute at HIGH.

Turnips

• Turnips have been eaten throughout history. When potatoes appeared, they quickly took over. I can assure you that turnips cooked in the microwave will surprise you by its delicate flavor, and it will not leave a smell in the kitchen.

Turnips "Nature"

To keep

• Simply place turnips in a loosely closed bag in the vegetable bin or on a shelf in the refrigerator.

• They will keep for as long as five to six weeks.

To peel

• As turnip skin is bitter, always peel it thickly.

• There is a very visible line between the skin and the pulp of the turnip. This line must be removed to avoid the bitterness.

• Then cut or prepare turnips as indicated in your recipe.

To cook

• Turnips can be cooked whole.

• Superb when wrapped in plastic wrap and micro-waved (see recipe), diced, sliced or even grated.

• Flavor with a pinch of sugar, a generous amount of pepper, dill seeds, or fresh dill when available, orange or lemon rind, bay leaves and allspice, after cooking.

A personal note: It is important, when cut or sliced, to stir turnip once or twice during the cooking period.

Wrapped Turnip

Preparation:	**5 m**
Cooking:	**12 m**
Standing:	**none**

A personal note: This is an easy and tasty way to microwave turnip. In summer, I replace the parsley with fresh chopped chives or dill weed or a head of dill.

Ingredients:

1   1-to-2-lb (500 g-1 kg) turnip
1/4 tsp (1 mL) sugar
1 tsp (5 mL) soft butter or margarine
Salt and pepper to taste

Method:

• Cut a 1-pound (500 g) turnip in half, a 2-pound (1 kg) turnip in four sections.

• Peel each one as for Turnips "Nature."

• If you wish to use parsley and butter, place the parsley on a piece of plastic wrap.

- Place turnip on top.

- Spread the soft butter on the cut side.

- Sprinkle with sugar.

- Wrap each piece of turnip separately, making sure it is all covered.

- Place on a microwave-safe rack.

- Microwave 3 minutes per quarter at HIGH, which would be 3 minutes for one quarter of turnip, 6 minutes for two, and so on, so four quarters would microwave in 12 minutes.

- To serve, unwrap, slice or mash. Salt and pepper to taste.

- It may also be reheated about 2 minutes at MEDIUM-HIGH.

Mashed Turnip

Preparation: . . . . **9 m**
Cooking: . . . . **from 15 to 18 m**
Standing: . . . . **none**

A personal note: The French always add potatoes to their mashed turnip, which gives it quite a different texture and flavor.

Ingredients:

1   1½-to-2-lb (750 g-1 kg) turnip
4 medium-sized potatoes, peeled and sliced
1/2 cup (125 mL) consommé or water
1/2 tsp (2 mL) sugar
1/4 tsp (1 mL) pepper
1 tsp (5 mL) savory
2 to 3 tbsp (30 to 50 mL) butter

Method:

• Peel the turnip and cut into thin slices as for Turnips "Nature."

• Add to the potatoes. Pour the consommé or the water on top.

• Add the sugar, pepper and savory. Stir to mix. Cover. Microwave at HIGH 12 to 14 minutes.

• Stir after 10 minutes and check the tenderness of the vegetables. When done, drain through a sieve, reserving the liquid.

• Add the butter and mash the vegetables. Adjust salt and pepper. If a little liquid is needed, use the reserved cooking water, adding a spoonful at a time.

• This can be prepared ahead of time and kept at room temperature.

• To warm, microwave at MEDIUM-HIGH 3 to 4 minutes, uncovered.

Helpful hint: To prepare croutons, place 2 cups (500 mL) of bread cubes in a pie plate and microwave 3 to 4 minutes at HIGH, stirring a few times.

My Mashed Turnip

Preparation: . . . . **8 m**
Cooking: . . . . **from 15 to 17 m**
Standing: . . . . **none**

A personal note: I always enjoy sour cream with mashed vegetables, including turnip. To serve as a vegetarian main course, I add to the mashed turnip a container of cottage cheese.

Ingredients:

1 medium-sized turnip
1/2 tsp (2 mL) sugar
1/2 cup (125 mL) water
2 tbsp (30 mL) butter
1/4 tsp (1 mL) pepper
3 tbsp (50 mL) sour cream
Salt to taste
3 tbsp (50 mL) minced parsley

Method:

• Peel the turnip as for Turnips "Nature" and slice thinly. Place in a microwave-safe dish with the sugar and water. Cover. Microwave at HIGH 12 to 14 minutes. Stir after 10 minutes and check the doneness. When cooked, drain.

• Add the remaining ingredients to the turnip. Mash and beat until creamy. Adjust pepper and salt.

• Turnip can take quite a bit of pepper.

• To reheat, microwave covered 3 minutes at MEDIUM.

Frank's Honeyed Turnip

Preparation: . . . . 7 m
Cooking: . . . . from 15 to 20 m
Standing: . . . . none

• This recipe is from a friend who is a pretty good cook besides producing the best honey I have ever tasted and the biggest, most perfect blueberries.

Ingredients:

1   1-to-1½-lb (500 g-750 g) turnip
1/2 cup (125 mL) water
3 tbsp (50 mL) honey
Grated rind of 1/2 a lemon
1 tbsp (15 mL) fresh lemon juice
1 tbsp (15 mL) butter
Salt and pepper to taste

Method:

• Pare as for Turnips ''Nature'' and slice the turnip into thin slices. Place in a microwave-safe dish with all the ingredients, except the salt and pepper.

• Stir well, cover. Microwave at HIGH 10 to 14 minutes, depending on the size of the turnip. Stir twice during the cooking period, and check doneness of the turnip.

• Drain the liquid from the cooked turnip into a microwave-safe bowl. Microwave the liquid at HIGH until it is reduced to about 1/4 cup (60 mL).

• Pour over the turnip. Salt and pepper to taste.

Onions

- All the kitchens of the world use onions. They are surely the most universal of all vegetables. Way back, even before the dawn of civilization, mankind was eating onions. They are an integral part of medicinal folklore and rare are those who have never used them.

- The onion family comprises more than one kind of onion. The stronger yellow or white types are used in cooking. The red onion has a sweeter flavor and is used in salads or dishes calling for raw onions to give a light flavor. Then come the green onions — small, mild and very tasty. They can be used raw in salads or in Chinese dishes. The French shallots, small onions with a deep yellow skin, are more difficult to find and usually are expensive. They have a mild garlic flavor and are not to be confused with small white pickling onions. They are superb and may be used raw or cooked.

- One pound (500 g) whole onions = 2 cups (500 mL) chopped onions.

German
Onion Pie

Convection or microwave cooking

• I was served this delicious pie in Germany, at the Canadian Army Officers' Mess. The cook graciously gave me his recipe. The pie was served as a light meal with a dish of hot bacon and wonderful rolls.

Ingredients:

**Pastry of your choice to cover a
   10-inch (25 cm) pie plate**

3 tbsp (50 mL) butter

**3 cups (750 mL) onions, peeled and thinly
   sliced**

**1/2 cup (125 mL) milk or half cream and
   half milk**

1½ cups (375 mL) sour cream

2 eggs, well beaten

3 tbsp (50 mL) flour

1 tsp (5 mL) dill seeds or thyme

7 or 8 bacon slices

Method:

• Line a microwave-safe pie plate with the rolled pastry of your choice.

• Preheat the convection section of your microwave oven to 400°F (200°C). Bake pastry 10 to 15 minutes or until golden brown. Or cook it in the microwave at HIGH for 3 minutes. It will not brown in the microwave, which is why I advise the convection method, if possible.

• Place the butter in an 8-cup (2 L) microwave-safe dish. Microwave at HIGH 3 minutes. The butter will be brown here and there.

• Add the sliced onions. Stir well and microwave 8 to 9 minutes at HIGH, stirring once. Pour onions into cooked pastry shell.

• Stir together the remaining ingredients, except the bacon slices. Pour over the onion mixture in the cooked pie shell. Bake in the microwave oven at MEDIUM until firm in the centre, which should take about 12 to 15 minutes.

Prepa
Cooki
Standi

• Place t
a single la
until crisp

• Place

Onions "Nature"

To keep

• Onions of all types should be stored in a dark, cool, dry place to prevent excess moisture that causes sprouting.

• They should be removed from plastic bags and placed in a basket or container. Under these conditions, they will keep as long as 3 months.

• Yellow onions can be stored the longest, which explains why they are always available in the winter. Do not refrigerate onions.

• Green onions will keep up to 2 weeks in a plastic bag, refrigerated in the vegetable bin. Untie them if they are bought in little bunches.

To prepare for cooking

• There are so many ways to cut an onion that you should simply follow the instructions given in the recipe. However, it is important to know how to peel it, depending on how you wish to use it.

• Cut off the end of the neck of the onion so that the top will be even and neat.

• Then cut a slice in the bottom and make a slit on one side of the onion and pull off the skin.

• Finally, chop, slice or whatever your recipe calls for.

• If the onion is to be used whole, proceed as follows: remove top of the onion as above, then remove the tiny core at the root end; the onion can then be cooked whole and will not break up.

To cook a whole onion

• Whether they are to be cooked whole with meat, to be added to a cooked dish or to be used as garnish, peel as above.

• Place the onions one next to the other in a microwave-safe pie plate or dish. Top each one with a little pinch of sugar and a small piece of butter.

• If you wish to add an herb flavor to the onion, add a pinch of savory or dill on top of the butter.

2 onions will take about 3 to 4 minutes at HIGH; however, check doneness after 2 minutes.

4 onions will take about 5 to 8 minutes at HIGH. Verify as above.

6 onions will take about 9 to 11 minutes at HIGH. Verify as above.

• When cooking any of the quantities given above, *but sliced,* microwave at HIGH for about the same times as given above, but stir twice during the cooking period.

To boil

• To boil small or medium-sized onions [1 pound (500 g) left whole], cover to half with hot water, cover dish, microwave at HIGH 7 to 9 minutes.

• Test doneness with the point of a small knife when 2 minutes are left.

Melted Onions

Preparation: . . . . 10 m
Cooking: . . . . from 6 to 8 m
Standing: . . . . none

A personal note: Delicious served "as is" or added to a white sauce or to the gravy of a roasted chicken or turkey, or to cooked carrots or turnips or noodles. In other words, this is a very versatile recipe.

Ingredients:

6 medium-sized yellow or red onions*
1/4 cup (60 mL) butter or margarine
1/2 tsp (2 mL) sugar
1/4 tsp (1 mL) pepper
Salt to taste

Yellow onions are stronger than red onions, so choose the onions according to your preference.

Method:

• Peel the onions as for Onions "Nature" and cut into round slices, thinly or thickly, as you prefer.
• Place the butter or margarine in an 8-cup (2 L) microwave-safe dish and melt at HIGH 3 minutes. The butter will be golden brown.
• Microwave only 1 minute if you prefer to have just melted butter with a natural color.
• Add the onions, sugar and pepper.
• Stir well, cover and microwave 6 to 8 minutes at HIGH, stirring once after 5 minutes.
• The onions should be soft but not mushy.
• When ready, salt to taste.
• Serve or use as suggested above.

Oni...

Convec...

Prepar...
Cookin...

Standi...

A perso...
for this
contrast
ions are

Ingredi...

1/4 cup (
4 cups (1
2 eggs, b
1 cup (25
Salt and
2/3 cup (

Method...

• Place th
plate and
• The but
• Add the
• Microw
ring once
• Beat to
pepper.
• Add to
• Adjust
• Microw
• To bake
preheat the
the oven

Onions Amandine

Preparation: . . . . 7 m
Cooking: . . . . from 18 to 24 m
Standing: . . . . none

A personal note: Melted onions topped with a white sauce and garnished with toasted almonds are perfect to serve with all fish dishes or roast chicken.

Ingredients:

4 large yellow onions, peeled and cut in half
4 tbsp (60 mL) butter

The sauce:

2 tbsp (30 mL) butter
2 tbsp (30 mL) flour
1 cup (250 mL) milk
1/2 cup (125 mL) Cheddar cheese, grated
2 tbsp (30 mL) vermouth or Madeira wine
Salt and pepper to taste
1/4 to 1/2 cup (60 to 125 mL) almonds, slivered

Method:

• Place onions in a 4-cup (1 L) microwave-safe dish with the 4 tablespoons (60 mL) butter.
• Cover and microwave at HIGH 6 to 8 minutes, stirring once.
• Place the 2 tablespoons (30 mL) butter in a microwave-safe bowl. Melt 1 minute at HIGH. Add the flour, mix well.
• Add the milk, stir. Microwave at MEDIUM-HIGH 3 to 4 minutes, or until creamy, stirring once.
• Add to the sauce the cheese, vermouth or Madeira wine. Salt and pepper to taste.
• Microwave 3 minutes at HIGH, stirring twice.
• Pour creamy sauce over the onions; do not mix.
• Place the almonds in a microwave-safe dish. Brown in the microwave at HIGH 3 to 4 minutes, stirring twice.
• Pour the browned almonds over the sauce.
• Microwave 3 to 4 minutes at MEDIUM-HIGH when ready to serve.

Boiled Onions with Currant Sauce

Preparation: . . . . 10 m
Cooking: . . . . from 15 to 17 m
Standing: . . . . none

A personal note: This is an unusual and very tasty way to serve onions with fried fish or roasted veal or sausages.

Ingredients:

6 to 8 medium-sized onions
1/2 cup (125 mL) dry currants
1½ cups (375 mL) water
2 tbsp (30 mL) butter
1½ tbsp (22 mL) flour
Juice and grated rind of 1 lemon

Method:

• Peel the onions. Cut into slices and break into rings. Place in a microwave-safe dish. Do not add any liquid.
• Cover and microwave 2 minutes at HIGH.
• To prepare Currant Sauce, place the currants and water in a microwave-safe dish, microwave 7 minutes at HIGH.
• Meanwhile, mix together the butter and flour. Add the lemon rind and juice to the currants, then stir in the flour and butter mixture. Mix well.
• Microwave at MEDIUM-HIGH 4 to 5 minutes, stirring twice.
• When sauce is creamy and cooked, pour over the onion slices.
• Salt to taste.
• These can be prepared ahead of time and kept at room temperature, covered.
• When ready to serve, reheat at MEDIUM-HIGH 2 to 3 minutes. Stir and serve.

Honey Glazed Onions

Preparation: . . . . 6 m
Cooking: . . . . from 16 to 18 m
Standing: . . . . none

A personal note: Serve these onions with roast pork or ham. They're also excellent with all types of roasted birds, especially duck and goose.

Ingredients:

6 to 8 medium-sized onions

2 tbsp (30 mL) water

1/4 cup (60 mL) honey

2 tbsp (30 mL) butter

Grated rind of 1/2 a lemon

1 tbsp (15 mL) lemon juice

1 tsp (5 mL) cider vinegar

Salt and pepper to taste

Method:

• Peel the onions, leaving them whole, as for Onions "Nature."

• Place in a 10-cup (2.5 L) microwave-safe dish.

• Add the water, cover and microwave 10 to 12 minutes at HIGH.

• Stir after 8 minutes of cooking.

• Test tenderness of onions with the point of a paring knife.

• Drain through a sieve, reserving the water.

• Place the remaining ingredients, except the salt and pepper, and the reserved water in the dish used for cooking the onions.

• Microwave 3 minutes at HIGH.

• Stir well. Add the well-drained onions, stir. Do not cover.

• Microwave 3 minutes at HIGH, stirring every minute.

• The onions should be soft, with a shiny glaze.

• Salt and pepper to taste.

• They are easy to reheat. Keep at room temperature and when ready to serve, microwave 3 minutes at MEDIUM, stirring once.

Smothered Onions

<table>
<tr><td>Preparation:</td><td>. **9 m**</td></tr>
<tr><td>Cooking:</td><td>. . . . . **from 6 to 8 m**</td></tr>
<tr><td>Standing:</td><td>. . . . .**none**</td></tr>
</table>

A personal note: Whenever you can find small white onions, especially in the autumn, serve these as they do in Belgium, with broiled beef patties and french fried tomatoes.

Ingredients:

2 lb (1 kg) small white onions

4 tbsp (60 mL) vegetable oil

4 tbsp (60 mL) bacon drippings

1/4 tsp (1 mL) celery salt

Salt and pepper to taste

1/4 cup (60 mL) fresh parsley, chopped fine (optional)

Method:

• Clean and remove skins from the small onions.

• This is quickly done if you cover them with boiling water, let them stand 5 minutes, drain and peel, cutting first the top and very little of the bottom so the onions do not break when cooking.

• Place the cleaned onions in a 4-cup (1 L) microwave-safe dish.

• Pour the oil and the bacon drippings on top.

• Cover and microwave at HIGH 6 to 8 minutes, stirring twice.

• It is important that the onions remain a little crunchy.

• Add the remaining ingredients, toss until well blended. Serve hot or tepid.

Onions Gratinés
Convection and microwave cooking

<table>
<tr><td>Preparation:</td><td>. . . . .**8 m**</td></tr>
<tr><td>Cooking:</td><td>. . . . . **from 28 to 33 m**</td></tr>
<tr><td>Standing:</td><td>. . . . .**none**</td></tr>
</table>

A personal note: If your microwave oven has a convection section, try these onions. One of the famous dishes of French cuisine, serve this with roast meat.

Ingredients:

6 to 8 medium-sized onions

2 tbsp (30 mL) butter

2 tbsp (30 mL) vegetable oil

Salt, pepper and nutmeg to taste

3 tbsp (50 mL) whipping cream

4 tbsp (60 mL) Swiss cheese, grated

1 tbsp (15 mL) butter

Method:

• Peel the onions as for Onions "Nature" and chop them fine.

• Place the 2 tablespoons (30 mL) butter in a 4-cup (1 L) microwave-safe dish. Add the oil and microwave 3 minutes at HIGH.

• Add the onions, stir until well mixed with the hot fat.

• Cover and microwave 3 minutes at HIGH.

• Stir well. Add salt, pepper and nutmeg to taste. Stir.

• Pour the whole into a Pyrex or Corning pie plate.

• Top with the grated cheese mixed with the cream and dot with the last tablespoon of butter.

• Preheat the convection section of your microwave oven to 400°F (200°C).

• Place onion dish on a rack and bake for 25 to 30 minutes or until the top cheese is a golden color.

Baked Onions with Dressing

Preparation: . . . . **12 m**
Cooking: . . . . **from 10 to 11 m**
Standing: . . . . **from 10 to 15 m**

A personal note: I often serve these garnished with buttered spinach, as a vegetable dish with roast pork or ham, or I serve them hot or at room temperature as a cooked salad.

Ingredients:

6 medium-sized onions
1 green pepper, cut into long strips
1/2 cup (125 mL) hot water
1 whole garlic clove, peeled
2 bay leaves

Dressing:

1/2 cup (125 mL) vegetable oil
Juice of 1/2 a lemon
1/2 tsp (2 mL) dry mustard
1/4 tsp (1 mL) each salt and pepper

Method:

• Peel the onions as for Onions ''Nature.'' Score each one on both sides with the point of a knife.

• Place them one next to the other in a microwave-safe dish. Cover with a lid or plastic wrap and microwave at HIGH 8 to 9 minutes. Let rest 10 minutes.

• In another microwave-safe dish place the green pepper, water, garlic and bay leaves. Microwave at HIGH 2 minutes.

• Drain and add to the onions.

• Mix the ingredients given for the dressing. Pour over the onions and green pepper. Stir gently and let rest at room temperature 10 to 15 minutes.

Green Onions on Toast

Preparation: . . . . **7 m**
Cooking: . . . . **6 m**
Standing: . . . . **none**

A personal note: This is a year-round pleasure, as fresh green onions are always available. Serve as an entrée or with cold cuts.

Ingredients:

2 to 3 bunches of green onions
2 tbsp (30 mL) butter
2 tbsp (30 mL) water
Salt and pepper to taste
3 tbsp (50 mL) chopped fresh parsley
4 pieces of buttered toast

Method:

• Cut onions so they will be just the right length to place on the toast. Clean them.

• Place butter in a microwave-safe dish long enough to place the onions without cutting them. An 8-inch (20 cm) Pyrex bread pan is what I like to use.

• Microwave 3 minutes at HIGH.

• Add the water, stir. Top with the prepared onions, all the white heads together.

• Salt and pepper to taste. Sprinkle with the parsley.

• Cover and microwave 6 minutes at MEDIUM-HIGH.

• Divide equally on the buttered toast.

Variation

• Pour a spoonful or two of grated cheese on top of each piece of toast.

• Place on a microwave rack.

• Microwave 1 minute 30 seconds at MEDIUM-HIGH. Serve.

My Favorite Onion Quiche

Convection and microwave cooking

Preparation: . . . . **15 m**
Cooking: . . . . **from 43 to 48 m**
Standing: . . . .**none**

A personal note: This is the perfect hot buffet dish. I find it is wise to make two instead of one.

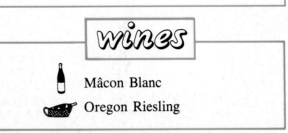

wines

Mâcon Blanc

Oregon Riesling

Ingredients:

Pastry of your choice for a 9 or 10-inch (23 or 25 cm) pie plate

4 tbsp (60 mL) butter

6 medium-sized onions

1 tsp (5 mL) salt

1/2 tsp (2 mL) pepper

1/4 tsp (1 mL) thyme

1 cup (250 mL) Gruyère cheese, grated

3/4 cup (190 mL) milk

3/4 cup (190 mL) cream

6 eggs

Method:

• Preheat the convection part of your microwave oven to 400°F (200°C).

• Line the microwave-safe pie plate with rolled pastry. Bake about 10 minutes or until golden brown.

• Place the butter in a 4-cup (1 L) microwave-safe dish and melt 1 minute at HIGH.

• Add the peeled and thinly sliced onions. Stir well. Microwave at HIGH 8 minutes, stirring once.

• Drain the onions if they have become watery.

• Add salt, pepper and thyme. Stir.

• Spread half the cheese on the cooked bottom crust. Pour half the onions over the cheese. Cover with the remaining cheese and top with the remaining onions.

• Beat together the milk, cream and eggs and pour over the onions. Bake at 400°F (200°C) 25 to 30 minutes or until custard is set.

• Serve hot or cooled, but not refrigerated.

Parsnips

• The parsnip is a member of the carrot family. It looks like a large white carrot, broad at the top and narrowing quickly.

Parsnips "Nature"

To buy

• Autumn is the beginning of the parsnip season, but it is only after the first frost that their starch changes to sugar, which makes them sweet and flavorful.

• Choose them firm, creamy white and without brown spots.

To keep

• If a bunch is tied together, untie them, leave 1 inch (2.5 cm) of green stem and place them loosely in a bag. Do not tie.

• They keep refrigerated from 3 to 6 weeks.

To prepare for cooking

• Cut a thick slice at the top so only creamy white

flesh remains. Do the same at the tip, then peel. Depending on the recipe, leave them whole or halve, slice or dice them.

To cook whole

• Use a microwave-safe loaf pan dish. Place the

parsnips so you alternate broad and narrow ends at both ends of the dish.

• Add **1/4 cup (60 mL) water.** Cover with waxed paper or plastic wrap.

• One pound (500 g) parsnips cooked whole will take about 9 to 10 minutes at HIGH. Check doneness with the tip of a pointed knife.

To cook them thinly sliced or cut into small sticks

• Place the parsnips in a microwave-safe dish. Add 1/4 cup (60 mL) water for each 2 to 3 cups (500 to 750 mL) of parsnips.

• Microwave 6 to 7 minutes at HIGH. Stir once during the cooking period.

Parsnips À l'Espagnole

Preparation: . . . . **10 m**
Cooking: . . . . **from 9 to 12 m**
Standing: . . . . **from 5 to 8 m**

A personal note: This is a very interesting way to serve parsnips. In Spain they use Seville bitter oranges, but as they are not readily available, I use whatever oranges I can find.

Ingredients:

6 to 8 medium-sized parsnips

1/4 cup (60 mL) water

2 tbsp (30 mL) butter

1 tsp (5 mL) cornstarch

1/4 cup (60 mL) brown sugar

1/2 tsp (2 mL) salt

1/4 tsp (1 mL) pepper

1/4 cup (60 mL) fresh orange juice

Grated rind of 1/2 an orange

Method:

• Wash and peel parsnips as for Parsnips "Nature."

• Cut into sticks. Place in a microwave-safe dish. Add the water. Stir well.

• Microwave 6 to 8 minutes at HIGH, stirring after 5 minutes of cooking. Check doneness with the point of a knife.

• When done, remove from microwave and let stand 5 to 8 minutes.

• Place the butter in a microwave-safe bowl and melt 1 minute at HIGH.

• Add the remaining ingredients, stir well. Microwave at HIGH 3 minutes, stirring twice. Drain the cooked parsnips. Pour orange sauce over. Stir well.

• When ready to serve, microwave 3 to 4 minutes at MEDIUM-HIGH, stirring once.

Mashed Parsnips

A personal note: Whenever I have medium, even-sized parsnips, I like to prepare them this way. I sometimes add 1 or 2 medium-sized potatoes, cooked and mashed.

Preparation: . . . . **8 m**
Cooking: . . . . **from 12 to 14 m**
Standing: . . . . **none**

Ingredients:

1 lb (500 g) medium-sized parsnips

2 medium-sized potatoes (optional)

6 green onions, chopped fine *or*
  1 small onion, chopped

1/4 cup (60 mL) water or chicken broth

1 tbsp (15 mL) flour

1/4 tsp (1 mL) savory or dill herb

Salt and pepper to taste

2 tbsp (30 mL) butter

2 tbsp (30 mL) cream or milk

Method:

• Pare, wash and slice the parsnips as for Parsnips "Nature." Peel and slice the potatoes, if to be added.

• Place in a microwave-safe dish the parsnips, potatoes, green onions or onion, water or chicken broth.

• Microwave at HIGH 7 to 8 minutes, stirring once.

• Drain, reserving the liquid. Mash the vegetables.

• Measure the cooking water. Microwave at HIGH until liquid is reduced to about 1 tablespoon (15 mL).

• Check a few times as it is cooking; it sometimes reduces very quickly.

• Sprinkle the flour over the cooked parsnips and potatoes.

• Add the savory or dill, salt and pepper. Add the butter and milk or cream.

• Beat until the whole is well mashed and creamy.

• Adjust seasoning.

• Place in a microwave-safe dish, cover.

• Microwave at MEDIUM 5 to 6 minutes or until piping hot.

• These can be prepared early in the morning and kept at room temperature until ready to serve.

• Warm, covered, at MEDIUM 6 to 9 minutes or until piping hot.

Sweet Potatoes

• The New World knew about sweet potatoes long before they ever reached the Old World. They are especially popular around Christmas and New Year's. They taste far better when microwaved rather than boiled.

Sweet Potatoes "Nature"

To buy

• Choose sweet potatoes of uniform shape. That is important for perfect results when more than one is cooked. Regardless of size, choose them of even size, with smooth skins. Be sure to avoid those that have become soft or have blemishes.

To prepare and cook

• Wash under cold running water. Prick them 3 or 4 times with the point of a knife.

• As they have a tendency to discolor when peeled, it is better to bake them whole, then scoop out the shells to mash or prepare the pulp.

• If only two sweet potatoes are cooked, place one in each half of the microwave oven. If 3, 6 or 8 are being cooked, place them in a circle around the edge of the turntable.

• Turn them over halfway through the cooking period. 4 to 6 medium-sized sweet potatoes should take from 10 to 14 minutes at HIGH, depending on their size.

• After 5 to 6 minutes, prick each potato with the point of a knife to see how advanced they are, turn them over and finish cooking.

Hawaiian Sweet Potatoes

Preparation: . . . . **7 m**
Cooking: . . . . **from 15 to 19 m**
Standing: . . . . **none**

A personal note: A microwaved ham steak and these sweet potatoes mixed with crushed pineapple and chopped nuts are almost a must for me!
I first cook the potatoes, then the ham. When ready to serve, I reheat the sweet potatoes 4 minutes at MEDIUM, covered.

Ingredients:

5 to 6 medium-sized sweet potatoes
1/2 cup (125 mL) crushed pineapple
3 tbsp (50 mL) chopped nuts of your choice
3 tbsp (50 mL) butter or margarine
3/4 cup (190 mL) mini marshmallows

Method:

• Wash and bake the sweet potatoes, as for sweet potatoes "Nature."

• When cooked, cut in half and remove pulp from skins with a spoon. Mash, then add the remaining ingredients except the marshmallows. Salt and pepper to taste. Mash all together.

• Place mixture in a buttered microwave-safe pie plate. Cover with the marshmallows.

• Microwave, uncovered, 5 minutes at HIGH. Serve.

Autumn Pleasure

Preparation: . . . . **30 m**
Cooking: . . . . **from 30 to 34 m**
Standing: . . . . **5 m**

A personal note: Sweet potatoes and apples are both at their best when a few nights of very cold weather have touched them, so this recipe is perfect for late fall. I usually make these to serve with roasted duck or chicken legs.

Ingredients:

6 medium-sized sweet potatoes
2 to 3 apples, peeled, cored and sliced
1/4 cup (60 mL) brown or maple sugar
1/2 tsp (2 mL) salt
1/3 cup (80 mL) melted butter
1/4 tsp (1 mL) nutmeg

Method:

• Wash and microwave the sweet potatoes, as for sweet potatoes "Nature."

• Let them cool about 20 minutes.

• Peel and slice thickly.

• Place half of them in a generously buttered 4-cup (1 L) microwave-safe dish. Top with half the apples and half the remaining ingredients.

• Repeat rows of potatoes, apples and remaining ingredients. Cover and microwave 20 minutes at MEDIUM-HIGH. Let stand 5 minutes. Serve.

407

Brandied Sweet Potatoes

Preparation: . . . . **11 m**
Cooking: . . . . **from 16 to 20 m**
Standing: . . . . **none**

A personal note: No better potatoes can be served with roasted turkey or a large chicken or roasted quail. They can be served in the orange shells or in a nice dish, which is less work.

Ingredients:

3 oranges

6 medium-sized sweet potatoes

1/3 cup (80 mL) butter

4 tbsp (60 mL) dark brown sugar

1/2 tsp (2 mL) salt

1 tbsp (15 mL) brandy*

1/4 tsp (1 mL) nutmeg or allspice

* Mont Blanc brandy is Canadian and it is the one I use in the kitchen because it is economical.

Method:

- Wash oranges, cut in half.
- Squeeze the juice and reserve.
- Clean the inside of the shells if to be used, and rub each one inside with soft butter.
- Microwave the sweet potatoes, as for sweet potatoes "Nature."
- When done, cut in half. Remove pulp from shell with a spoon.
- Add all the remaining ingredients and as much orange juice as needed to have a creamy texture.
- Stir until well blended.
- Place in a microwave-safe dish or in the buttered orange shells.
- When ready to serve, place the dish or the orange shells in a circle on the oven tray.
- Microwave 6 minutes at MEDIUM.

Peppers

- Peppers come in many sizes, shapes and colors. They go from hot and peppery to mild. The ones mentioned here are the most used — the mild green, red or yellow. Be careful if you do not know much about peppers. Ask about their flavors. Generally, the larger peppers are the mildest.

Green and Red Peppers "Nature"

To buy

• Look for deep green or red color, without brown stains, and preferably well shaped.

• The difference between the green and red peppers is only a degree of maturity; the red ones have matured longer.

• Do not buy a shrivelled pepper, as it has been on the counter too long and has lost its crisp freshness.

• *Chopped green peppers:* 1 pound (500 g) = 2 medium green peppers or 1 cup (250 mL) chopped.

To keep

• Place unwashed green or red peppers in a plastic bag. Keep in refrigerator vegetable bin.

• They will remain in excellent condition for 8 to 12 days.

To freeze

• If you have many and wish to freeze them, this is easy, as they require no blanching.

• Wash, clean, dice or cut in slivers, or in half ready to be stuffed.

• Place in plastic bag 1 or 2 cups (250 or 500 mL) at most.

• Even 1/4 cup (60 mL) can be frozen, to be used when a small quantity is required.

• To use, there is no need to defrost, except for the halves that are to be stuffed.

To parboil for stuffing

• If your recipe calls for parboiling the peppers before stuffing, it is important to do so, since they *do not always* cook as fast as the stuffing.

• Using a sharp knife, cut a wide circle around the stem and remove from the pepper.

• Save the top if your recipe specifies to cover after filling the pepper.

• Scoop out core and seeds, discard.

• It is not always necessary to parboil, although better results are obtained when green peppers are to be stuffed.

• Place the cleaned peppers standing in a microwave-safe high dish.

• Add 2 cups (500 mL) hot water or enough to cover

at least half the peppers. Cover and microwave 3 minutes at HIGH.

• Let stand 5 minutes. Drain in a colander. Let stand until cool enough to handle.

To melt green or red peppers

• This is a nice quick and easy way to prepare green or red peppers to add to a sauce or a cooked vegetable, such as cooked green peas or sliced carrots, or when they are diced and added to mashed potatoes or to a roast gravy or even a soup.

• Clean and sliver or dice as many red or green peppers as required.

• Place in a dish with 2 tablespoons (30 mL) of water for each cup (250 mL) of pepper used.

• Microwave 2 minutes at HIGH for each pepper used. When cooked, add to your chosen food.

• When adding to a gravy, use the cooking water as well as the pepper.

Stuffed Peppers

Preparation: . . . .**10 m**
Cooking: . . . . **from 20 to 22 m**
Standing: . . . .**none**

A personal note: If you have only half a pound (250 g) of ground beef, pork or lamb, or 2 cups (500 g) of any cooked meat, pass it through a meat grinder and serve as meat-stuffed peppers.

A personal note: The stuffed halves can be prepared ahead of time, covered and kept at room temperature. Microwave when ready to serve.

Ingredients:

About 1/2 lb (250 g) ground meat of your choice

1 onion, chopped fine

1/2 cup (125 mL) cracker crumbs, crushed

1/2 tsp (2 mL) salt

1/4 tsp (1 mL) pepper

1/4 cup (60 mL) quick cooking rice

1/4 cup (60 mL) water or consommé

1/2 tsp (2 mL) savory

3 to 4 green peppers

1 7½-oz (213 mL) can tomato sauce

1 garlic clove, chopped fine

Method:

• Place the meat in a microwave-safe bowl.

• If it is raw, separate it with a fork.

• Microwave at HIGH 2 minutes.

• Drain out clear fat. Crush meat with fork.

• Omit this step when using cooked leftover meat.

• Add the onion, crushed crackers, salt, pepper, quick cooking rice, water or consommé and savory. Mix well.

• Clean green peppers ready to be stuffed as for Green Peppers ''Nature.''

• Cut each green pepper in half lengthwise, and place in buttered pie plate with small ends toward the middle of the plate. Stuff each half with meat mixture.

• Mix together the tomato sauce and garlic and pour over the green peppers, dividing equally and making sure the filling of each half is covered with sauce.

• Cover with waxed paper or plastic wrap. Microwave at MEDIUM-HIGH 20 minutes. Serve.

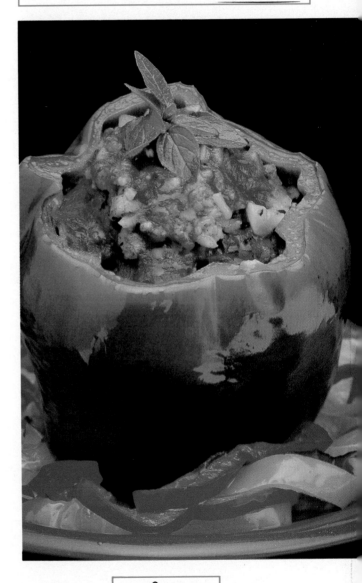

 Chianti

Sonoma Valley Cabernet Sauvignon

Green Peppers Italiano

Preparation: . . . . 8 m
Cooking: . . . . 7 m
Standing: . . . . none

A personal note: I like to serve these green or red peppers as a vegetable with roast chicken or pork. They're also very interesting served with sausages and mashed potatoes.

1/2 tsp (2 mL) sugar
Salt and pepper to taste

Ingredients:

3 tbsp (50 mL) olive or vegetable oil
3 green or red peppers, cut into slivers
2 onions, thinly sliced
2 garlic cloves, chopped fine
1 tsp (5 mL) basil

Method:

- Heat the oil in a 6-cup (1.5 L) microwave-safe dish 2 minutes at HIGH.
- Add the peppers, onions and garlic. Stir well.
- Microwave at HIGH 5 minutes. Stir again.
- Add the remaining ingredients.
- Stir and serve.

Leeks

- Of all the members of the onion family, leeks have the most delicate flavor and can be used in many ways. They are rather attractive — long, slim, half green and half white.

- The best leek season is from early September to the end of November, although they can be purchased almost all year round.

- If you wish to freeze or keep them longer, late autumn purchase is better.

Leeks "Nature"

To buy

• Select leeks with a fairly long white neck and very fresh-looking dark green tops.

To keep

• Separate the green from the white part by cutting right through without separating the leaves.

• Place the green tops in one plastic bag, the white bottoms in another. Do not wash.

• Close bags, leaving a small space on top.

• Prepared this way and refrigerated, they will keep 8 to 10 weeks.

To freeze

• Again, separate white from green.

• Fill sink with cold water and wash green parts, separating the leaves.

• Let them drain for a few minutes, then shake them to remove as much water as possible.

• Take as many leaves as needed. According to the size of your container, place them evenly together.

• Melt **1 teaspoon (5 mL) butter or margarine** 30 seconds at HIGH; do this right in the container if it is microwave-safe.

• Add as many sliced green tops as your container will take. Stir. Add a good pinch of sugar — NO SALT —.

• Microwave at HIGH 2 minutes.

• Stir, cover, and freeze.

• The white part of the leek can be prepared and frozen in the same manner as the green.

To use

• Add leeks to soups and to carrots, Brussels sprouts or cabbage before cooking them in the microwave.

• They can also be added to chicken or turkey stuffing, to rice or noodles.

• The quantity depends on your taste.

• I love to melt white leeks and add some to mashed potatoes instead of onions.

My Mother's Leeks and Tomatoes

Preparation: . . . . **10 m**
Cooking: . . . . **7 m**
Standing: . . . . **none**

A personal note: My mother was very fond of leeks and this creation of hers was very popular with family and friends. She served it hot, with rice or noodles or roast chicken.

Ingredients:

4 to 6 leeks, depending on size

3 tbsp (50 mL) olive oil

1 large onion, chopped fine

1/2 cup (125 mL) carrots, peeled and grated

1 cup (250 mL) fresh tomatoes, diced

1 tsp (5 mL) sugar

1/2 tsp (2 mL) basil or tarragon

Salt and pepper to taste

Method:

• Clean the leeks and separate the white from the green as for Leeks "Nature." Cut the white with **only 1 green top** into 1-inch (2.5 cm) pieces.

• Pour the oil into an 8-cup (2 L) microwave-safe dish, heat 1 minute at HIGH.

• Add the onion and carrots. Stir to coat with the oil. Microwave 3 minutes at HIGH.

• Add the remaining ingredients. Cover and microwave 4 minutes at MEDIUM-HIGH, stirring after 2 minutes of cooking. Serve.

wines

Muscadet

Chablis

Braised Leeks À la Française

Preparation: . . . . **10 m**
Cooking: . . . . **6 or 7 m**
Standing: . . . . **none**

A personal note: Use only the white part of small or medium-sized leeks to prepare this elegant dish. Serve hot as a vegetable, or cold tossed with a vinaigrette of your choice.

Ingredients:

6 medium-sized leeks, white part only

1/4 cup (60 mL) chicken consommé

2 bay leaves

3 tbsp (50 mL) parsley, minced

1/4 tsp (1 mL) salt

Pepper to taste

Method:

• Cut each leek at the line of green; only the white is used. See Leeks "Nature," on how to prepare the green part to use in another way or in soups.

• Cut each leek in four lengthwise slices. Wash carefully under cold running water and place neatly in a long microwave-safe dish.

• Add the chicken consommé and the bay leaves. Cover. Microwave 6 minutes at HIGH. Drain well*.

• To the well drained leeks add the parsley. Salt and pepper to taste.

To serve hot

• Add a piece of butter to the seasoned leeks. Microwave 1 minute at HIGH.

To serve cold

• Omit the butter. Simply toss, when the leeks are cooled, with a dressing of your choice.

* Add the "full of flavor" water to a soup or keep to add to a gravy or to microwave another vegetable.

Leeks
San Antonio

Preparation: . . . . **10 m**
Cooking: . . . . **from 11 to 13 m**
Standing: . . . . **2 m**

A personal note: This is an elegant and tasty Sicilian way to serve leeks with chicken or veal or to top microwaved long grain rice.

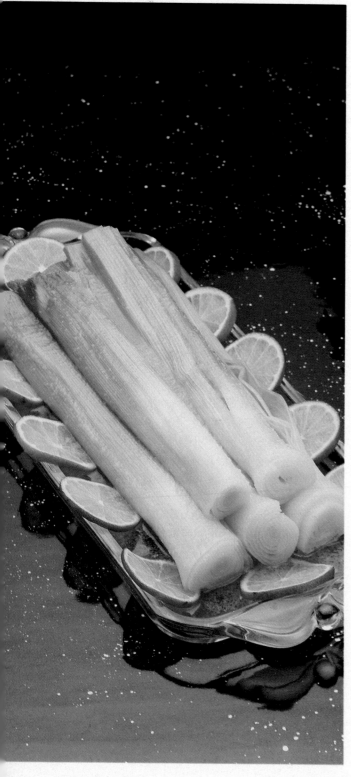

Ingredients:

4 medium-sized leeks

1/4 cup (60 mL) hot water

1 tbsp (15 mL) cornstarch

2 tbsp (30 mL) soft butter

Juice and rind of 1 lime or 1 small lemon

1/2 tsp (2 mL) salt

A good pinch of sugar

Method:

• Clean the leeks. Remove outer leaves and cut off half the green tops (can be used for soup or stew). Split the remaining green part in two from the white part up.

• Wash under running water, letting the water rush through the leaves, where sand is usually lodged. Drain well.

• Place the whole prepared leeks in an 8-inch (20 cm) square or oblong ceramic dish.

• Pour the hot water on top. Cover dish with waxed paper, microwave at HIGH 7 to 8 minutes. Let stand 2 minutes.

• Remove the cooked leeks to a platter.

• Mix together the cornstarch, soft butter, juice and rind of the lime or lemon, salt and sugar.

• Add this mixture to the water used to cook the leeks remaining in the dish. Stir well. Microwave at HIGH 3 minutes. Stir well.

• If too thick, add a bit of water. Stir well. Microwave again 1 or 2 minutes at HIGH. Stir well and pour over the cooked leeks.

• To reheat, if necessary, microwave about 1 minute at MEDIUM.

Welsh Leek Pie

Preparation: . . . . **12 m**
Cooking: . . . . **from 23 to 24 m**
Standing: . . . . **none**

A personal note: In Wales, this is a very good family dish. It is a sort of quiche without pastry. It is also holiday family fare served with cold roast chicken or turkey.

Ingredients:

6 medium-sized leeks

1/2 cup (125 mL) chicken consommé

Juice and grated rind of 1/2 a lemon

2 tbsp (30 mL) butter

4 eggs

1/4 cup (60 mL) cream of your choice

2 cups (500 g) cottage cheese

Salt and pepper to taste

3 tbsp (50 mL) finely crushed crackers

Method:

• Clean the leeks as for Leeks "Nature."

• Cut both the white and green parts into 1-inch (2.5 cm) pieces.

• Place in a microwave-safe dish the chicken consommé, lemon juice and rind and butter.

• Microwave at HIGH 8 to 9 minutes, stirring once.

• Strain, reserving the cooking stock.

• Beat together the eggs, cream and cottage cheese until well blended and creamy.

• Add 1/4 cup (60 mL) of the reserved cooking stock. Stir until well mixed.

• Salt and pepper to taste. Stir in the finely crushed crackers.

• Pour the whole into a 9 or 10-inch (23 or 25 cm) microwave-safe pie plate. Sprinkle with paprika.

• Microwave 15 minutes at MEDIUM. Serve as soon as ready.

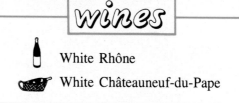

wines

White Rhône

White Châteauneuf-du-Pape

417

Green Peas

• Everyone agrees that fresh garden peas belong to the royalty of the vegetable world. The problem is that they must be prepared, cooked and eaten as fast as possible after being gathered from the garden. They are a rare treat when enjoyed at their peak.

Green Peas "Nature"

To buy

• In July and August, you will find good fresh green peas at the market.

• Buy those that have a deep green color, without any yellow spots, preferably the small types of pea pods. They are more tender.

• Cook them as soon as possible after buying.

• One pound (500 g) of peas in the pods = 1 to 2 cups (250 to 500 mL) shelled peas.

To keep

• Green peas deteriorate very rapidly after harvest.

• The peas inside the pod have a tendency to harden, so they should be used as soon as possible.

• If necessary to keep them, place unshelled peas in a plastic bag and refrigerate.

• They should not be kept for more than 24 hours before cooking.

To cook

• Shell peas only when ready to cook them.

• Wash 6 to 8 of the pods and place them in the bottom of a microwave-safe dish.

• Top with the peas and sprinkle with a good pinch of sugar and 3 tablespoons (50 mL) of water. Cover.

• Microwave at HIGH 6 to 8 minutes for 1 pound (500 g).

• Stir and check cooking after 5 minutes, since garden peas cook more quickly than bought ones.

• Drain. Salt to taste; do not pepper. Serve.

To cook frozen green peas

• Peas are one of the best of all frozen vegetables.

• Simply place the required amount, still frozen, in a microwave-safe dish. Do not add water.

• Cover. Microwave at HIGH. 1½ cups (375 mL) will take 4 to 5 minutes.

• In the summer, I gather a few leaves of fresh basil, mint or chives that I chop and add with a piece of butter to the cooked green peas.

• Stir and serve. Do not salt or pepper them.

Fresh or frozen green peas cooked by the Sensor method

• Shell fresh peas. Add a pinch of sugar and **2 tablespoons (30 mL) of butter** for each 2 to 3 cups (500 to 750 mL) of fresh or frozen peas.

• Place in a Micro-Dur dish. Cover. If you do not have such a dish, cover with plastic wrap.

• Set your Sensor at VEGETABLE HARD. Start the oven.

• When you hear the BEEP, remove dish from oven. Let stand, covered, 4 to 5 minutes.

• I always add any juice from the green peas to meat gravy. It makes a very good sauce.

Green Peas
À la Française

Preparation: . . . . **14 m**
Cooking: . . . . **6 m**
Standing: . . . . **5 m**

• This is one of the great vegetable dishes of the French cuisine ''répertoire.'' It's also the first vegetable recipe I cooked in the microwave many years ago, using my own green peas fresh from the garden. The color, flavor and texture were so perfect that since then I have never been able to eat green peas cooked any other way.

Ingredients:

3 tbsp (50 mL) butter

2 cups (500 mL) lettuce, coarsely shredded

1 tbsp (15 mL) fresh parsley, chopped fine

1 tbsp (15 mL) sugar

2 to 3 cups (500 to 750 mL) green peas*, shelled

12 small white pickling onions, peeled, *or* 6 green onions, chopped fine

* If you wish to replace the fresh green peas with frozen peas, use the same quantity. There is no need to defrost. Add to whole and microwave in the same manner.

Method:

• Place the butter in a 10-cup (2.5 L) microwave-safe dish and melt 1 minute at HIGH. Add the lettuce, parsley and sugar, blend well.

• Mix together the green peas and white onions or green onions. Place on top of lettuce. Cover. Microwave 6 minutes at HIGH. Let stand 5 minutes. Salt and pepper to taste. Serve.

> **Helpful hint:** Individual foods, such as baked potatoes, cupcakes and hors d'oeuvres, will cook more evenly if placed in the oven equal distance apart. When possible, arrange foods in a circular pattern. Similarly, when placing foods in a baking dish, arrange around the outside of dish, not lined up next to each other. Food should NOT be stacked on top of each other.

Minted Peas
À l'Anglaise

Preparation: . . . . **12 m**
Cooking: . . . . **from 8 to 9 m**
Standing: . . . . **5 m**

• This is one of my favorite ways to cook fresh garden peas. In winter, I use frozen green peas.

Ingredients:

2 tbsp (30 mL) butter

6 green onions, diced

2 cups (500 mL) fresh or frozen green peas

2 tbsp (30 mL) water*

2 tbsp (30 mL) fresh mint, chopped fine

1 tsp (5 mL) sugar

1 tsp (5 mL) lemon juice

* When using frozen green peas, omit the water.

Method:

• Place the butter in a 4-cup (1 L) microwave-safe dish and melt 1 minute at HIGH.

• Add the green onions. Stir until well coated with butter.

• Microwave at HIGH 3 minutes.

• Add the remaining ingredients. Cover and microwave at HIGH 5 to 6 minutes. Serve.

My Own Frozen Peas and Mushrooms

Preparation: . . . . **13 m**
Cooking: . . . . **7 m**
Standing: . . . . **none**

• When the fresh green peas season is over, I use frozen green peas, which I cook according to the following recipe.

Ingredients:

2 tbsp (30 mL) butter

3 green onions, chopped fine, *or*
  1 small or medium-sized leek, thinly sliced

1 can of sliced mushrooms

2 to 3 cups (500 to 750 mL) frozen green peas

1 tsp (5 mL) sugar

1/2 tsp (2 mL) basil

Salt to taste

Method:

• Place the butter in an 8-cup (2 L) microwave-safe dish and melt 1 minute at HIGH.

• Add the green onions or the leek. Stir well. Cover and microwave 2 minutes at HIGH.

• Stir and add the remaining ingredients. Stir well. Cover and microwave at HIGH 5 minutes. Salt to taste and serve.

Helpful hint: After defrosting a chicken, run cold water through the inside if it is still slightly frozen.

Quick and Easy
with Frozen Green Peas

• In my kitchen, I have a notebook where I jot down ideas for microwave cooking, the cooking times required and whether the results were good or extra good.

• The following are my notes on frozen green peas. I place an asterisk next to my favorites. You could do the same for yours.

Ingredients:

2 tbsp (30 mL) butter or margarine

4 cups (1 L) frozen green peas

1/2 tsp (2 mL) sugar

Method:

• Melt the butter 1 minute at HIGH in a 4-cup (1 L) microwave-safe dish.

• Add the peas and sugar.

• Choose your favorite variation. Stir.

• Cover and microwave 6 minutes at HIGH. Stir and serve.

Summer pleasure

• Omit the butter or margarine.

• Add **2 to 3 tablespoons (30 to 50 mL) minced chives** to the peas and sugar before cooking.

• Microwave same time as basic recipe.

• Stir in **1/3 cup (80 mL) sour cream.**

• Stir. Microwave 1 minute at HIGH. Serve.

Autumn delight

• Scrub or peel **10 to 12 small new potatoes.**

• Place in an 8-cup (2 L) microwave-safe dish.

• Add **1/4 cup (60 mL) water.**

• Cover and microwave 6 minutes at HIGH.

• I do not peel my potatoes, even after they are cooked.

• Add the 4 cups (1 L) frozen peas and the sugar. Stir.

• Cover and microwave at HIGH 3 minutes.

• Add butter to taste.

All year round

• Dice **8 to 12 green onions**, both white and green parts.

• Melt **2 tablespoons (30 mL) butter** 1 minute at HIGH.

• Add the green onions, stir well. Add the 4 cups (1 L) frozen green peas and the sugar. Stir.

• Microwave 6 minutes at HIGH.

• Season to taste. I use neither salt nor pepper. Serve.

English style

• Place **6 slices of bacon** on a sheet of white towelling. Set on a plate.

• Microwave at HIGH about 3 minutes or until crisp.

• Cool, then crumble. Microwave the 4 cups (1 L) frozen green peas as indicated in the basic recipe.

• Sprinkle bacon on top when ready to serve.

Autumn pleasure

• Make 4 incisions with the point of a knife in **a medium-sized green squash.**

• Microwave at MEDIUM 4 minutes.

• Set on a plate and let cool 10 minutes. Split in half, remove seeds* with a spoon.

• Add a piece of butter to each half and mash right in the shell.

• Fill each half with frozen green peas.

• Sprinkle peas with a few pinches of sugar. Set on a plate.

• Microwave at HIGH 6 minutes.

• The squash can be prepared ahead of time and kept at room temperature.

• When ready to serve, add the green peas and cook as indicated above.

* I give the seeds to the birds. They love them. Simply place them in a little dish or right on the grass or over the snow.

Potatoes

- Potatoes are eaten all over the world, ranking eighth in importance in world food crops.

- The English word potato came to us from the North American Indian "batata" by way of the Spanish "patata."

The potato is an important food

- The potato is a good food and should not be neglected. It is not the potato that is fattening; it is the butter, cream, etc., that we add to it. Anyone on a diet will appreciate the flavor of a microwaved potato. I often enjoy a broiled piece of meat with a microwaved potato. I do not put butter on the potato, yet it is most tasty and moist.

- Do not forget that potatoes are high in Vitamins A and C and in iron and calcium, so they are an important part of our diet.

Potatoes "Nature"

To buy

• Choose uniformly shaped potatoes. A mixture of large and small can be useful at times.

• Avoid potatoes that have started to sprout and those with blemishes. Wash with a stiff brush.

• If you see "eyes" or blemishes, remove them.

To keep

• Place potatoes in a basket or a large bowl.

• Keep in a cool, dark, moist place.

• Too much light can cause green spots, which should be removed when peeling.

• Do not bake a potato with green spots.

• Once the spots have been removed, potatoes may be boiled.

• When potatoes are properly stored, they will keep for 2 to 3 months.

To cook

• Here is an approximate time board that will help:

Approximate cooking time board	
Large or medium large	**at HIGH**
1 potato	4 to 5 minutes
2 potatoes	7 to 8 minutes
3 potatoes	10 to 12 minutes
4 potatoes	14 to 16 minutes
6 potatoes	17 to 19 minutes

A personal note: Potatoes are done when they are a little tender to the touch, but still firm. Remember that the potatoes soften quite a bit during the "standing" time.

• Potatoes are the exception to the rule of prolonged cooking for older vegetables. Of course, there are differences between new potatoes and old potatoes. Surface cells in new potatoes are ripe, but they still have a hard and firm texture.

• Fast boiling allows heat to penetrate interior starch. In old potatoes, surface cells have become enlarged to accommodate the starch granules that are expanding. If the cells are cooked too fast, the cellulose breaks up, the starch bursts and the potato falls to pieces.

• With this bit of knowledge, you will be able to serve fine and tasty potatoes, and you will understand why winter potatoes may be microwaved without adding water, whereas to microwave new potatoes, 1/4 cup (60 mL) water must be added.

• Microwaved potatoes retain moisture. If you prefer drier potatoes, prick each potato in 4 or 5 places with a long-tined fork. This permits the excess moisture to escape. Two to three slashes in each potato are also sufficient, but the potato will not be as dry.

• When microwaving large potatoes, make sure they are all the same size.

• If your oven has the Sensor method, prepare same as above, cover with a lid if you have a plastic dish, or cover dish of your choice with plastic wrap, pressing to make sure it adheres all around. Cook on " Sensor A6 " or at whatever your oven requires.

• Let stand 5 minutes, covered, after the cooking period is over.

• Whichever way you cook the potatoes, if they become gummy or wrinkled, it means they are overcooked.

French fried potatoes

• They cannot be done in the microwave oven. However, they warm up very well when fresh fried or frozen.

• Potatoes should be arranged like the spokes of a wheel, with the heavy end of each potato placed on the outside and the smaller end toward the middle.

• Another important point is to allow 4 to 5 minutes standing time after the potatoes are cooked, which allows the potatoes to finish cooking. The potato will soften quite a bit during the standing time.

• When a potato is overcooked, it is gummy inside and has a wrinkled appearance outside.

• Potatoes, peeled, then halved, sliced or diced, require 1/4 cup (60 mL) of water for 6 to 8 medium-sized potatoes to be cooked. Cover.

• Microwave at HIGH for the same time as given in the chart.

• Spread fresh or frozen french fries in a microwave-safe dish, large enough to keep them in a single layer.

• To heat frozen french fried potatoes: set them on DEFROST cycle for 2 to 3 minutes, for 3 to 4 cups (750 mL to 1 L).

• Stir well, then microwave 2 to 3 minutes at HIGH to give them some crispness.

• When you wish to reheat freshly deep fried potatoes, spread them in a microwave-safe dish, microwave at HIGH 2 to 3 minutes for each 3 to 4 cups (750 mL to 1 L) of french fried potatoes.

425

Baked Potatoes Country Style

Preparation: . . . . **10 m**
Cooking: . . . . **from 17 to 19 m**
Standing: . . . . **from 4 to 5 m**

A personal note: You'll get quick, easy, perfect results every time, once you have acquired the know-how. Remember that time may vary slightly, depending on the size and the variety of the potatoes. Test with the point of a paring knife.

Ingredients:

6 medium-sized potatoes

1 tsp (5 mL) coarse salt

1 tbsp (15 mL) soft butter or margarine

Method:

• Choose potatoes of equal size.

• Scrub with a brush under cold running water.

• Wipe with a paper towel.

• Make 4 to 5 incisions in each potato with the point of a knife.

• Place the salt on a plate or a paper towel.

• Place the butter or margarine in the palm of your left hand.

• Roll each potato in your hands until it is greasy.

• Then roll it in the coarse salt.

• The quantity of butter or margarine and salt given above is sufficient for 6 potatoes.

• Place the potatoes in a circle on the oven tray.

• Bake according to the chart for Potatoes "Nature."

Helpful hint: To give whipped cream a rich flavor, fold a spoonful of honey into it.

Potatoes Persillées

Preparation: . . . . **8 m**
Cooking: . . . . **from 12 to 18 m**
Standing: . . . . **none**

A personal note: Make this dish with small potatoes. When I buy a large bag of potatoes, I take out the small ones to make this recipe. In summer, I use the first small new potatoes from my own garden.

Ingredients:

6 to 9 small potatoes, peeled

1/4 cup (60 mL) water

2 tbsp (30 mL) butter

1/4 cup (60 mL) parsley, minced

3 green onions, chopped fine

Salt and pepper to taste

Method:

• Wash and peel the potatoes.

• Place them in a 4-cup (1 L) microwave-safe dish, add the water.

• Cover and microwave at HIGH 6 to 9 minutes or until tender, stirring twice during the cooking period.

• Drain the potatoes, reserving the water. Place the reserved water in a microwave-safe dish, add the remaining ingredients. Microwave 4 to 6 minutes at HIGH or until liquid is thick. Stir until well mixed.

• Add the cooked potatoes and stir gently until coated with the parsley mixture, cover.

• When ready to serve, microwave 2 to 3 minutes at MEDIUM-HIGH.

Helpful hint: ¼ teaspoon (1 mL) of dried herb is the equivalent of 1 teaspoon (5 mL) of any fresh herb.

Scalloped Potatoes

Preparation: .7 m
Cooking: . . . . from 26 to 33 m
Standing: . . . . .none

• When cooked in the microwave, Scalloped Potatoes are creamy, tasty, and so quickly prepared as compared with ordinary cooking.

Ingredients:

3 tbsp (50 mL) butter

1 onion, peeled and chopped fine

1 tsp (5 mL) salt

1/4 tsp (1 mL) pepper

1 tsp (5 mL) savory or dill

3 tbsp (50 mL) flour or arrowroot

2 cups (500 mL) milk*

4 cups (1 L) potatoes, peeled and thinly sliced

* You can also use 1 cup (250 mL) milk and 1 cup (250 mL) chicken broth.

Method:

• Place in a microwave-safe bowl the butter, onion, salt, pepper and savory or dill.

• Microwave at HIGH 2 minutes.

• Stir in the flour or arrowroot, mix thoroughly. Add the milk. Stir well.

• Microwave 6 to 8 minutes at MEDIUM, stirring twice.

• When creamy, adjust seasoning.

• Place the thinly sliced potatoes in a large microwave-safe pie plate or a 4-cup (1 L) microwave-safe dish in layers. Pour sauce over all.

• Move potatoes here and there with the point of a knife, so the sauce will be evenly divided among the sliced potatoes.

• Sprinkle top with a bit of paprika here and there.

• Microwave at MEDIUM 20 to 25 minutes, testing the doneness of the potatoes with the point of a knife.

• This recipe gives you 6 good helpings and can easily be divided in half; for a smaller quantity, reduce cooking period by about 10 minutes.

How to reheat leftovers

• Place leftovers in a smaller microwave-safe dish, being careful not to mix the layers.

• Cover. Keep refrigerated.

• To serve, microwave at MEDIUM, covered, until hot.

• Time depends on quantity, so test every 3 minutes.

Stuffed Baked Potatoes

• I make these potatoes in the morning, ready to be warmed up at lunch or dinner. They are always a success.

Preparation: . . . . **15 m**
Cooking: . . . . **from 18 to 23 m**
Standing: . . . . **none**

Ingredients:

6 medium equal-sized potatoes

3 tbsp (50 mL) butter

1/3 cup (80 mL) sour cream or plain yogourt

1/2 tsp (2 mL) salt

1/4 tsp (1 mL) pepper

1/2 tsp (2 mL) savory (optional)

2 green onions, chopped fine

Paprika to taste

Method:

• Scrub potatoes under cold running water.

• Place them in a circle in the microwave oven.

• Microwave 14 to 16 minutes at HIGH.

• Check doneness with the point of a knife after 14 minutes. Let cool 5 minutes.

• Cut an oval slice on top of each potato and scoop out the pulp with a spoon, or cut each potato in half and empty shell.

• Add to the potato pulp the remaining ingredients except the paprika.

• Mash until smooth and creamy.

• Fill each potato shell with the mashed potato. Sprinkle with paprika.

• Place in the microwave oven in a circle.

• Microwave at MEDIUM-HIGH 4 to 7 minutes or until potatoes are piping hot.

A personal note: These stuffed potatoes can be prepared in advance, ready to be warmed up. Do not refrigerate; keep on the kitchen counter covered with a bowl.

wines

Alsatian Sylvaner

Verdicchio

Broiled Rösti Potatoes

Convection and microwave cooking

Preparation: . . . . **30 m**
Cooking: . . . . **from 24 to 32 m**
Standing: . . . . **none**

A personal note: This is a delicious way to roast potatoes in the convection section of the microwave. They can also simply be microwaved, but will not have the same brown crust. To serve with chicken, I prefer to microwave them.

Ingredients:

6 to 8 medium-sized potatoes

4 tbsp (60 mL) butter

1/2 tsp (2 mL) salt

Method:

• Scrub potatoes under cold running water.

• Pierce each one 3 times with the point of a paring knife.

• Place in a circle on a microwave-safe rack.

• Microwave at HIGH 9 to 12 minutes; test the potatoes with the point of a knife. Let stand 20 to 30 minutes.

• When ready to use, peel potatoes and chop or shred coarsely on large grater.

• Place the butter in a 4-cup (1 L) microwave-safe dish and melt 4 minutes at HIGH. The butter will be golden brown.

• Add the potatoes and salt. Stir well.

• Press against the dish with the back of a fork.

• Preheat convection section of your microwave oven to 400°F (200°C).

• Place potatoes on a rack and bake for 15 to 20 minutes or until they are golden brown.

• Sprinkle top here and there with paprika. Serve.

Helpful hint: Chicken is done when juices are clear yellow and drumstick moves freely.

Gravy Browned Potatoes

Preparation: . . . . **5 m**
Cooking: . . . . **8 m**
Standing: . . . . **none**

A personal note: These potatoes are perfect to serve with all roasted meats. I microwave my potatoes and add them to the brown roast gravy. I also make this dish using leftover gravy to serve with slices of the cold roasted meat.

Method:

• Place the gravy fat and juice in a 10-cup (2.5 L) microwave-safe dish. Microwave 1 minute at HIGH.

• Add remaining ingredients and roll the potatoes in the mixture until they are well coated. Cover and microwave at HIGH 4 minutes.

• Stir well and microwave 4 minutes more or until potatoes are tender.

• Salt and pepper to taste. Serve.

Ingredients:

1/4 to 1/2 cup (60 - 125 mL) leftover fat and juice from roast gravy

1 tsp (5 mL) Kitchen Bouquet

1/4 tsp (1 mL) each paprika and savory

4 to 6 medium-sized potatoes, peeled

Helpful hint: To reheat sliced meat, arrange slices flat on a plate. Cover with waxed paper. Sauce or gravy may be poured over meat before reheating to help keep it moist.

Mashed Potatoes Parisienne

Preparation:	. . . . **12 m**
Cooking:	. . . . **from 8 to 10 m**
Standing:	. . . . **none**

A personal note: The addition of sour cream, savory, fresh parsley and green onions in the winter or chives in the summer makes these potatoes delicious and creamy. If your microwave has a Sensor, by all means use it to cook the potatoes.

Ingredients:

6 medium potatoes of even size, peeled and quartered

1 tsp (5 mL) salt

1/4 cup (60 mL) water

1/2 cup (125 mL) sour cream

1/4 cup (60 mL) butter or margarine

1 tsp (5 mL) savory

4 green onions, chopped fine *or*
   3 tbsp (50 mL) fresh chives, chopped

1/4 cup (60 mL) fresh parsley, chopped fine

Method:

• Wash potatoes under cold running water, peel and quarter.

• Place in a dish with the salt and water. Stir well.

• Cover and microwave at HIGH 8 to 10 minutes.

• Drain, mash, and add the remaining ingredients.

• Stir vigorously until all is smooth and well blended. Adjust seasoning.

• Place in a microwave-safe dish. Cover.

• Keep at room temperature and warm, when ready to serve, 2 to 5 minutes at MEDIUM, depending on how cool the potatoes are.

Baked Potatoes Oriental

Preparation:	. . . . **7 m**
Cooking:	. . . . **from 15 to 16 m**
Standing:	. . . . **none**

• These potatoes are very tasty. I first made them when looking for a flavorful microwaved potato to serve with Spareribs Oriental.

Ingredients:

1 tbsp (15 mL) vegetable Bovril

1 tbsp (15 mL) soy sauce

2 green onions, chopped fine

2 tbsp (30 mL) butter

6 medium-sized potatoes, peeled

Salt and pepper to taste

Method:

• In an 8-cup (2 L) microwave-safe dish place the vegetable Bovril, soy sauce, green onions and the butter.

• Microwave, uncovered, 3 minutes at HIGH, stirring after 2 minutes.

• Add the peeled potatoes, making sure they are all even-sized.

• Stir until coated with hot mixture.

• Microwave, uncovered, 10 minutes at HIGH.

• Stir, test doneness with the point of a knife.

• If necessary, microwave another 2 to 3 minutes. Serve piping hot.

Potato Skins

Preparation: . . . . **20 m**
Cooking: . . . . **from 22 to 26 m**
Standing: . . . . **none**

A personal note: This interesting hors d'oeuvre dates far back into our Canadian food background. It has suddenly become the fashion again all over the place. Six potatoes will give you 12 halves to serve as an entrée or 24 quarters to serve as cocktail nibbles.

Ingredients:

5 to 6 medium-sized potatoes
3 tbsp (50 mL) butter
1/2 tsp (2 mL) celery salt
1/2 tsp (2 mL) savory
1/2 cup (125 mL) grated cheese of your choice

Method:

• Wash potatoes. Make 3 to 4 gashes in each one with the point of a knife.

• Place in a circle on a microwave rack.

• Microwave 10 to 12 minutes at HIGH, turning each potato over after 5 minutes of cooking. Let stand 10 minutes after the cooking period.

• Cut each potato in half lengthwise.

• For smaller skins, cut each half potato lengthwise.

• Scoop out the potato pulp*.

• Place the skins on a round 9-inch (23 cm) pie plate (Pyrex or Corning).

• Place the butter in a small microwave-safe bowl. Melt 2 minutes at HIGH.

• Add the remaining ingredients except the cheese.

• Stir until well mixed.

• Brush the inside of each potato skin with this mixture.

• Sprinkle each piece of potato lightly with cheese.

• Sprinkle the whole with a bit of paprika.

• Microwave, uncovered, 10 to 12 minutes at HIGH. The skins will be crispy.

• Serve as soon as ready.

* Use the potato pulp that has been scooped out to make mashed potatoes. Cover and keep refrigerated if not needed on the same day. To reheat, microwave, covered, 8 to 9 minutes at MEDIUM-HIGH.

Tomatoes

• As everyone knows, tomatoes are the favorite vegetable around the world. You may be surprised to know that they belong to the Nightshade Family, which includes the potato, pepper and eggplant. They originated in Peru and from there covered the world.

Tomatoes "Nature"

To buy

• It isn't easy to buy good tomatoes, unless you are a very wise shopper, since most of our tomatoes are sold on plastic trays, tightly covered with plastic wrap, which makes it impossible to really feel their quality.

• However, medium-firm, brightly colored tomatoes, free of blemishes or brown spots, cracks or green areas, are the best. I also make sure they are heavy for their size.

• Do not buy over ripe or under ripe tomatoes, as their flavor will not be interesting. One will be watery, the other acid.

• They are at their peak of perfection in late spring and summer.

To keep

• When under ripe, keep them at room temperature, one next to the other. When ripe, place them in the same manner, but keep them refrigerated.

• When they are to be served raw, remove them from refrigerator one to two hours before serving.

To prepare for different uses

To peel

• Wash the tomatoes under cold running water. Dip them for a few seconds in boiling water, then in cold water.

• Remove the core on top with a small sharp, pointed knife. Then the peel will come off very easily.

• If the tomatoes are to be cooked, the skins should be left on.

• Do not peel whole tomatoes that are to be stuffed.

Note on cooking

• The ripeness and amount of liquid of a tomato is difficult to determine, so the microwave cooking period may vary. Check for doneness at the half time period.

• When they are to be cooked in halves, unpeeled, place cut-side down on a paper towel for 20 to 30 minutes, then prepare according to recipe.

434

Oriental Steamed Tomatoes and Zucchini

Preparation: . . . . **8 m**
Cooking: . . . . **7 m**
Standing: . . . . **none**

A personal note: Low in calories and easy to prepare and cook, this dish is excellent to serve with barbecued or broiled meats.

Ingredients:

2 medium-sized zucchini, unpeeled and sliced

2 medium-sized tomatoes, unpeeled

1 tbsp (15 mL) vegetable oil or butter

4 green onions, diced

1 bay leaf

1 tsp (5 mL) basil or savory

1 tsp (5 mL) soy sauce

1/4 tsp (1 mL) sugar

1 large garlic clove, chopped fine

Salt and pepper to taste

Method:

• Remove both ends of each zucchini, slice thinly. Cut each tomato into 6 wedges.

• Place the oil or butter in a 4-cup (1 L) microwave-safe dish and heat 2 minutes at HIGH.

• Add the green onions, stir well. Microwave 1 minute at HIGH.

• Add the zucchini, stir. Microwave at HIGH 2 minutes.

• Add the tomatoes, bay leaf, basil or savory, stir well. Cover and microwave 2 minutes at HIGH, stir well.

• Add the sugar, soy sauce and garlic.

• Salt and pepper to taste.

• When ready to serve, microwave at HIGH 2 minutes.

• Equally good served hot, warm or at room temperature.

435

Buttered Melted Tomatoes

Preparation: . . . . **10 m**
Cooking: . . . . **from 5 to 6 m**
Standing: . . . . **none**

A personal note: A grilled steak, a baked potato and these tomatoes equal a superb meal.

Ingredients:

2 lb (1 kg) firm tomatoes*

4 tbsp (60 mL) butter

1 tbsp (15 mL) sugar

1/2 tsp (2 mL) pepper

1/2 tsp (2 mL) thyme or marjoram

* 2 pounds (1 kg) tomatoes should give 4 to 6 medium-sized tomatoes.

Method:

• Pour boiling water over the tomatoes, let stand 2 minutes. Place in a bowl of cold water, then peel and cut each tomato in four.

• Place the butter in a 4-cup (1 L) microwave-safe dish. Microwave at HIGH 3 minutes. Add the tomatoes, placing them one next to the other.

• Mix the remaining ingredients in a bowl and sprinkle over the tomatoes. This can be prepared an hour or so ahead of time, but kept at room temperature.

• When ready to serve, microwave at MEDIUM-HIGH 2 to 3 minutes. Serve.

Scalloped Tomatoes

Preparation: . . . . **7 m**
Cooking: . . . . **13 m**
Standing: . . . . **none**

• This is a popular way to serve canned tomatoes as a vegetable dish. Quick and easy.

Ingredients:

One 19-oz (540 mL) can of tomatoes

1 medium-sized onion, chopped fine

1 tbsp (15 mL) sugar

1/2 tsp (2 mL) each of salt and savory

1/4 tsp (1 mL) rosemary

2 tbsp (30 mL) butter

1 cup (250 mL) bread, cut into 1/2-inch (2 cm) cubes

Method:

• Place in a 4-cup (1 L) microwave-safe dish the tomatoes, onion, sugar, salt, savory and rosemary. Mix well. Microwave 10 minutes at MEDIUM-HIGH, stir.

• Place the butter in a Pyrex or Corning pie plate and melt 1 minute at HIGH. Add the bread cubes, stir well and microwave 3 minutes at HIGH, stirring twice.

• The bread cubes should be brown here and there. Pour piping hot into the tomato sauce.

• Stir thoroughly. Salt and pepper to taste.

Broiled Tomatoes

Preparation: . . . . **5 m**
Cooking: . . . . **5 m**
Standing: . . . . **none**

A personal note: If your microwave oven has a broiler, why not use it for a favorite of many, broiled tomatoes?

Ingredients:

4 medium-sized tomatoes
1/2 tsp (2 mL) sugar
1/4 tsp (1 mL) salt
Pepper to taste
1/2 tsp (2 mL) thyme
1/3 cup (80 mL) sour cream

Variation:

1/2 cup (125 mL) fine breadcrumbs
3 tbsp (50 mL) soft butter
1/4 tsp (1 mL) curry powder *or*
   1 tbsp (15 mL) chili sauce

Method:

- Wash tomatoes. Remove cores but do not peel.
- Cut in half crosswise.
- Blend together the sugar, salt, pepper and thyme.
- Add the sour cream. Mix well.
- Top each half with some of this mixture.

Variation:

- Mix together the breadcrumbs, soft butter, curry powder or chili sauce.
- Spread over each tomato half.
- In either case, preheat the grill as indicated in your oven manual.
- When hot, place the tomatoes on the tray one next to the other.
- Broil 5 minutes. Serve.

Cooked Fresh Tomato Salad

Preparation: . . . . 12 m
Cooking: . . . . 16 m
Standing: . . . . none

A personal note: Serve hot, serve cold, depending on the season. When possible, use button mushrooms, easily available canned, more difficult to find fresh.

Ingredients:

1/2 lb (250 g) fresh button mushrooms

4 tbsp (60 mL) vegetable oil or margarine

1 large onion, minced

2 garlic cloves, chopped fine

2 tbsp (30 mL) cider or wine vinegar

1 tsp (5 mL) sugar

4 to 6 tomatoes, peeled and chopped

1/4 tsp (1 mL) thyme

2 bay leaves

2 tbsp (30 mL) fresh chopped parsley

Method:

• Cut stems from button mushrooms, wipe clean with a cloth. When using large mushrooms, cut stems, wipe clean and slice caps in four.

• Heat the oil or margarine in a 4-cup (1 L) microwave-safe dish 3 minutes at HIGH. Add the mushrooms, stir well. Microwave 2 minutes at HIGH.

• Add onion and garlic, stir. Microwave 3 minutes at HIGH. Stir well.

• Stir together the vinegar and sugar. Add to the tomato mixture. Microwave 4 minutes at HIGH.

• Add remaining ingredients and the mushrooms. Stir until well mixed. Microwave 4 minutes at HIGH.

• Serve hot or at room temperature.

Tomatoes St-Raphaël

Preparation:	. . . . **10 m**
Cooking:	. . . . **from 7 to 9 m**
Standing:	. . . . **none**

A personal note: These tomatoes are served hot with a dish of sliced hard cooked eggs, simply sprinkled with minced chives (green onions can be used), and a basket of hot French bread.

Ingredients:

4 medium-sized tomatoes

1/4 cup (60 mL) butter

1 small onion, chopped fine

1/2 tsp (2 mL) basil or tarragon

1/2 cup (125 mL) dried breadcrumbs

3 tbsp (50 mL) cheese, grated

2 tsp (10 mL) sugar

Salt and pepper to taste

2 green onions, chopped fine

Method:

• Try to choose tomatoes of even size. Wash, cut in half, place cut-side down on paper towel, let stand 10 minutes.

• Place the butter in a microwave-safe bowl and melt 2 minutes at HIGH.

• Add the onion, basil or tarragon. Stir well. Microwave 2 minutes at HIGH, stirring once.

• Add the breadcrumbs, stir. Microwave 2 to 3 minutes at HIGH, stirring once. The breadcrumbs will brown lightly.

• Place the tomatoes, cut-side up, in a 12 × 8-inch (30 × 20 cm) Pyrex or plastic dish. Sprinkle each half with 1/4 teaspoon (1 mL) sugar, salt and pepper to taste.

• Mix the browned breadcrumbs and grated cheese and divide equally on top of each tomato. Microwave, uncovered, 3 to 4 minutes at MEDIUM-HIGH.

• These can be prepared in advance and kept at room temperature, topping with the cheese mixture only when ready to serve.

Sautéed Cherry Tomatoes

Preparation: . . . . **8 m**
Cooking: . . . . **5 m**
Standing: . . . . **none**

• In the summer, when these elegant small tomatoes are on the market in quantity, try this favorite of mine. Quick and easy.

Ingredients:

8 to 12 cherry tomatoes
1/4 cup (60 mL) butter or margarine
1/2 tsp (2 mL) salt
1/4 tsp (1 mL) pepper
1 tsp (5 mL) sugar

Method:

• Wash tomatoes quickly in cold water, wipe dry.

• Cut the small core on top.

• Choose a microwave-safe pie plate or a dish large enough to hold the tomatoes one next to the other, core-side up.

• Mix the remaining ingredients.

• Divide equally over each little tomato.

• Microwave 5 minutes at MEDIUM-HIGH. Serve piping hot.

Gratiné Tomatoes

Convection or microwave cooking

| Preparation: .... **15 m** |
| Cooking: microwave: .... **from 8 to 10 m** |
| convection: .... **20 m** |
| Standing: .... **none** |

A personal note: In Florence, Italy, this dish is served as an hors-d'oeuvre with thin pasta. Cooked green pasta is placed in the middle of a white platter, then surrounded with the tomatoes. This is served with a bowl of grated cheese.

Ingredients:

6 medium-sized tomatoes

2 tbsp (30 mL) olive or vegetable oil

1 tsp (5 mL) basil

1/2 tsp (2 mL) oregano

2 garlic cloves, chopped fine

Salt and pepper to taste

1/4 cup (60 mL) grated Parmesan cheese

2/3 cup (160 mL) dry breadcrumbs

3 tsp (15 mL) sugar

Method:

• Slice the tomatoes in half crosswise and scoop up the pulp with a teaspoon, leaving a firm 1/4-inch (60 cm) wall. Remove the seeds from the tomato pulp. Chop the pulp coarsely and place in a bowl with all the liquid from the tomatoes.

• Add the oil, basil, oregano, garlic, salt, pepper, Parmesan and breadcrumbs. Stir until well blended.

• Sprinkle 1/4 teaspoon (1 mL) sugar inside each tomato. Salt and pepper lightly. Fill with an equal portion of stuffing.

• Place the tomato halves in a microwave-safe dish large enough to hold them one next to the other.

• Microwave at MEDIUM-HIGH 8 to 10 minutes. The time will vary, depending on the size of the tomatoes.

To cook by convection

• Preheat convection part of microwave oven to 350°F (180°C).

• Bake tomatoes 20 minutes. Serve hot.

wines

Valpolicella

Brunello di Montalcino

Super Tomato Mousse

Advance preparation: . . . . **12 h**
Cooking: . . . . **16 m**
Standing: . . . . **none**

A personal note: I serve this mousse as a salad, in a nest of watercress, or as a vegetable with cold poached salmon.

• Mix the unflavored gelatin with the cold water. Microwave 1 minute at MEDIUM. Stir. If gelatin is clear, it is ready to add to the tomato mixture. Stir well, while adding the gelatin.

• Whip the cream and fold into the tomato mixture. Adjust salt. Pour into an attractive mould or individual custard cups.

• Cover and refrigerate 12 hours before serving.

Ingredients:

6 medium-sized tomatoes
3 tbsp (50 mL) butter
1 tbsp (15 mL) sugar
1/2 tsp (2 mL) basil

White sauce:

2 tbsp (30 mL) butter
2 tbsp (30 mL) flour
1 cup (250 mL) milk
1 envelope unflavored gelatin
2 tbsp (30 mL) cold water
1 cup (250 mL) whipping cream

Method:

• Pour boiling water over tomatoes, let stand a few minutes. Peel as outlined in Tomatoes "Nature."

• Place the 3 tablespoons (50 mL) butter in a 4-cup (1 L) microwave-safe dish. Melt 2 minutes at HIGH. Add the peeled tomatoes, cut in four, sugar and basil. Stir well. Microwave 10 minutes at MEDIUM, stirring once.

• Make a white sauce in the following manner in a 4-cup (1 L) microwave-safe measuring cup or a bowl:

• Place the 2 tablespoons (30 mL) butter in the cup and melt 2 minutes at HIGH. Stir in the flour and add the milk. Microwave 2 minutes at MEDIUM-HIGH, stir well. Microwave 1 minute more at MEDIUM-HIGH, if sauce is not creamy enough.

• Salt and pepper to taste.

• Add to the tomatoes, mix thoroughly.

• Then pass the whole through a fine sieve or purée in a food processor.

Easy Tomato Sauce

Preparation: . . . . **9 m**
Cooking: . . . . **from 12 to 13 m**
Standing: . . . . **none**

A personal note: This versatile sauce can be cooked and frozen in small quantities to be added to gravy, or as a topping to cauliflower, cabbage or celery. Mixed with 2 cups (500 mL) of warm milk, you have a soup. Poured over cooked spaghetti and served with a bowl of grated cheese, you have a spaghetti sauce. Or it can be served instead of gravy with roasted pork or veal.

Ingredients:

3 tbsp (50 mL) butter or margarine

1 small onion, chopped fine

1 or 2 garlic cloves, chopped fine

2 celery stalks, diced

1 tsp (5 mL) sugar

1/2 tsp (2 mL) each thyme and basil

1 bay leaf

1   28-oz (796 mL) can of tomatoes

Salt and pepper to taste

Method:

• In a 6-cup (1.5 L) microwave-safe dish melt the butter or margarine 3 minutes at HIGH.

• Add the onion, garlic and celery. Stir well.

• Microwave 4 minutes at HIGH. Stir again.

• Add the remaining ingredients, stir well.

• Microwave 8 to 9 minutes at MEDIUM-HIGH.

• Stir well and use.

Helpful hint: When defrosting ground beef, let food stand for a time equal to the defrost time.

Green Tomato Sauce

Preparation: . . . . **12 m**
Cooking: . . . . **from 25 to 30 m**
Standing: . . . .**none**

• This sauce is an old Québec favorite. If you have tomatoes in your garden, this is a welcome recipe, as we always seem to have many green tomatoes. It freezes very well. Thawing it in the microwave oven is easy.

Ingredients:

6 to 8 green tomatoes

4 tbsp (60 mL) butter

4 medium-sized onions, thickly sliced

3 apples, peeled and sliced

1 tsp (5 mL) salt

1/2 tsp (2 mL) pepper

2 whole cloves

1/2 tsp (2 mL) cinnamon

1/2 tsp (2 mL) dry mustard

1 tbsp (15 mL) sugar

Method:

• Peel the tomatoes as for Tomatoes ''Nature'' and slice thickly.

• Place the butter in a 10 to 12-cup (2.5 to 3 L) microwave-safe dish and melt 2 minutes at HIGH.

• Add the tomatoes, onions and apples.

• Mix well with the butter. Add all the remaining ingredients. Mix well. Cover.

• Microwave 15 minutes at HIGH.

• Stir well and microwave 10 minutes at MEDIUM.

• The sauce should be creamy, with a nice texture.

• If the tomatoes are still a little hard, microwave another 5 minutes at MEDIUM.

• Serve.

Helpful hint: Always bring the cooked outside edges toward the center and the less cooked center portions toward the outside.

Tomato Juice Broth

Preparation: . . . . 7 m
Cooking: .20 m
Standing: . . . .**none**

A personal note: This broth is simple and quickly made. If desired, a half cup of fine vermicelli can be added.

Ingredients:

2 tsp (10 mL) butter or bacon fat
1 large onion, finely chopped
1/2 cup (125 mL) celery, diced
4 cups (1 L) tomato juice
1 bay leaf
1/2 tsp (2 mL) basil
1 tsp (5 mL) sugar
1 tsp (5 mL) salt
1/4 tsp (1 mL) pepper

Method:

• Place the butter or bacon fat in an 8-cup (2 L) microwave-safe bowl and melt 40 seconds at HIGH.

• Add the onion and celery. Microwave 5 minutes at HIGH, stir well, then add the remaining ingredients. Microwave 15 minutes at HIGH.

• Taste for seasoning. Serve hot or cold.

• The broth can be jellied by adding 2 envelopes of unflavored gelatin, soaked 5 minutes in an additional 1 cup (250 mL) cold tomato juice.

• Stir and add to the hot cooked soup. Stir well and microwave 2 minutes at HIGH.

• Cool and refrigerate.

Fresh Tomato Broth

Preparation: . . . . **8 m**
Cooking: . . . . **10 m**
Standing: . . . . **none**

A personal note: For a light brunch, serve this broth very hot with small hot rolls, accompanied by a good cheese sliced into individual pieces and a "café-cognac." One can't ask for better, and it's so easy for the hostess.

Ingredients:

2 cups (500 mL) fresh tomatoes, peeled and diced

2 cups (500 mL) beef consommé

1/2 tsp (2 mL) sugar

1 tbsp (15 mL) fresh lemon juice

1 tsp (5 mL) A-1 sauce

Salt and pepper to taste

1 tsp (5 mL) dill or basil*

Method:

• Place all the ingredients in a microwave-safe soup tureen.**

• Heat 10 minutes at HIGH.

* When possible, use fresh basil, finely minced.
** Use a soup tureen if you are serving at the table. A microwave casserole may be used if you are serving in the kitchen.

Fresh Tomato Bouillon

Preparation: . . . . 15 m
Cooking: . . . . 20 m
Standing: . . . . 20 m

A personal note: Use fresh tomatoes when you can, but when they're out of season, substitute a 19-oz (540 mL) can of tomatoes.

Ingredients:

2 tbsp (30 mL) butter

4 green onions *or* 1 small onion, chopped

1 large garlic clove, chopped

4 cups (1 L) fresh tomatoes, sliced

3 tsp (15 mL) sugar

1/4 tsp (1 mL) freshly ground pepper

1 celery stalk, sliced

1 cup (250 mL) water or beef consommé

1 tsp (5 mL) each of salt and basil

1/2 tsp (2 mL) oregano

Method:

• Place the butter in an 8-cup (2 L) microwave-safe bowl and melt 1 minute at HIGH. Add onions and garlic, mix and microwave at HIGH 4 minutes. Stir well; pieces here and there will be browned.

• Add remaining ingredients. Cover, microwave at HIGH 15 minutes.

• Let stand 20 minutes and strain through a fine sieve, pressing on the tomatoes.

• A nice garnish to the hot tomato bouillon are cubes of avocado and a few dices of crisp bacon.

• This bouillon can be served hot or cold.

Tomato Potage

Preparation: . . . . 12 m
Cooking: . . . . 26 m
Standing: . . . . none

• This is my favorite potage: rosy, creamy, flavorful and so easy to make.

Ingredients:

1/4 cup (60 mL) butter

2 medium onions, thinly sliced

4 ripe tomatoes, unpeeled and sliced

4 cups (1 L) boiling water

1/4 tsp (1 mL) pepper

1 tsp (5 mL) salt

1/2 tsp (2 mL) sugar

3 cups (750 mL) potatoes, peeled and sliced

1/2 cup (125 mL) cream

Method:

• Place the butter in a 12-cup (3 L) microwave-safe bowl and melt 1 minute at HIGH.

• Add the onions, microwave 5 minutes at HIGH; stir well.

• Add the tomatoes and stir to blend well with the onions.

• Add the remaining ingredients, except the cream. Microwave 20 minutes at HIGH.

• Purée in a vegetable mill or food processor.

• When ready to serve, add the cream and heat 1 minute at HIGH.

Creamed Tomato Dill Soup

Preparation: . . . . **10 m**
Cooking: . . . . **28 m**
Standing: . . . . **none**

A personal note: Cooked macaroni gives a creamy texture to this light cream soup; the fresh dill gives it character. It's perfect served cold, delectable served hot.

Ingredients:

3 fresh tomatoes, peeled and sliced
1 medium onion, peeled and sliced
1 garlic clove, crushed
1 tsp (5 mL) each of salt and sugar
1/4 tsp (1 mL) pepper
1 tbsp (15 mL) tomato paste
1/4 cup (60 mL) water
1/2 cup (125 mL) macaroni
2 cups (500 mL) boiling water
4 cups (1 L) chicken consommé
3/4 cup (200 mL) light cream
2 sprigs of fresh dill *or*
   1 tsp (5 mL) dried dill

Method:

• Place the tomatoes in a 12-cup (3 L) microwave-safe bowl.

• Add the onion, garlic, salt, sugar, pepper, tomato paste and water.

• Microwave 3 minutes at HIGH.

• In a second container, place the macaroni; cover with the 2 cups (500 mL) boiling salted water.

• Microwave at MEDIUM-HIGH 15 minutes, drain and add to the tomatoes. Mix.

• Pour the whole into a food processor or electric mixer.

• Start the machine and gradually add the chicken consommé, cream and dill. Process until creamy.

• Place in the microwave and cook 10 minutes at HIGH, or until the soup is very hot.

Cream of Fresh Tomatoes

Preparation: .... 9 m
Cooking: .... 17 m
Standing: .... none

A personal note: Use only fresh tomatoes, not canned for this soup. I make it when tomatoes are plentiful in my garden. It is light and smooth.

Ingredients:

6 to 8 tomatoes

2 cups (500 mL) boiling water

1 tbsp (15 mL) fresh minced basil

1/2 tsp (2 mL) salt

1 tsp (5 mL) sugar

1/2 cup (125 mL) unsalted butter

1 cup (250 mL) rich cream

1/2 cup (125 mL) milk

Chives, finely minced

Method:

- Cut the tomatoes into 5 or 6 pieces.

- Place in a 10-cup (2.5 L) microwave-safe bowl the boiling water, basil, salt and sugar. Microwave 15 minutes at HIGH, stirring well half-way through the cooking.

- Strain, pressing heavily on the tomatoes to extract as much juice as possible. Pour the juice into the bowl.

- Add the butter, in small pieces, stirring after each addition.

- Add the cream and milk gradually, beating with a wire whisk. Heat 2 minutes at HIGH.

- Garnish each bowl with finely minced chives.

- This soup may also be served chilled.

Pink Cream of Tomato

Preparation: . . . . **14 m**
Cooking: . . . . **from 29 to 34 m**
Standing: . . . . **none**

A personal note: This is my favorite tomato soup. At the end of the summer when tomatoes are at their best, I make about 40 2-cup (500 mL) containers of it, omitting the cream and the parsley, which I freeze. To serve, I defrost a container in the microwave, add cream and parsley, reheat and serve.

Ingredients:

3 medium tomatoes, unpeeled

2 leeks, thinly sliced

2 medium potatoes, peeled and diced

3 tbsp (50 mL) butter

Salt and pepper to taste

2 tsp (10 mL) sugar

3 cups (750 mL) chicken consommé or water

2 cups (500 mL) light or rich cream

2 tbsp (30 mL) parsley, finely minced

Method:

• Dice the tomatoes. Clean the leeks and slice both the white and green parts. Peel and dice the potatoes.

• Place the butter in a 12-cup (3 L) bowl. Heat 1 minute at HIGH.

• Add the leeks. Stir well and microwave 3 minutes at HIGH.

• Add the tomatoes and microwave another 3 minutes at HIGH.

• Stir well, add the potatoes; salt and pepper to taste.

• Add the sugar; stir until well blended.

• Add the chicken consommé or water.

• Cover, microwave 10 to 14 minutes at HIGH. Potatoes must be soft at this point.

• Purée in a food processor or food mill.

• Reheat 8 or 9 minutes at MEDIUM-HIGH.

• Add the cream and microwave 5 minutes at MEDIUM.

• Stir well and serve sprinkled with minced parsley.

Japanese Sea Vegetables

- I feel I should add a note here about the versatile sea vegetables of Japan, as so many of us are becoming increasingly aware of them.

- There is, for example, the Nori, Wakame and Kombu, which are readily available in Oriental food shops.

- They can be sautéed with vegetables or sprinkled over them instead of salt, or used to top a casserole of your choice or mixed with a sauce as a nutritional supplement with whatever vegetable you microwave.

- The big plus, of course, is the delicate, intriguing flavor and nutritional supplement they add to the vegetables. You will soon discover that they enhance the natural flavor of the vegetables without altering them.

Sauces for Vegetables

- Making sauce for vegetables in a microwave oven eliminates the difficulty, extra care and work required to prepare a sauce in the conventional manner. There are no lumps, burning or constant stirring. It is also interesting to remember that a sauce can be prepared early in the morning and warmed up when needed at meal time, particularly since warming up generally will take only from 1 to 3 minutes, depending on the amount.

- After making some of the following sauces, you will quickly learn to adapt your own favorites to microwave cooking.

- Do not worry about opening the microwave oven door to ckeck the cooking or to stir the sauce. As seconds can make quite a difference in microwave cooking, stirring is very important.

- Sauces are often an important adjunct to a good vegetable, since they garnish, extend or bind together the foods with which they are served.

Herb Butter

Preparation: . . . . **10 m**
Cooking: . . . . **none**
Standing: . . . . **none**

A personal note: As this butter may be kept for six months in the refrigerator and one year in the freezer, I suggest that you make it during the summer when aromatic herbs are plentiful.

4 green onions, chopped fine, both white and green parts

1/4 tsp (1 mL) fresh ground pepper

Grated rind of half a lemon

Ingredients:

1 cup (250 mL) unsalted butter*

1 tsp (5 mL) each of salt and dill

1/2 tsp (2 mL) tarragon

1/2 tsp (2 mL) savory

1/4 cup (60 mL) parsley, chopped

1 tsp (5 mL) powdered coriander (optional)

Method:

• Cream all the ingredients together, cool one hour in the refrigerator.

• Shape into small balls and refrigerate or freeze, as you wish.

* If you use salted butter, reduce the salt called for in the recipe to 1/4 teaspoon (1 mL).

Basic White Sauce

Preparation: . . . . 2 m
Cooking: . . . . from 4 to 5 m
Standing: . . . . none

Light sauce:

Medium sauce:

Ingredients:

1 tbsp (15 mL) butter or fat

1 tbsp (15 mL) flour

1 cup (250 mL) liquid

Ingredients:

2 tbsp (30 mL) butter or fat

2 tbsp (30 mL) flour

1 cup (250 mL) liquid

Thick sauce:

Light or Dark Brown Cream Sauce

Ingredients:

3 tbsp (50 mL) butter or fat
4 tbsp (60 mL) flour
1 cup (250 mL) liquid

Method:

• Place the butter or fat in a 4-cup (1 L) microwave-safe dish and melt 1 minute at HIGH.

• Add the flour, mix well. Add the liquid, stir well.

• Microwave 3 minutes at MEDIUM-HIGH, stir midway through cooking. Salt and pepper to taste. Microwave another 30 seconds to 1 minute or until creamy and well cooked.

• If you wish to have a browned sauce or a dark brown sauce, microwave the butter and flour together until you obtain the color you want.

Sauce Mornay

Preparation:	. . . . **5 m**
Cooking:	. . . . **from 5 to 6 m**
Standing:	. . . . **none**

A personal note: This French cheese sauce is very interesting to serve with root vegetables. In the winter, it gives an additional finish that is appreciated in cold weather. It's equally good with greens or colored vegetables.

Ingredients:

2 egg yolks

1/2 cup (125 mL) table cream

1 cup (250 mL) Medium White Sauce

1/2 cup (125 mL) grated cheese of your choice

Method:

• Beat the egg yolks and cream together.

• Cook White Sauce according to basic recipe.

• Add egg mixture to hot sauce, beating well.

• Beat in the cheese.

• Microwave, uncovered, 1 minute at HIGH. Stir and serve.

Sauce Soubise

Preparation:	. . . . **7 m**
Cooking:	. . . . **8 m**
Standing:	. . . . **none**

A personal note: This is an onion sauce, interesting to serve with cauliflower or cabbage, or over 2 cups (500 mL) of thinly sliced cooked carrots.

Ingredients:

1 tbsp (15 mL) butter

3 medium onions, thinly sliced

1 to 2 cups (250 to 500 mL) Medium White Sauce

A pinch of nutmeg

Salt and pepper to taste

Method:

• Place the butter in a medium-sized microwave-safe bowl and melt 2 minutes at HIGH. Add the onions, stir well. Cover and microwave 4 minutes at HIGH, stirring once.

• Add to 1 or 2 cups (250 or 500 mL) Medium White Sauce. Flavor with nutmeg, salt and pepper.

• When ready to serve, microwave at HIGH 2 minutes or until bubbly.

Parsley Sauce

Preparation:	. . . . **5 m**
Cooking:	. . . . **from 4 to 5 m**
Standing:	. . . . **none**

A personal note: A parsley sauce is nice over all summer vegetables or with cooked carrots.

Ingredients:

1 cup Medium White Sauce

2 tbsp (30 mL) parsley, chopped

1 green onion, chopped fine

1 tsp (5 mL) butter

Method:

• Make White Sauce.

• Add all remaining ingredients. Stir until butter is melted.

• Season to taste. Serve.

Sauce Béarnaise

Preparation:	. . . . **8 m**
Cooking:	. . . . **4 m**
Standing:	. . . . **none**

A personal note: A Béarnaise is a Hollandaise seasoned with tarragon and white wine vinegar. It is the ideal sauce to serve with green beans, new cauliflower, artichokes or melted leeks.

Ingredients:

3 tbsp (50 mL) white wine or cider vinegar

1 green onion, chopped

1 tsp (5 mL) tarragon

4 peppercorns, ground

1/3 cup (80 mL) butter

2 egg yolks, beaten

Method:

• Place the vinegar, onion and tarragon in a 2-cup (500 mL) microwave-safe measuring cup. Microwave, uncovered, 2 minutes at HIGH.

• Put through a sieve into an attractive microwave ovenware dish, pressing the onions.

• Add the ground peppercorns and butter. Microwave 1 minute at HIGH.

• Add the beaten egg yolks. Microwave, uncovered, 30 seconds at HIGH. Beat well. Microwave 20 seconds more, or until the sauce is creamy.

True Hollandaise

Preparation:	5 m
Cooking:	2 m
Standing:	none

A personal note: A sheer delight to make, this Hollandaise never fails. It's always perfect with the more delicate vegetables.

Ingredients:

1/3 to 1/2 cup (80 to 125 mL) salted or unsalted butter

2 egg yolks
Juice of 1 small lemon

Method:

• Place the butter in a small microwave-safe casserole or 2-cup (500 mL) measuring cup. Microwave 1 minute at MEDIUM-HIGH.

• Add egg yolks and lemon juice. Beat well with a small whisk. Microwave 20 seconds at MEDIUM-HIGH, beat well.

• If necessary, microwave 20 seconds more at MEDIUM-HIGH for the sauce to have a creamy texture.

• Whisk, salt to taste. Serve.

Sauce Mousseline

Preparation:	5 m
Cooking:	2 m
Standing:	none

Method:

• Beat **2 egg whites** stiff and add to the Hollandaise.

• For the sauce to be light and fluffy, add the egg whites immediately before serving.

Orange Sauce Maltaise

Preparation:	5 m
Cooking:	2 m
Standing:	none

Method:

• In the Hollandaise of your choice, replace the lemon juice with **4 tablespoons (60 mL) of the juice and the grated rind of one orange.**

Sour Cream Sauce

Preparation: . . . . **5 m**
Cooking: . . . . **3 m**
Standing: . . . . **none**

A personal note: Creamy, tasty, and easy to prepare, this sauce goes well with all vegetables.

Ingredients:

1 cup (250 mL) sour cream
1/2 tsp (2 mL) salt
1/2 tsp (2 mL) curry powder
1/8 tsp (0.5 mL) pepper

1 tbsp (15 mL) lemon juice
Grated rind of 1 lemon

Method:

• Combine all the ingredients in a 2-cup (500 mL) microwave-safe measuring cup.

• Microwave uncovered 2 minutes at MEDIUM-HIGH, stirring twice.

• If necessary, microwave 1 minute more at MEDIUM.

Mushroom Sauce

Preparation: . . . . **5 m**
Cooking: . . . . **7 m**
Standing: . . . . **none**

A personal note: Here's a recipe to use with summer or winter vegetables whenever you wish to serve a more elegant dish than family fare.

Ingredients:

3 tbsp (50 mL) butter or margarine

2 tbsp (30 mL) flour

1 tsp (5 mL) soy sauce *or*
  1 tbsp (15 mL) dry Madeira

3/4 cup (190 mL) light cream or milk

1/4 tsp (1 mL) salt

One 4-oz (112 g) can chopped mushrooms, undrained

1/4 tsp (1 mL) tarragon or curry powder

Method:

• Place butter or margarine in a 4-cup (1 L) microwave-safe glass bowl.

• Microwave 1 minute at HIGH.

• Add the flour, soy sauce or dry Madeira to the melted butter or margarine. Blend to a smooth paste.

• Add cream or milk, stir until smooth.

• Add salt, mushrooms, tarragon or curry powder.

• Microwave, uncovered, 2 minutes at HIGH. Stir well.

• Microwave another 4 minutes at HIGH. Stir well.

• By this time sauce should be thick and creamy.

• If it gets cold before you are ready to serve, stir well, microwave 1 minute at HIGH, uncovered.

White Wine Mushroom Sauce

Preparation: . . . . **10 m**
Cooking: . . . . **5 m**
Standing: . . . . **none**

• This is the perfect choice whenever you wish to serve a fine and elegant sauce with vegetables.

Ingredients:

1 tbsp (15 mL) butter

1 cup (250 mL), very full, mushrooms, thinly sliced

2 French shallots *or*
4 green onions, finely chopped

1 tbsp (15 mL) cornstarch

1/2 cup (125 mL) white wine *or*
juice of half a lemon

1 tbsp (15 mL) cream

Salt and pepper to taste

Method:

• Place the butter in a 4-cup (1 L) microwave-safe measuring cup and melt 1 minute at HIGH.

• Add the cleaned mushrooms, thinly sliced.

• Finely chop the shallots or green onions.

• Add to the mushrooms together with the cornstarch, mix well.

• Microwave 2 minutes at HIGH. Stir.

• Add the white wine or the lemon juice, cream, salt and pepper to taste, and microwave 2 minutes more at HIGH, stirring halfway through the cooking.

• This sauce reheats well, 2 minutes at MEDIUM.

Raisin Sauce

A personal note: A sauce I recommend to be used with vegetables having a slightly strong flavor, such as cabbage, turnip or parsnip.

Preparation: . . . .**5 m**
Cooking: . . . .**5 m**
Standing: . . . . **none**

Ingredients:

1/2 cup (125 mL) brown sugar

1 tbsp (15 mL) cornstarch

1 tsp (5 mL) dry mustard

2 tbsp (30 mL) each lemon juice and cider vinegar

Rind of half a lemon, slivered

1½ cups (375 mL) water

1/3 cup (80 mL) seedless raisins

1 tbsp (15 mL) butter

Method:

• In a 4-cup (1 L) microwave-safe measuring cup combine all ingredients, stirring until thoroughly mixed. Microwave, uncovered, 4 minutes at HIGH.

• Stir and microwave 1 or 2 minutes more if necessary.

464

own through the centuries, soup has been part of the heritage of many nations, representing an invitation for the whole family to sit around the table for a hearty meal. How many great artists have painted just such a table to please our eyes? Or perhaps they were simply hungry and dreaming of such fare.

I'm convinced soup meals are still a wonderful idea, whether at noon or suppertime. With a good loaf of bread, a piece of cheese and a basket of fruit, they make a tasty and nourishing meal. And they're a good way to help out a tight budget.

In many countries, soup still means a large soup kettle filled with meat, vegetables, macaroni and many other good things — a meal in a bowl.

Not so long ago, there were restaurants in Paris that served only soup, bread and cheese. The first one opened in 1765, serving only family-type soups and homemade bread — without butter. The rich soup was enough! Today Paris has the famous Androuet, which serves a superb onion soup and large trays of assorted cheeses to choose from. I remember its special menu for students, which cost so little and which we so enjoyed. But that was in the early 1900s. Today, it is elegance plus — in price, too. Still, it is worth it.

To my surprise, during a trip to Japan I found restaurants there that offer nothing but soup and rice. The soup is called Nabemono — from "nabe," a large pot. Nabemono contains meat or fish and a variety of vegetables cooked in a large iron pot called an "irori," which traditionally is suspended over a central fire that warms everyone sitting around it and makes it easy for everyone to help himself. Nabemono has been popular for more than 200 years.

Then there is the Japanese Shabu-Shabu, which also is essentially a soup. It comes in an earthenware bowl on a cast iron stand with a heater. The bowl is filled with boiling hot consommé and is served with a large, colorful plate filled with slivers of meat and vegetables and a dish of Japanese noodles. Everyone puts together his own soup to taste. A bowl of rice can complete the meal.

In North China, there is the very old custom of everyone sitting around a Mongolian Pot, a large round pan with a funnel in the middle that's filled with charcoal fire to heat the broth that surrounds it.

Sadly, in North America we have too often forsaken the "soupe de famille" for the commercial kind. They have their place, but we must not forget good homemade soups, particularly now that cooking them in the microwave oven can be as fast as preparing a commercial type. For example, a good consommé or bouillon can be cooked in 20 to 30 minutes and — believe it or not — their flavor actually is better than when they're cooked the regular way.

Without a doubt, soups are the most versatile item of the culinary repertoire. Hot, they nourish and warm the body and soul; during a heat wave, they can be served cold to refresh us. It's easy to experiment by choosing vegetables and herbs to suit one's taste.

I think it's important to have a varied repertoire of soups and "potages" to continually entice those who are at your table.

My aim in writing the following recipes has been to explain how to cook soups of all type quickly and easily, thanks to the microwave oven.

Family Chicken Soup

Preparation: . . . . 8 m
Cooking: . . . . 20 m
Standing: . . . . none

A personal note: A meal in a bowl, I have yet to meet a child who does not like this soup. It's a perfect way to use leftover chicken. When I roast a chicken, I remove bits and pieces from the carcass, make a microwave consommé with the bones. When both broth and chicken bits are on hand in the refrigerator, I can prepare this soup in only a few minutes.

Ingredients:

1/2 cup (125 mL) butter or margarine

1/2 cup (125 mL) flour

1 cup (250 mL) milk

6 cups (1.5 L) chicken consommé

1/2 cup (125 mL) cream of your choice

1 to 2 cups (250 to 500 mL) cooked chicken, diced

Salt and pepper to taste

6 green onions, diced (optional)

Method:

• Cream together the butter or margarine and the flour.

• Place in a 12-cup (3 L) microwave-safe bowl the milk and the chicken consommé.

• Microwave at HIGH 10 minutes.

• Add the butter-flour mixture to the cream.

• Mix with a whisk. Add to the hot liquid. Stir well.

• Microwave 10 minutes at HIGH, stirring 3 times.

• When creamy, add the chicken, salt and pepper to taste and the green onions. Serve.

• Sometimes I divide the chicken and green onions into the soup bowls, then fill with the cream of chicken soup.

Bulgarian Meatball Soup

Preparation: . . . . **15 m**
Cooking: . . . . **34 m**
Standing: . . . . **none**

A personal note: A soup of Bulgarian cuisine, this is a complete meal when served with hot homemade bread and butter.

Ingredients:

1 lb (500 g) ground beef

6 tbsp (90 mL) long grain rice, uncooked

1 tsp (5 mL) paprika

1 tsp (5 mL) savory

2 tsp (10 mL) salt

1/2 tsp (2 mL) pepper

6 cups (1.5 L) boiling water

2 beef bouillon cubes *or*
  2 tbsp (30 mL) liquid beef bouillon
  concentrate

6 to 8 green onions, diced

1 large green pepper, diced

2 medium carrots, peeled and thinly sliced

3 tomatoes, peeled and sliced

1/2 cup (125 mL) fresh parsley, minced

1 egg

Juice of 1 lemon

Method:

• Mix together the ground beef, rice, paprika, savory, salt and pepper. Shape into small 1-inch (2.5 cm) meatballs. Roll each one in flour.

• Place in a 12-cup (3 L) microwave-safe bowl the boiling water, beef bouillon cubes or beef concentrate, green onions, green pepper, carrots and tomatoes.

• Microwave at HIGH 25 minutes.

• Add the meatballs. Microwave at HIGH 8 minutes.

• Add the parsley and microwave another minute at HIGH.

• When ready to serve, beat the egg and lemon juice and add to the hot soup while stirring. Serve.

467

Andrea's Ham Soup

Preparation: . . . . **10 m**
Cooking: . . . . **30 m**
Standing: . . . . **none**

A personal note: This is an interesting way to use up leftover cooked ham. The soup can also be prepared with a thin slice of raw ham.

Ingredients:

6 cups (1.5 L) boiling water

2 tbsp (30 mL) tomato paste

1 tsp (5 mL) each coarse salt and tarragon

3/4 cup (200 mL) vermicelli, cut in short
   pieces

1 cup (250 mL) ham, cooked or raw, cut in
   thin strips

2 egg yolks

2 tbsp (30 mL) cream

Method:

• Place water in a 10-cup (2.5 L) microwave-safe bowl. Bring to boil 10 minutes at HIGH.

• Add the salt, tomato paste, tarragon and vermicelli.

• Cover and microwave at HIGH 15 minutes.

• Stir twice during the cooking period.

• Add the strips of ham to the bouillon. Microwave 5 minutes at HIGH.

• Beat the egg yolks and the cream in the bottom of a soup tureen, and pour the cooked soup all over the eggs and cream, stirring constantly. Serve immediately.

468

Barley, Ground Lamb Soup

Preparation: . . . . 10 m
Cooking: . . . . 55 m
Standing: . . . . none

A personal note: You can use ground beef instead of ground lamb in this soup, which makes a light meal. In summer, I sprinkle minced garden fresh chervil on the soup when it's ready to be served.

Ingredients:

3 tbsp (50 mL) butter or bacon fat

1¼ cups (300 mL) carrots, finely diced

1/2 cup (125 mL) turnip, finely diced

8 cups (2 L) hot water

3/4 cup (200 mL) pearl barley

1/2 lb (250 g) ground lamb

Salt and pepper to taste

Parsley, chervil or chives, minced

Method:

• Place the fat in a large microwave-safe bowl and melt 1 minute at HIGH.

• Add the diced carrots and turnip, stir well.

• Add the hot water, barley and ground lamb. Stir well

• Add salt and pepper.

• Cover and microwave 10 minutes at HIGH. Reduce the heat to MEDIUM-HIGH and microwave 45 minutes.

• Stir twice during the cooking period.

• Serve with chopped chervil, parsley or chives.

Indonesian Soup

Preparation: . . . . **10 m**
Cooking: . . . . **50 m**
Standing: . . . . **from 30 to 40 m**

A personal note: A rice soup with small meatballs and chicken wings, this is served thick as a main meal. It's different and interesting.

Ingredients:

1/2 cup (125 mL) long grain rice

1/2 lb (250 g) ground beef or lamb

1/4 tsp (1 mL) ground coriander

A good pinch of nutmeg

1 tsp (5 mL) salt

1 egg yolk

6 chicken wings

4 cups (1 L) chicken bouillon

2 cups (500 mL) boiling water

Method:

• Place half the rice in the bottom of a 10-cup (2.5 L) microwave-safe bowl.

• Mix the ground meat, coriander, nutmeg, salt and egg yolk. Shape into small meatballs and place on the rice.

• Place the chicken wings over the meatballs. Pour the remaining rice over.

• Pour the chicken bouillon and water over all. Cover. Microwave 20 minutes at HIGH, then 30 minutes at MEDIUM-HIGH. Let stand, without uncovering, 30 to 40 minutes.

• The meat and rice will form a sort of meat cake while cooking.

• Cut into portions and add to each bowl with a chicken wing.

470

Oriental Soup

Preparation: . . . . **16 m**
Cooking: . . . . **from 30 to 38 m**
Standing: . . . . **none**

A personal note: If you're looking for a light meal all in one dish, here is just the recipe. You need a microwave browning dish to make this soup in the microwave.

Ingredients:

1 cup (250 mL) vermicelli

4 cups (1 L) bouillon of your choice

1/4 tsp (1 mL) powdered ginger

1/2 tsp (2 mL) salt

4 thin slices lemon

1/2 lb (250 g) ground beef

Paprika

2 tbsp (30 mL) vegetable oil

Method:

• Bring 3 cups (750 mL) water to the boil 10 to 15 minutes at HIGH.

• Add the vermicelli. Microwave 6 minutes at HIGH. Drain.

• Place the bouillon in a 10-cup (2.5 L) microwave-safe bowl.

• Add the ginger, salt and lemon.

• Microwave 6 minutes at HIGH.

• Make a flat pancake with the ground meat. Sprinkle with paprika on one side.

• Preheat a microwave browning dish 6 minutes at HIGH.

• Without removing the dish from the oven, pour in the vegetable oil and place the ground meat pancake, paprika side down, on the dish.

• Microwave 3 minutes at HIGH.

• Remove from oven, cut into 6 wedges or squares, and place a piece in the bottom of each bowl. Cover with vermicelli.

• Add the very hot soup.

• The meat and vermicelli can be microwave ahead of time (do not refrigerate).

• When ready to serve, heat the bouillon and pour over the meat and vermicelli.

• If necessary, microwave 2 minutes at HIGH.

White Wine Onion Soup

Preparation: . . . . 11 m
Cooking: . . . . 16 m
Standing: . . . . none

A personal note: Delicious, different and light, this soup's classic garnish is a sprig of crisp watercress.

Ingredients:

4 tbsp (60 mL) butter

4 to 6 onions, peeled and thinly sliced, in rings

1/4 tsp (1 mL) thyme

3 cups (750 mL) chicken consommé

1 cup (250 mL) dry white wine

1/2 tsp (2 mL) sugar

1 tsp (5 mL) salt

1/4 tsp (1 mL) freshly ground pepper

2 cups (500 mL) light cream

1½ cups (375 mL) Swiss cheese, grated

Method:

• Place the butter in a 10-cup (2.5 L) microwave-safe bowl and melt 2 minutes at HIGH.

• Add the onions and thyme, stir well. Microwave, uncovered, 5 minutes at HIGH.

• Stir, add the chicken consommé, wine, sugar, salt and pepper.

• Microwave 8 minutes at HIGH.

• Add the cream, microwave 3 minutes at HIGH.

• Serve hot with a bowl of grated Swiss cheese; each person can add cheese to taste.

Helpful hint: For carefree barbecues, partially cook chicken, ribs, etc. in the microwave oven. Season and finish on the grill.

Port Wine Onion Soup

Preparation: . . . . **8 m**
Cooking: . . . .**15 m**
Standing: . . . . **from 1 to 2 m**

A personal note: This is quite different from onion soup au gratin. You pour hot onion soup over fine strips of bread sprinkled with grated Gruyère or Parmesan cheese in the bottom of a soup tureen or bowl.

Ingredients:

3 tbsp (50 mL) butter

2 large onions, finely chopped

1 tbsp (15 mL) flour

4 cups (1 L) boiling water

Salt and pepper to taste

1/2 cup (125 mL) dry port wine

4 to 5 slices of bread, cut in fine strips

1 cup (250 mL) Gruyère or Parmesan cheese, grated

Method:

• Place the butter in an 8-cup (2 L) microwave-safe bowl and melt 2 minutes at HIGH.

• Add the onions, stir well. Heat 5 minutes at HIGH.

• Add the flour, mix well. Add the boiling water, stir until well mixed. Add salt and pepper.

• Microwave 10 minutes at HIGH. Add the port.

• In a soup tureen or large bowl place half the bread strips, cover with the grated cheese and place the remaining strips of bread over the cheese.

• Pour the hot soup over it all. Let stand 1 or 2 minutes. Serve.

473

Shepherd's Onion Soup

Preparation: . . . . **7 m**
Cooking: . . . .**16 m**
Standing: . . . . **none**

• Very nourishing and tasty, this is a sort of onion soup with a water base. The recipe was given to me by a young shepherd in the Pyrenees Mountains, where he spent the summer taking care of his sheep. This soup was his nightly supper. I adapted it to the microwave.

Ingredients:

2 tbsp (30 mL) butter

4 onions, peeled and sliced

2 garlic cloves, sliced

3 to 4 cups (750 mL to 1 L) water

Salt and pepper to taste

6 thin slices of wholewheat or rye bread

A full cup (250 mL) grated Cheddar cheese

Method:

• Place the butter in a 6-cup (1.5 L) microwave-safe bowl and melt 2 minutes at HIGH.

• Add the onions and the garlic. Stir well. Microwave 3 minutes at HIGH. Stir well, microwave another 2 minutes at MEDIUM-HIGH.

• Add the water. Add salt and pepper to taste. Stir well. Microwave 10 minutes at MEDIUM-HIGH.

• Place a slice of bread in each bowl. Divide grated cheese on top. Two layers of bread and cheese can be used, if you prefer a more nourishing soup.

• Pour some of the onion broth on top of the bread.

• Microwave each bowl 1 minute at HIGH.

Pepper Soup

Preparation: . . . . **15 m**
Cooking: . . . . **34 m**
Standing: . . . . **none**

A personal note: When I cut up a chicken, I reserve the two legs to make this soup. Otherwise, I buy a tray of wings or legs for the soup, which makes a complete meal.

Ingredients:

2 tbsp (30 mL) butter or margarine
1 celery stalk, finely diced
1/2 green pepper, finely diced
1 medium onion, minced
1 tbsp (15 mL) flour
4 cups (1 L) hot water
2 to 4 chicken legs*
Salt to taste
1/2 tsp (2 mL) savory
1/4 tsp (1 mL) peppercorns, crushed
2 medium potatoes, finely diced
1 tbsp (15 mL) butter
Parsley, finely chopped

The chicken legs can be diced and added to the soup, or a piece of chicken can be placed in each bowl of soup.

Method:

• Place the butter or margarine in a 10-cup (2.5 L) microwave-safe bowl and melt 2 minutes at HIGH.

• Add the celery, green pepper and onion.

• Microwave 2 minutes at HIGH, stir, then microwave another 2 minutes at HIGH.

• Add the flour, stir to mix well with the vegetables.

• Add the remaining ingredients, except the butter and parsley.

• Stir well, return to microwave and cook at HIGH 30 minutes.

• When ready to serve, add the butter and parsley.

Early Season Finnish Soup

Preparation: . . . . 12 m
Cooking: . . . . 13 m
Standing: . . . . none

• Each year I make this soup around mid-July with my own garden vegetables, or with the produce from our great farmers' markets.

Ingredients:

4 small carrots, thinly sliced

1/2 cup (125 mL) each celery and cucumber, diced

1 cup (250 mL) zucchini, diced

1/4 cup (60 mL) parsley, minced

2 tbsp (30 mL) dill, minced

2 tbsp (30 mL) butter

4 to 5 cups (1 to 1.25 L) chicken broth

Method:

Place all the ingredients except the chicken broth, in a 10-cup (2.5 L) microwave-safe bowl. Mix together.

• Cover and microwave 5 minutes at HIGH, stirring twice.

• Add the chicken broth. Add salt and pepper to taste.

• Microwave, uncovered, 8 minutes at HIGH. Stir once during the cooking.

• If desired, place **1/2 teaspoon (2 mL) unsalted butter** in the bottom of each soup bowl before pouring the soup.

Picardy Soup

Preparation: . . . . **15 m**
Cooking: . . . . **from 32 to 36 m**
Standing: . . . . **none**

> **A personal note:** A cheese and vegetable soup, this make a light, nourishing meal when served with a sandwich or a salad.

Ingredients:

2 cups (500 mL) raw potatoes,
  peeled and diced

1/4 cup (60 mL) onions, minced

1/2 cup (125 mL) celery, diced

2½ cups (625 mL) water

1 tsp (5 mL) salt

2 tbsp (30 mL) butter

2 tbsp (30 mL) flour

2 cups (500 mL) milk

3/4 cup (200 mL) mild Cheddar, grated

1/2 tsp (2 mL) dry mustard

1 tsp (5 mL) savory

Grated rind of 1/2 a lemon

Salt and pepper to taste

1 19-oz (540 mL) can tomatoes

1/2 tsp (2 mL) sugar

Method:

• Place in a 10-cup (2.5 L) microwave-safe bowl the potatoes, onions, celery, water and salt. Cover and microwave at HIGH 15 to 18 minutes or until vegetables are tender. Stir twice during cooking.

• Place the butter in a 4-cup (1 L) microwave-safe bowl and melt 1 minute at HIGH. Stir in the flour. Mix well and add the milk.

• Microwave at HIGH 6 to 8 minutes, stirring twice.

• When creamy, add the grated cheese, dry mustard, savory and the grated lemon rind.

• Stir well and add to the cooked vegetables. (Do not drain; the water is part of the soup.)

• Add tomatoes and sugar. Salt and pepper to taste.

• Microwave at HIGH 10 minutes, stirring twice.

• To serve, garnish with chopped parsley.

Cabbage Soup

Preparation: . . . . **10 m**
Cooking: . . . . **35 m**
Standing: . . . . **none**

A personal note: You can make this soup with leeks or onions. I make mine with defrosted frozen leeks, which I freeze at the end of summer, when they are at their best in quality and price.

Ingredients:

4 potatoes, peeled and grated

4 cups (1 L) green cabbage, minced

1 large leek *or* 2 onions, minced

6 cups (1.5 L) boiling water

2 tsp (10 mL) salt

1 tsp (5 mL) dill seeds

1/4 tsp (1 mL) pepper

1/2 cup (125 mL) cream

2 tbsp (30 mL) butter

Method:

• Place in a 20-cup (5 L) microwave-safe bowl all the ingredients, except the cream and butter. Microwave at MEDIUM-HIGH 30 minutes, stirring after half the cooking time.

• Add the cream and butter. Microwave at MEDIUM-HIGH 5 minutes. Test seasoning and serve.

Celery and Rice Soup

Preparation: . . . . **5 m**
Cooking: . . . . **from 12 to 14 m**
Standing: . . . . **none**

A personal note: If you have some beef consommé or chicken broth, this is the soup to make. It's light, elegant, and hardly any work.

Ingredients:

2 tbsp (30 mL) butter

4 tbsp (60 mL) celery, finely diced

4 tbsp (60 mL) instant rice

4 cups (1 L) beef consommé or chicken broth

2 tbsp (30 mL) parsley or chives, minced

Method:

• Place the butter in a 6-cup (1.5 L) microwave-safe bowl and melt 1 minute at HIGH.

• Add the remaining ingredients. Microwave at HIGH 12 to 14 minutes.

Prague Mushroom Soup

Preparation: . . . . 17 m
Cooking: . . . . 37 m
Standing: . . . . none

A personal note: A delicious traditional soup of Central Europe, Prague Mushroom Soup usually is made with wild mushrooms, fresh or dry. They give the soup a very special flavor. Even 3 to 6 dry mushrooms added to fresh mushrooms will change the flavor.

Ingredients:

1/2 cup (125 mL) butter

1 cup (250 mL) each diced celery and carrots

1 large onion, finely chopped

2 medium tomatoes, unpeeled, diced

1 cup (250 mL) potatoes, finely diced

3 cups (750 mL) mushrooms, thinly sliced

6 cups (1.5 L) consommé of your choice

1/2 tsp (2 mL) thyme

1/2 tsp (2 mL) tarragon *or*
  1 tsp (5 mL) fresh dill

Salt and pepper to taste

Method:

• Place the butter in a 12-cup (3 L) microwave-safe bowl and melt 2 minutes at HIGH.

• Add the vegetables except the mushrooms.

• Stir well in the butter.

• Microwave, covered, 10 minutes at MEDIUM-HIGH, stirring halfway through the cooking.

• Add mushrooms, stir.

• Add the remaining ingredients.

• Cover and microwave 25 minutes at MEDIUM-HIGH. Stir well.

• This soup will keep 4 to 5 days refrigerated and will freeze 6 to 9 weeks without losing its flavor.

Swiss Mountain Soup

Preparation: . . . . 8 m
Cooking: . . . . 12 m
Standing: . . . . none

A personal note: In Switzerland, this soup is made with wild mushrooms, which give it a very distinct flavor. Cultivated mushrooms also give it an interesting taste. Minced chives and parsley are used as a garnish in Switzerland.

Ingredients:

2 tbsp (30 mL) butter

4 green onions, minced

2 tbsp (30 mL) flour

1/2 tsp (2 mL) curry powder

1 cup (250 mL) chicken broth

2 cups (500 mL) milk

Salt and pepper to taste

1/2 lb (250 g) mushrooms, minced

1 egg yolk

1/4 cup (60 mL) cream

Chives and parsley to taste

Method:

• Place the butter in a 6-cup (1.5 L) microwave-safe bowl, melt for 1 minute at HIGH.

• Add the green onions, flour and the curry powder, blend together.

• Add the chicken broth, milk, salt and pepper to taste.

• Add the mushrooms.

• Microwave 8 minutes at HIGH, stirring once at mid-cooking.

• Beat together the egg yolk, cream and 2 tablespoons (30 mL) of the hot soup. Pour into the soup, stirring constantly.

• Microwave at MEDIUM 4 minutes.

• Garnish with chives and parsley.

Cucumber Soup

Preparation: . . . . **14 m**
Cooking: . . . . **from 25 to 26 m**
Standing: . . . . **none**

A personal note: To serve hot, prepare this soup with milk. To serve it cold, replace the milk with chicken broth.

Ingredients:

3 cups (750 mL) cucumbers, peeled and sliced

1 medium onion, finely chopped

2 tbsp (30 mL) butter

3 tbsp (50 mL) flour

1 tsp (5 mL) salt

2 cups (500 mL) milk or chicken broth

Juice of 1/2 a lemon

1/4 tsp (1 mL) dried dill *or*
 1 tsp (5 mL) fresh dill

1 cup (250 mL) sour cream

1 small cucumber, peeled, seeded and grated

Method:

• Place in an 8-cup (2 L) microwave-safe bowl the sliced cucumbers, onion and butter. Sprinkle with the flour. Stir well and microwave at HIGH 10 minutes, stirring well after 5 minutes.

• Add the salt and milk or broth. Microwave 10 minutes at HIGH.

• Add the lemon juice and dill.

• Make a purée by passing the mixture through a vegetable mill or in a food processor. Add the sour cream, beat well.

• To serve hot, stir well and microwave at MEDI-UM 5 to 6 minutes. Check during the cooking, since this soup must not boil after the sour cream has been added.

• To serve cold, spread grated cucumber in each bowl, then pour in the soup.

481

Red Cabbage Soup

Preparation:	10 m
Cooking:	18 m
Standing:	none

A personal note: This soup can be served hot or cold. Garnish it with a dollop of sour cream when hot, and with finely chopped chives and walnuts when cold.

Ingredients:

1/4 cup (60 mL) butter or bacon fat

1 leek, cleaned and thinly sliced

1/4 tsp (1 mL) allspice

1/4 tsp (1 mL) ground cloves

2 garlic cloves, chopped fine

2 tbsp (30 mL) brown sugar

1/4 cup (60 mL) cider or Japanese vinegar

3 cups (750 mL) red cabbage, finely shredded

1 19-oz (540 mL) can tomatoes

2 cups (500 mL) chicken bouillon

Salt and pepper to taste

Method:

• Place the butter or bacon fat in an 8-cup (2 L) microwave-safe bowl and melt 1 minute at HIGH.

• Stir in the leek. Microwave 4 minutes at HIGH.

• Add the allspice, cloves and garlic, stir well. Microwave 1 minute at HIGH.

• Add the brown sugar and the vinegar and stir until the sugar is softened.

• Add the shredded cabbage and tomatoes. Cover and microwave 5 minutes at HIGH.

• Stir well, add the chicken bouillon. Salt and pepper to taste. Microwave at HIGH 8 minutes. Stir and serve.

Parsnip Soup

Preparation: . . . . **12 m**
Cooking: . . . .**25 m**
Standing: . . . . **5 m**

• This old recipe from Quebec has almost been forgotten, yet it's so good. Also almost forgotten are parsnips, sometimes called "carottes blanches" (white carrots) in France.

Ingredients:

5 strips of bacon
1 cup (250 mL) onions, minced
2 cups (500 mL) parsnips, diced
2 cups (500 mL) potatoes, diced
1 cup (250 mL) boiling water
3 cups (750 mL) milk
3 tbsp (50 mL) butter
1 tsp (5 mL) salt
1/4 tsp (1 mL) pepper
1/2 cup (125 mL) cream
Parsley, finely chopped

Method:

• Cut the bacon into small pieces. Place in a 12-cup (3 L) microwave-safe bowl.

• Microwave 3 minutes at HIGH, stirring after half the cooking time.

• Remove the cooked bacon with a perforated spoon, let cool on absorbent paper.

• To the remaining fat in the dish add the onions, stir well. Microwave 2 minutes at HIGH.

• Add the parsnips and potatoes. Mix well with the onions.

• Pour the boiling water over all. Microwave 10 minutes at HIGH.

• Add the milk, butter, salt, pepper and cream, stir well and microwave 10 minutes at MEDIUM-HIGH.

• Let stand 5 minutes.

• Serve, sprinkled with the finely chopped parsley.

Traditional Pea Soup

Preparation: . . . . **30 m**
Cooking: . . . . **1 h**
Standing: . . . . **1 h**

A personal note: With a microwave oven there is no need to soak dry peas overnight. Place the dried peas, in a large microwave-safe bowl, add the 8 cups (2 L) of hot water. Cover and microwave at HIGH 15 minutes. Let stand covered for one or two hours. Drain if any water is left, then finish recipe as follows:

Ingredients:

1 to 1½ cups (250 to 375 mL) dry yellow peas *

8 cups (2 L) tepid or hot water

2 onions, minced

2 garlic cloves, chopped fine

**1/2 lb (250 g) salt pork, in one piece *or*
8 slices of bacon, diced ****

1 tsp (5 mL) savory

1/2 tsp (2 mL) pepper

1/2 cup (125 mL) celery leaves, minced

Salt to taste

Method:

• Place the soaked peas and all the other ingredients in a 16-cup (4 L) microwave-safe bowl, cover. Microwave 30 minutes at HIGH. Stir, then microwave 30 minutes at MEDIUM. Stir. Let stand 1 hour, covered. Warm up when ready to serve.

* Use dried peas that were soaked previously according to instructions given in caption.
** Salt pork gives the original Eastern Canada flavor, but bacon can be used. In that case, the soup is then referred to as "New England Pea Soup."

Lentil Soup

Preparation: . . . . **50 m**
Cooking: . . . . **1 h 30 m**
Standing: . . . . **1 h**

A personal note: This is a very nourishing meatless soup; cooked on the stove it requires 3 hours; in the microwave, it cooks in an hour and a half. Use whole brown lentils.

Ingredients:

1 cup (250 mL) lentils

5 cups (1.25 L) boiling water

1 tbsp (15 mL) coarse salt

1/4 tsp (1 mL) pepper

1/2 cup (125 mL) butter or margarine

1 28-oz (796 mL) can tomatoes

1 large onion, minced

1 tbsp (15 mL) dill seeds

2 garlic cloves, crushed

2 bay leaves

Method:

• Rinse lentils under running water.

• Place in a bowl, cover with hot water and let soak 40 minutes.

• Drain, then place in an 8-cup (2 L) microwave-safe baking dish.

• Add the other ingredients, cover. Microwave 15 minutes at HIGH, stir, then microwave, uncovered, at MEDIUM-HIGH 45 minutes to 1 hour.

• Stir well. Continue to microwave at the same intensity if necessary.

• Let stand 1 hour.

• To serve, microwave in the bowl or in individual plates, 1 minute per plate; 3 to 4 plates can be reheated together.

Sugar Pea Soup

Preparation:	. . . .**1 h**
Cooking:	. . . .**20 m**
Standing:	. . . .**none**

A personal note: Dried mushrooms and sugar peas give this soup a very special flavor. It is not economical to prepare, since dried mushrooms and sugar peas are luxury foods, but if you wish to serve a special soup, I recommend this one.

Ingredients:

1/3 cup (80 mL) dried mushrooms, broken in small pieces

4 cups (1 L) chicken broth or consommé

1/2 lb (250 g) sugar peas (*mange-tout*)

Rind of 1/2 a lemon

4 green onions, minced (green and white parts)

1/4 cup (60 mL) dry vermouth

Salt to taste

Method:

• Soak the dried mushrooms in the chicken broth or consommé for 1 hour, then, with scissors, cut them into strips and return them to the bouillon. Remove the sugar peas' two ends, then cut them in two lengthwise. Add to the bouillon with the remaining ingredients.

• Microwave 20 minutes at HIGH. Serve.

Chinese Watercress Soup

Preparation:	. . . .**10 m**
Cooking:	. . . .**10 m**
Standing:	. . . .**none**

A personal note: To be successful with this delicate and savory soup, it is important to use a good homemade chicken broth.

Ingredients:

4 green onions, diced (white and green parts)

4 cups (1 L) chicken broth

2 eggs, lightly beaten

1 tsp (5 mL) soy sauce

1 cup (250 mL) watercress leaves

Salt to taste

Method:

• Add the green onions to the chicken broth in a 6-cup (1.5 L) microwave-safe bowl. Cover and microwave at HIGH 10 minutes.

• Beat the eggs with the soy sauce. Slowly pour this mixture into the hot broth, stirring constantly.

• The eggs will form long filaments and will cook very quickly, simply from the heat of the broth.

• Add the watercress leaves. Serve immediately.

• The soup will resemble scrambled eggs.

Sunshine Soup

Preparation: . . . . **9 m**
Cooking: . . . . **25 m**
Standing: . . . . **none**

• An interesting combination of carrots and peanuts, this soup is flavored with nutmeg and savory.

Ingredients:

2 cups (500 mL) hot water

2 cups (500 mL) milk

2 tbsp (30 mL) butter

1 large onion, finely chopped

4 medium carrots, thinly sliced

2 tbsp (30 mL) peanut butter

1/4 tsp (1 mL) nutmeg

1 tsp (5 mL) savory

1 garlic clove, finely chopped

1 tsp (5 mL) salt

1/2 tsp (2 mL) pepper

Method:

• Place all the ingredients in an 8-cup (2 L) microwave-safe bowl.

• Cover and microwave at MEDIUM-HIGH 25 minutes.

• Serve as is or pass through a vegetable mill or blend in a food processor to make a creamed soup.

Mountaineer Bread Soup

Preparation: . . . . **5 m**
Cooking: . . . . **10 m**
Standing: . . . . **none**

A personal note: The Italian shepherds in the high mountains make this very interesting and nourishing soup over a wood fire. Whenever I have a chicken broth made with the bones of a roasted chicken, I like to make this soup.

Ingredients:

5 slices of bread, diced
1 large garlic clove, peeled and cut
4 cups (1 L) chicken broth
Fresh parsley or chervil, chopped

Method:

• If your oven has a tray, place the slices of either fresh or stale bread on it.

• The bread can be buttered on one side.

• Dry at HIGH 1 minute; some bread may take 1.5 minutes.

• When you take the bread out of the oven, rub one side with the cut garlic clove. Some of the garlic will melt on the bread.

• Set aside until ready to serve.

• Microwave the chicken broth at HIGH until boiling hot.

• Place a slice of bread in each soup bowl. Slowly fill the bowl with the boiling broth.

• Microwave at HIGH 30 seconds for each bowl.

• If you wish to use cheese, place a thin slice of a cheese of your choice on top of the dry bread. Then proceed as above.

• When ready to serve, sprinkle soup with the minced parsley or chervil.

Helpful hint: To warm baby bottles, remove cap and nipple from bottle. Microwave at MEDIUM 30 to 60 seconds, until it is lukewarm.

Avgolemono Soup

Preparation: . . . . 7 m
Cooking: . . . . 23 m
Standing: . . . . none

A personal note: This wonderful Greek soup is difficult to achieve if you do not have an electric mixer or a food processor. The soup is perfect served before a roasted chicken or leg of lamb.

Ingredients:

8 cups (2 L) chicken broth

1/2 cup (125 mL) short grain rice

4 eggs, beaten

Juice of 2 lemons

1/4 cup (60 mL) parsley, minced

Method:

• Place in a large microwave-safe bowl the chicken broth and rice. Microwave at HIGH 10 minutes, stirring once. Then microwave 10 minutes at MEDIUM-HIGH. Stir well.

• Beat together the eggs and lemon juice.

• Gradually add to the egg mixture 2 cups (500 mL) of the hot soup, beating constantly. Or, if you have a mixer or food processor, place the eggs and lemon juice in the machine, beat at high speed for 1 minute, then gradually add 1 cup (250 mL) of the hot broth. Beat and add the remaining hot soup, beating constantly. Microwave 3 minutes at MEDIUM.

• Add the parsley and serve.

Old-fashioned Celery Soup

| Preparation: .12 m |
| Cooking: . . . . .28 m |
| Standing: . . . . .none |

• In the old days, celery was an autumn delight, since we couldn't get any after November. To give flavor to soups and stews during the winter, celery seeds replaced it. This soup was one of our favorite autumn soups.

Ingredients:

3 tbsp (50 mL) butter

2 full cups (500 mL) celery, diced

1 large onion, diced

3 cups (750 mL) milk

1 blade mace

1 bay leaf

3 tbsp (50 mL) flour

3 tbsp (50 mL) butter

Salt and pepper to taste

2 egg yolks

1/4 cup (60 mL) cream

1/2 cup (125 mL) cooked ham, minced (optional)

Parsley or chives, chopped (optional)

Method:

• Place the first 3 tablespoons (50 mL) butter in a microwave-safe bowl and melt 2 minutes at HIGH.

• Add the celery and onion.

• Stir well, microwave 15 minutes at MEDIUM, stirring twice. Purée in a blender or food processor.

• Microwave the milk with the mace and bay leaf 3 minutes at HIGH. Cool.

• Melt the second 3 tablespoons (50 mL) butter 1 minute at HIGH.

• Stir in the flour, add the cooled milk. Stir and cook 5 minutes at HIGH, stirring well after 3 minutes.

• When sauce is creamy, add the puréed celery and onion. Salt and pepper to taste. Microwave 2 minutes at HIGH.

• Beat the egg yolks with the cream, add the minced ham. Add to the hot soup.

• When ready to serve, microwave 1 minute at HIGH. Stir well and serve.

• Sprinkle top of soup with minced parsley or chives.

Old Country Cabbage Soup

Preparation: . . . . **15 m**
Cooking: . . . .**27 m**
Standing: . . . .**none**

• This is a simple and economical yet tasty family soup. When cooked in the microwave, it takes on a special flavor that you just can't get when you cook it on the stove.

Ingredients:

4 to 5 cups (1 to 1.25 L) cabbage, finely chopped

3 tbsp (50 mL) butter or margarine

2 tbsp (30 mL) flour

4 cups (1 L) chicken or beef consommé

1 tsp (5 mL) dill or parsley

3 to 4 frankfurters, thinly sliced

Method:

• In a 12-cup (3 L) microwave-safe bowl melt the butter or margarine at HIGH 2 minutes.

• Add the cabbage, stir well. Cover and microwave at HIGH 5 minutes, stirring once during the cooking period.

• Stir in the flour. When well mixed, add the remaining ingredients, except the frankfurters. Microwave at HIGH 20 minutes, stirring after the first 10 minutes.

• When cooked, add the frankfurters. Microwave 1 minute at HIGH and serve.

Classic Oxtail Soup

Preparation: .... **from 6 to 12 h**
Cooking: .... **from 1 h to 2 h**
Standing: .... **none**

A personal note: This superb, delicate soup requires a bit of work, but is well worth the trouble. In the microwave, it can be cooked in 2 hours compared to the classic way, which requires 4 to 6 hours.

Ingredients:

1 oxtail, cut into sections
2 tbsp (30 mL) butter
1 large onion, sliced
3 carrots, peeled and sliced
2 celery stalks, diced
8 to 9 cups (2 to 2.25 L) beef consommé or water
6 whole peppercorns
1 tsp (5 mL) salt
2 bay leaves
1/2 tsp (2 mL) thyme
1 tsp (5 mL) dill or marjoram
3 to 4 slices of lemon peel
1/4 cup (60 mL) dry sherry

Method:

• Place the butter in a large microwave-safe bowl and melt 1 minute at HIGH.

• Add the onion, carrots and celery, stir well.

• Microwave 3 minutes at HIGH. Stir well and microwave another 3 minutes at HIGH.

• Add the oxtail. Stir to mix.

• Add the beef consommé or water.

• Add the peppercorns, salt, bay leaves, thyme, dill or marjoram, and the lemon peel. Mix well.

• Cover, microwave 1 hour at MEDIUM-HIGH.

• Stir and microwave at HIGH 25 to 35 minutes or until meat on oxtail is tender.

• Pour into a bowl, cover and refrigerate 6 to 12 hours.

• Reheat 20 minutes at HIGH.

• Remove oxtail and pass soup through a fine sieve.

• Add the oxtail and the sherry.

• Warm up at HIGH when ready to serve.

• Place a piece of oxtail in each bowl.

Roquebrune Fish Soup

Preparation: . . . . **15 m**
Cooking: . . . . **20 m**
Standing: . . . . **none**

• Roquebrune is a pretty corner in the South of France. Fish of all types are abundant there and different kind are used each time the soup is made. You may use any fish you like.

Ingredients:

3 tbsp (50 mL) olive oil

1 garlic clove, finely chopped

1 medium onion, minced

1/2 tsp (2 mL) thyme

A pinch of saffron (to taste)

1½ lb (750 g) fish fillets of your choice

1/2 tsp (2 ml) salt

1/4 tsp (1 mL) pepper

1 cup (250 mL) dry white wine

3 cups (750 mL) boiling water

1/3 cup (80 mL) tomato paste

1/2 tsp (2 mL) fennel seeds

3 tbsp (50 mL) brandy

2 cups (500 mL) cream

Method:

• Heat the olive oil in a 12-cup (3 L) microwave-safe bowl 2 minutes at HIGH.

• Add the garlic, onion, thyme and saffron. Mix well.

• Add the fish cut into 1-inch (2.5 cm) pieces.

• Stir and add the salt and pepper, white wine, boiling water, tomato paste and fennel seeds.

• Cover and microwave at HIGH 15 minutes.

• Add the brandy and cream.

• Microwave at HIGH 5 minutes.

Rijeka Fish Soup

Preparation: . . . . **10 m**
Cooking: . . . . **from 12 to 16 m**
Standing: . . . . **none**

A personal note: This easy-to-prepare fish soup is most delicious when cooked in the microwave. Hungarian white wine is the best to use.

Ingredients:

1/4 cup (60 mL) olive oil

1 medium onion, finely minced

1/2 cup (125 mL) fresh tomatoes, peeled and diced

1½ cups (375 mL) clam juice *

1/2 lb (250 g) fish fillets of your choice

2 cups (500 mL) dry white wine

1/4 cup (60 ml) long grain rice

1/4 tsp (1 mL) curry powder

Salt to taste

* *Bottled clam juice may be used.*

Method:

- Place the olive oil in an 8-cup (2 L) microwave-safe bowl, microwave 3 minutes at HIGH.
- Add the onion and the tomatoes. Mix well.
- Microwave 4 minutes at HIGH.
- Add the remaining ingredients.
- Stir and microwave 8 to 12 minutes at HIGH. Salt to taste.

Yugoslav Fish Soup

Preparation: . . . . **10 m**
Cooking: . . . . **from 14 to 16 m**
Standing: . . . . **none**

A personal note: This is a delicate and savory soup. For perfect results, use olive oil rather than vegetable oil and a fairly dry fruity white wine. If possible, use fresh fish.

Ingredients:

1/4 cup (60 mL) olive oil

1/2 cup (125 mL) onions, finely chopped

1/2 cup (125 mL) tomatoes, peeled and diced

1 8-oz (250 mL) bottle clam juice

1/2 lb (250 g) fish fillets, fresh or frozen

2 cups (500 mL) white wine *or*
  1 cup (250 mL) white wine *and*
  1 cup (250 mL) water

1/4 cup (60 mL) instant rice

1/4 tsp (1 mL) curry powder

Salt to taste

Method:

• Place the olive oil, onions and tomatoes in an 8-cup (2 L) microwave-safe bowl, stir well. Microwave 4 minutes at HIGH.

• Add the remaining ingredients. Microwave 10 to 12 minutes at HIGH, stirring halfway through the cooking.

• Serve with crackers that have been buttered and generously sprinkled with sesame seeds.

• Place in a circle on a paper plate, toast 1 minute at HIGH for each 6 crackers, let cool on a rack.

Venetian Soup

Preparation: . . . . **6 m**
Cooking: . . . . **10 m**
Standing: . . . . **none**

A personal note: This quickly prepared Italian soup makes an interesting light meal served with a green salad.

Ingredients:

1 tbsp (15 mL) butter or olive oil
1 tbsp (15 mL) flour
1/2 cup (125 mL) water
1 cup (250 mL) canned tomatoes
1/2 tsp (2 mL) basil or thyme
1/2 tsp (2 mL) celery salt
1 tsp (5 mL) sugar
1/4 tsp (1 mL) pepper
1 10-oz (284 mL) can consommé
1 cup (250 mL) water
1 hard-cooked egg, sliced or diced
Croutons to taste

Method:

• Melt the butter or heat the olive oil 1 minute at HIGH in a 6-cup (1.5 L) microwave-safe dish.

• Add the flour and mix thoroughly.

• Add the water, tomatoes, basil or thyme, celery salt, sugar and pepper.

• Microwave 10 minutes at HIGH, stirring after 5 minutes.

• Add the consommé, water and the hard-cooked egg. Microwave 2 minutes at HIGH. The croutons should be served separately.

Helpful hint: To get more juice from oranges, lemons and limes, microwave fruit, one at a time, 30 seconds at MEDIUM before squeezing.

Chicken or Turkey Carcass Bouillon

Preparation: . . . . 10 m
Cooking: .50 m
Standing: . . . . 2 h

A personal note: You will be surprised how tasty a bouillon you can make with poultry bones and skin that are usually thrown out. Microwave cooking makes all the difference, as it seems to bring out every bit of flavor left in the bones.

Ingredients:

**1 chicken or turkey carcass from
a cooked bird**

Stuffing and gravy leftovers, if any

8 cups (2 L) water

**1 cup (250 mL) celery leaves *or*
4 celery stalks**

2 medium onions, cut in four

1 large carrot, cut in four

1 tbsp (15 mL) coarse salt

10 whole peppercorns

1 tsp (5 mL) thyme

2 bay leaves

3 thin slices of lemon peel (optional)

Method:

• Place all the ingredients in a 16-cup (4 L) round high microwave-safe bowl, with lid. Cover.

• Microwave 20 minutes at HIGH.

• Stir and microwave 30 minutes at MEDIUM. Let stand 2 hours.

• Strain through a fine sieve or through a sieve lined with a J-Cloth.

• Keep refrigerated, well covered.

• The bouillon freezes well, losing none of its flavor for 3 to 5 months.

• Defrost uncovered on the Defrost cycle of your oven.* Time varies according to the amount being defrosted. Start with 15 minutes and add more time, as necessary.

* For quicker defrosting, microwave uncovered 10 to 15 minutes at HIGH, according to quantity.

Creamy Turkey Consommé

Advance preparation: . . **from 12 to 24 h**
Cooking: . . . . **30 m**
Standing: . . . . **4 h**

A personal note: This is the soup to make when a turkey carcass, stuffing and gravy are on hand.

Ingredients:

1 turkey carcass
Remaining stuffing and sauce
8 cups (2 L) boiling water
1/2 tsp (2 mL) savory
2 tbsp (30 mL) flour
4 tbsp (60 mL) cold broth

Method:

• Place in a 12-cup (3 L) microwave-safe bowl the carcass, remaining stuffing and gravy.
• Pour the boiling water on top and add the savory.

• Microwave at MEDIUM-HIGH 30 minutes.
• Cover and let stand 4 hours.
• Strain. Refrigerate 12 to 24 hours.

To make a creamed or garnished "Cream of Turkey"

• Remove the layer of fat that coagulates on top of the consommé.
• Mix the flour with the 4 tablespoons (60 mL) cold broth. Add to the consommé.
• Microwave at MEDIUM-HIGH 20 minutes. Stir well and serve.
• **1 cup (250 mL) small noodles or instant rice** can be added to the consommé at the same time as the flour.
• Microwave for same period mentioned above.

498

Beef Consommé

Advance preparation:.... **from 4 to 5 h**
Cooking: ....**1 h 35 m**
Standing:.....................**none**

A personal note: One or two pounds (500 g or 1 kg) of uncooked or cooked beef bones or half beef and half veal bones will make a savory consommé ready to be served as is or garnished. The onion peel gives the consommé a golden color.

Ingredients:

2 lb (1 kg) beef bones, or beef and veal bones

6 cups (1.5 L) hot water

3 whole cloves

2 tsp (10 mL) coarse salt

3 medium onions, unpeeled, cut in four

1 celery stalk, cut in four

2 medium carrots, unpeeled, cut in three

1/2 tsp (2 mL) each dry mustard and thyme

1/2 tsp (2 mL) celery seeds

Method:

- Place all the ingredients in a 16-cup (4 L) microwave-safe casserole.
- Cover. Microwave 35 minutes at HIGH.
- Stir and microwave 1 hour at LOW.
- Let cool 4 to 5 hours. Strain through a fine sieve.
- Keep in the refrigerator, or freeze.

Beef Consommé du Chef

A personal note: This recipe is the classic way to make a tasty consommé, which can be served as is or used whenever a consommé is required.

Advance preparation: . . . . **from 3 to 4 h**
Cooking: . . . . **1 h 30 m**
Standing: . . . . **none**

Ingredients:

2 tbsp (30 mL) diced beef fat or butter

2 lb (1 kg) brisket or shoulder of beef (in one piece)

1 lb (500 g) veal knuckle or beef bones

8 cups (2 L) tepid water (tap water will do)

3 medium onions, unpeeled, cut in four

2 carrots, peeled and sliced in four

3 whole cloves

1 tbsp (15 mL) coarse salt

1/2 tsp (2 mL) each thyme *and* dry mustard

1 cup (250 mL) celery leaves, coarsely chopped

Method:

• Place the beef fat or butter in a large microwave-safe casserole.

• Melt at HIGH 3 minutes.

• Add the brisket or shoulder of beef, the veal knuckle or beef bones. Stir well.

• Microwave at HIGH 10 minutes.

• Add the remaining ingredients.

• Cover and microwave 20 minutes at HIGH.

• Stir and microwave 1 hour at MEDIUM.

• Cool 3 to 4 hours at room temperature, then strain through a fine sieve or one covered with a cloth (I like to use a J-Cloth), which gives a clear consommé.

• Pour into a jar, cover and refrigerate.

• The fat will rise to the top of the consommé, which will keep it fresh and clear for as long as one month.

• To use, make an opening in the fat and take out as much consommé you require.

• It can also be frozen once the fat is removed.

• The fat, which is clear and very tasty, can be used whenever a recipe calls for a "fat of your choice."

Curried Chicken Consommé

Preparation: . . . . **8 m**
Cooking: . . . .**20 m**
Standing: . . . .**none**

A personal note: One of my favorite lunches is this curried chicken consommé, a chicken salad, a bowl of watercress, and a maple syrup baked apple.

Ingredients:

2 slices bacon

2 tbsp (30 mL) butter

1 medium onion, minced

1 tbsp (15 mL) flour

1 tsp (5 mL) curry powder

6 cups (1.5 L) chicken consommé

1/3 cup (80 mL) long grain rice

Parsley, minced

Method:

• Place bacon on a microwave-safe plate. Microwave at HIGH, 2 minutes.

• Set the bacon on a paper towel, pour fat into an 8-cup (2 L) microwave-safe bowl.

• Add the butter. Melt 1 minute at HIGH.

• Add the onion, stir well, microwave 2 minutes at HIGH.

• Add the curry and the flour, mix well. Add the chicken consommé and the rice.

• Stir and microwave 15 minutes at HIGH.

• Dice bacon, add to it an equal quantity of minced parsley.

• Add to soup. Adjust seasoning and serve.

Consommé Messin

Preparation: . . . . **10 m**
Cooking: . . . . **24 m**
Standing: . . . . **none**

• This is a delicious consommé garnished with a Swiss cheese surprise at the bottom of the bowl. It's one of my favorites.

Ingredients:

4 cups (1 L) beef consommé

2 onions, thinly sliced in rings

3 medium tomatoes, peeled or unpeeled, thinly sliced

2 celery stalks, diced

1 garlic clove, thinly chopped

1/2 cup (125 mL) vermicelli

1 cup (250 mL) grated cheese

Method:

• Add to the consommé the onions, tomatoes, celery and garlic.

• Microwave 15 minutes at HIGH. Stir.

• Add the vermicelli. Microwave 5 minutes at HIGH, stirring twice.

• Divide the grated cheese equally in the soup bowls.

• To serve, pour the hot broth over the cheese.

• Microwave 3 bowls at a time 4 minutes at HIGH.

Consommé Madrilène

Advance preparation: . . . . **1 h**
Cooking: . . . . **55 m**
Standing: . . . . **none**

A personal note: This is an elegant consommé that can be served hot or cold. The classic garnish for hot Madrilène is small green noodles, cooked separately and added to taste when ready to serve. Served cold, Madrilène can be garnished with grated peeled cucumber or whipped cream or a bit of caviar.

Ingredients:

4 cups (1 L) hot water

1 28-oz (796 mL) can tomatoes

2 lb (1 kg) veal shank, cut in pieces

1 large onion, cut in four

1 carrot, cut in two lengthwise

1 bay leaf

1 tbsp (15 mL) sugar

1/2 tsp (2 mL) thyme

1 garlic clove, crushed

1/2 lb (250 g) minced beef

1 tsp (5 mL) salt

10 peppercorns

Method:

• Place all the ingredients in a 16-cup (4 L) microwave-safe bowl.

• Cover and microwave 25 minutes at HIGH.

• Stir and microwave 30 minutes at MEDIUM.

• Cool for 1 hour. Strain through a fine sieve. Serve.

To make a jellied Madrilène

• Heat 2 cups (500 mL) of cooked Madrilène 10 minutes at HIGH.

• Soak 1 envelope of unflavored gelatin in 1/2 cup (125 mL) cold Madrilène for 1 minute.

• Add to the hot broth.

• Stir well, microwave 2 minutes at HIGH. Pour into cups.

• Refrigerate 6 to 12 hours. Garnish to taste.

Consommé Quimper

Preparation: . . . . **8 m**
Cooking: . . . . **15 m**
Standing: . . . . **none**

A personal note: Use chicken broth or beef consommé to make this light, colorfully garnished consommé. It's excellent served before roasted meat.

1 small garlic clove, minced
4 cups (1 L) chicken consommé

Ingredients:

2 tbsp (30 mL) butter
1/4 cup (60 mL) mushrooms, thinly sliced
1/2 cup (125 mL) celery, finely diced
1/4 cup (60 mL) small carrots, thinly sliced
1/4 cup (60 mL) green onions, finely chopped

Method:

• Place the butter in an 8-cup (2 L) microwave-safe bowl and melt 1 minute at HIGH.

• Add all the vegetables, cover. Microwave the vegetables at HIGH for 3 minutes, stir well.

• Microwave another 2 minutes at HIGH.

• Add the consommé, cover and heat 10 minutes at HIGH.

• It reheats very well.

Quick Beef Consommé

Preparation: . . . . **5 m**
Cooking: . . . . **25 m**
Standing: . . . . **none**

A personal note: This is a dual consommé that is prepared in 30 minutes. It can be served as is, with a garnish of your choice, or it can be used as a base for sauces, etc.

Ingredients:

1/2 lb (250 g) minced beef

1 egg white

1 leek, finely chopped

1 medium carrot, grated

1 10-oz (284 mL) can beef consommé

6 cans hot water

1 tsp (5 mL) thyme

Method:

• Mix the minced beef with the egg white, leek and carrot, place in a microwave-safe casserole, add the remaining ingredients.

• Cover and microwave at HIGH 25 minutes.

• Let cool and strain through a fine sieve or one covered with a cloth. Refrigerate.

• Serve this consommé hot with a garnish of your choice or use it in a recipe requiring consommé, or as a base.

A personal note: With the meat and vegetables remaining in the sieve you can make a Shepherd's Pie.

Consommé Pavase

• In Italy, all restaurants serve this soup. To make it successfully, it's important to start with a good chicken or beef consommé.

Preparation: . . . . **5 m**
Cooking: . . . . **15 m**
Standing: . . . . **none**

A personal note: It is important to use a good chicken or beef consommé.

Ingredients:

4 slices Italian or French bread
4 tbsp (60 mL) Parmesan cheese
4 eggs
4 cups (1 L) consommé of your choice

Method:

• Toast the slices of bread. Cover with the cheese.

• Place on a microwave rack, heat 40 seconds at HIGH.

• Remove from microwave.

• Microwave the consommé 10 minutes at HIGH.

• Meanwhile, break an egg into each of 4 microwave-safe bowls. Pierce each yolk.

• Place a slice of toast on each egg.

• Pour equal quantities of hot consommé over each egg.

• Place the bowls in a circle in the microwave.

• Microwave 4 minutes at MEDIUM-HIGH. Serve.

Jellied Bouillon Rouge

Advance preparation: . . . . **12 h**
Cooking: . . . . **17 m**
Standing: . . . . **none**

A personal note: My favorite jellied bouillon, this is easy to make and economical. Garnish with a dollop of sour cream; for special occasions top cream with a spoonful of caviar.

Ingredients:

4 cups (1 L) beef consommé *or*
  1 10-oz (284 mL) can bouillon *and*
  2 cups (500 mL) water
4 fresh beets, uncooked
2 envelopes gelatin
1/3 cup (80 mL) sherry or port wine
1 tbsp (15 mL) fresh lemon juice
Salt and pepper to taste
Nutmeg to taste

Method:

- Pour beef consommé or beef bouillon and water into an 8-cup (2 L) microwave-safe bowl.
- Peel beets and slice thinly, add to liquid. Microwave at HIGH 15 minutes.
- Let stand 10 minutes, strain through a fine sieve. Discard beets.
- Add gelatin to the sherry or port.
- Let stand 2 minutes, add to strained consommé.
- Microwave at HIGH 2 minutes. Stir well.
- Add lemon juice, salt and pepper to taste.
- Pour into individual cups or bowls.
- Sprinkle with a little nutmeg. Refrigerate 12 hours.
- To serve, break up jelly and garnish.

Guadeloupe Consommé

Preparation: . . . . .5 m
Cooking: . . . . .18 m
Standing: . . . . .none

• I learned how to make this consommé on a trip to Guadeloupe. Do not let its simplicity fool you; you will be delightfully surprised.

Ingredients:

Recipe for Consommé Madrilène
Juice and grated rind of 2 oranges
2 tbsp (30 mL) orange liqueur of your choice

Method:

• Warm the consommé Madrilène 15 minutes at HIGH.

• When ready to serve, add the juice and grated rind of the 2 oranges and the liqueur.

• Microwave 3 minutes at HIGH.

• Serve hot in the winter, cold in the summer.

Curried Cream Soup

Preparation: . . . . 5 m
Cooking: . . . . 13 m
Standing: . . . . none

A personal note: In India, they serve this cream cold or hot. It is often garnished with small fresh shrimp.

Ingredients:

1½ cups (375 mL) chicken or beef consommé

1 cup (250 mL) light cream

1/2 tsp (2 mL) curry powder

1 tbsp (15 mL) parsley, minced

1/4 tsp (1 mL) salt

2 eggs, beaten

1/2 cup (125 mL) white wine

Roasted almonds (optional)

Method:

• Place in a 4-cup (1 L) microwave-safe bowl, the chicken or beef consommé and cream.

• Mix the curry powder with a few teaspoons of the liquid and add to the consommé with the parsley and salt. Microwave 10 minutes at HIGH.

• Break the eggs into a separate bowl, beat them, then add the white wine. Pour into the hot broth, while stirring with a wire whisk.

• Return to the microwave and cook 2 minutes at MEDIUM. Stir with the wire whisk, then microwave for 1 more minute.

• Add a few roasted almonds to each soup bowl, then serve.

Green Cream Soup

A personal note: You can make this cream soup with fresh or frozen spinach but it is finer in flavor when prepared with fresh spinach. The bottled clam juice can be found where imported products are sold.

Ingredients:

1 lb (500 g) fresh spinach *or*
   2 12-oz (340 g) packages frozen spinach
1 cup (250 mL) rich cream
1 cup (250 mL) light cream
1 8-oz (250 mL) bottle clam juice
1/4 tsp (1 mL) nutmeg
Salt and pepper to taste

Method:

• Wash the fresh spinach. Place in an 8-cup (2 L) microwave-safe bowl, cover, microwave at HIGH 3 minutes.

• Purée (its water included) in a food processor or electric mixer.

• Return the green purée to the bowl.

• Add the remaining ingredients. Salt and pepper to taste.

• Microwave 4 minutes at HIGH.

• Stir well and serve.

Mountain Cream Soup

Preparation: . . . . **12 m**
Cooking: . . . . **from 20 to 22 m**
Standing: . . . . **none**

A personal note: This is the best cheese soup of Swiss cuisine. It is served very hot, accompanied by French bread that has been heated to make it crusty. The first time I ate this soup in Switzerland, it was served very hot over a crust of bread, accompanied by a glass of well-chilled white wine.

Ingredients:

2 cups (500 mL) chicken broth

1 medium onion, finely chopped

1 medium carrot, peeled and finely diced

1 celery stalk, finely diced

2 tbsp (30 mL) butter

3 tbsp (50 mL) flour

2 cups (500 mL) cream of your choice

1/2 cup (125 mL) Parmesan cheese, grated

1/2 cup (125 mL) Gruyère cheese, grated

Salt and pepper to taste

Method:

• Place in an 8-cup (2 L) microwave-safe bowl the chicken broth, onion, carrot and celery. Microwave at HIGH 15 minutes.

• Pass the vegetables through a fine sieve, reserving the broth.

• Place the butter in the bowl and melt 1 minute at HIGH.

• Add the flour; stir well. Add the cream and reserved broth.

• Stir and microwave at HIGH 5 to 7 minutes, stirring after half the cooking time.

• Add the cheeses while stirring, and the reserved vegetables. The soup is generally hot enough to melt the cheese.

• If necessary, microwave at MEDIUM 1 minute.

• Garnish each soup bowl with buttered croutons.

Creamed Carrot Vichyssoise

Preparation: . . . . **10 m**
Cooking: . . . . **15 m**
Standing: . . . . **none**

A personal note: An interesting soup, this is good hot or cold — it follows the seasons. In the summer, I prepare it with carrots and chives from the garden and serve it cold. In the winter, I replace the chives with parsley and serve it hot.

Ingredients:

2 tbsp (30 mL) butter

6 to 8 green onions, minced

2 cups (500 mL) carrots, sliced

2 cups (500 mL) chicken consommé

1½ cups (375 mL) boiling water

1/2 tsp (2 mL) salt

1 tsp (5 mL) basil or tarragon

6 peppercorns, crushed

1/2 cup (125 mL) light cream or milk

Method:

- Place the butter in an 8-cup (2 L) microwave-safe bowl and melt 1 minute at HIGH.

- Add the green onions and carrots; stir well.

- Microwave at HIGH 5 minutes.

- Add the chicken consommé, boiling water, salt, crushed peppercorns, basil or tarragon.

- Cover and microwave at HIGH 10 minutes.

- Purée in a food processor or blender.

- Add the cream or milk. Mix well, heat and serve or refrigerate.

- Very easy to reheat.

Creamed Spinach Soup

Preparation: . . . . **9 m**
Cooking: . . . . **13 m**
Standing: . . . . **none**

A personal note: This soup is a beautiful shade of green — a bit of spring in your bowl. In the summer I add a cup of chopped sorrel from my garden to the spinach and omit the dry vermouth or white wine.

Ingredients:

1 package fresh spinach

1/2 tsp (2 mL) sugar

2 tbsp (30 mL) chicken concentrate (Bovril)

1 cup (250 mL) each milk and cream of your choice

1/4 cup (60 mL) dry vermouth or white wine

1 tsp (5 mL) lemon rind

1/2 tsp (2 mL) mace or nutmeg

Salt and pepper to taste

Method:

• Wash the spinach with cold water. Place in an 8-cup (2 L) microwave-safe bowl, sprinkle with the sugar.

• Cover, microwave at HIGH 3 minutes, stirring once during the cooking period.

• Purée the cooked spinach and its water, either in a food processor or with an electric beater.

• Add the chicken concentrate to the spinach.

• Add the milk, cream, vermouth or white wine and lemon rind; stir well.

• Add the mace or nutmeg. Cover, microwave at HIGH 10 minutes.

• Salt and pepper to taste, and serve

The Senegalese

A personal note: One of the beautiful classic soups, what makes it different is the combination of chicken broth, apples and curry powder. Serve it hot or cold before a roast beef, partridge, duck or quail.

Preparation: . . . . **14 m**
Cooking: . . . . **from 20 to 22 m**
Standing: . . . . **none**

Ingredients:

4 tbsp (60 mL) butter

2 medium onions, chopped

3 celery stalks, diced

2 tsp (10 mL) curry powder

6 cups (1.5 L) chicken broth

1 bay leaf

2 apples, peeled and diced

1 cup (250 mL) light cream

1 cup (250 mL) cooked white chicken*

You can cook half a chicken breast in the soup, adding it at the same time as the onions and celery.

Method:

• Place the butter in a 12-cup (3 L) microwave-safe bowl and melt 1 minute at HIGH.

• Add the onions and celery.

• Stir well and add the curry powder; stir once more.

• Microwave 5 minutes at HIGH.

• Add the chicken broth, bay leaf and apples.

• Microwave 10 minutes at HIGH. Pass through a fine sieve.

• When ready to serve, add the cream and chicken, sliced in thin strips.

• Microwave 5 to 7 minutes at HIGH. Serve.

Cold Cucumber Cream Soup

Preparation: . . . . **10 m**
Cooking: . . . . **18 m**
Standing: . . . . **none**

A personal note: This is the perfect cold soup for hot summer nights. I like to serve it before a barbecue. You can prepare it 3 to 4 days ahead. Keep it refrigerated, well-covered.

Ingredients:

3 medium-small cucumbers
1 leek
2 tbsp (30 mL) butter
2 bay leaves
1 tbsp (15 mL) flour
3 cups (750 mL) chicken broth
1 tsp (5 mL) salt
1 cup (250 mL) whipping cream
1 tbsp (15 mL) lemon juice
1 tbsp (15 mL) fresh dill
Sour cream to taste

Method:

• Peel 2 of the cucumbers, cut into thin slices, reserve the other one.

• Clean the leek and slice the green and white parts thinly.

• Place the butter in an 8-cup (2 L) microwave-safe bowl and melt 1 minute at HIGH.

• Add the 2 sliced cucumbers and the leek; stir well. Add the bay leaves. Microwave 3 minutes at HIGH. Stir well.

• Add the flour, stir and add the chicken broth and salt. Microwave 15 minutes at HIGH, stirring after half the cooking time.

• Remove the bay leaves. Pass through a food processor or blender. Refrigerate until ready to serve.

• When ready to serve, add the third cucumber, peeled and grated, the cream, lemon juice and chopped dill. Salt to taste.

• Serve in broth cups with a small spoonful of sour cream in each cup.

Creole Cream of Onion Soup

Preparation: . . . . **8 m**
Cooking: . . . . **from 22 to 24 m**
Standing: . . . . **none**

A personal note: This is a very unusual soup, but most delectable. Serve it before a light salad or as a soup and dessert lunch.

Ingredients:

1 cup (250 mL) heavy cream

2 cups (500 mL) light cream or milk

1½ cups (375 mL) chicken bouillon

3 tbsp (50 mL) butter

2 large onions, thinly sliced

1 tbsp (15 mL) flour

1 tsp (5 mL) curry powder

Salt to taste

Method:

• Place the heavy cream and the light cream or milk and the chicken bouillon in an 8-cup (2 L) microwave-safe bowl.

• Stir and microwave 10 minutes at HIGH.

• Place the butter in an 8 × 8-inch (20 × 20 cm) microwave-safe dish and melt 2 minutes at HIGH.

• Add the onions, stir well. Microwave at HIGH 4 minutes, stirring once.

• Remove onions from the butter with a slotted spoon. Reserve.

• To the remaining butter add the flour; stir to mix. Add the curry powder; stir well.

• Add to the hot cream mixture.

• Mix well and microwave at MEDIUM-HIGH 8 to 10 minutes, stirring twice. The soup should be like a light cream sauce at this point.

• Add the softened onions. Stir well, salt to taste. Serve.

Cream of Zucchini

Preparation: . . . . **13 m**
Cooking: . . . . **40 m**
Standing: . . . . **none**

A personal note: At the end of each summer, when zucchini is plentiful, I make a large recipe of this soup and freeze it for the winter. It is easy to make half the recipe if you prefer.

Ingredients:

4 lb (2 kg) zucchini

8 cups (2 L) chicken consommé

1 tbsp (15 mL) each marjoram and fresh dill

4 tbsp (60 mL) butter

1/2 cup (125 mL) flour

4 cups (1 L) milk

1 cup (250 mL) cream

Salt and pepper to taste

1/2 cup (125 mL) parsley, chopped

Method:

• Peel and dice the zucchini and place in a large microwave-safe bowl with the chicken consommé, marjoram and dill.

• Microwave at HIGH 20 minutes.

• Then purée in a food mill (which is faster than a food processor when large quantities are involved) or a food processor.

• In another microwave-safe bowl, melt the butter 2 minutes at HIGH.

• Add the flour. Stir until well mixed.

• Add the milk and cream. Stir well.

• Microwave 20 minutes at HIGH, stirring 3 times during that period.

• Add the puréed zucchini. Mix well. Salt and pepper to taste.

• Add the parsley.

• It is not necessary to reheat the soup after adding the puréed zucchini. Stir well.

• Adjust seasoning.

• Place in container. Freeze.

• When you wish to serve some, simply reheat the required quantity at HIGH.

Cream of Broccoli

A personal note: I really like this cream of broccoli soup. In winter, I serve it hot; in summer, chilled. One of my favorite lunches is this soup, served cold, with tomatoes that I pick in my garden all hot from the sun, a basket of sorrel sprigs, a few basil leaves and a bunch of chives. I place a small pair of scissors in a basket with the herbs and everyone chooses and cuts herbs to taste into the soup.

Preparation: .9 m
Cooking: .12 m
Standing: .none

Ingredients:

1 large cluster of broccoli *or*
  3 small clusters of broccoli
4 tbsp (60 mL) cold water
3 tbsp (50 mL) butter
1 medium onion, chopped fine
3 tbsp (50 mL) flour
1/2 tsp (2 mL) salt
1/4 tsp (1 mL) pepper
3 cups (750 mL) milk
1/2 cup (125 mL) cream
2 tsp (10 mL) concentrated chicken broth (Bovril)

Method:

• Clean the broccoli and cut the stems and flowerets into 2-inch (5 cm) lengths.

• Place in a microwave-safe dish with the cold water.

• Cover and microwave 4 minutes at HIGH.

• Pour the whole into a blender jar or a food processor and blend.

• Place the butter in a 6-cup (1.5 L) microwave-safe bowl and melt 1 minute at HIGH.

• Add the onion; mix. Microwave 2 minutes at HIGH.

• Add the flour, salt, pepper; stir.

• Add the milk, the blended broccoli and the cream; mix.

• Add the concentrated chicken broth.

• Microwave 5 minutes at HIGH. Stir. Salt and pepper to taste.

• Serve hot or cold.

Helpful hint: Honey, a natural food and sweetening ingredient for thousands of years, is easier to digest than sugar and it gives a quick lift when you are tired.

Cold Vichyssoise

Preparation: . . . . **14 m**
Cooking: . . . . **18 m**
Standing: . . . . **none**

A personal note: This recipe is the creation of French chef Louis Diat, who made the reputation of the Ritz-Carlton in New York in the '20s. During that period, French cuisine was scarcely known in the United States. Louis Diat made ''potage parmentier'' — the hot potato soup of France — and served it cold, calling it Cold Vichyssoise.

Ingredients:

4 tbsp (60 mL) butter

4 medium leeks, thinly sliced

1 large onion, sliced

5 medium potatoes, peeled and thinly sliced

4 cups (1 L) chicken broth

1 tsp (5 mL) salt

1 cup (250 mL) each milk *and* cream

Chives or parsley, minced

Method:

• Place the butter in a 12-cup (3 L) microwave-safe bowl and melt 1 minute at HIGH.

• Add the leeks and onion, stir well.

• Microwave 3 minutes at HIGH.

• Stir and add the potatoes, chicken broth and the salt.

• Microwave at HIGH 15 minutes.

• Purée in a food mill or food processor. Cover and refrigerate.

• When ready to serve, add 1 cup (250 mL) of the milk and the cream, salt to taste. You can add more milk for a lighter consistency.

• Beat with a whisk and serve, sprinkled with minced chives or parsley.

Cream St-Germain

Preparation:	8 m
Cooking:	22 m
Standing:	none

• This is a beautiful deep green soup of the classic French repertoire.

Ingredients:

2 cups (500 mL) frozen green peas

1 medium leek, sliced, both the green and the white

10 to 12 lettuce leaves, chopped

10 to 12 spinach leaves, chopped

1 tsp (5 mL) salt

1/2 tsp (2 mL) sugar

1 cup (250 mL) water

4 cups (1 L) chicken consommé

1/2 cup (125 mL) cream

Method:

• Place in an 8-cup (2 L) microwave-safe bowl the first seven ingredients.

• Cover, microwave at HIGH 12 minutes.

• Purée in a food processor or blender.

• Add the chicken consommé and the cream. Mix well.

• Microwave 10 minutes at HIGH. Serve.

Cream of Cauliflower Magnani

Preparation: . . . . 10 m
Cooking: . . . . 33 m
Standing: . . . . none

• A good friend of mine from Bologna, who was a marvellous cook, taught me how to make this unusual and tasty cream soup.

Ingredients:

1 medium-sized cauliflower

2 tbsp (30 mL) butter

4 medium-sized tomatoes, diced

1 large onion, thinly sliced

1 tbsp (15 mL) lemon juice

Grated rind of half a lemon

4 cups (1 L) chicken consommé

1 tsp (5 mL) sugar

Salt and pepper to taste

2 tbsp (30 mL) cream

Method:

• Wash and break the cauliflower into flowerets. Chop a few of the small green leaves.

• Place in a microwave-safe bowl, add 2 tablespoons (30 mL) water. Microwave 10 minutes at HIGH.

• To cook by "Sensor," prepare in the same manner, then cover dish with plastic wrap or use a plastic dish and its cover. Microwave at "A8," or as your own oven dictates.

• When the cauliflower is cooked, mash or blend it until smooth. Set aside.

• Melt the butter 1 minute at HIGH. Add the onion, microwave 3 minutes at HIGH, stirring once.

• Add the tomatoes. Stir well and microwave 3 more minutes at HIGH.

• Add the remaining ingredients, except the cream and add the cooked cauliflower. Stir well. Microwave 15 minutes at HIGH, stirring twice.

• Taste for seasoning. Add the cream. Microwave at HIGH, 2 minutes.

Cream Soup Vert Pré

Preparation:	7 m
Cooking:	8 m
Standing:	none

• A speciality of the Pré-Catalan restaurant in Paris, this soup was created in the early '40s when France started to can her famous green peas.

Ingredients:

1/2 lb (250 g) fresh mushrooms, thinly
   sliced

2 tbsp (30 mL) butter

1 can no 4 green peas, drained

2 cups (500 mL) milk

Salt and pepper to taste

Method:

• Place the butter in a microwave-safe bowl and melt 1 minute at HIGH.

• Add the mushrooms, stir well. Microwave 4 minutes at HIGH, stirring once after 2 minutes of cooking.

• Add the milk.

• Drain the peas, reserving the liquid, then purée them in a blender or food processor.

• Add to the milk; stir well. Salt and pepper to taste. Microwave 4 minutes at HIGH, stirring once.

• If soup is too thick, thin it with some of the liquid from the green peas.

Cream of Noodles Ali-Bab

• This soup was created by an engineer who became a famous chef and who wrote in the '20s a still most interesting cookbook.

Ingredients:

4 cups (1 L) chicken consommé

1 cup (250 mL) fine noodles

2 tbsp (30 mL) butter

1 tbsp (15 mL) flour

2 tbsp (30 mL) grated Swiss or Cheddar cheese

2 egg yolks, beaten

1 cup (250 mL) light cream

Salt and pepper to taste

Grated cheese

Preparation:	**10 m**
Cooking:	**30 m**
Standing:	**none**

Method:

• Bring the consommé to boil in a 6-cup (1.5 L) microwave-safe bowl 10 minutes at HIGH.

• Add the noodles broken into 1-inch (2.5 cm) pieces. Microwave 10 minutes at HIGH.

• Mix together the butter, flour and grated Swiss or Cheddar cheese.

• Add to the cooked noodle consommé, stirring constantly. Microwave 6 minutes at HIGH, stirring once.

• Beat the egg yolks with the cream. Add to the hot consommé; stir well. Salt and pepper to taste. Microwave 4 minutes at MEDIUM stirring once.

• Serve with a bowl of grated cheese.

Cream of Lettuce Soup

Preparation: . . . . **8 m**
Cooking: . . . . **17 m**
Standing: . . . . **none**

• This soup is the speciality of several Parisian restaurants. To try it is to adopt it. Use the lettuce of your choice.

Ingredients:

1/4 cup (60 mL) butter or margarine

4 cups (1 L) lettuce, minced

1 large onion, finely chopped

4 cups (1 L) chicken broth

3 egg yolks

1/2 to 1 cup (125 to 250 mL) Parmesan or Gruyère cheese, grated

Method:

• Place the butter or margarine in a 10-cup (2.5 L) microwave-safe bowl. Melt at HIGH 1 minute.

• Add the lettuce and onion; stir well.

• Add the chicken broth. Microwave 12 minutes at HIGH.

• Mix the egg yolks with the grated cheese. Add to the hot soup, stirring constantly, preferably with a wire whisk.

• Microwave 5 minutes at MEDIUM-LOW.

• Beat well with the whisk before serving.

My Favorite Cream of Mushroom

Preparation: . . . . **25 m**
Cooking: . . . . **30 m**
Standing: . . . . **none**

• Quick and easy to prepare, what makes this soup special is the consommé made with the tails and peelings of the mushrooms. I have enjoyed this soup for years, but enjoy it even more when it's cooked in the microwave, which seems to give it a very special flavor.

Ingredients:

1/2 lb (250 g) fresh mushrooms

3 cups (750 mL) water

1/2 tsp (2 mL) salt

2 tbsp (30 mL) butter

1 medium onion, chopped fine

3 tbsp (50 mL) butter

3 tbsp (50 mL) flour

1 cup (250 mL) light cream

Salt and pepper to taste

Method:

• Peel and remove tails of mushrooms.

• Place peelings and tail ends in a bowl with the water and salt. Cover, microwave at HIGH 20 minutes.

• Let stand 15 minutes. Strain, reserving the liquid.

• Melt the 2 tablespoons (30 mL) butter 1 minute at HIGH.

• Thinly slice the peeled mushrooms, then add them and the onion. Stir and microwave 5 minutes at HIGH, stirring once.

• In another microwave-safe bowl, place 3 tablespoons (50 mL) butter and melt 1 minute at HIGH.

• Stir in the flour and the cream. Microwave 4 minutes at HIGH, stirring twice.

• Add this sauce to the mushroom consommé and the melted mushrooms and onion.

• Stir well. Season to taste.

• When ready to serve, microwave 4 minutes at HIGH. Stir well and serve.

Cream of Crab

Preparation: . . . . **12 m**
Cooking: . . . . **18 m**
Standing: . . . . **none**

A personal note: An elegant and tasty soup this is best made with canned crabmeat. I always keep a tin on hand, to use when an emergency arises and I need a soup that is a gourmet beginning to a meal.

Ingredients:

- 4 tbsp (60 mL) butter
- 2 thick slices of fresh ginger root
- 3 green onions, diced, both green and white parts
- 1/2 cup (125 mL) shredded crabmeat
- 1/4 tsp (1 mL) salt
- 2 tbsp (30 mL) sherry
- 4 cups (1 L) chicken consommé
- 2 egg whites, beaten
- 4 tbsp (60 mL) light cream
- 2 tbsp (30 mL) chicken consommé
- 1½ tsp (8 mL) cornstarch

Method:

- Place the butter in an 8-cup (2 L) microwave-safe bowl and melt 1 minute at HIGH. Add the fresh ginger and green onions. Stir well and microwave 1 minute at HIGH.

- Add crabmeat, salt and sherry. Microwave 2 minutes at MEDIUM.

- Add chicken consommé; stir well. Microwave 10 minutes at HIGH. Discard the ginger.

- Combine the egg whites, lightly beaten, with the cream, the 2 taplespoons (30 mL) of chicken consommé and the cornstarch.

- Gradually add this to the hot crabmeat soup. Mix well. Microwave at HIGH 5 minutes, stirring twice.

Helpful hint: When you wish to serve crisp hot crackers with your soup, microwave the crakers 45 to 60 seconds at HIGH.

Scandinavian Fish Cream Soup

Preparation: . . . . **10 m**
Cooking: . . . . **30 m**
Standing: . . . . **none**

A personal note: This is a very elegant soup to serve before a seafood dish or a roast of veal.

Ingredients:

3 cups (750 mL) boiling water

3 medium potatoes, diced

3 green onions, cut into 1/2-inch (1 cm) pieces

1 bay leaf

3/4 cup (200 mL) cream

2 tbsp (30 mL) flour

1 lb (500 g) salmon or trout

1 tbsp (15 mL) butter

1 tsp (5 mL) salt

1/4 tsp (1 mL) pepper

1/8 tsp (0.5 mL) allspice

Method:

- Place in an 8-cup (2 L) microwave-safe bowl the boiling water, potatoes, onions and bay leaf.
- Microwave at HIGH 20 minutes.
- Remove the bay leaf. Mix the flour with the cream.
- Add to the soup, stirring constantly.
- Add the fish, cut into 1-inch (2.5 cm) pieces.
- Microwave 10 minutes at HIGH, stirring halfway through the cooking.
- Add the butter, salt, pepper and allspice. Serve.

Venetian Fish Cream Soup

Preparation:	. . . . 14 m
Cooking:	. . . . 15 m
Standing:	. . . . **none**

A personal note: The secret of this cream soup is the combination of two kinds of fish of your choice — e.g. halibut and sole, or haddock and cod — and the saffron. All you need is a pinch — but it counts. You can find saffron in specialty grocery shops.

Ingredients:

2 lb (1 kg) fish of your choice

2 tomatoes, unpeeled and diced

2 medium onions, chopped fine

3 celery stalks, diced

1 medium parsnip, peeled and diced

A pinch of saffron

Salt and pepper to taste

6 cups (1.5 L) hot water

Method:

• Place in a 10-cup (2.5 L) microwave-safe bowl the fish (left whole, with its skin, if they are not fillets), the tomatoes, onions, celery, parsnip, saffron, salt and pepper.

• Pour in the hot water. Cover and microwave at HIGH 15 minutes.

• Remove the bones and skin, if need be.

• Remove the fish and vegetables from the broth with a perforated spoon. Pour the solids into a food processor or electric mixer.

• Purée, then add to the broth. Taste for seasoning.

• This soup can be prepared ahead of time. Reheat 5 to 6 minutes at HIGH, without covering.

Chicken Broth

Advance preparation: . . . . **from 2 to 3 h**
Cooking: . . . . **50 m**
Standing: . . . . **none**

A personal note: I like to make chicken broth by simmering a 3-to-4-pound (1.5-2 kg) chicken in the microwave. It is done quickly and the flavors of both the chicken and the broth are superior to those produced by the conventional cooking method. The chicken meat is juicy and white, providing lovely slices to serve hot or cold as well as meat for the chicken pie or salad.

Ingredients:

1 3-to-4-lb (1.5 - 2 kg) chicken
6 cups (1.5 L) hot water
1 medium carrot, peeled and sliced
2 celery stalks, diced
1 garlic clove, minced
2 bay leaves
20 peppercorns
1 tsp (5 mL) coarse salt
1 large onion, finely chopped
1 tsp (5 mL) thyme

Method:

• Cook the chicken whole or cut in pieces. Place it in a 12-cup (3 L) round high microwave-safe bowl with cover.

• Add the remaining ingredients. Cover and microwave 25 minutes at HIGH, stir. Microwave another 25 minutes at MEDIUM.

• If you're cooking the chicken whole, turn it after the first 25 minutes at HIGH.

• Cool 2 to 3 hours in its own juices.

• Remove the chicken, strain the broth.

• To serve the chicken jellied, strain the broth and boil at HIGH for 10 minutes.

• Pour hot over the chicken — whole, cut in four or sliced thinly — and refrigerate 6 to 12 hours.

• Some fat may rise to the top, but it is easy to remove once the jellied consommé has set.

White Stock

Preparation: . . . . 12 m
Cooking: . . . . 50 m
Standing: . . . . 1 h

A personal note: White stock is light colored and light flavored, perfect to finish a veal or chicken gravy, to make a light white sauce or to use as a delicate base for mild vegetable soup, such as asparagus, fresh green pea, etc.

Ingredients:

2 lb (1 kg) veal knuckles or meaty veal bones

2 onions, peeled, cut in four

2 celery stalks *or*
3/4 cup (200 mL) celery leaves, chopped

6 peppercorns *or* 1/2 tsp (2 mL) pepper

1 tsp (5 mL) coarse salt

2 bay leaves

1/2 tsp (2 mL) thyme

A bunch of fresh parsley stems, if available
8 cups (2 L) cold water

Method:

• Ask butcher to cut meat or chop bones, when possible; if not, use as is.

• Place all the ingredients in a 20-cup (5 L) microwave-safe bowl, cover, microwave 20 minutes at HIGH.

• Stir and microwave 30 minutes at MEDIUM. Let stand 1 hour.

• Strain through a fine sieve.

• Keep refrigerated.

Quénafes Broth

Preparation: . . . . **8 m**
Cooking: . . . . **20 m**
Standing: . . . . **none**

• *Quénafes,* small dumplings that are cooked in broth, are a specialty of the north of France and of Alsace.

Ingredients:

6 cups (1.5 L) beef broth

1 whole egg

2 egg yolks

2/3 cup (160 mL) flour

Grated nutmeg to taste

Salt and pepper to taste

Method:

• Place the beef broth in a 10-cup (2.5 L) microwave-safe bowl and boil 15 minutes at HIGH.

• Mix in a bowl the whole egg, yolks and flour. Stir with a metal whisk until well mixed. Add the nutmeg, salt and pepper.

• Drop this dough by small teaspoonfuls into the hot broth. To keep the dough from sticking, dip the spoon in the hot broth before dipping it in the dough. Cover and heat 5 minutes at HIGH.

• Sprinkle with finely chopped parsley before serving.

Japanese "Suimono" Broth

Preparation: . . . . 50 m
Cooking: . . . . .25 m
Standing: . . . . 15 m

• Delicate, savory, elegant!

Ingredients:

1 lb (500 g) chicken wings

3 tbsp (50 mL) Sake*

2 green onions, cut in four

1 inch (2.5 cm) fresh ginger root

1 tsp (5 mL) salt

4 cups (1 L) hot water

6 thin slices of lime

* *A dry sherry can replace the Sake (Japanese wine).*

Method:

• Soak the chicken wings in the Sake 40 minutes.

• Place all the ingredients in an 8-cup (2 L) microwave-safe bowl.

• Cover and microwave at HIGH 25 minutes.

• Let stand 15 minutes. Remove the skin from the wings, chop fine, return to the broth.

• Serve in small cups.

• I like to garnish mine with 2 to 4 small pieces of diced Tofu.

Vegetable Bouillon

Preparation: . . . . **15 m**
Cooking: . . . .**30 m**
Standing: . . . .**none**

A personal note: Full of nourishment, this bouillon can be garnished as you please once it's strained. I like to add small noodles. You can use this to replace meat bouillon in other recipes.

Ingredients:

2 tbsp (30 mL) butter

2 medium onions, diced

1 leek, white and green parts, sliced

2 to 3 carrots, thinly sliced

1 or 2 parsnips, peeled and sliced

1 small celery root, peeled and diced (optional)

1 tsp (5 mL) each thyme and coarse salt

2 bay leaves

8 peppercorns

12 cups (3 L) hot water

Method:

• Place the butter in a large microwave-safe bowl and melt 2 minutes at HIGH.

• Add the prepared vegetables.

• Stir well and microwave 15 minutes at HIGH. Stir again.

• Add the remaining ingredients, cover and microwave 15 minutes at HIGH.

• Let cool, then pass through a fine sieve lined with cheesecloth.*

• This bouillon will keep refrigerated 3 to 4 weeks or in the freezer 6 to 8 months.

The strained vegetables can be served with meat as creamed vegetables by adding 1 cup (250 mL) of medium white sauce; or they can be added, without the sauce, to a stew.

Polish Borsch

Preparation:	15 m
Cooking:	25 m
Standing:	10 m

• There are several ways of preparing a "borsch,", which can be served hot or cold. This one is a bright rose colored consommé, light and savory, that is perfect served before roasted meat.

Ingredients:

4 cups (1 L) raw beets, peeled and grated*

1 large onion, minced

1 tsp (5 mL) salt

1/4 tsp (1 mL) pepper

4 cups (1 L) boiling water

1/4 tsp (1 mL) marjoram

2 tsp (10 mL) sugar

2 tsp (10 mL) cider or wine vinegar

1 cup (250 mL) sour cream

A bit messy to do by hand on a grater, beets are very easy to grate in a food processor.

Method:

• Place all the ingredients, except the sour cream, in a 6-cup (1.5 L) microwave-safe bowl.

• Microwave 15 minutes at HIGH, then 10 minutes at MEDIUM-HIGH.

• Let stand 10 minutes. Strain through a fine sieve.

• Add the sour cream to the broth, beat with a wire whisk or an electric beater until well mixed.

To serve cold

• Adjust seasoning.

• Refrigerate until ready to serve.

To serve hot

• If Borsch is cold, microwave 8 minutes at MEDIUM or until very hot. You must avoid boiling. Add sour cream.

Mushroom Potage

Preparation: . . . . **12 m**
Cooking: . . . . **12 m**
Standing: . . . . **none**

• This soup is reasonable in price and elegant in presentation besides being interesting in terms of taste.

Ingredients:

4 tbsp (60 mL) butter

2 medium onions, finely chopped

1/2 tsp (2 mL) sage

1 tsp (5 mL) basil

1 tbsp (15 mL) tomato paste

2 tbsp (30 mL) parsley, minced

1 garlic clove, minced

1/2 lb (250 g) mushrooms, thinly sliced

4 cups (1 L) boiling water

2 egg yolks

1/2 cup (125 mL) rich or light cream

1 tbsp (15 mL) flour

Method:

• Place the butter in an 8-cup (2 L) microwave-safe bowl and melt 1 minute at HIGH.

• Add the onions, sage, basil, tomato paste, parsley, garlic and salt and pepper to taste.

• Stir well into the melted butter. Microwave 3 minutes at HIGH.

• Add the mushrooms, stir well.

• Add the boiling water. Microwave at HIGH 6 minutes.

• Beat the yolks, cream and flour in a bowl.

• Add to the mushroom broth, stirring constantly with a wire whisk.

• Return to the microwave, heat at MEDIUM-HIGH 3 minutes. Stir and serve.

535

Cauliflower Potage *Diablotins*

Preparation: . . . . **10 m**
Cooking: . . . .**24 m**
Standing: . . . .**none**

A personal note: *Diablotins* are small bread cubes toasted in butter just before they are added to the soup. I serve my soup in bowls and add to each one a few diablotins.

Ingredients:

4 cups (1 L) boiling water
1 tsp (5 mL) coarse salt
1/4 tsp (1 mL) nutmeg
1 medium cauliflower
3 tbsp (50 mL) cornstarch
4 tbsp (60 mL) cold milk
2/3 cup (160 mL) cream

"Diablotins":
2 tbsp (30 mL) butter
1 cup (250 mL) croutons

Method:

• Place in a 6-cup (1.5 L) microwave-safe bowl the boiling water, coarse salt, nutmeg and cauliflower cut into small bouquets.

• Microwave 15 minutes at HIGH.

• Remove the cauliflower with a perforated spoon and purée in a food processor or blender.

• Dilute the cornstarch in the cold milk.

• Add to the broth, as well as the cauliflower and cream; stir well.

• Return to the microwave for 5 minutes at HIGH stirring twice during the cooking time.

• You will obtain a light cream soup.

• To make the *diablotins*, melt the butter 2 minutes at HIGH, add the croutons, stir well.

• Return to the microwave 1 to 2 minutes at HIGH, until they are golden.

• Stir once during the cooking time.

• Add to the soup.

Parisian Potage

Preparation:	**14 m**
Cooking:	**35 m**
Standing:	**15 m**

• I have never been able to make this leek and potato potage better than when I make it in the microwave. The butter replaces the broth.

Ingredients:

4 cups (1 L) leeks, thinly sliced

3 to 4 cups (750 mL - 1 L) potatoes

1/4 cup (60 mL) butter

2 tsp (10 mL) salt

1 tsp (5 mL) pepper

**6 cups (1.5 L) boiling water or
 chicken consommé**

Method:

• Peel the leeks, leaving a portion of the green part.

• Make an incision in the green part and wash under cold running water to remove the sand.

• Then slice the white and green parts.

• Peel the potatoes, cut them into small strips. Do not mix with the leeks.

• Place the butter in a 16-cup (4 L) microwave-safe bowl and melt 1 minute at HIGH.

• Add the leeks, stir well and microwave 5 minutes at HIGH covered, stirring after half the cooking time.

• Add the potatoes, salt and pepper; stir together.

• Add the boiling water or chicken consommé.

• Microwave 30 minutes at HIGH, covered, stirring after half the cooking time. Let stand 15 minutes before serving.

• Pass through a vegetable mill, purée in a food processor or serve it in the Parisian style, by adding 1 cup (250 mL) cream when ready to serve.

• If necessary, reheat in the microwave before serving.

Bologna Potage

• Do not hesitate to make this soup for company. Although it seems quite simple, it is very tasty and different.

Preparation: . . . . 15 m
Cooking: . . . . 30 m
Standing: . . . . 15 m

Ingredients:

2 tbsp (30 mL) olive or vegetable oil

4 tomatoes, peeled and cut in four

2 cups (500 mL) potatoes, diced

2 celery stalks with leaves, diced

1 tsp (5 mL) tarragon or oregano

1/2 tsp (2 mL) chervil (if possible)

4 green onions, finely chopped
  (white and green)

1 tsp (5 mL) each of sugar and salt

1/2 tsp (2 mL) pepper

6 cups (1.5 L) boiling water or chicken broth

1/4 to 1/2 cup (60 to 125 mL) cream

Method:

• Heat the oil in a 12-cup (3 L) microwave-safe bowl 2 minutes at HIGH.

• Add the tomatoes, potatoes; stir together well.

• Microwave 10 minutes at HIGH.

• Stir and add the remaining ingredients, except the cream.

• Cover and microwave 20 minutes at HIGH. Stir after half the cooking time.

• Add the cream. Stir well, cover and let stand 15 minutes before serving.

• If necessary, reheat 5 minutes at HIGH.

Sorrel Potage

Preparation:	**11 m**
Cooking:	**from 20 to 25 m**
Standing:	**none**

• I know it isn't easy to find sorrel, but if you have a garden, it is easy to grow and it's a perennial that lasts a long time, even with our rigorous winters. When the leaves have reached maturity, they are ugly to look at but that does not stop them from being delicious. Sorrel gives a pronounced lemon flavor. In cooking, the green leaves become bronze in color.

Ingredients:

1 large onion, cut in four

2 handfuls of sorrel leaves, minced

3 tbsp (50 mL) butter

3 large potatoes, peeled and sliced

4 cups (1 L) boiling water

1 tsp (5 mL) coarse salt

1/2 cup (125 mL) cream

Method:

• Place in an 8-cup (2 L) microwave-safe bowl the onion, sorrel and butter. Microwave 3 minutes at HIGH. Stir once during the cooking time.

• Add the potatoes, salt and boiling water; stir well. Microwave 15 minutes at HIGH. Test the potatoes; if necessary, microwave an additional 3 to 4 minutes at HIGH.

• Pass through a sieve or purée in a food processor.

• When ready to serve, add the cream and reheat in the microwave 3 to 5 minutes at MEDIUM-HIGH.

Lettuce Potage

Preparation:	**6 m**
Cooking:	**11 m**
Standing:	**none**

A personal note: In Paris, this is the spring "potage." I make it year round by replacing the fresh peas with frozen green peas.

Ingredients:

1/2 cup (125 mL) butter

1 head of Boston lettuce broken up into pieces

1½ cups (375 mL) frozen small green peas

1 tsp (5 mL) salt

1 tbsp (15 mL) sugar

3 cups (750 mL) boiling water

1 cup (250 mL) watercress (optional)

Method:

• Place the butter in a 6-cup (1.5 L) microwave-safe bowl and melt 1 minute at HIGH.

• Add the lettuce and green peas, microwave 3 minutes at HIGH.

• Add the remaining ingredients.

• Microwave 8 minutes at HIGH.

• Mix in a food processor or electric mixer. Salt to taste and serve.

• You can add **1/2 cup (125 mL) rich cream**.

Potage
St-Germain

Preparation:....................1 h
Cooking:.....................50 m
Standing:......................none

• A green split pea soup, this is excellent family fare, nourishing and tasty.

Ingredients:

2 cups (500 mL) dried green peas, split

6 cups (1.5 L) broth of your choice

1 leek, thinly sliced *or* 6 green onions

1 cup (250 mL) onions, finely chopped

1 carrot, thinly sliced

4 to 5 bacon slices, diced

3 tbsp (50 mL) butter

2 bay leaves

1/4 tsp (1 mL) thyme

1/4 tsp (1 mL) marjoram or savory

Salt and pepper to taste

1/4 cup (60 mL) rich cream or milk

Method:

• Soak the dried green peas 1 hour, covered with warm water. Drain and place in a 12-cup (3 L) microwave-safe bowl. Add the broth. Microwave 15 minutes at HIGH. Skim, if necessary.

• In another dish, melt 1 tablespoon (15 mL) of the butter 1 minute at HIGH.

• Add the leek or green onions, onions, carrot and bacon.

• Stir well. Microwave 3 minutes at HIGH, stirring after half the cooking time.

• Add the drained green peas and broth, bay leaves, thyme, marjoram or savory, salt and pepper. Mix well. Microwave 30 minutes at MEDIUM-HIGH.

• Purée in a food processor or food mill.

• Add the cream or milk and the 2 tablespoons (30 mL) of remaining butter.

• Adjust seasoning and serve.

Polish Lentil Potage

Advance preparation: . . . . 1 h
Cooking: . . . . 28 m
Standing: . . . . none

A personal note: For a light supper, serve this potage with a salad and a piece of cheese. It freezes very well.

Ingredients:

1/2 cup (125 mL) green lentils

4 cups (1 L) water

1 carrot, diced

1 medium potato, peeled and diced

1 large onion, minced

1 celery stalk, diced

1 tbsp (15 mL) dill (preferably fresh)*

2 garlic cloves, finely minced

4 smoked sausages, thinly sliced

1 tsp (5 mL) salt

6 slices of lemon

2 tbsp (30 mL) butter

Method:

- Rinse the lentils under cold running water.
- Place in an 8-cup (2 L) microwave-safe bowl.
- Add 2 cups (500 mL) water.
- Cover and microwave 10 minutes at HIGH.
- Remove from microwave and let stand 1 hour.
- Add the remaining 2 cups (500 mL) of water together with the carrot, potato, onion, celery, dill and garlic. Stir to mix.
- Cover and microwave 15 minutes at HIGH, stirring mid-way through the cooking.
- Add the remaining ingredients, cover and cook at HIGH 3 minutes.

In winter, replace fresh dill with 1 teaspoon (5 mL) dill seeds.

Pumpkin Potage

Preparation: . . . . **16 m**
Cooking: . . . . **37 m**
Standing: . . . . **none**

A personal note: Not many North Americans are aware of this smooth, delicate cream soup, which is so popular in France all year round. Try it. Canned pumpkin can replace the fresh, but it loses some of its delicate flavor.

Ingredients:

3 cups (750 mL) pumpkin, peeled and diced
1 large onion, sliced
3 cups (750 mL) hot water
3 cups (750 mL) milk
2 tbsp (30 mL) heavy cream
1/4 tsp (1 mL) nutmeg
Salt and pepper to taste
2 eggs, lightly beaten
1 tbsp (15 mL) butter

Method:

• Place in a 12-cup (3 L) microwave-safe bowl the pumpkin, onion and hot water.

• Microwave 20 minutes at HIGH. Drain reserving the water.

• Purée in a food mill or food processor.

• Return the purée to the saucepan. Add the milk, cream, nutmeg, salt and pepper to taste.

• Stir well; the mixture should have the consistency of cream. If too thick, add some of the reserved water.

• Microwave 15 minutes at MEDIUM, stirring twice during that period.

• Beat the eggs with 2 tablespoons (30 mL) of the soup. Beat into the soup, add the butter.*

• When ready to serve, heat 2 minutes at HIGH, stirring after 1 minute. Serve.

The soup can be prepared up to addition of the eggs and will keep for 2 days refrigerated, covered. To serve, reheat 4 to 6 minutes at HIGH and beat in the eggs and butter.

Corn Chowder

A personal note: This is a traditional Old South recipe. I prefer to use frozen corn, but canned corn kernels are also very good. In summer, you can use corn on the cob removed from the cob before cooking.

Preparation: . . . . **10 m**
Cooking: . . . . **16 m**
Standing: . . . . **none**

Ingredients:

2 cups (500 mL) water

3 chicken bouillon cubes

1 cup (250 mL) corn of your choice

1/2 tsp (2 mL) salt

1/4 tsp (1 mL) pepper

1/4 tsp (1 mL) curry powder

1 medium onion, finely minced

1 tbsp (15 mL) flour

1 cup (250 mL) milk

1/2 cup (125 mL) cream

2 beaten egg yolks

Method:

• Place the water in a 10-cup (2.5 L) microwave-safe bowl.

• Cover and microwave 5 minutes at HIGH. Add the bouillon cubes, microwave 1 minute at HIGH, stir well.

• Add the corn, salt, pepper, curry powder and onion.

• Microwave 5 minutes at HIGH.

• Mix the flour with the milk and cream.

• Beat the egg yolks with 1/4 cup (60 mL) of the milk-cream mixture. Blend into the creamed corn.

• Microwave 5 minutes at MEDIUM-HIGH, stirring 3 times during the cooking to obtain a smooth and creamy mixture.

• Adjust seasoning and serve.

Mushroom Chowder

Preparation: . . . . 15 m
Cooking: . . . . from 18 to 20 m
Standing: . . . . none

A personal note: Completely different from mushroom Potage, this soup can be served as a light meal with a good slice of bread and cheese.

Ingredients:

1/3 cup (80 mL) butter or margarine

1 large onion, finely chopped

1 cup (250 mL) celery, diced

1 cup (250 mL) carrots, thinly sliced

1/2 to 1 lb (250 to 500 g) mushrooms

2 medium tomatoes, diced

4 cups (1 L) broth of your choice

2 cups (500 mL) hot water

1/2 tsp (2 mL) thyme

1 tsp (5 mL) tarragon

3 tbsp (50 mL) parsley, minced

Salt and pepper to taste

Method:

• Place the butter or margarine in a 12-cup (3 L) microwave-safe bowl and melt 1 minute at HIGH.

• Add the onion and mix well into the butter. Microwave 2 minutes at HIGH.

• Stir well and add the remaining ingredients. Cover. Microwave at HIGH 15 to 18 minutes.

• Garnish to taste with chopped parsley and serve.

New England Vegetable Chowder

Preparation: . . . .**8 m**
Cooking: . . . .**15 m**
Standing: . . . .**none**

• This is a very nourishing and tasty chowder.

Ingredients:

4 slices bacon, diced

1 medium-sized onion, diced

1 cup (250 mL) hot water

1 cup (250 mL) shredded carrots

2 10-oz (284 mL) cans cream of chicken soup

2 cups (500 mL) milk

1 cup (250 mL) corn niblets

Salt and pepper to taste

1 tsp (5 mL) soy sauce

A bowl of cracker crumbs

Method:

• Microwave the diced bacon in a 12-cup (3 L) microwave-safe bowl 3 minutes at HIGH.

• Add the onion. Microwave 2 minutes at HIGH. Stir well.

• Add the hot water and the carrots.

• Microwave 5 minutes at HIGH.

• Add the remaining ingredients, except the cracker crumbs.

• Microwave at HIGH 5 minutes, stirring twice.

• To serve, place a spoonful of cracker crumbs in each bowl, then fill with soup.

Corn and Potato Chowder

Preparation: . . . . 14 m
Cooking: . . . . .30 m
Standing: . . . . 15 m

A personal note: This chowder gains flavor when it is refrigerated for 6 to 12 hours after being cooked and then reheated when ready to be served.

Ingredients:

4 medium potatoes, peeled and thinly sliced

3 cups (750 mL) boiling water

1 tsp (5 mL) coarse salt

2 tbsp (30 mL) chicken concentrate (Bovril)

1 tbsp (15 mL) butter

1 large onion, finely chopped

4 to 6 bacon slices

3 cups (750 mL) milk

1½ cups (375 mL) frozen corn

1/2 tsp (2 mL) curry powder or sage

Method:

• Place the potatoes and boiling water in an 8-cup (2 L) microwave-safe bowl. Add the coarse salt and chicken concentrate, cover and microwave at HIGH 10 minutes.

• Let stand 5 minutes. Drain, reserving 2 cups (500 mL) of the cooking water.

• Mash the potatoes.

• Place the butter in a microwave-safe bowl and melt 2 minutes at HIGH.

• Add the onion, stir and microwave 3 minutes at HIGH.

• Place the bacon slices on a sheet of paper towel, cover with another sheet of paper towel, place in the microwave and cook 4 minutes at HIGH.

• Remove from paper and let cool. Cut into small pieces and add to the onions.

• Pour over the mashed potatoes; mix well. Add the 2 cups (500 mL) reserved water, the milk, frozen corn, curry powder or sage.

• Mix well, cover and microwave 10 minutes at HIGH.

• Let stand 15 minutes before serving.

Smoked Sausage Chowder

Preparation: . . . . **16 m**
Cooking: . . . . **30 m**
Standing: . . . . **none**

A personal note: This is a family soup that makes a meal. Serve with crackers and finish with a good medium or mild Cheddar.

Ingredients:

1/2 lb (250 g) smoked sausages (hot dogs)

2 tbsp (30 mL) butter or margarine

1 cup (250 mL) onion, chopped

2 medium potatoes, peeled and diced

2 large carrots, thinly sliced

3 cups (750 mL) boiling water

1 tsp (5 mL) salt

1 tsp (5 mL) thyme or sage

1 tbsp (15 mL) H.P. or Worcestershire sauce

1½ cups (375 mL) milk or light cream

1 cup (250 mL) frozen or canned corn

3 tbsp (50 mL) parsley, finely chopped

Method:

• Cut sausages into thin slices.

• Place the butter or margarine in a 12-cup (3 L) microwave-safe bowl and melt 1 minute at HIGH.

• Add the onion, potatoes, carrots, boiling water, salt, thyme or sage and H.P. or Worcestershire sauce. Mix well. Microwave 20 minutes at HIGH.

• Add the milk or cream, frozen or canned corn (do not drain the canned corn). Microwave 10 minutes at HIGH.

• Add the parsley and serve.

• This soup reheats very well.

Billi-Bi

Preparation: . . . . **15 m**
Cooking: . . . . **16 m**
Standing: . . . . **none**

• This is a delicious soup to serve for a certain special dinner.

Ingredients:

2 lb (1 kg) fresh mussels
2 French shallots, peeled and chopped
1 small onion, cut in four
2 sprigs of parsley
1 tsp (5 mL) salt
1/2 tsp (2 mL) pepper
1 cup (250 mL) dry white wine
2 tbsp (30 mL) butter
1/2 bay leaf
1/4 tsp (1 mL) thyme
2 cups (500 mL) rich cream
1 egg yolk, slightly beaten

Method:

• Wash the mussels several times in cold water. Place in a 10-cup (2.5 L) microwave-safe bowl.

• Add the shallots, onion, parsley, salt, pepper, white wine, butter, bay leaf and thyme. Cover and microwave 5 minutes at HIGH.

• Remove from microwave. Remove the mussels from their open shells. Do not use those whose shells have remained closed.

• Place a cloth in a sieve and pass through the cooking broth.

• Rinse the casserole, pour in the drained liquid. Add the cream. Microwave 10 minutes at HIGH.

• Chop the mussels, add the beaten yolk.

• Pour all into the cooked broth, stirring constantly. Microwave 1 minute at HIGH and serve.

Quick garnishes for your soups

- Bouillon, cream or vegetable soups can be served as is or garnished to taste.
- The following suggestions can bring color, flavor and texture to the soup of your choice. Add when ready to serve.
- Popcorn
- Little dots of peanut butter
- Paper-thin slices of carrot or radish
- Chopped chives, dill or basil
- Diced green onions, the white and green parts
- Minced celery leaves
- Tiny cubes of fresh tomato
- Small cheese cubes (any cheese you like)
- Sliced olives
- Crumbled crisp bacon
- A thin slice of lemon, lime or orange
- A spoonful of shoestring potatoes
- A large potato chip on top of soup
- A spoonful of sour cream or yogurt
- A spoonful of whipped cream, lightly salted

Wine in soup

- To *potages,* cream of mushroom, chicken or fish soup add **2 to 3 tablespoons (30 to 50 mL) sherry or dry Madeira wine** when ready to serve.
- Add **1 tablespoon (15 mL) Chablis or Rhine wine** to each bowl of oyster soup just before serving.
- **Dry sherry, dry Madeira wine and light red wine** are all good with all kinds of soups.

Golden Strands

- A creation of Chinese cuisine, which is several hundred years old, Golden Strands are the perfect garnish for a consommé or clear soup.

Ingredients:

2 eggs
3 tbsp (50 mL) flour
1/2 tsp (2 mL) salt

Method:

- Beat the eggs, add the flour and salt. Beat to obtain a perfect mixture. Pass through a sieve. This can be done ahead of time.
- To serve, bring the broth or consommé or soup to a boil in the microwave at HIGH.
- Remove from the microwave. Immediately pour the egg mixture into the hot broth, through a perforated spoon; the filaments will cook as they fall into the hot consommé.
- Then heat the consommé 1 to 2 minutes at HIGH, if necessary.

Snowballs

- Mix a few spoonfuls of sour cream with fresh and finely chopped parsley, chives or chervil.
- Place a scoop in the centre of each bowl of soup when ready to serve.
- Snowballs are particularly good with tomato and cream soups.

Canned Soups

• Canned soups or dehydrated soup mixes certainly have a place in our busy lives. They are good tasting and, with a little imagination and know-how, are easily adaptable to all kinds of variations.

• The following ideas will help you create new recipes that your microwave will allow you to cook in a jiffy.

To prepare canned soups in the microwave

• Pour the canned soup of your choice into a microwave-safe bowl.

• Add an equal amount of water or milk. Stir well.

With water

• Microwave 3 to 4 minutes at HIGH, uncovered, for a 10-ounce (284 mL) can.

• Stir after half the cooking time.

With milk

• Microwave 6 to 8 minutes at MEDIUM, covered, for a 10-ounce (284 mL) can.

• Stir after half the cooking time.

To prepare dry soup mixes

• Some boxes contain 2 envelopes (84 g) of mix. For two envelopes, use 8 cups (2 L) of hot water in a 10-cup (2.5 L) microwave-safe bowl.

• For one envelope, use 4 cups (1 L) hot water in a 6-cup (1.5 L) microwave-safe bowl.

A personal note: Always start with hot water, which gives a better flavor to the soup.

• Microwave at HIGH 4 to 8 minutes, depending on whether one or two envelopes are used. Stir once during the cooking period.

A few variations and garnishes for canned soup

• Replace the water with chicken broth or consommé or tomato juice.

• Add a little nutmeg to cream of chicken or mushroom soup; a pinch of curry to chicken rice soup; marjoram or oregano to tomato soup.

• Add to any kind of soup fresh chives or parsley or an herb of your choice, such as basil, thyme, marjoram, tarragon, savory, etc. — 1/4 teaspoon (1 mL) is sufficient.

• Sprinkle grated cheese on the soup or mix the cheese with the soup before heating it.

• Garnish cream soup with a spoonful of whipped cream, lightly salted, just before serving.

• Garnish with small strips of ham or chicken.

• Add small dumplings, prepared as follows:

• Cream **2 tablespoons (30 mL) butter.**

• Add **2 eggs, 1/4 teaspoon (1 mL) salt and 6 tablespoons (90 mL) flour.** Mix well.

• Drop by small spoonfuls into the very hot soup, microwave 3 minutes at HIGH, covered.

• It is preferable to have the soup in an 8-cup (2 L) microwave-safe dish to keep the dumplings well separated.

Oxtail Soup

Preparation: . . . . **5 m**
Cooking: . . . . **13 m**
Standing: . . . . **none**

A personal note: This nourishing soup takes on a certain elegance when it is garnished with thin slices of lemon sprinkled with minced parsley placed on top of the soup in each bowl.

Ingredients:

2 10-oz (284 mL) cans oxtail soup

1 10-oz (284 mL) can consommé

3 cups (750 mL) water

4 green onions *or*
  1 small onion, finely chopped

1/4 cup (60 mL) sherry

Method:

• Place in an 8-cup (2 L) microwave-safe bowl the soup, consommé, water and onions.

• Microwave 12 minutes at HIGH.

• Add the sherry. Heat 1 minute at HIGH. Serve.

Cream of Celery Soup

Preparation: .5 m
Cooking: .10 m
Standing: .none

Ingredients:

1 10-oz (284 g) can cream of celery soup

1 10-oz (284 g) can chicken consommé

1/2 cup (125 mL) each rich cream and milk

1/3 cup (80 mL) celery with leaves,
   finely chopped

1 cup (250 mL) water

Method:

• Place all ingredients in a microwave-safe bowl with a cover.

• Cover, microwave at MEDIUM-HIGH 10 minutes, stirring 3 times during the cooking.

552

Madras Cream

Preparation:	8 m
Cooking:	10 m
Standing:	none

Ingredients:

1 10-oz (284 g) can cream of green pea soup

1 10-oz (284 g) can cream of tomato soup

1 can of milk

1/2 can of water

1/2 cup (125 mL) rich or light cream

1 tsp (5 mL) curry powder

1/4 cup (60 mL) cream, whipped (optional)

1/2 cup (125 mL) butter croutons

Method:

• Place in a baking microwave-safe dish the two soups, milk, water, cream and curry powder. Microwave at HIGH 10 minutes, stirring twice during the cooking.

• Garnish each bowl with a bit of whipped cream and a few croutons.

Cucumber Cream of Celery

Preparation:	10 m
Cooking:	5 m
Standing:	none

• This summer soup is prepared in 10 minutes. It is good hot, excellent cold.

Ingredients:

2 10-oz (284 mL) cans cream of celery soup

1 small cucumber, peeled and diced

2 sprigs of watercress *or* 1/4 cup (60 mL) parsley

6 green onions, finely chopped

2 cups (500 mL) milk

1 cup (250 mL) water

Method:

• Place in a baking dish the cream of celery soup, cucumber, watercress or parsley and green onions. Add the milk and water, stir well. Microwave 5 minutes at HIGH.

• Purée in a blender or a food processor. Refrigerate.

• Serve garnished with a spoonful of sour cream.

Cucumber Soup

Preparation: . . . . 7 m
Cooking: . . . . .5 m
Standing: . . . .**none**

A personal note: Be sure to serve the toasted croutons with this soup. They give it a finishing touch.

Ingredients:

1 small cucumber

1 10-oz (284 g) can cream of green pea soup

1 can milk

1/2 can of water

1/2 cup (125 mL) toasted croutons

Method:

• Peel the cucumber, cut in two lengthwise, remove the seeds and grate on a fine grater.

• Place in a microwave-safe casserole and add the remaining ingredients, except the croutons.

• Microwave 5 minutes at HIGH, stir well. Garnish with croutons and serve.

Quick Port Consommé

Preparation: . . . . 5 m
Cooking: .5 m
Standing: . . . . **none**

• It's impossible to tell that the base is canned consommé in this easy and quickly made soup. It can be served hot or jellied.

Ingredients:

2 10-oz (284 mL) cans consommé

2 cups (500 mL) water

1/2 cup (125 mL) dry port

1/4 tsp (1 mL) curry powder

1 cup (250 mL) mushrooms, thinly sliced

Method:

• Place in a 6-cup (1.5 L) microwave-safe bowl the undiluted consommé, water, port and curry powder. Microwave 4 minutes at HIGH.

• Add the mushrooms. Microwave 1 minute at HIGH. Serve.

To serve jellied

• Add **2 envelopes of unflavored gelatin** to 1 cup (250 mL) cold water, let stand 2 minutes.

• Add to the other ingredients. Microwave 4 minutes at HIGH; stir well.

• Add the mushrooms. Microwave 3 minutes at HIGH (the cooking time is longer than mentioned above since the gelatin must melt completely). Stir.

• Cover and refrigerate 6 to 12 hours before serving.

Onion Soup au Gratin

Preparation: . . . . **14 m**
Cooking: . . . . **18 m**
Standing: . . . . **none**

A personal note: For perfect results when cooking this soup in the microwave, you need a browning dish (Corning).

Ingredients:

4 to 5 large onions, peeled and thinly sliced

1/4 cup (60 mL) butter

1 10-oz (284 mL) can chicken broth

1 10-oz (284 mL) can consommé

1/2 tsp (2 mL) thyme

2 cups (500 mL) boiling water

4 to 6 slices of toasted bread

1 cup (250 mL) Swiss or Cheddar cheese, grated

1/4 cup (60 mL) Parmesan, grated

Method:

• Heat the browning dish 6 minutes at HIGH. Without removing it from the oven, add the onions and butter. Microwave at HIGH 5 minutes, stir well and pour into a 6-cup (1.5 L) microwave-safe bowl.

• Add the chicken broth, consommé and thyme; mix well.

• Add the boiling water. Cover and microwave at HIGH 9 to 10 minutes.

• Toast the bread in a toaster.

• Pour the soup into 4 to 6 bowls. Place a slice of toasted bread in each bowl.

• Mix the cheese and sprinkle evenly over the soup. Melt the cheese 3 minutes at MEDIUM.

• If the soup must be reheated, place the bowls, without the bread and cheese, in a circle in the microwave and heat 5 minutes at HIGH.

• Cover with the bread and cheese and melt as indicated above.

To *gratiné* in a combined microwave-convection oven

• Cook the soup in the microwave as indicated above, until you're ready to add the bread.

• Place the bowls garnished with the toasted bread and cheese on the lower rack, and brown at 425°F (220°C), which will take 2 to 4 minutes.

• Serve very hot.

Meatball Soup

Preparation: . . . . 15 m
Cooking: .30 m
Standing: . . . . 10 m

A personal note: A very popular family soup, serve this hot in the winter, cold in the summer. In winter, I serve the soup with a basket of toast. In summer, I prefer sesame seed crackers, buttered with parsley or chives butter.

Ingredients:

Meatballs:

1 lb (500 g) ground beef

1/4 cup (60 mL) breadcrumbs

1 egg slightly beaten

1 tsp (5 mL) salt

1 large garlic clove, chopped fine

1/4 tsp (1 mL) thyme

2 tbsp (30 mL) butter

Soup:

2 10-oz (284 mL) cans beef consommé

2 cups (500 mL) water

2 7½-oz (213 mL) cans tomato sauce

2 celery stalks with leaves, chopped fine

1 large carrot, peeled and grated

1 tsp (5 mL) oregano or basil

1 tsp (5 mL) sugar

Salt and pepper to taste

1/2 cup (125 mL) curly macaroni

Method:

• Combine in a bowl all the ingredients for the meatballs, except the butter. Form into small round balls.

• Place the butter in an 8 × 8-inch (20 × 20 cm) ceramic dish and melt 3 minutes at HIGH.

• Add the meatballs, stir to coat with the hot butter. Microwave 10 minutes at HIGH, stirring once. Pour into a 12-cup (3 L) microwave-safe bowl.

• Add the remaining ingredients. Stir well. Microwave at HIGH 20 minutes, stirring once.

• Let stand 10 minutes and serve.

Quick Vegetable Soup

Preparation:	3 m
Cooking:	5 m
Standing:	none

• Three minutes preparation time, five minutes cooking time and this soup is ready to serve.

Ingredients:

4 cups (1 L) boiling water

1 2½-oz (68 g) packet dehydrated chicken noodle soup

1 onion, peeled and diced

1 tbsp (15 mL) butter

1 19-oz (540 mL) can diced vegetables

1/2 tsp (2 mL) basil

1/4 tsp (1 mL) savory

Bowl of grated cheese

Method:

• Pour the contents of the packet of chicken noodle soup into the boiling water. Add the onion and butter.

• Drain the vegetables and add to the soup with the basil and savory. Microwave at HIGH 5 minutes. Stir well and serve with a bowl of grated cheese for each one to use to taste.

Boula

Preparation:	3 m
Cooking:	from 6 to 7 m
Standing:	none

A personal note: A very simple soup, this is often served in elegant restaurants. Turtle consommé can be found in gourmet groceries.

Ingredients:

1 10-oz (284 mL) can cream of green pea soup

1 12½-oz (380 mL) can turtle consommé

1 tbsp (15 mL) dry sherry

1/4 cup (60 mL) whipping cream

Method:

• Place in a microwave-safe casserole the soup, consommé and sherry.

• Mix together. Heat 6 minutes at HIGH; stir.

• The Boula must be very hot, but it must not boil.

• If necessary, heat another minute.

• Whip the cream. Place a spoonful in each bowl of hot soup.

Croutons

• These small golden and crispy bread cubes, with the taste of butter, are an interesting garnish for all kinds of soups.

Ingredients:

2 cups (500 mL) diced bread

1 tbsp (15 mL) butter

1 tbsp (15 mL) vegetable oil

1/2 tsp (2 mL) paprika

Method:

• Remove the crusts from the bread. Cut each slice into 1/2-inch (1 cm) strips, and each strip into small squares.

• Place the oil and butter in an 8 × 8-inch (20 × 20 cm glass or porcelain baking dish. Microwave 2 minutes at HIGH.

• Mix the bread with the paprika. Without removing the dish from the microwave, add the bread to the hot fat; stir together well. Fry 2 to 3 minutes at MEDIUM-HIGH, stirring after 2 minutes.

• These croutons will keep well in a covered plastic box, refrigerated.

• It is not necessary to heat them before using them.

Cheese Croutons

A personal note: These croutons are made from small round slices of a *baguette* of French bread or cubes of white bread.

Italian Croutons

A personal note: If possible, prepare these croutons with a *baguette* of French bread, which will give you small round slices. If not, use bread cubes.

Ingredients:

12 to 24 small round slices of bread

2 garlic cloves, unpeeled

Olive or vegetable oil

Method:

• Place 6 to 8 slices of bread on a microwave rack. Microwave at HIGH 1 minute.

• Remove a small slice of each unpeeled garlic clove, and rub each slice of dried bread on both sides with the garlic. You will see it melt on the bread.

• Then brush each slice with a bit of olive or vegetable oil. Place on the rack, microwave 40 seconds at HIGH. Let cool.

• Keep in a well-covered container, but do not refrigerate.

Ingredients:

1/4-inch (6 mm) thick slices of bread

Soft butter

Cheddar (or other kind) cheese, grated

Method:

• Butter each slice of bread. Cover, to taste, with cheese. Different cheeses give different flavors.

• Place on a microwave rack. Microwave 1 minute at MEDIUM-HIGH.

• Will keep 10 days in a cool place.

Butter Balls

Preparation: . . . . **4 m**
Cooking: . . . . **5 m**
Standing: . . . . **none**

• Light and tasty, these small balls of dough cooked in a hot broth please many a gourmet.

Ingredients:

2 tbsp (30 mL) butter
2 eggs
1/4 tsp (1 mL) salt
6 tbsp (90 mL) flour
A pinch of aniseeds or caraway seeds, to taste

Method:

• Cream the butter. Add the remaining ingredients; mix well.

• Drop by small spoonfuls into very hot broth.

• Microwave at HIGH 5 minutes. This quantity of dough will be sufficient for 4 to 8 cups (1 to 2 L) of broth or consommé.

Bread Boulettes

Preparation: . . . . **8 m**
Cooking: . . . . **13 m**
Standing: . . . . **none**

A personal note: There are many ways to make *Boulettes.* I prefer this Hungarian way. Any clear broth or bouillon can be used. For a full meal, add *Boulettes* to a thick vegetable soup.

Ingredients:

2 thick slices of brown bread, diced
1 tbsp (15 mL) chicken or bacon fat
1 garlic clove
1 small onion, chopped fine
2 tsp (10 mL) parsley, finely chopped
Grated rind of half a lemon
Salt and pepper to taste
1/2 tsp (2 mL) savory or fresh dill
1 egg, lightly beaten
Fine breadcrumbs

Method:

• Place bread in a bowl, cover with cold water, let soak 10 minutes.

• Squeeze as dry as possible and mash in a bowl with a fork.

• Heat the chicken or bacon fat 2 minutes at HIGH.

• Add the onion and the garlic. Stir well. Microwave 3 minutes at HIGH, stirring after 2 minutes.

• Add the soaked bread, lemon rind, salt and pepper, savory or fresh dill. Mix well.

• Add the beaten egg, stir until well mixed. If mixture is too wet to form a neat little ball, add enough dry breadcrumbs to give it the right texture. Roll the mixture into tiny balls, set on a plate. Refrigerate until ready to use.

• Bring consommé or bouillon to boil. Add to the hot liquid as many *boulettes* as you wish, one by one. Cover and microwave 10 minutes at MEDIUM-HIGH.

Poultry

Whichever way you choose to cook your poultry or small game, from roasted to poached, the microwave makes it simple and ensures success.

Chicken is an excellent meat, and a source of high-quality protein, niacin and iron. One very interesting point is that 3½ ounces (100 g) of white chicken meat, skinned, contains only 166 calories.

We also have game farms that all year round produce ducks, quail, pheasant, etc., sold fresh or frozen.

To defrost poultry and game

• To cook a frozen chicken to perfection, it must first be defrosted completely. Personally, I favor slow defrosting by placing the chicken in a dish and letting it stand in the refrigerator, without unwrapping, for 12 to 24 hours. This allows the flesh to slacken and excess moisture can be removed easily.

• Of course, emergencies arise that don't allow sufficient time for slow defrosting. That is when your microwave oven comes to the rescue!

1. Remove chicken from original wrapper.

2. Place a microwave-safe rack in the bottom of a

dish. Set the chicken on it. Do not cover.

3. Set DEFROST. A whole chicken up to 4 pounds (2 kg) will require 12 to 14 minutes per pound (24 to 28 minutes per kg). A cut-up chicken, 8 to 10 minutes per pound (16 to 20 minutes per kg). A boned chicken breast, 10 to 12 minutes per pound (20 to 24 minutes per kg).

4. IMPORTANT: The whole chicken or cut-up chicken must be turned over three to four times during defrosting.

5. As soon as possible, break apart the chicken pieces before completion of the DEFROST cycle.

6. As the chicken or cut-up chicken is removed from the microwave oven, rinse under cold water.

• My favorite method is to wash the defrosted chicken with a cloth soaked in fresh lemon juice, white wine, sherry or brandy.

• Whatever liquid you use, do not wipe after moistening.

• Spread the pieces or set the chicken on a sheet of absorbent paper and let stand 20 to 30 minutes before cooking.

Auto Weight Defrost

• Some ovens feature a defrost system referred to as Auto Weight Defrost — another wonder of microwave ovens.

• Read the instructions in your oven manual for Auto Weight Defrost. The defrosting is automatic.

• These guidelines apply to all types of Auto Weight Defrost:

• Remove wrapper, because the wrap will hold steam and juice close to the food, which can cause the outer surface of the food to cook.

• I like to place the meat on a microwave-safe rack set in a dish. Then, I simply set the control.

After Defrosting

• Whole poultry may still be icy in the centre. Run cold water into cavity. If the giblets are inside, they will then be easily removed.

- Small items can stand 10 to 20 minutes after defrosting.

To test the doneness of a chicken

- In a properly cooked chicken, the breast will be white throughout, showing no brilliant spots when sliced. The brown meat will slice easily and show no tinge of pink.

- A chicken should never be cooked rare. On the other hand, overcooking chicken leaves it dry and tasteless.

- Each of the following recipes gives a specific cooking time, but since wattage varies in microwaves, cooking periods may vary. Here is the way to test the doneness of birds:

A. With a meat thermometer

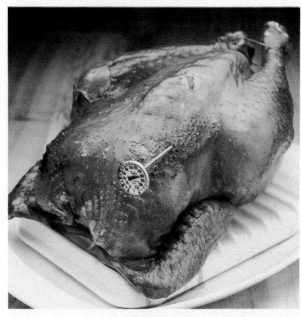

- Stop the oven, insert the tip of the thermometer into the thickest part of the white meat, being sure it does not touch bones, which would give a higher reading. Poultry is done at 180° - 185°F (82° - 85°C).

B. By touch

- Test lightly with thumb and index finger. If cooked, the poultry will have a springy feel, slightly resistant to indentation.

C. Move the leg bone: When cooked, it is even possible to pull it off.

Types of poultry and game

- There are many reasons why chicken is a year-round favorite. It is easy to prepare, easy on the budget, and it can be served in dozens of ways.

- I think the only dilemma chicken poses for those who enjoy cooking is the question of what type to buy.

- The answer is easy if you know how you wish to prepare it and how many people you will be serving.

- I usually allow half a pound (250 g) per serving. The type of chicken you choose indicates the age and approximate size, so choose one that meets your specific needs.

Broiler-fryers

- They are all-purpose chickens, ideal for frying, roasting, stewing.

- They are about 9 weeks old and weigh from 2 to 4 pounds (1 to 2 kg).

Roasters

- Best choice for roast chicken or roast stuffed chicken.

- Larger than broiler-fryers, they are about 12 weeks old and weigh 3½ to 5 pounds (1.75 to 2.5 kg).

Capons

- They are "deluxe" chickens. They have more white meat than other chickens and are very tender.
- Usually roasted, these young de-sexed male chickens weigh from 4 to 7 pounds (2 to 3.5 kg).
- When a large chicken salad is needed for a buffet or special party, they are the best buy, as they offer the most meat for the price.

Goose

- It should weigh between 10 and 14 pounds (5 to 7 kg) to be at its best.
- Heavier types are very fat.
- Most geese come to the market frozen.
- When possible do get a fresh one.
- Goose is at its best roasted, stuffed or unstuffed.

Turkeys

- Young females of 10 to 13 pounds (5 to 6.5 kg) are the best for flavor and texture.
- They are best for roasting in the microwave when they weigh from 8 to 13 pounds (4 to 6.5 kg).

Cornish hens

- Sometimes called game hens, they are the smallest members of the chicken family.

- They are delicate, tasty and elegant.
- They weigh from 1 to 2 pounds (500 g to 1 kg).
- Usually a 1-pound (500 g) bird is used for each serving, a 2-pound (1 kg) one is cut in half.
- They are at their best when stuffed and roasted. They are often cooked or served with fresh fruit.

Chicken

Poached Chicken

Preparation	**17 m**
Cooking :	**from 35 to 40 m**
Standing :	**none**

A personal note : This is a classic French cuisine recipe that I have adapted very successfully to microwave cooking. The cooked chicken can be served with a sauce of your choice, made into a pie or salad or simply sliced. The very concentrated broth makes excellent soup.

Ingredients :

2 medium carrots, thinly sliced
1 medium onion, sliced

1 medium leek, minced
2 celery stalks, diced
3 tbsp (50 mL) butter
2 bay leaves
1 tsp (5 mL) tarragon
1/2 tsp (2 mL) thyme
6 sprigs of parsley, minced
1 tbsp (15 mL) coarse salt
1/2 tsp (2 mL) freshly ground pepper
3 lb (1.5 kg) chicken parts *or*
   1   3-to-4-lb (1.5 - 2kg) chicken
1 cup (250 mL) white wine (optional)
2 cups (500 mL) chicken broth

Method :

• In a 14-cup (3.5 L) microwave-safe casserole-dish place the carrots, onion, leek, celery, butter, bay leaves, tarragon, thyme, parsley, salt and pepper. Stir together. Cover and microwave 10 minutes at HIGH. Stir well. The vegetables will be glossy and have lost their firmness.

• Add the chicken pieces or whole chicken, covering the chicken here and there with the vegetables.

• Add 1/4 cup (60 mL) of wine or chicken broth. Cover and microwave at HIGH 20 to 25 minutes or until the chicken is tender. Stir twice during the cooking period, allowing the chicken to absorb all the flavor from the vegetables and herbs.

• Add the remaining wine and the chicken broth. Microwave at HIGH 5 minutes.

• Serve directly from the casserole dish or cool in its juice, strain and use as you wish.

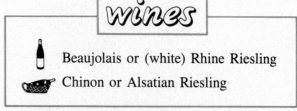

wines

Beaujolais or (white) Rhine Riesling
Chinon or Alsatian Riesling

Chicken Teriyaki

Advance preparation . . . . . . **from 2 to 8 h**	
Cooking . . . . **26 m**	
Standing . . . . **5 m**	

Canadian Riesling or Liebfraumilch
Californian or Rhine Riesling Spätlese

• It takes a lot of experience and a knowledge of Japanese cuisine to be able to cook Japanese recipes to perfection. This recipe is an adaptation, but a good one, and easy to prepare.

Ingredients:

3 lb (1.5 kg) chicken breast or chicken legs

1/2 cup (125 mL) soy sauce*

1 tsp (5 mL) sesame oil

1/4 cup (60 mL) Sake or dry sherry

1 large garlic clove, chopped fine

1 tbsp (15 mL) dark brown sugar

1 tbsp (15 mL) freshly grated ginger root

* Use Kikkoman soy sauce when available; it is lighter and milder than Chinese soy sauce.

Method:

• Wash chicken, place it in plastic bag.

• Mix the remaining ingredients and pour over the chicken. (If you place the bag in a bowl, it is easy to pour in the liquid.) Tie the bag and stir all around so the chicken is coated with the marinade.

• Refrigerate 2 to 8 hours.

• To cook, remove chicken from bag, reserving the marinade.

• Place the chicken in an oblong microwave-safe dish. Cover the tip of the legs with little pieces of aluminum foil.

• Microwave 15 minutes at HIGH. Baste generously with the marinating liquid.

• Microwave another 10 minutes at MEDIUM. Let stand 5 minutes.

• Serve with plain boiled rice.

• Add the remaining marinade to the pan drippings. Heat at HIGH 1 minute.

• Serve as a sauce, to pour over the chicken and the rice.

Small Broiler, Ivory Sauce

Preparation . . . .**20 m**
Cooking . . . .**from 22 to 26 m**
Standing . . . .**none**

A personal note: This is the perfect recipe to cook a small 2½-to-3-lb (1.2 - 1.5 kg) broiler. It is also the recipe to follow when you wish to steam any type of small bird. It's excellent if you are on a diet, as you can simply reduce the butter and omit the cream. It's also recommended when you want to serve creamed chicken in a pie or in puff pastry shells.

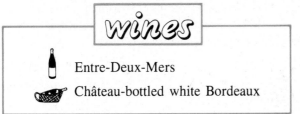

wines

Entre-Deux-Mers

Château-bottled white Bordeaux

Ingredients:

1   2½-to-3-lb (1.2 - 1.5 kg) chicken

1 tsp (5 mL) salt

1/2 tsp (2 mL) pepper

2 tbsp (30 mL) butter

1 leek or large onion, sliced

1 medium carrot, sliced

1/2 cup (125 mL) celery, diced

1/2 cup (125 mL) water

1/2 tsp (2 mL) tarragon

Method:

• Rub the chicken cavity with the salt and pepper. Fold wings under and tie legs together.

• Melt the 2 tablespoons (30 mL) butter in a microwave-safe dish large enough to take the chicken.

• Add the leek or onion, the carrot and the celery.

• Microwave 4 minutes at HIGH, stir well. Add the water and tarragon, stir well.

• Place the prepared chicken breast-side down in the dish. Cover. Microwave at HIGH 10 minutes. Baste chicken, then microwave at MEDIUM-HIGH 3 minutes per pound (500 g).

• Turn chicken breast-side up after the first 3 minutes. Cut up chicken.

Ivory Sauce:

Ingredients:

3 tbsp (50 mL) butter

1/4 cup (60 mL) flour*

The bouillon from the cooked chicken

1/3 cup (80 mL) light cream

Enough milk to measure 2 cups (500 mL)

Salt and pepper to taste

Method:

• Place 3 tablespoons (50 mL) butter in a 4-cup (1 L) microwave-safe measuring cup and melt 1 minute at HIGH.

• Add the flour, stir well. Add the drained bouillon from the cooked chicken, stir.

• Add the cream and enough milk for 2 cups, stir.

• Microwave at HIGH 2 minutes, stir well. Repeat cooking if sauce is not sufficiently cooked.

• Salt and pepper to taste. Pour over the chicken and vegetables.

• Stir well and serve.

* I like to use instant flour, which gives a creamier and lighter sauce, but any flour will do.

Lemon Chicken Barcelona

Preparation: ....10 m
Cooking: ....from 24 to 30 m
Standing:.....................none

A personal note: A lemon-steamed chicken with a delicious light gravy. Serve Lemon Chicken Barcelona with small dumplings cooked in chicken stock, or with rice stirred with parsley and toasted almonds.

Ingredients:

1 3-lb (1.5 kg) broiler
1 tsp (5 mL) salt
1/2 tsp (2 mL) pepper
1/2 tsp (2 mL) paprika
1 lemon, unpeeled, thinly sliced
3 tbsp (50 mL) butter

  Vina Sol (white from the Penedes region) or Aligoté

  Chablis or Mosel Riesling Kabinett

Method:

• Wash chicken, wipe as dry as possible.

• Mix the salt, pepper and paprika. Rub chicken all over with the mixture.

• Fill cavity with the slices of lemon. Tie legs together. Close cavity.

• Place the butter in an 8 × 8-inch (20 × 20 cm) microwave-safe dish. Microwave at HIGH 3 to 4 minutes or until butter is browned.

• Place chicken breast-side down in browned butter.

• Microwave at HIGH 10 minutes. Turn chicken. Baste with drippings.

• Microwave at MEDIUM 10 minutes. Test for doneness; if necessary, microwave another 5 minutes.

• Remove chicken to a hot platter.

• Add a few spoonfuls of hot water or chicken broth to the juice in the pan.

• Microwave at HIGH 1 minute. Stir well. Pour over chicken or serve in a sauceboat.

Norwegian
Citron Chicken

Advance preparation: . . . . 24 h
Cooking: . . . . from 42 to 55 m
Standing: . . . . from 4 to 5 h

A personal note: A very interesting cold chicken, this is a perfect buffet dish. In Norway, they surround it with steamed prawn or lobster, but the chicken by itself is tasty and interesting.

Ingredients:

6 cups (1.5 L) hot water

1   3-lb (1.5 kg) chicken

1 tsp (5 mL) coarse salt

15 peppercorns

6 to 8 celery leaves tied together

8 to 10 parsley stems tied together

1/2 tsp (2 mL) thyme

3 egg yolks

3 tbsp (50 mL) flour

1 cup (250 mL) light cream

2 tbsp (30 mL) dry sherry

2 tbsp (30 mL) grated lemon rind

Salt and pepper to taste

2 cups (500 mL) shredded lettuce or watercress

1 lb (500 g) cooked shrimp or lobster meat (optional)

Method:

• Place the first 7 ingredients in a 20-cup (5 L) microwave-safe saucepan. Cover. Microwave at HIGH 30 to 40 minutes or until chicken is tender.

• Remove from oven. Let stand until cool, 4 to 5 hours.

• Remove chicken from the bouillon. Remove and discard the skin. Slice all the meat. Set on an attractive serving dish.

• Beat the egg yolks with the flour, cream and sherry. Add the lemon rind. Microwave 10 minutes at MEDIUM, beat with a whisk. If necessary, microwave 2 to 5 minutes at MEDIUM-HIGH or until creamy. Salt and pepper to taste. Stir well.

• While hot, pour over the chicken set on the serving dish. Refrigerate overnight.

• To serve, surround the dish with shredded lettuce or watercress. If you wish, place pieces of cooked seafood over the lettuce.

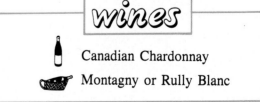

wines

Canadian Chardonnay

Montagny or Rully Blanc

571

Chicken Montagnard

• I was taught how to make this chicken by an old shepherd in the French Alps. It's simple, unusual and interesting.

Ingredients:

1 2-to-4-lb (1 - 2 kg) chicken
3 slices of dry bread
1 large garlic clove, unpeeled
1/4 cup (60 mL) parsley, minced
Grated rind of 1 lemon
1/2 tsp (2 mL) salt
1/4 tsp (1 mL) pepper
1 tbsp (15 mL) soft butter
2 tsp (10 mL) vegetable oil
1 tsp (5 mL) paprika

Method:

• Wrap paper towel around 2 slices of bread. Place in the microwave on a rack. Microwave at HIGH 1 minute. Touch the bread to see if it is dry. If necessary, microwave another 30 seconds to 1 minute. Cool 1 minute.

• Cut a small slice at the end of the clove of garlic and rub hard on the dried bread. The garlic will melt into the bread. Dice the bread.

• Mix the parsley, lemon rind, salt and pepper. Add the diced bread, mix.

• Stuff into the chicken. Secure the opening with toothpicks.

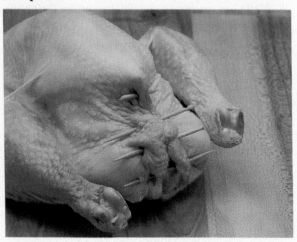

| Preparation . . . . .15 m |
| Cooking : the meal : . . .10 m per pound (500 g) |
| the sauce : . . . . .6 m |
| Standing . . . . .none |

• Blend together the butter, oil and paprika. Rub all over the chicken with your hands. Pour remaining mixture, if any, on top of chicken.

• Place chicken on a rack set on a microwave-safe dish, breast-side down. Microwave 10 minutes per pound (500 g) at MEDIUM-HIGH.

• After 15 minutes of cooking, place chicken breast-side up and finish the cooking period.

• When done, remove chicken to a hot platter. Cover and keep warm.

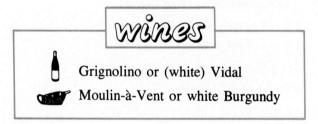

Grignolino or (white) Vidal
Moulin-à-Vent or white Burgundy

The sauce :

Ingredients:

2 tbsp (30 mL) butter
2 tbsp (30 mL) flour
1 small onion, chopped fine
1 clove garlic, chopped fine
1/2 cup (125 mL) chicken bouillon
1/2 cup (125 mL) white wine or cream
1/4 tsp (1 mL) tarragon

Method:

• Mix the butter and flour. Add to the chicken drippings, mix well.

• Add the remaining ingredients. Stir and microwave at HIGH 3 minutes. Stir well, then microwave another 3 minutes. Adjust seasoning. Serve in a sauceboat.

• I like to pour a few tablespoons of this creamy sauce over the chicken before serving.

Milk Fried Chicken

• A delight of my youth, this is an old-fashioned way to brown and cook a chicken, then finish it in milk sauce. My mother served it with hot buttered French bread and a bowl of minced chives or parsley that we used as we liked.

• This recipe is proof that even old, traditional recipes can be adapted to microwave cooking.

Ingredients:

1 3-lb (1.5 kg) chicken
1/4 cup (60 mL) flour
2 tsp (10 mL) salt
1/4 tsp (1 mL) each pepper and turmeric
2 tbsp (30 mL) butter or bacon fat
3 tbsp (50 mL) flour
2 cups (500 mL) milk

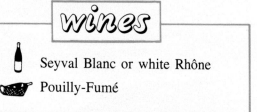

wines

Seyval Blanc or white Rhône
Pouilly-Fumé

Method:

• Cut the chicken into individual pieces. Wipe with absorbent paper.

• Mix together the flour, salt, pepper and turmeric.

Preparation: . . . . .15 m
Cooking: the meal . . . . .from 21 to 25 m
           the sauce . . . . .from 4 to 6 m
Standing: . . . . .none

• Roll each piece of chicken in this mixture until well coated. Place the butter or bacon fat in an 8 × 8-inch (20 × 20 cm) microwave-safe dish and melt 5 minutes at HIGH; the butter will brown, the bacon fat will be very hot.

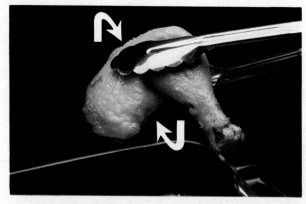

• Place the chicken pieces skin-side down in the fat. Brown 8 to 10 minutes at HIGH.

• Turn pieces, then microwave at MEDIUM-HIGH 8 to 10 minutes.

• Remove chicken to a warm dish.

• Cover and let stand while making the sauce.

To make the sauce:

• Add the flour to the fat in the dish, mix well, scraping brown pieces.

• Add the milk, mix well.

• Microwave 4 to 6 minutes at HIGH, stirring twice.

• When creamy, salt and pepper to taste, then pour over the chicken. Serve.

574

Glazed Roasted Chicken

Preparation: . . . . .18 m
Cooking: . . . . . . .7 m per pound (500 g)
Standing: . . . . .from 8 to 10 m

The glaze:
3 tbsp (50 mL) butter
1½ tsp (7 mL) paprika
1 tsp (5 mL) Kitchen Bouquet
1/4 tsp (1 mL) thyme or tarragon

The gravy:
2 tbsp (30 mL) Madeira or port or cold tea
Salt and pepper to taste

Method:

• Fill the chicken cavity with the onion, lemon slices, celery and thyme.

• Tie the chicken legs and wings as usual.

• Place a microwave-safe rack in an 8 × 10-inch (20 × 25 cm) microwave-safe dish.

• To make the glaze: Place the butter, paprika, Kitchen Bouquet and thyme in a microwave-safe measuring cup and microwave 1 minute at HIGH.

• Mix the glaze thoroughly and brush all over the chicken.

• Put the chicken on the rack breast-side down. Microwave 7 minutes per pound (14 minutes per kg) at HIGH, turning it halfway through the cooking.

• Baste with the juice in the pan and finish cooking.

• Let stand 8 to 10 minutes. Place on a warm dish.

• To make gravy: Add the Madeira, port or cold tea. Stir well and microwave 1 minute at HIGH. Serve in a sauceboat.

• A liquid glaze brushed over the chicken before cooking gives the skin a delicious flavor. It is an old French method that I have adapted to the microwave.

Ingredients:

1 3-to-4-lb (1.5 - 2 kg) chicken
1 onion, chopped
3 lemon slices, unpeeled
1 celery stalk
1 tsp (2 mL) thyme

wines

Alsatian Pinot Blanc
Pouilly-Fumé

Bread Stuffing

Preparation: . . . . .17 m
Cooking: . . . . .18 m
Standing: . . . . .1 h

A personal note: One of the best all-purpose bread stuffing recipes I know, this can be reduced or doubled without changing the flavor and quality. I prefer to cook it in a baking dish rather than in the bird's cavity. But you are free to use it as a stuffing or as a casserole.

Ingredients:

4 cups (1 L) brown or rye bread, toasted and diced

2 cups (500 mL) onions, chopped fine

2 cups (500 mL) diced celery and leaves

1 tsp (5 mL) thyme

1 tsp (5 mL) savory

1 tsp (5 mL) salt

1/2 tsp (2 mL) pepper

1/2 cup (125 mL) butter or margarine, melted

1/3 cup (80 mL) sherry, brandy or chicken broth

Method:

• Mix together the toasted bread cut into small dice, the onions, celery, thyme, savory, salt and pepper.

• Melt the butter or margarine 1 minute at HIGH, add the liquid of your choice. Microwave at HIGH 2 minutes.

• To stuff the poultry, place some of the bread mixture in the neck, pour half of the hot liquid mixture over the stuffing. Fill cavity with remainder. Repeat. Sew the opening with strong thread.

To cook as a casserole

• Use the same ingredients.

• Place half the bread mixture in the bottom of a microwave-safe loaf pan.

• Pour half the liquid on top. Repeat. Cover with waxed paper or a lid. Let stand 1 hour at room temperature.

• Then microwave, covered, 18 minutes at MEDIUM.

Variations

• If you like meat in the stuffing, pass giblets through a mincer, then add **1/2 pound (250 g) minced pork.**

• Melt **2 tablespoons (30 mL) butter** 1 minute at HIGH.

• Add the meats. Stir well.

• Cover and microwave 3 minutes at MEDIUM-HIGH.

• Add meat to bread mixture.

• Then proceed same as above — either to stuff the turkey or make a casserole.

Quebec Potato Stuffing

Preparation :	. . . .	**10 m**
Cooking :	. . . .	**from 34 to 36 m**
Standing :	. . . .	**none**

• This is one of the most traditional stuffings of Quebec cuisine. It is full of flavor.

Ingredients :

The heart, gizzard and liver from the chicken*
1 tbsp (15 mL) chicken fat or other fat, chopped
3 medium-sized onions, finely chopped
1 garlic clove, minced
4 cups (1 L) cooked potatoes, peeled
2 tsp (10 mL) savory
1 tbsp (15 mL) salt
1/2 tsp (2 mL) pepper
1 tbsp (15 mL) butter

Method :

• Put the heart, gizzard and liver through a meat grinder.

• Melt the chopped fat 5 minutes at HIGH. Stir after 2 minutes.

• Add the minced giblets, stir. Microwave 3 minutes at MEDIUM-HIGH.

• Add the onions, garlic, savory, salt and pepper. Stir well. Microwave 2 minutes at HIGH.

• To microwave the potatoes add 1/4 cup (60 mL) water, cover and microwave 14 to 16 minutes at HIGH. Mash them and mix with the cooked giblets. Add the butter and stir well.

• Place in a microwave-save dish, cover with lid or waxed paper. Microwave 10 minutes at MEDIUM-HIGH.

* If you prefer, replace the chopped giblets with 1 pound (500 g) minced pork, or use the two meats for a richer stuffing.

Crisp Quartered Chicken

Preparation : . . . . **10 m**
Cooking : the meal : . . . . **15 m**
        the sauce : . . . . **30 s**
Standing : . . . . **10 m**

A personal note : I roast this chicken in the microwave, cut into quarters, or I sometimes use a few pounds of chicken wings or 6 to 8 chicken legs, instead.
I recommend using Flavored Breadcrumbs, which are economical and very tasty.

Ingredients :

1 cup (250 mL) homemade coating*
1 3-lb (1.5 kg) chicken, cut in four
1 egg white, lightly beaten
1 tsp (5 mL) cold water or white wine
3 tbsp (50 mL) butter

Method :

• Place the coating of your choice on a square of waxed paper.

• In a large plate, beat together with a fork the egg white and cold water or wine.

• Roll the pieces of chicken in the egg white-water mixture, then in the coating, until every part of the chicken is well covered.

• Place the chicken pieces one next to another in a glass or ceramic baking dish.

• Melt the butter 1 minute at HIGH. Spoon all over the chicken pieces.

• Roast at HIGH 10 minutes, then 5 minutes at MEDIUM. Let stand 10 minutes and serve as is or with Lemon Caper Sauce.

A commercial coating may be used, if you wish.

Seyval Blanc or Mâcon Blanc
Alsatian Riesling

To make the sauce :

Ingredients :

2 tbsp (30 mL) butter
Grated rind of half a lemon
2 tbsp (30 mL) fresh lemon juice
1 tbsp (15 mL) capers

Method :

• Place butter in a microwave-safe dish and melt 1 minute at HIGH. Add the remaining ingredients. Microwave 30 seconds at HIGH. Add to chicken gravy. Stir well.

Chicken Madeira

Preparation : . . . . .15 m
Cooking : . . . . .from 25 to 27 m
Standing : . . . . .none

A personal note : This is a classic recipe of Portuguese cuisine. Try to use Portuguese Madeira wine, as it gives a beautiful flavor and color to the dish.

Ingredients :

3 tbsp (50 mL) butter

3 French shallots, minced *or*

   6 green onions, chopped fine

1/2 lb (500 g) fresh mushrooms, sliced

1 tsp (5 mL) tarragon

Salt and pepper to taste

1/4 cup (60 mL) dry Madeira wine

6 to 8 chicken breasts, boned

White Rhône or Canadian Chardonnay

White Burgundy or Australian Chardonnay

Method :

• Place the butter in a microwave-safe dish large enough to hold the chicken breasts in one layer and melt 1 minute at HIGH.

• Add the shallots or green onions. Microwave at MEDIUM 3 minutes, stir well.

• Add the mushrooms and tarragon, stir well. Microwave at HIGH 2 minutes, stir.

• Add salt and pepper to taste and the Madeira wine. Microwave at HIGH 2 minutes.

• Place each breast on a wooden board or between sheets of waxed paper.

• Pound with a mallet to thin them out.

• Roll each breast, tie with thread and place it in the hot sauce in the dish. Microwave at MEDIUM-HIGH 15 minutes. Test with a fork for doneness.

• If necessary, microwave another 3 to 5 minutes. Remove from oven.

• Set on serving dish, keep warm.

• Pour gravy remaining in dish over the chicken.

Chicken Breasts Soubise

Preparation: . . . .**10 m**
Cooking: . . . .**25 m**
Standing: . . . .**none**

A personal note: Soubise means onions. And these chicken breasts cook on a bed of onions flavored with white vermouth. Serve with fine parsleyed noodles or buttered rice.

Ingredients:

2 large onions, sliced into rings

1/2 tsp (2 mL) salt

4 chicken breast halves

3 tbsp (50 mL) soft butter

1/4 tsp (1 mL) each pepper and thyme

1 tsp (5 mL) paprika

1/4 cup (60 mL) white vermouth

2 tbsp (30 mL) cream of your choice

Method:

• Place the onion rings in the bottom of an 8 × 8-inch (20 × 20 cm) ceramic or Micro-Dur dish.

• Shape the breasts nicely and place one in each corner of the dish.

• Mix together the salt, soft butter, pepper, thyme and paprika. Spread over the top of each breast, preferably with your fingers.

• Microwave uncovered 10 minutes at HIGH.

• Remove the breasts from the dish without turning them.

• Add the vermouth and stir well. Microwave 3 minutes at HIGH.

• Return the breasts to the dish. Cover and microwave at HIGH 10 minutes.

• Set the chicken on a warm serving dish.

• Discard the onions

• Add the cream to the sauce. Beat with a metal whisk or an electric beater. Adjust seasoning.

• Microwave at HIGH 2 minutes. Pour over the chicken breasts or all around.

 wines

 Vidal or White Rhône

White Burgundy or Australian Chardonnay

Chicken Breasts Autumn Leaves

• A stuffing of nuts and apples gives an autumn air to this chicken dish.

Preparation : . . . . **18 m**
Cooking : the meal : . . . . from **14 to 15 m**
the sauce : . . . . from **6 to 7 m**
Standing : . . . . **5 m**

Ingredients :

4 chicken breasts, boned, cut in half

2 cups (500 mL) crustless bread, diced

1 tsp (5 mL) tarragon or thyme

1 tsp (5 mL) salt

1/4 tsp (1 mL) pepper

1/2 tsp (2 mL) garlic, crushed

1/3 cup (80 mL) walnuts or pecans, chopped

1/2 cup (125 mL) sultana raisins

3 tbsp (50 mL) melted butter

2 apples, peeled and grated

1/2 cup (125 mL) apple juice

Grated rind of 1 lemon

3 tbsp (50 mL) soft butter

Method :

• Wipe the boneless chicken breasts with a cloth dipped in **port wine or orange juice.**

• Mix all the remaining ingredients except the last

3 tablespoons (50 mL) of butter. Blend thoroughly to make a sort of paste. Divide evenly on the chicken half breasts, forming a little roll in the middle of each. Roll and secure each piece of chicken with toothpicks.

• Roll each one lightly in **1 tablespoon (15 mL) of flour stirred with 1 teaspoon (15 mL) paprika.**

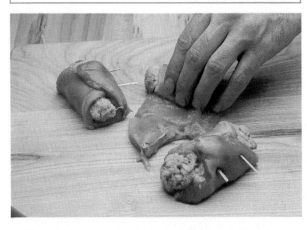

• Preheat a browning dish 6 minutes at HIGH.

• Rub each piece of chicken with the remaining 3 tablespoons (50 mL) soft butter.

• Without removing the browning dish from the oven, place the rolls in it. Microwave at HIGH 8 minutes. Turn rolls over.

• Microwave at MEDIUM-HIGH 6 to 7 minutes. Let stand 5 minutes.

• Set rolls on a hot platter.

To make the sauce :

• Add **one small onion** chopped fine to the fat in the dish.

• Add **1 teaspoon (5 mL) butter** and **1 cup (250 mL) thinly sliced mushrooms.** Stir well. Microwave 3 minutes at HIGH.

• Add **1 tablespoon (15 mL) flour** and mix well.

• Add **3 tablespoons (50 mL) brandy or Madeira wine** and **2/3 cup (160 mL) cream.** Stir.

• Microwave at HIGH 3 to 4 minutes. Stir well. Pour over the chicken.

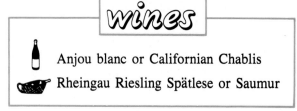

wines

Anjou blanc or Californian Chablis
Rheingau Riesling Spätlese or Saumur

583

Chicken Breasts Milano

Preparation: ....20 m
Cooking: the meal: ....25 m
          the sauce: ....from 6 to 7 m
Standing: ....10 m

A personal note: A specialty of Italian cuisine, this dish is even better when cooked in the microwave. When I serve it hot, I top the chicken with a mushroom sauce. If I serve it cold, I omit the sauce. I slice the cold stuffed breast, which I set around a rice salad; the green of the spinach is very colorful.

Ingredients:

4 whole chicken breasts, boned

Stuffing:

Salt and pepper to taste
1 package fresh spinach
1/2 cup (125 mL) fine breadcrumbs
1/2 tsp (2 mL) savory
1 tsp (5 mL) basil
1 egg
1/4 cup (60 mL) soft butter
6 green onions, chopped fine
1 large garlic clove, chopped fine

Seasoned sherry:

1/4 tsp (1 mL) salt
1/4 cup (60 mL) dry sherry
1/4 cup (60 mL) melted butter
1 tsp (5 mL) paprika

Method:

• Salt and pepper the inside of the chicken breasts.

• Wash the spinach, removing hard stems, then pour boiling water on it. Let stand 10 minutes. Drain thoroughly, chop.

• Add the next 7 ingredients. Mix well. Spread mixture equally over the inside of each breast. Roll, close with wooden picks. Place in a pie plate, breast-side up.

• Blend together the ingredients for the seasoned sherry.

• Microwave chicken breasts 15 minutes at HIGH.

• Pour 1 teaspoon (5 mL) of seasoned sherry over each breast. Microwave at MEDIUM another 10 minutes. Let stand covered 10 minutes.

To make the sauce:

Ingredients:

2 tbsp (30 mL) butter
2 tsp (10 mL) cornstarch
1/4 cup (60 mL) cream or milk
1/2 lb (250 g) fresh mushrooms, sliced

Method:

• Melt the butter 1 minute at HIGH. Blend in the cornstarch and add the cream or milk.

• Microwave 3 minutes at HIGH. Stir once while cooking.

• Add the mushrooms and any of the drippings from the cooking of the chicken breast. Microwave at MEDIUM-HIGH 3 to 4 minutes. Stir well, then serve separately.

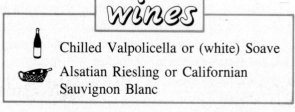

wines

Chilled Valpolicella or (white) Soave

Alsatian Riesling or Californian Sauvignon Blanc

Glazed Chicken Breasts, Country Inn

Preparation: .20 m
Cooking: . . . . .from 23 to 24 m
Standing: . . . . .none

A personal note: Three-star chef Alain Chapel created this recipe. He was amused by my adaptation of it to microwave cooking and he strongly encouraged me to add it to my other recipes. His tomato "coulis" is superb. It may also be served with a roast of veal or poached sole fillets.

Beaujolais Villages or Baco Noir
Alsatian Pinot Noir

Ingredients:

Tomato "coulis"

4 red tomatoes

3 tbsp (50 mL) olive oil

1 garlic clove, unpeeled, cut in two

2 tsp (10 mL) sugar

Chicken

2 chicken breasts, cut in two

Salt, pepper and paprika to taste

2 tsp (10 mL) red wine vinegar

1 tbsp (15 mL) Japanese or white wine vinegar

2 tsp (10 mL) Dijon mustard

1/4 cup (60 mL) white wine or white vermouth

3 tbsp (50 mL) tomato "coulis"

1 tsp (5 mL) butter

Method:

- Cut the tomatoes in four.
- Heat the oil in microwave-safe baking dish 1 minute at HIGH.

- Add the unpeeled garlic, stir in the oil and brown lightly 2 minutes at HIGH. Stir. Add the tomatoes and sugar, microwave 5 minutes at HIGH.

- Stir well and microwave at HIGH 4 or 5 minutes or until the tomatoes have lost most of their juice and have a somewhat creamy texture. Put through a fine sieve.

- Cut each breast in two so you have four pieces.
- Preheat a browning dish 6 minutes at HIGH.
- Sprinkle each piece of chicken with salt, pepper and paprika.
- Without removing the hot dish from the oven, place the chicken pieces in it skin-side down. Brown 5 minutes at HIGH.
- Turn the chicken. Pour the red wine vinegar and Japanese or white wine vinegar on top. Microwave 4 minutes at HIGH.
- In the meantime, mix together the Dijon mustard, white wine or vermouth and tomato "coulis." Set chicken on a hot serving dish.
- Add the above mustard mixture to the juice in the baking dish. Mix well. Microwave 3 minutes at HIGH, stir.
- Add the butter and mix thoroughly. Pour over the chicken.
- If the chicken has cooled, it is easy to reheat by placing the serving dish in the microwave 3 to 5 minutes at MEDIUM. Serve with a bowl of rice.

Portuguese Glazed Chicken Breast

Preparation: . . . . .15 m
Cooking: . . . . .29 m
Standing: .10 m

A personal note: Chicken "nouvelle cuisine" is a very lengthy preparation on top of the stove but is quick and easy in the microwave. It's the perfect dish for an elegant dinner, served with fine green noodles or asparagus.

Ingredients:

2 tbsp (30 mL) butter
4 chicken breast halves
1 cup (250 mL) leeks, thinly sliced
2 French shallots, minced
1 bunch watercress or parsley, whole
1/3 cup (80 mL) port wine
2/3 cup (160 mL) chicken broth
2 egg yolks
3 tbsp (50 mL) cold water
Salt and pepper to taste

Method:

• Place the butter in a microwave-safe baking dish and melt 1 minute at HIGH.

• Add the leeks and shallots. Stir well. Microwave 4 minutes at MEDIUM-HIGH, stirring halfway through cooking.

• Add the watercress or parsley, the port and chicken broth. Microwave uncovered 3 minutes at HIGH. Stir.

• Roll up each half breast like a sausage. Salt and pepper to taste.

• Place the chicken in the port sauce and baste. Cover with lid or plastic wrap.

• Microwave 18 minutes at MEDIUM. Let stand 10 minutes. Remove breasts to a hot serving plate.

• Pour the hot sauce mixture into the processor or blender bowl.

• Beat the egg yolks lightly with the cold water, add. Cover and beat to obtain a creamy sauce.

• Pour into a microwave-safe dish and microwave 2 minutes at HIGH, stirring well after 1 minute. You will have a lovely green sauce.

• Pour over the chicken breast. Reheat 2 minutes at MEDIUM. Serve.

wines

Dao red or Maréchal Foch
Vintage Spanish Rioja red

Chicken Breasts or Legs California

Preparation: . . . . **12 m**
Cooking: . . . . **from 27 to 35 m**
Standing: . . . . **none**

A personal note: Chicken breasts are wonderful cooked over a bed of melted onions and served with a creamy sauce and parsleyed rice. I sometimes replace the breast with chicken legs, which are more economical but just as easy to make.

Ingredients:

2 good-sized chicken breasts, boneless, *or*
  6 to 8 chicken legs
1/2 to 3/4 cup (125 - 190 mL) onion, thinly sliced
1/4 cup (60 mL) butter or margarine
1/2 tsp (2 mL) thyme or tarragon
3 thin slices of lemon, unpeeled
1/3 cup (80 mL) heavy or light cream
Salt and pepper to taste
1 tbsp (15 mL) flour

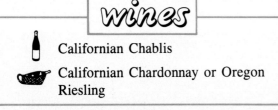

wines

Californian Chablis

Californian Chardonnay or Oregon Riesling

Method:

• I prefer to cut each chicken breast in half. When time permits, I bone the chicken legs and turn them into neat rolls, but they can also be cooked whole.

• Place the butter or margarine in a microwave-safe dish large enough to hold the chicken pieces one next to the other and melt 3 minutes at HIGH.

• Add the onions, thyme or tarragon and lemon slices to the melted butter. Stir well. Microwave at HIGH 3 minutes, stirring once. This will soften the onions.

• Stir well and place the pieces of chicken over the onions. Pour the cream over all. Salt and pepper to taste.

• Cover the dish with a lid or plastic wrap. Microwave at MEDIUM-HIGH 20 minutes for chicken breasts, 25 to 28 minutes for chicken legs.

• Remove dish from microwave and place chicken on a warm platter.

• Strain the onions from the liquid with a perforated spoon. Place them over the chicken.

• To the liquid left in the pan add the flour, mix well.

• Add the cream, stir. Microwave 4 minutes at MEDIUM-HIGH, stirring after 2 minutes.

• Salt and pepper to taste. Pour over the chicken and onions.

Glaze for Roasted Birds

- A glaze brushed on chicken, large or small, before cooking, gives it a shiny coating and a delicious flavor.
- It is good to brush the under part of the chicken when it is turned over as some recipes call for.
- If you have never used a glaze, try one on chicken legs or wings. Since these parts are less expensive than chicken breasts, you will learn how to do it and see the result.
- Duck, quail, turkey, etc., can be glazed as well as chicken.
- Whenever I use one of the following glazes, I like to brush it all over the bird when it is cooked, just before serving.
- I usually add **1 tablespoon (15 mL) of brandy, scotch, rye or rum** to the last touch of glaze.

Oriental Glaze

Preparation:	....................2 m
Cooking:	.......................2 m
Standing:	......................**none**

A personal note: This can be used with all types of birds except turkey.

Ingredients:

2 tsp (10 mL) cornstarch
1/4 cup (60 mL) soy sauce
1 tbsp (15 mL) sesame oil
2/3 cup (160 mL) water

Method:

- Combine the cornstarch and soy sauce in a microwave-safe bowl. Stir in the sesame oil and the water. Microwave at HIGH 2 minutes, stirring twice.
- Use this sauce before, during and after roasting the bird of your choice.

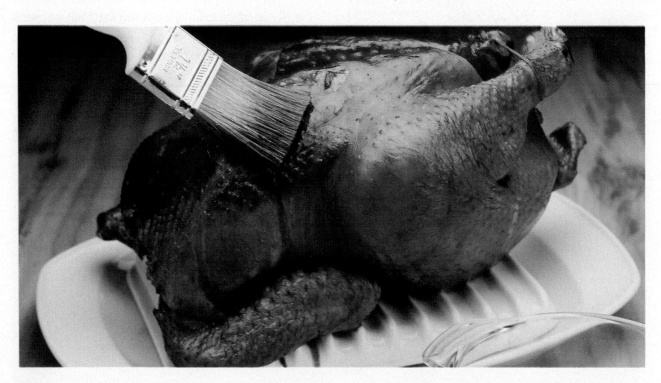

Mayonnaise chaud-froid

Advance preparation : . . . . 35 m
Cooking : . . . . from 1 to 2 m
Standing : . . . . none

A personal note : A " chaud-froid " is used to coat cold slices of cooked chicken or any other type of bird. It's an elegant way to serve cold poultry at any time.

Ingredients :

1 tbsp (15 m) unflavored gelatin

2 tbsp (30 mL) cold water or white wine

2 cups (500 mL) mayonnaise of your choice

Method :

• Measure the cold water or white wine into a microwave-safe cup. Add the gelatin, let stand 1 minute.

• Microwave at MEDIUM 1 to 2 minutes or until mixture is like clear water. Pour slowly into the cold mayonnaise, stirring vigorously with a whisk.

• Place slices of cooked chicken on a piece of waxed paper and coat with the mayonnaise, spreading it with a spatula. Lift meat and place in dish. Refrigerate to set about 30 minutes.

• Surround chicken with watercress or crisp lettuce leaves or parsley.

• In the summer, when I have fresh tarragon leaves or dill, I add about 1 tablespoon (15 mL) of either herb when adding the gelatin.

591

Giblet Gravy

Preparation : . . . .**5 m**
Cooking : . . . .**from 6 to 8 m**
Standing : . . . .**none**

Ingredients :

1/2 cup (125 mL) fat from roasted fowl drippings
1/3 cup (80 mL) all-purpose or instant flour
1 garlic clove, crushed or chopped fine
1 ½ cups (375 mL) strained giblet broth
1/4 cup (60 mL) sherry or Madeira or red wine

Method :

- When roasted, set bird on a warm plate.
- Pour drippings into a bowl. Let the fat rise to the top, this should take 3 to 4 minutes.
- Skim off 1/2 cup (125 mL) of the fat on top, add the flour, stir until well mixed.
- Add the garlic and giblet broth

- Remove all fat left in drippings.
- Add remaining juice to flour mixture. Microwave at HIGH 6 to 8 minutes, stirring twice. It will give a light, creamy gravy. Adjust salt.

Variations — Add any of the following :

- **1 cup (250 mL) thinly sliced mushrooms** to the gravy, before the last 4 minutes of cooking **or**
- **1 cup (250 mL) thinly sliced onions.** Cook same as above ; **or**
- **1 cup (250 mL) canned, unsweetened chestnuts chopped coarsely** **or**
- **1/2 cup (125 mL) cranberry sauce or diced orange.**

Chicken Wings
with Bacon

Preparation : . . . . .8 m
Cooking : . . . . .20 m
Standing : .none

A personal note : Equally good hot or cold and always popular, these chicken wings are perfect to serve cold on a picnic or to a crowd watching baseball or hockey. Serve them with hot buttered French bread.

Ingredients :

6 bacon slices

6 chicken wings

2 tbsp (30 mL) flour

1/2 tsp (2 mL) paprika

1/2 tsp (2 mL) savory or thyme

Salt and pepper to taste

1 tbsp (15 mL) flour

1/2 cup (125 mL) apple juice, water, cream or white wine

Method :

• Dice bacon. Place in an 8 × 8-inch (20 × 20 cm) microwave-safe dish. Microwave 2 minutes at HIGH.

• Combine 2 tablespoons (30 mL) flour with seasonings. Roll wings in the mixture.

• Place wings with rounded part down in the hot bacon. Microwave 10 minutes at HIGH.

• Turn the wings and stir the bacon that sticks to the dish. Continue cooking at MEDIUM 5 minutes or until chicken is tender. Remove wings.

• Add the 1 tablespoon (15 mL) flour to fat in the dish and stir.

• Add water, apple juice or the liquid of your choice and stir well. Microwave 3 minutes at MEDIUM-HIGH. Pour over the chicken wings.

Bacon Noir or (white) Canadian

Chilled Morgon or Californian Chenin Blanc

Orange Marmalade Chicken Wings

Preparation:	.... **10 m**
Cooking:	.... **18 m**
Standing:	.... **5 m**

A personal note: These are beautifully glazed chicken wings. I sometimes replace the marmalade with homemade apple jelly flavored with orange rind. Serve hot with small parsleyed noodles or cold with a green salad.

Ingredients:

8 to 10 chicken wings

2 tbsp (30 mL) butter

1/2 tsp (2 mL) tarragon or basil

1 tsp (5 mL) salt

1/4 tsp (1 mL) pepper

1/4 tsp (1 mL) paprika

1/2 cup (125 mL) orange marmalade

Grated rind of 1 orange

Method:

• Wash wings and dry with paper towelling. Tuck the tips under the larger joints to form a triangle.

• Place the butter in an 8 × 12-inch (20 × 30 cm) microwave-safe dish and melt 2 minutes at HIGH.

• Mix together the tarragon or basil, salt, pepper and paprika. Season the wings with this mixture. Place in the hot butter, with the small points of wings on top. Microwave 10 minutes at HIGH, turn wings over and microwave another 6 minutes at HIGH.

• Spread wings with the orange marmalade or apple jelly mixed with orange rind. Microwave another 2 minutes at HIGH. Let stand 5 minutes.

• Baste 3 times while standing with the juices accumulated in the bottom of the dish.

• Equally good served hot or cold.

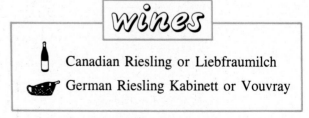

wines

Canadian Riesling or Liebfraumilch

German Riesling Kabinett or Vouvray

Chicken Wings Dijon

Preparation:	. . . .	10 m
Cooking:	. . . .	10 m
Standing:	. . . .	10 m

A personal note: The combination of honey, curry and mustard makes these chicken wings golden brown and gives them an intriguing flavor. Serve with boiled long grain rice mixed with lots of chopped green onions.

Ingredients:

2 to 3 lb (1 to 1.5 kg) chicken wings

1 tbsp (30 mL) Dijon mustard

Juice of 1 lemon or 2 limes

1/2 tsp (2 mL) curry powder

1/4 tsp (1 mL) salt

3 tbsp (50 mL) honey

Method:

• Place in a microwave-safe dish large enough to hold the chicken wings in one layer the mustard, lemon or lime juice, curry powder, salt and honey.

• Microwave at HIGH 2 minutes.

• Fold each chicken wing in a triangle and roll in the hot mixture.

• Place wings one next to the other.

• Cover and microwave 10 minutes at MEDIUM-HIGH.

• Let stand covered 10 minutes before serving.

• There will be enough sauce to pour some on each serving of wings.

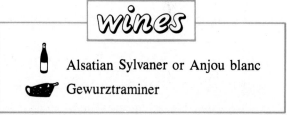

Alsatian Sylvaner or Anjou blanc

Gewurztraminer

Baked Chicken La Jolla

• I ate this chicken in California and enjoyed it so much I adapted it to microwave cooking.

Preparation: . . . . .12 m
Cooking: . . . . .from 22 to 25 m
Standing: . . . . .from 5 to 8 m

Ingredients:

1   2½-to-3-lb (1-1.5 kg) chicken pieces

1 tsp (5 mL) basil

1/2 tsp (2 mL) freshly ground pepper

Rind of half a lemon

6 green onions, chopped fine

Juice of half a lemon and half an orange

1/2 tsp (2 mL) crushed or powdered coriander

1/2 tsp (2 mL) paprika

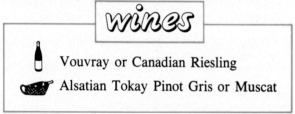

Vouvray or Canadian Riesling

Alsatian Tokay Pinot Gris or Muscat

Method:

• Pat chicken pieces with a paper towel, as dry as possible.

• Place on a piece of waxed paper the basil, pepper and lemon rind. Rub mixture into the chicken parts.

• Arrange chicken in a microwave-safe 10-inch (25 cm) round dish, placing small parts like drumsticks toward the middle of the dish. Sprinkle chopped green onions on top.

• Combine the lemon and orange juice, the coriander seeds and the paprika. Pour over the chicken. Cover, microwave 10 minutes at HIGH.

• Baste chicken with juices in the bottom of the dish. Microwave 12 to 15 minutes at MEDIUM-HIGH. Let stand 5 to 8 minutes.

• Baste with juices after 4 minutes.

• Serve with parsleyed rice or green noodles.

Chicken Wings Teriyaki

Preparation : . . . . .8 m
Cooking : the meal : . . . . .from 12 to 15 m
the sauce : . . . . .from 5 to 6 m
Standing : . . . .**none**

• In Japanese cuisine, Teriyaki implies a mildly sweet soy-base sauce to be added to lightly grilled meat. Teriyaki sauce is sold in specialty and food import shops.

• This sauce, which I have adapted to microwave cooking, is delicious and so easy to make. The recipe was given to me by a young Japanese girl in Hawaii.

Teriyaki sauce :

Ingredients :

7 tbsp (105 mL) Sake

7 tbsp (105 mL) mirin (mild wine)

7 tbsp (105 mL) soy sauce

1 tbsp (15 mL) sugar

Method :

• Place all the ingredients in a large microwave-safe measuring cup.

• Microwave 5 to 6 minutes at HIGH. Stir well.

• Pour into a glass bottle.

• Cool and refrigerate. Use as needed.

Liebfraumilch or Californian Chablis

Rhine Riesling Spaetlese

Chicken wings :

Ingredients :

10 to 12 chicken wings

Paprika

2 tbsp (30 mL) peanut oil

1 medium onion, thinly sliced

1 celery stalk, diced fine

1/4 cup (60 mL) chili sauce

1/3 cup (80 mL) Teriyaki sauce

Method :

• Fold the wings. Sprinkle generously with paprika.

• Heat the peanut oil 2 minutes at HIGH in a microwave-safe baking dish.

• Without removing dish from oven, add the chicken wings, placing them one next to the other. Stir to coat them with the oil.

• Microwave 6 to 7 minutes at HIGH. Stir the wings.

• Add the remaining ingredients. Stir thoroughly. Microwave 6 to 8 minutes at HIGH. Stir. Serve with rice.

Boiled Chicken with Dumplings

Preparation :	. . . .	.20 m
Cooking :	. . . .	.35 m
Standing :	. . . .	.none

A personal note : The chicken can be cooked a few hours ahead of time. It reheats in 15 minutes at MEDIUM. You then remove chicken parts with a perforated spoon, cook the dumplings in the hot liquid, and serve.

Ingredients :

The chicken :

1   3-lb (1.5 kg) chicken, cut up *or*
   3 lb (1.5 kg) chicken legs or wings
2 cups (500 mL) chicken broth
1 large onion, chopped
2 celery stalks with leaves, diced
4 medium carrots, sliced
2 tsp (10 mL) salt
1/2 tsp (2 mL) pepper
1/2 tsp (2 mL) tarragon or savory
1/4 tsp (1 mL) thyme
1 garlic clove, chopped fine
1/2 cup (125 mL) cold water

Dumplings :

1½ cups (375 mL) flour
1 tsp (5 mL) dried parsley (optional)
1/4 tsp (1 mL) savory
2 tsp (10 mL) baking powder
1/2 tsp (2 mL) salt
2/3 cup (160 mL) milk
1 egg
2 tbsp (30 mL) vegetable oil

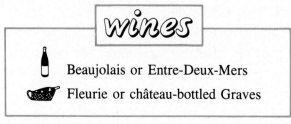

Beaujolais or Entre-Deux-Mers
Fleurie or château-bottled Graves

Method :

The chicken :

• Place all the ingredients in a large 16-cup (4 L) microwave-safe bowl, cover and microwave at MEDIUM-HIGH 30 minutes or until the chicken is tender. Stir well.

• Remove chicken from broth with a perforated spoon. Cover to keep warm.

Dumplings :

• Mix together the flour, parsley, savory, baking powder and salt.

• In another bowl, beat the remaining ingredients together. When ready to cook, add to the flour mixture and beat just enough to blend.

• Drop by spoonfuls into the broth.

• Cover and microwave 5 minutes at HIGH or until the dumplings are puffed and cooked.

• Place the cooked dumplings around the chicken. Pour a tablespoon or two (15-30 mL) of the juice over the chicken. Serve.

Napa Creamed Chicken

Preparation: .... 14 m
Cooking: the meal: .... from 16 to 18 m
        the sauce: .... 8 m
Standing: .... none

A personal note: This delicious cooked chicken with cream sauce can be served with rice, with a basket of hot biscuits or cooked as a pie.

Ingredients:

2 tbsp (30 mL) butter

1/4 cup (60 mL) water or chicken consommé

1 medium onion, chopped

2 carrots, thinly sliced

2 medium potatoes, cut in matchsticks

2 celery stalks, finely diced

2 to 3 cups (500 - 750 mL) cooked chicken, diced

1/2 tsp (2 mL) dried thyme

1/2 cup (125 mL) fresh parsley, minced, *or*
   3 tbsp (50 mL) parsley, dried

1/4 tsp (1 mL) nutmeg

Salt and pepper to taste

The sauce:

3 tbsp (50 mL) butter

4 tbsp (60 mL) flour

2½ to 3 cups (625 - 750 mL) chicken consommé

Method:

• Place in a bowl the 2 tablespoons (30 mL) butter and the 1/4 cup (60 mL) water or chicken consommé. Add the onion, carrots, potatoes and celery. Stir well. Cover and microwave 10 minutes at MEDIUM-HIGH, stir well.

• Add the diced cooked chicken, stir well. Add the thyme, parsley and grated nutmeg, stir well. Salt and pepper to taste.

To make the sauce:

• Place the 3 tablespoons (50 mL) butter in a microwave-save dish and melt 2 minutes at HIGH.

• Add the flour, stir well. Add the chicken consommé, stir. Microwave 4 minutes at HIGH, stir well. Microwave another 2 minutes at HIGH or until creamy. Stir. Adjust seasoning and pour over the chicken. Mix.

• Serve, or cover if prepared ahead of time. Keep on kitchen counter and warm up 6 to 8 minutes at MEDIUM-HIGH, covered, when ready to serve.

wines

Californian or Australian Chardonnay

Fine Napa Valley Chardonnay

Chicken À la King

• An old recipe of mine, this is still the best for using leftover chicken or turkey. Through the years, I have tried many ways of making Chicken à la King. This is my favorite recipe and I find it even better when prepared in the microwave oven.

Ingredients:

2 tbsp (30 mL) butter

1/2 cup (125 mL) green pepper, diced

1 cup (250 mL) mushrooms, sliced

3 tbsp (50 mL) flour

2 cups (500 mL) light cream or milk

1/4 tsp (1 mL) salt

1/2 tsp (2 mL) tarragon *or*
  1/4 tsp (1 mL) thyme

3 cups (750 mL) cooked chicken, diced*

3 egg yolks

1/4 tsp (1 mL) paprika

3 tbsp (50 mL) soft butter

1 small onion, chopped fine

1 tbsp (15 mL) lemon juice

2 tbsp (30 mL) sherry

* You can use 2 or 3 cups (500 or 750 mL) of cooked chicken, or you can simmer a small 3-pound (1.5 kg) chicken 40 minutes at MEDIUM, cut it and prepare it à la King.

Method:

• Place the first 2 tablespoons (30 mL) of butter in a 4-cup (1 L) microwave-safe bowl and melt 1 minute at HIGH.

• Add the green pepper and the mushrooms, stir well. Microwave 3 minutes at HIGH.

• Push the vegetables to one side, pressing out the butter. Stir the flour into the butter until well blended, then add the cream or milk.

• Stir with the vegetables until well mixed. Microwave 3 minutes at HIGH, stir well. Microwave another 3 to 6 minutes or until creamy. Salt to taste. Add the chicken, mix well. Microwave 1 minute at HIGH, stir again.

• Mix together the egg yolks, paprika, soft butter, onion, lemon juice and sherry.

• Add to chicken mixture. Stir until well mixed. Microwave at MEDIUM 6 to 7 minutes, stirring after 3 minutes. It should be creamy and cooked.

• Serve in puff pastry shell, make into a pie or serve in a nest of cooked rice.

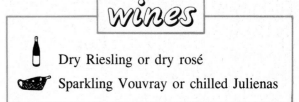

wines

Dry Riesling or dry rosé

Sparkling Vouvray or chilled Julienas

Chicken Stock

Advance preparation : . . . . .**from 3 to 6 h**

Cooking : . . . .**30 m**

Standing : . . . .**none**

A personal note : When liquid is needed to steam or boil chicken, the canned type can be used, but homemade chicken stock will double the quality and flavor of a sauce or boiled chicken. It freezes well. I like to freeze mine in 2-cup (500 mL) containers for convenience's sake, then uncover it and defrost at HIGH for 5 to 7 minutes, whenever I need it. To make about 12 cups (3 L), you will need 3 pounds (1.5 kg) of chicken parts such as wings, back, neck and any piece of skin available. You can buy these from your market, if you ask the butcher to set them aside for you.

I have a box in my freezer where I put such pieces as I cook chicken or turkey. I make 3-pound (1.5 kg) bags and set them together in the box. When needed, I place a 3-lb (1.5 kg) frozen package in a baking dish, add the other ingredients and cook it 20 minutes longer.

Ingredients :

3 lb (1.5 kg) bony chicken parts such as back, neck, end of wings, fat*

1 veal bone, when available

12 cups (3 L) hot water

1 large yellow onion, unpeeled

4 whole cloves

2 celery stalks with leaves, cut in half

2 carrots, peeled, cut in four

12 crushed peppercorns

A handful of fresh parsley, with stems

1 bay leaf

1 tbsp (15 mL) thyme

1/2 tsp (2 mL) savory

1 tsp (5 mL) tarragon

Method :

• Place the ingredients in a 16-cup (4 L) microwave-save bowl. Cover and microwave 30 minutes at HIGH.

• Let cool in the bowl, which may take from 3 to 6 hours.

• Strain through a fine sieve. Salt to taste, preferably with coarse salt.

• Keep refrigerated or freeze.

• Yield : 12 cups (3 L).

You may replace the chicken parts with a cooked poultry carcass, the gravy and vegetables added to the broth. Cooking time remains the same. Cool in the cooking dish. Strain and keep in the refrigerator or freezer.

Giblet Broth

Preparation : .8 m
Cooking : .30 m
Standing : .1 h

A personal note : To make a tasty turkey or roasted chicken gravy, use cooked giblet broth as part of the liquid. The slight effort required to make it means the difference between a dull and a tasty gravy.

Ingredients :

Giblets and neck from turkey

1/2 a lemon

1 tsp (5 mL) salt *and* 8 peppercorns

2 whole cloves *and* 1 bay leaf

1/2 tsp (2 mL) thyme

1 medium onion, cut in four

1/2 cup (125 mL) celery with leaves, chopped

1 small carrot, sliced

3 cups (750 mL) boiling water

Method :

• Remove heart, liver, gizzard and neck from turkey or chicken. Rinse in cold water and rub all over with half a lemon.

• Place in an 8-cup (2 L) microwave-safe saucepan all the remaining ingredients. Microwave at HIGH 10 minutes.

• Remove the liver and set aside. Cover the dish and microwave at HIGH 20 minutes.

• Let stand one hour, then strain through a fine sieve.

• Chop the giblets which are tender. Add the liver. Add to the broth, if you wish.

• This can be cooked, strained, chopped, etc., then refrigerated covered, overnight.

603

Duck

Chinese Duck

Convection cooking

Advance preparation : . . . .**12 h**
Cooking : the meal : . . . .**from 35 to 60 m**
       the sauce : . . . .**1 m**
Standing : . . . .**none**

> **A personal note :** This recipe is an adaptation of the classic Chinese lacquered duck. This one is cut up ; the Chinese way, it is cooked whole. The 12 hours of marinating is important.

Ingredients :

1   **4-to-4½-lb (2-2.2 kg) domestic duck**

Marinating mixture

4 tbsp (60 mL) sugar

1 tbsp (15 mL) salt

4 tbsp (60 mL) honey

3 tbsp (50 mL) soy sauce

1/3 cup (80 mL) consommé

4 tbsp (60 mL) cold water

Method :

• Quarter the duck.

• Mix together in a large bowl the sugar, salt, honey, soy sauce and the consommé.

• Wipe the pieces of duck with lemon juice. Add to the marinating mixture. Mix well to coat the duck with the sauce. Cover and marinate 12 hours in the refrigerator.

• To roast the duck, remove from the marinade and put the pieces in a baking dish.

• Add the cold water. Do not cover.

• Preheat the convection oven 15 minutes at 350°F (180°C).

• Place a rack in the oven ceramic tray and put the baking dish on it.

• Cook 35 minutes to 1 hour, turning the pieces of duck halfway through the cooking.

To make gravy :

• Add a few spoonfuls of **port wine and cream** to the drippings in the baking dish.

• Remove the fat on top and heat the gravy 1 minute at HIGH in the microwave. Serve.

 Californian Chenin Blanc or
Canadian Riesling
Saumur or Juancon

Duck À l'orange

Preparation: . . . .**40 m**
Cooking: the meal: . . . .**from 40 to 45 m**
       the sauce: . . . .**4 m**
Standing: . . . .**15 m**

A personal note: This recipe works for wild as well as domestic duck. The only difference is that the wild duck must be tested often for doneness, because cooking time varies according to age and type of duck.

Ingredients:

1 4-to-5-lb (2-2.5 kg) duck
Juice of 1 lemon
1 tsp (5 mL) salt
2 medium apples, unpeeled, cut in eighths
1 tbsp (15 mL) brown sugar
Rind of 1 orange
1 garlic clove
8 to 10 peppercorns
1 slice of bread

Method:

• Clean the duck inside and outside with the lemon juice. Salt inside the cavity.

• Cut apples into eighths and mix together with the brown sugar, orange rind, garlic and peppercorns. Stuff the cavity with the mixture and close it with the slice of bread.

• Tie the legs with a wet string.
• Wrap the tips of the wings and legs with strips of foil.

• Place the duck, breast-side down, over an inverted saucer or a microwave rack placed in the baking dish. Microwave 20 minutes at HIGH. Turn the duck on its back.

• Cover with waxed paper and roast 20 minutes at MEDIUM-HIGH. Test doneness. It is sometimes necessary to microwave 5 minutes more.

• Put the duck on a serving dish, cover with a bowl or waxed paper and let stand 15 minutes.

• In the meantime, prepare the orange sauce.

The sauce:

Ingredients:

2 tbsp (30 mL) brown sugar
1 tbsp (15 mL) cornstarch
Rind of 1 orange
2/3 cup (160 mL) orange juice
3 tbsp (50 mL) gravy, strained
3 tbsp (50 mL) brandy

Method:

• Mix together in a large microwave-safe measuring cup or a bowl the brown sugar and the cornstarch.

• Add to it the orange rind and juice. Strain the drippings.

• Remove the fat on top and add the brown juice to the orange juice mixture. Mix thoroughly and microwave 2 minutes at HIGH. Stir and microwave 2 minutes at HIGH.

• Add the brandy and serve.

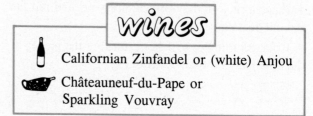

Californian Zinfandel or (white) Anjou
Châteauneuf-du-Pape or Sparkling Vouvray

Cantonese Roasted Duck

A personal note: A browning dish is a must to succeed with this Chinese way to roast duck. Serve with rice or small dumplings.

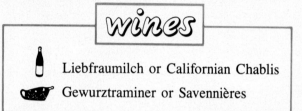

Liebfraumilch or Californian Chablis
Gewurztraminer or Savennières

Ingredients:

1 3-to-4-lb (1.5-2 kg) domestic duck
2 garlic cloves, chopped fine
1/2 cup (125 mL) green onions, chopped
2 tbsp (30 mL) each dry sherry and soy sauce
1 tsp (5 mL) ground cardamom
2 tbsp (30 mL) fresh ginger, thinly sliced
1 tsp (5 mL) brown sugar
1 tsp (5 mL) vegetable oil

Basting sauce:

1 tbsp (15 mL) each honey and water
1 tsp (5 mL) rice vinegar*

Japanese rice vinegar is readily available in Oriental food shops. It is mild, slightly sweet and pungent. It may be replaced with cider vinegar.

Method:

• Place in a glass measuring cup the basting sauce ingredients. Microwave 1 minute at HIGH. Stir well.

• Wash duck under cold running water, wipe inside and out with paper towels. Place on a dry paper towel. Let stand 2 hours, without covering, for the skin to dry.

• Combine in a small bowl the garlic, onions, sherry, soy sauce, cardamom, ginger and brown sugar.

Advance preparation: ....2 h
Cooking: the meal: ....25 m
          the sauce: ....2 m
Standing: ....10 m

• Preheat browning dish 7 minutes at HIGH. Do not remove dish from oven. Add the vegetable oil and microwave 40 seconds at HIGH.

• Add the garlic-onion mixture to the hot oil and stir for at least 30 to 40 seconds and pour sauce into the duck. Sew opening so most of the sauce will remain in the duck.

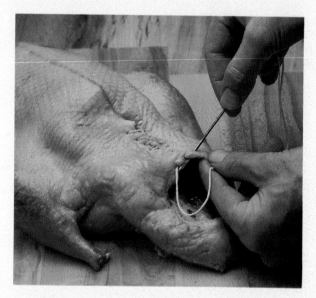

• Wipe the browning dish and preheat again for 7 minutes. Place the duck in the browning dish, breast-side down. Brush all over with basting sauce. Microwave 10 minutes at HIGH. Turn.

• Remove drippings from dish and place duck breast-side up on a microwave rack or an inverted plate placed in the dish. Baste again and repeat cooking at MEDIUM for 15 minutes more.

• Let duck stand covered for 10 minutes before serving.

To make gravy:

• Add **1 tablespoon (15 mL) cornstarch** to the gravy in the dish, stir well.

• Add **2 tablespoons (30 mL) water**. Mix well. Microwave 2 minutes at HIGH. Stir well. Serve with duck.

608

Plum Sauce Duck

Convection cooking

Preparation: . . . . 35 m
Cooking: the meal: . . . . . from 1 h to 1 h 15 m
       the sauce: . . . . .2 m
Standing: . . . . 15 m

 wines

 Liebfraumilch

German Riesling Spaetlese or (red) Recioto della Valpolicella

A personal note: This is the easiest of all ways to cook wild or domestic duck. Serve with boiled rice stirred with diced cooked beets, green onions and finely chopped parsley. The pinkish color of the rice is attractive and the mixture of flavors is interesting.

Ingredients:

1   3-to-4-lb (1.5-2 kg) duck

1 medium-sized onion, cut in four

1 unpeeled orange, cut in four

1/2 cup (125 mL) Oriental plum sauce

1 garlic clove, chopped fine

Salt and pepper to taste

Grated rind and juice of 1 orange

1 tsp (5 mL) each sugar and cornstarch

3 tbsp (50 mL) red wine or port

Method:

• Rinse duck under cold running water. Dry inside and out with paper towel. Place the onion and orange wedges in duck cavity. Tie legs over the cavity with a string.

• Preheat convection part of your microwave oven to 375°F (190°C).

• Place low rack in the oven. Set a Pyrex or ceramic plate under rack to catch the dripping.

• Blend together the plum sauce and all the remaining ingredients. Roll duck in the mixture, pouring a few spoonfuls of it into the cavity.

• Place duck on rack in preheated oven. Roast 1 hour to 1 hour 15 minutes, basting twice with some of the drippings in the plate.

• Let stand 15 minutes before serving.

To make sauce:

• Mix **1 teaspoon (5 mL) cornstarch** with **3 tablespoons (50 mL) of red wine or port wine**. Add to gravy in the plate. Stir well. Microwave 2 minutes at HIGH. Stir until creamy. Serve.

Duck Hymettus

A personal note: A walnut stuffing gives this duck an interesting flavor. I like to serve it with a big bowl of fresh, crisp watercress, which complements the walnut-bread stuffing. Pour the gravy over the stuffing when serving.

Preparation : . . . .**20 m**
Cooking : the meal : . . . . **from 35 to 40 m**
            the sauce : . . . . **from 4 to 7 m**
Standing : . . . . **15 m**

Ingredients:

1 domestic duck

The stuffing:

1 tbsp (15 mL) butter

1/2 cup (125 mL) onion, chopped fine

3/4 cup (190 mL) walnuts, chopped

Grated rind of 1 lemon

1 cup (250 mL) fresh bread, diced

3 tbsp (50 mL) parsley, chopped

1 tsp (5 mL) sage

1/2 tsp (2 mL) thyme

1/2 tsp (2 mL) cinnamon or allspice

1/2 tsp (2mL) ground cardamom (if available)

Salt and pepper to taste

1 egg, lightly beaten

2 tbsp (30 mL) butter

4 tbsp (60 mL) honey

Paprika

Juice of 1 lemon *or* 1/4 cup (60 mL) brandy, rum or orange liqueur

The gravy:

1 tbsp (15 mL) flour

3/4 cup (190 mL) chicken consommé

Method:

• To prepare the stuffing, place the butter in a microwave-safe bowl and melt 1 minute at HIGH. Add the onion and microwave 2 minutes at HIGH. Stir well.

• Add the walnuts, mix and microwave 3 minutes at HIGH.

• Add the remaining stuffing ingredients. Adjust seasoning. Mix well and stuff into the duck.

• Sew opening with heavy thread, tie legs with a string. Cream together the butter and honey and rub it on the breast and legs of the duck.

• Place duck on rack set in a 12 × 12-inch (30 × 30 cm) ceramic (Corning) dish or other microwave-safe dish large enough to hold rack and duck. Sprinkle breast of duck with paprika. Microwave at HIGH 15 minutes.

• Add lemon juice, brandy, rum or orange liqueur. Baste with the pan juices and turn the bird.

• Microwave at MEDIUM 15 to 25 minutes, or until breast meat is soft and leg bones can be moved slightly when twisted.

• Place duck on a warm platter and cover with foil. Let stand 15 minutes.

To make gravy:

• Add the flour to the drippings. Stir well.

• Add the chicken consommé. Stir and microwave 3 to 5 minutes at MEDIUM. Stir well.

• Microwave 1 minute or 2 more if necessary. The gravy should be smooth and light. Stir well.

Canadian Riesling or Californian French Colombard

Côteaux du Layon

Ballottine of Duck

Preparation: . . . . .45 m
Cooking: the meal: . . . . .from 24 to 28 m
        the sauce: . . . . .from 7 to 8 m
Standing: . . . . .none

A personal note: Without experience, it is somewhat difficult to bone a duck. Ask your butcher, or cut through the middle of the back, fold down with your hands, and start by removing the inside bones, which are very flexible, cutting through here and there. This can be done quickly.

Method:

To make the stuffing:

- Combine butter and onion in a glass bowl. Microwave 1 minute at HIGH. Combine with ground meat, breadcrumbs, parsley, sage and sherry. Mix in the beaten egg. Add salt and pepper to taste.

- Stuff the duck, alternating ham, walnuts and stuffing mixture; this makes an interesting design when the duck is served. Shape the ballottine in a cylinder, as long and as narrow as possible.

- Sew up with a trussing needle and heavy white thread, threading and tying at regular intervals to keep the ballottine in shape.

- Place in a long, narrow glass or earthenware dish. Microwave 14 to 18 minutes at MEDIUM-HIGH, then 10 minutes at LOW. Refrigerate when cooled. Slice when cold.

- If you wish to serve it hot, reheat covered with a lid or waxed paper 5 minutes at MEDIUM.

- If you have a temperature probe: Once you have placed the ballottine in the dish, insert the probe and set for 160°F (68°C). The oven does the work. When it stops, the duck is cooked. (Consult your oven manual.)

To make the sauce:

- Combine the broth, carrot and onion in a microwave-safe bowl and microwave 5 minutes at MEDIUM-HIGH, stirring once. Strain, pressing with a rubber spatula to extract all the juices.

- Mix the cornstarch and Madeira and stir until smooth. Add to the sauce, stir. Add the mushrooms and microwave 2 minutes at HIGH, stir. If sufficiently creamy, it is ready; if not, microwave another minute at HIGH.

- The sauce can be poured over the sliced duck before it is refrigerated covered, which will form a glaze. To serve hot, pour the hot sauce over the sliced or unsliced ballottine.

Ingredients:

1 4-to-5-lb (2-2.5 kg) duck, deboned

Stuffing:

2 tbsp (30 mL) butter

1 onion, peeled and chopped fine

3/4 lb (375 g) ground pork

3/4 cup (190 mL) white breadcrumbs

1 tsp (5 mL) sage

6 to 8 sprigs parsley, minced

3 tbsp (50 mL) dry sherry

1 egg, beaten

2 thin slices cooked ham, julienned

2 tbsp (30 mL) walnuts, coarsely chopped

Salt and freshly ground pepper to taste

Sauce:

1/2 cup (125 mL) chicken broth, homemade or
  canned condensed

1/2 carrot, thinly sliced

1/2 small onion, peeled and sliced

1 tsp (5 mL) cornstarch

1/4 cup (60 mL) Madeira

1/3 lb (160 g) mushrooms, sliced

Salt and freshly ground pepper to taste

Red Burgundy or (white) Canadian Chardonnay

Saint-Joseph or (white) Meursault

Wild Rice Stuffing

Preparation: . . . . .15 m
Cooking: . . . . .36 m
Standing: .10 m

A personal note: Use with duck or quail. Double for roasted chicken.

Ingredients:

The bird liver *or*
  1/2 lb (250 g) chicken liver
3 tbsp (50 mL) butter
6 green onions, chopped
4 tbsp (60 mL) chicken consommé
1 cup (250 mL) wild rice
1/4 tsp (1 mL) curry powder

Method:

• Chop the liver into small pieces with a sharp knife.

• Place the butter in a microwave-safe dish and melt 2 minutes at HIGH; it will brown. Add the liver. Cover and microwave 3 minutes at HIGH.

• Add green onions, stir well. Add the chicken consommé.

• Microwave 3 minutes at HIGH. Salt and pepper to taste. Set aside.

• Bring 4 cups (1 L) of water to boil 10 minutes at HIGH.

• Add the wild rice and curry. Stir well.

• Cover and microwave 30 minutes at MEDIUM. Let stand 10 minutes.

• When rice is ready, add the green onion mixture. Mix well. Adjust salt and serve.

Port Wine Sauce for Duck

Preparation: . . . .**8 m**
Cooking: . . . .**from 26 to 27 m**
Standing: . . . .**none**

A personal note: Use this to reheat leftovers or to serve as an extra sauce with your favorite duck recipe.

Ingredients:

1/2 cup (125 mL) port wine

4 green onions, chopped

1/4 tsp (1 mL) thyme

1/2 cup (125 mL) fresh orange juice

1 cup (250 mL) chicken consommé

Salt and pepper to taste

2 tsp (10 mL) cornstarch

Grated rind of 1 orange

1 orange cut into sections

Method:

• Place in a microwave-safe bowl the port wine, green onions, thyme and orange juice. Stir until well mixed.

• Boil at HIGH about 20 minutes or until reduced to half. Stir 2 to 3 times during the cooking period.

• Add 1/2 cup (125 mL) of chicken consommé. Boil 3 minutes at HIGH. Salt and pepper to taste.

• Mix together the cornstarch, the remaining chicken consommé, orange rind and sections.

• Add to wine mixture and stir.

• Microwave 3 to 4 minutes at HIGH, stirring once.

• The sauce should be light and creamy.

617

Basting Sauce

Preparation: .5 m
Cooking: . . . . .none
Standing: .none

A personal note: Simply place cleaned bird, split in half or legs tied, in a ceramic (Corning) dish and cook by microwave or by convection. I sometimes use this sauce over chicken breasts.

Ingredients:

1/2 cup (125 mL) fresh orange juice

1/2 cup (125 mL) chili sauce

1/4 cup (60 mL) each honey *and* Worcestershire sauce

3 garlic cloves, chopped fine

1 small onion, chopped fine

1/4 tsp (1 mL) pepper

Method:

• Mix all the ingredients together. Brush generously inside and outside the bird (chicken, quail, duck, pheasant, turkey.

• Follow instructions given for cooking chosen bird by convection or microwave.

• Each type of bird will have a different flavor, although the same basting sauce is used.

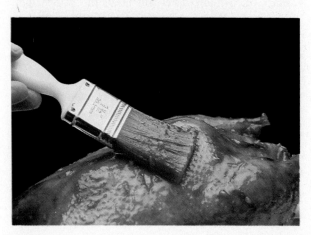

Orange Sauce for Duck

Preparation: .4 m
Cooking: . . . . .5 m
Standing: .none

A personal note: I serve this sauce with roast duck but also use it often to warm up thinly sliced leftover duck.

Ingredients:

1 cup (250 mL) fresh orange juice

1 tbsp (15 mL) cornstarch

3 tbsp (50 mL) sugar

2 tbsp (30 mL) Grand Marnier or other orange liqueur

Grated rind of 1/2 an orange

Method:

• Mix the cornstarch with the orange juice.

• Add the sugar, stir well. Microwave at MEDIUM 3 minutes, stirring after 2 minutes; add the orange rind and the liqueur. Stir well.

• Microwave 1 minute at HIGH. Serve.

Quails

Aberdeen Quails

Preparation : . . . .**15 m**
Cooking : . . . .**from 27 to 29 m**
Standing : . . . .**none**

• Scots are very fond of wild birds, so they are masters at cooking them. We have farm-bred quails, but they nonetheless retain a certain "wild flavor." Roasted in the microwave the Aberdeen way, they are super.

Ingredients :

3 to 4 quails

Stuffing :

1 cup (250 g) wholewheat bread, diced

1 or 2 wild mushrooms, chopped fine

1/2 cup (125 mL) light cream, heated

2 tbsp (30 mL) whisky of your choice

1 tsp (5 mL) tarragon or rosemary

1/2 tsp (2 mL) salt

1/4 tsp (1 mL) pepper

Coating :

1 tsp (5 mL) dark brown sugar

1 tsp (5 mL) Kitchen Bouquet

1/2 tsp (2 mL) paprika

1 tsp (5 mL) dry mustard

1 tbsp (15 mL) soft butter

Method :

• Reserve quail livers for gravy. Wash quail under running water. Drain well. Wipe inside and out with paper towelling.

Prepare stuffing :

• Place all the ingredients in a bowl. Mash and stir together until thick.

• Divide into 3 or 4 portions. Stuff each quail with a portion.

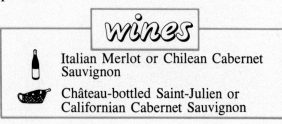

Italian Merlot or Chilean Cabernet Sauvignon

Château-bottled Saint-Julien or Californian Cabernet Sauvignon

• Fold the wings under. Tie the bird with a string.

Coating :

• Mix the coating ingredients together. Rub all over the quail with your hands.

• Preheat a browning dish 5 or 6 minutes at HIGH. Without removing the dish from the oven, place each quail on the dish, breast-side down. Microwave 5 minutes at HIGH. Turn quail over. Microwave 5 minutes at HIGH. Turn birds once again. Microwave 10 minutes at MEDIUM-HIGH. Test for doneness, as sometimes 5 or 6 more minutes are needed, depending on size of the quail. Remove to a hot platter.

To make gravy :

• To the residue in the dish add the **quail livers, chopped fine**, and **3 tbsp (50 mL) white wine or whisky**. Scrape dish.

• Add **1 tsp (5 mL) instant flour**. Stir well. Microwave 2 to 3 minutes at HIGH, stirring once.

• Remove from oven. Stir well. Serve with the quail.

Quails Comice

A personal note: When the season for ripe pears is at its peak in the South of France, they prepare these delicious quails with fresh pears and pear liqueur. Traditionally, they are served with two elegant vegetables and hot, crusty French bread.

Preparation:	18 m
Cooking:	32 m
Standing:	none

Ingredients:

6 medium-sized quails

6 small garlic cloves

4 slices of bacon, diced

2 tbsp (30 mL) soy sauce*

1/2 tsp (2 mL) paprika

2 tbsp (30 mL) soft butter

3 tbsp (50 mL) brandy or white wine

1 cup (250 mL) pears, peeled and thinly sliced

3 tbsp (50 mL) cream

1 tbsp (15 mL) flour

3 tbsp (50 mL) brandy

* When possible use Japanese "Kikkoman" Soy sauce which is milder than the Chinese.

Method:

• Wash quails inside and out with a little brandy. Stuff each with a clove of garlic and a bit of diced bacon.

• Mix together the soy sauce and the paprika. Rub all over the quail, then spread the 2 tablespoons (30 mL) of soft butter evenly over each breast.

• Place in a microwave-save baking dish large enough to hold the quails one next to the other.

• Add the 3 tablespoons (50 mL) of brandy or white wine and the pears in the bottom of the dish.

• Microwave 10 minutes at HIGH.

• Baste with juice in bottom of dish. Microwave at MEDIUM 20 minutes more or until birds are tender.

• Test breast meat with the point of a knife or move, the little leg bones, which should be flexible.

• Place birds on warm platter. Cover to keep warm.

• Mix together the cream, flour and brandy.

• Add to the juice and pears left in the dish. Stir until well blended.

• Microwave 2 minutes at HIGH. Stir.

• When creamy, serve.

• No salt or pepper is used in this classic recipe.

Quails
À la Bruxelloise

Advance preparation :	12 h
Cooking :	48 m
Standing :	none

• Cracked black pepper, fresh or dried thyme and fresh green grapes are combined to give flavor and elegance of taste to dainty quails.

Ingredients :

6 small quails, split in half

1 tsp (5 mL) salt

1 tsp (5 mL) thyme

1/3 cup (80 mL) butter

1 cup (250 mL) white wine or white grape juice

30 to 40 fresh green grapes

Marinade

1/2 cup (125 mL) olive or peanut oil

12 black peppercorns, cracked

6 sprigs of thyme *or* 1 tsp (5 mL) dried thyme

1/4 cup (60 mL) parsley coarsely chopped

Method :

• Mix the marinade ingredients in Pyrex bowl.

• Roll each half quail in mixture. Cover and refrigerate overnight to marinate.

• Remove quails from marinade. Pat dry with paper towels. Season with the salt and thyme.

• Place the butter in a ceramic (Corning) 12-inch (30 cm) square dish and melt 5 minutes at HIGH. The butter will be golden brown. Place each quail half in the hot butter, breast-side down.

• Microwave, uncovered, 15 minutes at HIGH. Turn quails skin-side up. Microwave at MEDIUM-LOW 20 minutes. Turn quails once more. Microwave at HIGH 5 minutes.

• Remove quails from dish. Keep warm.

• To the juice and fat remaining in the pan, add the grape juice or white wine. Microwave 5 minutes at HIGH.

• Add the grapes one by one, left whole or split in half. Stir well in the juice. Microwave 3 minutes at HIGH. Stir well and pour over the quail.

• Serve with tiny cooked pasta of your choice.*

* I use little star-shaped pasta that I buy at an Italian shop.

Chilean Cabernet Sauvignon or red Spanish Rioja

Château-bottled red Bordeaux

Plum Glaze for Duck, Quail and Pheasant

Preparation : .3 m
Cooking : . . . . .2 m
Standing : .none

Ingredients :

1 can purple plums
3 tbsp (50 mL) corn syrup
2 tbsp (30 mL) lemon juice
Rind of 1 orange

Method :

- Wash and drain all the plums.
- Add all the other ingredients in a microwave-safe bowl.
- Microwave at HIGH for 2 minutes. Stir well.
- Use this sauce before, during and after roasting the bird of your choice.

Turkey

Roasted Turkey

Preparation : . . . .**20 m**
Cooking : the meal : . . . .**2 h 30 to 3 h 15 m**
         the sauce : . . . .**3 m**
Standing : . . . .**20 m**

A personal note : The ideal weight for a microwave-roasted turkey is 8 to 13 pounds (4 to 6.5 kg). My favorite weight is a 10-pound (5 kg) turkey with short, stubby legs.

A microwave-roasted turkey **does** brown, despite what many say. The difference with a microwave-roasted turkey is that the skin has a beautiful color but is not as crisp. As far as health is concerned, it is much better, since hard-to-digest fat does not penetrate the white meat.

However, if you do wish to have a crisp, browned skin, place the cooked turkey in a roaster and set it in a preheated 400°F (200°C) oven. It will take about 10 to 15 minutes for the skin to become crisp. Before placing the turkey in the oven, baste 5 to 6 times with the drippings. If you have a combined microwave-convection oven, place the turkey on a rack in the preheated 400°F (200°C) oven. (See your oven manual.) The skin will crisp ; it may take 10 minutes more than a regular oven.

Ingredients :

1 **10-to-13-lb (5 - 6.5 kg) turkey**

1 tsp (5 mL) coarse salt

1/4 tsp (1 mL) pepper

1/2 tsp (2 mL) nutmeg

1 tsp (5 mL) tarragon

1/4 cup (60 mL) brandy

1 large onion, cut in half

1 celery stalk

2 garlic cloves, cut in half

1/4 tsp (1 mL) nutmeg

1/3 cup (80 mL) butter, melted

1 tsp (5 mL) paprika

2 tsp (10 mL) Kitchen Bouquet

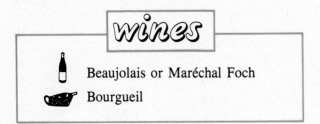

Beaujolais or Maréchal Foch
Bourgueil

Method :

• Wash turkey under cold running water. Dry with paper towelling.

• Mix the salt, pepper, nutmeg, tarragon and brandy. Pour into cavity.

• Stuff the onion, celery and garlic into the cavity.

• Push wings under the turkey. Tie legs together with a string.

• Rub skin all over with the 1/4 teaspoon (1 mL) of nutmeg.

• Mix the melted butter with paprika and Kitchen Bouquet and brush turkey all over with the mixture.

• Place breast-side down on a rack. Set in the oven tray or on a dish if tray has no sides to catch the gravy.

• Roast at MEDIUM-HIGH 9 minutes per pound (500 g). Turn turkey over.

• Cover ends of legs and top of breast with a small strip of foil wrap to prevent turkey legs and top of breast from drying.

• Roast at MEDIUM-HIGH 6 minutes per pound (500 g). Remove foil.

• Let stand 20 minutes, covered with waxed paper, before carving.

• Inner heat of the cooked turkey should be 180° to 185°F (80° to 82°C). Check with a meat thermometer.

To make gravy :

• Pour the juices accumulated in the dish into a microwave-safe saucepan or bowl.

• Add **2 tablespoons (30 mL) instant flour or pastry flour,** stir well with a whisk. Microwave at HIGH 2 minutes.

• Stir again with the whisk and microwave at HIGH another minute, stirring once.

• Add **1/4 cup (60 mL) brandy.** Stir well.

• Microwave another minute or until hot.

12 49
M.HIGH

10	1	10	1
Defrost	Power	Stand Timer	Auto Start

Auto Weight Defrost

Category	1.0 lb	0.1 lb

1 : Beef Pork Lamb Ground Meats
2 : Chicken Turkey Cornish Hens
3 : Shrimp Sea Scallops Whole Fish

Auto Sensor Control

Cook	Cook Warm	Froz Cook	Froz Cook Warm

Cook (+Warm)	Froz-Cook(+Warm)
A1 : Reheat Pasta	: Froz.Con.Foods(1-11oz)
A2 : Beef-Well Pork	: Froz.Con.Foods(12-22oz)
A3 : Beef-Med	: Pot Roast
A4 : Beef-Rare	: Chicken Pieces
A5 : Stews	: Precooked Stews
A6 : Potatoes Carrots	: Hamburgers
A7 : Vegetables-Soft	: Vegetables
A8 : Fish Vegs-Firm	: Fish Filets Scallops

Doneness Control	More	Less

	Clock	Start

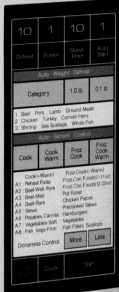

Panasonic

us

Roasted Turkey

Convection cooking

Preparation : . . . .**25 m**
Cooking : the meal : . . . **15 m per pound (500 g)**
            the sauce : . . . .**4 m**
Standing : . . . .**none**

A personal note : If your microwave also has the convection method, this recipe will result in a crisp, browned turkey.

A decided advantage is that it can be roasted an hour before being served. Cover hot turkey with a towel topped with foil wrap.

To reheat when ready to serve, uncover, baste all over with drippings and reheat at MEDIUM-LOW 15 minutes.

 Young red Bordeaux

Alsatian Pinot Noir or Tavel rosé

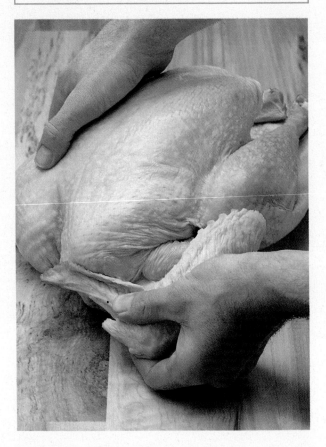

Ingredients :

1   **10-to-12-lb (5-6 kg) turkey**

1 tbsp (15 mL) butter

1 tbsp (15 mL) vegetable oil

1 tsp (5 mL) Dijon or dry mustard

**A large handful of fresh parsley or
    celery leaves**

Grated rind of one lemon

1 tsp (5 mL) savory

2 tsp (10 mL) coarse salt

1 large onion, cut in four

Method :

• Wash turkey under cold running water. Dry with paper towelling.

• Mix together the butter, vegetable oil and mustard. Set aside.

• Place the remaining ingredients in the cavity. Tie legs together with a string. Fold wings under the turkey.

• Butter the whole turkey with the butter and oil mixture.

• Preheat oven at 350°F (180°C). Set prepared turkey on low rack. Place a pie plate under the rack to catch the drippings. Microwave 15 minutes per pound (500 g) at 350°F (180°C).

To make gravy :

• Mix **2 tablespoons (30 mL) flour** with **1/4 cup (60 mL) chicken consommé** and add to the juices accumulated in the dish placed under the turkey. Mix well. Microwave at HIGH 2 minutes. Stir.

• Add another **1/4 cup (60 mL) chicken consommé** and **1/4 cup (60 mL) port wine or Madeira.**

• Microwave 2 minutes at HIGH.

Roasted Turkey

Convection and microwave cooking

A personal note: For cooks whose microwave ovens also feature convection cooking, here is a third successful method of cooking a turkey in the microwave. This recipe alternates microwave and convection cooking.

Preparation: . . . . **18 m**
Cooking: . . . . . . **15 m per pound (500 g)**
Standing: . . . . **15 m**

wines

Chinon or Canadian Cabernet
Château-bottled Saint-Julien

Ingredients:

1 8-to-14-lb (4 - 7 kg) turkey
1 large garlic clove
Half a lemon
Fat taken from the turkey
2 tbsp (30 mL) flour
1 tbsp (15 mL) dry mustard
1 tsp (5 mL) paprika
1 tsp (5 mL) coarse salt

Method:

• Wash the turkey and dry it thoroughly. Rub the skin with the garlic clove and the lemon half.

• Cut the fat into small pieces. Spread out in the bottom of a glass or ceramic dish.

• Microwave at HIGH 2 to 3 minutes, stirring once during the cooking. Remove the browned pieces.

• Add the flour, mustard and paprika to the fat.

• Spread this mixture over the turkey breast and legs. Put the coarse salt in the cavity. Truss the bird.

• Place a rack in the oven ceramic tray.

• Set the turkey on the rack.

• Place a microwave-safe pie plate under the rack to catch the drippings. Roast at 350°F (180°C) 15 minutes per pound (500 g). The turkey will cook to perfection.

• Let stand 15 minutes before serving.

To make gravy:

• Remove the turkey from the oven. Place it on a serving dish and cover.

• Remove the rack and scrape the brown particles into the pie plate, stirring them into the accumulated fat.

• Mix thoroughly. Add **2 tablespoons (30 mL) of flour**, mix into the juices and add **3/4 cup (190 mL) chicken broth or half broth and half wine of your choice or Madeira.**

• Mix thoroughly and microwave 2 minutes at HIGH.

• Stir well. Pour into a sauceboat.

• If the turkey has cooled, warm up at MEDIUM as necessary.

631

A turkey in a cooking bag

Preparation: . . . . .16 m
Cooking: the meal: . . . .7 to 8 m per lb (500 g)
           the sauce: . . . . .4 m
Standing: . . . . .15 m

Ingredients:

1 10-to-12-lb (5 - 6 kg) turkey

A personal note: A large cooking bag is needed (clear plastic). Make sure the turkey is completely defrosted. Cover the tips of the wings and legs with strips of aluminum foil. Place inside the turkey **1 large onion, cut in four, 1 tsp (5 mL) salt, 1/2 tsp (2 mL) pepper, 2 bay leaves and 1 tsp (5 mL) thyme or tarragon.**

• Spread the following mixture over the breast, legs and wings:

1/2 cup (125 mL) butter, melted
1 tsp (5 mL) paprika
1/4 tsp (1 mL) each pepper and garlic, powdered

Method:

• Mix all the ingredients together in a microwave-safe bowl. Microwave 1 minute at HIGH.

• Spread mixture over the whole turkey.

• Place the turkey in the bag, sprinkle with the mixture and tie the bag loosely with a string so the turkey can be moved inside the bag.

• Place the bag in a 12-cup (3 L) glass cooking dish, breast-side down. Make 4 or 5 slits in the top of the bag. Microwave at HIGH 7 to 8 minutes per pound (500 g).

• Midway through the cooking, turn the bag so turkey is breast-side up. Continue cooking at MEDIUM-HIGH 8 minutes per pound (500 g).

• The turkey is cooked when it reaches 160°F (70°C) on the thermometer.

• Remove from bag, place on a warm serving dish, cover with a cloth or a paper and let stand. After 15 minutes, the thermometer should register 170°F (75°C).

Meanwhile, make the gravy:

• Pour into the dish the juice and fat accumulated in the bag. Remove surface fat if you wish.

• To the juice add **2 to 3 tablespoons (30 to 50 mL) flour**, stir well. Add **1/2 cup (125 mL) white wine, cider or chicken broth**. Mix well.

• Microwave 4 minutes at HIGH, stir well. If necessary, microwave one more minute for a light and creamy gravy.

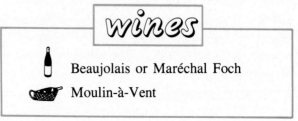

wines

Beaujolais or Maréchal Foch
Moulin-à-Vent

Roast Turkey Breast

Preparation: . . . . .10 m
Cooking: . . . . .from 23 to 25 m
Standing: . . . . .10 m

A personal note: At our markets we can now find cut-up turkey — either whole breasts, legs or wings. These are quickly prepared and very tasty. They are usually cut from smaller turkeys. The breast weighs about 2 to 2½ pounds (1 to 1.25 kg), enough to serve up to 4 people.

Ingredients:

1 turkey breast, boned

3 tbsp (50 mL) butter or margarine

1 tsp (5 mL) salt

1/2 tsp (2 mL) pepper

1 tsp (5 mL) thyme or sage

1 tbsp (15 mL) scotch or brandy

1 egg white, lightly beaten

2 tbsp (30 mL) cold water

2 tbsp (30 mL) fine dry breadcrumbs

Method:

• Cream together the butter or margarine, salt, pepper, thyme or sage and scotch or brandy. Spread inside the boned breast. Roll and tie loosely with string.

• Mix together in a plate the egg white and cold water, and place the dry breadcrumbs on a piece of waxed paper.

• Roll the breast in the egg white mixture, then in the fine breadcrumbs.

• Place on a rack. Set rack on a 9-inch (23 cm) microwave-safe pie plate.

• Microwave 15 minutes at HIGH. Baste lightly with drippings and microwave another 8 to 10 minutes at MEDIUM-HIGH or until tender. (Test with a fork or the point of a paring knife.)

• Serve hot or cold.

• When served hot, cover and let stand 10 minutes before serving.

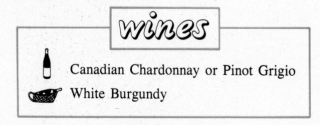

wines

Canadian Chardonnay or Pinot Grigio

White Burgundy

Turkey Wings Oriental

Preparation: ....10 m
Cooking: ....22 m
Standing: ....10 m

A personal note: Four whole turkey wings will weigh about 4 pounds (2 kg). I cut each wing into two and I reserve the tips to make turkey stock.

wines

Liebfraumilch or Californian Chablis

Rhine Riesling Spaetlese or Vouvray

Ingredients:

4 whole turkey wings

Paprika

1/3 cup (80 mL) peanut oil

Sauce:

1 cup (250 mL) soy sauce

3 tbsp (50 mL) Sake or sherry

2 tbsp (30 mL) fresh ginger root, grated

2 garlic cloves, chopped fine

Grated rind of 1 orange and 1 lemon

1 tbsp (15 mL) brown sugar

Method:

• Cut each wing into two parts, reserving the wing tips to make stock. Sprinkle each piece with paprika. Dip each part into the oil.

• Place in an 8 × 10-inch (20 × 25 cm) microwave-safe dish the cut part placed toward the middle. Microwave 10 minutes at HIGH. Move the pieces around in the dish.

• Place the sauce ingredients in a microwave-safe measuring cup. Microwave 2 minutes at HIGH. Pour over the turkey wings, cover with waxed paper. Microwave at HIGH another 10 minutes. Baste with sauce in the dish.

• Cover and let rest 10 minutes before serving. Serve with rice.

Scalloped Turkey
À l'Italienne

Preparation :	. . . .	10 m
Cooking : the meal :	. . . .	15 m
the sauce :	. . . .	from 5 to 6 m
Standing :	. . . .	none

• Nobody will ever know this is made with leftovers. In Verona, Italy, where I first ate this dish, the noodles were homemade green noodles, but any type of noodle can be used.

Ingredients :

8 oz (250 g) fine noodles

Leftover turkey, sliced or diced, and stuffing

4 tbsp (60 mL) butter

4 tbsp (60 mL) flour

1 cup (250 mL) milk

1 cup (250 mL) turkey or chicken broth*

1/4 cup (60 mL) parsley, finely chopped

Salt and pepper to taste

3 tbsp (50 mL) butter, melted

3 tbsp (50 mL) fine breadcrumbs

1/4 tsp (1 mL) nutmeg, grated

* You can make the broth with the turkey bones.

Method :

• To cook the noodles, bring 6 cups (1.5 L) water to boil, 7 to 8 minutes at HIGH in a 12-cup (3 L) microwave-safe bowl. Add the noodles and microwave, uncovered, 5 to 6 minutes at HIGH. Drain thoroughly.

• Place cooked noodles in a casserole, top with sliced or diced turkey, top turkey with leftover stuffing, if any.

• Place butter in a 4-cup (1 L) microwave-safe measuring cup and melt 1 minute at HIGH.

• Add the flour, stir well. Add the milk and broth.

• Stir and microwave 2 minutes at HIGH. Stir and microwave another 2 minutes or until creamy. The time may vary slightly, depending on how cold the milk is.

• Add the parsley. Salt and pepper to taste.

• Pour over the noodles and turkey until well covered.

• Melt the butter 1 minute at HIGH.

• Add the fine breadcrumbs and nutmeg. Mix well and spread over the sauce.

• Microwave 10 minutes at MEDIUM. Serve hot.

Chilled Valpolicella or (white) Soave

Alsatian Pinot Noir

636

Turkey Casserole

Preparation: . . . .**10 m**
Cooking: . . . .**14 m**
Standing: . . . .**none**

• It's useful to have good recipes for leftover turkey. This casserole is a pleasant and tasty family dish.

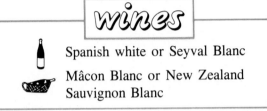

wines

Spanish white or Seyval Blanc

Mâcon Blanc or New Zealand Sauvignon Blanc

Ingredients:

About 3 cups (750 mL) leftover turkey, sliced or diced

2 tbsp (30 mL) butter

2 tbsp (30 mL) flour

1 cup (250 mL) chicken consommé or turkey broth

1 cup (250 mL) cream

2 tbsp (30 mL) sherry

2 egg yolks, beaten

Buttered breadcrumbs

Method:

• Place the butter in an 8-cup (2 L) microwave-safe casserole and melt 1 minute at HIGH. Stir in the flour.

• Add the chicken consommé or turkey broth. Mix well. Microwave at HIGH 2 minutes. Stir well and microwave another minute or until creamy.

• Add the cream and sherry. Mix well. Stir in the egg yolks. Whisk until well blended with the sauce. Microwave at MEDIUM 1 minute. Stir and season to taste.

• Place a layer of turkey meat in the bottom of a baking dish, cover with half the sauce, make another layer of turkey meat and top whole with the remaining sauce.

• Sprinkle buttered breadcrumbs on top. Cover.

• Microwave 8 minutes at MEDIUM. This can be prepared in advance and cooked when ready to serve, simply add 2 minutes cooking time.

Topping variations:

• Crush **6 soda crackers**. Add **2 tablespoons (30 mL) melted margarine or butter, 1/2 teaspoon (2 mL) paprika** or **1 teaspoon (5 mL) sesame seeds**. Sprinkle on top of casserole and microwave the same time as above.

English Bread Stuffing

Preparation:	12 m
Cooking:	6 m
Standing:	none

A personal note: Enough to stuff a 10-to-12-pound (5-6 kg) turkey.

Ingredients:

1 cup (250 mL) butter or turkey fat, diced

1 tbsp (15 mL) savory or sage

1½ tsp (7 mL) salt

1/4 tsp (1 mL) pepper

1/2 cup (125 mL) fresh parsley, minced

3/4 cup (190 mL) celery with leaves, chopped

3 cups (750 mL) onions, chopped

10 to 11 cups (2.5 - 2.75 L) dry bread, diced

Method:

• Melt in a large bowl the butter or diced turkey fat 2 minutes at HIGH for the butter, 4 minutes at HIGH for the diced fat, stirring once.

• Add the savory or sage, salt, pepper, parsley, celery and onions. Mix well. Microwave 6 minutes at MEDIUM-HIGH, stirring once.

• Pour over the diced bread. Mix well. Adjust seasoning.

Dutch Bread and Potato Stuffing

Preparation:	15 m
Cooking:	3 m
Standing:	none

A personal note: This can be used with chicken, turkey, duck or pheasant. When using this stuffing with any kind of bird, wash bird inside and out with Dutch Gin (Geneva Gin).

Ingredients:

2 eggs

2 cups (500 mL) milk

4 cups (1 L) coarse breadcrumbs

1/4 tsp (1 mL) pepper

1 tsp (5 mL) salt

2 cups (500 mL) cooked potatoes, mashed

1/2 cup (125 mL) celery, chopped fine

1/4 cup (60 mL) butter

1 large onion, chopped *or*
   10 green onions, chopped fine

Method:

• Beat the eggs until light. Add the milk and pour over the dry breadcrumbs.

• Add the salt, pepper, mashed potatoes and celery. Mix together.

• Place the butter in a microwave-safe bowl and melt 2 minutes at HIGH. Add the onion or green onions, stir until well coated with the butter. Microwave at HIGH 3 minutes, stirring once.

• Pour over the mixture.

• Mix well and use to stuff turkey, chicken, duck or pheasant.

French Cuisine Turkey Stuffing

Preparation:	**3 m**
Cooking:	**none**
Standing:	**none**

A personal note: This is a way to flavor the inside of a turkey that permeates the whole bird as it cooks. It's especially recommended for a turkey weighing from 9 to 12 pounds (4.5 to 6 kg). Furthermore, it is quick and easy. This stuffing can also be used for a chicken 5 pounds (2.5 kg) or more or for a 4-pound (2 kg) duck.

Ingredients:

2 garlic cloves, chopped fine

10 peppercorns, crushed

1 tsp (5 mL) sage

3 tbsp (50 mL) margarine

1   6-inch (15 cm) length of French bread

Method:

• Mix together the garlic, peppercorns, sage and margarine.

• Spread all over the French bread.

• Place as is in the turkey cavity and roast according to the recipe you are following.

Smoked Oyster Stuffing

Preparation:	**8 m**
Cooking:	**none**
Standing:	**none**

A personal note: A Scandinavian way to stuff turkey, this recipe features smoked oysters coupled with raisins and walnuts. I sometimes use it with quail or pheasant.

Ingredients:

1½ cups (375 mL) bread croutons

1 cup (250 mL) milk

1 cup (250 mL) celery, coarsely chopped

1 large onion, chopped fine

1/2 cup (125 mL) raisins

1/2 cup (125 mL) walnuts, chopped

1   3.62-oz (104 g) can smoked oysters

1/2 cup (125 mL) butter or margarine, melted

Method:

• Place all the ingredients in a large bowl, toss together until well mixed. Add salt to taste. Fill cavity loosely, as the dressing expands while cooking. This quantity is sufficient for a 7-to-12-pound (3.5 - 6 kg) turkey.

Goose

Classic Roasted Goose

Advance preparation : . . . . .24 h
Cooking : the meal : . . . .5 m per pound (500 g)
            the sauce : . . . . .from 8 to 11 m
Standing : . . . . .none

• I adapted this classic way to roast goose to micro-wave cooking. The goose skin is crisp and fat free, the meat, juicy and tender.

A personal note : If desired, it can be stuffed with Apple Raisin Stuffing, or simply seasoned inside the cavity.

Ingredients :

1 10-to-12-lb (5 - 6 kg) young goose

Juice of 2 lemons

1 onion, thinly sliced

1 large garlic clove, cut in half

6 whole cloves

1/2 tsp (2 mL) thyme

1 tsp (5 mL) basil

1/3 cup (80 mL) parsley, chopped

Method :

• Wipe the goose inside and out with a cloth dipped in vinegar (I like to use cider vinegar).

• Mix the remaining ingredients well in a large bowl and roll the goose all over in the mixture.

• Cover the bowl with a cloth or with foil and marinate 24 hours, refrigerated or in a cool place.

• Then, stuff the bird as you wish or simply put into the cavity 4 unpeeled apples cut in thick slices and the ingredients used to marinate the goose.

• Tie legs with wooden picks, place wings under the neck skin.

• Place on a rack set in a microwave-safe dish large enough to hold the goose.

• Cover tips of legs with small pieces of foil.

• Add **2 cups (500 mL) water or apple juice** on top of the bird.

• Sprinkle generously all over with **paprika**, then rub breast with **2 tablespoons (30 mL) melted butter or margarine**, stirred with **1 tablespoon (15 mL) Kitchen Bouquet**.

• Cover the goose with a large piece of buttered waxed paper.

• Roast 5 minutes per pound (500 g) at HIGH.

• Baste with the juice in the bottom of the pan every 20 minutes.

• Prick the wings and legs after 40 minutes with the point of a knife to let fat escape.

• Then continue roasting at MEDIUM. Test for doneness with a fork.

To make gravy :

• Remove goose to a warm platter. Remove excess fat from pan. This is easy, as fat stays on top.

• Place in a small microwave-safe bowl **3 table-spoons (50 mL) of the top clear fat**. Add **3 to 4 tablespoons (50 - 60 mL) flour**. Mix well.

• Microwave at MEDIUM-HIGH 3 to 6 minutes, stirring every minute, until mixture reaches a nice brown color.

• Remove from the roasting dish any fat that remains on top.

• Add the browned flour mixture to the remaining gravy. Stir well.

• Add **1 cup (250 mL) port wine or orange juice or strong tea**. Stir well.

• Microwave 5 minutes at MEDIUM, stirring once ; it should then be bubbling and creamy. Serve in a sauceboat.

• Excellent served with Port Wine Jelly or English Tart Applesauce.

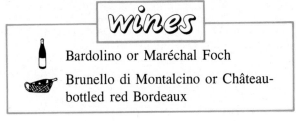

wines

Bardolino or Maréchal Foch

Brunello di Montalcino or Château-bottled red Bordeaux

Goose Apple Stuffing

Preparation : . . . . 7 m
Cooking : . . . . 2 m
Standing : . . . . **none**

A personal note : This is one of my favorites. I sometimes add **1/2 cup (125 mL) chopped pears.** Cut the recipe in half and use to stuff a duck or pheasant.

Ingredients :

2 cups (500 mL) soft breadcrumbs

4 tbsp (60 mL) butter

1 small onion, chopped fine

1 cup (250 mL) walnuts or pecans, chopped

1 tsp (5 mL) basil or oregano

2 tbsp (30 mL) milk

2 unpeeled apples, grated

Salt to taste

Method :

• Use centre of loaf (no crust) to make crumbs.

• Place butter in a microwave-safe bowl and melt 2 minutes at HIGH. Add the onion and chopped nuts, stir well. Microwave 2 minutes at HIGH.

• Add the basil or oregano, milk, breadcrumbs and apples. Mix well. Salt to taste.

• Stuff the bird loosely, as this stuffing expands.

Helpful hint : **To blanch nuts,** cook in boiling water at HIGH for 30 seconds to 1 minute, then strain and remove skins by rubbing between paper towels.

Apple Raisin Goose Stuffing

Preparation: . . . . **10 m**
Cooking: . . . . **4 m**
Standing: . . . . **none**

A personal note: If you like apples and raisins in bread stuffing, try this one. For me, there is none better.

Ingredients:

1/4 cup (60 mL) soft butter

1 cup (250 mL) onion, chopped

1 cup (250 mL) celery, finely diced

1 tsp (5 mL) salt

1/2 tsp (2 mL) pepper

3 cups (750 mL) toasted bread, diced

2 tsp (10 mL) aniseeds

2 cups (500 mL) unpeeled apples, grated

4 tbsp (60 mL) Madeira or port wine

2/3 cup (160 mL) raisins

Method:

- Place the butter in an 8-cup (2 L) microwave-safe bowl and melt 2 minutes at HIGH.
- Add the onion and celery, stir well.
- Microwave 4 minutes at HIGH, stirring twice.
- Add all the remaining ingredients. Stir well.
- Stuff the goose, sew up with thread.

Helpful hint: To soften or flavor candied fruit or raisins required for recipe, place the required amount of fruit or raisins in a bowl and pour over the liquor or other liquid called for in the recipe. Microwave 2 minutes at HIGH. Cool before using.

643

English Tart Applesauce

Preparation: .8 m
Cooking: . . . . .from 13 to 19 m
Standing: . . . . .none

A personal note: I was given this most interesting sauce in Lambourn, England, by a race horse trainer. It is a perfect hot fruit sauce to serve with goose.

Ingredients:

6 to 8 apples

2 tbsp (30 mL) butter

1/2 tsp (2 mL) curry powder

2 tbsp (30 mL) flour

1 cup (250 mL) milk

1 tsp (5 mL) cider or wine vinegar

2 tbsp (30 mL) fresh mint, chopped

Method:

• Peel, core and slice the apples.

• Place the butter in a microwave-safe bowl and melt 1 minute at HIGH.

• Add the curry powder and stir until well blended. Stir in the flour and add the milk. Stir well. Microwave at MEDIUM-HIGH 3 to 4 minutes, or until creamy and smooth, stirring twice during the cooking period.

• Add the apples, mix well. Cover and microwave at MEDIUM-LOW about 10 to 15 minutes, stirring twice.

• Then beat until the apples are reduced to a pulp.

• Adjust seasoning and add the cider or wine vinegar and the chopped mint. Serve hot.

• This sauce can be made 4 to 5 days in advance and kept refrigerated.

• When ready to serve, reheat 2 to 4 minutes at MEDIUM-HIGH. Stir well and serve.

French Glaze for Turkey and Large Chicken

Preparation:	**7 m**
Cooking:	**2 m**
Standing:	**none**

Ingredients:

1/2 cup (125 mL) butter

2 tsp (10 mL) savory

2 tsp (10 mL) tarragon

2 tsp (10 mL) thyme

1 tsp (5 mL) Kitchen Bouquet

1 tbsp (15 mL) chicken Bovril

Method:

• Place all the ingredients in a microwave-safe bowl. Microwave 2 minutes at HIGH. Stir well.

• Brush on turkey or large roasting chicken just before putting it into the microwave oven. Roast as directed by your recipe. Baste once halfway through the roasting period and once when bird is ready.

Port Wine Jelly

Advance preparation:	**time to set**
Cooking:	**5 m**
Standing:	**none**

A personal note: To me, this is a must with roast goose. It can be made in advance, as it will keep 10 to 15 days refrigerated. The best port wine to use is a Portuguese type, but a good-quality Canadian port will do.

Ingredients:

1/2 cup (125 mL) sugar

1 cup (250 mL) water

Grated peel and juice of 1 lemon

1 envelope unflavored gelatin

1 cup (250 mL) port wine

Method:

• Place in a large microwave-safe measuring cup the sugar, water and grated lemon rind. Microwave at HIGH 4 minutes. Stir well.

• Meanwhile, soak the gelatin in the lemon juice. Add the soaked gelatin to the hot mixture. Stir well. Microwave 1 minute at MEDIUM-HIGH.

• Let cool 10 minutes, then add the port wine. Stir well. Pour into an attractive serving dish.

• Cover and refrigerate until set.

Partridge

Cabbage Partridge

Preparation: . . . . .18 m
Cooking: . . . . . .from 1 h 20 to 1 h 40 m
Standing: .20 m

A personal note: This is always a choice dish. When I am ready to serve, I toast 4 to 6 slices of bread on the convection oven rack at 400°F (200°C). I place a whole or half a partridge on each slice of bread and I surround it with cabbage. The bread is delicious. In France, I was served partridge cooked in this manner, but the slice of bread was soaked with cognac before the partridge was placed on it.

wines

Alsatian Pinot Blanc or red Burgundy

Alsatian Tokay Pinot Gris or (red) Côte-de-Beaune-Villages

Ingredients:

4 to 5 partridges

1/2 lb (250 g) fat salt pork

Paprika

4 to 6 large onions, sliced

Garlic

4 cups (1 L) green cabbage, chopped

1 tsp (5 mL) coarse salt

1/2 tsp (2 mL) pepper, fresh ground

1 tsp (5 mL) thyme

1 cup (250 mL) white wine or red burgundy, cider or apple juice

Method:

• Clean the partridges with the lemon juice. Set aside.

• Slice the fat salt pork thinly. Place in a microwave-safe baking dish. Brown one side 10 minutes at HIGH, stirring once. Turn.

• Sprinkle the partridges with paprika. Place them over the browned salt pork, stir. Microwave 15 minutes at HIGH, turning the partridges once during the cooking. Remove from dish.

• Add the onions, garlic and cabbage to the drippings. Stir well. Cover and microwave 15 minutes at HIGH, stirring halfway through the cooking.

• Bury the partridges in the cabbage, add salt, pepper, thyme and the chosen liquid. Cover and microwave at MEDIUM-LOW 40 to 60 minutes.

• Check doneness of partridges in last 20 minutes of cooking. As for all wild birds, cooking time will vary.

• Let stand 20 minutes.

• Place partridges on toasted bread slices. Surround with the cabbage.

647

Partridge Casserole

A personal note: If you are not sure how tender the partridge is, this is the perfect recipe to use. The Italians cook them this way, but serve them with a lightly sweetened "Zabaglione." Unusual and delicious.

Ingredients:

2 partridges rubbed with orange juice

4 slices of bacon, diced

1 cup (250 mL) small white onions

1 cup (250 mL) mushrooms, thinly sliced

1/4 cup (60 mL) Madeira wine

1/2 cup (125 mL) chicken consommé

Juice of 1/2 lemon

Preparation:	**14 m**
Cooking:	**44 m**
Standing:	**none**

Method:

• Rub the cleaned partridges with the orange juice inside and outside. Tie the legs together with a string.

• Line an 8 × 8-inch (20 × 20 cm) Corning or Pyrex dish with the diced bacon. Place the partridges on top.

• Mix the small onions and the sliced mushrooms. Stuff into the partridge cavities.

• Pour on top the Madeira wine and the consommé. Salt and pepper to taste. Cover with plastic wrap.

• Microwave at HIGH 20 minutes, uncover, baste the partridges with the juice in the dish.

• Place birds breast-side down and microwave another 20 minutes at MEDIUM. Test for doneness after 15 minutes; it may take a few minutes more or a few minutes less, depending on the tenderness of the bird.

• Add the lemon juice to the gravy.

• Add the onions and the mushrooms from inside the partridges. Heat at HIGH 2 minutes. Serve with wild rice.

If you wish to serve with "Zabaglione"

• Beat the **yolks of 3 eggs with 2 tablespoons (30 mL) sugar** in a 4-cup (1 L) microwave-safe measuring cup. Add **a full wine glass of Madeira or Marsala wine**. Beat again until well mixed.

• Microwave 2 minutes at HIGH, beat with a whisk. Microwave 1 minute at MEDIUM-HIGH, beat again. Microwave another minute at MEDIUM-HIGH.

• If the sauce is not creamy, repeat operation once more, as the coldness of the eggs can make a difference in the cooking time. The sauce should be slightly creamy. Serve hot.

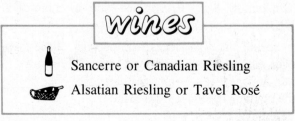

wines

Sancerre or Canadian Riesling

Alsatian Riesling or Tavel Rosé

Pheasant

Pheasant
À la Normande

Convection cooking

Preparation: . . . . .12 m
Cooking: . . . . .1 h
Standing: .none

A personal note: In French cuisine, "à la Normande" always implies apples and very strong cider. This pheasant recipe follows suit. Roasted in the convection section of the microwave oven it is a real success.

 Vidal or Vouvray

Sparkling Vouvray or château-bottled white Graves

Ingredients:

1 pheasant

1 tsp (5 mL) paprika

2 tsp (10 mL) butter

6 to 8 apples, peeled and thinly sliced

3 tbsp (50 mL) butter, melted

1/2 cup (125 mL) cream

Salt and pepper to taste

3 tbsp (50 mL) brandy

2 egg yolks, beaten

Method:

• Clean and truss the pheasant with a wet string.

• Mix together the paprika and the 2 teaspoons (10 mL) butter. Rub the wings and breast of the pheasant with this mixture.

• Preheat the convection oven 15 minutes at 375°F (190°C).

• Line a baking dish with half the apples. Pour the melted butter on top.

• Set the pheasant on this bed of apples. Place the remaining apples all around. Salt and pepper to taste.

• Place the dish on the roasting rack. Cook at 375°F (190°C) 1 hour or until the pheasant is golden brown on top and the meat is tender.

• When cooked, put the pheasant on a warm serving dish.

• Add the cream and brandy to the apples, mix well.

• Add the beaten egg yolks. Cook at MEDIUM about 3 minutes in the microwave, stirring halfway through the cooking. You will have a smooth sauce.

• Salt to taste. Serve in a sauceboat.

Pheasant Fines-Herbes

Preparation : . . . . .10 m
Cooking : . . . . .from 20 to 30 m
Standing : .none

A personal note : The combination of rosemary, thyme and dry white wine gives pheasant a very special flavor that I think of as "elegant."

wines

Seyval Blanc or Entre-Deux-Mers

Alsatian Tokay Pinot Gris or Californian Fumé Blanc

Ingredients :

2 tbsp (30 mL) butter

6 green onions, chopped fine

1 tsp (5 mL) thyme

1/2 tsp (2 mL) rosemary

1/2 tsp (2 mL) paprika

1/2 tsp (2 mL) pepper

1/2 cup (125 mL) dry white wine or vermouth

1 2-lb (1 kg) pheasant, quartered

2 tsp (10 mL) cornstarch

1 cup (250 mL) sour cream

Method :

• Put in a microwave-safe measuring cup or bowl the butter, green onions, thyme, rosemary, paprika, pepper and white wine or vermouth.

• Microwave at HIGH 4 minutes, stirring twice. This is the basting sauce.

• Place pheasant pieces, skin-side down, in a 10-inch (25 cm) microwave-safe dish without overlapping.

• Baste lightly with a bit of the hot sauce.

• Microwave 10 minutes at MEDIUM-HIGH. Turn pheasant over.

• Baste again with the basting sauce. Microwave 7 minutes at HIGH.

• Check for doneness with a fork, as it varies.

• If necessary, microwave another 10 minutes at MEDIUM. Remove pheasant to a hot platter.

• Add remaining basting sauce to drippings.

• Mix the cornstarch with 1 tablespoon (15 mL) of cold water and stir in. Mix well.

• Microwave at HIGH 2 minutes, stirring after 1 minute of cooking.

• Beat in the sour cream, stirring constantly. Place pheasant in sauce. Sprinkle with salt.

• Cover and microwave 1 minute at MEDIUM. Serve.

Simple Port Wine Sauce

Preparation:	4 m
Cooking:	2 m
Standing:	none

A personal note: This sauce is simple but delicious with all types of birds, especially pheasant.

Ingredients:

1/2 cup (125 mL) port wine
2 large green onions, chopped fine
Juice of 1/2 a lemon

Method:

• Mix the ingredients in a microwave-safe bowl. Microwave at HIGH 2 minutes.

• Add to any bird gravy or pour over leftover meat, thinly sliced. Cover with waxed paper and microwave 1 to 2 minutes at MEDIUM-HIGH. Time depends on quantity.

Flavored Breadcrumbs

Preparation:	5 m
Cooking:	30 s
Standing:	10 m

A personal note: This coating replaces commercial mixes. It keeps for several months, refrigerated in a jar or plastic container. This recipe yields 2 cups (500 mL).

Ingredients:

2 cups (500 mL) breadcrumbs
2 tbsp (30 mL) peanut oil
2 tsp (10 mL) pepper
1/2 tsp (2 mL) salt
1 tsp (5 mL) paprika
1/4 tsp (1 mL) garlic powder
1/2 tsp (2 mL) thyme
1 tsp (5 mL) savory
1/2 tsp (2 mL) each turmeric and curry powder

Method:

• Mix all the ingredients together in a microwave-safe bowl. Microwave 30 seconds at HIGH. Stir thoroughly.

• Let stand 10 minutes. Pour into a clean and dry container. Cover and refrigerate.

Rabbit

Rabbit
À la Française

• The rabbit, diced salt pork fat, onions, white wine and leeks all contribute to the delightful enjoyment of this dish.

Advance preparation : . . . .**from 6 to 12 h**
Cooking : . . . .**from 58 to 70 m**
Standing : . . . .**15 m**

Ingredients :

1 young rabbit, cut up

1 cup (250 mL) white wine or cider

1 medium onion, thinly sliced

2 garlic cloves, minced

1 bay leaf

1/2 tsp (2 mL) thyme

3 whole cloves

1/2 cup (125 mL) salt pork fat, diced

1 tbsp (15 mL) butter

20 small onions, peeled

1 tsp (5 mL) Dijon mustard

1/4 cup (60 mL) flour, browned

1 tsp (5 mL) savory

3 tbsp (50 mL) parsley, minced

3 small leeks, thinly sliced

Method :

• Place the pieces of rabbit in a bowl.

• Add the white wine or cider, onion, garlic, bay leaf, thyme and cloves. Mix together, cover and marinate 6 to 12 hours, refrigerated.

• Place the diced salt pork and the butter in a microwave-safe baking dish. Brown at HIGH 8 to 10 minutes, stirring twice during the cooking.

• Drain the rabbit from the marinade and put it in the baking dish. Stir well. Cover and microwave 10 minutes at HIGH.

• Stir and add the small onions and the mustard. Sprinkle with the browned flour, mix well.

• Strain the marinating liquid and pour over the rabbit. Add the savory, parsley and leeks. Mix together. Cover and simmer 40 minutes at MEDIUM. Stir twice.

• Check doneness of rabbit and if necessary microwave 10 minutes more at MEDIUM.

• Let stand 15 minutes before serving.

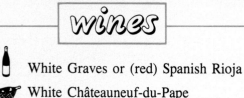

wines

White Graves or (red) Spanish Rioja
White Châteauneuf-du-Pape

Hare or Rabbit Baden-Baden

Preparation: . . . . .15 m
Cooking: . . . . .from 36 to 47 m
Standing: . . . . .20 m

• I tasted this dish in Germany on a trip to the Black Forest. I was so intrigued with the taste of the diced prunes and beer that I asked for the recipe. Adapting it to microwave cooking made it even better.

A personal note: To cut rabbit, remove 4 legs, cut each one in two at joint. Cut the back into 4 pieces.

wines

Brown ale or Canadian Riesling

German Riesling Spaetlese

Ingredients:

1/2 lb (250 mL) dried prunes

Juice of 1 orange

1 rabbit cut into pieces

3 tbsp (50 mL) flour, browned

1/2 tsp (2 mL) salt

1/4 tsp (1 mL) pepper

1 tsp (5 mL) thyme

2 tbsp (30 mL) bacon fat

6 small onions peeled, left whole

2 bay leaves

Salt and pepper to taste

1 cup (250 mL) light beer of your choice

1 tbsp (15 mL) brown sugar

Method:

• Soak the prunes in the orange juice 10 minutes.

• Place in a bag the browned flour, salt, pepper and thyme. Add the pieces of rabbit and shake in bag until well coated with the seasoned flour.

• Put the bacon fat in a 12 × 12-inch (30 × 30 cm) microwave-safe dish and microwave at HIGH 4 minutes. The fat must be very hot.

• Add the floured rabbit pieces one by one to the hot fat. Microwave 5 minutes at HIGH on one side. Turn, microwave 3 minutes at HIGH. Turn each piece of rabbit again.

• Add the onions, the undrained prunes, bay leaves, salt and pepper; pour the beer all around. Sprinkle the brown sugar over the liquid.

• Cover and microwave at HIGH 5 minutes.

• Reduce heat to MEDIUM and microwave 20 to 30 minutes or until meat is tender. Test with a fork.

• Let stand covered 20 minutes.

• Sauce can be thickened by adding **1 tablespoon (15 mL) of flour** to the gravy, beating with a whisk. Microwave at MEDIUM 3 to 4 minutes or until creamy.

• Serve in sauceboat.

Terrine of Rabbit

Advance preparation: . .**from 2 to 3 days**
Cooking: . . . . **37 m**
Standing: . . . . **20 m**

A personal note: A bit of work is involved to make this terrine, but when you want a special pâté for a buffet, I strongly recommend this one, which is always a success. A great plus is that it can be made 2 to 3 days ahead and it will keep refrigerated for 8 days. I surround mine with crisp green watercress and serve it with marinated fresh mushrooms and hot French bread.

wines

Beaujolais or Maréchal Foch

Bourgueil or Portuguese Bairrada

Ingredients:

1 3-to-4-lb (1.5 - 2 kg) rabbit

1/2 lb (250 g) pork, minced

1/4 lb (125 g) salt pork, minced

1/2 cup (125 mL) milk

1/2 cup (125 mL) breadcrumbs

2 eggs, well beaten

1/4 tsp (1 mL) each of thyme, marjoram, savory, nutmeg, cloves and pepper

1 tsp (5 mL) salt

1/2 cup (125 mL) parsley, chopped

1 bay leaf

2 tbsp (30 mL) brandy or port wine

Method:

• Remove the rabbit meat from the bones and put through a meat chopper, together with the rabbit liver and kidneys.

• Add the minced pork and salt pork; mix together until very well blended.

• Heat the milk, 2 minutes at HIGH.

• Add the breadcrumbs. Mix to make a paste. Press hard to remove excess milk, if any.

• Add the bread paste to the meat.

• Beat the eggs with thyme, marjoram, savory, nutmeg, cloves, pepper, salt and parsley.

• Pour into the meat mixture with the bay leaf and brandy or port. Beat together until thoroughly blended.

• Pack into a 9 × 5-inch (23 × 13 cm) microwave-safe bread pan, well buttered.

• The bottom of pan can be lined with very thin slices of salt pork. Cover top with a buttered paper.

• Bake at HIGH 10 minutes, then at MEDIUM 25 minutes.

• Let stand in oven for 20 minutes when cooking time is over. Cover with foil.

• Cool and refrigerate 2 to 3 days before unmolding.

Rice

ice is the oldest and most cultivated grain in the world. The Chinese date their first cultivation of rice back 5000 years. By the 4th century BC, rice had reached Egypt by way of Persia, like so many of the foods and customs we take for granted today.

In 1686, a ship from Madagascar, landing in a South Carolina city for repairs, expressed its gratitude by leaving a bag of rice. The city fathers quickly planted it, as they had been instructed, in a swamp near their city and, to their amazement, it yielded almost enough to feed the colony. And so the U.S.A. had entered into rice production. Today, Texas, Arkansas, Louisiana and California are the major American rice producers.

Rice has through the centuries circled the earth and has played a vital role in the history of mankind. It will no doubt continue to do so in the future, feeding millions of people.

Think of the famous Rissoto Milanese of Italy, which, by the way, cooks beautifully in the microwave oven. It was first made in the Po Valley, where they started to grow rice in the 15th century.

In Japan, rice planting is a time of happy celebration. In Osaka, a dozen country girls are chosen each June 14 to perform the ceremony of transplanting seedlings in the rice paddy fields of Sumihochu Shrine. I am happy to have had the privilege of seeing this celebration.

Another interesting fact is that the Japanese word for rice, "gohan", is also used for meals, since in Japan no meal is complete without a bowl of rice.

Varieties of rice

1. Short grain rice

• The shorter the grain, the shorter the growing time, the higher the yield and the lower the cost.

• Short grain rice is moister than the long grain version, takes less water to cook and the grains cling more to each other.

• It is the best of all types of rice for puddings, rice croquettes and rice rings.

2. Long grain rice

• Long grain rice is 3 to 4 times longer and is whiter than the short grain type. Properly cooked, the grains separate from each other.

• Long grain rice may be used whenever you wish to serve rice, but it is especially good for salads, to serve mixed with vegetables or as a substitute for potatoes.

• It is more costly than short grain rice.

3. Parboiled rice

• Parboiled or converted rice is steamed or put through a hot water processing before being polished, which allows water soluble proteins to permeate the starch part of the rice and remain there. It has a light golden color and requires more cooking time.

• It can be used in the same manner as long grain rice.

• It is the most costly of all rice.

4. Brown rice

• The kernels in brown rice are unpolished, which gives them their light brown color.

• It is important to know that brown rice retains much of its bran layers, which contain its natural oil, proteins and vitamins.

- It has a chewier consistency than polished or long grain rice and also has a nutty flavor, of which I am personally very fond, especially when served with roasted or broiled meats.

- Brown rice takes somewhat longer to cook than polished rice.

5. Quick cooking or instant rice

- The best quick cooking or instant rice available is the long grain type.

- Pre-steamed, it needs only to be heated quickly in boiling water. It is ready to use or serve in just minutes.

6. Wild rice

- Wild rice is not really rice at all, but the seed of a marsh grass.

- The grains are long, dark greenish in color and more chewy when cooked than other rice.

- Considered a gourmet delicacy, wild rice is gathered by hand, which explains its high cost. It is gathered from lakes in the deep green forests of Minnesota, Wisconsin and all the neighboring parts of Canada.

- In the spring, limp shoots of the aquatic grass appear in these lakes. By late fall, they stand tall and produce an edible seed, the "wild rice." Indians as early as the 1st century AD were harvesting, drying and threshing the seeds. It was the major source of carbohydrate in their diet.

- The commercialization of wild rice began in the early 1600s, when the voyageurs, coureurs de bois and fur traders began to follow the natural eating habits of the Indians living in the lake region — a diet of game, fish, wild rice and wild berries. Since the mid-1970s, 95 per cent of wild rice has been cultivated in the wild rice paddies of the U.S.A. and Canada.

- Wild rice is low in calories and fat, yet high in fibre and good-quality protein. It also has a variety of minerals and vitamins and no or very few preservatives.

The advantages of rice

• An important fact is that rice has a wonderful and almost unique quality : it is able to absorb the impact of heavy food, so you can eat more without that too-full feeling. I hope you will enjoy the following rice recipes, which can be cooked so quickly and so easily with perfect results in a microwave oven. You will also, I am sure, appreciate the versatility and outstanding nutritional value of rice.

• As there are small variations in the cooking of rice, depending on the brand used, it is advisable to read the directions on the package.

• What is fascinating about rice is its extraordinary versatility. It can be used in soups, served as a vegetable, as a main course, as a dessert, as baby food, etc.

To cook rice automatically

• If your oven has an Automatic or Instamatic setting, use it to cook your rice. The time is of little concern, since the oven itself will determine that. Consult your oven manual for instructions.

• The quantity of rice and water remain the same as in the Rice Cooking Chart. The dish must be covered during the cooking period.

Rice Cooking Chart					
Item	Container	Amount of hot water	Approx. time to boil water at HIGH (in minutes)	Approx. time to cook rice at MEDIUM-LOW (in minutes)	Stand time (in minutes)
Long grain 1 cup (250 mL)	8-cup (2 L) casserole	2 cups (500 mL)	4 to 5	14 to 16	10
Short grain 1 cup (250 mL)	8-cup (2 L) casserole	2 cups (500 mL)	4 to 5	10 to 12	10
Quick cooking 1 cup (250 mL)	4-cup (1 L) casserole	1 cup (250 mL)	2 to 3	5	5
Brown rice 1 cup (250 mL)	8-cup (2 L) casserole	3 cups (750 mL)	5 to 6	45 to 50	15
Wild rice* 1 cup (250 mL)	8-cup (2 L) casserole	4 cups (1 L)	6	30 to 40	15

* Depending on the type of wild rice, cooking time can vary from 25 minutes to 40 minutes. Stir once, halfway through the cooking time.
When cooking time is finished, let stand 10 minutes, stir with a fork. Taste.
If you prefer a softer wild rice, **add 1/2 cup (125 mL) hot water**, stir with a fork. Microwave another 8 to 10 minutes at MEDIUM-HIGH. Let stand 15 minutes. Stir with a fork and finish according to your recipe.

To cook rice starting with cold water

Preparation : . . . . .2 m
Cooking : . . . . .from 25 to 30 m
Standing : . . . . .from 10 to 15 m

A personal note : If you consider cooking rice a mystery, try this method. It will never fail you. It will show you how easy it is to cook rice in a microwave oven.

Ingredients :

2 cups (500 mL) water, at room temperature

1/2 tsp (2 mL) salt

1 tbsp (15 mL) vegetable or olive oil

1 cup (250 mL) short or long grain rice

Method :

• Put the water, salt and oil in an 8-cup (2 L) microwave-safe dish with a cover. Stir in the rice.

• Microwave, uncovered, 10 minutes at HIGH. Stir well.

• Cover and microwave 15 minutes at MEDIUM for short grain, 20 minutes at MEDIUM for long grain.

• Let stand, covered, without stirring, 10 to 15 minutes.

• Add butter or herbs or cooked vegetables only after standing time. Stir with a fork.

Interesting variations

• Use homemade or diluted **canned consommé or tomato juice** instead of water.

• Add to the water **2 tablespoons (30 mL) dried soup vegetables** or **1 tablespoon (15 mL) of a dried herb of your choice**.

• Use **apple juice** instead of water to make curried rice.

To cook wild rice

Preparation: ....3 m
Cooking: ....from 26 to 41 m
Standing: ....35 m

• This method for cooking wild rice, referred to as the New Quick-Soak Method, was developed by food specialists at the Ontario Food Council. It is the best method I have ever used, since it best preserves the flavor and texture of the wild rice.

Ingredients:

1 cup (250 mL) wild rice
3 cups (750 mL) water
1 tsp (5 mL) salt

Method:

• Place rice in a sieve and rinse under cold running water until the water runs clear.

• Measure the water in a 6-cup (1.5 L) microwave-safe dish. Microwave 6 minutes at HIGH.

• Add the rice and salt. Stir well. Cover and microwave 20 to 30 minutes at MEDIUM. Stir with a fork.

• Cover and let stand 25 minutes.

• Taste. If it needs more cooking, give it another 5 minutes at MEDIUM.

• Let stand 10 minutes. Serve.

Interesting variations on plain boiled rice

Any type of rice can be used

1. For a golden colored rice, add **1/4 teaspoon (1 mL) of turmeric** to the water before adding the rice.

Excellent and colorful with fish and egg dishes.

2. To **3 cups (750 mL) of cooked rice**, add **2 tablespoons (30 mL) fresh lemon juice, 1 teaspoon (5 mL) grated lemon rind** and salt to taste. Serve with chicken, veal or meat loaf.

3. Toss cooked rice with butter to taste. Add **chives or parsley, 4 to 5 slices of diced microwaved bacon, and 1 tablespoon (15 mL) sour cream**. Serve with roast chicken, veal or pork.

663

4. Vegetarian Rice, to serve as is or with veal roast or boiled chicken.

Ingredients:

3 cups (750 mL) cooked rice*

1 cup (250 mL) raw mushrooms, thinly sliced

1/4 cup (60 mL) black olives, sliced

1/4 cup (60 mL) almonds, slivered

1/2 cup (125 mL) cheese of your choice, grated

1/4 teaspoon (1 mL) salt; pepper to taste

* *1 cup (250 mL) uncooked rice will give you 3 cups (750 mL) cooked rice.*

Method:

• Add all the ingredients to the cooked rice.

• Serve as is or shape into a ring by simply buttering a ring mold and packing the cheese mixture into it.

• If the shaped rice is cold and you would prefer to have it hot, cover with waxed paper when ready to serve and microwave 4 minutes at MEDIUM, in its mold.

• Unmold on serving dish. Fill to your taste.

To reheat cooked rice

- Place cold cooked rice in a microwave-safe dish.
- Drizzle on top **1 tablespoon (15 mL) cold water for each cup of cooked rice**. Do not stir.
- Cover dish and warm 6 to 8 minutes at MEDIUM. Stir with a fork. Test. If not hot enough, heat for another minute or 2.

Another method

- Place the cooked rice in a plastic sieve. Place over a dish of hot water. Top with waxed paper.
- Warm 2 to 3 minutes, depending on the quantity of rice, at MEDIUM. Stir with a fork.

Cooking yields different types of rice

1 cup (250 mL) uncooked	=	cooked
long, medium or short grain rice	=	3 cups (750 mL)
converted or parboiled	=	4 cups (1 L)
instant or quick cooking	=	2 cups (500 mL)
wild rice	=	3 to 4 cups (750 mL to 1 L)

To freeze rice

- Rice freezes well, but takes as long to thaw and reheat as to cook from raw.
- Plain cooked rice placed in a well-covered dish will keep for 5 to 6 months in the freezer.
- To use, thaw one to two hours at room temperature.
- Or place **1 or 2 cups (250 or 500 mL)** in a plate at room temperature for 20 minutes, then in the microwave oven for 10 minutes at LOW.

Stir with a fork and repeat operation, if necessary, while checking the rice after 5 minutes.

Coconut Water

Preparation: . . . .**2 m**
Cooking: . . . .**3 m**
Standing: . . . .**none**

A personal note: Rice to be used for curried rice or dessert is excellent when it's cooked in Coconut Water.

Ingredients:

1 cup (250 mL) milk

1 cup (250 mL) water

1 cup (250 mL) unsweeted coconut*, grated

* *You can buy a fresh coconut and grate it. Use the coconut milk as part of the milk required in the recipe.*

Method:

• Combine in a microwave-safe bowl all the ingredients.

• Microwave 3 minutes at MEDIUM.

• Let cool, then strain through a fine sieve, pressing hard on the coconut.

• Use as part of the liquid demanded by the recipe.

• Yield: 2 cups (500 mL).

Risi Pisi

A personal note: Risi Pisi is an Italian speciality that comes from Venice. I always make it when the first green peas are available, usually at the end of June. Serve it with chicken, sausages or liver. It's especially good with chicken livers.

Ingredients:

3 slices bacon, diced

4 green onions, peeled and diced

2 tbsp (30 mL) butter

1 tbsp (15 mL) vegetable oil

1 cup (250 mL) long grain rice

2 cups (500 mL) fresh green peas*

1/4 cup (60 mL) fresh parsley, minced

3 cups (750 mL) hot water or
    chicken consommé

Method:

- Place the bacon in an 8-cup (2 L) microwave-safe dish.
- Microwave 1 minute at HIGH.

Preparation: . . . . .12 m
Cooking: . . . . .from 23 to 28 m
Standing: . . . . .5 m

Italian Chardonnay
Pouilly-Fumé

- Add the green onions and the butter. Microwave 2 minutes at MEDIUM-HIGH. Stir well.
- Add the vegetable oil and the rice. Stir until the whole is well mixed. Add the green peas, stir again.
- Add the parsley and hot water or chicken consommé. Stir again. Cover and microwave 20 minutes at MEDIUM. Stir with a fork.
- Test the doneness of the green peas and the rice. If necessary, microwave another 5 minutes at MEDIUM.
- Let stand 5 minutes. Serve.

When fresh green peas are not available, substitute an equal quantity of unthawed frozen green peas. Do not change the cooking period.

Akni Rice Water and Pilaff

Preparation : . . . . 12 m
Cooking : . . . . 15 m
Standing : . . . . none

• India gave us this super recipe for cooking rice. The Akni water in which the rice is cooked gives it a delicate, exciting flavor. A pilaff is a dish with rice that has been tossed in melted butter, then flavored and cooked.

Ingredients :

Akni Rice Water

1 onion cut in half, thinly sliced
2 or 3 garlic cloves, crushed
1 2-inch (5 cm) piece of fresh ginger root
1 tbsp (15 mL) fennel seeds
1 tbsp (15 mL) coriander seeds
1/2 tsp (2 mL) cardamom seeds
4 cups (1 L) water

Method :

Akni :

• Place in a microwave-safe bowl the sliced onion, the garlic and fresh ginger. Tie loosely in a piece of cotton or cheesecloth the fennel, coriander and cardamom seeds and add to the onion mixture.

• Pour the water on top. Microwave 5 minutes at HIGH. Cool. Remove spice bag when ready to use.

Ingredients :

Akni Rice Pilaff

1 to 2 tbsp (15 to 30 mL) butter
1 medium-sized onion, thinly sliced
4 whole cloves
1/2 tsp (2 mL) cardamom
1 or 2-inch (2.5 or 5 cm) cinnamon stick
2 cups (500 mL) long grain rice

Method :

Pilaff :

• Place the butter in an 8-cup (2 L) microwave-safe dish and melt 1 minute at HIGH. Add the onion, whole cloves, cardamom and cinnamon stick.

• Stir in the uncooked rice until the grains are coated. Add the 4 cups (1 L) of Akni Rice Water. Cover and microwave 15 minutes at MEDIUM-HIGH, stirring after 5 minutes of cooking. Depending on the type of rice used, the cooking period can vary, so check the rice.

• When it is cooked, add a piece of butter to taste and serve.

• This Akni Rice Pilaff freezes very well, so prepare the full recipe, which will give you 6 cups (1.5 L) when cooked. Use what you require and freeze the rest in a microwave-safe dish.

• To thaw, simply place the dish with the frozen rice in the microwave oven for 4 to 6 minutes at HIGH, stirring once.

• As the rice is already cooked, be careful not to overcook it when reheating.

wines

Gewurztraminer
Rheingau Spätlese Halbtrocken

Turkish Pilaff

Preparation : . . . . 7 m
Cooking : . . . . 25 m
Standing : . . . . none

A personal note : Turkish Pilaff is perfect to serve with roast lamb or pork and all types of chicken dishes.

Ingredients :

1/4 cup (60 mL) butter or vegetable oil

1 medium-sized onion, chopped fine

1 cup (250 mL) long grain rice

1/4 tsp (1 mL) cinnamon

A pinch of allspice or cloves

2 cups (500 mL) hot chicken consommé

1 tsp (5 mL) salt, pepper to taste

1/4 cup (60 mL) each currants and chopped nuts

Method :

• Melt the butter or heat the oil 2 minutes at HIGH in a 6-cup (1.5 L) microwave-safe dish.

• Add the onion, stir well. Microwave 2 minutes at HIGH.

• Add the rice. Stir until well coated with the onion butter.

• Microwave 3 minutes at HIGH, stirring after 2 minutes of cooking.

• Add all the remaining ingredients, except the chopped nuts.

• Microwave 20 minutes at MEDIUM-LOW.

• Add the chopped nuts. Stir the whole with a fork. Serve.

wines

Gewurztraminer

Condrieu

Dried Fruit Pilaff

Preparation: ....14 m
Cooking: ....25 m
Standing: ....none

A personal note: If you roast a large chicken or barbecued meat in summer, try this Indian Dried Fruit Pilaff with it.

Ingredients:

3 tbsp (50 mL) butter

1 cup (250 mL) long grain or parboiled rice

2 cups (500 mL) hot water

1/2 tsp (2 mL) salt

2 tbsp (30 mL) butter

1/3 cup (80 mL) dried apricots, slivered

1/3 cup (80 mL) dried prunes, quartered

1/4 cup (60 mL) dried currants

1 tbsp (15 mL) honey

2 tbsp (30 mL) hot water

Method:

• Place the butter in an 8-cup (2 L) microwave-safe dish and melt 2 minutes at HIGH.

• Stir in the rice until well buttered. Add the hot water and salt.

• Cover and microwave 20 minutes at MEDIUM. Let stand.

• In another microwave-safe dish, place the remaining butter and melt 1 minute at HIGH.

• Add the slivered apricots, the quartered dried prunes and the currants. Stir well.

• Add the honey and hot water.

• Cover and microwave at MEDIUM-LOW 5 minutes.

• Stir, then pour over the hot rice. Serve.

• Serve warm with meat or cool as a dessert with a topping of yogurt.

Liebfraumilch

California Late-Harvest Riesling

Minty Rice

Preparation: . . . . **10 m**
Cooking: . . . . **from 47 to 52 m**
Standing: . . . . **none**

A personal note: A friend of mine who is very involved in vegetarian health food cuisine serves this dish as a light luncheon dish with a bowl of crunchy watercress. I serve it hot with cold or hot thinly sliced chicken, or as a garnish for sliced cooked ham.

wines

Mâcon Blanc

Condrieu

Ingredients:

3 tbsp (50 mL) butter or margarine

1 onion, peeled and thinly sliced

1 cup (250 mL) brown rice

2½ cups (625 mL) chicken consommé

1/4 cup (60 mL) fresh mint leaves, chopped

1/4 cup (60 mL) parsley, chopped

3/4 cup (190 mL) natural yogurt

Salt and pepper to taste

Method:

• Place the butter in an 8-cup (2 L) microwave-safe dish and melt 1 minute at HIGH.

• Add the onion, stir until well coated with the butter. Microwave 2 minutes at HIGH, stir.

• Add the brown rice, chicken consommé, mint and parsley. Cover and microwave 45 to 50 minutes at MEDIUM-LOW.

• When cooked, add the yogurt, salt and pepper to taste. Stir with a fork. Serve.

Rice and Cheese Casserole

Convection cooking

> **A personal note:** Quick and simple to prepare, this casserole can be served as a main dish with a green salad or with hard cooked eggs in white sauce or with cold thinly sliced meat.

Ingredients:

1 cup (250 mL) short grain rice

2 cups (500 mL) Cheddar cheese, grated

1/2 cup (125 mL) milk

1/2 cup (125 mL) light cream

1/4 cup (60 mL) parsley, chopped

4 green onions, chopped fine

3 tbsp (50 mL) butter, melted

1 cup (250 mL) coarse breadcrumbs

Method:

• Microwave the rice according to the directions in the Rice Cooking Chart.

• Butter an 8 × 8-inch (20 × 20 cm) microwave-safe dish. Make alternate layers of rice and cheese until all is used.

• Mix the milk and cream with the parsley and green onions. Pour over the rice and cheese.

• Stir the breadcrumbs with the melted butter. Spread over the rice and cheese.

• Preheat the convection part of your microwave oven to 350°F (180°C). Bake casserole about 30 minutes, or until light brown on top. Serve hot.

wines

Red Burgundy

Côtes de Nuits

Preparation: . . . . .10 m
Cooking: . . . . .from 44 to 46 m
Standing: . . . . .none

Broccoli and Rice Casserole

Preparation: . . . . .8 m
Cooking: . . . . .9 m
Standing: .none

A personal note: This recipe was especially developed to use quick cooking rice. Any other vegetable can be used instead of broccoli.

Ingredients:

2 cups (500 mL) hot water

1 envelope onion soup mix

2 cups (500 mL) quick cooking rice

2 tbsp (30 mL) butter or margarine

1 tsp (5 mL) salt

1/2 tsp (2 mL) pepper

Juice and grated rind of one lemon

1 lb (500 g) fresh broccoli

Method:

• Mix together the hot water and soup mix in a microwave-safe bowl. Add the rice, butter or margarine, salt and pepper. Stir together.

• Add the lemon juice and grated rind. Cover and microwave 2 minutes at HIGH. Let stand 5 minutes.

• Wash the broccoli, break up into flowerets and place in a microwave-safe dish with 1/2 cup (125 mL) water. Cover and microwave 5 minutes at HIGH. Drain.

• Place cooked broccoli in a microwave-safe baking dish, pour the rice mixture on top, sprinkle with grated cheese to taste. Microwave 2 minutes at HIGH. Serve.

Sauvignon Blanc

Château-bottled white Bordeaux

Bacon and Green Pepper Rice

Preparation : . . . . **11 m**
Cooking : . . . . **from 25 to 27 m**
Standing : . . . . **none**

A personal note : This is an interesting flavored rice casserole to serve as a light meal or to accompany a roast of pork or veal.

Ingredients :

4 to 6 slices of bacon

3 tbsp (50 mL) bacon drippings*

1 medium-sized onion, chopped fine

1 medium-sized green pepper, diced

1 19-oz (540 mL) can tomatoes

1/2 tsp (2 mL) sugar

1/2 tsp (2 mL) thyme or savory

1/2 cup (125 mL) long grain rice

1/2 cup (125 mL) Cheddar cheese, grated

* Bacon drippings may be replaced by butter or any other fat.

Method :

• Place slices of bacon in a dish. Microwave 2 to 3 minutes at HIGH. Place cooked bacon on paper towelling.

• To the fat remaining in the dish add the onion and green pepper. Microwave 3 minutes at HIGH. Stir well.

• Add the tomatoes, sugar, thyme or savory, stir. Add the rice, stir. Cover and microwave 20 minutes at MEDIUM, stirring after 15 minutes and testing for doneness, cooking 5 minutes more if necessary.

• When rice is tender, sprinkle top of casserole with the grated cheese.

• Crumble reserved bacon over all. Microwave 1 minute at HIGH. Serve.

Valpolicella

Barbaresco

Cheese Rice Ring

Preparation: .4 m
Cooking: . . . . .from 15 to 17 m
Standing: . . . . .none

 ## wines

(with meat) Valpolicella
(with fish) Soave
(with meat) Côte de Beaune-Villages
(with fish) Saint-Véran

A personal note: This is an elegant accompaniment to creamed leftover meat, chicken or fish. Or fill the ring with cooked fresh garden vegetables in summer, or simply top it with a cheese sauce.

Ingredients:

2 cups (500 mL) short grain rice uncooked

1/2 cup (125 mL) cheese of your choice, grated

1/4 cup (60 mL) butter, melted

Salt to taste

Method:

• Microwave the rice according to the Rice Cooking Chart.

• To the hot rice add the grated cheese, melted butter and salt. Stir with a fork until the whole is well blended.

• Butter a microwave-safe ring mold and fill with the rice, bringing it right to the top of the mold. This is important, because if the mold is not properly filled, the ring can break when turned out.

• Let stand 5 minutes. When ready to unmold, place the mold in a microwave-safe pan. Add hot water.

• Microwave 5 minutes at MEDIUM to warm up the rice. Loosen rice around the edges and unmold by inverting QUICKLY onto a hot platter.

• Fill as you choose. Serve.

Molded Rice

Preparation: . . . . 20 m
Cooking: . . . . from 28 to 30 m
Standing: . . . . 5 m

A personal note: This is an easy way to make a rice ring, which you can fill with creamed chicken, steamed seafood or cooked vegetables, or, as a dessert, fill with poached fruit or a chocolate, lemon or orange cream.

Ingredients:

2 cups (500 mL) cold water

1/2 tsp (2 mL) salt

2 tsp (10 mL) butter or margarine

1 cup (250 mL) short grain rice

1/4 tsp (1 mL) grated nutmeg *or*
    grated rind of 1 lemon

1/4 cup (60 mL) butter

Method:

• Place the cold water, 1/2 teaspoon (2 mL) salt and the 2 teaspoons (10 mL) butter or margarine in an 8-cup (2 L) microwave-safe bowl. Microwave 10 minutes at HIGH.

• Add the rice and the grated nutmeg or the grated lemon rind. Cover and microwave 10 to 12 minutes at MEDIUM-LOW. Stir gently with a fork. The water should all be absorbed and the grains soft.

• Cover, let stand 15 minutes.

• Butter a microwave-safe ring mold. Press the cooked rice into it.

• Melt the remaining butter 2 minutes at HIGH. Pour over the molded rice. Cover with a plate or a square of waxed paper. Microwave 8 to 9 minutes at MEDIUM. Let stand 5 minutes.

• Loosen the edges and turn out onto a platter.

• Fill centre as you please.

Variation:

• **Add a spoonful or two of diced pimento or minced chives or fresh tarragon to taste, or 1/2 or 3/4 cup (125 or 190 mL) of cooked frozen green peas.**

Brown Rice Salad

Preparation: . . . .**14 m**
Cooking: . . . .**from 51 to 56 m**
Standing: . . . .**none**

A personal note: Totally different from Summer Rice Salad, this rice salad is perfect with barbecued meat, hamburgers or shish kebabs.

Ingredients:

1 cup (250 mL) brown rice, uncooked

2 tbsp (30 mL) oil of your choice

1 small onion, peeled and thinly sliced

1 medium green pepper, cut into thin strips

1 small red pepper, cut into thin strips

1 tbsp (15 mL) red wine vinegar or tarragon vinegar

Salt and pepper to taste

1/4 tsp (1 mL) marjoram or basil

Method:

• Microwave the brown rice according to directions for brown rice in the Rice Cooking Chart.

• In a 4-cup (1 L) microwave-safe dish heat the oil 2 minutes at HIGH. Add the onion, green and red peppers. Stir — always with a fork in this recipe — until well coated with the oil. Microwave 4 minutes at MEDIUM-HIGH, stir well.

• Add the cooked brown rice and the remaining ingredients, stir again. Microwave 2 minutes at MEDIUM, stir. Adjust seasoning.

• Serve hot or at room temperature, but not refrigerated.

Summer Rice Salad

Preparation: . . . . 16 m
Cooking: . . . . from 14 to 16 m
Standing: . . . . none

A personal note: For me this salad is a summer-long pleasure, as it seems to be the perfect companion to all our summer foods. It's super with cold boiled salmon.

Ingredients:

1 cup (250 mL) long grain rice*, uncooked

2 raw carrots, peeled and grated

4 to 6 green onions, thinly sliced

1/4 cup (60 mL) parsley, chopped

1/2 cup (125 mL) celery and leaves, diced

1 cup (250 mL) green peas, cooked

Dressing:

1/2 tsp (2 mL) salt

1/4 tsp (1 mL) each pepper and dry mustard

A good pinch of sugar

2 tbsp (30 mL) cider or wine vinegar

4 tbsp (60 mL) oil of your choice

Method:

• Microwave rice according to the instructions for long grain rice in the Rice Cooking Chart. Cool.

• Cook and cool the green peas.

• Add to the cool rice the grated raw carrots, green onions, parsley, celery and leaves, and the cooked and cooled green peas.

• Blend together the ingredients for the dressing. Pour over the rice mixture, toss lightly with a fork. Place in a bowl.

• To taste, top with **a good spoonful of capers or 2 tablespoons (30 mL) of chopped nasturtium seeds****, or with nasturtium flowers, which are edible and have a very nice peppery flavor, or with **a good handful of minced lovage**, or a **handful of chopped walnuts**.

• All are very nice on this salad.

• This recipe yields 4 cups (1 L) of salad.

* Short grain rice can replace the long grain rice. Cook according to Rice Cooking Chart.

** Nasturtium seeds appear when the bloom falls. They may be kept in vinegar like pickles.

Helpful hint: To plump dried fruits: When a recipe (even one baked the conventional way) calls for dried fruits and nuts to be soaked 12 to 24 hours with a quantity of rum or brandy, use same quantity of fruits, nuts and rum or brandy. Mix in a large microwave-safe bowl. Microwave 5 minutes, covered, at MEDIUM. No amount of ordinary cooking can make them as moist or as tasty. I use this with all my favorite festive fruitcakes.

Kedgeree

• When the English were in India, Kedgeree became one of their favorite dishes. The English used long grain rice, although in Indian cuisine they prefer short grain rice. You will have to decide. This recipe was given to me by an English Canadian friend who made the best Kedgeree I ever tasted.

Ingredients:

1 cup (250 mL) long grain rice

6 hard boiled eggs

1 cup (250 mL) each milk and water

1/2 to 1 lb (250 to 500 g) smoked salmon

4 tbsp (60 mL) butter

Advance preparation:	. . . . **24 h**
Cooking:	. . . . **from 22 to 24 m**
Standing:	. . . . **none**

Method:

• The day before you're going to serve the Kedgeree, microwave rice according to basic instructions in the Rice Cooking Chart.

• Hard boil the eggs.

• Place fish in a microwave-safe dish, cover with milk and water. Cover and heat 4 minutes at HIGH. Let stand 15 minutes.

• Drain fish in colander 15 minutes. Break up in pieces and add to the rice.

• Chop the hard boiled eggs into small pieces and add to the rice and fish.

• Place the butter in a small microwave-safe dish and microwave 2 minutes at HIGH.

• Pour into the rice mixture and stir with two forks to blend. Add pepper to taste. Refrigerate overnight.

• To serve, lightly butter a microwave-safe dish. Pour in the rice and fish mixture.

• Cover with waxed paper. Microwave 8 minutes at MEDIUM, stir lightly with a fork.

• Adjust seasoning.

• If the rice is not hot enough, heat 2 minutes at a time at MEDIUM.

A personal note: 1 tablespoon (15 mL) of **chicken bouillon powder** and **2 tablespoons (30 mL) of butter** may be added to the rice before cooking.

wines

Gewurztraminer

Brut champagne

Chinese Fried Rice

Preparation: ....8 m
Cooking: ....from 3 to 4 m
Standing: ....none

A personal note: A quick lunch, Chinese Fried Rice is easy to make with leftover cooked rice and leftover cooked meat.

Ingredients:

4 tbsp (60 mL) vegetable oil or bacon fat

1 cup (250 mL) rice, cooked

4 green onions, chopped

1/2 tsp (2 mL) salt

1/2 to 1 cup (125 to 250 mL) cooked
    pork, veal or beef, thinly sliced

1 or 2 eggs

2 tbsp (30 mL) soy sauce

Method:

• I like to use a browning dish to make this dish in the microwave oven.

• Preheat a browning dish 6 minutes at HIGH.

• Add the oil or bacon fat, heat 2 minutes at HIGH.

• Add the rice, stir until well coated with the oil.

• Add the green onions, salt and meat of your choice. Stir well.

• Make a hole in the centre, break 1 or 2 eggs into the hole.

• Microwave 1 or 2 minutes* at MEDIUM, then stir the eggs into the rice and meat.

• Add the soy sauce, stir again.

• Microwave 2 minutes at MEDIUM. Stir and serve.

Microwave 1 minute for one egg and 2 minutes for 2 eggs.

wines

Gewurztraminer

Rhine Riesling Spätlese

Confetti Rice

Preparation:	10 m
Cooking:	10 m
Standing:	10 m

A personal note: This recipe is full of color and flavor. Any combination of fresh or leftover vegetables can be used. Confetti Rice is perfect with pork, veal or lamb. A special advantage is that it can be prepared hours ahead of time and reheated when ready to be served.

Ingredients:

2 cups (500 mL) boiling water

1 tsp (5 mL) salt

1 cup (250 mL) long grain rice

2 carrots, peeled and shredded

1/2 cup (125 mL) celery, finely diced

4 green onions, chopped fine

1 cup (250 mL) *or* 1/2 box frozen green peas *or* 1/4 cup (60 mL) green pepper, diced

1 tbsp (15 mL) butter or margarine

Fresh parsley, chives or dill to taste

Method:

• Place all the ingredients in an 8-cup (2 L) microwave-safe baking dish. Stir well.

• Cover and microwave 10 minutes at HIGH, stirring once.

• Check doneness and microwave one or two minutes more, if necessary.

• Let stand 10 minutes. Stir. Adjust seasoning. Serve.

Beaujolais

Chinon

My Own Wild Rice Chasseur

Preparation: . . . . .7 m
Cooking: . . . . .from 35 to 45 m
Standing: . . . . .none

A personal note: My mother made this casserole using brown rice and served it with roast wild duck or deer steak. I use wild rice and serve it with roast duck, beef or pork. If you prefer, you can use half wild rice, half brown rice, following the same directions.

wines

Pinot Blanc

Riesling

Ingredients:

1½ cups (375 mL) wild rice*, cooked

2 tbsp (30 mL) brandy

1 tsp (5 mL) curry powder

4 tbsp (60 mL) chutney of your choice

1/4 cup (60 mL) butter

Salt and pepper to taste

Or half wild rice and half brown rice

Method:

• Microwave 3/4 cup (190 mL) wild rice or half wild rice and half brown rice according to instructions for wild rice in the Rice Cooking Chart.

• Place in a microwave-safe dish the brandy, curry powder and chutney. Microwave 1 minute at MEDIUM.

• Add to the cooked wild rice. Stir well with a fork.

• Add the butter, salt and pepper to taste. Stir.

• When ready to serve, cover and microwave 4 minutes at MEDIUM.

Wild Rice
À la Ferguson

Convection cooking

• Many years ago, one of my friends gave me the recipe for this wild rice casserole, the best I have ever tasted. I consider it a great gift, since I am able to pass it on to many others. May it be your turn to enjoy it.

Ingredients:

1 cup (250 mL) wild rice

3 tbsp (50 mL) butter

1 medium-sized onion, chopped fine

2 celery stalks, diced

1/2 cup (125 mL) parsley, chopped

1/4 tsp (1 mL) thyme

3 medium carrots, grated

1 ½ cups (375 mL) chicken consommé

1 ½ cups (375 mL) Cheddar cheese, grated

2 tbsp (30 mL) butter, melted

Advance preparation : . . . . .2 h
Cooking : . . . . . .from 1 h 35 to 1 h 45 m
Standing : .none

Method:

• Wash the wild rice under cold running water. Spread on a towel and let dry for 2 hours.

• Microwave the rice according to directions for wild rice in the Rice Cooking Chart.

• Place butter in a 6-cup (1.5 L) microwave-safe dish. Melt 2 minutes at HIGH.

• Add the onion, stir well. Microwave 3 minutes at HIGH, stirring once after 2 minutes.

• Add the celery, parsley, thyme, carrots. Stir until well mixed.

• Butter an 8 × 8-inch (20 × 20 cm) or a 6-cup (1.5 L) microwave-safe baking dish. Fill with alternate layers of the cooked wild rice, vegetable mixture and grated cheese.

• Pour the chicken consommé over all. Cover with the dish lid or a piece of foil.

• Preheat the convection part of your microwave at 350°F (180°C). Bake the casserole for 1 hour. Serve.

A personal note : If you need your oven for other dishes to be cooked for the meal, bake the wild rice casserole first. Covered and set on a wooden board, it will remain hot for 35 to 45 minutes. Or bake it and keep on kitchen counter for an hour or two, then warm when ready to serve by covering with plastic wrap and heating in the microwave 8 minutes at MEDIUM-HIGH.

Red Burgundy

Côte de Beaune-Villages

Wild Rice Vegetable Casserole

A personal note: This casserole is super to serve as a luncheon casserole. All you will need to finish the meal is an interesting fruit dessert.

Preparation :	. . . .	15 m
Cooking :	. . . .	46 m
Standing :	. . . .	none

wines

White Bordeaux

White Graves

Ingredients:

1 cup (250 mL) wild rice

3 cups (750 mL) water

1 tsp (5 mL) salt

1/4 cup (60 mL) butter

1 large onion, chopped fine

1/2 lb (250 g) mushrooms, thinly sliced

1 cup (250 mL) carrots, peeled and shredded

1/4 tsp (1 mL) pepper

1 tsp (5 mL) salt

1/2 cup (125 mL) light cream

1 egg, lightly beaten

2 tbsp (30 mL) brandy

1/4 cup (60 mL) parsley, minced

Method:

• Wash the wild rice thoroughly. Place the water in an 8-cup (2 L) microwave-safe pan. Add the salt. Microwave 5 minutes at HIGH.

• Add the wild rice. Microwave 20 minutes at MEDIUM.

• Place the butter in a microwave-safe bowl and melt 2 minutes at HIGH. Add the chopped onion, stir. Microwave 2 minutes at HIGH.

• Add the mushrooms. Microwave 2 minutes at HIGH, stir.

• Add onion and mushrooms to the cooked wild rice, stir well with a fork.

• Add the shredded carrots, salt and pepper.

• Mix together the remaining ingredients. Stir into the cooked wild rice. Cover and microwave 20 minutes at MEDIUM. Adjust seasoning and serve.

My Four-Bowl Rice Cream

Preparation :	. . . .	**5 m**
Cooking :	. . . .	**13 m**
Standing :	. . . .	**none**

• Whenever I serve this dessert for a buffet, everyone comments on it and is intrigued with the four bowls of garnishes, which they can use one at a time or in any combination.

Ingredients :

1/4 cup (60 mL) short or long grain rice

2 cups (500 mL) light cream

2 egg yolks

4 tbsp (60 mL) sugar

1 tsp (5 mL) vanilla

2 egg whites

2 tbsp (30 mL) sugar

Method :

• Short grain rice gives a creamier pudding ; long grain gives a light pudding.

• Place the rice of your choice and cream in a large microwave-safe bowl.

• Microwave 10 minutes at MEDIUM-HIGH, stirring once.

• Beat the egg yolks with the 4 tablespoons (60 mL) sugar and the vanilla until light and foamy.

• Add to the cooked rice. Stir to mix thoroughly.

• Beat the egg whites with the 2 tablespoons (30 mL) sugar, fold into the cooked rice cream. Microwave 1 minute at MEDIUM. Stir well.

• Pour into an elegant serving dish and around it place four attractive bowls filled as follows :

Asti Spumante

Sauternes

Bowl I

• **Thinly sliced canned peaches**, drained and flavored with a **few spoonfuls of sherry or brandy**.

Bowl II

• Toasted slivered almonds, prepared as follows in the microwave oven: place **1/2 cup (125 mL) (or more, to your taste) of slivered almonds** in a bowl with **2 tablespoons (30 mL) of butter**. Microwave 1 to 2 minutes at HIGH. Stir well. They should be golden in color.

Bowl III

• **Shredded coconut**, sprinkled with a bit of **nutmeg**.

Bowl IV

• **Strawberry or raspberry jam.**

Sweet Rice

Preparation: . . . .**6 m**
Cooking: . . . . **from 27 to 30 m**
Standing: . . . .**none**

A personal note: Sweet Rice is a super break-fast cereal, with little work and a short cooking period. You can prepare it the day before and simply reheat it in a plate, 1 to 3 minutes at MEDIUM. As a dessert, serve it at room temperature topped with cream and maple syrup. As a variation, sprinkle top with chopped nuts of your choice or peeled and diced fresh fruit, such as peaches, pears, apples, oranges or pitted cherries.

wines

Sweet Anjou
Coteaux du Layon

Ingredients:

1/2 cup (125 mL) short grain rice

1½ cups (375 mL) milk

3 tbsp (50 mL) butter

4 tbsp (60 mL) sugar or brown or maple sugar

**1/4 tsp (1 mL) nutmeg or cinnamon *or*
   grated rind of 1 orange**

Method:

• Put the rice and the milk in a 4-cup (1 L) microwave-safe bowl. Cover and microwave 20 minutes at MEDIUM.

• Add the butter, sugar or brown or maple sugar, the spice of your choice or the orange rind.

• Stir well with a fork. Cover and microwave 5 to 8 minutes at MEDIUM.

• Stir with a fork when ready to serve. Equally good hot or cold

• To reheat, pour a spoonful or two of milk or cream over the rice. Do not stir. Cover and microwave 2 to 3 minutes, depending on the quantity, at MEDIUM.

Pasta

Italy and Pasta seem to be synonymous, since for centuries the Italians have been growing the right type of semolina flour needed to make pasta.

The Chinese, however, had made pasta for centuries before it was known to the Italians and the 13th century explorer Marco Polo brought back various types from his first trip to Egypt. Ravioli was eaten in Rome as early as 1284.

An amusing pasta fact is the importance in Northern China of preparing very long noodles, their length being a sign of longevity. They also make noodles from shrimp, rice, peas, corn and ming beans.

The Japanese are also enthusiastic noodlers, creating theirs from wheat, rice and buckwheat. Japanese noodles fall into two categories — **Udon** noodles and **Sôneb** (wheat flour noodles) and **Soba** noodles, eaten cold in the summer and so delicious. Japanese noodles are delicate, with a gentle flavor. They are excellent if you are on a diet as they are low in calories.

The Japanese also make **Green Tea Leaf** noodles and **Green Spinach** noodles, unusual textures and tastes make them well worth the effort of searching for.

To buy pasta

• Basically, all pasta is made in the same way, although each type is different and permits many variations.

• Any type of pasta can substitute for the one called for in a recipe.

• Pasta comes mostly in 500 g packages which are the most economical and practical size to buy, since pasta has a long shelf life and is always ready for a quickly prepared meal.

To peel and seed tomatoes

• Many pasta tomato sauce recipes call for the tomatoes to be peeled. Here is the easy way to do it.

• Bring some water to boil. It takes 5 minutes at HIGH to boil 4 cups (1 L) of water.

• Drop tomatoes two at a time into the boiling water. Let stand about 10 seconds.

• Remove from the boiling water and cool under run-

ning cold water to stop the cooking and facilitate handling.

• Cut off the stem with a sharp, pointed, vegetable knife and peel off the skin.

• Cut the peeled tomato in half and scoop out the seeds carefully with your fingers. (The seeds give the tomatoes an acid flavor.)

• The tomatoes are now ready to use as the recipe demands.

690

Pasta Cooking Chart

Pasta	Container	Amount of hot water	Approx. time to boil water at HIGH (in minutes)	Approx. time to cook pasta at HIGH (in minutes)	Stand time (in minutes)
Vermicelli 8 oz (250 g)	12-cup (3 L) casserole	6-cup (1,5 L)	7 to 8	4 to 5	3
Egg noodles medium width 8 oz (250 g)	12-cup (3 L) casserole	6 cups (1.5 L)	7 to 8	5 to 6	3
Elbow macaroni 8 oz (250 g)	12-cup (3 L) casserole	6 cups (1.5 L)	7 to 8	7 to 8	3
Lasagne noodles Long or square 8 oz (250 g)	12 × 8-inch (30 × 20 cm) baking dish	6 cups (1.5 L)	7 to 8	13 to 15	3
Spaghetti 8 oz (250 g)	12 × 8-inch (30 × 20 cm) baking dish	8 cups (2 L)	8 to 9	7 to 8	3
Specialty noodles Bows, shells, etc. 8 oz (250 g)	12-cup (3 L) casserole	6 cups (1.5 L)	7 to 8	10½ to 11	3

Basic way to work with pasta

• Follow directions given above for recommended dish size, amount of water and cooking time.

• Add pasta to boiling water, with **1 teaspoon (5 mL) salt** and **1 tablespoon (15 mL) oil**.

• Microwave, covered, at HIGH. Stir twice.

• Test pasta for doneness and, if necessary, add a little more time.

• Stir cover and let stand 3 minutes. Drain, if necessary.

• If necessary to reheat after standing time, cover and microwave 1 or 2 minutes at MEDIUM-HIGH.

Monique's Fifteen-Year Pasta

Convection cooking

A personal note: My daughter Monique gave all kinds of amusing names to her creations. Quickly prepared, her Fifteen-Year Pasta has particular characteristics — the taste of sharp, top-quality Cheddar cheese and basil.

Preparation:	. . . .**20 m**
Cooking:	. . . .**from 50 to 60**
Standing:	. . . .**none**

Ingredients:

8 oz (250 g) elbow or other macaroni

1 tbsp (15 mL) vegetable oil

1 19-oz (540 mL) can tomatoes

1 tbsp (15 mL) basil

1 tsp (5 mL) sugar

Salt and pepper to taste

1 to 2 cups (250 - 500 g) strong Cheddar cheese, diced*

2 eggs, beaten

1 cup (250 mL) milk

* Use more or less cheese according to your taste.

Method:

• Microwave macaroni according to the Pasta Cooking Chart.

• Drain. To the cooked macaroni add the oil, stir with a fork until well blended.

• Place in buttered 8 × 8-inch (20 × 20 cm) or 6-cup (1.5 L) microwave-safe dish.

• Add the tomatoes, basil, sugar, salt and pepper. Mix the whole with a fork. Stir in the cheese.

• Stir together the beaten eggs and the milk and pour over the macaroni and cheese.

• Preheat the convection part of your microwave oven at 350°F (180°C).

• Set the prepared dish in the oven.

• Bake 40 to 45 minutes, or until golden brown on top.

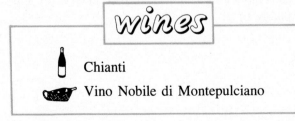

wines

Chianti

Vino Nobile di Montepulciano

Tomato and Cheese Macaroni

Microwave or convection cooking

Preparation : . . . . **15 m**
Cooking : microwave : . . . . **from 15 to 20 m**
        convection : . . . . **from 35 to 40 m**
Standing : . . . . **none**

A personal note : Pour this tasty sauce over cooked macaroni, noodles or any other pasta of your choice. There is enough sauce for 1/2 a pound (250 g) of cooked pasta. Enjoy !

Red Rhône

Châteauneuf-du-Pape

Ingredients :

1 28-oz (796 mL) can tomatoes

1 tsp (5 mL) sugar

1 tsp (5 mL) dry mustard

1/2 tsp (2 mL) pepper

1/2 tsp (2 mL) each savory and thyme

1 tsp (5 mL) paprika

1/2 cup (125 mL) celery leaves, minced

1/2 cup (125 mL) tomato paste

1/2 lb (250 g) macaroni, cooked

1 cup (250 mL) cheese of your choice, grated

1/3 cup (80 mL) fine breadcrumbs

A few spoonfuls of butter or margarine

Method :

• Butter an 8-cup (2 L) microwave-safe casserole or brush with oil.

• Mix together the tomatoes, sugar, dry mustard, pepper, savory, thyme, paprika, celery leaves and tomato paste.

• Make alternate layers of the tomato mixture, the cooked macaroni and the grated cheese.

• Sprinkle with the breadcrumbs and dot with butter to taste. Cover dish with waxed paper.

• Microwave 15 to 20 minutes at MEDIUM. Or pre-heat the convection part of your microwave at 350°F (180°C).

• Set prepared dish in the oven and bake 35 to 40 minutes, or until top is golden brown.

Cottage Cheese Macaroni

Microwave and convection cooking

A personal note: I like to use elbow macaroni to make this casserole. If you prefer another type of pasta, simply use an equal quantity. In summer, I use fresh chives and basil from my herb garden.

Ingredients:

4 cups (1 L) water

1 medium-sized onion, peeled and cut in two

1 tsp (5 mL) salt

2 cups (500 mL) elbow macaroni

2 eggs

1 cup (250 mL) milk

1½ cups (375 mL) cottage cheese

1/4 cup (60 mL) parsley or chives, chopped fine

2 tbsp (30 mL) soft butter

1/4 tsp (1 mL) salt

1/4 tsp (1 mL) pepper

1/2 tsp (2 mL) sweet basil or oregano

Preparation: . . . . **12 m**

Cooking: . . . . **from 48 to 50 m**

Standing: . . . . **none**

wines

Australian Chardonnay

Dry Vouvray

Method:

• Place in a large microwave-safe bowl the water, onion and the teaspoon of salt. Microwave 10 minutes at HIGH.

• Add the macaroni, stir. Microwave 12 to 14 minutes at HIGH.

• Strain into a fine sieve. Set aside.

• Beat the eggs until light. Add the milk and cottage cheese. Mix together with a fork and add the remaining ingredients.

• Add to the macaroni, stir until the whole is well mixed.

• Pour into a well-buttered baking dish.

• Preheat the convection part of your microwave oven at 350°F (180°C). Place the dish in the oven.

• Bake, uncovered, 35 minutes, or until golden brown here and there. Serve warm or at room temperature, but not refrigerated.

Milanese Macaroni

Preparation: . . . . **10 m**
Cooking: . . . . **from 17 to 18 m**
Standing: . . . . **10 m**

A personal note: In Milan, this macaroni is accompanied by a green salad or a bowl of cooked shrimp, served cold in their shells. The shrimp are shelled at the table and eaten with spoonfuls of hot macaroni.

Ingredients:

1 cup (250 mL) macaroni
1 cup (250 mL) Cheddar cheese, grated
1/2 tsp (2 mL) dry mustard
1/4 tsp (1 mL) fresh ground pepper
1 cup (250 mL) milk
1/2 cup (125 mL) cream of your choice

Method:

• Microwave the macaroni according to the Pasta Cooking Chart.

• Mix together the cheese, mustard and pepper.

• Butter an 8 × 8-inch (20 × 20 cm) microwave-safe baking dish and fill with layers of macaroni and cheese mixture. Pour the milk and cream over all, mix well.

• You may, to taste, sprinkle with either paprika, finely minced chives, 3 to 4 minced green onions or fresh minced parsley. Microwave, uncovered, 10 minutes at MEDIUM.

• Let stand 10 minutes before serving.

wines

Chianti
Château-bottled Saint-Émilion

Sour Cream Macaroni

Preparation: . . . . **12 m**
Cooking: . . . . **from 15 to 18 m**
Standing: . . . . **none**

A personal note: This dish is a meal-in-one, although you may want to add a salad or a cooked vegetable served cold with French dressing.

Ingredients:

2 cups (500 mL) macaroni
1 cup (250 mL) Cheddar cheese, grated
1 cup (250 mL) cottage cheese
1/2 cup (125 mL) sour cream or plain yogurt
Salt and pepper to taste
4 green onions, minced
Parsley, minced (to taste)
2 tbsp (30 mL) butter

Method:

• Microwave the macaroni according to the Pasta Cooking Chart.

• Mix together the Cheddar and cottage cheese.

• Butter an 8 × 8-inch (20 × 20 cm) microwave-safe baking dish. Put half the cooked macaroni in it and sprinkle with half the cheese.

• Repeat with the remaining macaroni and cheese.

• Mix together the sour cream or yogurt, salt, pepper and green onions. To taste, add minced parsley.

• Dot with butter. Spread over the macaroni.

• Microwave, uncovered, 8 to 10 minutes at MEDIUM.

wines

Red Burgundy
Oregon Pinot Noir

Old-Fashioned Macaroni

Microwave or convection cooking

| Preparation : . . . .**30 m** |
| Cooking : microwave : . . . .**from 15 to 18 m** |
| convection : . . . .**38 m** |
| Standing : . . . .**none** |

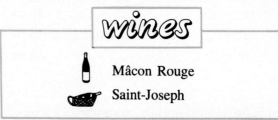

Mâcon Rouge
Saint-Joseph

A personal note : This dish is especially good when baked by convection. Do not let its simplicity stop you from making it. You will be surprised at the results. I sometimes mix in bits and pieces of leftover cheese.

Ingredients :

8 oz (250 g) macaroni of your choice

1/2 lb (250 g) strong Cheddar cheese or any other type of cheese, grated

1 cup (250 mL) sour cream

3 tbsp (50 mL) butter

Paprika to taste

Method :

• Microwave macaroni according to the Pasta Cooking Chart.

• Butter a 6-cup (1.5 L) microwave-safe baking dish. Place half the cooked macaroni in the dish, sprinkle with half the cheese, top with half the sour cream and dot with half the butter.

• Repeat with remaining ingredients. Sprinkle with paprika. Microwave, uncovered, 8 to 10 minutes at MEDIUM.

• Or preheat the convection part of your microwave at 350°F (180°C).

• Set prepared macaroni dish in the oven and bake 20 to 30 minutes, or until top is golden.

Delight of the Sea Macaroni Salad

Preparation: . . . . .15 m
Cooking: . . . . .from 7 to 8 m
Standing: .none

A personal note: Whether made with canned, fresh or leftover fish, this salad is always interesting, particularly as a buffet dish.

Ingredients:

2 cups (500 mL) macaroni, cooked

1 to 2 cups (250 to 500 mL) cooked or canned fish, flaked*

1 green pepper, diced

1 small red pepper, slivered (optional)

1/2 cup (125 mL) celery, diced

3/4 cup (190 mL) sour cream

2 tbsp (30 mL) light cream or milk

Juice of 1/2 a lemon

1 tbsp (15 mL) fresh dill, chopped *or* 1 tsp (5 mL) dried dill

* Use canned tuna or lobster or a cooked fish of your choice or well-drained canned clams, using the liquid as part of the water to cook the macaroni.

Method:

• Microwave the elbow macaroni according to the Pasta Cooking Chart. Drain and cool.

• Place cooked macaroni in a bowl. Add the flaked fish, green and red pepper and diced celery. Stir the whole with a fork.

• Blend the remaining ingredients, then mix with the macaroni mixture. Toss lightly. Serve in a nest of lettuce or surround with watercress.

• In summer, I sometimes use the mixture to stuff fresh tomatoes.

• Do not refrigerate but keep in a cool place until ready to serve.

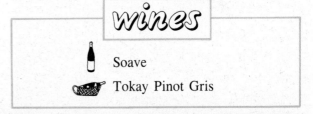

Soave

Tokay Pinot Gris

Macaroni Salad
À la Vinaigrette

Preparation : . . . . **15 m**
Cooking : . . . . **from 7 to 8 m**
Standing : . . . . **none**

A personal note : This salad is attractive served in a nest of lettuce or watercress. Decorate the whole with cherry tomatoes.

Ingredients :

2 cups (500 mL) macaroni, cooked
1 small yellow onion, diced
1/3 cup (80 mL) fresh parsley, minced
1 cucumber, peeled and diced

Dressing :*

1/3 cup (80 mL) oil of your choice
1/4 cup (60 mL) fresh lemon juice
1/4 tsp (1 mL) sugar
1/4 tsp (1 mL) pepper
1 garlic clove, split in half
1/4 tsp (1 mL) dry mustard
1 tsp (5 mL) salt

* This dressing will keep for 2 to 3 months at room temperature. Shake well before using. Yield : 1 cup (250 mL).

Method :

• Place all the dressing ingredients in a jar. Shake thoroughly before using.

• Microwave the macaroni of your choice according to the Pasta Cooking Chart. Cool.

• To cool macaroni add the diced onion, parsley and cucumber. Mix lightly with two forks.

• Shake prepared dressing and add as much as you like to the macaroni mixture. Toss well and place in a nest of greens. Do not refrigerate as the salad will loose much of its quality.

• When tossed with the dressing, this salad will keep 4 to 6 hours at room temperature and will be even tastier for it.

Noodle and Cottage Cheese Casserole

Preparation :	. . . . **8 m**
Cooking :	. . . . **from 5 to 6 m**
Standing :	. . . . **none**

A personal note : This most tasty casserole can easily be prepared in the morning and warmed up for dinner, without losing any of its flavor. Serve with a green salad or a thinly sliced tomato salad.

wines

Italian Chardonnay
White Burgundy

Ingredients :

2 cups (500 mL) noodles of your choice

3/4 cup (190 mL) plain yogurt or sour cream

1 cup (250 mL) cottage cheese

3 tbsp (50 mL) butter or margarine

Salt and pepper to taste

1/3 cup (80 mL) parsley, chopped

3 to 4 green onions, chopped fine

1 egg, lightly beaten

Method :

• Microwave the noodles in boiling water, according to the Pasta Cooking Chart. Drain.

• Mix the cooked noodles in a large bowl with all the remaining ingredients. Toss together with a fork.

• In summer, serve at room temperature with a green salad.

• To serve hot, pour into a microwave-safe well-buttered dish, microwave 10 minutes at MEDIUM. If not hot enough, microwave another 4 to 5 minutes.

• Depending on the type of noodles used, a little more cooking may be required to make them piping hot.

Alfredo's Pasta

• Alfredo is one of the famous restaurants in Italy and its special way of serving pasta is world-renowned. Do not let the simplicity of the dish fool you; the taste is wonderful.

Preparation: . . . .**5 m**
Cooking: . . . .**from 6 to 7 m**
Standing: . . . .**none**

Ingredients:

1/2 lb (250 g) fine egg noodles

3/4 cup (190 mL) butter, unsalted

1 cup (250 mL) Parmesan cheese, grated

Salt and pepper to taste

Chianti

Brunello di Montalcino

Method:

• Microwave the noodles according to the Pasta Cooking Chart. Drain.

• Place the cooked noodles in a warm dish.

• Slice the butter over the noodles, microwave 30 seconds at HIGH. Stir to mix the butter.

• Add the grated Parmesan, salt and pepper to taste. Stir again.

• You will have a creamy sauce around the noodles.

• Serve at once.

700

Côte d'Azur Noodles

Preparation : . . . .**10 m**
Cooking : . . . .**from 13 to 14 m**
Standing : . . . .**none**

• Pasta of all kinds is very popular in the south of France. This recipe is one of my favorites. It's quickly prepared and can be served with any type of pasta.

Ingredients :

5 cups (1.25 L) cold water

3 cups (750 mL) medium-sized pasta bows*

1 tsp (5 mL) salt

3/4 cup (190 mL) cooked chicken cut into match sticks

3/4 cup (190 mL) fresh mushrooms, thinly sliced

1/2 cup (125 mL) whipping cream

1/2 cup (125 mL) Parmesan cheese, grated

* Or any other type of pasta.

Barbaresco

Châteauneuf-du-Pape

Method :

• Place the cold water in an 8-cup (2 L) microwave-safe bowl. Microwave 8 minutes at HIGH.

• Add the pasta and the salt, stir. Microwave 10 minutes at MEDIUM. Drain.

• Add the remaining ingredients to the hot pasta. Stir well with a fork. Cover and microwave 3 minutes at MEDIUM. Stir again and serve.

Chopped Beef Noodle Casserole

Preparation: ....15 m
Cooking: ....from 32 to 33 m
Standing:.....................none

A personal note: This casserole will give you 10 servings. I make the whole recipe, then divide it in two — one half to serve, the other half to freeze. I then have an emergency casserole that can go from the freezer to my microwave oven. It takes about 10 minutes at DEFROST to thaw, 10 minutes at MEDIUM-HIGH to heat up.

Ingredients:

2 tbsp (30 mL) butter or margarine

1 large onion, peeled and chopped

1 cup (250 mL) celery, diced

1 large garlic clove, chopped fine

1 lb (500 g) ground beef

1   10-oz (284 mL) can sliced mushrooms, undrained

1   7½-oz (213 mL) can tomato sauce

1/2 cup (125 mL) chicken consommé or water

1 tsp (5 mL) salt

Pepper to taste

Grated rind of 1 lemon

1 tsp (5 mL) lemon juice

8 oz (250 g) egg noodles

1 cup (250 mL) Cheddar cheese, grated

Method:

• Microwave noodles according to Pasta Cooking Chart.

• Combine butter or margarine and onion in a large microwave-safe casserole. Microwave at HIGH 1 minute, stir. Add the celery and garlic. Microwave at HIGH 1 minute. Stir well.

• Add crumbled ground beef, stir to mix. Microwave at HIGH 5 minutes. Stir well.

• Add the remaining ingredients except the cheese. Mix thoroughly. Cover and microwave at HIGH 10 minutes, stir.

• Add the cheese, stir until well blended. Microwave at MEDIUM 10 minutes. Serve.

Beaujolais-Villages

Chianti Classico Riserva

Rice and Noodle Pilaff

Preparation : .3 m
Cooking : . . . . .from 6 to 8 m
Standing : . . . . .none

A personal note : Fine noodles and quick cooking rice combine in a tasty casserole that can be served with roast chicken or pork and is also elegant served as a vegetarian dish for a buffet or a light lunch. This pilaff is a classic of Armenian cuisine.

Ingredients :

4 tbsp (60 mL) butter or margarine

1/2 cup (125 mL) fine noodles or
  small pasta shells

1 cup (250 mL) quick cooking rice

1 tsp (5 mL) salt

2 cups (500 mL) chicken broth or water, hot

Method :

• Place the butter or margarine in a 4-cup (1 L) microwave-safe dish and melt 3 minutes at HIGH.

• Add the fine noodles or pasta shells and the quick cooking rice. Stir together until both are well buttered.

• Add the salt and the hot chicken broth or water. Stir. Microwave, uncovered, 6 minutes at HIGH.

• Depending on the type of pasta used, it is sometimes necessary to microwave 1 or 2 minutes more or less.

• This is a basic recipe that lends itself to many variations.

Variation 1 :

• Add to the cooked pilaff **1 cup (250 mL) more or less of canned peas.**

• I use the water drained from the peas as part of the liquid to cook the pilaff.

Variation 2 :

• Dice an **unpeeled tomato**, sprinkle with **a good pinch of sugar and basil**.

• Microwave 1 minute at HIGH. Add to pilaff when adding the butter.

• Stir well and finish cooking as in the recipe.

Variation 3 :

• Slice thinly **1/2 pound (250 g) fresh mushrooms** and **2 green onions**.

• Melt **1 tablespoon (15 mL) butter** in a dish. Add the mushrooms and green onions. Stir well.

• Microwave 1 minute at HIGH. Pour over the rice and noodle pilaff just before cooking it. Stir well.

• Microwave according to time given for pilaff.

A personal note : When **chives** and **parsley** are readily available in summer, **add 1/4 cup (60 mL)** of each to the hot pasta. Stir with a fork until well blended.

Italian Chardonnay

White Burgundy

Barley Pilaff

Preparation : . . . . .12 m
Cooking : . . . . .22 m
Standing : . . . . .none

A personal note: This is a most convenient dish. It can be served successfully with chicken, goose, duck or lamb and it is delicious served with nothing but a green salad. You can prepare the pilaff early in the day, let it stand covered on the kitchen counter, and reheat it 5 minutes at MEDIUM just before serving.

wines

Mâcon Rouge

Old Barolo

Ingredients :

1 ¾ cups (440 mL) barley

4 tbsp (60 mL) butter

2 onions, minced

1/2 lb (250 g) mushrooms, chopped

3 ½ cups (875 mL) consommé

1/2 tsp (2 mL) salt

Method :

• Place 2 tablespoons (30 mL) of the butter in a microwave-safe bowl and melt 1 minute at HIGH.

• Add the onions and mushrooms and microwave 1 minute at HIGH.

• Remove onions and mushrooms from butter, draining them well, and place in a microwave-safe baking dish.

• Add the remaining 2 tablespoons (30 mL) of butter to the melted butter and microwave 1 minute at HIGH.

• Stir in the barley. Microwave 1 minute at HIGH, stir. Add the barley to the onions and mushrooms together with the consommé and salt, stir. Cover and microwave 20 minutes at MEDIUM, stirring midway through the cooking.

• Add a little hot water, if necessary.

Leeks and Shells
À la Parisienne

Preparation : . . . . .10 m
Cooking : . . . . .12 m
Standing : . . . . .none

• All over France during mid-summer, when fresh leeks are at their luscious best, the French make a very simple leek sauce to pour over hot noodles and serve with grated Swiss cheese.

Ingredients :

3 to 4 leeks

1/3 cup (80 mL) butter

Salt and pepper to taste

3 cups (750 mL) small egg noodle shells*

Cheese of your choice, grated

* The shells and leeks can be cooked a few hours ahead of time, stirred together, covered and warmed up 4 minutes at MEDIUM-HIGH when ready to serve. Stir well after 2 minutes of cooking.

Method :

• Clean leeks and cut them, the white and most of the green, in 1/2-inch (1 cm) lengths.

• Place the butter in a 6-cup microwave-safe dish and melt 3 minutes at HIGH.

• Add the leeks, stir until well buttered. Let stand.

• To cook the small egg noodle shells, measure 6 cups (1.5 L) water in a large microwave-safe dish. Microwave 6 minutes at HIGH.

• Add the noodles. Microwave 5 minutes at HIGH.

• Drain, add to the melted leeks. Stir well.

• Add salt and pepper to taste. Microwave 1 minute at HIGH.

• Serve as soon as ready with a bowl of grated cheese.

wines

German Riesling (dry)

Tokay Pinot Gris

Pasta Salad
À la Capri

Advance preparation : . . . . .**from 1 to 2 h**
Cooking : . . . .**from 4 to 5 m**
Standing : . . . .**none**

• This is a perfect salad in summer, when tomatoes and basil are abundant and fragrant. In Capri, Italy, it is referred to as Penne à la Capresa. It is a great summer delight to serve this uncooked cold sauce over hot pasta. Try it. It is a delightful experience.

Ingredients :

4 large tomatoes

3 tbsp (50 mL) fresh basil leaves *or*
   2 tsp (10 mL) basil leaves, dried

2 garlic cloves, chopped fine

1/2 tsp (2 mL) sugar

Salt and pepper to taste

A few spoonfuls of olive oil*

1 lb (500 g) vermicelli

1 cup (250 mL) cheese, grated**

* Or any oil of your choice.

** I prefer fresh-grated Mozzarella cheese, but you can use whatever cheese you prefer. My second choice is a good mild Cheddar.

Method :

• Peel and dice the tomatoes into 1/2-inch (1.25 cm) pieces.

• Place in a bowl and add the basil, garlic, sugar, salt and pepper. Mix gently, add the olive oil.

• Leave on kitchen counter to marinate for 1 to 2 hours. The flavors will mix and juice will form.

• When ready to serve, cook vermicelli according to Pasta Cooking Chart. Drain well.

• Pour into a serving bowl and add the tomato mixture, stir to mix.

• Top with the grated cheese. Serve cooked vermicelli as soon as ready.

Valpolicella

Amarone

Summer Stars

• This recipe gets its name because it is prepared with tiny star pasta and summer fresh parsley. I like to serve Summer Stars when the parsley in my garden is in full bloom. Excellent served as a side dish.

Preparation: .8 m
Cooking: . . . . .from 6 to 7 m
Standing: . . . . .none

Ingredients:

1/2 cup (125 mL) each butter and margarine

1 large garlic clove, chopped fine

1 cup (250 mL) fresh parsley, chopped

1/2 cup (125 mL) Parmesan cheese, grated

2 or 3 cups (500 or 750 mL) stars or any
   small pasta of your choice

Chianti

Brunello di Montalcino

Method:

• Place the butter and margarine in a microwave-safe bowl. Microwave 2 minutes at HIGH.

• Add the garlic, microwave another minute at HIGH.

• Add the parsley and the cheese. Stir to mix. Set aside.

• Place 4 cups (1 L) water in a microwave-safe bowl and bring to a boil, 5 minutes at HIGH. Add the pasta.

• Cover and microwave 6 to 7 minutes at HIGH. Let stand until ready to serve.

• It will remain hot for 10 to 15 minutes.

• Drain pasta if necessary, add to the cheese mixture. Stir well and serve.

Monique's Meatless Lasagne

Microwave and convection cooking

Preparation : .20 m
Cooking : . . . .**from 1 h 30 to 1 h 40**
Standing : . . . .**none**

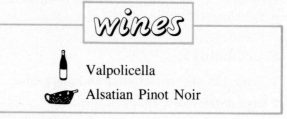

Valpolicella

Alsatian Pinot Noir

A personal note : This large recipe serves 10 to 12. For smaller numbers, you can make it in two dishes, freeze one and serve the other. Use the frozen one within 6 to 8 weeks. A large microwave-safe bowl is required to cook the noodles or you can cook them in two batches. The recipe includes instructions for making the lasagne.

Ingredients :

12 cups (3 L) water

1 tbsp (15 mL) salt

1 tbsp (15 mL) vegetable oil

1 box (500 g) lasagne noodles

2 lb (1 kg) cottage cheese

1 cup (250 mL) sour cream

2 eggs

1/2 tsp (2 mL) each pepper and oregano

Salt to taste

1 lb (500 g) Mozzarella cheese, thinly sliced

3 tbsp (50 mL) vegetable oil

2 large onions, chopped fine

1/4 cup (60 mL) celery, diced

1 28-oz (796 mL) can tomatoes

2 6-oz (260 mL) cans tomato paste

1/4 tsp (1 mL) pepper

1 tsp (5 mL) basil

2 tsp (10 mL) sugar

2 10-oz (384 mL) cans mushroom stems and pieces

For a lasagne with meat

1½ lb (750 g) ground beef

Method :

• Pour water into a large microwave-safe bowl, add the salt and the vegetable oil. Microwave at HIGH 10 to 12 minutes.

• Place lasagne noodles one by one into the water. Microwave at HIGH 10 minutes. Test for tenderness with a fork or the point of a knife. Depending on the brand, it could take 5 to 9 minutes more for the lasagne to become tender. Place the container in the sink and let cold water run into it until the noodles have cooled. Drain.

• Meanwhile, mix the cottage cheese, sour cream, eggs, pepper and oregano with salt to taste.

• Butter a large oblong baking dish or two 8 × 8-inch (20 × 20 cm) microwave-safe dishes. Separate the slices of Mozzarella cheese.

• Microwave 2 tablespoons (30 mL) of the oil in a microwave-safe dish 4 minutes at HIGH.

• Add the onions and the celery. Microwave 2 minutes at HIGH, stir well. Microwave 2 minutes more at HIGH. The onions should be golden brown here and there.

• Strain the tomatoes to remove the seeds, pressing the pulp through the sieve. Add tomato pulp and juice to the onions and celery, stir. Add the tomato paste, pepper, basil and sugar.

To make a lasagne with meat

• When using ground meat, heat the remaining tablespoon of vegetable oil in a microwave-safe dish 1 minute at HIGH.

• Add the ground beef to the hot oil. Salt and pepper to taste. Microwave 2 minutes at MEDIUM-HIGH, stir well with a fork to break up the meat. Microwave another 2 minutes at MEDIUM-HIGH.

• Add to the onion and celery mixture. Add the mushrooms. Adjust seasoning.

To prepare the lasagne

• Place a layer of the cooked noodles in long strips to cover the bottom of the dish. Top with a layer of the creamed cheese mixture, then the slices of Mozzarella, then the sauce. Repeat these four layers until dish is filled, ending with noodles, sauce and a topping of sliced cheese.

• Preheat the convection part of your oven at 325°F (160°C). Whatever the size of the dish, bake, uncovered, for 1 hour 15 minutes per dish.

• If prepared ahead of time, when ready to serve place the lasagne on a rack in the microwave oven and reheat 10 minutes at MEDIUM for each dish. Serve.

Lasagne Italiano

Microwave or convection cooking

Preparation: ....40 m
Cooking: microwave: ...from 1 h 13 to 1 h 23
         convection: ...from 1 h 23 to 1 h 33
Standing: ....none

• A famous Italian chef from Florence taught me how to make this lasagne. Since then I have tried many recipes, but none was ever better. It is easily prepared in the microwave oven.

A personal note: The recipe makes 5 to 6 servings. For enough lasagne to serve 10 to 12 portions, make the recipe twice in two separate dishes. I like to prepare mine in the morning, microwave both of them and keep the cooked dishes covered at room temperature.

To warm, cover top of first dish with waxed paper, microwave 15 minutes at MEDIUM. While serving it, warm the second dish in the same way.

For a large party, I prepare 4 to 6 recipes of baked lasagne in separate dishes. I warm up one while serving the other. It works very well.

Ingredients:

1. The sauce:

1/4 cup (60 mL) oil of your choice

1 large onion, peeled and chopped fine

1 to 3 garlic cloves, chopped fine

1 28-oz (796 mL) can tomatoes

1/4 cup (60 mL) fresh parsley, minced

1 tsp (5 mL) basil

1 tsp (5 mL) thyme

1 5½-oz (156 mL) can tomato paste

1 tbsp (15 mL) sugar

Salt and pepper to taste

2. The meat mixture:

1/2 lb (250 g) each beef and pork, minced

1/3 cup (80 mL) parsley, minced

1 tsp (5 mL) oregano or savory

2 eggs, lightly beaten

3 tbsp (50 mL) cheese, grated

Salt and pepper to taste

3. The pasta:

1 lb (500 g) mini or long lasagne

8 cups (2 L) water

2 tbsp (30 mL) salt

1 tbsp (15 mL) vegetable oil

4. The cheese:

1/2 lb (250 g) Mozzarella cheese, thinly sliced

1 lb (500 g) cottage cheese

2 tbsp (30 mL) hot water

1/2 cup (125 mL) Parmesan, grated

Method:

1. To cook the sauce

• Heat the oil in a 4-cup (1 L) microwave-safe dish 2 minutes at HIGH.

• Add the onion and garlic, stir well. Microwave 3 minutes at MEDIUM-HIGH. Add the can of tomatoes and the remaining ingredients.

2. To cook the meat mixture

• In another bowl mix the minced beef and the minced pork.

• Add the parsley, oregano or savory, the lightly beaten eggs, the grated cheese, salt and pepper to taste. Pour into the tomato sauce, mix thoroughly. Cover, microwave 20 minutes at MEDIUM.

3. To cook the pasta

• Measure the water in a 10 to 12-cup (2.5 - 3 L) microwave-safe dish. Microwave 20 minutes at HIGH; the water must boil rapidly.

• Add the salt and oil. Put in the lasagne.

• When using the long, wide lasagne, place them one at a time in the water. As each one softens, add another one until you have used the pound (500 g).

• Do not cover. Microwave at MEDIUM-HIGH 15 to 20 minutes. Check the tenderness of the pasta after 15 minutes. If necessary, give it another 5 minutes. Drain thoroughly.

4. To cook the lasagne

• Oil a 10 × 10-inch (25 × 25 cm) Pyrex or Corning dish.

• Place 6 to 7 tablespoons (90 - 105 mL) of the sauce (1) in the bottom of the dish.

• Cover with a layer of cooked lasagne, top with thin slices of Mozzarella.

• Mix the cottage cheese with the hot water, spread a layer of it on the Mozzarella cheese.

• Then spoon 1/4 of the sauce over the cottage cheese.

• Repeat until all of the ingredients have been used. Sprinkle top with the grated Parmesan. Let stand until ready to serve. Microwave 15 minutes at MEDIUM and serve. Or, if you wish to brown the top, preheat the convection part of your microwave oven 10 minutes at 350°F (180°C).

• Set the prepared lasagne in the oven. Bake 20 to 30 minutes and serve.

Chianti

Brunello di Montalcino

Japanese Noodles

- In Japan, "menrui" or noodles are eaten winter and summer.

- They are served either very hot in special broths or very cold with different types of dipping sauces and garnishes.

- There are different types of Japanese noodles and all are available in our part of the world in shops specializing in Japanese food.

The Udon type noodles

- The udon medium-sized wheat noodle type are slim, white or wholewheat noodles that cook in a minute or two in boiling liquid, to be served over hot vegetables. They are superb with chicken.

The Hiyamugi type noodles

- Hiyamugi noodles are usually served cold on a bed of finely crushed ice, with a cold dipping sauce.

- I love the cold noodles with steamed shrimp or scallops, served either hot or cold. I also enjoy them topped with chopped cold hard-boiled eggs.

- If you wish to serve a choice of flavoring or seasoning with any type of cooked Japanese noodles, peel and grate fresh ginger to taste.

Add to chopped green onions with roast chicken or seafood.

Add to toasted sesame seeds with lamb stew or roast.

Add to chopped watercress with steak

Add to chopped watercress tossed with **1 tablespoon of salad oil** with fish.

- With all types of cooked chicken, toss with fine cooked noodles **grated ginger to taste** and **2 tablespoons (30 mL) of Sake** (rice wine). Instead of Sake, I like to use Mirin, which is a sweet rice wine, also available in Japanese food shops.

- It's super served with cooked shrimp and Japanese soy sauce, the best one being Kikkoman soy sauce.

Fried Noodles (Yakisoba)

Preparation : . . . . .10 m
Cooking : .6 m
Standing : . . . . .none

A personal note : Cabbage and cooked ham combine with fried noodles to make an interesting meal for family or guests. A fried egg can top each portion of noodles before serving.

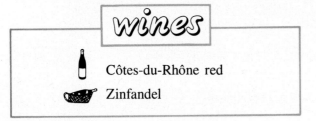

Côtes-du-Rhône red

Zinfandel

Ingredients :

8 oz (250 g) small egg noodles*

6 cups (1.5 L) water

3 tbsp (50 mL) vegetable oil

Salt and pepper to taste

3 cups (750 mL) cabbage, finely shredded

2 thin slices of cooked ham

1 medium-sized onion, thinly sliced

1 small green pepper, cut into small strips

Sauce :

1/4 cup (60 mL) ketchup or chili sauce

2 tbsp (30 mL) HP Sauce

There are different types of small egg noodles to choose from.

Method :

• Bring the water to boil, about 10 minutes at HIGH. Place the noodles gently into the water. Microwave 3 minutes at HIGH. Pour into a large sieve, drain thoroughly.

• Pour the oil into a microwave-safe bowl, microwave 1 minute at HIGH.

• Add the well-drained noodles and stir until they are

well coated with the oil. Add salt and pepper to taste. Pour into a dish, cover to keep warm.

• Slice into thin shreds the cabbage, ham, onion and green pepper. Mix together in a bowl.

• Place 1 tablespoon (15 mL) of oil in another microwave-safe bowl and microwave 1 minute at MEDIUM-HIGH.

• Stir in the vegetable and ham mixture. Microwave 2 minutes at MEDIUM-HIGH. Add to the hot noodles.

• Mix together the sauce ingredients. Pour over the noodles, stir. Microwave 1 minute at HIGH. Serve.

713

Sauces

Spaghetti Sauce

Preparation: . . . . **12 m**
Cooking: . . . . **12 m**
Standing: . . . . **10 m**

A personal note: You can make this spaghetti sauce in no more than 12 minutes. Sometimes, before the sauce is set aside to stand, I add 1 cup (250 mL) diced cheese — either one kind or a mixture. The heat of the sauce will melt the cheese.

Ingredients:

8 oz (250 g) spaghetti

8 oz (250 g) beef or pork, minced

1 large onion, chopped

1/2 cup (125 mL) celery with leaves, diced

1 carrot, grated (optional)

1 tsp (5 mL) basil

1 tsp (5 mL) savory

1 19-oz (540 mL) can tomatoes

1 tsp (5 mL) salt

1 tsp (5 mL) sugar

1/2 tsp (2 mL) fresh ground pepper

Method:

• Microwave the spaghetti according to the Pasta Cooking Chart.

• Place in a microwave-safe baking dish the minced beef or pork, break it up with a fork.

• Add the onion, celery, carrot, basil and savory. Mix together. Microwave, uncovered, 8 minutes at HIGH, stirring 2 or 3 times.

• Add the remaining ingredients. Mix thoroughly. Microwave 4 minutes at HIGH.

• Cover and let stand 10 minutes. Serve.

Pork Spaghetti Sauce

Preparation: . . . . **8 m**
Cooking: . . . . **12 m**
Standing: . . . . **none**

Ingredients:

2 pork chops, minced

2 medium onions, minced

2 celery sticks, diced

1 carrot, grated

1/2 tsp (2 mL) basil or oregano

1 bay leaf

1 19-oz (540 mL) can tomatoes

1 tsp (5 mL) salt

1 tsp (5 mL) sugar

1/2 tsp (2 mL) pepper

Method:

• Place all the ingredients in a 4-cup (1 L) casserole.

• Microwave at HIGH 8 minutes, stirring twice.

• Add the can tomatoes, salt, sugar and pepper. Stir well and microwave at HIGH 4 minutes.

A personal note: This sauce is sufficient to serve with 8 ounces (250 mL) cooked spaghetti.

Chicken Liver Spaghetti Sauce

Preparation: . . . . 15 m
Cooking: . . . . 16 m
Standing: . . . . none

• A speciality of Verona, Italy, this famous Italian pasta sauce can be prepared in 20 minutes and turns out perfectly. Fresh tomatoes are sometimes quite costly. I believe the quality of the sauce is worth the expense.

Ingredients:

2 tbsp (30 mL) butter

1 lb (500 g) chicken livers, diced

2 tbsp (30 mL) butter

2 garlic cloves, chopped fine

2 large onions, chopped fine

1/2 cup (125 mL) fresh mushrooms, sliced

1 tsp (5 mL) salt

1/2 tsp (2 mL) pepper

1/2 tsp (2 mL) dry mustard

2 fresh tomatoes, peeled and diced

3 tbsp (50 mL) tomato paste

1 tbsp (15 mL) flour

1 cup (250 mL) canned consommé, undiluted

1 tsp (5 mL) basil

1/2 tsp (2 mL) rosemary or marjoram

Method:

• Place the first 2 tablespoons (30 mL) butter in a 4-cup (1 L) microwave-safe dish. Microwave at HIGH 2 minutes.

• Add the diced chicken livers. Stir well. Microwave at HIGH 3 minutes, stirring once. Remove the livers from the dish.

• Melt the second 2 tablespoons (30 mL) butter in the same dish 2 minutes at HIGH.

• Add the garlic and onions. Microwave at HIGH 4 minutes. Stir.

• Add the mushrooms. Mix well. Microwave 1 minute at HIGH.

• Add the salt, pepper and dry mustard. Stir well.

• Add the diced tomatoes, stir again. Microwave at HIGH 4 minutes.

• Stir together the tomato paste and the flour. Add to the tomato mixture. Stir in the consommé, basil and rosemary or marjoram. Microwave 4 minutes at HIGH, stirring once.

• This sauce will keep 4 to 6 days refrigerated, covered. Warm at MEDIUM, as needed. The time will depend on the quantity.

• This sauce freezes very well and may be kept frozen for 3 to 4 months. When you wish to use it, just place it frozen in the microwave and warm at MEDIUM-HIGH, uncovered, until hot.

Italian Vegetable Spaghetti Sauce

Preparation:	....................**14 m**
Cooking:	.....................**15 m**
Standing:	......................**none**

• There are few meatless spaghetti sauces. This is a very tasty one that can be prepared with oil or with melted bacon fat.

Ingredients:

8 oz (250 g) spaghetti

1/2 cup (125 mL) olive or vegetable oil

2 medium carrots, grated

2 large onions, sliced thin

2 medium leeks, sliced

1 28-oz (796 mL) can of tomatoes

1 tbsp (15 mL) sugar

1 tsp (5 mL) salt

1 tbsp (15 mL) oregano or savory

Method:

• Microwave the spaghetti according to the Pasta Cooking Chart.

• There may be slight variations in the cooking time, depending on the brand of pasta used. Stir and check doneness.

• Place the oil in an 8-cup (2 L) microwave-safe baking dish and microwave 3 minutes at HIGH.

• Add the vegetables, the tomatoes, sugar, salt and oregano or savory. Mix thoroughly. Cover and microwave 15 minutes at HIGH.

• Pour as a sauce over the spaghetti and serve.

Helpful hint: Sauce or gravy may be poured over cooked meat before reheating to help keep meat moist.

Fresh Tomato Sauce for Pasta

Preparation:	....................**7 m**
Cooking:	..........**from 19 to 25 m**
Standing:	......................**none**

• I can never resist making this super fresh tomato sauce with the first tomatoes in my garden. I like to pour the sauce over a delicate cooked pasta like fine noodles or little stars.

Ingredients:

3 large ripe tomatoes, unpeeled

1 tbsp (15 mL) butter or olive oil

1 tsp (5 mL) sugar

1 tbsp (15 mL) basil

2 cups (500 mL) fine noodles or star pasta

Salt to taste

Method:

• Cut the unpeeled tomatoes into 6 to 8 pieces and mash. Place in a Pyrex or Corning dish.

• Microwave at HIGH 8 to 10 minutes, or until sauce has thickened, stirring two or three times during the cooking period. The texture should be like that of a thick but creamy sauce.

• Add the remaining ingredients, except the pasta and salt. Stir until creamy.

• Microwave the fine noodles or star pasta according to Pasta Cooking Chart.

• Add the tomato sauce and salt. Stir well.

• Serve or warm later at MEDIUM for 3 or 4 minutes.

Helpful hint: To measure honey, dip spoon into hot water, it will slip off the spoon easily.

Year-round Pasta Tomato Sauce

Preparation: ....10 m
Cooking: ....from 12 to 14 m
Standing:......................none

1 5½-oz (156 mL) can tomato paste
1 bay leaf
1/2 tsp (2 mL) thyme
1 tsp (5 mL) basil or oregano
2 tsp (10 mL) sugar

A personal note: This is a sauce for all seasons and, I would add, for all emergencies. Equally interesting made with fresh or canned tomatoes, it freezes well but should be thawed out slowly. I defrost mine on the kitchen counter overnight, on folded towelling. When in a hurry, thaw in your microwave oven on DEFROST.

Method:

- Place the oil of your choice in a large microwave-safe dish, the ideal size being 6 cups (1.5 mL).

- Microwave at HIGH 2 minutes.

- Add the onion and garlic. Stir until well coated with the oil.

- Microwave 4 minutes at MEDIUM-HIGH, stirring once. The onion should be tender but not browned.

- Add the remaining ingredients. Stir to mix well.

- Microwave 8 to 10 minutes at MEDIUM-HIGH, stirring after 5 minutes of cooking.

- There is enough sauce to serve with 8 ounces (250 g) of cooked pasta of your choice.

Ingredients:

1/4 cup (60 mL) olive or vegetable oil
1 large onion, finely chopped
1 garlic clove, finely chopped
1 28-oz (796 mL) can tomatoes *or*
   6 fresh tomatoes, peeled and diced

The Simplest of All Fresh Tomato Sauces

Preparation:	. . . . .5 m
Cooking:	. . . . .4 m
Standing:	. . . . .none

A personal note: Not only is this the simplest fresh tomato sauce, it is also one of the best, quick and easy. I sometimes use it mixed gently with 2 cups (500 mL) of cooked brown rice, serve it as a main dish with a bowl of grated cheese or add it to a roasted meat gravy.

Ingredients:

1 ½ to 2 cups (375 to 500 mL) ripe, unpeeled
  tomatoes, thickly sliced
1 tbsp (15 mL) butter or olive oil
1 tsp (5 mL) sugar
1/2 tsp (2 mL) basil or oregano or thyme

Method:

• Place the tomatoes in a microwave-safe dish, microwave at HIGH 2 to 4 minutes, stirring after 2 minutes.

• When ready, the tomatoes should have a nice, creamy texture, stir in the remaining ingredients until the mixture is light and smooth.

• I learned how to make this sauce in the south of France, where they serve it over pasta, rice or to top poached or fried fish. I like it best served over small pasta.

• In summer, when basil is at its best, place a few stems in a jar and set it on the table with a pair of scissors.

• Each person cuts the fresh basil onto the cooked pasta sauce when ready to eat. Super!

Tomato Sauce Bonne Santé

Microwave and convection cooking

Preparation:	. . . . .10 m
Cooking:	. . . . .from 24 to 30 m
Standing:	. . . . .none

• This tasty and colorful sauce could also be called Summer Delight because it is at its best when gardens are filled with fresh vegetables.

Ingredients:

1 10 oz (384 g) fresh spinach
1/4 cup (60 mL) chives, chopped fine, *or*
  4 green onions, diced
1 egg, lightly beaten
1/2 cup (125 mL) Cheddar, grated
4 large tomatoes
2 tbsp (30 mL) butter
Salt and pepper to taste

Method:

• Wash the spinach, place in a microwave-safe bowl, microwave 2 minutes at HIGH. Pour into a sieve, press with a spoon to remove excess water. When well drained, chop with two knives. Salt and pepper to taste. Add the chives or green onions. Mix well. Microwave 2 minutes at MEDIUM.

• Beat the egg with the cheese. Add to the spinach mixture. Mix thoroughly.

• Cut tops off tomatoes, hollow out. Squeeze each tomato gently to remove some of the seeds. Sprinkle a little sugar into each tomato shell. Dice the pulp from inside the tomatoes and add to the spinach mixture. Fill the hollowed tomatoes with the mixture. Replace tops removed from the tomatoes.

• Preheat the convection part of your microwave oven at 375°F (190°C). Place tomatoes on a plate, bake 20 to 25 minutes, depending on their size.

• Serve with cooked pasta of your choice, microwaved according to basic instructions in Pasta Cooking Chart, and a bowl of grated cheese.

Simone's Eggplant Sauce

Preparation: . . . .**15 m**
Cooking: . . . . **from 20 to 21 m**
Standing: . . . .**none**

A personal note: My friend Simone always said she could not cook, but every time she did, the result was perfect and delicious, including this sauce, which can be served over rice or noodles, to top a casserole or with small pasta. It is superb poured over fried fillets of fish.

Ingredients:

1 medium eggplant, peeled and diced

2 tbsp (30 mL) bacon fat or oil

1 large garlic clove, chopped fine

1 medium or large green pepper, diced

1 tsp (5 mL) sweet basil

1 19-oz (540 mL) can tomatoes

1 tsp (5 mL) salt

1/4 tsp (1 mL) pepper

1 tsp (5 mL) sugar

3 cups (750 mL) elbow macaroni, cooked

Method:

• Soak the eggplant in cold water for 10 minutes, then drain it thoroughly.

• Place the bacon fat or oil in a microwave-safe dish. Microwave 2 minutes at HIGH.

• Add the garlic, green pepper and basil. Microwave 3 minutes at MEDIUM-HIGH, stir.

• Add the tomatoes, salt, pepper and sugar, stir.

• Add the well-drained eggplant. Stir. Microwave 10 minutes at MEDIUM-HIGH.

• Add the elbow macaroni. Microwave according to instructions in the Pasta Cooking Chart.

• Serve with a bowl of grated cheese of your choice.

720

Sienna Sauce

Preparation: . . . .**10 m**
Cooking: . . . .**15 m**
Standing: . . . .**none**

• A very good vegetarian pasta sauce, Sienna Sauce will keep 4 to 6 days refrigerated, 2 to 3 months frozen.*

Ingredients:

1/2 cup (125 mL) vegetable oil

2 medium-sized carrots, grated

2 large onions, chopped fine

2 medium-sized leeks, thinly sliced

1 28-oz (796 mL) can tomatoes

2 tsp (10 mL) sugar

1 tsp (5 mL) salt

Method:

• Place the oil in a 6-cup (1.5 L) microwave-safe dish. Microwave 2 minutes at HIGH.

• Add the remaining ingredients, stir well.

• Microwave 15 minutes at MEDIUM-HIGH.

• Serve over cooked pasta or rice.

If you wish to use only small quantities at a time, divide the cooked sauce into 2 or 3 containers and freeze.

Eggs

Egg wisdom

- The egg has inside its shell "what we all need to keep us healthy and well." Treat it accordingly, which is easy to do when you are aware of a few basic facts.

- Eggs are bursting with vitamins, good for young and old.

- Microwave eggs at MEDIUM, MEDIUM-LOW or LOW.

- Eggs do not have to be just eggs. A poached egg on toast is a nourishing, tasty meal; served on a thin slice of ham, it's a man's favorite; topped with Hollandaise sauce, it becomes an elegant dish, and so forth. Try some of the following egg recipes. I hope they will inspire you to adapt your own favorites to microwave cooking.

- Keep eggs cool by placing them in the refrigerator, preferably out of the box.

- It does not matter if the shell is brown or white, all that counts is freshness.

- You will find it very easy to separate the white from the yolk when the eggs are cold.

- Do not wash eggs before placing them in the refrigerator, as they have a protective coating that will help keep them fresh until ready to use.

- To obtain a good, fluffy volume when beating egg whites, let them stand at room temperature 20 to 30 minutes before beating.

- Egg whites keep for weeks when stored in a well-covered jar — jam jars are perfect — and refrigerated.

- I hope you will find the recipes in this chapter an incentive to prepare eggs the easy microwave way.

- Eggs are essential in custards, omelettes, mousses and mayonnaise, to bind meat loaves, for the golden, tender quality of cakes and pastry, and to clarify consommé.

- For me, what is most interesting is that although there are 1,001 different dishes in which eggs are an essential ingredient, there are only a few basic ways to use or cook them.

- Some people won't buy eggs with yellow shells; others stay away from eggs with white shells. Yet the color of an eggshell is determined by the breed of hen and has absolutely nothing to do with the flavor or quality of the egg.

Cooking eggs in a microwave oven

• You really have to be knowledgeable to cook eggs in a microwave oven. But if you follow the methods I have developed, you will soon learn to cook eggs successfully in your microwave oven.

• There can be seconds of difference in the cooking time in a recipe, depending on the size of eggs you buy and their temperature. Even whether they are refrigerated on open shelves or in their closed box can change the cooking time by one or two seconds.

Three important rules

1. Do not ever microwave a whole egg in the shell, since the egg is sure to explode and make a mess in your oven.

2. Do not try to reheat a hard-cooked egg in its shell, for the same reason. Peel it, place it in a bowl, cover with hot water to the top and microwave 30 seconds at HIGH.

3. When cooking any type of egg whole — fried, poached, etc. — make 2 or 3 holes in the white and the yolk with the point of a small knife to break the invisible skin covering the egg and prevent it from exploding in the oven. It isn't dangerous but it sure is messy.

• I strongly advise against cooking eggs at HIGH. MEDIUM power (70%) is best.

• If your oven has only one setting, which would be HIGH, place a 2-cup (500 mL) measure of cold water in the microwave oven alongside the egg. The water will absorb some of the microwaves.

• Another important factor to be aware of is that the high fat content of the yolk makes it cook faster than the white, which is the reverse of the conventional way.

• If you wish to have microwaved egg yolks remain soft, remove the dish from the microwave oven before the whites are completely cooked. Cover with waxed paper and let stand 1 to 2 minutes. They will not get cold, but the whites will firm.

To fry bacon before cooking eggs

1. If you do not wish to keep the melted bacon fat, place the bacon slices in a layer on a piece of white paper towelling on a serving plate.

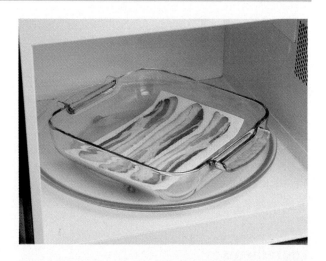

• Microwave 1 to 3 slices 35 to 45 seconds or slightly more, depending on how well you want it cooked. Set aside while cooking the eggs.

2. If you wish to keep the fat, microwave the bacon on a small plate without paper. As soon as it's done, remove the bacon to a piece of paper towelling and place the fat in a jar and refrigerate. To reheat bacon, microwave 30 seconds at MEDIUM-HIGH.

Fried Eggs

Preparation : .1 m
Cooking : . . . . .from 25 to 30 s
Standing : . . . . .none

A personal note : Cooked in a small plate, the egg will have no color. But if you use a marvellous small browning pan (Corning), you can control the color of the butter while making a perfect fried egg or two at a time. Fried Eggs are quick and easy to prepare in a browning pan.

Ingredients :

1 tsp (5 mL) butter or bacon fat
1 egg
Salt and pepper to taste

Method :

• Place the butter or bacon fat in the browning pan and melt 30 to 40 seconds at HIGH.

• Break the egg into the melted fat.

• Pierce the yolk and the white gently with the point of a knife 3 to 4 times.

• Microwave at MEDIUM-HIGH 25 to 30 seconds.

• The timing will depend on the size of the egg.

• To fry 2 eggs, simply microwave 10 to 20 seconds longer to melt the fat and cook the eggs.

Bacon and Eggs

Preparation: . . . .**3 m**
Cooking: . . . .**from 4 to 5 m**
Standing: . . . .**none**

• A favorite breakfast for so many, Bacon and Eggs takes only a minute or so to prepare directly on one's plate.

Ingredients:

1, 2 or 3 slices of bacon

1 or 2 eggs

Parsley or chives to taste

Method:

• To cook the bacon (See beginning of chapter: to fry bacon before cooking eggs).

• When the bacon is cooked, remove from plate and break 1 or 2 eggs into the hot fat on the plate.

• Pierce the yolk and the white of the egg 2 to 3 times with the point of a knife.

• Microwave 1 egg 20 to 25 seconds, 2 eggs 25 to 35 seconds to 1 minute at MEDIUM, depending on the size and temperature of the egg and how well you want it done.

• Add the cooked bacon and serve.

Scrambled Eggs

Preparation: .... 2 m
Cooking: .... from 4 to 5 m
Standing: .... none

• If you need to serve more than one or two eggs, this is a good, easy way to prepare them.

Ingredients:

4 eggs
1/4 tsp (1 mL) salt
1/4 cup (60 mL) light cream or milk
2 tbsp (30 mL) butter

Method:

• Break the eggs into a bowl. Add the salt and cream or milk and beat with a fork, just enough to blend.

• Place the butter in a glass or ceramic pie plate and melt 2 minutes at HIGH. It will be golden brown.

• Pour the beaten eggs into the hot butter. Microwave 1 minute at MEDIUM. Stir gently.

• If necessary, microwave another minute.

• The easy way is to pour the soft portion over the partly cooked portion and move lightly with the fork.

• Depending on how cold the eggs and liquid were, it could take a few more seconds of cooking.

• Keep in mind that even after 2 minutes out of the microwave oven, the eggs are still cooking.

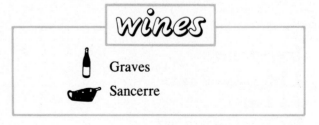

wines

Graves
Sancerre

Poached Eggs

• If you prefer to eat eggs without any type of fat, poached eggs are perfect. They are easy to cook in a microwave oven.

Preparation : . . . .**2 m**
Cooking : . . . .**from 30 to 40 s**
Standing : . . . .**none**

Ingredients :

1/2 cup (125 mL) water
1/4 tsp (1 mL) vinegar or lemon juice
1 egg

Method :

• Place in a small microwave-safe dish or teacup the water and vinegar or lemon juice.

• Microwave 1 minute at HIGH.

• Break the egg into a saucer. Pierce the yolk and the white of the egg with the point of a knife, then gently pour the egg into the hot water.

• Microwave at MEDIUM 30 to 40 seconds, depending on how well done you like it cooked.

• Remove egg from the water with a slotted spoon. Place egg on buttered toast or on an English muffin cut in half.

• In the summer, try sprinkling the egg or the toast with chives.

A personal note : To poach 2 eggs at a time, heat 2 cups (500 mL) water 5 minutes at HIGH. Pierce the yolk and the white of the eggs with the point of a knife. Microwave the 2 eggs together 1 minute at MEDIUM-HIGH. Cover and let stand 1 minute. Serve. I do not advise poaching more than 2 eggs at a time, as some parts will be overcooked, others undercooked.

wines

Entre-Deux-Mers
Tokay Pinot Gris

Mushroom Poached Eggs

Preparation : . . . .**5 m**
Cooking : . . . .**5 m**
Standing : . . . .**none**

• I always keep a can of condensed mushroom soup on a shelf and some English muffins in my freezer, so if an emergency arises I am ready to serve these poached eggs topped with a mushroom sauce within minutes.

Ingredients :

2 tbsp (30 mL) butter
1 can condensed cream of mushroom soup
1/3 cup (80 mL) milk or white wine
4 eggs
Salt and pepper to taste
2 English muffins, toasted and buttered

Method :

• Place the butter in a ceramic or Pyrex pie plate and melt 1 minute at HIGH.

• Add the soup and the milk or wine. Stir well.

• Microwave at MEDIUM-HIGH 2 minutes, or until sauce is hot, stirring once.

• Break the eggs, one at a time, onto a small plate.

• Gently slide the eggs into the creamy sauce, 1 by 1, until all 4 are in the hot sauce.

• Make an incision once in the yolks, once in the whites, with the point of a knife.

• Then, with a spoon, carefully ladle some of the hot sauce over the eggs. Salt and pepper.

• Cover with waxed paper. Microwave 3 minutes at HIGH.

• Check doneness of the eggs. Microwave another 20 to 30 seconds more.

• To serve, place one egg with some of the sauce on one half of a toasted and buttered English muffin.

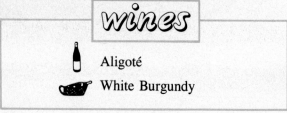

Aligoté
White Burgundy

A personal note : In summer, I sprinkle the butter with minced chives ; in winter, I use fresh parsley or dried tarragon.

Hua Eggs
in Red Sauce

Preparation: .7 m
Cooking: . . . . .from 12 to 14 m
Standing: . . . . .none

• These eggs are poached in a quickly made tomato sauce. You need a browning dish for this recipe.

Ingredients:

3 tbsp (50 mL) olive or vegetable oil

2 small onions, chopped fine

1 garlic clove, minced

1 16-oz (454 g) can tomatoes

1 tbsp (15 mL) parsley, minced

1/2 tsp (2 mL) each salt and marjoram

1/4 tsp (1 mL) each pepper and sugar

4 to 6 eggs

wines

Chianti

Rioja red

Method:

• Pour the oil into a browning dish, microwave 2 minutes at HIGH.

• Add the onions and garlic, stir well. Microwave 2 minutes at HIGH, stirring once.

• Add the tomatoes, parsley, salt, marjoram, pepper and sugar, stir well. Microwave 6 minutes at HIGH, stirring once after 4 minutes.

• Break the eggs one at a time into a small dish, pierce the white and yolk of each egg with the point of a knife, then slip them one at a time into the hot sauce, spooning a bit of sauce gently over each egg. Cover and microwave at MEDIUM 1 minute per egg.

• An elegant way to serve the eggs is to toast split English muffins or the bread of your choice, lift a poached egg onto each toast with a perforated spoon and pour sauce over all.

Baked Eggs and Cheese

Preparation : .5 m
Cooking : . . . . .2 m
Standing : .1 m

• This is a simple, easy, quick way to make a good breakfast or light supper. Serve with toast and a watercress salad. These eggs are baked in custard cups.

Ingredients :

4 thin slices of the cheese of your choice

4 eggs

1/4 cup (60 mL) chili sauce

1/4 tsp (1 mL) curry powder

2 tsp (10 mL) sherry or Madeira

Minced chives or parsley to taste

Method :

• Line each of 4 ramekins with a slice of cheese.

• Break an egg on top of each slice of cheese.

• Pierce the white and the yolk of each egg with the point of a knife.

• Mix together the chili sauce, curry powder, sherry or Madeira.

• Divide equally over the eggs.

• Microwave 2 ramekins at a time 40 to 45 seconds at MEDIUM. Let stand on kitchen counter covered with waxed paper while you microwave the other two, also 40 to 45 seconds at MEDIUM.

wines

Red Rhône

Amarone

Baked Eggs
À la Française

Preparation : .3 m
Cooking : . . . . .from 35 to 60 s
Standing : . . . . .none

A personal note : Serve these eggs as a light lunch or supper. My favorite way is to top them with fresh minced chives. For a light meal, serve with a salad and a poached fruit for dessert. This dish is elegant when baked and served in ceramic ramekins.

Ingredients :

2 eggs
2 tsp (10 mL) milk or cream
1 tsp (5 mL) butter
Salt and pepper to taste
Parsley or chives, minced

Method :

• Bake in glass custard cups or French ceramic ramekins.

• Break each egg into a ramekin.

• Pierce each yolk and white carefully with the point of a little knife.

• Pour 1 teaspoon (5 mL) of milk or cream over each egg.

• Place 2 ramekins at a time in the microwave oven. Microwave 35 to 40 seconds at MEDIUM.

• Depending on the power of your oven and the size of the eggs, you may need to cook them 10 to 12 seconds longer.

• To check, simply look at and touch the white part of the eggs.

• To taste, top with the minced parsley or chives. Serve.

731

Ham, Eggs and Potatoes

Preparation .6 m
Cooking . . . . .14 m
Standing . . . . .none

• Serve this dish with a tossed salad and you have a delicious luncheon in a jiffy.

Ingredients:

3 medium potatoes

1 tbsp (15 mL) butter

3 green onions, finely chopped

Fresh ground pepper to taste

A dash of curry powder (optional)

1 cup (250 mL) ham, cooked and diced

3 eggs

1/4 cup (60 mL) milk

Method:

• Scrub potatoes, do not peel, make 2 or 3 incisions in each with the point of a knife.

• Microwave 7 minutes at HIGH.

• Peel the potatoes, dice and place in a microwave-safe baking dish.

• Place the butter in a microwave-safe dish and melt 1 minute at HIGH, add the green onions. Microwave another minute at HIGH.

• Sprinkle with pepper and curry to taste. Stir, pour over the potatoes, add the ham, stir to mix.

• Beat the eggs with the milk and pour over all.

• Stir lightly and microwave 3 to 4 minutes at HIGH, stirring once. Serve.

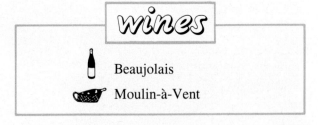

Beaujolais

Moulin-à-Vent

Helpful hint: To separate cold bacon slices easily, heat package at HIGH 30 seconds. It will separate easily.

Quiche Lorraine

Microwave or convection cooking

Preparation: . . . . 10 m
Cooking: convection: . . . . 30 m
           microwave: . . . . from 8 to 9 m
Standing: . . . . none

A personal note: The classic quiche is prepared with diced bacon or salt pork and Swiss cheese. Here is my favorite version, using diced bacon or salt pork and mild or strong Cheddar cheese. You can omit the pie crust; simply pour the mixture directly into the pie plate and cook as indicated.

wines

Alsatian Pinot Blanc

Château-bottled Graves

Ingredients:

Lard pie crust

6 slices bacon or salt pork, diced

3 eggs

1 cup (250 mL) heavy cream

1/2 tsp (2 mL) salt

1/4 tsp (1 mL) pepper

1/4 tsp (1 mL) nutmeg

1 cup (250 mL) Cheddar cheese, grated

Method:

• Cut the bacon or salt pork into 1-inch (2.5 cm) pieces.

• Place a sheet of paper towelling on a plate and place the diced bacon or salt pork on it. Microwave 2 or 3 minutes at HIGH.

• Beat together in a bowl the eggs, cream, salt, pepper and nutmeg. Add the grated cheese. Mix together.

• Line a pie plate with the rolled dough*.

• Spread the diced bacon or salt pork over the crust and pour the cheese mixture over all. Sprinkle with a little grated cheese, if desired.

• Microwave 8 to 9 minutes at MEDIUM. Or preheat the convection part of your microwave oven at 400°F (200°C). Place the prepared quiche on the oven rack and bake 30 minutes.

• Check for doneness with the point of a knife. If not cooked, bake a few minutes more or until done. Serve hot or tepid.

To microwave the quiche, precook the crust 3 minutes at HIGH. Cool before filling with the cheese mixture.

733

Omelette Variations

- There are so many ways to vary an omelette that there is no excuse for always serving it the same way.

- I hope you will be tempted by the following ideas.

How to make an omelette in a browning dish

Preparation: 4m
Cooking: . . . . .from 1 to 2 m
Standing: . . . . .none

• If you have a browning dish (Corning), here is the way to make an omelette that will be brown when folded, just as if it had been cooked in a frying pan.

Ingredients:

2 eggs, lightly beaten

2 tbsp (30 mL) milk, cream or water

1/2 tsp (2 mL) salt

2 tsp (10 mL) butter

Method:

• Place the browning dish in the microwave oven. Microwave 3 minutes at HIGH.

• Mix in a bowl the eggs, milk, cream or water and salt.

• Place the butter in the hot browning dish. It will sizzle and brown in just a few seconds. Swirl the melted butter so as to cover the whole bottom of the dish.

• Beat the eggs with the remaining ingredients. Pour into the hot browning dish. Microwave 1 minute at MEDIUM-HIGH.

• If necessary, push the cooked part of the omelette to the middle of the dish and microwave 30 to 35 seconds more at MEDIUM. Serve as is or top with a garnish or sauce of your choice.

735

Omelette Fermière

A personal note: Quick and easy to prepare, this dish can be served with buttered noodles or cooked potatoes for a light meal. The ham can be replaced by bacon.

Preparation: . . . . .5 m
Cooking: . . . . .from 2 to 3 m
Standing: .1 m

Ingredients:

3 eggs

3 tbsp (50 mL) milk

Salt and pepper to taste

2 tbsp (30 mL) parsley, minced

1 thin slice of ham

2 tsp (10 mL) butter

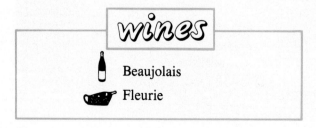

Beaujolais

Fleurie

Method:

• Beat the eggs and milk together, salt and pepper to taste. Add the parsley and stir thoroughly.

• Dice the ham, removing fat if any. Stir into the beaten eggs.

• Melt 1 teaspoon (5 mL) of the butter in an 8-inch (20 cm) ceramic or Pyrex pie plate 1 minute at HIGH.

• Pour in the omelette mixture. Cover with plastic wrap.

• Microwave 30 seconds at HIGH. Lift wrap and gently stir the cooked part of the omelette, allowing the uncooked part to flow under.

• Cover again, microwave 1 minute 10 seconds at MEDIUM.

• Let stand 1 minute and serve.

736

My Favorite 3-Egg Omelette

Preparation: .... 2 m
Cooking: .... from 4 to 5 m
Standing: .... none

• You can serve this omelette just as it is, with a filling of your choice or with one of the suggested variations. It is easy and quick to make.

Ingredients:

3 eggs
3 tbsp (50 mL) sour cream
Salt and pepper to taste

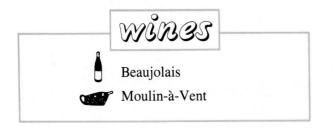

wines

Beaujolais
Moulin-à-Vent

Method:

• Break the eggs into a bowl. Add the sour cream, salt and pepper. Mix all together.

• Butter generously a 9-inch (23 cm) ceramic pie plate and pour in the egg mixture.

• Cover with waxed paper. Microwave 2 minutes at MEDIUM.

• Stir lightly, moving the outer portions of the omelette to the centre of the plate.

• Microwave another 2 minutes at MEDIUM.

• Place your choice of filling or sauce in the middle and fold the omelette over.

• Microwave 30 seconds more at MEDIUM-LOW. Serve.

Scandinavian Omelette

Preparation: ....5 m
Cooking: ....from 3 to 4 m
Standing: ....none

A personal note: This light, fluffy, 3-egg omelette is filled with salmon, green onions and dill. The salmon can be replaced by an equal quantity of chopped cooked shrimp.

Alsatian Riesling

Pouilly-Fumé

Ingredients:

3 eggs, separated

2 tbsp (30 mL) milk or water

1 tbsp (15 mL) butter

1/2 cup (125 mL) cooked salmon

4 green onions, chopped fine

1 tsp (5 mL) dill, chopped fine

Method:

• Beat the egg whites until they form soft peaks. Beat the egg yolks with the milk or water. Gently fold the whites into the yolks.

• Place the butter in a 9-inch (23 cm) Pyrex or Corning pie plate and melt 1 minute at HIGH.

• Pour the egg mixture into the hot butter.

• Microwave at MEDIUM 3 to 4 minutes, or until eggs are set.

• While the eggs are cooking, mix together the cooked salmon, green onions and dill.

• Pour over the cooked omelette. Fold in half and serve.

Spanish Omelette

Preparation: .8 m
Cooking: . . . . .from 8 to 9 m
Standing: .5 m

A personal note: For a perfect Spanish Omelette, fresh tomatoes are a must. Without them I would not consider making this omelette. This is an interesting light luncheon dish served with a bowl of watercress or a rice salad, followed by poached fruit, in season. Very Spanish! Excellent for the weight watcher.

Ingredients:

1 tbsp (15 mL) olive or vegetable oil

1/2 green pepper, chopped fine

2 to 4 green onions, chopped fine

1/4 cup (60 mL) celery, diced

A good pinch of thyme

2 fresh tomatoes, unpeeled and diced

1 tsp (5 mL) sugar

1/2 tsp (2 mL) salt

3 tbsp (50 mL) parsley, fresh chopped

1 3-egg omelette (see *My Favorite 3-Egg Omelette.*)

Method:

• Place the oil in a ceramic or Pyrex pie plate and microwave 1 minute at HIGH.

• Add the green pepper, onions, celery and thyme, mix well.

• Microwave 4 minutes at MEDIUM-HIGH, stirring once.

• Add the tomatoes, sugar, salt and parsley, mix well. Cover and microwave 2 minutes at HIGH. Let stand 5 minutes.

• In the meantime, prepare the omelette. Pour over the vegetables and serve.

wines

Valdepenas

Rioja red

Albertans' Favorite Omelette

Preparation : . . . .**5 m**
Cooking : . . . . **from 4 to 5 m**
Standing : . . . .**none**

Ingredients :

1 tsp (5 mL) butter or bacon fat

1/2 cup (125 mL) cooked ham, diced

1 small onion, chopped fine

1/4 cup (60 mL) red or green pepper, slivered

Salt and pepper to taste

1   3-Egg omelette (see *My Favorite 3-Egg Omelette*)

Method :

• Place the butter or bacon fat in a 1-cup (250 mL) glass measuring cup or a microwave-safe bowl and melt 1 minute at HIGH.

• Add the ham, onion and red or green pepper. Stir well.

• Microwave 2 minutes at HIGH, stirring once. Salt and pepper to taste.

• Add a small pinch of sugar.

• Make the omelette.

wines

Rhône red

Cornas

Swiss Mountain Special Omelette

Preparation: .... 6 m
Cooking: .... from 6 to 7 m
Standing: .... none

• A garnish of fresh mushrooms and Swiss or mild Cheddar cheese makes this omelette quite special.

Ingredients:

1 cup (250 mL) fresh mushrooms, sliced

1/4 cup (60 mL) green onions, chopped fine

2 tbsp (30 mL) butter

Salt and pepper to taste

1/2 cup (125 mL) Swiss or mild Cheddar cheese, grated

1 3-Egg omelette (see *My Favorite 3-Egg Omelette*)

Method:

• Place in a microwave-safe bowl the fresh mushrooms, green onions and butter. Cover and microwave 2 minutes at HIGH. Stir well. Salt and pepper to taste.

• Make the omelette. Fill omelette with the mushroom and green onions mixture.

• Top with the grated cheese. Serve.

Red Burgundy

Côte de Nuits

Fines-Herbes Omelette

Preparation: . . . . .5 m
Cooking: . . . . .from 4 to 5 m
Standing: . . . . .none

• In summer, when fresh herbs are available, try this omelette. I grow my own herbs, so as soon as they are ready, I make sure to have my first Fines-Herbes Omelette for lunch. I serve it with hot French bread and a salad.

Ingredients:

1 3-egg omelette (see *My Favorite 3-Egg Omelette*)

3 tbsp (50 mL) parsley, chopped

2 tbsp (30 mL) fresh chives, chopped fine

1 tbsp (15 mL) basil, chopped

1 tbsp (15 mL) dill, chopped

Method:

• Prepare the omelette, adding to the egg mixture the parsley, chives, basil and dill.

• Stir until well mixed.

• Microwave as indicated in the recipe. Serve.

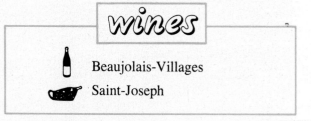

Beaujolais-Villages

Saint-Joseph

To whip butter

• The whipped butter will keep for a month in the refrigerator, so it's worth doing a pound (500 g) at a time. It's better to use unsalted than salted butter.

• Place 1 pound (500 g) unsalted butter in the freezer for 12 to 24 hours. Unwrap it, place in a microwave-safe bowl and microwave 1 minute at HIGH. Let stand 1 minute, by which time the butter should be soft. If not, microwave another 30 seconds at HIGH. Then beat with a wire whisk or a hand beater until creamy. Place in a bowl, making large swirls on top, or in a wide-molded jar. Refrigerate, covered. Even cold, the whipped butter will melt instantly on hot pancakes, waffles or toast.

Omelette À la Reine

Preparation: .5 m
Cooking: . . . . .from 6 to 7 m
Standing:. .none

A personal note: This is a classic French way to serve an omelette. It's excellent even when made with leftover chicken. Serve with a green salad or hot buttered spinach.

Ingrédients:

Ingredients:

2 tbsp (30 mL) butter

1 cup (250 mL) cooked chicken, slivered

1/2 tsp (2 mL) dried tarragon

Salt and pepper to taste

1 3-egg omelette (see *My Favorite 3-Egg Omelette*)

Method:

• Place the butter in a 9-inch (23 cm) microwave-safe pie plate and melt 1 minute at HIGH.

• Add the chicken, stir well.

• Add the tarragon, salt and pepper to taste. Stir again. Cover and microwave 2 minutes at MEDIUM.

• Prepare the omelette.

• When cooked, fill with the chicken, fold and top, to taste, with Sauce Velouté also flavored with a bit of tarragon.

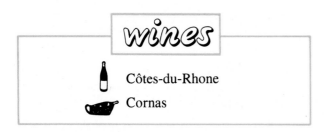

wines

Côtes-du-Rhone

Cornas

Chicken Liver Omelette

Preparation : .8 m
Cooking : . . . . .from 8 to 10 m
Standing : . . . . .none

• I'm always assured of a success when I serve this omelette. Enjoy it with a bowl of fresh, crisp watercress.

Ingredients :

2 tbsp (30 mL) margarine or butter

1/2 lb (250 g) fresh chicken liver, slivered

1 tsp (5 mL) flour

Salt and pepper to taste

2 tbsp (30 mL) sherry of your choice

3 green onions, chopped fine

1 3-egg omelette (see *My Favorite 3-Egg Omelette*)

Method :

• Place the butter or margarine in a 9-inch (23 cm) microwave-safe pie plate. Microwave 2 minutes at HIGH (the butter must sizzle).

• Add the slivered chicken liver. Stir well. Sprinkle with the flour, salt and pepper to taste. Microwave 2 minutes at MEDIUM.

• Add the sherry and the green onions. Microwave 2 minutes at MEDIUM.

• Make the omelette.

• Garnish with the hot chicken liver mixture.

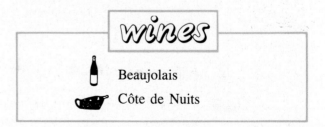

Beaujolais

Côte de Nuits

Cheese Omelette

Preparation: . . . . **4 m**
Cooking: . . . . **from 3 to 4 m**
Standing: . . . . **2 m**

wines

Côtes-du-Rhône red

Crozes-Hermitage

• This omelette is made in a browning dish.

Ingredients:

4 eggs

1/4 cup (60 mL) milk

1/4 tsp (1 mL) salt

A dash of pepper

2 tsp (10 mL) butter

1/2 cup (125 mL) cheese, grated

Method:

• Combine eggs, milk, salt and pepper in a medium-sized bowl; beat until well blended.

• Heat a browning dish for 3 minutes at HIGH. Place butter in the browning dish. When melted, add the egg mixture.

• Cover with lid or waxed paper and microwave at MEDIUM 3 to 3½ minutes, or until omelette is almost set in the centre.

• Sprinkle with cheese, cover and let stand for 2 minutes.

• Loosen eggs with rubber spatula, tilt browning dish and roll omelette on to serving plate.

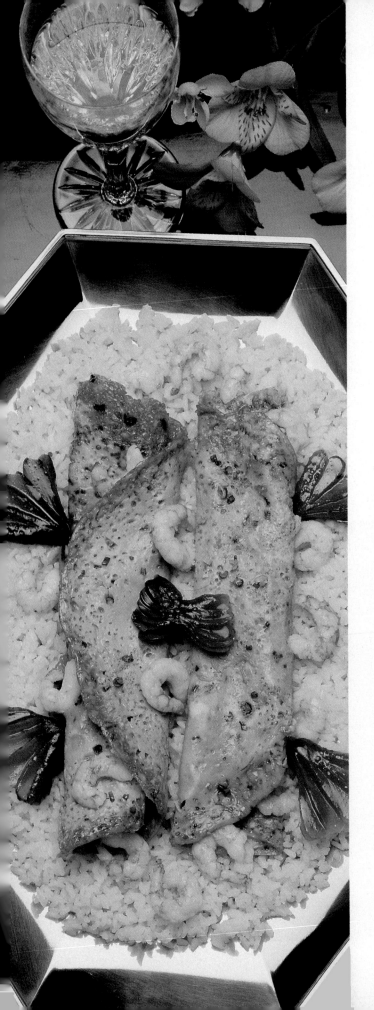

Rolled Omelette (Tamago Yaki)

Preparation : . . . .**3 m**
Cooking : . . . .**from 2 to 3 m**
Standing : . . . .**none**

A personal note : Simple and quick to make in the microwave oven, this recipe will give you a very nourishing, non-fattening dish.

Ingredients :

2 green onions, finely chopped
4 eggs (preferably at room temperature)
2 tsp (10 mL) Japanese soy sauce
2 tbsp (30 mL) vegetable oil

Method :

• Beat together with a fork the green onions, eggs and soy sauce.

• Pour 1 tablespoon (15 mL) of the oil into an 8-inch (20 cm) microwave-safe pie plate. Microwave 1 minute at HIGH.

• Pour half the egg mixture into the hot plate. Quickly spread mixture into a thin coating covering the bottom of the plate.

• Microwave 1 minute at MEDIUM-HIGH. Halfway through cooking stir.

• Microwave 40 to 60 seconds at MEDIUM.

• Roll up the omelette, slip on to a warm plate. Repeat for the other half of the mixture.

• I sometimes cut 6 cooked and shelled shrimp into thin slices, which I divide evenly over the omelette before rolling.

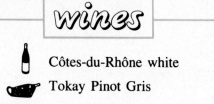

wines

Côtes-du-Rhône white
Tokay Pinot Gris

Florentine Spinach Filling

Preparation : . . . . .10 m
Cooking : . . . . .from 5 to 6 m
Standing : . . . . .none

• There are many different ways of serving an omelette, either plain or with a sauce.

Ingredients :

1 lb (500 g) fresh spinach
A pinch of freshly grated nutmeg
Salt and pepper to taste
Velouté Sauce

Method :

• Wash spinach under cold running water. Place in a microwave-safe dish.

• Microwave 2 to 3 minutes at HIGH, stirring after 2 minutes. Some spinach may take only 2 minutes to cook.

• Drain well in a colander, reserving the liquid.

• Add enough light cream to the reserved liquid to obtain the 3/4 cup (190 mL) of liquid required to prepare the Velouté Sauce.

• Microwave 3 minutes at MEDIUM. Season to taste. Stir well.

• Add the well-drained, cooked spinach. Mix well.

• If necessary to warm, microwave 2 minutes at MEDIUM. Pour over the cooked omelette.

Sauces

Velouté Sauce

Preparation : . . . . .2 m
Cooking : . . . . .from 2 to 3 m
Standing : .none

A personal note : To this basic sauce, you can add melted leeks, green onions, cooked spinach, chopped fresh herbs, etc. Simply pour the variation of your choice over the cooked omelette.

Ingredients :

4 tbsp (60 mL) butter

3 tbsp (50 mL) flour

3/4 cup (190 mL) light cream or milk or chicken stock

Method :

• Place the butter in a microwave-safe bowl and melt 1 minute at HIGH.

• Add the flour. Stir to mix.

• Add the liquid of your choice. Stir to mix.

• Microwave 2 minutes at HIGH. Stir.

• If necessary to obtain a creamy sauce, microwave at MEDIUM another minute.

• Pour over the cooked omelette.

Basic White Sauce

Preparation: .2 m
Cooking: . . . . .from 2 to 3 m
Standing: . . . . .none

Ingredients:

2 tbsp (30 mL) butter or bacon fat

2 tbsp (30 mL) flour

1 cup (250 mL) milk or consommé

Salt and pepper to taste

Method:

- Place butter or bacon fat in a microwave-safe bowl and melt 40 seconds at HIGH.

- Add the flour, stir until well mixed.
- Add the milk or consommé. Stir.
- Microwave 2 minutes at HIGH. Stir well. Season to taste.
- If necessary, microwave another minute at MEDIUM.

Variations:

Dill Sauce

Ingredients:

1 or 2 tbsp (15 or 30 mL) fresh or dried dill

A dash of nutmeg

Method:

- To Basic White Sauce add the ingredients.
- Mix well. Microwave 2 minutes at MEDIUM.

Mushroom Sauce

Ingredients:

1 tbsp (15 mL) butter

1 cup (250 mL) mushrooms, thinly sliced

1 or 2 green onions, thinly sliced

1 tbsp (15 mL) flour

1 cup (250 mL) milk or chicken consommé

Method:

- Place the butter in a microwave-safe dish and melt 1 minute at HIGH. Add the mushrooms. Stir until the mushrooms are coated with the melted butter.
- Add the onions. Mix well. Add the flour, stir until well mixed.
- Add the milk or consommé. Stir. Microwave 4 minutes at MEDIUM-HIGH, stirring once during the cooking period. Season to taste.

Tomato Sauce or Spanish Red Sauce

Ingredients:

3 tbsp (50 mL) tomato purée or paste
   (the purée is lighter than the paste,
   but more difficult to find).

Method:

- Add the tomato purée or paste. Mix. Microwave 2 minutes at HIGH.

Cheese Sauce

Ingredients:

1/4 tsp (1 mL) dry mustard
1/2 cup (125 mL) cheese of your choice, grated

Method:

- Add the ingredients to Basic White Sauce.

Curry Sauce

Ingredients:

1/2 to 1 tsp (2 to 5 mL) curry powder
1 green onion, diced

Method:

- To Basic White Sauce add the ingredients.
- Microwave 2 minutes at MEDIUM.

Creamed Leek Sauce

Preparation : .5 m
Cooking : . . . . .2 m
Standing : . . . . .none

Ingredients :

1 leek, the white part and some of the green
2 tbsp (30 mL) butter
Salt and pepper to taste
Velouté Sauce

Method :

• Clean the leek. Remove a few inches of the green, or leave it all if it has been cut at the shop. Slice thinly.

• Place the butter in a microwave-safe bowl and melt 1 minute at HIGH.

• Stir in the leek. Salt and pepper to taste.

• Microwave 2 minutes at MEDIUM-HIGH.

• Add to the Velouté Sauce. Stir to mix.

• Adjust seasoning. Pour over the cooked omelette.

Desserts

he one subject on which any group of people will immediately take up verbal arms is the subject of desserts. Some people can't live without them, while others argue that they're old fashioned and "passé." Others refuse them categorically because they're dieting. But desserts are usually the winners — especially with men.

Recipes abound for delectable, elegant sweets that, happily, are neither difficult nor tedious to prepare, especially in a microwave oven.

In this book I discuss cakes, pies, muffins, creams, mousses, cold and hot soufflés, poached fruits, jams, etc. — all, from the simple to the dramatic, quick and easy to make in a microwave oven.

I admit that some desserts need to be cooked by the convection method. And why not?!

Light Creamy Desserts

Lemon Mousse

Advance preparation : . . . . **from 6 to 12 h**
Cooking : . . . . **from 3 to 4 m**
Standing : . . . . **none**

• Lemon Mousse is an elegant, light, cool dessert to serve in the heat of summer, or any time throughout the year after a rich meal.

Ingredients :

1/2 cup (125 mL) sugar

1 envelope unflavored gelatin

1/4 tsp (1 mL) salt

1/2 cup (125 mL) each water and lemon juice

Grated rind of 1 lemon

3 eggs, separated

1/3 cup (80 mL) sugar

1 cup (250 mL) whipping cream

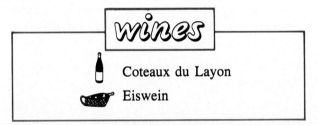

wines

Coteaux du Layon

Eiswein

Method :

• Mix together in a 4-cup (1 L) microwave-safe bowl the sugar, gelatin, salt, water, lemon juice and rind.

• Beat the egg yolks and add to the mixture.

• Microwave, uncovered, 2 minutes at MEDIUM-HIGH, stir well.

• Microwave 2 more minutes at MEDIUM-HIGH.

• Cool for mixture to thicken, about 30 minutes.

• Beat the egg whites until frothy. Beat in the remaining 1/3 cup (80 mL) sugar, then fold into the cooled lemon mixture.

• Whip cream and fold into mixture.

• Pour into an attractive serving bowl.

• Refrigerate 6 to 12 hours or until ready to serve.

Nassau Chocolate Mousse

Advance preparation: ....from 3 to 12 h
Cooking:.....................5 m
Standing:.....................none

A personal note: Serve this mousse in small cups or as a pie filling with chocolate cookie crumb crust.

Ingredients:

2 1-oz (24 g) squares semi-sweet chocolate

1/3 cup (80 mL) vanilla or plain white sugar

1 envelope unflavored gelatin

3 egg yolks

A pinch of salt

1 cup (250 mL) milk

3 tbsp (50 mL) rum or brandy

3 egg whites

1/3 cup (80 mL) sugar

1 cup (250 mL) whipping cream

Method:

• Melt the chocolate in a microwave-safe bowl 2 minutes at MEDIUM.

• Add the first 1/3 cup (80 mL) sugar and the gelatin, stir.

• Beat in the egg yolks and salt. Stir in the milk and rum or brandy, mix well.

• Microwave 4 minutes at HIGH, or until mixture is slightly thickened, stirring 3 times during the cooking period.

• Cool 30 to 40 minutes.

• Beat the egg whites until foamy. Gradually add the other 1/3 cup (80 mL) sugar and beat until stiff. Fold into the cold chocolate cream.

• Whip the cream until stiff and fold the chocolate mixture into it.

• Spoon into 6 to 8 individual dessert cups or into an 8-inch (20 cm) crumb or cookie crust.

• Refrigerate 3 to 12 hours before serving.

Cold Lemon Soufflé

Advance preparation: . . . . .2 h
Cooking: . . . . .30 s
Standing: .none

A personal note: Cold Lemon Soufflé is super served with lightly sweetened strawberries or raspberries. You can also cover and place in the freezer for 12 hours to obtain a frozen soufflé.

Ingredients:

3 egg yolks

1 cup (250 mL) sugar

1 envelope unflavored gelatin

1/4 cup (60 mL) cold water

1/3 cup (80 mL) fresh lemon juice

Grated rind of 1 lemon

1½ cups (375 mL) whipping cream

3 egg whites, beaten

Method:

• Beat egg yolks until pale yellow. Add the sugar gradually, beating thoroughly. The mixture will be light and creamy.

• Meanwhile add the fresh lemon juice and rind to the egg yolk mixture.

• Soak the gelatin 2 minutes in the cold water. Microwave the gelatin 30 seconds at HIGH, then add it to the creamed mixture, stirring as it is added. Stir to mix thoroughly.

• Refrigerate until mixture has the texture of egg whites.

• Whip the cream. Beat the egg whites. Gradually add both to the lemon mixture. Pour into a serving dish.

• Refrigerate at least 2 hours before serving. The soufflé can be refrigerated 2 to 3 days before being served.

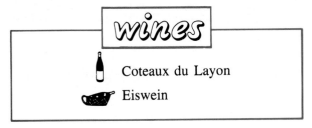

Coteaux du Layon

Eiswein

Helpful hint: To make a creamy cake topping, make the cake filling, then refrigerate overnight or place for 1 hour in the freezer. Fold in whipped cream to taste.

Helpful hint: To make a tasty cake filling with dried apricots, put them in a microwave-safe bowl with just enough cream to cover. Microwave 6 minutes at MEDIUM, then let stand 3 to 5 minutes. Purée in a blender with a small spoonful of butter. Cool and use.

Snow Eggs

- An old-fashioned dessert made the world over, this dish is sometimes caramelized when an elegant dessert is desired. It is very good without the caramel.

Preparation :	. . . . **30 m**
Cooking :	. . . . **from 8 to 10 m**
Standing :	. . . . **none**

Asti Spumante

Sweet champagne

Ingredients :

1½ cups (375 mL) milk

1/2 cup (125 mL) light cream

1/4 cup (60 mL) sugar

1 tsp (5 mL) vanilla

2 egg whites

1/4 cup (60 mL) sugar

A pinch of salt

1/2 tsp (2 mL) vanilla

3 egg yolks

Method :

- Place in a 6-cup (1.5 L) microwave-safe dish the milk, cream and the first 1/4 cup (60 mL) sugar. Mix well.

- Microwave 5 minutes at MEDIUM-HIGH, or until milk boils. Add the 1 teaspoon (5 mL) vanilla.

- Beat egg whites with the remaining sugar and a pinch of salt until stiff.

- Add the 1/2 teaspoon (2 mL) vanilla.

- Drop 6 to 8 tablespoons of the mixture on the boiling milk to form 6 to 8 mounds. Microwave, uncovered, 2 minutes at MEDIUM-HIGH.

- Turn meringues over and microwave at MEDIUM-HIGH another 30 seconds.

- Remove meringues from the milk with a slotted spoon into a serving dish.

- If necessary, repeat until all the egg white is cooked.

- To the remaining milk add the well-beaten egg yolks. Microwave at MEDIUM 2 to 3 minutes, stirring well after each minute. You should have a light, creamy, golden sauce.

- Beware of overcooking, as the sauce will curdle.

- Stir well and pour over the cooked egg whites.

- Serve warm or cool, then refrigerate.

Maple Syrup Parfait

Advance preparation: . . . . . **from 4 to 5 h**
Cooking: . . . .**3 m**
Standing: . . . .**none**

A personal note: This is a quick and easy way to prepare a parfait.

Ingredients:

2 cups (500 mL) vanilla ice cream

2 egg yolks

1/2 cup (125 mL) maple syrup

1/4 cup (60 mL) nuts, chopped (optional)

2 egg whites

1/2 tsp (2 mL) salt

Method:

• Uncover the ice cream and let it soften at room temperature.

• Beat the egg yolks in a microwave-safe bowl. Gradually add the maple syrup while beating.

• Microwave 2 minutes at MEDIUM, stir well.

• Microwave 1 more minute at MEDIUM, stir again. The sauce should be smooth and creamy.

• Cool, then add to the softened ice cream together with the nuts.

• Stir well. An electric beater may be used.

• Beat the egg whites stiff with the salt.

• Fold into the ice cream. Pour into a mold.

• Cover and refrigerate 4 to 5 hours before serving.

wines

Sainte-Croix-du-Mont, Château Coulac

Anjou, Moulin Touchais (recent vintage)

759

Dover Chocolate Pudding

Preparation : . . . . .20 m
Cooking : . . . . .6 m
Standing : .15 m

• No one will dare call this very interesting English dessert a bread pudding.

Ingredients :

3 tbsp (50 mL) butter

1 1-oz (28 g) square unsweetened chocolate

1/2 cup (125 mL) sugar

3 eggs

1 cup (250 mL) light cream or milk

1 ½ cups (375 mL) soft white breadcrumbs

1/4 cup (60 mL) toasted almonds, slivered

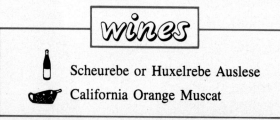

Scheurebe or Huxelrebe Auslese

California Orange Muscat

Method :

• Place the butter and unsweetened chocolate in a microwave-safe bowl and microwave 2 minutes at MEDIUM-HIGH, stirring once.

• When the chocolate is melted, add the sugar and stir until well mixed.

• Beat the eggs until fluffy.

• Add to chocolate mixture while stirring. Add the cream or milk and stir to mix thoroughly.

• Microwave 2 minutes at HIGH, stirring once.

• If needed, microwave 40 seconds more. Timing depends on how cold the cream or milk was.

• When creamy, let stand a few minutes, then stir in the breadcrumbs.

• Microwave, uncovered, 2 minutes at HIGH.

• Let stand 15 minutes before serving.

• Sprinkle the toasted almonds on top.

Pulled Bread Chocolate Pudding

Preparation: . . . . 20 m
Cooking: . . . . 15 m
Standing: . . . . 10 m

• The fact that the soft centre of bread slices is pulled into small pieces gives an almost soufflé texture to this bread pudding.

Ingredients:

2 cups (500 mL) milk or light cream

4 to 5 slices fresh white bread

1/3 cup (80 mL) unsweetened cocoa

1/2 cup (125 mL) brown sugar

1/2 tsp (2 mL) salt

1/4 cup (60 mL) butter

2 eggs well beaten

1 tsp (5 mL) vanilla

Method:

• Pour the milk or light cream into a microwave-safe bowl and microwave 5 minutes at HIGH.

• Remove crust from bread and pull the white, soft bread into small pieces. Put them into the hot milk. Mix. Let cool to tepid.

• Mix the cocoa, brown sugar and salt. Add to the softened bread and stir until well mixed.

• Place the butter in a microwave-safe dish and melt 2 minutes at HIGH. Add to the bread mixture. Stir well.

• Beat the eggs with the vanilla. Add to the bread. Mix well. Pour into a microwave-safe serving dish. Microwave 6 minutes at MEDIUM-HIGH.

• Let stand 10 minutes in the microwave oven.

• Test for doneness with the point of a knife. If middle is still a bit uncooked, microwave 1 minute at HIGH. Let stand until just tepid.

• Serve as is or with plain cream or whipped cream.

Scheurebe or Huxelrebe Auslese

Malvasia delle Lipari

Strawberry Pudding

Convection cooking

Preparation : .20 m
Cooking : . . . . .from 25 to 30 m
Standing : . . . . .none

Late Harvest Riesling
Sweet champagne

• The famous English summer pudding made with raspberries and served cold was the inspiration for this. I prefer to serve it tepid, as the fruit flavor is more pronounced.

Ingredients :

4 cups (1 L) strawberries

Juice of 1/2 a lemon

2/3 cup (160 mL) brown sugar

4 cups (1 L) toasted bread cubes

1/4 cup (60 mL) white sugar

Grated rind of 1 lemon

2 tbsp (30 mL) butter

Method :

• Wash and hull the berries and mix them with the lemon juice and brown sugar. Place mixture in a shallow 6-cup (1.5 L) pan.

• Mix the bread cubes, white sugar and lemon rind.

• Sprinkle over the strawberries, but do not mix. Dot with butter.

• Preheat the convection part of microwave oven at 350°F (180°C). Bake pudding 25 to 30 minutes in preheated oven.

• Serve warm or tepid with cold rich cream or sour cream.

Custard with Jam

Preparation : . . . . .10 m
Cooking : . . . . .from 6 to 9 m
Standing : . . . . .5 m

A personal note : If you wish to make a dessert in a jiffy with ingredients usually on hand in any kitchen, try this one. The cooking period varies, depending on how cold the milk and eggs are, so make sure to check doneness after 6 minutes.

Method :

- Place all the ingredients, except the jam, in a 4-cup (1 L) measuring cup or bowl. Stir well.
- Pour into a Pyrex or ceramic pie plate.
- Microwave 6 to 9 minutes at MEDIUM-HIGH.
- Let stand 5 minutes, cover with the chosen jam and serve.

Ingredients :

1¾ cups (440 mL) milk

1/4 cup (60 mL) sugar

3 eggs

1/4 tsp (1 mL) salt

1/2 tsp (2 mL) vanilla

1/3 tsp (1.5 mL) nutmeg

Jam of your choice

Monbazillac

Muscat Beaumes-de-Venise

Homemade Pudding Mix

Preparation: . . . .**4 m**
Cooking: . . . .**none**
Standing: . . . .**none**

• This is a very handy mix that allows you to prepare an economical and delicious dessert in less than five minutes. The flavoring is up to you.

Ingredients:

2½ cups (625 mL) powdered milk
1 cup (250 mL) sugar
3/4 cup (190 mL) cornstarch
1 tsp (5 mL) salt

For Chocolate Pudding Mix:

• Add
3/4 cup (190 mL) unsweetened cocoa
1 tsp (5 mL) instant coffee

For Caramel Pudding Mix:

• Replace the sugar in the basic recipe with an equal amount of brown sugar, i.e. **1 cup (250 mL).**
• Add **1/4 tsp (1 mL) cinnamon.**

Method:

• Place all the ingredients in a bowl and mix thoroughly.
• Place in a container or a plastic bag and close tightly.
• Keep in a cool place. You do not have to refrigerate the mix.
• It keeps for 3 to 4 months.

Homemade Pudding

Preparation: . . . .**10 m**
Cooking: . . . .**4 m**
Standing: . . . .**30 m**

Ingredients:

3/4 cup (190 mL) Homemade Pudding Mix
1 cup (250 mL) water
1/4 cup (60 mL) milk or cream

Method:

• Place all the ingredients in a 4-cup (1 L) microwave-safe measuring cup, mix. Microwave 4 minutes at HIGH, stirring twice during the cooking.

To flavor:

• Add one of the following to the cooked pudding:
1 tsp (5 mL) vanilla *or*
Rind of one orange or lemon *or*
2 tbsp (30 mL) rum or brandy

Omelette Tropicale

Advance preparation: ....1 h
Cooking: ....from 2 to 4 m
Standing: ....none

A personal note: This is a very easy dessert to prepare. It can be made with as many or as few eggs as you wish. The other ingredients are easily increased or decreased according to your needs.

Ingredients:

1 banana, peeled and sliced

2 tbsp (30 mL) rum

1 tbsp (15 mL) butter

1 tsp (5 mL) slivered almonds

3 eggs

1 tbsp (15 mL) sugar

3 tbsp (50 mL) cold water

1 tbsp (15 mL) currant jelly

Method:

• Soak sliced banana in rum 1 hour before making the omelette.

• Melt the butter in a microwave-safe pie plate 30 seconds at HIGH.

• Add the almonds. Microwave 30 to 60 seconds or until golden brown, stirring once.

• Beat the eggs with the sugar and cold water.

• Pour over the almonds. Microwave at MEDIUM-HIGH 1 or 2 minutes. Depending on number of eggs used, cooking time may range from 30 seconds to 3 minutes.

• Place the currant jelly in the middle, fold the omelette over.

• Pour the cold rum bananas on top. Enjoy!

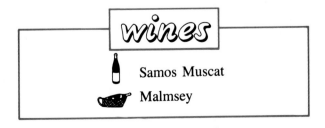

Samos Muscat

Malmsey

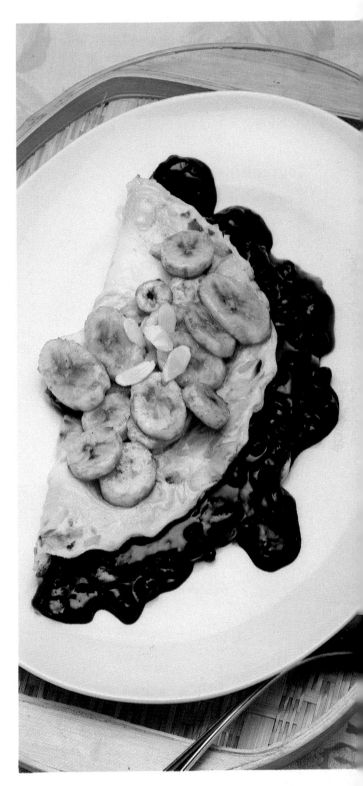

Red Wine Jelly

Advance preparation : . . . . **12 h**
Cooking : . . . . **7 m**
Standing : . . . . **none**

A personal note : Red Wine Jelly is a cool dessert that can be made a day or two ahead of time. In the summer, I like to serve it with sweetened raspberries, whipped cream or plain cream.

Asti Spumante

Banyuls

Ingredients :

1 envelope unflavored gelatin

1/4 cup (60 mL) cold water

2 pieces of lemon peel

1 cup (250 mL) water

1/2 cup (125 mL) sugar

1 cup (250 mL) jam of your choice

1 cup (250 mL) dry red wine

2 tbsp (30 mL) brandy or lemon juice

Method :

- Soak gelatin in the cold water for 5 minutes.
- Place in a microwave-safe bowl the lemon peel, water, sugar and jam.
- Microwave 5 minutes at HIGH, stir well.
- Microwave 2 minutes at MEDIUM, stir well.
- Add the gelatin and stir until it is dissolved.
- Add the remaining ingredients. Stir well.
- Pour into a mold or into a glass dish.
- Refrigerate 12 hours before serving.

Zabaglione

Preparation:	.....................5 m
Cooking:	......................1 m
Standing:	.....................none

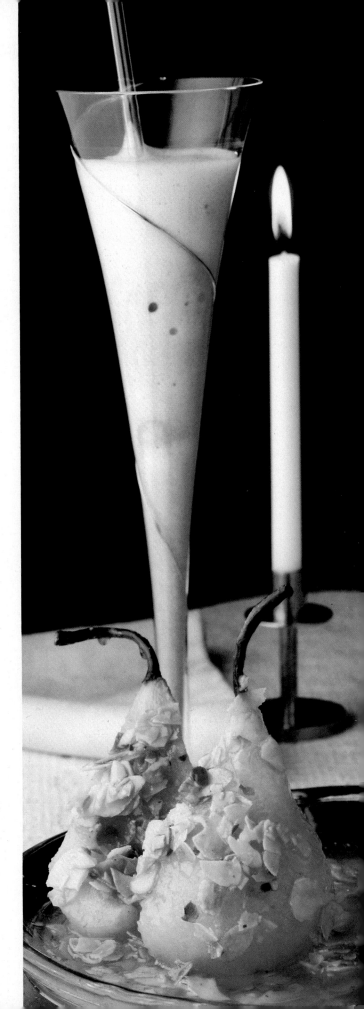

• Zabaglione is the most delicate and exciting of all the Italian desserts. To make it to perfection, you must follow the instructions exactly as given. I like to make this in front of my guests, with the microwave oven set on a rolling table in the dining room.

Ingredients:

6 egg yolks
1/4 cup (60 mL) fine granulated sugar
1/2 cup (125 mL) Marsala or Port wine

Method:

• Beat the egg yolks and the sugar with an electric beater until thick and yellow.

• Slowly add the wine, while beating all the time. I add a full tablespoon (15 mL) at a time.

• Microwave, uncovered, 30 seconds at MEDIUM, then beat mixture again with electric beater until smooth and frothy.

• Repeat this operation twice more, beating well each time, then microwave again at MEDIUM for 15 seconds.

• This foamy, delicate cream should now be ready to serve but, depending on the starting temperature of the eggs, it could require another 15 seconds of cooking at MEDIUM.

• Pour into individual glasses.

• Serve hot by itself or with small meringues.

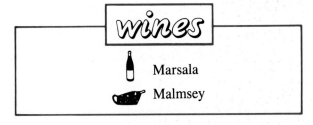

wines

🍾 Marsala

🥄 Malmsey

Zabaglione and Pears Florentine →

Jams

Jams in the Microwave

- One day, facing an emergency that had to be dealt with immediately, I had a problem. I had just finished cleaning some strawberries to make jam. I knew it meant an hour of work. Suddenly, I happened to look at my microwave oven and said: "Why not?" Then and there I started to work — "somewhat in the dark" — and discovered I could make the jam, from fruit cleaning to jam-in-the-jar, in 30 minutes. Really happy about it, I decided to test other types of fruit. That was in 1982. At the end of that summer, I had a full shelf of all types of jams, labelled and waiting!

- In 1985, I started to open some to sample flavor, color and keeping quality. I could not believe what I saw and tasted.

- Whether I tried the 1982 or 1983 or 1984-1985, they were all fragrant, with perfect texture and flavor. "Never again," I said to myself, "shall I ever make another jar of jam other than cooked in the microwave."

How to sterilize jars

- Uncover each jar and fill with hot or cold water.

- Place covers in a microwave-safe bowl, cover with hot or cold water. Place in the middle of the microwave oven.

- Place all the jars around the bowl — 6 to 8 jars is usually what is comfortable to use in a microwave oven.

- Microwave 20 minutes at HIGH.

- Using a cloth, as they are very hot, remove each jar to a tray. Pull covers from the water, place on tray. Cover the whole with a clean cloth.

- Repeat operation until all the jam jars you wish to use are sterilized.

- It does not matter if the water in the jars cools. What is important is to keep them covered with the cloth and empty the jars only when they are to be filled with the boiling hot jam or syrup and fruits.

- Sterilize all the glasses you need before you start making the jam or preserve.

A few "how-tos" to remember

- Because microwaved jam relies on the natural pectin of the fruit with the help of the citric acid in fresh lemon, these jams are lower in calories.
Example: Most microwaved jams have 16 calories per tablespoon (15 mL), as compared with most commercial and old-fashioned jams, which have about 50 calories per tablespoon (15 mL).

- Microwaved jams, made according to the following recipes, will keep 2 to 3 years in a cool, dark place, such as a cool pantry.

- Make sure all fruit are well washed before cooking. When washing strawberries, raspberries or any small, soft fruit, wash them before removing stem as gently as possible under running cold water, with the fruit in a colander. Let the fruit drain in the colander set over a tray. Remove stem when ready to make the jam.

- Do not double the recipes given for jam; the results will not be perfect. The cooking period gives you just enough time to measure the sugar and prepare the fruit for the next batch. You need not wash the cooking pot between recipes, even if it is sort of sticky.

- The following recipes will give 5½ to 6 8-oz (250 mL) jars.

Raspberry or Strawberry Jam

Advance preparation : . . .**from 10 to 12 h**
Cooking : . . . .**20 m**
Standing : . . . .**none**

A personal note : Raspberries and strawberries cook in the same way in this recipe. I recommend using small strawberries, such as the Vercor type, for making jam, as they do not break up when cooking and big strawberries have less fragrance.

Ingredients :

3 cups (750 mL) sugar

4 cups (1 L) strawberries or raspberries

Juice of 1/2 a lemon

Method :

• Place sugar in a 12-cup (3 L) microwave-safe bowl. Top with the strawberries or raspberries. Pour the lemon juice over all. Do not stir or cover. Microwave 10 minutes at HIGH.

• Stir thoroughly. All the sugar will be at the bottom of the bowl and it must be well stirred with the fruits. Use a rubber spatula or a plastic spoon to stir, so the fruit does not get crushed. Microwave, uncovered, another 10 minutes at HIGH.

• Remove water from sterilized jars when you are ready to fill. Fill with the boiling jam. Cover tightly without delay.

• Place filled jars upside down on a cloth. Let stand 10 to 12 hours or until cold.

• Label, store. For your own information, mark the date.

Fine Shredded Marmalade

Advance preparation: . . . . **12 h**
Cooking: . . . . **45 m**
Standing: . . . . **none**

- I have microwaved this marmalade for the last four years and never lost a jar.

Ingredients:

1 orange

1 grapefruit

1 lemon

Water

Sugar

Method:

- Remove rind of well washed orange, grapefruit and lemon with zester knife in very small shreds, without any of the white part.

- Cover rind with boiling water. Microwave at HIGH 5 minutes. Drain.

- Cut fruit into very thin slices, discarding seeds. Add slices to peel, and measure. Place the whole in a large microwave-safe bowl, add 1/4 cup (60 mL) of water for each cup of fruit. Microwave at HIGH 20 minutes.

- Add 1 cup (250 mL) of sugar for each cup of fruit mixture. Microwave at HIGH 15 to 20 minutes or until thick and amber colored. Stir a few times. Cool 5 minutes.

- Pour into hot sterilized jars.

- Cover and invert jars. Let stand 12 hours or more before labelling.

- Keep in a cool, dark place.

Helpful hint: Food containing a lot of fat or sugar reheats very fast in the microwave.

Honeyed Peach Jam

Advance preparation:............12 h
Cooking:....................25 m
Standing:....................none

A personal note: Superb with hot croissants, this jam is equally good served with roasted duck or quail.

Ingredients:

3 lb (1.5 kg) fresh peaches*

2 inches (5 cm) cinnamon stick

1 tsp (5 mL) whole cloves

1/2 tsp (2 mL) allspice, whole or ground

2 cups (500 mL) honey

3 tbsp (50 mL) fresh lemon juice

1/4 cup (60 mL) fresh orange juice

1/4 cup (60 mL) hot water

1/4 tsp (1 mL) salt

* The fruit must be weighted for this jam, as size and texture of peaches vary quite a bit.

Method:

• Pour boiling water over the peaches to cover, then peel and pit them.

• Chop the peaches finely or pass through food processor for 2 seconds.

• Tie loosely in a cheesecloth or a piece of cotton the cinnamon stick and whole cloves and allspice. Place in the jam container with the peaches and the remaining ingredients.

• Microwave 10 minutes at HIGH.

• Stir well and microwave at HIGH 10 minutes more.

• Depending on the maturity of the peaches, this jam sometimes needs 5 minutes more at HIGH.

• Bottle and cool as for Strawberry Jam.

Autumn Plum Jam

Advance preparation : . . . . .12 h
Cooking : . . . . .35 m
Standing : . . . . .none

A personal note : There's no need to remove plum pits, since they float to the top when jam is cooked. They are then easy to remove. Fresh mint leaves are at their best when those fragrant little blue plums are at the market in the fall.

- Wash apples, peel and remove cores.
- Place sugar in a large microwave-safe bowl, add the fruit and top with the mint leaves.
- Microwave, uncovered, 15 minutes at HIGH. Stir well.
- Microwave 10 minutes at HIGH, stir. Microwave 10 minutes at MEDIUM.
- Pour into sterilized jars, as for Strawberry Jam.

Ingredients :

1½ lb (750 g) blue autumn plums

1 lb (500 g) sour or wild apples, sliced or chopped

4 cups (1 L) sugar

1 cup (250 mL) fresh mint leaves

Method :

- Wash plums and cut around them ; do not peel.

A personal note : Serve this deep purple jam with roast lamb or chicken or use it to sweeten your fruit salads. It's also a treat served with cottage cheese and toasted English muffins. In other words, it's a " must " in your fruit cupboard.

Green Apple Jam

Advance preparation : . . . . .2 days
Cooking : . . . . .25 m
Standing : . . . . .none

• The recipe for this old fashioned apple jam was given to me by my grandmother, who inherited it from her mother. I hope today's mothers will give favorite recipes to their daughters, who can later talk about them.

• This jam is made with the season's first green apples. Adapted to microwave cooking, it turns out perfectly, with an even better color and flavor.

Ingredients :

4 cups (1 L) green apples, unpeeled and chopped
4 cups (1 L) first young rhubarb, diced
1 cup (250 mL) canned crushed pineapple, drained
1 cup (250 mL) seedless raisins or currants
Grated rind and juice of 1 orange and 1 lemon
4 cups (1 L) sugar
1/2 tsp (2 mL) salt
1/2 tsp (2 mL) each nutmeg and allspice
1/4 cup (60 mL) of the drained pineapple juice

Method :

• Place all the ingredients in a large microwave-safe bowl.

• Stir well and let stand overnight on the kitchen counter.

• Microwave 15 minutes at HIGH, stir well. Microwave 10 minutes at HIGH.

• Pour while hot into sterilized jam jars.

• Cover, turn upside down on counter.

• Let cool 10 to 12 hours.

Old-Fashioned Gooseberry Jam

Advance preparation:	.........2 days
Cooking:	....................20 m
Standing:	....................none

• Gooseberries and apples were a must in jam making in the '20s. Whenever I can find gooseberries, I hurry to make this tasty jam. I adapted the recipe to microwave cooking with great ease and improved color and flavor, even though I sincerely believed the old way could never be improved.

Ingredients:

1 ¼ lb (625 g) gooseberries*

3 large apples

3 cups (750 mL) sugar

Juice of 1 lemon

Red and green gooseberries are equally good.

Method:

• Clean the gooseberries by removing the small tails and wash. Mash with a potato masher or chop in a food processor.

• Sprinkle with half the sugar.

• Cover with a cloth and let stand on the kitchen counter for 12 hours.

• Peel, core and dice the apples and mix thoroughly with the gooseberries.

• Place in a large dish with the sugar and lemon juice.

• Microwave 10 minutes at HIGH, stir well.

• Microwave another 10 minutes at HIGH, stir.

• Pour into sterilized jars.

• Cover and let stand 12 hours, upside down, on a tray or on the kitchen counter.

Dutch Pumpkin Jam

Advance preparation : . . . . 2 days
Cooking : . . . . 30 m
Standing : . . . . none

A personal note : My mother would sometimes use some of the Halloween pumpkin to make this autumn jam. For perfect results with this one, use a scale.

Ingredients :

2 lb (1 kg) pumpkin, peeled and diced*

3 cups (750 mL) sugar

1 tsp (5 mL) fresh ginger root, grated

1/4 tsp (5 mL) allspice

Grated peel of 1 lemon

Juice of 1 lemon

1/2 cup (125 mL) sweet Dutch gin**

* Weigh the pumpkin after it has been peeled and diced.

** The best Dutch gin for this jam is De Kuyper.

Method :

• Peel and remove seeds from pumpkin, then weigh the 2 pounds (1 kg).

• Place in a microwave-safe bowl the sugar and the pumpkin, in alternate layers.

• Cover with a cloth and let stand 24 hours in a cool place.

• To cook, add the remaining ingredients to the pumpkin, except the gin. Microwave 10 minutes at HIGH, stir well.

• Microwave 10 minutes more at HIGH, stir.

• Add the gin. Microwave 10 minutes at MEDIUM, stir well.

• Pour into sterilized jars. Cover.

• Let cool 12 hours, upside down.

Apple Rum Chutney

Advance preparation : . . . . **12 h**
Cooking : . . . . **from 20 to 25 m**
Standing : . . . . **none**

A personal note : Every year I make this chutney. Since the older it gets, the better it is, be sure to date it. I have some that are seven years old.

1½ tsp (7 mL) salt
1/2 tsp (2 mL) dried red pepper
1 cup (250 mL) cider or Japanese vinegar
1/2 cup (125 mL) dark rum

Ingredients :

5 cups (1.25 L) apples, pared, cored and chopped
1 lemon, seeded and chopped
1 cup (250 mL) brown sugar
1 cup (250 mL) granulated sugar
1½ cups (375 mL) seedless raisins
2 tbsp (30 mL) candied ginger

Method :

• Combine in a large microwave-safe saucepan all the ingredients. Cover and microwave for 10 minutes at HIGH.

• Stir well. Microwave at HIGH 10 to 15 minutes, or until thick and syrupy.

• Let stand 15 minutes. Bottle, cover and invert the jars. Let stand 12 hours to cool.

Candies

Chocolate Bark

Preparation : . . . .**5 m**
Cooking : . . . .**4 m**
Standing : . . . .**none**

• This microwaved sweet is made in 5 minutes, ready to be served in 10.

Ingredients :

1 package (350 g) semi-sweet chocolate chips
1 tbsp (15 mL) butter
3/4 cup (190 mL) nuts of your choice, chopped
1/2 cup (125 mL) raisins

Method :

• Place the chocolate chips and the butter in a microwave-safe bowl. Microwave 4 minutes at MEDIUM-HIGH, stirring once.

• When all the chips have melted, add the nuts and raisins, stir. Spread on a piece of waxed paper set on a cookie sheet. Cool on kitchen counter.

• To serve, break up in pieces.

• Will keep 2 to 3 weeks in covered box in a cool place.

Marshmallow Treats

Preparation:	...................15 m
Cooking:	.............from 4 to 5 m
Standing:	......................none

Ingredients:

1 8-oz (250 g) bag of marshmallows

1/4 cup (60 mL) butter or margarine

5 cups (1.25 L) Rice Krispies cereal

Method:

• In a large microwave-safe dish combine the marshmallows and the butter or margarine. Microwave 4 to 5 minutes at HIGH, stirring twice.

• Add the cereal and stir well to coat thoroughly with the marshmallow mixture. Press into buttered dish.

• Cool and cut into squares.

Nanaimo Bars

Advance preparation:	.............1 h
Cooking:	.......................2 m
Standing:	......................none

• In the '70s, everyone was cooking these, which were called both cookies and candy bars. To me, they are candy. Quick, easy to make and delicious.

Ingredients:

1/2 cup (125 mL) butter or margarine

5 tbsp (75 mL) sugar

5 tbsp (75 mL) unsweetened cocoa

1 egg

1 tsp (5 mL) vanilla

2 cups (500 mL) graham cracker crumbs

1 cup (250 mL) coconut

1/2 cup (125 mL) walnuts, chopped

1/2 cup (125 mL) chocolate chips

Method:

• Place butter or margarine in a microwave-safe bowl and melt 1 minute at HIGH.

• Add sugar, cocoa, egg and vanilla. Stir until very well mixed.

• Add graham cracker crumbs, coconut and walnuts. Stir until well mixed.

• Pour into an ungreased 8 x 8-inch (20 x 20 cm) square microwave-safe pan.

• Spread equally.

• Wet your hands and press batter into pan.

• Sprinkle chocolate chips over all. Microwave 2 minutes at MEDIUM. Cool.

• Cover with plastic wrap. Refrigerate at least 1 hour or overnight.

• Cut into squares. Serve.

Nanaimo Bars →

Homemade Granola

Preparation: . . . .**30 m**
Cooking: . . . .**10 m**
Standing: . . . .**none**

• Making your own granola is more economical than buying it and the flavor certainly is better. It will keep in a well-covered container for 6 to 8 months. Serve as a cereal or make your own healthy sweets.

Ingredients:

4 cups (1 L) oatmeal

1 cup (250 mL) coconut

3/4 cup (190 mL) wheat germ

1/2 cup (125 mL) sesame seeds

1/2 cup (125 mL) nuts of your choice, chopped

1/2 cup (125 mL) brown sugar

1/2 cup (125 mL) honey

1/2 cup (125 mL) margarine or butter, melted

1/2 tsp (2 mL) salt

1 tsp (5 mL) vanilla

1/2 cup (125 mL) raisins

Method:

• Blend all the ingredients except the raisins, in a large glass bowl.

• Microwave at HIGH 10 minutes, or until the ingredients are toasted, stirring every 4 minutes.

• Stir in the raisins at the last 2 minutes of cooking.

• Cool, sprinkled on cookie sheet.

• Store in covered container. Yield: 6 cups (1.5 L)

Helpful hint: To clarify honey that has turned to sugar, uncover its jar and microwave 30 seconds to 1 minute at HIGH, depending on the amount of honey. Remove from oven as soon as liquefied.

Granola Bars

Advance preparation : ..**from 40 to 60 m**
Cooking :.....................**5 m**
Standing :.....................**none**

Ingredients :

1/4 cup (60 mL) sesame seeds

1/2 cup (125 mL) honey or corn syrup

3/4 cup (190 mL) peanut butter, crunchy style

3 cups (750 mL) homemade granola

1/2 cup (125 mL) nuts of your choice, chopped

1/3 cup (80 mL) dried apricots, chopped

1/4 cup (60 mL) sunflower seeds (optional)

1/4 cup (60 mL) wheat germ

Method :

• Spread the sesame seeds in a microwave-safe baking dish.

• Microwave at HIGH 4 to 5 minutes, or until golden brown, stirring often. Set aside.

• Measure honey or corn syrup in a large glass bowl, cover with waxed paper. Microwave 1 minute at HIGH.

• Blend in the peanut butter. Microwave 30 seconds at HIGH.

• Stir in the remaining ingredients and the toasted sesame seeds.

• Press evenly on a 7 × 11-inch (18 × 28 cm) cookie sheet. Cover.

• Refrigerate 40 to 60 minutes.

• Cut into bars.

Helpful hint : To rehydrate apricots to make jam or cake filling, you don't have to soak them for hours ever again. Just put the required amount in a bowl with just enough water or other liquid of your choice to cover. Heat 6 minutes at MEDIUM in your microwave oven and let stand 3 to 5 minutes.

Syrup for Frozen Fresh Fruit

Preparation : . . . . **15 m**
Cooking : . . . . **from 12 to 17 m**
Standing : . . . . **none**

• For the last six years I have prepared all varieties of fruit for freezing, to enjoy through the winter months.

Ingredients :

Thin syrup :

2 cups (500 mL) sugar

4 cups (1 L) water

• Microwave 12 minutes at HIGH

Medium syrup :

3 cups (750 mL) sugar

4 cups (1 L) water

• Microwave 14 minutes at HIGH

Heavy syrup :

5 cups (1.25 L) sugar

4 cups (1 L) water

• Microwave 17 minutes at HIGH

Method :

• Place the sugar and the water in a microwave-safe bowl large enough to prevent syrup from boiling over.

• Stir well after 6 minutes of cooking.

• The syrup must cool before the fruit is added.

• Place prepared fruit, such as peeled peaches cut in half, in jars, with one hard pit in every jar.

• Top with the cooled syrup. Cover, label and freeze.

Helpful hint : To melt chocolate, place 1-ounce (28 g) squares of chocolate in their waxed paper wrappers, seam side up, on a plate and microwave 1 minute at MEDIUM. Scrape chocolate from paper with a rubber spatula. No chocolate will be lost on the sides of a pan — and there's no pan to wash.

Fruit Desserts

Honey Bee Apples

Preparation: . . . . **10 m**
Cooking: . . . . **10 m**
Standing: . . . . **none**

• Do not let the simplicity of this dessert deceive you. It is an elegant dessert that can be served to company.

Ingredients:

6 baking apples
2/3 cup (160 mL) honey
Grated rind of 1 orange
1/2 tsp (2 mL) nutmeg
2 tbsp (30 mL) rum
Juice of 1/2 an orange

Method:

• Core the apples and, starting at the stem end, pare them one-third of the way down.

• Place them in a 2 × 8-inch (5 × 20 cm) microwave-safe baking dish.

• Mix together the honey, orange rind and nutmeg and fill each cavity with the mixture.

• Mix the rum with the orange juice and pour over the apples.

• Microwave 6 minutes at HIGH.

• Baste apples with the juice in the bottom of the dish.

• Microwave at MEDIUM 4 to 5 minutes, or until the apples are tender.

• Serve hot or cold.

Sweet Vouvray
Moulin Touchais

Apple Allegro

Preparation: . . . . **10 m**
Cooking: . . . . **10 m**
Standing: . . . . **none**

A personal note: There are two pleasant ways to serve these apples — warm, with whipped cream on top or over ice cream, or cold, on top of sponge cake.

Ingredients:

6 medium apples
2 tbsp (30 mL) butter, melted
Lemon juice
4 tbsp (60 mL) brown sugar
2 tsp (10 mL) brandy
1/2 tsp (2 mL) cinnamon

Method:

• Peel the apples, cut them into quarters and core.

• Arrange in a single layer, core-side down, in a buttered microwave-safe baking dish.

• Brush with melted butter. Sprinkle with lemon juice to taste, brown sugar, brandy and cinnamon.

• Microwave 10 minutes at HIGH.

• Baste several times with the juice in the bottom of the dish. Serve.

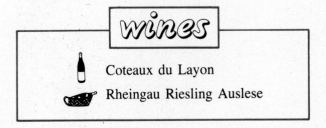

Coteaux du Layon
Rheingau Riesling Auslese

Poached Apples

A personal note: I make this dessert when apples are past their prime, at the middle or end of winter. Quick and easy to prepare, Poached Apples are most tasty.

Ingredients:

5 to 6 apples
1/2 cup (125 mL) brown sugar
1/2 cup (125 mL) water or apple juice
Grated rind and juice of 1/2 a lemon or orange
2 tbsp (30 mL) jam of your choice
2 tbsp (30 mL) sherry (optional)

Method:

• Peel the apples and cut them into quarters.

• Place in a microwave-safe bowl the brown sugar, water or apple juice, the lemon or orange grated rind and juice. Microwave at HIGH 3 minutes.

• Stir well. Add the apples, stir. Microwave at HIGH 5 to 7 minutes, stirring once during the cooking period.

• Remove the apples to a serving dish with a slotted spoon, draining as much syrup as possible.

• Add the remaining ingredients to the syrup. Stir. Microwave at HIGH 1 minute. Pour over the apples.

• Cool, cover and refrigerate until ready to serve.

Coteaux du Layon
Moulin Touchais

Maple Poached Apples

• This is a truly Canadian recipe. Maple syrup and apples are usually on hand in most households.

Ingredients:

4 to 5 apples
1/3 cup (80 mL) maple syrup
3 tbsp (50 mL) butter
A pinch of allspice (optional)

Method:

• Place in a 9-inch (23 cm) pie plate (ceramic or Pyrex) the maple syrup, butter and allspice. Microwave 2 minutes at HIGH.

• Peel and core apples, cut in four. Roll in the hot syrup. Microwave 3 minutes at HIGH.

• Turn the apple quarters. Microwave 4 to 5 minutes at HIGH.

• Serve hot or cold, but do not refrigerate.

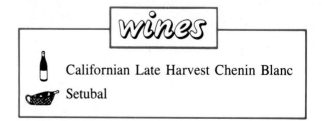

Californian Late Harvest Chenin Blanc
Setubal

Caramel Apples

Preparation: . . . . .15 m
Cooking: . . . . .from 9 to 12 m
Standing: . . . . .1 h

• I like to make these quick and easy apples all year round, but especially when the first Melba apples are available. Melbas have a very short season and are not good keepers, but they are worth looking for.

Ingredients:

4 to 6 apples

1/3 cup (80 mL) butter or margarine

1 cup (250 mL) brown sugar

1/2 tsp (2 mL) cinnamon or allspice

2 tbsp (30 mL) cream

1 tsp (5 mL) vanilla extract

Method:

• Peel the apples, cut them into quarters and core.

• Place the butter or margarine in a 9-inch (23 cm) microwave-safe pie plate.

• Microwave at HIGH 2 minutes. Stir in the brown sugar and the spice of your choice until well mixed.

• Place the apples over this sugar mixture.

• Microwave 6 to 7 minutes at HIGH, depending on the variety of apples used — they should be soft when touched with the point of a knife, but not mushy.

• Remove the cooked apples to a serving dish.

• Add the cream and vanilla extract to the syrup in the plate.

• Microwave 3 to 5 minutes at HIGH, stirring twice.

• When the syrup has thickened, pour over the apples.

• Let stand about 1 hour at room temperature before serving.

• If you wish to make these early in the day, simply warm them up 1 minute at HIGH when ready to serve.

wines

Cream sherry

Hungarian Tokay

Apple Crisp

Preparation : . . . . **15 m**
Cooking : . . . . **18 m**
Standing : . . . . **none**

A personal note : Depending on the occasion, I like to serve this Apple Crisp hot topped with very cold ice cream, cold with a creamy butter-scotch sauce, or with a small decanter of hot rum for each one to use to taste.

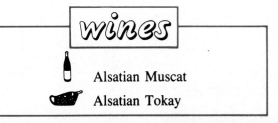

Alsatian Muscat
Alsatian Tokay

Ingredients :

4 cups (1 L) apples

1/3 cup (80 mL) sugar

2 tbsp (30 mL) flour

1/2 tsp (2 mL) cinnamon *or*
    1/4 tsp (1 mL) ground cardamom

1 tbsp (15 mL) margarine or butter

2 tbsp (30 mL) lemon juice

Topping :

3/4 cup (190 mL) brown sugar

3/4 cup (190 mL) flour

1/3 cup (80 mL) butter

2 tbsp (30 mL) nuts, chopped

A pinch of salt

A pinch of cinnamon or cardamom

Method :

• Peel the apples and slice them into an 8 × 8-inch (20 × 20 cm) microwave-safe dish.

• Mix together the sugar, flour, cinnamon or carda-mom and margarine or butter and sprinkle over the apples. Pour lemon juice over all.

• Mix the topping ingredients together. Sprinkle over the apples. Press down all over with a knife.

• Microwave 10 minutes at HIGH, and 8 or 9 minutes at MEDIUM-HIGH, until the topping is cooked and lightly browned.

English Galette

Preparation : ....10 m
Cooking : ....12 m
Standing : ....10 m

A personal note : An old-fashioned English luncheon dessert, Galette is served with a bowl of cinnamon sugar, prepared by mixing together **1 teaspoon (5 mL) cinnamon** and **1 cup (250 mL) sugar.**

Ingredients :

4 medium apples

2 eggs, beaten

1½ cups (375 mL) milk

1½ cups (375 mL) flour

2 tsp (10 mL) baking powder

2 tbsp (30 mL) sugar

1/2 tsp (2 mL) salt

2 tbsp (30 mL) butter

Juice and grated rind of 1 lemon

Method :

• Peel the apples, core them and chop or coarsely grate.

• Add beaten eggs to milk, beat a few seconds.

• Mix together the flour, baking powder, sugar and salt. Add to milk mixture, stir.

• Place the butter in a small microwave-safe bowl and microwave 40 seconds at HIGH. Stir the melted butter into the mixture.

• Mix together the grated or chopped apples, the lemon juice and rind. Add to batter, mix well. Place in a round 10½-inch (26 cm) microwave-safe dish. Microwave at HIGH 10 minutes. There may be a spot in the middle that is still soft. If so, microwave another 2 minutes at HIGH.

• Sprinkle top with a spoonful or two of dark brown sugar, let stand 10 minutes.

Asti Spumante

Sweet sparkling Vouvray

790

Pink or Purple Applesauce

Preparation : . . . .**15 m**
Cooking : . . . .**13 m**
Standing : . . . .**none**

• One day I found a cup of cranberries in my freezer that somehow never had been used. I took them out and — looking for something to do with them — spied six apples in my fruit basket. Why not try cooking them together in the microwave oven? The result was an applesauce with a beautiful color and a very interesting taste.

Ingredients :

6 apples
1 cup (250 mL) cranberries, uncooked
1 cup (250 mL) sugar
1 tbsp (15 mL) fresh lemon juice
Freshly grated nutmeg, to taste*

Method :

• Peel, core and slice the apples. Place in a 4-cup (1 L) microwave-safe dish the apples, cranberries, sugar and lemon juice.

• Microwave at HIGH 10 minutes. Stir well.

• Microwave 2 to 3 minutes at MEDIUM. Stir again.

• Pour into a serving dish.

• Top with the grated nutmeg.

* It is much more economical to buy whole nutmeg and a nutmeg grater — and grate whatever you require — than to buy ground nutmeg. The nutmeg will keep fragrant, whole, for 2 to 3 years.

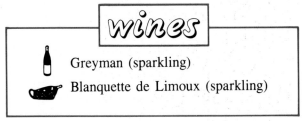

Greyman (sparkling)
Blanquette de Limoux (sparkling)

Jellied Rhubarb

Advance preparation : . . . . .**from 2 to 3 h**
Cooking : . . . .**from 8 to 9 m**
Standing : . . . .**none**

• In the winter when only frozen rhubarb is available, I enjoy making this fast, easy and tasty dessert.

Ingredients :

1 lb (500 g) frozen rhubarb*
1/3 cup (80 mL) water
1 package 6 oz (175 g) strawberry or peach Jell-O or other jelly powder

Method :

• Place in a microwave-safe bowl the frozen rhubarb and the water.

• Microwave at HIGH 8 to 9 minutes, stirring well after 5 minutes of cooking.

• Place the Jell-O or other jelly powder in a serving dish. Pour the hot rhubarb over and stir until thoroughly mixed. The heat of the rhubarb is sufficient to dissolve the granulated gelatin.

• Refrigerate until ready to serve as is or topped with cream, whipped cream or ice cream.

* The frozen rhubarb I like best is sold in 2 pounds (1 kg) bags. Half the bag is used to make this dessert.

Asti Spumante
Coteaux du Layon

Baked Rhubarb

Preparation :	. . . . **10 m**
Cooking :	. . . . **4 m**
Standing :	. . . . **3 m**

A personal note : You may become addicted to this, just as I am. I sometimes use 10 to 12 wild rose petals chopped fine with rose water or chopped fresh wild roses (2 or 3 are sufficient).

Ingredients :

2 cups (500 mL) rhubarb

2 tbsp (30 mL) water

A pinch of salt

1/2 cup (125 mL) sugar

1/8 tsp (0.5 mL) rose water*

* Rose water is sold in drugstores and in speciality food shops.

Method :

• Clean and cut the rhubarb in 1/2-inch (1 cm) pieces. Place in an 8-cup (2 L) microwave-safe dish. Add water and salt. Microwave 4 minutes at HIGH, stirring once.

• Add sugar, rose water or chopped wild roses.

• Let stand 3 minutes. Stir thoroughly.

Variation :

• Sugar may be replaced by **an equal amount of honey.**

• Sprinkle top with **grated rind of 1 orange** and **a dash of nutmeg.**

Asti Spumante

Sweet Anjou

Rhubarb Crisp

Preparation :	. . . . **10 m**
Cooking :	. . . . **15 m**
Standing :	. . . . **none**

• An old Canadian favorite. For my family, it isn't spring until I make this old Canadian favorite with fresh-cut rhubarb from the garden.

Ingredients :

2 cups (500 mL) rhubarb

2 tbsp (30 mL) lemon juice

1/2 cup (125 mL) sugar

Grated rind of 1/2 a lemon

1 cup (250 mL) brown sugar

3/4 cup (190 mL) flour

1/4 cup (60 mL) rolled oats

1/2 cup (125 mL) soft butter

Method :

• Wash and cut rhubarb into 1/2-inch (1 cm) pieces.

• Add lemon juice and sugar. Mix well.

• Place in an 8 × 8-inch (20 × 20 cm) baking dish. Sprinkle lemon rind on top.

• Mix together brown sugar, flour, rolled oats and butter until crumbly. Sprinkle on top of the rhubarb.

• Microwave 10 minutes at HIGH and 5 minutes at MEDIUM.

• Serve hot or at room temperature.

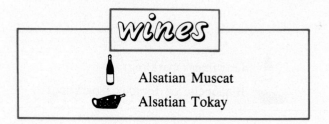

Alsatian Muscat

Alsatian Tokay

Rhubarb and Strawberry Compote

Preparation : . . . . .10 m
Cooking : . . . . .5 m
Standing : . . . . .from 2 to 3 h

• An old classic dessert in France, England, Italy and surely in Canada. I consider it an annual must.

Ingredients :

4 cups (1 L) fresh rhubarb

1/2 cup (125 mL) fresh orange juice

1 cup (250 mL) sugar

2 cups (500 mL) fresh strawberries

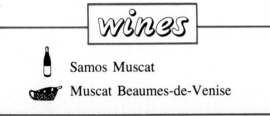

Samos Muscat

Muscat Beaumes-de-Venise

Method :

• Clean and cut the fresh rhubarb into 1/2-inch (1 cm) pieces.

• Place in an 8-cup (2 L) microwave-safe dish. Add the orange juice and the sugar, stir.

• Microwave at HIGH 4 to 5 minutes, stirring twice.

• Clean the strawberries and cut each in half. When the rhubarb is cooked and hot, add the strawberries. Stir gently. Cover with a plate or a paper.

• Let stand 2 to 3 hours at room temperature.

• Serve as is or with cream or over ice cream.

• I prefer it served with a bowl of sour cream.

Strawberry Compote

Advance preparation: . . . . . **from 3 to 4 h**
Cooking: . . . . **2 m**
Standing: . . . . **none**

wines

Monbazillac

Sauternes

• The strawberries don't cook but they absorb the warm honey-orange syrup and become very tasty.

Ingredients:

About 4 cups (1 L) fresh strawberries
1/4 to 1/2 cup (60 to 125 mL) honey
Grated rind and juice of 1/2 an orange

Method:

• Wash and hull the strawberries. Place in a microwave-safe bowl and microwave 40 seconds at HIGH.

• Pour the honey over the berries. Add the grated orange rind and juice. Microwave 1 minute at HIGH. Stir gently.

• Cover and refrigerate 3 to 4 hours.

Jiffy Strawberry Compote

Preparation: . . . . **10 m**
Cooking: . . . . **2 m**
Standing: . . . . **none**

• A simple easy dessert with a delectable flavor. I like to serve it with small meringue cookies.

Ingredients:

3 to 4 cups (750 mL to 1 L) fresh strawberries
1/2 cup (125 mL) fruit sugar
Grated rind of 1 orange
Juice of 1/2 an orange
1 tbsp (15 mL) orange liqueur or sherry (optional)

Method:

• Mix all the ingredients together. Place in a microwave-safe serving dish. Microwave 2 minutes at MEDIUM-LOW.

• Stir gently by shaking the bowl, rather than by stirring with a spoon.

• Keep at room temperature until ready to serve.

wines

Monbazillac

Sauternes

Strawberry Mousse

Preparation: . . . . .15 m
Cooking: . . . . .3 m
Standing: .none

A personal note: This dessert is super and a favorite in many countries, including Italy, France, Germany and Switzerland. Each one has its own variation. Mine is the addition of **1 teaspoon (5 mL) of rose water or half a cup of chopped wild roses** (they must be the wild type) **or a small handful** that I microwave 3 minutes at HIGH, stirring once. Make it once and take it from there to create your own variation.

Ingredients:

4 cups (1 L) fresh strawberries

1 cup (250 mL) fruit sugar

2 tbsp (30 mL) fresh lemon juice

2 egg whites

1 cup (250 mL) whipping cream

1 tsp (5 mL) vanilla extract

2 envelopes unflavored gelatin

3/4 cup (190 mL) cold water

Method:

• Clean and slice the strawberries. Place in a bowl with the fruit sugar and lemon juice. Stir gently and set aside.

• Beat the egg whites until stiff and whip the cream. Add the vanilla, mix.

• Place the unflavored gelatin in a microwave-safe measuring cup, add the cold water. Microwave 2 to 3 minutes at MEDIUM. It is ready when all the gelatin is dissolved. Stir well and let cool slightly.

• Now that all is ready, you must work fast.

• Pour the gelatin over the strawberries and stir thoroughly. Blend in the beaten egg whites, folding them gently into the mixture, then fold in the whipped cream.

• Pour into an attractive cut glass dish. Cover and refrigerate until ready to serve.

• You can top the mousse with whole strawberries and sprinkle them lightly with fruit sugar.

Sweet Vouvray

Coteaux du Layon

Strawberries with Cream

Preparation: . . . .**10 m**
Cooking: . . . .**2 m**
Standing: . . . .**none**

A personal note: A hot syrup poured over fresh strawberries, then refrigerated to chill, is a "gourmet" experience. Do try them when in full season. I like to serve them with sweetened whipped cream or plain cream, flavored with a few drops of rose water.*

Method:

- Place the sugar, water or apple juice in a microwave-safe measuring cup. Microwave 2 minutes at MEDIUM-HIGH, stirring once.

- Add to the hot syrup the liqueur of your choice and a few drops of rose water; if you wish, omit the liqueur and use only the rose water.

- Mix well. Pour the hot syrup over the strawberries. Stir gently, preferably with your hands.

- Cover and refrigerate until ready to serve.

Ingredients:

1/4 cup (60 mL) sugar

1/4 cup (60 mL) water or apple juice

2 tbsp (30 mL) of a liqueur of your choice (optional)

A few drops of rose water

4 to 6 cups (1 to 1.5 L) fresh strawberries

Rose water may be purchased at certain drugstores and at speciality food shops.

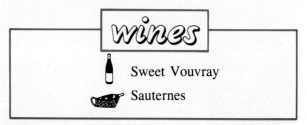

Sweet Vouvray

Sauternes

Strawberries Romanoff

Advance preparation: . . . . **1 h 40 m**
Cooking: . . . . **3 m**
Standing: . . . . **none**

• A super classic dessert, Strawberries Romanoff is quickly and easily made in a microwave oven without losing any of the delicate flavor of the fresh strawberries.

Ingredients:

3 to 4 cups (750 mL to 1 L) fresh strawberries

1/2 cup (125 mL) fruit sugar

1/4 tsp (1 mL) rose water *or*
   1/2 tsp (2 mL) vanilla extract

1 cup (250 mL) whipping cream

2 cups (500 mL) strawberry ice cream

2 tbsp (30 mL) brandy or rum

Method:

• Wash the strawberries quickly under running cold water (use a colander).

• Shake well, spread on a cloth to dry, about 30 minutes.

• Place strawberries in a microwave-safe bowl with the fruit sugar. Shake the bowl to distribute the sugar on the strawberries. Microwave 1 minute at MEDIUM. Shake the bowl gently and microwave another minute at MEDIUM-LOW.

• Refrigerate 1 hour.

• Whip the cream (do not sweeten) and refrigerate. (It can be refrigerated as long as the strawberries.)

• When ready to serve, remove the ice cream from the freezer, uncover and microwave 1 minute at MEDIUM-HIGH to soften. Place in a bowl, add the whipped cream and the brandy or the rum. Mix well and fold in the strawberries.

• Serve as soon as ready.

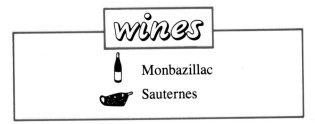

wines

Monbazillac
Sauternes

Mrs. Cooke's Strawberry Swirl

Advance preparation: . . . . . **from 3 to 5 h**
Cooking: . . . .**3 m**
Standing: . . . .**none**

• I found this recipe in a Nova Scotia cookbook entitled The Mixing Bowl. I adapted it to microwave cooking and have made it many times, always with the same pleasure.

Crust:

Ingredients:

1/4 cup (60 mL) butter

1 cup (250 mL) graham wafers, crushed

1 tbsp (15 mL) sugar

Method:

• Place the butter in an 8 × 8-inch (20 × 20 cm) ceramic dish or microwave-safe pie plate and melt 2 minutes at HIGH.

• Add the graham crackers and the sugar, mix well.

• Remove 1/3 cup (80 mL) and reserve for topping.

• Spread the remaining crumbs all over the dish or pie plate to make a crust.

• Place in a 4-cup (1 L) microwave-safe measuring cup:

1/2 cup (125 mL) milk

1/2 lb (250 g) marshmallows

• Microwave 3 minutes at MEDIUM.

• Stir well to make sure all the marshmallows have melted. Cool.

• Whip **1 cup (250 mL) cream**, fold into the cooled mixture.

• Mix well and pour over graham cracker crust.

Topping:

Ingredients:

1 package strawberry Jell-O or other brand
   of jelly powder

1 cup (250 mL) boiling water

1 cup (250 mL) cold apple juice or cold water

2 cups (500 mL) fresh sliced strawberries *or*
   1 box (245 g) thawed out sliced strawberries

Method:

• Mix the Jell-O or other powder with the boiling water until well dissolved. Add the apple juice or cold water. Refrigerate until barely set.

• Fold in the strawberries. Pour over the marshmallow filling already in the pie.

• Sprinkle remaining crumb mixture on top.

• Refrigerate 2 to 4 hours before serving.

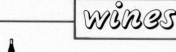

Asti Spumante

Californian Late Harvest Chenin Blanc

Fruit Cobbler

Preparation: ....35 m
Cooking: ....from 8 to 9 m
Standing: ....none

A personal note: This microwaved fruit cobbler can be served simply as fruit cooked in a syrup, using a single type of fruit or a mixture of your choice. Topped with batter, it becomes a cobbler pudding.

Ingredients:

1/3 cup (80 mL) sugar

1 tbsp (15 mL) water

2 cups (500 mL) fresh fruit, peeled (plums, peaches, apples or pears, etc.)

1 tbsp (15 mL) cornstarch

1/2 tsp (2 mL) vanilla or almond extract

Topping batter

1 cup (250 mL) all-purpose flour

1 tsp (5 mL) baking powder

1/2 tsp (2 mL) salt

2 tbsp (30 mL) brown sugar

1 egg

1/2 cup (125 mL) milk

1 tbsp (15 mL) soft butter or margarine

2 tsp (10 mL) brown sugar

1/4 tsp (1 mL) cinnamon

Method:

- Place in a microwave-safe dish the sugar and water.
- Microwave 2 minutes at HIGH.
- Add 1 cup (250 mL) of the peeled fruit left whole, sliced or cut in four.
- Stir the cornstarch into this mixture, mix well. Microwave 2 minutes at HIGH, stirring every minute.
- Some fruit may require an extra minute. The syrup will thicken almost instantly to form a glaze over the fruit, which is why it is important to stir well every minute.
- When the sauce is creamy and transparent, add the remaining cup of fruit and the vanilla or almond extract. Microwave 1 minute at HIGH.
- Serve as is for a fruit dessert, or place in an 8-inch (20 cm) round baking dish to make a cobbler.

Cobbler dough:

- Sift together the flour, baking powder and salt.
- Stir in the brown sugar.
- Beat the egg and the milk together.
- Add to mixture with the soft butter or margarine and stir.
- When dough forms a soft ball, drop dough by spoonfuls on top of the hot fruit compote (if fruit has cooled, microwave 1 minute at HIGH to heat).
- Mix the brown sugar and cinnamon, sprinkle over dough. Cover with waxed paper and microwave 4 to 5 minutes at MEDIUM-HIGH, turning casserole a quarter turn halfway through cooking period if your oven does not have a turntable.

wines

Asti Spumante

Sauternes

799

Blueberry Dumplings

Preparation :	. . . .	**30 m**
Cooking :	. . . .	**13 m**
Standing :	. . . .	**none**

A personal note : Treat yourself to this dessert at least once a year ! It's super served hot with vanilla ice cream.

Ingredients :

Sauce :

2½ cups (625 mL) fresh blueberries

1/3 cup (80 mL) sugar

A good pinch of salt

1 cup (250 mL) water

1 tbsp (15 mL) fresh lemon juice

Dumplings :

1 cup (250 mL) all-purpose flour

2 tbsp (30 mL) sugar

2 tsp (10 mL) baking powder

1/4 tsp (1 mL) salt

1 tbsp (15 mL) butter

1/2 cup (125 mL) milk

Method :

• Place in a 4-cup (1 L) microwave-safe bowl the blueberries, sugar, salt, water and lemon juice.

• Microwave 4 minutes at HIGH. Stir well.

• Sift together in a bowl the flour, sugar, baking powder and salt. Cut in the butter with a knife.

• Add the milk, all at once. Stir only until flour is dampened.

• Microwave the blueberry sauce 3 minutes at HIGH.

• Drop batter in the hot blueberries from a tablespoon (15 mL). You should have 6 to 7 dumplings.

• Cover and microwave 6 minutes at HIGH.

• Serve as is or with cream or ice cream.

wines

Late Harvest Riesling

Pineau des Charentes

Berry Crisp

Preparation: . . . . .20 m
Cooking: . . . . .from 7 to 8 m
Standing: .15 m

A personal note: Serve this crisp hot or tepid, with cream, whipped cream or yogurt. In the summer, I use fresh berries. In the winter, I replace them with frozen fruit.

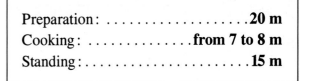

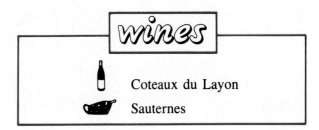

Coteaux du Layon

Sauternes

Ingredients:

3 cups (750 mL) Fresh strawberries, raspberries or blueberries *or* 1 15-oz (425 mL) package frozen berries of your choice

2 tbsp (30 mL) lemon juice

2/3 cup (160 mL) brown sugar

1/2 cup (125 mL) flour

2/3 cup (160 mL) rolled oats

1/3 cup (80 mL) margarine or butter

3/4 tsp (3 mL) cinnamon

1/4 tsp (1 mL) allspice

1/4 tsp (1 mL) salt

Method:

• Place the berries in an 8 × 8-inch (20 × 20 cm) microwave-safe baking dish.

• Pour the lemon juice on top.

• Mix the remaining ingredients, sprinkle over the fruit.

• Microwave 7 to 8 minutes at HIGH.

• Let stand 15 minutes before serving.

English Raspberry Pudding

Preparation : . . . . .15 m
Cooking : . . . . .4 m
Standing : .none

• A true English pudding almost as old as England. It has gone through many transformations. Here is another one, since I adapted it to microwave cooking. To me, this pudding is a must when raspberries are at their peak at the end of June or early July.

Method :

• Wash and hull the berries, mix them with the lemon juice and brown sugar. Pour into an 8 × 8-inch (20 × 20 cm) microwave-safe baking dish. (I like to use a Corning ceramic dish for this pudding.)

• Mix together the bread cubes, white sugar and grated lemon rind. Spread over the raspberries. Press mixture gently together, but do not stir. Dot all over with the butter. Microwave 4 minutes at HIGH.

• Serve hot or cool, but not refrigerated.

• Serve as is or top with ice cream or cream.

Ingredients :

4 cups (1 L) raspberries

Juice of 1/2 a lemon

2/3 cup (160 mL) light brown sugar

4 cups (1 L) toasted bread cubes

1/4 cup (60 mL) white sugar

Grated rind of 1 small lemon

2 tbsp (30 mL) butter

wines

Sweet Anjou

Sweet champagne

Fresh Raspberry Bavarian Cream

Advance preparation: . . . . . **from 3 to 6 h**
Cooking: . . . . **2 m**
Standing: . . . . **none**

• Bavarian Cream is a cool, creamy, summer delight. I never miss making this cream when fresh raspberries are in season.

Ingredients:

1 cup (250 mL) water
1 3-oz (74 g) package raspberry-flavored gelatin
2 cups (500 mL) vanilla ice cream
1 banana, sliced (optional)
1 cup (250 mL) fresh raspberries, mashed

Method:

• Place water in a 4-cup (1 L) microwave-safe measuring cup.

• Microwave at HIGH 2 minutes, or until it boils.

• Stir in the gelatin until dissolved.

• Add ice cream, stir until melted. Stir in the mashed fruit and the sliced banana.

• Pour into a nice glass dish.

• Refrigerate 3 to 6 hours.

• Unmold on a large plate, surround with sweetened berries.

wines

Monbazillac
Sauternes

Summer Pudding

Advance preparation: . . . . . **from 6 to 8 h**
Cooking: . . . . **6 m**
Standing: . . . . **none**

• An English classic, make this when fresh raspberries are in season.

Ingredients:

2 cups (500 mL) fresh raspberries
1/2 cup (125 mL) sugar
1 tsp (5 mL) lemon juice
6 thin slices white bread, buttered
Whipped cream

Method:

• Clean the raspberries and place them in a microwave-safe dish. Add the sugar.

• Microwave 6 minutes at HIGH, stirring twice.

• Add lemon juice, stir well. Do not strain.

• Place a few slices of buttered bread in the bottom of a serving dish. Cover with as much of the raspberry syrup as the bread will absorb. Repeat procedure until all is used.

• Cover and refrigerate 6 to 8 hours.

• Unmold or serve from dish with whipped cream.

wines

Monbazillac
Barsac

Sauce Parisienne

Preparation: ....15 m
Cooking: ....7 m
Standing: ....**none**

A personal note: Try to use vanilla bean* to make this sauce, or substitute **1 teaspoon (5 mL) of vanilla extract** that you add after the creamy custard is cooked.

Ingredients:

1/2 cup (125 mL) milk

1/2 cup (125 mL) whipping cream

2 inches (5 cm) of vanilla bean*

2 egg yolks

1/4 cup (60 mL) sugar

1 cup (250 mL) fresh raspberries

1 cup (250 mL) whipping cream

Method:

• Place in a microwave-safe bowl the milk, whipping cream and vanilla bean (if you do use it). Microwave 2 minutes at HIGH.

• Beat the egg yolks with the sugar and add to the hot milk. Stir until well mixed. Microwave 5 minutes at MEDIUM, stirring twice. It is sometimes necessary to microwave one minute more at MEDIUM.

• Remove the vanilla bean. At this point, add the liquid vanilla if you have not used the vanilla bean.

• Wash the raspberries and pass through a strainer to make a purée, or simply add them to the sauce.

• Whip the cream and fold into the sauce.

• Serve warm or at room temperature.

*You can buy vanilla bean at good speciality shops. Keep it well-buried in a box of fruit sugar. You can use as much as **2 cups (500 mL) of fruit sugar with only 1 vanilla bean**; all of the sugar will take the vanilla flavor. Use with fresh fruit or in any sauce you wish to flavor with vanilla. When you have used the vanilla stick in a liquid, as you do in this recipe, let it dry 6 to 8 hours on a paper towel then put it back in the sugar.*

How to make vanilla extract

Preparation: ....**1 m**
Cooking: ....**none**
Maturing time: ......**from 3 to 4 weeks**

• Once you try this you will always make it... The word superlative is not too much for it.

Ingredients:

1 bottle (341 mL) Bacardi rum (40 % alc.)

3 vanilla beans

Method:

• Add vanilla to rum. Shake well.

• Let ripen 3 to 4 weeks in a dark cupboard.

• Use in the same quantity as ordinary vanilla extract.

• When the bottle of rum is half full, simply fill with more rum and add another vanilla bean.

• When a recipe calls for a vanilla bean, simply take it out of the rum and add to your recipe.

• Remove it when ready, wash it and put it back into the rum.

• Vanilla made this way is far more economical than buying vanilla extract and many times more tasty.

Wine Poached Pears

Preparation: . . . . **20 m**
Cooking: . . . . **9 m**
Standing: . . . . **none**

Sweet Vouvray
Moulin Touchais

A personal note: Whenever I have leftover white wine or Sake, plus fresh pears, I make these delicious pears and serve them hot or at room temperature. In the winter, I defrost **a cup or two of unsweetened berries**, to which I add about **1/3 cup (80 mL) of sugar.** I mash them and serve them as a sauce to accompany the poached pears.

Ingredients:

4 to 5 pears
1 cup (250 mL) white wine or Sake
1/2 cup (125 mL) apple juice or soda water*
1/3 to 1/2 cup (80 to 125 mL) sugar

* Soda water may be replaced by Seven-Up, ginger ale or tonic.

Method:

• Peel, cut in half and core the pears.

• Place in a microwave-safe bowl all the ingredients except the pears. Stir and microwave 3 to 4 minutes at HIGH.

• Place the prepared pears in the syrup core-side down. Baste with the hot syrup. Microwave about 5 minutes at MEDIUM-HIGH.

• Baste the fruit with the syrup. Microwave another minute at MEDIUM-HIGH.

• Serve hot or cold.

Pears Glacées

Preparation: . . . . **20 m**
Cooking: . . . . **from 12 to 20 m**
Standing: . . . . **none**

A personal note: A famous recipe from the répertoire of the French chefs, Pears Glacées is easy to prepare. Glaze with apricot jam when ready to serve.

Ingredients:

1 cup (250 mL) sugar
1 cup (250 mL) water
Rind of 1 orange
6 whole fresh pears
1/2 cup (125 mL) apricot or strawberry jam
2 tbsp (30 mL) liqueur of your choice
Vanilla or strawberry ice cream (optional)

Method:

• Place in a microwave-safe dish the sugar, water and orange rind. Microwave 10 minutes at MEDIUM-HIGH.

• Peel the pears, cut in half, remove core and place in the hot syrup, basting them 8 to 10 times, so the pears are covered with the syrup. Microwave 6 to 8 minutes at HIGH. The pears should be tender, but not too soft. Remove pears from the syrup*. Place on a serving dish.

• Warm the apricot or strawberry jam with the liqueur 40 seconds at HIGH. Brush each pear with this jam glaze. Add about 1/2 cup (125 mL) of the hot syrup in the bottom of the dish. Serve cold, if you wish, over vanilla or strawberry ice cream.

* Keep the remaining syrup in a glass jar, refrigerated. It can be used to poach any fruit. It will keep 5 to 6 months.

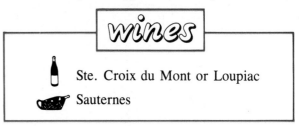

Ste. Croix du Mont or Loupiac
Sauternes

Pears Melba

Preparation: . . . . **20 m**
Cooking: . . . . **from 12 to 20 m**
Standing: . . . . **none**

A personal note: A colorful and delicious dessert of fresh pears, this is perfect when you are looking for a buffet dessert. This recipe was developed with Bosc winter pears, the very best pears to poach or microwave.

Ingredients:

1 10-oz (300 g) package frozen raspberries

1/2 cup (125 mL) sugar

1 tbsp (15 mL) cornstarch

2 tbsp (30 mL) lemon juice

1 tbsp (15 mL) brandy (optional)

4 to 6 pears

Method:

• Place the frozen raspberries in a 4-cup (1 L) microwave-safe dish. Microwave, uncovered, at HIGH 3 minutes. Turn over and microwave 2 to 3 minutes more.

• Blend together the sugar, cornstarch, lemon juice and brandy. Microwave 2 minutes at MEDIUM-HIGH.

• Add raspberries, stir.

• Peel the pears and cut in half. Place in a microwave-safe dish.

• Pour the fruit mixture over the pears and microwave, covered, at HIGH 5 to 9 minutes, depending on size and ripeness of pears. Check for doneness and if necessary, microwave 2 or 3 minutes more at HIGH.

• Serve warm or cold, as is or topped with whipped cream or ice cream.

Asti Spumante

Sweet champagne

Pears Florentine

Preparation: . . . . **25 m**
Cooking: . . . . **8 m**
Standing: . . . . **none**

A personal note: Here is another quick and delectable Italian dessert that can be served hot or at room temperature.

Ingredients:

1/3 cup (80 mL) almonds, slivered

1 tbsp (15 mL) butter

4 to 6 pears

1/2 cup (125 mL) sugar

1/4 tsp (1 mL) almond extract

1/2 cup (125 mL) white wine or vermouth

Method:

• Peel, cut in half and core the pears.

• Place the almonds and the butter in a microwave-safe saucer. Microwave about 2 minutes at HIGH, stirring once or twice. They should be browned lightly. If the almonds are very cold (I keep mine frozen), they may take 1 minute more to brown. However, that is easy to judge.

• Place the pears in a ceramic pie plate, core side up, the large end to the rim of the plate.

• Stir together the sugar, toasted almonds and the almond extract. Fill the cavity of each pear with some of this almond sugar.

• Pour the wine into the bottom of the plate. Microwave 6 minutes at HIGH. Serve at room temperature.

• For a spectacular dessert, serve with a Zabaglione as a sauce.

Monbazillac

Vin Santo

Pears in Lemon Cream

Preparation : . . . . .35 m	
Cooking : . . . . .from 16 to 17 m	
Standing : . . . . .none	

Monbazillac

Riesling Auslese

A personal note : This is a very elegant and tasty way to serve pears. They can be served simply poached and kept in their syrup, or topped with the lemon cream. Another variation is to replace the lemon with 4 to 6 slices of lime.

Ingredients :

6 pears

1 cup (250 mL) water or apple juice

1/2 cup (125 mL) sugar

6 slices lemon or lime, unpeeled

Lemon Custard :

1/4 cup (60 mL) sugar

1 tbsp (15 mL) cornstarch

1 cup (250 mL) light cream or milk

2 egg yolks

Method :

• Peel, cut in half and core the pears. Place in a round 8 or 9-inch (20 or 23 cm) ceramic dish the water or apple juice, sugar, slices of lemon or lime. Stir to mix. Microwave 10 minutes at HIGH. Stir well.

• Place the pears in the hot syrup, with the small end toward the middle of the dish. Baste pears with the hot syrup. Microwave 4 to 5 minutes at HIGH, or until pears are tender. Test with the point of a knife.

• Baste once after 3 minutes of cooking. Remove pears to a serving dish with a slotted spoon.

• Mix together the 1/4 cup (60 mL) sugar, the cornstarch and cream or milk. Add the egg yolks. Mix thoroughly.

• Add mixture to the hot pear syrup. Stir well. Microwave 1 minute at MEDIUM, stir well. Micro-

wave another 2 minutes, stirring once. The sauce should have a light, creamy texture. Pour hot over the pears.

• Cover and let stand until cooled, but do not refrigerate.

807

Fresh Peaches
À l'Anglaise

Preparation:	. . . . .10 m
Cooking:	. . . . .8 m
Standing:	. . . . .5 m

A personal note: Use your microwave oven to peel the peaches for this dessert in no time, with the greatest of ease. Place the peaches in a circle and microwave 15 seconds at HIGH. Let them stand 10 minutes on the counter, then peel.

Italian Moscato

Malvasia delle Lipari

Ingredients:

4 to 6 peaches

1 tbsp (15 mL) fresh lemon juice

2 tbsp (30 mL) sugar

1/4 cup (60 mL) almonds, slivered

2 pinches of nutmeg

2 tbsp (30 mL) brandy*

* I recommend using Mont Blanc White Brandy, which is economical and very good for cooking.

Method:

• Peel peaches, cut in half and remove pits. Coat lightly with lemon juice. Place peaches in an 8 × 8-inch (20 × 20 cm) microwave-safe baking dish, open side up. Sprinkle with the sugar.

• Mix together the almonds and nutmeg in a microwave-safe pie plate. Microwave, uncovered, 3 minutes at HIGH, stirring once. Fill peach cavities with the almonds. Microwave, uncovered, 5 minutes at HIGH. Pour brandy on top. Let stand 5 minutes.

Poached
Canned Peaches

Preparation:	. . . . .10 m
Cooking:	. . . . .5 m
Standing:	. . . . .none

A personal note: Poaching canned peaches in a creamy sauce takes away their canned feeling. I sometimes pour the hot peaches and their sauce over a light white cake, replacing the vanilla extract in the cake with an equal amount of almond extract.

Ingredients:

1/3 cup (80 mL) sugar

2 tbsp (30 mL) cornstarch

Grated rind of an orange

14 or 26-oz (398 or 796 mL) can peach halves

1/4 cup (60 mL) white wine or sherry

Method:

• Place in a microwave-safe bowl the sugar, cornstarch and orange rind. Stir until well blended.

• Drain the peaches and add 1/3 cup (80 mL) of the peach syrup to the cornstarch mixture. Stir again until well mixed. Microwave 2 minutes at HIGH, stir well.

• Add the wine or sherry. Microwave at MEDIUM-HIGH 2 to 3 minutes, or until sauce is creamy and transparent.

• Add the peaches to the hot syrup. Stir until well mixed. Pour into the serving dish.

• Serve warm or cold.

• The dish can be refrigerated, covered, without the peaches losing any of their flavor.

Asti Spumante

Beaumes-de-Venise

Creamy Peaches

Preparation: . . . . **15 m**
Cooking: . . . . **from 8 to 10 m**
Standing: . . . . **none**

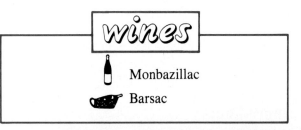

Monbazillac

Barsac

A personal note: Another French delight, this is a super dessert. The peaches are barely cooked and the light pudding on top can be served either cold or at room temperature.

Ingredients:

2 cups (500 mL) fresh peaches

3 eggs

1/2 cup (125 mL) sugar

1/2 tsp (2 mL) ground nutmeg

1/4 cup (60 mL) flour

1 tsp (5 mL) vanilla

1 cup (250 mL) light or heavy cream

1/2 cup (125 mL) dry white wine or vermouth

1/4 cup (60 mL) jelly or jam of your choice

Method:

• Peel the fresh peaches and slice into an 8-inch (20 cm) baking dish (Corning or Pyrex).

• Place the remaining ingredients, except the jam, in a bowl. Mix thoroughly with a rotary beater, pour over the peaches. Microwave at MEDIUM-HIGH, uncovered, 6 to 8 minutes.

• Check doneness with the point of a knife, especially in the middle of the dish. If necessary, microwave 1 or 2 minutes longer. Cool.

• When ready to serve, melt the jelly or jam of your choice 40 seconds at HIGH in the microwave and pour over the peaches.

A personal note: I strongly recommend the use of nutmeg bought whole and grated finely according to your needs. (Nutmeg graters are found in kitchenware boutique.) It is readily available at spice counters, and will keep indefinitely. Whole nutmeg, freshly grated, is highly superior in flavor to ground nutmeg, and much more economical.

Madeira Peaches

Ingredients:

4 to 5 peaches

1/3 cup (80 mL) butter

2/3 cup (160 mL) sugar

1/3 cup (80 mL) Madeira wine

Method:

• Peel peaches, cut in half and remove pits.

• Place the butter in a 9-inch (23 cm) microwave-safe pie plate and melt 2 minutes at HIGH. The butter will brown lightly here and there. Stir in the sugar. Microwave at HIGH 1 minute, stir. Microwave another 1 to 2 minutes, or until sugar caramelizes.

Preparation: . . . . **20 m**
Cooking: . . . . **from 9 to 12 m**
Standing: . . . . **none**

• Add the Madeira wine, stir. Microwave 1 minute at MEDIUM.

• Place peach halves in this syrup rounded side up. Baste 3 to 4 times with the syrup, then microwave at MEDIUM-HIGH 3 to 4 minutes, basting the peaches with the syrup after 2 minutes of cooking. Remove peaches from the syrup.

• Microwave syrup 2 minutes at MEDIUM-HIGH. Pour over the peaches.

• Serve cold as is or over ice cream or topped with cream.

• Make sure this dessert is well covered when placed in the refrigerator.

Setubal

Malmsey

Deep Dish Peach Pie

Convection cooking

A **personal note:** I make this when fresh peaches are available. When the season is over, I use the good, dependable apple. Both are good. This pie is best when cooked in the convection part of the microwave oven.

Ingredients:

6 to 8 fresh peaches

1 tbsp (15 mL) lemon juice

1/4 cup (60 mL) soft butter or margarine

1/4 cup (60 mL) flour

1 cup (250 mL) brown sugar

1/2 tsp (2 mL) almond extract

Pastry of your choice for a 9-inch (23 cm)
   pie crust

1 egg yolk, beaten

2 tsp (10 mL) water

1 tsp (5 mL) sugar

Method:

• Peel and slice the peaches. Sprinkle with the lemon juice. Toss together gently. Melt the butter or margarine 1 minute at HIGH and mix with the flour and brown sugar.

• Add to the sliced peaches, stir. Add the almond extract.

• Place mixture in a 9-inch plate (23 cm) 2½-inch (7 cm) deep.

• Top with the pastry of your choice.

• Brush the pastry with the egg yolk beaten with the water.

• Sprinkle the teaspoon (5 mL) of sugar on top.

• Preheat the convection part of your microwave oven at 375°F (190°C).

Preparation:	45 m
Cooking:	45 m
Standing:	none

• Place pie on rack and bake 45 minutes or until golden brown. Cool on rack.

• Serve warm or at room temperature, with whipped or plain cream, yogurt, sour cream or ice cream.

Variation:

• When this deep dish pie is made with apples, peel and slice the apples.

• Replace the almond extract with **vanilla extract** or use **lemon or orange rind**.

• About **1/2 teaspoon (2 mL) ground cardamom or coriander** may be added.

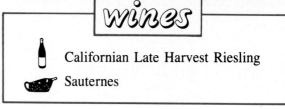

wines

Californian Late Harvest Riesling

Sauternes

Simone's Oriental Pumpkin

Preparation :	. . . . **20 m**
Cooking :	. . . . **9 m**
Standing :	. . . .**none**

• This recipe came to me from a dear friend from Egypt, who was an impulsive cook and created many fascinating dishes.

Ingredients :

3 cups (750 mL) pumpkin
1/2 cup (125 mL) water
1/2 cup (125 mL) brown sugar
1/2 tsp (2 mL) cinnamon
1/4 tsp (1 mL) nutmeg
Grated rind and juice of 1 orange
Butter

Method :

• Peel pieces of pumpkin and measure 3 cups (750 mL).

• Cut into thin half moons and place in an 8-inch (20 cm) microwave-safe dish. Add the water.

• Microwave, covered, 5 minutes at HIGH.

• Mix the brown sugar with the cinnamon and nutmeg, sprinkle on the pumpkin.

• Sprinkle the orange juice and rind on top. Dot with butter.

• Cover with waxed paper. Microwave 3 minutes at HIGH. Stir. Microwave 1 minute at HIGH.

• Serve hot or cold with cream or ice cream or, as the Orientals do, topped with a 1-inch (2.5 cm) layer of crushed ice, which the guests remove as soon as served.

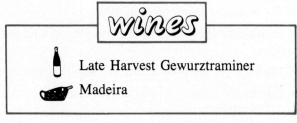

wines

Late Harvest Gewurztraminer
Madeira

Coated Fresh Fruit

• A creamy orange flower water sauce poured hot over fresh, uncooked fruit. Surprising and delectable.

Preparation: . . . . **20 m**
Cooking: . . . . **5 m**
Standing: . . . . **none**

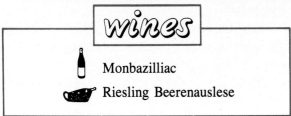

Monbazilliac
Riesling Beerenauslese

Ingredients:

2 tbsp (30 mL) butter

2 tbsp (30 mL) flour

1/2 cup (125 mL) cream

1/2 cup (125 mL) milk

1/2 cup (125 mL) plain or vanilla sugar

1 tsp (5 mL) orange flower water*

3 cups (750 mL) fresh peeled and sliced fruit of your choice**

2 tbsp (30 mL) plain or vanilla sugar

Orange flower water can be purchased in speciality food shops or drugstores.
*** A mixture of fruit — such as peaches, pears, oranges, especially when fresh — is more interesting. The canned fruit can be of one type.*

Method:

• Place the 2 tablespoons (30 mL) butter in a 4-cup (1 L) microwave-safe dish and melt 1 minute at HIGH. Stir in the flour.

• Add the cream, milk and the 1/2 cup (125 mL) sugar, stir to mix. Microwave 1 minute at HIGH, stir well. Microwave 2 minutes at HIGH, stirring once. If necessary, microwave another minute at HIGH. Sauce should be creamy.

• Add orange flower water.

• Peel and slice the fruit of your choice into a nice serving dish.

• If fresh fruit is not available, well drained canned fruit may be used, but it will not be as delicate in flavor and texture.

• Sprinkle the fruit with the 2 tablespoons (30 mL) sugar.

• A pleasant addition, when available, is chopped fresh mint leaves.

• Pour the hot sauce over the fruits. Do not mix. Cover and refrigerate until cold.

Creole Bananas

• Creole Bananas is another quick and easy dessert. In the summer, I enjoy them over ice cream.

Preparation :	. . . .	5 m
Cooking :	. . . .	4 m
Standing :	. . . .	1 m

Ingredients :

3 tbsp (50 mL) butter
1/3 cup (80 mL) brown sugar
2 tbsp (30 mL) cream
1/4 tsp (1 mL) cinnamon
1/4 tsp (1 mL) nutmeg
4 to 5 bananas
1/4 cup (60 mL) rum

Method :

• Melt the butter 1 minute at HIGH in a microwave-safe dish large enough to hold all the ingredients.

• Add the brown sugar, cream, cinnamon and nutmeg. Mix thoroughly.

• Slice the peeled bananas lengthwise in quarters, then in half.

• Add to the brown sugar mixture. Stir well. Microwave, uncovered, 3 minutes at HIGH, or until the syrup boils.

• Add the rum and let stand 1 minute before serving.

wines

Samos Muscat

Hungarian Tokay

How to peel and section citrus fruit

• Whether orange, grapefruit, lemon or lime, cut off all the rind and the white skin (as it is bitter). This is easy to do if you use a fairly large sharp knife, and work around and around the fruit over a bowl to catch any of the juices.

• To section the fruit whole, peel, then cut down each wedge on both sides of each section, as close to the membrane as possible and push the section into the bowl.

• Of course, remove any seeds.

Rum Grapefruit

Preparation :	10 m
Cooking :	5 m
Standing :	none

A personal note : Surprise your family and guests with hot grapefruit served as an entrée or, if you prefer, as a dessert. The dish can be prepared an hour or so ahead of time, then microwaved when ready to serve. The important ingredient in this recipe is the fresh ginger, as the powdered type is not half as tasty.

Ingredients :

1 large grapefruit
2 tsp (10 mL) brown sugar
1 tsp (5 mL) fresh ginger root, grated
1 tsp (5 mL) butter
Rum (optional)

Method :

• Cut grapefruit in half. Remove seeds if necessary. Cut around sections. Place each half on a serving dish. Mix together the brown sugar and ginger and sprinkle on each half.

• Dot with butter and pour 1 teaspoon (5 mL) of rum over each half, if you wish. Prepare as many as you require.

• To microwave, place grapefruit in a circle, microwaving 4 at a time, uncovered, 5 minutes at HIGH. If you wish to serve them hot, they will remain hot for 8 to 10 minutes.

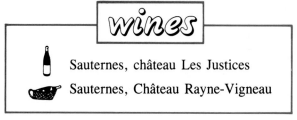

wines

Sauternes, château Les Justices
Sauternes, Château Rayne-Vigneau

Irish Sweet Oranges

Preparation :	10 m
Cooking :	3 m
Standing :	none

• A tasty dessert, equally good hot or cold, Irish Sweet Oranges can be prepared very quickly.

Ingredients :

3 to 5 oranges
3 tbsp (50 mL) orange marmalade
2 to 4 tbsp (30 to 60 mL) whisky or brandy

Method :

• Slice the oranges into a serving bowl.

• Place the marmalade and whisky or brandy in a microwave-safe bowl and microwave 3 minutes at MEDIUM-HIGH. Stir, then pour over the oranges.

• Refrigerate to cool completely or serve tepid.

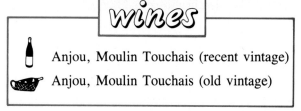

wines

Anjou, Moulin Touchais (recent vintage)
Anjou, Moulin Touchais (old vintage)

Poached Orange or Grapefruit

Advance preparation : . . . .**from 4 to 12 h**
Cooking : . . . .**2 m**
Standing : . . . .**none**

A personal note : Simply poached in a plain syrup or a liqueur-flavored type. I like to serve mine in a cut glass dish, either at room temperature or refrigerated for 4 to 12 hours.

 Sauternes, Château du Pick

Sauternes, Château Gilette

Ingredients :

6 oranges *or*
  2 to 3 grapefruit (depending on size)
3/4 cup (190 mL) sugar
1/2 cup (125 mL) water
Grand Marnier, brandy or a liqueur of your choice

Method :

• Using a potato peeler, cut the top thin rind from 2 oranges or 1 grapefruit. Be careful not to take any of the white skin. With a small, sharp knife, cut the rind into long, thin slivers.

• Place in a microwave-safe measuring cup the sugar and water. Add the orange or grapefruit rind. Stir well, microwave at HIGH 2 minutes, stirring once.

• Peel and section the rest of the fruit, place in a serving bowl.

• Add the hot syrup with rind. Stir gently.

• Add the liqueur of your choice. Stir again gently. Cover, refrigerate 4 to 12 hours.

• Remove from the refrigerator one hour before serving.

About cake making

• Like pies, cake can be cooked very quickly by microwave, or cooked by the convection method in your microwave oven, which will take the usual time. Whatever method you choose, I am sure you will enjoy the quality of the finished cakes.

Important bits of information

• The first thing to do, whatever recipe you are making, is to choose the right pan and to prepare it as required.

• To microwave, use Pyrex, Corning or a plastic type pan. To cook by convection, metal pans can be used. In fact, they are preferable for baking cakes.

• For the best results, have all ingredients at room temperature.

• Butter and margarine are the best fats to use in cake making, followed by vegetable fats such as Crisco.

• When your recipe calls for brown sugar, pale or dark, make sure the measuring cup is firmly packed.

• Perhaps the most important part of cake making is the creaming of the butter or other fat — before and after the addition of the sugar. The way I like to work this part is by beating the room-temperature butter or other fat with a hand or electric beater until the fat is fluffy and creamy. Then I add a few spoonfuls at a time of the measured sugar, beating until creamy after each addition. I keep beating until I do not feel any grains of sugar when tested between the tips of my fingers. This takes a little more time than just mixing, but it makes all the difference between a perfect light cake and just a cake.

• When the recipe calls for beaten egg whites to be folded into the batter, do not use an electric mixer. Do it by hand. It takes a little longer, but it does a great deal for the quality of the finished cake.

• Whether a cake is baked by microwave or by convection, it should always be placed on a rack to bake as well as to cool to allow air to circulate all around. This keeps it light and perfect.

• Beat egg whites only to the stiff, shiny stage. If beaten too long, they become granular.

Folding

• It is an important part of cake making. When the recipe tells you to " fold the beaten egg whites into the batter, " this is how to proceed:

• Beat the egg whites, then fold about one-third of the beaten whites into the cake batter, mixing thoroughly, even folding with a wire whisk or an egg beater.

• Use a rubber spatula to place the remaining beaten whites on top of the cake mixture. Then cut the spatula down from the centre to the bottom of the bowl, running over the bottom of the bowl and against the edge of the bowl, rotating it as you work.

• Keep gently repeating this process until all the beaten whites have been folded in.

Helpful hints for cakes

To beat and fold egg whites into batter

1. Separate the eggs carefully, making sure that no yolk particles are mixed in with the whites.

2. You will get a greater volume of beaten whites if they have been standing at least one hour at room temperature before beating.

3. "BEAT TO SOFT PEAK" means that when air is added to egg whites, through the beating process, the whites first expand and become fluffy and sort of creamy or opaque. If the recipe calls for sugar to be added "to the soft peak beaten egg whites," this is the point at which it should be added gradually.

• "BEAT TO MEDIUM PEAK" means the mixture should form rounded, glossy peaks when the beater is lifted from the bowl. Egg whites at this stage hold their shape and they are stiff and dry.

• "BEAT TO STIFF PEAK" means to continue beating after reaching the "medium peak" stage to obtain stiffer and larger peaks. This stage is used for meringue, pie topping, frosting, etc.

• Beating further than indicated will only result in a dry and somewhat useless meringue.

On flour

• When a recipe calls for sifted flour, measure the demanded amount from flour that is sifted. This is important, as the weight and texture of the flour is different when sifted.

1 cup (250 mL) all-purpose flour unsifted	=	4 ¼ ounces (140 g)
1 cup (250 mL) all-purpose flour sifted	=	3 ⅞ ounces (118 g)

Measure fats like a chef

• This is truly the ONLY accurate method for measuring butter or any type of fat.

• Referred to as Water Displacement, it is very easy

to do. First, check your needs in the following chart:

butter or shortening	cold water
3/4 cup (190 mL)	1/4 cup (60 mL)
2/3 cup (160 mL)	1/3 cup (80 mL)
1/2 cup (125 mL)	1/2 cup (125 mL)
1/3 cup (80 mL)	2/3 cup (160 mL)
1/4 cup (60 mL)	3/4 cup (190 mL)

Place the proper amount of cold water given in the table above for the amount of fat you have to measure, then add the fat until the water reaches the 1-cup (250 mL) level.

Preparing the cake pan

• Some recipes call for a special way to prepare the cake pan.

• Here is how to do it.

To grease the pan

• It takes about **1 teaspoon (5 mL) of shortening** to grease an 8 or 9 or 10-inch (20 or 23 or 25 cm) pan.

• Spreading it with fingers is better than with paper, as too much of the fat gets into the paper and the greasing is not equally done.

To flour a cake pan

• Dust a bit of flour in the bottom of the pan and

shake the pan until the flour is well distributed. NOT DONE FOR MICROWAVING.

To line a pan with paper

• Place the pan over waxed or white or brown un-

glazed paper and trace around the edge with a pencil. Cut a bit outside the pencil mark. It will fit to perfection in the bottom of the pan.

• But before placing the paper in the pan, grease one side of it and lightly grease the pan. Place the paper greased side down in the pan, then grease the top side.

• Remember that some cakes cannot be cooked successfully by the microwave method — for example, angel food, sponge cakes, etc. But, of course, they can be baked in the convection part of your microwave oven.

• Always cool cooked cake on a rack.

• Upside down-type cakes are really the most successful when done by microwave, as the top of a microwaved cake always remains pale yellow or whitish. An upside down cake when unmolded looks very good.

• For plain cakes, top the batter with **2 to 3 spoonfuls of chopped nuts mixed** with **3 tablespoons (50 mL) of brown sugar** before cooking to give it a very nice appearance.

Homemade Cake Mix

Preparation: . . . . .5 m
Cooking: . . . . .none
Standing: .none

A personal note: This old recipe is free of all preservatives, yet it will keep for two to three months in your kitchen cupboard, as long as it is stored in a tightly covered container.

One recipe will give you 13 cups of mix, which makes it extraordinarily economical when compared to commercial mixes.

Ingredients:

12 cups (3 L) all-purpose flour
1/4 cup (60 mL) + 2 tbsp (30 mL) baking powder
2 tbsp (30 mL) salt
1⅓ cups (330 mL) instant powdered milk

Method:

• Sift the measured flour. Add the baking powder and the salt, sift a second time. Add the powdered milk and mix thoroughly.

• Place in a container with tight fitting lid.

Commercial-type cake

• To prepare the cake, add **3 tablespoons (50 mL) vegetable oil** for each cup (250 mL) of the mix.

• Use water instead of the milk required in the recipe, flavor to taste.

• Use standard measuring cups and spoons for perfect results.

• When preparing a cake or other recipe with this mix, put it in the measuring cup with a spoon. Do not sift it before use and do not pack it in the cup.

• If the recipe calls for eggs, remove them from the refrigerator 5 to 10 minutes before making the cake.

• Make sure that the molds you have are microwave-safe, or use Pyrex or Corning dishes.

• The ideal size is 8 inches (20 cm).

• For perfect results when baking a cake in the microwave oven, it is sometimes necessary to place a small inverted Pyrex dish in the middle of the mold and to pour the dough all around it.

• Choose a ring mold as a special mold for microwave baking.

• Remember that special plastic molds for microwave cooking must not be used in a conventional oven.

Stir and Bake Cake

Preparation: ....10 m
Cooking: ....from 4 to 5 m
Standing: ....4 m

A personal note: This quick cake can be stirred in the mold and microwaved in no time

Ingredients:

2/3 cup (160 mL) Homemade Cake Mix

1/2 cup (125 mL) sugar

2 tbsp (30 mL) instant powdered milk

1/4 cup (60 mL) vegetable oil

1 egg

1/4 cup (60 mL) + 2 tbsp (30 mL) water

1/2 tsp (2 mL) vanilla

Method:

• Place in a bowl the mix, sugar and powdered milk.

• In another bowl, mix together the oil, egg and water.

• Pour over the dry ingredients together with the vanilla. Beat together for 1 minute.

• Pour into an 8-inch (20 cm) microwave-safe mold. Microwave 4 to 5 minutes at HIGH.

• Let stand 4 minutes, then unmold.

Variations:

• To make cupcakes, use paper cups placed in small microwave-safe molds and fill to half with the dough.

• Microwave 1 ½ to 2 minutes at HIGH.

Chocolate

• To the cake recipe add **3 tablespoons (50 mL) cocoa** with **1 tablespoon (15 mL) brown sugar** and **1 tablespoon (15 mL) more vegetable oil.**

Lemon or Orange

• To the cake recipe add either **2 tablespoons (30 mL) lemon or orange juice** and **the grated rind of 1/2 a lemon** or **1/2 an orange.**

• Omit the 2 tablespoons (30 mL) water from the recipe.

Spicy

• Substitute **brown sugar** for the white sugar in the cake recipe and add **1/4 teaspoon (1 mL) each allspice, cinnamon and nutmeg** and, if desired, **1/4 cup (60 mL) chopped nuts.**

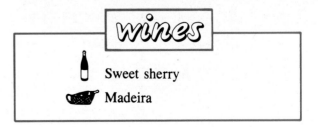

wines

Sweet sherry

Madeira

Chocolate Brownies with Cake Mix

Preparation : . . . . from 10 to 12 m
Cooking : . . . . 6 m
Standing : . . . . 20 m

Ingredients :

3/4 cup (190 mL) Homemade Cake Mix
1 cup (250 mL) sugar
6 tbsp (90 mL) cocoa
1/4 cup (60 mL) vegetable oil
2 eggs
1/2 cup (125 mL) nuts, chopped
1 tsp (5 mL) vanilla
1/4 cup (60 mL) butter or margarine

Method :

• In a 4-cup (1 L) measuring cup, stir together with a fork the basic mix, sugar and cocoa.

• Place the butter or margarine in a 6 × 10-inch (15 × 25 cm) Pyrex or Corning dish and microwave 40 seconds at HIGH.

• Pour over the dry ingredients the oil and the eggs while stirring with a fork.

• Add the nuts and vanilla.

• Pour the mixed ingredients into the melted butter. Mix together for a few minutes with the fork, smooth the top of the cake.

• Microwave 6 minutes at HIGH, turning the dish once during the cooking if you do not have a turntable.

• When cooked, let stand for 20 minutes on a cake rack before cutting into squares.

• To taste, roll each square in icing sugar.

• These brownies freeze very well. To thaw, place one square on a white paper towel and microwave 30 seconds at HIGH.

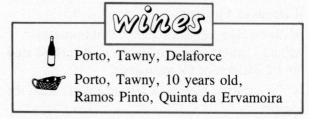

wines

Porto, Tawny, Delaforce

Porto, Tawny, 10 years old,
Ramos Pinto, Quinta da Ervamoira

Maple Upside-Down Cake

Preparation: . . . . 20 m
Cooking: . . . . from 4 to 5 m
Standing: . . . . 10 m

• This 3-minute microwaved upside down cake is tasty and light. The top remains pale yellow, but unmolded, it is very attractive.

Ingredients:

1 cup (250 mL) maple syrup

2 to 3 tbsp (30 to 50 mL) nuts, chopped (optional)

1 tbsp (15 mL) soft butter

3 tbsp (50 mL) sugar

1 egg

1 cup (250 mL) all-purpose flour

2 tsp (10 mL) baking powder

1/4 tsp (1 mL) salt

1/4 tsp (1 mL) nutmeg or cinnamon

1/2 cup (125 mL) milk

Method:

• Butter an 8 × 8-inch (20 × 20 cm) microwave-safe baking dish. Pour in the maple syrup and nuts to taste. Microwave 3 minutes at HIGH.

• Blend together until creamy the butter, sugar and egg.

• Stir together the flour, baking powder, salt, nutmeg or cinnamon. Add to the creamed mixture, alternating with the milk. Stir until well blended.

• Divide dough into four large balls and place in the hot syrup, then stretch dough with two forks until it is all joined together. This is easy, as the dough gets very soft when it comes in contact with the hot syrup, and it joins completely when cooking.

• Place pan on a rack, microwave at MEDIUM-HIGH 4 to 5 minutes, or until the top of the cake looks dry and the middle well done. Sometimes the middle looks a little softer, but when the cake stands on the counter, residual heat finishes the cooking.

• Any leftover may be kept in the baking dish, covered, at room temperature, or unmolded with the syrup, which penetrates the cake and enhances the flavor.

• It will keep for several days.

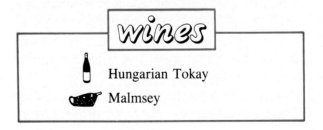

wines

Hungarian Tokay

Malmsey

A Perfect One-egg Cake

Preparation : . . . . .15 m
Cooking : . . . . .6 m
Standing : .none

A personal note: This is a very old recipe that I adapted to microwave cooking. If you make the cake without the garnish, you will have a plain butter cake to serve as is or to top with sweetened fresh fruit, such as strawberries, raspberries or blueberries. If you microwave the cake with the given garnish or a variation of your choice in the bottom of the pan, you will have an attractive and tasty upside down cake when unmolded.

Ingredients:

The batter:

1/2 cup (125 mL) butter or margarine
 or shortening

1 cup (250 mL) sugar

1 egg

1 tsp (5 mL) almond or vanilla extract

1⅔ cups (410 mL) flour

2 tsp (10 mL) baking powder

1/4 tsp (1 mL) salt

1/2 cup (125 mL) milk

Walnut mixture:

3 tbsp (50 mL) butter or margarine

1/2 cup (125 mL) pale brown sugar

2 tbsp (30 mL) all-purpose flour

1/2 cup (125 mL) walnuts, chopped

3 tbsp (50 mL) water or brandy or white wine

Method:

• Beat in a bowl the butter, margarine or shortening until creamy.

• Add the sugar, egg and vanilla or almond extract and beat together until light and fluffy.

• Mix together with a spoon the flour, baking powder and salt. Beat alternately with the milk into the creamed mixture.

• When well blended, if you wish to make a plain cake, pour the batter into an 8 × 8-inch (20 × 20 cm) microwave-safe baking dish. Place on a rack and microwave 6 minutes at MEDIUM-HIGH, checking doneness after 4 minutes.

• When done, cool on rack.

To make an upside down cake

• Make the walnut mixture by creaming together the 3 tablespoons (50 mL) butter or margarine, the brown sugar and the 2 tablespoons (30 mL) flour.

• Add the chopped walnuts and the water, brandy or white wine. Stir. Generously butter the bottom of the baking dish, then spread in the walnut mixture. Spoon the cake batter over this.

• Place the baking dish on a rack, microwave 3 minutes at MEDIUM-HIGH. Give the cake a quarter turn and bake another 3 minutes.

• Test doneness same as for an oven-baked cake. The finished cake will be creamy yellow on top, and when unmolded will have an attractive nut caramel topping.

Variation — Blueberry mixture

Ingredients:

2 to 3 cups (500 to 750 mL) blueberries

1/2 cup (125 mL) sugar

Grated rind of 1/2 a lemon

1/4 tsp (1 mL) ginger or cinnamon

Method:

• Mix all the ingredients together in the bottom of the baking dish and substitute for the walnut mixture.

• Spoon the cake batter over this mixture and microwave as for an upside down cake.

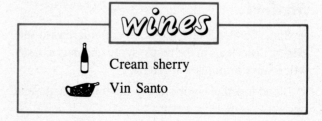

Cream sherry
Vin Santo

Hélène's Quick Quick Cake

Preparation : . . . . .10 m
Cooking : . . . . .from 8 to 9 m
Standing : .15 m

• Quick to make and quick to bake, this cake has many variations. A must in your cake répertoire. A big plus is that canned fruit and fresh fruit make it equally flavorful.

A personal note: You can replace canned fruit with nuts and coconut to taste or with about **3 tablespoons (50 mL) raisins** or with **2 or 3 cups (500 or 750 mL) fresh fruit**, such as **strawberries, raspberries, blueberries**, etc., sprinkled with **1/2 to 3/4 cup (125 to 190 mL) white sugar**. In this case, omit the 3 tablespoons (50 mL) white wine or liquid as fresh fruit is juicy.

Ingredients:

The batter:

1½ cups (375 mL) flour

3 tsp (15 mL) baking powder

1 cup (250 mL) sugar

2 eggs + enough milk to give 1 cup (250 mL) of liquid

To flavor

Add *one* of the following *to the flour:*

1/2 tsp (2 mL) nutmeg or allspice

1 tsp (5 mL) ground cardamom or cinnamon

Grated lemon or orange rind

OR

Add *one* of the following *to the milk:*

1 tsp (5 mL) vanilla extract

1/2 tsp (2 mL) almond extract or rose water

2 tsp (10 mL) liqueur of your choice

The garnish:

2 tbsp (30 mL) butter

2/3 cup (160 mL) pale brown sugar

3 tbsp (50 mL) white wine or liquid drained from canned fruit

Canned fruit of your choice (apricots, peaches, pineapple, etc.), drained

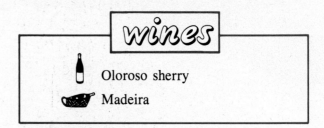

Oloroso sherry

Madeira

Method:

To prepare the batter

• Mix together in a bowl the flour, baking powder, sugar and one of the dry flavorings, such as nutmeg, if you wish.

• Place the eggs in a 1-cup (250 mL) measuring cup and fill with milk.

• Add the liquid flavoring, such as vanilla.

• Pour into the dry ingredients and beat thoroughly with an electric beater.

To make an upside down cake

• Place a small custard cup, open side down, in the middle of an 8 × 8-inch (20 × 20 cm) microwave-safe cake pan.

• Add the 2 tablespoons (30 mL) butter and microwave 1 minute at HIGH.

- Sprinkle the brown sugar over the butter, add the white wine or liquid drained from the canned fruit. Stir.

- Top with the chosen fruit.

- Pour the batter over all.

- Place the cake pan on a microwave-safe rack and microwave 5 minutes at HIGH. Check doneness and microwave 2 or 3 minutes more at MEDIUM.

- Remove from oven and let stand 15 minutes on rack.

- Remove custard cup so that the juice accumulated under it will spread into the garnish.

- To serve, cut into portions with the fruit mixture or other chosen garnish on top, or pass a knife around the cake and unmold.

Sliced Apple Cake

Preparation : . . . .**15 m**
Cooking : . . . .**from 6 to 7 m**
Standing : . . . .**10 m**

A personal note : This moist cake will keep a week in its baking pan, covered with plastic wrap, or as long as two weeks in the refrigerator, either molded or unmolded, covered with plastic wrap. To serve, I warm up each piece 40 seconds at MEDIUM-HIGH.

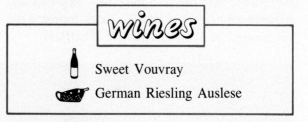

wines

Sweet Vouvray

German Riesling Auslese

Ingredients :

2 eggs

3/4 cup (190 mL) brown sugar

1/2 cup (125 mL) vegetable oil

1 tsp (5 mL) vanilla

3 cups (750 mL) thinly sliced apples, peeled

1¾ cups (440 mL) all-purpose flour

1/2 tsp (2 mL) salt

1 tsp (5 mL) baking soda

1/2 tsp (2 mL) cinnamon

1/2 tsp (2 mL) nutmeg

1/4 tsp (1 mL) allspice (optional)

Method :

- Beat together the eggs and brown sugar.
- When light, add the oil, vanilla and apples. Mix thoroughly.
- Sift together the flour, salt, soda and spices.
- Add to the apple mixture, blend thoroughly.
- Pour into an 8 × 8-inch (20 × 20 cm) ceramic dish.
- Microwave at HIGH 4 minutes.
- Let stand 3 minutes, without removing from oven.
- Microwave 2 to 3 minutes more at MEDIUM-HIGH.
- Check doneness in the middle of the cake after 2 minutes.
- Let stand 10 minutes on a rack before unmolding.
- This cake can also be left in the baking dish and cut into squares as needed.
- Keep covered.

Lemon Cake

Convection or microwave cooking

Preparation : . . . . **15 m**
Cooking : microwave : . . . . **6 m**
    convection : . . . . **45 m**
Standing : . . . . **none**

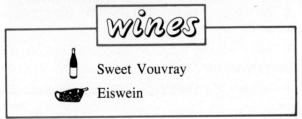

wines

🍾 Sweet Vouvray

🥮 Eiswein

Ingredients :

2 tbsp (30 mL) butter or margarine

1 cup (250 mL) sugar

2 eggs

1¼ cups (300 mL) flour

1/2 tsp (2 mL) salt

2 tsp (10 mL) baking powder

1/2 cup (125 mL) yogurt

Grated rind of 1 lemon

3 tbsp (50 mL) sugar

Juice of 1 lemon

• A simple cake full of flavor, this Lemon Cake has excellent keeping quality. It is one of my favorites.

Method :

• Beat 2 minutes with an electric mixer the butter or margarine, sugar and eggs. Add the remaining ingredients except the 3 tablespoons (50 mL) sugar and lemon juice. Mix well.

• Preheat the convection part of your microwave oven at 325°F (160°C). Place the cake on a rack and bake 45 minutes.

• Microwave the lemon juice and the 3 tablespoons (50 mL) sugar together 1 minute at MEDIUM, stir well. Pour hot over the cake in the mold as it is removed from the oven. I leave my cake in the mold, covered, and I cut it as needed. It keeps very well, when cooled, covered with plastic wrap.

• This cake can be microwaved, 6 minutes at HIGH, checking for doneness after 4 minutes. The microwave version is very tasty, but not quite as perfect.

829

My Mother's Rhubarb Cake

Preparation:	**15 m**
Cooking:	**8 m**
Standing:	**none**

A personal note: As soon as the first fresh, deep pink rhubarb appeared in the springtime garden, my mother made stewed rhubarb and this cake. It was a treat! In those days, we always had sour milk. Today, I sour milk with vinegar or I use buttermilk or plain yogurt. When we had guests, my mother topped the squares of her rhubarb cake with homemade ice cream. How good it was!

Ingredients:

1 ½ cups (375 mL) dark brown sugar

1/2 cup (125 mL) soft butter (unsalted when possible)

2 eggs

1 cup (250 mL) sour milk or buttermilk or plain yogurt

1 tsp (5 mL) soda

1 tsp (5 mL) salt

2⅓ cups (580 mL) flour

1 ½ to 2 cups (375 to 500 mL) rhubarb, washed, peeled and cut into small dice

Method:

• Cream brown sugar and butter of your choice, using an electric beater or a hand beater.

• When creamy, add the eggs slightly beaten and all at once the sour milk, or buttermilk or plain yogurt.

• Stir together the soda, salt and flour. Blend into the creamed mixture.

• Add the rhubarb. Stir by hand until well blended with the creamed mixture.

• Grease a 9 × 13-inch (23 × 33 cm) microwave-safe pan.

• Pour batter into the pan and microwave 5 minutes at MEDIUM, then 3 minutes at HIGH.

• Check for doneness. Cool on a cake rack.

• When cooled, unmold. Serve as is or with ice cream or ice with the glaze as in Canadian Carrot Cake.

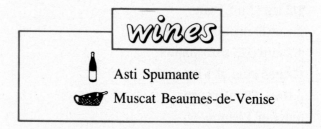

wines

Asti Spumante

Muscat Beaumes-de-Venise

Leyden Gingerbread

Convection cooking

Preparation : . . . . .10 m
Cooking : . . . . .from 50 to 60 m
Standing : . . . . .none

• Dutch women are very talented in the use of spices. For centuries, spices have had a priority in their kitchens because of The Netherlands' association with Indonesia. The coriander seeds called for in this recipe are fairly easy to find.

Ingredients :

1/3 cup (80 mL) pure lard
1/2 cup (125 mL) brown sugar
1 egg
2/3 cup (160 mL) molasses
Grated rind of 1 orange
2½ cups (625 mL) all-purpose flour
2 tsp (10 mL) baking powder
1/2 tsp (2 mL) salt
2 tsp (10 mL) ground ginger
1 tsp (5 mL) coriander seeds, crushed (optional)
1 tsp (5 mL) baking soda
1 cup (250 mL) boiling water

Method :

• Cream together the lard, brown sugar and egg until light and foamy.

• Add molasses and orange peel.

• Sift together the flour, baking powder, salt, ginger, crushed coriander seeds and soda.

• When all is well mixed and creamy, add the boiling water. Mix until well blended. Do not worry if batter seems thin ; it should be thin.

• Preheat the convection part of your microwave oven at 325°F (160°C). Pour batter into a greased pan and bake 50 to 60 minutes.

wines

Vin Santo

Malvasia delle Lipari

Swiss Carrot and Nut Cake

Convection cooking

Ingredients:

1 cup (250 mL) very fine breadcrumbs

1/2 tsp (2 mL) cinnamon

1/4 tsp (1 mL) ground cloves

2/3 cup (160 mL) peeled carrots, finely grated

1¼ cups (315 mL) almonds or filberts, with skins

6 egg yolks, beaten

1¼ cups (315 mL) sugar

Grated rind and juice of 1 lemon

6 egg whites, beaten

Method:

How to make fine breadcrumbs in your microwave

• Break up 4 to 5 slices of white, brown or raisin bread. Place on a microwave-safe rack.

• Microwave 3 to 5 minutes at HIGH. Start looking at the bread after 3 minutes.

• It is easy to see how dry it is. Give it another minute at a time, if necessary.

• Let the bread cool on the table or on a plate. This is also quick; 3 to 5 minutes does it.

• Then make fine breadcrumbs with a rolling pin, or a blender or a food processor.

Advance preparation:	. . from 2 to 3 days
Cooking:	. . . . from 45 to 55 m
Standing:	. . . . none

• Measure the needed cup and set aside about 3 spoonfuls for the cake mold.

• Add the cinnamon and ground cloves to the breadcrumbs in the cup and stir. Set aside.

• Any leftover breadcrumbs will keep, refrigerated in a covered bowl, for up to 12 months.

• Grate the peeled carrots and the nuts, set aside until needed.

How to prepare the pan

• Butter bottom and sides of a round 8 or 9-inch (20 or 23 cm) microwave-safe cake pan.

• Sprinkle with the 3 spoonfuls reserved breadcrumbs.

• Shake all around until butter is all covered. Then turn pan over and give it a shake to remove any excess crumbs.

How to make the cake

• Combine in a bowl the egg yolks, sugar and lemon juice.

• Beat with an electric or hand beater until thick and creamy.

• Add the breadcrumbs mixed with the cinnamon and cloves. Mix well.

• Stir in the carrots, the nuts and lemon rind.

• Beat the egg whites until stiff. Add 1/3 of the beaten whites to the batter, mix thoroughly. Then carefully fold in the remaining egg whites with a rubber spatula.

• Preheat the convection part of your microwave oven at 350°F (180°C).

• Spoon the batter gently into the prepared pan, place on a rack and bake 45 to 55 minutes, or until a toothpick inserted in the centre comes out dry. Cool on rack.

• Then unmold and wrap in foil. Let the cake ripen 2 to 3 days, refrigerated.

• Serve as is or cover with a glaze made as follows:

The glaze

• This glaze can also be used on other cakes.

Ingredients:

2 cups (500 mL) sifted icing sugar

4 tbsp (60 mL) cold water or orange juice

1/2 tsp (2 mL) lemon extract or fresh lemon juice

Method:

• Mix all the ingredients together until very creamy and light, then pour over the cooled cake. Smooth top with a knife, and let dripping fall naturally around the cake.

wines

Samos Muscat

Malvasia delle Lipari

Canadian Carrot Cake

Preparation :	. . . . **20 m**
Cooking :	. . . . **8 m**
Standing :	. . . . **none**

• Much simpler to make than the original Swiss Carrot and Nut Cake I make it by the microwave method because the brown sugar and spices sprinkled on top give it a nice finish.

Ingredients :

1 cup (250 mL) sugar

3/4 cup (190 mL) vegetable oil*

3 eggs

1½ cups (375 mL) flour

1/2 tsp (2 mL) salt

1½ tsp (7 mL) baking soda

1 tsp (5 mL) cinnamon

1/4 tsp (1 mL) nutmeg

2 cups (500 mL) carrots, peeled and grated fine

Grated rind of 1/2 a lemon (optional)

* The vegetable oil can be replaced by shortening at room temperature.

Method :

• Place sugar and vegetable oil in a bowl.

• Add eggs, one at a time, beating well at each addition. It is important to have this part of the recipe very well beaten. (I use an electric hand beater or my mixer.)

• Sift together the flour, salt, soda, cinnamon and nutmeg. Add to the creamed mixture, along with the grated carrots and the lemon rind. Mix the whole until well blended. Pour into a well greased, microwave-safe 8 × 8-inch (20 × 20 cm) pan.

• Sprinkle top of cake with **1/2 cup (125 mL) dark brown sugar**. Microwave at MEDIUM 5 minutes, then 3 minutes at HIGH. Test for doneness.

• Cool 10 to 15 minutes on rack. Unmold.

• Serve as is or use glaze as given after recipe for Swiss Carrot and Nut Cake.

wines

🍾 Oloroso sherry

🥄 Malmsey

Lovers' Apple Cake

Preparation: . . . . .20 m
Cooking: . . . . .from 5 to 8 m
Standing: . . . . .10 m

- Let stand 10 minutes in the oven.

- Check doneness in the middle of the cake. If it is still a little soft, microwave the cake at MEDIUM another 3 minutes.

- Cool on rack. Unmold when cooled, or cut into squares. Serve.

- If you wish to warm up a piece of cake, set it on a plate and microwave 30 to 40 seconds at MEDIUM-HIGH.

A personal note: On Saint Valentine's Day, tie a red ribbon around the cake. Pour 1/4 to 1/2 cup (60 to 125 mL) hot brandy or rum on top of the cooled cake. You don't need an icing; simply place two red roses on top of the cake.

Ingredients:

1/4 cup (60 mL) soft butter

1 cup (250 mL) sugar

1 tsp (5 mL) vanilla

1 egg

2 cups (500 mL) apples, peeled and cut into small dice

1 cup (250 mL) flour

1/2 tsp (2 mL) each baking powder and baking soda

1 tsp (5 mL) cinnamon

1/2 tsp (2 mL) ground cloves

1/2 cup (125 mL) walnuts, chopped (optional)

2 tsp (10 mL) unsweetened or semi-sweet cocoa

Method:

- Place in a bowl the butter, sugar, vanilla and egg.

- Beat with an electric mixer until fluffy and creamy. Stir in the apples.

- In another bowl, sift together the flour, baking powder, soda, cinnamon and cloves.

- Add to the creamed mixture.

- Sprinkle the chopped walnuts over the whole and blend thoroughly.

- Pour into a square 8-inch (20 cm) ceramic or plastic dish. Sprinkle top with the cocoa.

- Place on microwave-safe rack. Microwave 5 minutes at HIGH.

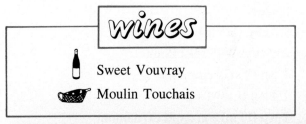

wines

Sweet Vouvray

Moulin Touchais

My Finnish friend Marta's Cardamom Cake

Preparation: . . . .**15 m**
Cooking: microwave: . . . .**from 5 to 8 m**
        convection: . . . .**from 40 to 50 m**
Standing: . . . .**none**

Microwave or convection cooking

• A delicious sort of pound cake, I often enjoy this cake, especially in the afternoon with a cup of coffee.

Ingredients:

1/2 cup (125 mL) soft unsalted butter or margarine
1 cup (250 mL) sugar
2 eggs
1/2 cup (125 mL) molasses
2½ cups (625 mL) flour
1 tsp (5 mL) cinnamon
1/4 tsp (1 mL) salt
2 tsp (10 mL) ground cardamom
2 tsp (10 mL) baking soda
2 cups (500 mL) sour cream
1/2 cup (125 mL) walnuts, chopped
3/4 cup (190 mL) seedless raisins

Method:

• Butter two 9 × 5-inch (23 × 13 cm) microwave-safe loaf pans or a 10-inch (25 cm) Bundt pan.

• Cream the butter or margarine at high speed with an electric mixer.

• Gradually add the sugar. Beat until light and creamy.

• Add eggs, one at a time, beating well at each addition.

• Add molasses. Beat at high speed just enough to blend the whole.

• Sift together the flour, cinnamon, salt, cardamom and soda.

• Add all at once to the creamed mixture and pour the sour cream on top. Then beat at high speed for 2 minutes.

• Add walnuts and raisins and beat by hand until well mixed into the batter.

• Divide the batter equally between the prepared loaf pans or pour into the Bundt pan.

To bake

• Microwave in loaf pans, one at a time, 3 minutes at HIGH, 2 minutes at MEDIUM-HIGH.

• Test for doneness; it may require 2 to 3 minutes more at MEDIUM-HIGH.

• Cool on rack before unmolding.

The Bundt pan cake

• I prefer this large cake baked in the convection part of the microwave oven preheated at 325°F (160°C).

• Set the cake on a rack and bake 40 to 50 minutes. Test for doneness.

• Cool on cake rack. Unmold. Wrap.

• It will keep fresh in a cool place for up to two weeks.

Strawberry Shortcake

Convection cooking

> **A personal note:** A true shortcake is not made with sponge cake, but a sort of rich biscuit type of cake that is split, buttered and filled and topped with fresh strawberries. Although it can be microwaved, to be perfect this shortcake should be baked in the convection part of the microwave oven.

```
Preparation: ................30 m
Cooking:  ..........from 12 to 14 m
Standing: ....................none
```

Ingredients:

2 to 3 cups (500 to 750 mL) **fresh strawberries**

2 cups (500 mL) flour

1/4 cup (60 mL) sugar

4 tsp (20 mL) baking powder

1/2 tsp (2 mL) salt

A good pinch of nutmeg

1/2 cup (125 mL) butter

2 egg yolks

1/3 cup (80 mL) milk

1 cup (250 mL) whipping cream

3 tbsp (50 mL) icing sugar

Method:

• Butter generously an 8 or 9-inch (20 or 23 cm) round microwave-safe cake pan. Set aside. Wash and hull the strawberries. Drain in a colander while making and baking the shortcake.

• Preheat the convection part of your microwave oven at 450°F (230°C).

• Sift together in a bowl the flour, sugar, baking powder, salt and nutmeg.

• Cut in the butter with two knives and work it into the dry ingredients until the mixture looks mealy.

• Beat the egg yolks with the milk. Stir into the flour mixture, stirring only until all the flour has disappeared. Do not try to beat until all is smoothed out.

• Spoon batter into the prepared pan. Dip a metal spatula in milk or water and smooth the top of the batter, but it should retain a rugged appearance.

• Set on a rack and bake about 12 to 14 minutes, or until golden brown on top.

• When tested with the point of a knife, the cake should be dry.

• Lightly crush the strawberries. Add the icing sugar.

• Cut the warm shortcake in half with a sharp knife to make two equal layers. Butter the bottom layer with soft butter. Pour the sweetened berries on top. Cover with the other half of the cake.

• To taste, sprinkle top with icing sugar and garnish with strawberry halves and whipped cream if the shortcake is to be eaten at one meal.

• If not, sprinkle top and strawberries with icing sugar. Serve with a bowl of whipped cream.

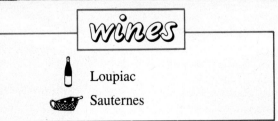

Loupiac

Sauternes

5-Minute Cheesecake

A personal note: Delicious, creamy and light, this cheesecake can be served with sweetened strawberries or raspberries or a creamy fresh blueberry sauce. Yummy!

Preparation: . . . . **10 m**
Cooking: . . . . **from 3 to 5 m**
Standing: . . . . **none**

Ingredients:

The crust:

1/4 cup (60 mL) butter or margarine

1 cup (250 mL) graham cracker crumbs
  (about 12 biscuits)

2 tbsp (30 mL) sugar

A good pinch of nutmeg

The filling:

1 8-oz (250 g) package cream cheese

1/3 cup (80 mL) sugar

1 egg

1 tbsp (15 mL) fresh lemon juice

Topping:

1 cup (250 mL) sour cream

3 tbsp (50 mL) sugar

Method:

• Microwave butter or margarine in an 8-inch (20 cm) round glass or ceramic pie plate 30 seconds to 1 minute at HIGH, until melted.

• Stir in the graham cracker crumbs, sugar and nutmeg.

• Mix well and press over bottom and half an inch (1.25 cm) up sides of plate.

• In a microwave-safe bowl microwave cream cheese at MEDIUM, 6 to 8 seconds, or until softened. Stir well. Beat in sugar and egg. Blend in the lemon juice and pour on crust.

• Microwave uncovered at HIGH 2 to 3 minutes, or until set around the edges, rotating the dish twice while cooking, unless you have a turntable.

• Combine sour cream and sugar for topping.

• Spoon over hot cheesecake, spreading with a spatula to completely cover the baked cheese.

• Microwave at HIGH 1 to 1½ minutes, or until topping is hot.

• Cool. Refrigerate until ready to serve.

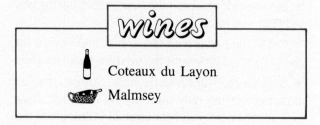

wines

Coteaux du Layon

Malmsey

Hawaiian Banana Bread

Preparation: . . . . **15 m**
Cooking: . . . . **7 m**
Standing: . . . . **none**

• A few years ago I visited a banana plantation in Hawaii. I was invited afterwards to taste their favorite banana cake and coffee. Both were delicious.

Ingredients:

1 cup (250 mL) bananas, mashed
1/4 cup (60 mL) vegetable oil
1/4 cup (60 mL) white sugar
1/4 cup (60 mL) brown sugar, firmly packed
2 eggs
1/2 tsp (2 mL) each of vanilla and almond extract
1½ cups (375 mL) flour
1/2 tsp (2 mL) baking soda
1/4 tsp (1 mL) baking powder
1/4 tsp (1 mL) salt
1/2 cup (125 mL) walnuts, chopped
2 tbsp (30 mL) dark brown sugar
1/4 tsp (1 mL) nutmeg

Method:

• Beat the first 6 ingredients until creamy and light.

• Sift together the next 4 ingredients. Add to the banana mixture. Stir in the walnuts.

• Pour the batter into an 8 × 4-inch (20 × 10 cm) microwave-safe loaf pan. (It is not necessary to grease pan.)

• Blend together the brown sugar and the nutmeg. Sprinkle on top of the cake.

• Microwave 4 minutes at HIGH. Rotate the pan and microwave another 3 minutes at MEDIUM.

• Cool cake on a rack for 20 to 30 minutes before unmolding.

Sweet sherry
Hungarian Tokay

Christmas Plum Pudding

Preparation : .20 m
Cooking : . . . . .from 8 to 15 m
Standing : .15 m

• Did you ever bake a Christmas Plum Pudding in 15 minutes that will keep well wrapped in a cool place for 10 to 12 months in perfect condition? Try this one…

Ingredients :

1/2 cup (125 mL) candied fruit

1 cup (250 mL) raisins

1/2 cup (125 mL) currants

1/2 cup (125 mL) rum

1 cup (250 mL) minced beef suet

1 tbsp (15 mL) cinnamon

2 tsp (10 mL) ginger

1/2 tsp (2 mL) each nutmeg, allspice and salt

1 cup (250 mL) sugar

1 cup (250 mL) jam or marmalade

2 cups (500 mL) fine breadcrumbs

3 eggs

2 tbsp (30 mL) milk

1/2 cup (125 mL) rum, wine or fruit juice

Method :

• Mix together in a microwave-safe bowl the candied fruit, raisins, currants and rum.

• Microwave 2 minutes at HIGH.

• Combine in a second bowl the suet, cinnamon, ginger, nutmeg, allspice, salt, sugar, jam or marmalade and breadcrumbs. Add to the fruit mixture.

• Beat together the eggs, milk and wine, rum or fruit juice and blend into the batter.

• Mix well and pour into one or two microwave-safe bowls. Cover with plastic wrap so pudding steams.

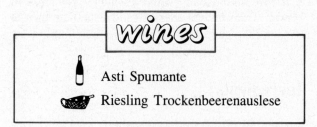

Asti Spumante

Riesling Trockenbeerenauslese

• Microwave one at a time at MEDIUM-HIGH 8 to 15 minutes depending on size of bowl used. ·

• Test with a wooden pick and microwave 1 minute more if necessary.

• Remove plastic wrap and let stand 15 minutes on kitchen counter before unmolding.

• You can make individual puddings in custard cups. Microwave 5 minutes for 6 cups at HIGH. Test as above.

To glaze

• Microwave **1/2 cup (125 mL) jam of your choice** at HIGH 15 seconds.

• Brush over pudding and sprinkle with icing sugar.

To reheat

• Place pudding in a microwave-safe bowl and reheat at MEDIUM 4 to 10 minutes, depending on size.

To flame

• Heat **1/3 to 1/2 cup (80 to 125 mL) rum** 30 seconds at HIGH. Pour over pudding and flame.

To enhance the flavor of your pudding

• Wrap it in a cloth dipped in rum, wine or whatever alcoholic beverage you choose to let it ripen until Christmas, and up to several months thereafter.

Noël Fruit Cake

Preparation : . . . . **35 m**
Cooking : . . . . **7 to 10 m**
Standing : . . . . **none**

A personal note : This cake will keep for months. When cooled, wrap it first in a cloth — dipped in rum, wine or other spirits if you choose — then in aluminum foil and keep in a cool place or refrigerate. When ready to use, let the cake stand at room temperature for 3 to 4 hours before serving.

Ingredients :

1/2 lb (250 g) candied cherries, cut up

4 oz (125 g) dates, coarsely chopped

4 oz (125 g) mixed candied peel, chopped

1/2 lb (250 g) candied pineapple, cut up

4 oz (125 g) candied orange peel

4 oz (125 g) seedless raisins

1/2 cup (125 mL) rum or brandy

2 cups (500 mL) walnuts

1 cup (250 mL) Brazil nuts or other nuts of
    your choice, coarsely chopped

1/2 cup (125 mL) sugar

1 cup (250 mL) all-purpose flour

1 tsp (2 mL) baking powder

1/4 tsp (1 mL) salt

1 tsp (5 mL) ground cardamom

3 tbsp (50 mL) Dutch cocoa powder (optional)

1/2 cup (125 mL) butter

4 eggs, well beaten

1 tsp (5 mL) pure vanilla extract

1 tsp (5 mL) almond extract

Method :

• Using a large microwave-safe bowl, combine cherries, dates, mixed candied peel, pineapple, orange peel, raisins and rum or brandy.

• Microwave at HIGH for 2 minutes, to flavor the fruit with the alcohol. Mix in the nuts.

• Sift together sugar, flour, baking powder, salt and cardamom, and cocoa powder if you wish, and blend into fruit until pieces are well coated.

• Cream butter and blend it thoroughly into the fruit mixture.

• Combine eggs, vanilla and almond extract, fold into the batter, stirring everything together until well blended.

• Pour into a buttered glass loaf pan 9 × 5 inches (23 × 13 cm) or two 8½ × 4½-inch (22 x 11 cm) microwave-safe pans.

• Microwave at HIGH 6 to 8 minutes for the larger pan. Test doneness with a wooden pick.

• If necessary, microwave 1 or 2 minutes more, testing again after 1 minute.

• For two pans, microwave one at a time at HIGH 5 to 6 minutes. Test for doneness as above.

• Let stand on kitchen counter. Cake will continue to cook as it cools.

• Unmold, wrap and store.

wines

Asti Spumante

Sweet champagne

Baking Powder Substitution

If your recipe calls for baking powder and you find you've run out, you can substitute the following mixture :

Ingredients :
2 tsp (10 mL) cream of tartar

1 tsp (5 mL) baking soda

1/4 tsp (1 mL) salt

Method :
• Mix well and use this amount for each 2 cups (500 mL) of flour called for in your recipe.

Honey-Ginger Sauce

Preparation: .3 m
Cooking: . . . . .from 4 to 5 m
Standing: . . . . .none

A personal note: This sauce was originally used on top of a sweet dumpling, but I have enjoyed it for many years on top of plum pudding.

Ingredients:

1/2 cup (125 mL) honey

1 cup (250 mL) water or white wine

3 tbsp (50 mL) ginger root, grated

2 tbsp (30 mL) arrowroot flour or cornstarch

Juice and grated rind of 1 lime

Method:

• Place all the ingredients in a microwave-safe dish or bowl, stir. Microwave 1 minute at HIGH, stir. Microwave 3 minutes more at HIGH, stirring once. It sometimes takes 1 minute more; do it at MEDIUM-HIGH.

• When sauce is creamy and transparent, it is ready.

Hélène's Sauce

Preparation: .5 m
Cooking: . . . . .from 5 to 6 m
Standing: . . . . .none

• Hélène has been a constant companion of mine for 28 years, writing, testing, tasting — always with a smile, which I have greatly appreciated.

• This is my very favorite sauce to serve with plum pudding.

Ingredients:

1 cup (250 mL) sugar

1 cup (250 mL) unsalted butter, softened

4 egg yolks, beaten

1 cup (250 mL) milk or cream

1/4 cup (60 mL) white wine

1/4 cup (60 mL) brandy

Method:

• Mix together the sugar, butter, beaten egg yolks and milk or cream. Microwave 3 minutes at MEDIUM, uncovered. Beat well and microwave 1 to 2 minutes at MEDIUM, or until sauce has thickened.

• Add wine and brandy and microwave another 30 seconds at MEDIUM.

• Serve warm or cold, with hot plum pudding.

Rum Glaze

Preparation: . . . . .5 m
Cooking: . . . . .2 m
Standing: . . . . .none

A personal note: Pour this glaze over a cake while it is still warm. It makes any cake — white, sponge, chocolate, etc. — moist and flavorful.

Ingredients:

1/2 cup (125 mL) butter or margarine

1 cup (250 mL) sugar

Grated rind of 1/2 a lemon or 1/2 an orange

1/4 cup (60 mL) rum of your choice

Method:

• Place the butter or margarine in a 4-cup (1 L) microwave-safe measuring cup and melt 2 minutes at HIGH.

• Stir in the sugar, the grated lemon or orange rind and the rum. Mix well.

• Microwave 2 minutes at HIGH.

• Stir until sugar is all melted.

• Pour warm over warm unmolded cake.

Liqueur Glaze

Preparation: . . . . .5 m
Cooking: . . . . .2 m
Standing: . . . . .from 2 to 3 h

A personal note: Somewhat different in texture from the Rum Glaze, this is the glaze to use when you wish to have a special liqueur flavor.

Ingredients:

1/2 cup (125 mL) butter or margarine

1/2 cup (125 mL) sugar

1/4 cup (60 mL) liqueur of your choice

1/4 cup (60 mL) water or apple juice

Method:

• Place the butter or margarine in a 4-cup (1 L) microwave-safe measuring cup and melt 2 minutes at HIGH.

• Add sugar, liqueur and water or apple juice. Microwave 2 minutes at HIGH, stirring after 1 minute of cooking.

• Make slits here and there in the cake with a pointed knife and pour glaze over the cake. Let stand on a rack 2 to 3 hours before unmolding.

Super Chocolate Pecan Cake Frosting

Preparation :	. . . . .5 m
Cooking :	. . . . .1 m 30 s
Standing :	. . . . .none

A personal note : I always enjoy this frosting on nut cakes. When the cake is made with walnuts, use walnuts ; if there are pecans in the cake, use pecans. The quantity remains the same.

Ingredients :

2 1-oz (28 g) squares semi-sweet chocolate
1/2 cup (125 mL) soft margarine
1 egg, beaten
1 tsp (5 mL) fresh lemon juice
1½ cups (375 mL) icing sugar
1/2 cup (125 mL) nuts of your choice, chopped

Method :

• Place chocolate in a 4-cup (1 L) microwave-safe measuring cup or bowl and melt 1 minute 30 seconds at HIGH, stirring after 30 to 40 seconds.

• Add margarine and egg to hot chocolate. Mix thoroughly.

• Add lemon juice and icing sugar. Beat until creamy. Fold in the chopped nuts.

• Frost cooled cake as soon as icing is ready.

Fresh Strawberry Glacé

Preparation :	. . . . .10 m
Cooking :	. . . . .3 m
Standing :	. . . . .none

• The "glacé" is the French way of flavoring and topping cakes, mousse, fruit pies, fresh fruit, etc. This one is beautiful to look at and very fragrant with the strawberry flavor.

Ingredients :

4 cups (1 L) fresh strawberries
1 cup (250 mL) sugar
1 tbsp (15 mL) cornstarch
1 tsp (5 mL) lemon rind, grated
1 tbsp (15 mL) lemon juice

Method :

• Crush 1½ cups (375 mL) of the strawberries with a fork.

• Add the sugar, cornstarch, lemon rind and juice. Stir together until well blended. Microwave 3 minutes at HIGH, stirring 3 to 4 times. Pour hot over your chosen dessert.

Glazed Fresh Fruit

- A quick and easy superlative dessert, try Fresh Strawberry Glacé during the peak of the season on any fruit — strawberries, raspberries, peaches or other.
- Simply fill a dish with about 4 cups (1 L) of the fresh chosen fruit.
- Pour enough of the warm strawberry glaze over the fruit to completely cover it.

Sliced Oranges in the Pink

- Peel **4 to 6 oranges** and slice as thinly as possible.
- Place them in a cut glass dish.
- Top with Fresh Strawberry Glacé.
- Cover and leave overnight at room temperature.
- Stir together just before serving.

Nutty Coconut Cake Topping

Preparation :	....................**5 m**
Cooking :	.......................**2 m**
Standing :	.....................**none**

A personal note : Frost your cake with this crunchy topping when the cake is unmolded but still hot.

Ingredients :

1/2 cup (125 mL) nuts of your choice
1/2 cup (125 mL) coconut
1 cup (250 mL) brown sugar
1/2 cup (125 mL) rich cream or evaporated milk
1 tsp (5 mL) vanilla extract

Method :

- Place nuts and coconut in a 4-cup (1 L) microwave-safe bowl.
- Microwave 2 minutes at HIGH, stirring once. This will toast the coconut.
- Add brown sugar, cream or milk and vanilla.
- Mix until well blended. Spread on cake.

Fluffy Chocolate Cake Topping

Preparation:	.....................5 m
Cooking:	.............from 2 to 3 m
Standing:	.....................none

• This creamy, light, chocolate topping is good on any cake. There is no sugar in it; semi-sweet chocolate is used.

Ingredients:

2 tbsp (30 mL) hot water

1 tbsp (15 mL) dry instant coffee

4 1-oz (28 g) squares semi-sweet chocolate

1/4 cup (60 mL) whipping cream

Method:

• Place the water in a microwave-safe bowl, microwave 1 minute at HIGH.

• Add the instant dry coffee, stir until well mixed. Add the chocolate.

• Microwave 2 to 3 minutes at MEDIUM, stirring once. Cool.

• Whip the cream and fold into the cooled chocolate mixture.

• Fluff on top of a cooled cake.

Substitutions for chocolate squares

3 tbsp (50 mL) cocoa + 1 tbsp (15 mL) butter = 1 square or 1 ounce (28 g) unsweetened chocolate

3 tbsp (50 mL) cocoa + 1 tbsp (15 mL) butter + 1 ½ tsp (7 mL) sugar = 1 square or 1 ounce (28 g) sweet chocolate

Canned Pear Topping

Preparation:	.....................3 m
Cooking:	.....................6 m
Standing:	.....................none

A personal note: This topping makes a quick, attractive dessert poured hot over ice cream or a square of lemon cake, or simply as is, served in a small fruit dish.

Ingredients:

2 tbsp (30 mL) butter

1/3 cup (80 mL) brown sugar

1/4 tsp (1 mL) each cinnamon and nutmeg

1/4 tsp (1 mL) ginger

1 28-oz (796 mL) can pear halves*

* The pear halves can be sliced, to taste.

Method:

• Combine in a 9-inch (23 cm) microwave-safe pie plate the butter, brown sugar and spices.

• Microwave, uncovered, 2 minutes at MEDIUM-HIGH, stirring once.

• Drain pears, stir into the hot syrup and microwave, covered, 4 minutes at MEDIUM-HIGH.

Pies

All about pies

- In restaurants, pie seems to be the great "national favorite." And this is true not only in Canada but virtually the world over.
- In France, you will find the bottom crust type; in Italy, it is often an almond crust as well as a pastry type. In Canada and the United States, the English double crust pie is the favorite.
- As for filling, apples are the winner!
- For centuries, the expression "as easy as pie" has been used. I sometimes wonder about that, since only good knowledge and "savoir-faire" concerning pie baking make it easy. Read the basic instructions regarding pies carefully and if you learn to apply the rules, it will soon become "as easy as pie."

About flour

- A well-made pastry should be tender and flaky.
- So it is important to know something about flour.
- All wheat flour contains "gluten," a stretchy elastic cell wall that develops as soon as the wheat proteins are mixed with liquid, giving the flour what is needed for a tender and flaky pastry.
- All-purpose flour and pastry flour are used for pie crust.
- Pastry flour gives a more tender crust, but an all-purpose flour of good quality also gives satisfactory results.
- All-purpose or pastry flour is always specified on the bags. Remember that both can be used.

About the fat in pastry making

1. The use of unsalted butter or a combination of unsalted butter and good-quality shortening is excellent for a delicate pie — but costly.
2. A pastry made only with high-fat shortening will be good and flaky, but flat in flavor.
3. Pastry made with pure lard, which is 100% animal fat, plus a certain percentage of water makes a marvellously tender and flaky pastry.

How to bake a pie in the microwave

- There are two ways to bake a pie:
a) By the microwave method
b) By the convection method

The microwave method

- Use a microwave-safe plate (Corning or Pyrex or special type plastic).
- The pastry does not brown when baked by the microwave method, but the doneness, flavor and texture are quite acceptable.

- Butter the pie plate lightly and line with the pastry of your choice, making sure the dough is firmly set on the edges as well as on the bottom of the pie plate.

- Prick pastry all over with the point of a paring knife or with a fork. Place pastry-lined plate on a microwave-safe rack. Microwave 3 to 4 minutes at HIGH, depending on the type of pastry you are using; it could also take 4 to 5 minutes at HIGH. It is easy to judge the doneness by the appearance of the pastry.

- Even though not browned, the flavour and texture of the pastry are quite acceptable. After all, when the pie crust is filled, it is the texture that is important.

- I prefer a pre-baked single crust for any type of pie when baked by microwave.

The convection method

1. Preheat the convection part of your microwave oven, as required by the recipe.

2. Make the pie according to the recipe. Bake in preheated oven according to the time required by the recipe.

3. Make sure it is placed on a rack.

4. When done, cool on a rack.

Helpful hint: To adapt a recipe for microwave cooking reduce the amount of liquid in the original recipe by one quarter [3/4 cup (190 mL) for 1 cup (250 mL)].
Reduce cooking time to a quarter of the time required: 15 minutes in microwave = one hour in conventional oven.
Increase cooking time gradually as the amount of food is increased. It need not be necessary to double the time.

All-Purpose Pastry

Advance preparation:	**30 m**
Cooking:	**none**
Standing:	**none**

A personal note: To prepare this dough, you can use shortening, margarine or butter in combination with the pure lard.

Ingredients:

2 cups (500 mL) all-purpose flour

3/4 tsp (4 mL) salt

1/3 cup (80 mL) butter

1/4 cup (60 mL) pure lard

About 6 tsp (90 mL) *very* cold water

1 tbsp (15 mL) fresh lemon juice or white vinegar

Method:

• Place in a bowl the flour, salt, butter and pure lard. Working quickly and lightly with the tips of your fingers, stir together until mixture resembles grains of rice.

• Add the remaining ingredients. Combine all lightly, working with the tips of your fingers or a blending fork. As soon as the dough seems to cling together, form into a ball with your hands.

• Place in a bowl or wrap in waxed paper, refrigerate 20 to 30 minutes or overnight.

• Chilling relaxes the dough and prevents shrinking during the baking period, whether baked by the microwave or convection method.

• When rolling the dough, use as little flour as possible on the board, as too much hardens the pastry.

Helpful hint: You can bake a pie in a metal pie plate in the convection part of the microwave oven.

Pure Lard Pastry

Preparation:	**10 m**
Cooking:	**none**
Standing:	**none**

A personal note: My favorite type of pastry, Pure Lard Pastry is quickly prepared and will keep 3 to 4 weeks wrapped in plastic wrap in the refrigerator. Wrapped in plastic wrap, then foil and frozen, it will keep for 4 to 6 months. Cut the ball of dough in four. Each package will make a double 8-inch (20 cm) or 9-inch (23 cm) pie.

Ingredients:

5 cups (1.25 L) all-purpose flour

1 tsp (5 mL) salt

1 tbsp (15 mL) sugar

1/4 tsp (1 mL) baking soda

1 lb (500 g) pure lard

1 egg

3 tbsp (50 mL) fresh lemon juice or white vinegar

Cold water

Method:

• Stir together in a large bowl the flour, salt, sugar and baking soda. Mix well. Add the pure lard in 2-inch (5 cm) pieces and cut in with two knives.

• Beat together in a 1-cup (250 mL) measuring cup the egg, fresh lemon juice or vinegar and fill with cold water. Add to the flour mixture. Then work the whole with your fingers until you have a nice ball of dough. It is sometimes necessary to add a few tablespoons of cold water. Do so one at a time.

• Then turn the ball of dough onto a floured table and knead for 1 minute or 2. You will then have a ball of nice soft dough.

• The dough is as easy to roll cold out of the refrigerator as it is fresh and soft. The only difference is that the soft type takes a little more flour on the table and rolling pin.

My Homemade Pie Crust Mix

Preparation: . . . . **10 m**
Cooking: . . . . **none**
Standing: . . . . **none**

A personal note: I always keep some of this mix ready to be used when I'm in a hurry. Store it in any container with a tight-fitting lid.

Ingredients:

6 cups (1.5 L) all-purpose flour

1 tbsp (15 mL) salt

1 lb or 2⅓ cups (500 g or 580 mL) vegetable shortening*

* Pure lard can also be used. It will give you a more delicate pastry.

Method:

• Mix flour and salt together, then cut in shortening with 2 knives until mixture is crumbly.

• Pour into container. Cover.

For a one-crust pie

• Measure 1½ cups (375 mL) of mix and 2 to 3 tablespoons (30 to 50 mL) cold water.

• Work together with a fork just long enough for the mixture to hold together.

For a two-crust pie

• Measure 2¼ cups (560 mL) of the mix with 3 to 4 tablespoons (50 to 60 mL) cold water.

• In both cases, the quantity of water may vary with the weather, so use a little less and add as needed.

• Form the dough into a ball, wrap in waxed paper and refrigerate 30 minutes.

• Roll, form and bake dough as any other type.

French Pastry
for tart shells

Preparation : . . . .**10 m**
Cooking : . . . .**none**
Standing : . . . .**none**

A personal note : This is a difficult pastry to roll, but worth the effort. It's super for tart shells. It becomes a golden color when microwaved.

Ingredients :

1 cup (250 mL) sifted all-purpose or pastry flour
1/8 tsp (0.5 mL) salt
1/4 cup (60 mL) sugar (full)
1 egg yolk, lightly beaten
1/4 cup (60 mL) soft butter

Method :

• Sift together the sifted flour, salt and sugar.

• Make a hole in the centre, put in the egg yolk and butter.

• Mix the whole with a fork until smooth. Unlike other pastry, it must be blended smooth and creamy.

• Form into a ball, wrap and refrigerate 2 to 3 hours.

• It is delicate to roll, but will be appreciated.

854

Egg Pastry

Preparation : . . . .**10 m**
Cooking : . . . .**none**
Standing : . . . .**none**

• This interesting pastry comes out a golden color when baked by microwave. I find it is good with any pie filling.

Ingredients :

3 cups (750 mL) all-purpose flour
1 tsp (5 mL) salt
1 cup (250 mL) butter or margarine
1 egg, lightly beaten
1/2 tsp (2 mL) lemon rind, grated
1/3 cup (80 mL) *ice* water

Method :

• Place the flour and salt in a large bowl. Stir with a spoon until fluffy and well mixed. Cut in the butter or margarine until the pieces of fat are small.

• Mix together the egg, the lemon rind and ice water, add to the flour mixture.

• Stir the whole together with a fork until the dough forms a ball.

• Refrigerate 30 minutes before rolling.

Graham Cracker Pie Shell

Advance preparation : . . . . . **from 1 to 3 h**
Cooking : . . . . **none**
Standing : . . . . **none**

• This recipe is sufficient for a pie shell. It is perfect to bake by microwave.

Ingredients :

1 cup (250 mL) graham cracker crumbs

3 tbsp (50 mL) brown sugar

1 tbsp (15 mL) honey

3 tbsp (50 mL) melted butter
    (1 minute at HIGH)

Method :

• Blend thoroughly the graham cracker crumbs and the brown sugar. Stir in the honey and melted butter.

• Press into pie plate with your fingers.

• Refrigerate 1 to 3 hours before filling.

A personal note : If the honey is very sugary, uncover and microwave 20 to 30 seconds at HIGH. It will then be soft enough to measure easily.

Spiced Crumb Crust

Preparation : . . . . **5 m**
Cooking : . . . . **from 1 to 1½ m**
Standing : . . . . **none**

A personal note : Powdered cinnamon or allspice or cloves is added to the dry ingredients to change the flavor. I like cinnamon with apples and allspice with pears.

Ingredients :

1/4 cup (60 mL) butter

1¼ cups (310 mL) fine breadcrumbs*

1/2 cup (125 mL) sugar

1/2 tsp (2 mL) cinnamon or other spice
    of your choice

* You can use stale bread crushed with a rolling pin or in a blender.

Method :

• Place the butter in a Pyrex or Corning pie plate. Microwave 1 minute at HIGH.

• Add remaining ingredients, blend well with a fork.

• Then press evenly over bottom and sides of the pie plate.

• Microwave at HIGH 1 to 1½ minutes. Cool.

Food Processor Crunchy Pie Crust

Preparation: . . . .**10 m**
Cooking: . . . .**1 m**
Standing: . . . .**none**

A personal note: This crust must be prepared in a food processor. Otherwise, the All Bran remains too coarse and tends to harden when microwaved.

Ingredients:

1/4 cup (60 mL) butter or margarine
3/4 cup (190 mL) Bran Flakes
3/4 cup (190 mL) All Bran
1/4 cup (60 mL) brown sugar
1/4 cup (60 mL) walnuts

Method:

• Place butter or margarine in a microwave-safe pie plate and melt 1 minute at HIGH.

• Place the two brans in food processor with the brown sugar and walnuts, blend on and off until it reaches a coarse texture.

• Add to melted butter in pie plate. Mix well.

• Press evenly on bottom and sides of pie plate.

• Place pie plate on a microwave-safe rack and microwave 1 minute at HIGH.

• Set aside to cool and fill according to taste.

Microwaved Open-Face Apple Pie

Preparation : . . . .**20 m**
Cooking : microwave : . . . . **from 8 to 9 m**
             convection : . . . . **from 40 to 50 m**
Standing : . . . .**10 m**

Microwave or convection cooking

• This is the first one-crust fruit pie I ever made in my microwave oven — and I still make it. I have not yet decided whether I prefer cinnamon or ground cardamom as a flavor for the pie. I sometimes use one, then the other.

Ingredients :

Pastry of your choice

5 to 6 cups (1.25 to 1.50 L) peeled apples, thinly sliced

1/2 cup (125 mL) white sugar

1/2 cup (125 mL) dark or light brown sugar

3 tbsp (50 mL) flour

1/4 cup (60 mL) butter

1/2 tsp (2 mL) salt

1/2 tsp (2 mL) cinnamon or ground cardamom

2 tbsp (30 mL) fresh lemon juice *or*
   1/2 tsp (2 mL) vanilla

1/3 cup (80 mL) light cream or milk

Method :

• Line the pie plate with the pastry, and microwave according to directions for baking pie shells by microwave. Cool.

• Fill cooled pie shell with the sliced apples.

• Blend together the white and brown sugars, the flour, butter, salt, cinnamon or cardamom until you have a crumbly mixture.

• Pour half this mixture over the apples and stir lightly to blend, being careful not to puncture the bottom crust.

• Mix the lemon juice or vanilla with the cream or milk, pour over the apple mixture and top with the remaining crumbs.

• There are two ways to bake this pie :

By microwave

• Sprinkle top of pie with **1 tablespoon (15 mL) of sifted cocoa.**

• Place pie on rack.

• Microwave 8 to 9 minutes at MEDIUM-HIGH.

• Let stand 10 minutes in the microwave.

• Serve hot or cold.

By convection

• Preheat the convection part of your microwave oven at 350°F (180°C).

• Place the pie on a rack. Bake 40 to 50 minutes.

• Cool on rack on the kitchen counter.

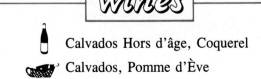

wines

Calvados Hors d'âge, Coquerel

Calvados, Pomme d'Ève

Rum Raisin Pie

Convection cooking

Preparation: . . . . 15 m
Cooking: . . . . from 12 to 18 m
Standing: . . . . 1 h

A personal note: Heating the rum and raisins in the microwave oven makes them soft, rummy and delicious. The rum may be replaced by fresh orange juice.

Ingredients:

3/4 cup (190 mL) seedless raisins
1/4 cup (60 mL) rum or fresh orange juice
1 egg
1 tsp (5 mL) cornstarch
1/2 cup (125 mL) sugar
1/2 cup (125 mL) sour cream
1/4 tsp (1 mL) cardamom or cinnamon
1 tbsp (15 mL) fresh lemon juice
Pastry for a 9-inch (23 cm) pie shell

Method:

• Place the raisins, rum or fresh orange juice in a microwave-safe cup or bowl. Microwave at HIGH 3 minutes. Let stand until just cooled.

• Place the egg, cornstarch, sugar, sour cream, cardamom or cinnamon and fresh lemon juice in a bowl, stir until well mixed. Microwave at MEDIUM-HIGH 2 minutes, stir well. Microwave another minute or two at MEDIUM-HIGH, or until creamy. Stir well.

• Add the rum-soaked raisins, mix well. Let stand while the pastry is baked.

• Place baking rack in lower part of your oven. Preheat convection part of your microwave oven at 400°F (200°C).

• Line a 9-inch (23 cm) pie plate with the rolled pastry. Crimp the edges.

• Cover with a square of waxed paper, pour in a cup of uncooked rice.* Put the prepared pie plate on the rack, bake 5 to 8 minutes.

• Remove pie plate from oven, gently remove the waxed paper with the rice.

• Return pie shell to oven until golden brown, about 5 to 10 minutes more. Cool.

• When cooled, fill with the rum raisin filling. Let stand about one hour at room temperature. Serve.

This method prevents the pastry from shrinking in the plate.

wines

Asti Spumante
California Orange Muscat

Spring Lemon Mincemeat

Convection cooking

Ingredients:

1/2 cup (125 mL) fresh lemon juice

3 cups (625 mL) unpeeled apples, grated

1 cup (250 mL) raisins of your choice

1/2 cup (125 mL) nuts of your choice, chopped

1/4 cup (60 mL) marmalade of your choice

2 cups (500 mL) sugar

1/2 tsp (2 mL) salt

2 tsp (10 mL) cinnamon

1 tsp (5 mL) ground cloves

1 tsp (5 mL) ginger

1 tsp (5 mL) ground cardamom (optional)

Grated rind of 2 oranges

Method:

• Combine all the ingredients in the order given. Mix thoroughly.

• Keep in glass jar, covered, in the refrigerator.

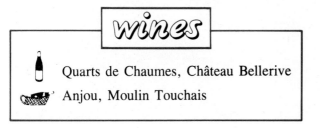

Quarts de Chaumes, Château Bellerive

Anjou, Moulin Touchais

Preparation:	20 m
Cooking: mincemeat:	none
pie:	from 30 to 40 m
Standing:	none

To bake a Lemon Mincemeat Pie by the convection method

• Add **1/4 cup (60 mL) melted butter** for each 2 cups (500 mL) of mincemeat used.

• Line a pie plate with a pastry of your choice. Fill with mincemeat.

• Bake in the convection part of your microwave oven preheated at 400°F (200°C). Place pie on a rack.

• Bake 30 to 40 minutes or until golden brown.

• Serve warm topped with ice cream or serve cooled but not refrigerated.

Elizabeth's Mincemeat

Convection cooking

Preparation :	**20 m**
Cooking : mincemeat :	**none**
pie :	**from 30 to 40 m**
Standing :	**none**

> **A personal note:** If you like mincemeat without any spices, this one is for you. It will keep in perfect condition, well covered and refrigerated, up to one year.

Ingredients :

1 lb (500 g) currants

1 lb (500 g) raisins

1 lb (500 g) apples, peeled and chopped (about 5 medium-sized apples)

1 lb (500 g) sugar

1/2 lb (250 g) suet, minced

1/2 lb (250 g) mixed peel

Rind and juice of 2 lemons

1/2 cup almonds (optional)

Method :

- Mix all the ingredients together thoroughly.
- Place in well-covered containers and refrigerate.

To make a pie

- Just line a pie plate with the pastry of your choice, and fill with about 2 cups (500 mL) of mincemeat.

- You can top the mincemeat with one apple, peeled and sliced, and sprinkle a few spoonfuls of rum or brandy over all.

- Cover with dough.

- Place the pie on a rack in the convection part of your microwave oven preheated at 400°F (200°C).

- Bake 30 to 40 minutes or until golden brown.

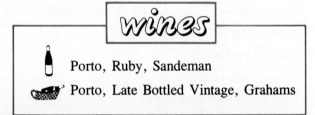

Porto, Ruby, Sandeman

Porto, Late Bottled Vintage, Grahams

Lean Mincemeat

Preparation:	. . . .	15 m
Cooking:	. . . .	35 m
Standing:	. . . .	none

• In the old days, when no household dared be without homemade mincemeat, this meatless type was the great favorite. I have been making it for years and have kept it in my cold pantry for as long as a year, or refrigerated for up to two years, and I have never lost even a spoonful of it.

Ingredients:

1 large orange

1 large lemon

2 cups (500 mL) seeded raisins

2 cups (500 mL) golden raisins

1 cup (250 mL) pitted dates, chopped

10 medium-sized apples (a firm apple is best)

1½ cups (375 mL) apple cider or juice

3 cups (750 mL) firmly packed brown sugar

1 tsp (5 mL) salt

1 tsp (5 mL) allspice

1 tsp (5 mL) nutmeg

1 tsp (5 mL) ground cloves

2 tsp (10 mL) ground cardamom (optional)

1 tbsp (15 mL) vanilla *or*
  1/4 cup (60 mL) rum or brandy (optional)

Method:

• Slice orange and lemon, unpeeled. Remove the seeds. Cut slices in half and chop fine in a food processor or blender.

• Place in a large microwave-safe dish, add the raisins and the dates. Stir to mix.

• Do not peel the apples, but remove cores and seeds. Cut into small dice. Add to the orange-lemon mixture.

• Add the apple cider or juice. Stir until well mixed.

• Microwave, uncovered, 20 minutes at HIGH, stir thoroughly. Microwave another 10 minutes at MEDIUM.

• Add the brown sugar, salt, spices and vanilla. Stir until well mixed. Microwave at MEDIUM 5 minutes.

• Add the rum or brandy. Stir thoroughly.

• Cool for about 15 minutes.

• Pack into glass jars.

• Cover tightly and put aside to ripen, or use when cooled.

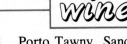

Porto Tawny, Sandeman

Porto Tawny, 20 years old, Ramos Pinto, Quinta da Ervamoira

Lemon Meringue Pie

Microwave and convection cooking

Preparation: . . . . .20 m
Cooking: . . . . .from 36 to 50 m
Standing: . . . . .none

A personal note: This recipe will show you how to use both the microwave and convection functions of your oven for the same recipe.

Filling:

Ingredients:

1 cup (250 mL) sugar

1 ¼ cups (310 mL) cold water

1 tbsp (15 mL) butter

1/4 cup (60 mL) cornstarch

3 tbsp (50 mL) cold water

Grated rind of 1/2 a lemon

Juice of 1 lemon

3 egg yolks

2 tbsp (30 mL) milk

Pastry of your choice for a 9-inch (23 cm)
  pie shell

Method:

• Combine in a microwave-safe bowl the sugar, the 1 ¼ cups (310 mL) cold water and the butter.

• Microwave at HIGH 3 to 4 minutes or until sugar is dissolved, stirring once.

• Mix the cornstarch with the 3 tablespoons (50 mL) cold water. Add to the above, stirring well.

• When mixed, microwave at HIGH 2 minutes, stir. Microwave at HIGH another 2 to 4 minutes or until creamy, stirring once or twice.

• Add the lemon rind and juice, stir.

• Beat the egg yolks with the milk. Add to mixture. Microwave at MEDIUM-HIGH 3 to 4 minutes, stirring twice.

• If necessary to obtain a creamy filling, microwave another minute or two.

• Cool while baking the pie shell.

• Place a rack in your oven.

• Preheat the convection part of a microwave at 400°F (200°C).

• Line a pie plate with the rolled pastry.

• Cover with a square of waxed paper, pour in a cup of uncooked rice.*

• Place pie plate in preheated oven. Bake 5 to 8 minutes.

• Remove plate from oven, gently remove the waxed paper with the rice. Put shell back into the oven, bake until golden brown all over, about 8 to 10 minutes more.

• Cool. Pour cooled filling into cooled pie shell.

* This method prevents the pastry from shrinking in the plate.

Meringue:

Ingredients:

3 egg whites

6 tbsp (90 mL) sugar

1 tsp (5 mL) lemon juice *or*
  1/4 tsp (1 mL) vanilla

A pinch of salt

Method:

• Beat the egg whites with a whisk or an egg beater until they form soft peaks when the beater is lifted.

• Gradually add the remaining ingredients, one at a time, beating well at each addition.

• Spread over the lemon filling, making sure it is spread to the edges of the filling. Place pie with meringue on rack.

• Brown at 400°F (200°C) until golden, about 15 to 20 minutes.

• Cool and serve. Do not refrigerate.

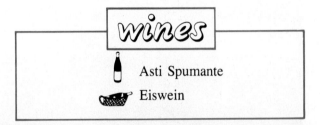

wines

Asti Spumante

Eiswein

Sugar Pie

Convection cooking

Preparation: . . . . .10 m
Cooking: . . . . .from 30 to 35 m
Standing: . . . . .none

• There is no need to pre-cook the crust of this pie, which is a most popular winter dessert.

Ingredients:

1   9-inch (23 cm) unbaked pie shell

1 cup (250 mL) brown sugar

1/4 cup (60 mL) all-purpose flour

1 cup (250 mL) milk

1 cup (250 mL) cream

1 tsp (5 mL) maple extract

3 tbsp (50 mL) butter or margarine

A good pinch of nutmeg

Method:

• Preheat the convection part of your microwave oven at 400°F (200°C).

• Line a pie plate with the unbaked pie shell of your choice.

• Mix the brown sugar and flour, spread in the bottom of the pastry.

• Mix the milk, cream and maple extract, pour over the brown sugar mixture. Dot with butter or margarine. Sprinkle with nutmeg.

• Place on a rack in the preheated oven and bake 30 to 35 minutes, or until the crust is golden brown. Cool and serve.

Bernard's Favorite

Convection cooking

Preparation: . . . .**20 m**
Cooking: . . . .**35 m**
Standing: . . . .**none**

• My husband and I both eat quite a bit of cottage cheese and yogurt. One day I tried a pie with cottage cheese, and it became a favorite. Use a graham cracker crust or a pastry of your choice.

Ingredients:

Pie shell of your choice
1/2 cup (125 mL) jam of your choice
1½ cups (375 mL) cottage cheese
1 tbsp (15 mL) flour
1/4 tsp (1 mL) salt
1 cup (250 mL) heavy or light cream
1/3 cup (80 mL) sugar
3 eggs, separated
Grated rind of 1 lemon
2 tbsp (30 mL) fresh lemon juice

Method:

• Line a pie plate with pastry of your choice.

• Spread the jam of your choice in the bottom of the pie crust.

• Blend together the remaining ingredients, except the egg whites.

• Beat the egg whites until stiff, then fold into the cottage cheese mixture. Pour the whole over the jam.

• Preheat the convection part of your microwave oven at 400°F (200°C).

• Place pie on a rack, reduce heat to 350°F (180°C) and bake about 35 minutes or until mixture is firm when tested with the blade of a knife.

• Serve hot or at room temperature.

Monbazillac
Barsac

Walnut Crust Chocolate Pie

Advance preparation : . . . . . **from 4 to 5 h**
Cooking : . . . . **4 m**
Standing : . . . . **none**

• If you are looking for a very special dessert, though slightly expensive, try this pie. It can be made six to 12 hours ahead of time.

Ingredients :

Crust :

1 ¼ cups (310 mL) walnuts, finely minced

2 tbsp (30 mL) brown sugar

2 tbsp (30 mL) soft butter

Filling :

6 tbsp (90 mL) butter

4 oz (112 g) unsweetened chocolate

1 cup (250 mL) sugar

3 eggs, lightly beaten

2 tbsp (30 mL) brandy

1 tsp (5 mL) vanilla extract

A pinch of salt

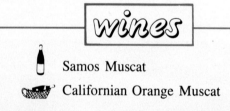

wines

Samos Muscat

Californian Orange Muscat

Method :

• If you have a blender or food processor, use it to mince the walnuts fine but not powdered. A sharp knife can be used but it takes longer.

• Blend the chopped walnuts, brown sugar and the 2 tablespoons (30 mL) soft butter.

• Press mixture into an 8-inch or 9-inch (20 or 23 cm) microwave-safe pie plate, covering evenly the bottom and the side of the plate. Microwave at HIGH 1 minute.

• Mix together the 6 tablespoons (90 mL) butter, the unsweetened chocolate and sugar.

• Microwave 2 minutes at HIGH, stir.

• If the chocolate is not all melted, microwave one more minute at HIGH, stir well.

• Add the lightly beaten eggs*, brandy, vanilla and salt.

• Stir until well blended. Pour into cooled pie shell.

• Refrigerate at least 4 to 5 hours before serving.

The eggs are added raw to the hot mixture. Well beaten, they cook without any further heat. If possible, have them at room temperature for one hour before use.

Meringue Pie Shell

Convection cooking

Preparation:	. . . . .20 m
Cooking:	. . . . .2 h
Standing:	. . . . .none

A personal note: Four egg whites and a little time equals a beautiful, tasty meringue pie shell. Both meringue and filling can be done in the morning and put together when ready to be served for dinner.

The meringue base of this pie **must** be cooked in the convection part of your microwave oven. The filling can be microwaved before or after baking the meringue base

Ingredients:

Meringue:

4 egg whites

A good pinch of cream of tartar

A pinch of salt

1/4 tsp (1 mL) vanilla extract

3/4 cup (190 mL) sugar

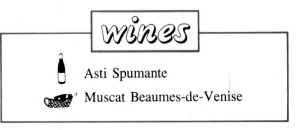

Asti Spumante

Muscat Beaumes-de-Venise

Method:

- If you have an electric mixer, by all means use it, as it makes all of it so easy, or use a hand beater.

- Beat the egg whites in a bowl until frothy.

- Add the cream of tartar and keep on beating for about half a minute.

- Add the salt and vanilla and beat again at medium speed while adding the sugar half a teaspoon (2 mL) at a time, until the whites form shiny firm peaks. This should take about 5 minutes in a mixer.

- Oil bottom, sides and rim of a 9 or 10-inch (23 or 25 cm) Pyrex or Corning pie plate.

- Mound meringue in the pie plate, using a rubber spatula to bring the meringue to the edges of the plate. If you can, place the meringue about 1½ inches (4 cm) above the rim of the plate, which gives you a deep pie shell that can be filled generously when baked.

- Preheat convection part of microwave oven at 200°F (100°C).

- Place meringue plate on a rack. Bake 2 hours.

- Let it cool on wire rack in the oven (if you do not need your oven), or on the kitchen counter.

Cream Filling for Meringue Pie

Advance preparation : . . . . .3 h
Cooking : . . . . .from 5 to 7 m
Standing : . . . . .none

• Little changes are made to this basic cream to produce a different pie each time. Here are a few of them. You can easily create your own.

Ingredients :

4 egg yolks
1/2 cup (125 mL) sugar
1 tbsp (15 mL) fresh lemon juice
3 tbsp (50 mL) of a liqueur of your choice
1 cup (250 mL) heavy cream, whipped
Toasted almonds, thinly sliced to garnish

Method :

• In a 4-cup (1 L) microwave-safe measuring cup, combine the egg yolks and sugar. Mix well. I use a wire whisk, which makes the work quick and easy.

• Microwave at MEDIUM 2 minutes, beating after 1 minute of cooking.

• Beat again after another minute and microwave 1 minute more, if necessary. It should have the consistency of mayonnaise. Slow cooking and lots of stirring are necessary to prevent the eggs from turning.

• When creamy, remove from microwave, add lemon juice, mix. Add liqueur, mix well. Cool.

• Whip the cream and fold into the cooled yolk mixture. Mix well.

• Pour into the cold meringue shell, sprinkle top with toasted almonds and refrigerate at least 3 hours.

Toasted almonds :

• Place **1/3 cup (80 mL) thinly slivered almonds** on a plate.

• Microwave at HIGH 3 to 4 minutes, stirring twice, or until almonds are golden brown.

• Cool for 10 minutes and sprinkle over top of cream in the pie.

Variations on Liqueur

Mint Liqueur:

• Add a dash of green coloring to the filling or, in the summer, chop very fine **1/2 cup (125 mL) fresh mint leaves** and use to replace liqueur called for in the recipe.

Raspberry:

• Give the cream a pale pink shade with a bit of red food coloring.

• Top with **fresh raspberries**, enough to completely cover the cream.

• Very attractive when placed in a circle on the cream.

Orange Cream:

• Add **2 tablespoons (30 mL) Grand Marnier** or **Cointreau** to the filling.

• Add 2 drops each of red and yellow coloring for a pale yellow color.

Chocolate Cream:

• Melt **2 to 3 ounces (56 to 74 g) of semi-sweet chocolate.**

• Place the wrapped squares on a plate. Microwave about 2 minutes at HIGH. It is then easy to scrape from the paper the melted chocolate and to add it to the filling.

• Garnish top of pie with a few grated slivers of semi-sweet chocolate.

Rum Raisin Cream:

• Place in a bowl **1/2 cup (125 mL) raisins** of your choice and **4 tablespoons (60 mL) rum.**

• Microwave 1 minute at HIGH. Cool.

• Mix with the basic cream filling.

• Garnish top with little fans of thinly sliced unpeeled oranges.

Molasses Apple Pie

Convection cooking

Preparation : . . . .**20 m**
Cooking : . . . .**from 35 to 45 m**
Standing : . . . .**none**

• This traditional Canadian apple pie recipe is used across Canada.

Ingredients :

Pastry of your choice for a 2-crust pie
5 to 6 apples
1/4 cup (60 mL) brown sugar
1/4 cup (60 mL) molasses
2 tbsp (30 mL) butter or margarine
1/4 tsp (1 mL) each cinnamon and allspice

Method :

• Preheat convection part of your microwave oven at 400°F (200°C).

• Meanwhile, line a 9-inch (23 cm) pie plate with pastry.

• Peel the apples and slice them or grate them, un-peeled. Mix the apples with the remaining ingredients, fill pie plate.

• Cover with the top crust. Crimp the edges.

• Make a few cuts in the top crust with the point of a knife. Rub dough with a little milk.

• Place on a rack in the preheated oven. Bake about 35 to 45 minutes, or until a golden color.

• Serve hot or at room temperature.

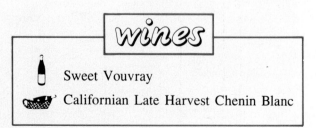

wines

Sweet Vouvray

Californian Late Harvest Chenin Blanc

Honey Apple Pie

Preparation: . . . . .20 m
Cooking: . . . . .from 13 to 14 m
Standing: . . . . .none

A personal note: One of my favorite apple pies, Honey Apple Pie can be made with one crust or with a bottom and a top crust, the top crust brushed with sour cream or yogurt and sprinkled with brown sugar. It has a nice gold crust cooked by microwave.

Ingredients:

Pastry of your choice

5 to 8 apples

1/2 cup (125 mL) sour cream or yogurt

1/4 cup (60 mL) honey

1/4 cup (60 mL) light brown sugar

A pinch of salt

1 tsp (5 mL) cinnamon

1/2 tsp (2 mL) nutmeg

Grated rind of 1/2 an orange

Method:

• Line a pie plate with pastry.

• Peel, core and slice the apples, fill pie plate.

• Mix the rest of the ingredients and pour over the apples.

• Cover with the top crust, make a few slashes on top.

• Brush top crust with a bit of sour cream or yogurt, and sprinkle with about **1 tablespoon (15 mL) of dark brown sugar.**

• Place pie on a rack. Microwave at HIGH 8 minutes. Lower heat to MEDIUM and microwave another 5 to 6 minutes.

• Place on a rack to cool on the kitchen counter.

Helpful hint: To soften ice cream, microwave at WARM 1 to 2 minutes. Check, and repeat if necessary.

wines

Samos Muscat

German Auslese

Irish Apple Pie

Convection cooking

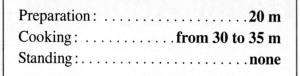

Sweet Vouvray

Sauternes

| Preparation : . . . . **20 m** |
| Cooking : . . . . **from 30 to 35 m** |
| Standing : . . . . **none** |

A personal note : A very popular pie in Ireland, flavored with Irish Whisky. I often replace the whisky with an equal amount of rum, which is more readily available in our kitchen. This pie must be cooked in the convection part of the microwave oven.

Ingredients :

6 to 8 apples
1/4 cup (60 mL) butter
1 cup (250 mL) sugar
Rind and juice of 1 orange
1/4 cup (60 mL) Irish Whisky or rum
Enough pastry of your choice to cover top of dish

Method :

• Place the butter in an 8 × 8-inch (20 × 20 cm) by 2 inches (5 cm) high microwave-safe dish, microwave 2 minutes at HIGH.

• Add the sugar, orange rind and juice and stir.

• Peel the apples, core and cut in eighths. Stir in the apples and blend well with the flavored butter.

• Roll the pastry. Cut three holes in it and place over the apples. Press pastry over the edges of the dish, trim if necessary.

• Preheat the convection part of your microwave oven at 450°F (230°C).

• Place pie on a rack and bake 30 to 35 minutes, or until the pastry is golden brown.

• When the pie is baked, pour the alcohol of your choice equally into each hole on top of the pie, using a funnel.

• Serve warm or tepid with thick sour cream or yogurt.

Strawberry Rhubarb Pie

Microwave or convection cooking

Preparation: . . . .**20 m**
Cooking : microwave : . . . .**9 m**
convection : . . . .**from 20 to 25 m**
Standing : . . . .**none**

Convection cooking

• Preheat the convection part of your microwave oven at 425°F (210°C).

• Place pie on rack, bake 20 to 25 minutes or until crust is golden brown and the filling creamy.

A personal note : May and June are the perfect months to enjoy the super flavor of this pie. A favorite of so many. This recipe will show you how to make use of both the microwave and the convection part of your combined microwave oven. It is a one-crust pie.

Ingredients :

Pastry of your choice for a 9-inch (23 cm) pie plate

2 eggs

3/4 cup (190 mL) white sugar

2 tbsp (30 mL) flour

1/2 cup (125 mL) rich cream

2 cups (500 mL) fresh rhubarb, diced

2 cups (500 mL) fresh strawberries, sliced

1/4 cup (60 mL) brown sugar

1/4 cup (60 mL) flour

Grated rind of 1/2 an orange

2 tbsp (30 mL) butter

Method :

• Roll pastry and line pie plate. Any type of pastry can be used.

• Beat together until smooth the eggs, white sugar, 2 tablespoons (30 mL) flour and cream.

• Stir in the rhubarb and strawberries. Pour into the pie shell.

• Mix in a bowl the brown sugar, the 1/4 cup (60 mL) flour, the grated orange rind and the butter.

• When mixture is crumbly, sprinkle over the fruit in the pie shell.

• Place on a rack, microwave 9 minutes at HIGH. Remove pie plate from microwave.

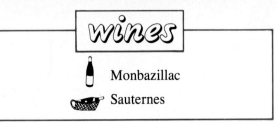

wines

🍾 Monbazillac

🐟 Sauternes

Blueberry Pie

Convection cooking

• Blueberry pie has a sort of old-fashioned air. I usually try to make this pie at least twice while blueberries are in season. This is my mother's recipe. I have never found a tastier one.

Ingredients:

Pastry of your choice for a 2-crust pie
4 well-packed cups (1 L) fresh blueberries
1/2 cup (125 mL) white sugar
1/2 cup (125 mL) light brown sugar
1/3 cup (80 mL) maple syrup or sugar
4 tbsp (60 mL) flour
3 tbsp (50 mL) cornstarch or rice flour
1/4 tsp (1 mL) allspice
1/4 tsp (1 mL) nutmeg
3 tbsp (50 mL) melted butter
2 tbsp (30 mL) lemon juice

Preparation:	.................20 m
Cooking:	..........from 35 to 40 m
Standing:	......................none

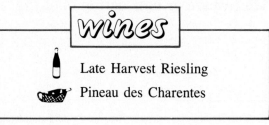

🍾 Late Harvest Riesling
🥤 Pineau des Charentes

Method:

• Line a plate with the rolled pastry.

• Brush crust with a little melted butter.

• Mix all the ingredients thoroughly. Pour into pie shell.

• Top with pastry. Sprinkle top with 1 tablespoon (15 mL) sugar.

• Preheat the convection part of your microwave oven at 400°F (200°C).

• Place pie on a rack. Bake 35 to 40 minutes, or until golden brown.

The Best of Pumpkin Pies

Convection cooking

Preparation: . . . . **20 m**
Cooking: . . . . **from 30 to 35 m**
Standing: . . . . **none**

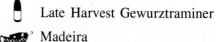

Late Harvest Gewurztraminer

Madeira

A personal note: When fresh pumpkin is not available, I use canned pumpkin. Easy and quick to make.

Ingredients:

2 cups (500 mL) cooked pumpkin or squash

1/2 cup (125 mL) sugar

2 eggs, lightly beaten

1/4 tsp (1 mL) salt

1½ cups (375 mL) milk

1/4 cup (60 mL) molasses

2 tbsp (30 mL) melted butter

1 tsp (5 mL) ginger

1/2 tsp (2 mL) nutmeg

1 tsp (5 mL) cinnamon

**Pastry of your choice for a 9-inch (23 cm)
  2-crust pie**

Method:

• Preheat the convection part of your microwave oven at 400°F (200°C).

• Mix all the ingredients of the pie in a bowl. Stir well.

• Line a pie plate with the rolled pastry. Fill with pumpkin or squash mixture.

• Top with another rolled pastry. Crimp the edges.

• Make a few cuts in the top crust with the point of a knife. Brush top with a little cream or milk.

• Place on a rack in the preheated oven. Bake at 400°F (200°C) for 30 to 35 minutes.

• Serve at room temperature.

Frozen Desserts

Creamy, Speedy Frozen Ice Cream

Preparation:	. . . . **10 m**
Cooking:	. . . . **from 2 to 3 m**
Standing:	. . . . **none**

• This ice cream is quick and easy to prepare with ingredients that are usually on hand.

Ingredients:

15 large marshmallows

1 tbsp (15 mL) milk

1 cup (250 mL) sour cream

1 package (425 g) frozen strawberries, thawed

Method:

• Place marshmallows and milk in a microwave-safe bowl. Microwave 2 to 3 minutes at MEDIUM, stir. The marshmallows should be melted.

• Add the sour cream and the thawed strawberries, mix thoroughly. Pour into a mold, cover and place in the freezer.

Strawberry Ice Cream

Advance preparation : . . . . 5 h
Cooking : . . . . none
Standing : . . . . none

A personal note : This ice cream is at its best when served immediately, but it can be stored in the freezer for as long as one week.

Ingredients :

4 cups (1 L) fresh strawberries, washed and hulled*

3/4 cup (190 mL) icing sugar

3/4 cup (190 mL) whipping cream

1 tbsp (15 mL) orange liqueur (optional) *or*
Grated rind of 1 orange

* Frozen unsweetened strawberries can be substituted for fresh berries, in equal quantity.

Method :

• At least five hours before serving, place strawberries on a baking sheet in a single layer and freeze until firm.

• Just before serving, put frozen berries and icing sugar in a food processor or blender and chop finely.

• Without stopping, add the cream and orange liqueur or grated rind. Process until mixture is smooth and creamy, stopping several times to scrape.

• When the ice cream has been stored in the freezer, process it until it is smooth and creamy before serving.

Helpful hint : To reheat a piece of cake or pie place it on a paper plate and microwave 10 to 40 seconds. The filling and the icing will be warmer than the pastry.

Florentine Coffee Ice

Preparation: . . . . 15 m
Cooking: . . . . 7 m
Standing: . . . . from 5 to 10 m

• Everyone in Florence seems to enjoy this delightful ice in the summer.

Ingredients:

4 tbsp (60 mL) instant coffee
2 cups (500 mL) water
1/4 to 1/2 cup (60 to 125 mL) sugar
1 tsp (5 mL) vanilla

Method:

• Combine in a microwave-safe bowl the instant coffee, water and sugar, use more or less to your taste.

• Microwave 5 minutes at HIGH, stir well. Microwave 2 minutes at HIGH.

• Cool and add vanilla.

• Pour mixture into an ice tray or just place mixing bowl in the freezer. Cool, stir well and freeze until firm.

• To serve, pour the frozen coffee into a bowl, break up the pieces. Let stand 5 to 10 minutes, then beat with an electric beater until mixture is all broken up but still icy. It should have the consistency of sherbet.

• Serve in small demi-tasses or glasses.

• If you wish, top it with whipped cream, sweetened or plain.

Champagne Glass Granite

Preparation: . . . . **15 m**
Cooking: . . . . **8 m**
Standing: . . . . **none**

A personal note: A granite is a fruit-flavored ice similar to a sherbet and most delectable. Following are my favorite mixtures.
For a very elegant dinner, serve it after the entrée and before the meat as a palate cleanser. "Very elegant Europe."

Ingredients:

Lemon Granite:

2 cups (500 mL) water
1 cup (250 mL) sugar
1 cup (250 mL) fresh lemon juice
Grated rind of 2 lemons

Orange Granite:

2 cups (500 mL) water
3/4 cup (190 mL) sugar
1 cup (250 mL) fresh orange juice
Juice of 1 lemon
Grated rind of 1 orange

Strawberry Granite:

1 cup (250 mL) water
1/2 cup (125 mL) sugar
2 cups (500 mL) mashed strawberries
2 tbsp (30 mL) fresh lemon juice

Method:

• Measure the water and sugar demanded by the chosen granite.

• Microwave at HIGH 5 minutes, stirring after 3 minutes of cooking.

• After the 5 minutes of cooking, stir thoroughly. Microwave again 3 minutes at HIGH. Cool the syrup.

• Stir in the fruit juices or the fruit purée, depending on the recipe.

• Pour mixture into a pudding dish (I use a deep pie plate) and freeze.

• While it is freezing, stir every 30 minutes, scraping into the mixture all of the small ice particles that form around the edges.

• When ready, the ice should have a fine, snowy texture. Serve in glasses or on plates.

• When you have made the ice the day before or early in the day, remove it from the freezer about 30 minutes before serving.

Helpful hint: To heat the liqueur used to flambé a dessert, pour it into a glass container and microwave 15 to 30 seconds at HIGH. Pour over dessert and flambé.

Muffins

- Freshly baked, hot muffins are very popular. They can be served at breakfast or enjoyed as a snack anytime during the day. They are marvellously easy to blend and bake, with almost endless variations! All types of muffins will warm in the microwave oven 6 to 9 seconds at HIGH for 1 or 2.

Muffin "know-how"

- The liquid ingredients should be measured in one bowl.
- The dry ingredients should be measured in another bowl.
- The LIQUID ingredients should be poured all at once over the dry ingredients.
- Then, the liquid ingredients should be stirred into the dry ingredients until they are moistened but still lumpy.
- As the batter should never be beaten, it should be worked quickly. So be sure to have everything ready, even the molds.

- Butter the molds or spray lightly with Pam or use muffin paper cups placed in a plastic muffin mold.

- Muffins do not brown in the microwave oven, although they cook to perfection.

To brown, use one of the following topping ideas:

- Brown sugar mixed with **1 teaspoon (5 mL) of cocoa**, simply sprinkled on top of each muffin

- cinnamon sugar or chocolate chips

- cranberry sauce or a little swirl of red jam on top of the batter makes them attractive.
- A muffin paper cup placed in each section of a muffin pan is the easiest and most attractive way to bake microwaved muffins.
- When the recipe contains brown sugar or molasses, the muffins will brown naturally.

Basic Muffins I

Preparation: . . . . .8 m
Cooking: . . . . .from 2 to 3 m
Standing: . . . . .none

Helpful hint: To toast coconut in the microwave oven, simply place the required coconut on a plate. Microwave 2 to 3 minutes at HIGH, stirring twice. Do not brown too much. The coconut will brown more when the muffins are microwaved.

- I have two favorite basic microwaved muffin recipes that can be varied almost endlessly. Use your own ideas or preferences once you know how to make them.

Ingredients:

The 2-egg Batter

2 cups (500 mL) flour

2½ tsp (12 mL) baking powder

1/2 tsp (2 mL) salt

3 tbsp (50 mL) sugar

2 eggs

3/4 cup (200 mL) cold milk

1/4 cup (60 mL) butter or margarine, melted

Method:

- Sift together in a bowl the flour, baking powder, salt and sugar.

- Beat together the eggs and milk, pour over the flour mixture. Stir to just moisten the dry ingredients.

- Melt the butter or margarine 2 minutes at HIGH.

- Pour over the batter and stir until the dry ingredients are thoroughly moistened but still lumpy. In other words, just enough to blend the two.

- Pour into prepared muffin pans, only 2/3 full.

- To taste, sprinkle top lightly with **finely chopped nuts** or **cinnamon** and **sugar mixed together** or **toasted coconut** or **1 teaspoon (5 mL) each of brown sugar** and **cocoa** mixed together.

- For 6 muffins, microwave at HIGH 2 to 3 minutes. The variation in baking time depends on the type of muffins. Serve hot.

Helpful hint: To peel peaches, microwave 15 to 20 seconds at MEDIUM, depending on their size. Let stand 10 minutes, then peel.

Basic Muffins II

Preparation: .8 m
Cooking: . . . . .from 2 to 3 m
Standing: . . . . .none

• The ingredients and the quantities are almost the same as for Muffins I. Yet when baked they are different. I was never able to decide which one I prefer. I sometimes make No. I, at other times no. II.

Ingredients:

The 1-egg Batter

1⅔ cups (410 mL) flour

1/2 cup (125 mL) sugar

2 tsp (10 mL) baking powder

1/2 tsp (2 mL) salt

1/4 tsp (1 mL) nutmeg or cinnamon or allspice

1/3 cup (80 mL) vegetable oil

3/4 cup (200 mL) milk

1 egg

Method:

• Combine in a bowl the flour, sugar, baking powder, salt, nutmeg or cinnamon or allspice. Stir until well mixed.

• Mix together the oil, milk and egg.

• Pour into dry ingredients and stir just enough to moisten the dry ingredients.

• Choose a topping of your choice.

• Microwave 6 muffins 2½ to 3 minutes at HIGH.

Helpful hint: A cake is done when a toothpick inserted in the centre comes out clean or if the sides of the cake recede from the pan.

Variations to use with either Basic Muffins recipe

Cheese Muffins

• Add **1/2 cup (125 mL) grated cheese** of your choice to the dry ingredients.

Bacon Muffins

• Microwave **4 to 6 slices of bacon** on a piece of white towelling 4 minutes at HIGH.

• Cool and crumble.

• OMIT sugar in the muffin recipe and add the crumbled bacon to the dry ingredients.

Health Muffins

• Replace 1 cup (250 mL) of the flour called for in the recipe with **1 cup (250 mL) wholewheat or graham or buckwheat flour.**

• Use dark brown sugar instead of white sugar in the same quantity as called for in the basic recipe.

• Bake same as for plain muffins.

Apple Muffins

• Add **1 cup (250 mL) peeled and finely chopped apples** to dry ingredients.

Dried Fruit Muffins

• Use brown sugar in batter instead of white sugar, and add **1/4 to 1/2 cup (60 to 125 mL) dried currants or raisins or soft dried diced apricots or dried chopped apples.**

Oatmeal Muffins

• Replace 1 cup (250 mL) flour with **1 cup (250 mL) quick-cooking oatmeal.**

Sour Cream Muffins

• I love these! Use **1 to 1¼ cups (250 to 310 mL) sour cream** in place of milk and melted butter.

• Decrease baking powder to 1/2 teaspoon (2 mL) and add **1/2 teaspoon (2 mL) soda.**

Jam Muffins

• Make batter of your choice.

• Microwave 2 minutes at HIGH.

• Quickly place **1 teaspoon (5 mL) of a jam of your choice** and **2 teaspoons (10 mL) finely chopped nuts** (optional) on top of each muffin.

• Microwave 30 to 40 seconds at HIGH.

Bran Muffins

Preparation : .5 m
Cooking : . . . . .from 4 to 5 m
Standing : . . . . .none

A personal note : I sometimes use all natural bran or I mix half bran flakes and half natural bran. These are butterless, perfect for a fat-free diet.

Ingredients :

3 cups (750 mL) natural whole bran

1/2 cup (125 mL) dark brown sugar

1 tsp (5 mL) baking soda

.1½ cups (375 mL) flour

2 cups (500 mL) buttermilk or sour milk

Method :

• Place the bran and brown sugar in a bowl and stir to mix.

• Sift together the baking soda and flour.

• Add to bran mixture with the buttermilk or sour milk. Stir just enough to blend.

• Pour into muffin pan. Microwave 4 to 5 minutes at HIGH. Serve hot, with honey.

 Rémy Pannier (sparkling)

Blanquette de Limoux, Sieur d'Arques

Quick Blueberry Muffins

Preparation: .5 m
Cooking: . . . . .from 2 to 3½ m
Standing: . . . . .none

• I make these all year round. In summer, I use fresh blueberries; in winter, I replace them with my own frozen blueberries. There is hardly any difference between the two, if you freeze your own blueberries.

Ingredients:

1½ cups (375 mL) flour

1/2 cup (125 mL) sugar

2½ tsp (12 mL) baking powder

1/4 tsp (1 mL) salt

1 egg

3/4 cup (200 mL) milk

1/3 cup (80 mL) melted butter

1 cup (250 mL) blueberries

Grated rind of 1/2 a lemon

2 tbsp (30 mL) sugar

Method:

• Sift together the flour, sugar, baking powder and salt.

• In another bowl, beat the egg, add the milk and the melted butter.

• Pour over the dry ingredients, stir just enough to moisten the whole. Stir in the blueberries.

• Spoon into microwave-safe muffin pan lined with paper baking cups.

• Mix together the lemon rind and sugar. Sprinkle a bit on each muffin.

• For a 6-muffin mold, microwave at HIGH 2 to 2½ minutes. Test doneness.

• If necessary, microwave another minute at MEDIUM.

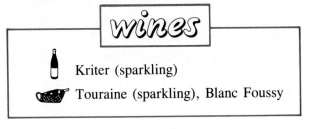

Kriter (sparkling)

Touraine (sparkling), Blanc Foussy

Helpful hint: To freeze your own blueberries:

• Wash them and dry them on a cloth.

• Place **1 teaspoon (5 mL) sugar** in the bottom of each container or freezer bag. (Do not freeze more than 2 cups (500 mL) per container).

• Place prepared berries on top of sugar. Do not mix. Cover with a little square of crumpled waxed paper. Cover container or close bag. Freeze.

• Prepared this way, the thawed blueberries look like fresh ones.

All-Season Blueberry Muffins

Preparation:	. . . . **10 m**
Cooking:	. . . . **from 4 to 5 m**
Standing:	. . . . **none**

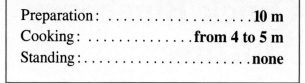

wines

Vin Fou (sparkling), Henri Maire

Clairette de Die, Vins Fins du Diois-Die

A personal note: In winter, I replace the fresh blueberries with frozen blueberries — not thawed — or with an equal amount of well-drained crushed pineapple.

Ingredients:

1/4 cup (60 mL) butter

3 tbsp (50 mL) margarine

2/3 cup (160 mL) sugar

1 egg, lightly beaten

1 cup (250 mL) milk

1½ cups (375 mL) fresh blueberries

2¼ cups (560 mL) all-purpose flour

1 tsp (5 mL) salt

4 tsp (20 mL) baking powder

Method:

• Cream together the butter, margarine and sugar.

• When light and creamy, add the egg and the milk. Beat until well blended. Add the blueberries.

• Sift together the flour, salt and baking powder.

• Add all at once to the creamed mixture. Mix JUST ENOUGH to blend and fold in the blueberries.

• Pour into microwave-safe muffin pan. Top each muffin with 3 to 4 blueberries.

• Microwave 4 to 5 minutes at HIGH, or until done.

• Serve with butter whipped until creamy. If you wish, top with sweetened blueberries.

Cranberry Muffins

Preparation : . . . . 10 m
Cooking : . . . . from 3 to 4 m
Standing : . . . . none

• I found this recipe in the Farm Journal, which I read faithfully. I keep on making them. They have a sort of Christmas feeling.

Ingredients :

1 cup (250 mL) fresh cranberries

1/4 cup (60 mL) sugar

1½ cups (375 mL) flour

1/4 cup (60 mL) sugar

2 tsp (10 mL) baking powder

1 tsp (5 mL) salt

1/2 tsp (2 mL) cinnamon

1/4 tsp (1 mL) allspice

1 egg, beaten

Grated rind of 1/2 an orange

3/4 cup (200 mL) orange juice

1/3 cup (80 mL) butter

1/4 cup (60 mL) nuts of your choice, chopped (optional)

Method :

• Coarsely chop raw cranberries with a sharp knife on a piece of waxed paper.

• Pour into a bowl and sprinkle with 1/4 cup (60 mL) of the sugar, set aside.

• Place in a bowl the flour, the remaining 1/4 cup (60 mL) sugar, baking powder, salt, cinnamon and allspice. Make a well in the centre of the mixed dry ingredients.

• Combine the egg, grated orange rind and orange juice.

• Melt the butter 1 minute at HIGH, add to the orange juice mixture.

• Pour the whole all at once into the flour mixture. Stir just enough to blend.

• Fold in the chopped sweetened cranberries.

• Fill microwave-safe muffin pans a little more than half. Microwave at HIGH 3 to 4 minutes, or until dry on top.

Helpful hint : An excellent way to learn cooking times is to weigh the food, and to count an average 6 to 7 minutes per pound (500 g).

 Coteaux du Layon, Château Bellevue

Muscat de Beaume-de-Venise, Caves des Vignerons

Super Strawberry or Raspberry Muffins

Preparation : . . . . 7 m
Cooking : . . . . from 2¹/₂ to 3 m
Standing : . . . . none

A personal note : In summer, I add about 1 ½ cups (375 mL) of fresh strawberries or raspberries to the batter in place of the frozen berries called for. It does not change the baking time.

Ingredients :

1 ¾ cups (440 mL) flour

1/3 cup (80 mL) sugar

2 tsp (10 mL) baking powder

1/2 tsp (2 mL) salt

1/3 cup (80 mL) vegetable oil

1 egg

1 package (425 mL) frozen strawberries or
  raspberries, thawed

Method :

• Make sure the microwave-safe muffin pan is well oiled or use cupcake paper cups.

• Place in a mixing bowl the flour, sugar, baking powder and salt.

• Mix together in another bowl the oil, egg and 1 cup (250 mL) of the strawberries or raspberries and juice. Add to the dry ingredients and stir just enough to moisten the whole.

• Fill the muffin pans only half full with the batter.

• Microwave at HIGH 2 ½ to 3 minutes or until done.

• Serve with strawberry or raspberry butter.

Strawberry or Raspberry Butter :

• Blend together 1/2 cup (125 mL) soft butter or **margarine and the remaining strawberries or raspberries and their juice.**

• Refrigerate and use to butter top of hot muffins when ready to serve.

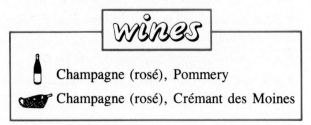

Champagne (rosé), Pommery

Champagne (rosé), Crémant des Moines

890

Upside - Down Muffins

Microwave or convection cooking

A personal note: These super and unusual muffins must be baked in a microwave-safe muffin pan without holes. They are a sort of upside down muffin. They are also very good baked in the convection part of the microwave oven, which permits you to use any metal muffin pan.

Ingredients:

2 tbsp (30 mL) butter

1/2 cup (125 mL) maple syrup

1/4 cup (60 mL) walnuts, coarsely chopped

2 cups (500 mL) flour

3 tsp (15 mL) baking powder

1 tsp (5 mL) cinnamon or allspice

1/2 tsp (2 mL) salt

3 tbsp (50 mL) maple syrup

1 cup (250 mL) milk

1/4 cup (60 mL) vegetable oil

1 egg

Method:

• Place butter and the 1/2 cup (125 mL) maple syrup in a measuring cup. Microwave 3 minutes at HIGH.

• Place 1 teaspoon (5 mL) of hot syrup in the bottom of each muffin pan.

• Then sprinkle 1 teaspoon (5 mL) of chopped walnuts over the syrup.

• Sift together in a large bowl the flour, baking powder, cinnamon or allspice and the salt.

• Stir together the remaining maple syrup, milk, oil and egg. Pour into the dry ingredients all at once and stir just until moistened.

• Fill each cup only 2/3 full over the syrup.

Preparation:	..................30 m
Cooking: microwave:	........from 2½ to 3 m
convection:	................20 m
Standing:	......................none

Gewurztraminer

Gewurztraminer, Vendanges tardives

By convection:

• Preheat convection part of your microwave oven at 425°F (225°C).

• Place muffin pan on rack and bake 20 minutes, or until golden brown.

By microwave:

• Microwave at HIGH 2½ to 3 minutes for 6 muffins.

• As soon as muffins are baked by either method, unmold on a sheet of waxed paper. Otherwise, the syrup will harden.

891

Cookies

Cookie "know-how"

Regardless of the type of cookie you wish to make, the following hints will assure you of perfect success.

1. Cookies can be baked in microwave or convection part of your microwave oven.

2. Read your recipe, then gather together all the utensils and ingredients required.

3. Make sure all ingredients are at room temperature.

4. When the cookies are to be baked in the convection part of your microwave oven, preheat the oven for 15 minutes at the temperature demanded by the recipe.

5. Rolled cookies

• If you have to roll the cookie dough, the flour used for dusting should be used sparingly, and any flour remaining on the cut cookies should be brushed off before putting them on the baking sheet. This type of dough is easier to work with if refrigerated before rolling.

6. Sheet Cookies

• They are quick and easy to prepare, but when time permits, they will be perfect in texture and flavor if they are refrigerated an hour or so before being rolled.

7. With any type of cookie

• Always give careful attention to the baking time, which can be a minute more or less, depending on the temperature of the ingredients and the kind of flour used.

8. To keep cookies crisp

• Keep in a container with a loose cover.

• Pack cookies with a sheet of waxed paper between each layer.

• Keep in a cool place when possible.

9. To keep cookies soft

• Use an airtight container. Pack cookies as above with a sheet of waxed paper between each row.

• Place 3 or 4 slices of unpeeled apple on the top sheet. Change the slices from time to time to ensure freshness.

• Here are a few of my favorite, easy to make, cookie recipes.

893

Brown Sugar Bars

Preparation: . . . . .7 m
Cooking: . . . . .4 m
Standing: .none

Helpful hint: If your brown sugar has hardened, add a few drops of water, about 1/4 teaspoon (1 mL), to the sugar. Microwave 10 to 15 seconds at HIGH. Surprise! You will find it very easy to measure. Repeat operation if it hardens again.

 Porto, Ruby, Sandeman
Porto, Tawny, Delaforce

Ingredients:

1/2 cup (125 mL) butter

1/2 cup (125 mL) dark brown sugar

1¼ cups (310 mL) flour

1/4 tsp (1 mL) salt

1/2 cup (125 mL) chocolate chips

1/4 cup (60 mL) nuts of your choice, chopped

Method:

• Cream butter and sugar. Add flour and salt. Stir until well mixed.

• Place evenly in an 8 × 8-inch (20 × 20 cm) microwave-safe dish. Microwave at HIGH 3 minutes.

• Melt chips in a cup 30 to 40 seconds at HIGH.

• Spread on cooked biscuits.

• Sprinkle with finely chopped nuts.

• Cool. Cut into bars.

Spiced Cookies In-A-Hurry

Advance preparation: . . . . . **from 1 to 2 h**
Cooking: . . . . **6 m**
Standing: . . . . **none**

A personal note: When your time is limited, try these. They are blended, dropped on waxed paper, chilled and ready to eat!

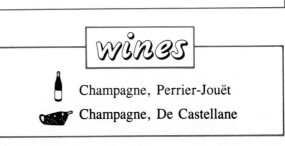

wines

Champagne, Perrier-Jouët
Champagne, De Castellane

Ingredients:

1/2 cup (125 mL) butter or margarine

1/2 cup (125 mL) milk

2 cups (500 mL) sugar

1/4 cup (60 mL) unsweetened cocoa

1/4 tsp (1 mL) salt

1 tsp (5 mL) vanilla or almond extract

1/2 cup (125 mL) peanut butter

3 cups (750 mL) quick-cooking oatmeal

Method:

• Place in a microwave-safe bowl the butter or margarine and milk. Microwave 1 minute at HIGH. Stir.

• Add sugar, cocoa and salt. Microwave 4 minutes at HIGH. Stir well.

• Microwave 1 more minute at HIGH.

• Add vanilla or almond extract and peanut butter. Stir until well mixed.

• Add the oatmeal. Stir well and drop by teaspoons on waxed paper or cookie sheet.

• Refrigerate 1 to 2 hours.

Butter Crunch Cookies

• This recipe will give you 4 to 5 dozen health cookies. They are very easy to make.

Preparation: . . . . 15 m
Cooking: . . . . from 4 to 5 m
Standing: . . . . none

Ingredients:

3/4 cup (200 mL) butter or margarine
3/4 cup (200 mL) sugar
1 egg
1 tsp (5 mL) almond extract
1½ cups (375 mL) flour
1/2 tsp (2 mL) baking powder
1/4 tsp (1 mL) salt
1/2 cup (125 mL) oatmeal
1/2 cup (125 mL) Grape Nut cereal

Method:

• Cream the butter or margarine. Gradually add the sugar.

• When well mixed, add the egg and almond extract. Mix thoroughly.

• Sift together the flour, baking powder and salt. Add to first mixture, mix.

• Add the oatmeal and Grape Nut. Mix thoroughly.

• Shape into small balls. Place well apart on waxed paper set on a cardboard.

• Flatten each cookie with the bottom of a floured glass. Do not place too close, as they spread.

• Microwave 4 to 5 minutes at MEDIUM-HIGH. Check doneness.

• When ready, remove cookies from the paper by sliding them off. Repeat for the remaining cookies.

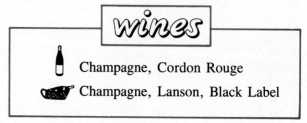

Champagne, Cordon Rouge
Champagne, Lanson, Black Label

Tea-time Currant Dainties

Microwave or convection cooking

Preparation: . . . . **10 m**
Cooking: microwave: . . . . **from 3 to 4 m**
           convection: . . . . **from 12 to 14 m**
Standing: . . . . **none**

• These dainty cookies are nice to serve at tea time. Baked in the convection part of the microwave oven, they are a deeper golden color. When in a hurry, I microwave them.

Ingredients:

1/2 cup (125 mL) butter
1/2 cup (125 ml) sugar
3 eggs
Grated rind of 1/2 an orange
2 cups (500 mL) flour
1/3 cup (80 mL) currants

Method:

• Cream butter until very soft. Add the sugar and beat again.

• Add the eggs and beat the whole 1 or 2 minutes with an egg beater.

• Add the orange rind, then fold in the flour and the currants. Beat until thoroughly mixed.

• Drop cookies on the prepared pan.*

• Microwave 3 to 4 minutes at MEDIUM-HIGH. Do not overcook, as they will be hard when cooled.

* A stiff cardboard topped with waxed paper makes a good cookie sheet for the microwave oven.

By convection:

• Preheat convection part of your microwave oven at 350°F (180°C).

• Place cookies on a sheet, bake 12 to 14 minutes.

 Porto, Ruby, Sandeman
 Porto, Late Bottled Vintage, Taylor

Helpful hint: To soften raisins, pour a little water over them, then microwave, uncovered, 3 minutes at MEDIUM. Let stand 2 minutes. Drain and use.

Lemon Pecan Dainties

Convection cooking

Advance preparation : . . . . **from 6 to 24 h**
Cooking : . . . . **10 m**
Standing : . . . . **none**

• An elegant tea time cookie !

Ingredients :

3/4 cup (200 mL) butter

1 cup (250 mL) sugar

1 egg

Grated rind of 1 lemon

1 tbsp (15 mL) lemon juice

2 cups (500 mL) all-purpose flour

1 tsp (5 mL) baking powder

1/2 tsp (2 mL) salt

1/4 tsp (1 mL) mace or nutmeg

3/4 cup (190 mL) pecans or walnuts, chopped

Method :

• Cream the butter with the sugar, then add the egg, lemon rind and juice.

• Combine dry ingredients and add to the creamed mixture. Mix well.

• Stir in pecans or walnuts. Shape into rolls.

• Wrap in waxed paper and chill 6 to 24 hours.

• Slice thinly and place on ungreased baking sheet.

• Preheat convection part of microwave oven at 375°F (190°C).

• Bake 10 minutes or until golden brown.

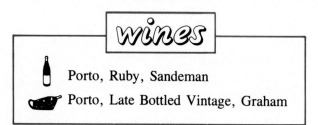

wines

Porto, Ruby, Sandeman

Porto, Late Bottled Vintage, Graham

Jam Squares

Preparation: . . . . **20 m**
Cooking: . . . . **from 7 to 8 m**
Standing: . . . . **10 m**

A personal note: If you have small amounts of jam in several jars, this is a good way to use it up. I often mix jam, jelly and marmalade or I use any one type. No matter which, the squares are nice and tasty.

Champagne (rosé), Pommery

Champagne (rosé), Lanson

Ingredients:

1/4 cup (60 mL) margarine

1/4 cup (60 mL) sugar

1 egg

1/2 cup (125 mL) flour

Grated rind of 1/2 a lemon

1/4 cup (60 mL) nuts of your choice, chopped

1/4 tsp (1 mL) cinnamon

A good pinch of salt

1/2 cup (125 mL) strawberry or raspberry jam

Topping:

1/2 cup (125 mL) flour

1/4 cup (60 mL) brown sugar

3 tbsp (50 mL) butter or margarine

Method:

• Beat the margarine and sugar until creamy.

• Add the egg, flour, lemon rind, nuts, cinnamon and salt. Mix until well blended.

• Pour into an 8 × 8-inch (20 × 20 cm) microwave-safe baking dish.

• Microwave 4 to 5 minutes at HIGH, or until the middle part is slightly firm.

• Let stand 10 minutes.

• Spread top of cooked cake with the jam.

• Mix the topping ingredients until granulated. Sprinkle evenly over the jam.

• Microwave 3 minutes at HIGH.

• Cool on rack. Cut into squares or bars.

Enjoy!

Youngsters' Delight

Preparation : . . . .**15 m**
Cooking : . . . .**from 8 to 9 m**
Standing : . . . .**15 m**

• And good for them, too, as this treat is made with grated carrots. Quick and easy to prepare.

Ingredients :

1/2 cup (125 mL) margarine
1 cup (250 mL) dark brown sugar, well packed
2 eggs
1 cup (250 mL) flour
1 tsp (5 mL) baking powder
1 tsp (5 mL) cinnamon
1/4 tsp (1 mL) salt
1½ cups (375 mL) carrots, peeled and grated

Method :

• Place margarine in a microwave-safe bowl. Melt 2 minutes at HIGH.

• Add the brown sugar and the eggs, stir until well mixed.

• Stir together the flour, baking powder, cinnamon and salt.

• Add to creamed mixture, stir until well mixed.

• Add the grated carrots. Stir until well mixed in the batter.

• Grease an 8 × 8-inch (20 × 20 cm) microwave-safe square dish. Pour prepared mixture into it.

• Microwave 8 minutes at MEDIUM-HIGH, check doneness with the point of a knife.

• If necessary, microwave another minute.

• Let stand 15 minutes on kitchen counter.

• To serve, cut into squares.

• Covered with foil, they will keep fresh 4 to 6 days.

Helpful hint : Do not salt foods before microwaving. Salt tends to dehydrate the food and it also distorts the microwaves.

900

Chocolate Brownies

Preparation: . . . .**10 m**
Cooking: . . . .**7 m**
Standing: . . . .**none**

A personal note: I sometimes top these with thinly rolled almond paste. Super delicious. Almond paste is not readily available and somewhat costly, so it's good to know the brownies are also very nice without the almond paste.

Ingredients:

1/3 cup (80 mL) shortening

2 oz (56 g) unsweetened chocolate

1 cup (250 mL) sugar

3/4 cup (200 mL) flour

1/2 tsp (2 mL) each baking powder and salt

2 eggs

1/3 cup (80 mL) almonds, thinly sliced.

Method:

• Place shortening and chocolate in an 8 × 8-inch (20 × 20 cm) Pyrex or Corning dish.

• Microwave 3 minutes at MEDIUM-HIGH, or until chocolate is melted.

• Add the remaining ingredients, stir well.

• Spread batter evenly in the baking dish.

• Microwave 4 minutes at MEDIUM. Check doneness with a toothpick.

• If necessary, microwave another minute at MEDIUM-HIGH.

• Cool, cut into bars or squares.

Carrot and Pineapple Petits Fours

A personal note: I make these in paper cups placed in a microwave-safe muffin pan. I cover them with frosting or simply sprinkle icing sugar over them. They can also be microwaved in small Pyrex cups.

 Sauternes, Château Suduiraut

 Sauternes, Château d'Arche

Ingredients:

1⅓ cups (330 mL) flour

1 cup (250 mL) sugar

1 tsp (5 mL) cinnamon

3/4 tsp (3 mL) soda

1/2 tsp (2 mL) salt

1/4 tsp (1 mL) nutmeg

1 cup (250 mL) carrots, finely grated

1/2 cup (125 mL) vegetable oil

1/2 cup (125 mL) crushed pineapple, well drained

2 eggs

1/4 cup (60 mL) nuts, chopped (optional)

Method:

• Mix together the flour, sugar, cinnamon, soda, salt and nutmeg.

• Add the remaining ingredients and mix thoroughly.

• Pour the batter either into paper cups placed in a microwave-safe muffin pan or into small Pyrex cups placed in a circle in the microwave oven.

• Microwave 2 minutes at HIGH.

• If your oven does not have a turntable, give the pan or the cups half a turn midway through the cooking.

• Microwave 1 minute at HIGH.

• One or two of the petits fours may seem soft. Do not microwave further; the cooking will continue during standing time.

• Let stand 2 minutes on the kitchen counter, then unmold and place on a rack. Ice or sprinkle with icing sugar.

Swiss Chocolate Squares

Advance preparation: ....1 h
Cooking: ....from 8 to 9 m
Standing: ....none

• The Swiss and chocolate are inseparable, and their chocolate is super good! Try these squares, you will enjoy them. As a plus, they are good keepers — if you hide them.

Ingredients:

1/2 cup (125 mL) butter

3 tbsp (50 mL) pure cocoa

1 cup (250 mL) sugar

2 large eggs

1 tsp (5 mL) vanilla

3/4 cup (200 mL) flour

1 tsp (5 mL) baking powder

1 cup (250 mL) almonds, slivered or walnuts, chopped

1 Swiss chocolate bar of your choice
use a bar of about 3½ oz (100 g)

Method:

• Grease an 8 × 8-inch (20 × 20 cm) Pyrex or Corning baking dish with shortening.

• Place the butter in a microwave-safe bowl, micro-wave 1 minute at HIGH. To this melted butter add the cocoa, sugar, eggs and vanilla. Stir until well mixed.

• Mix flour and baking powder. Add to first mixture.

• Add the nuts of your choice. Stir the whole to blend thoroughly.

• Pour batter into the prepared dish. Spread evenly with a knife. Microwave 8 to 9 minutes at MEDIUM. Test doneness with the point of a knife.

• If necessary, give it 30 to 40 seconds more.

• Break the chocolate bar into pieces and place evenly over the surface of the baked squares.

• Cover pan and let stand on kitchen counter for 8 to 12 minutes, then smooth melted chocolate over the squares.

• Cool about 1 hour before cutting into bars or squares.

Sauces

Soft Custard Sauce

Preparation: ....10 m
Cooking: ....from 5 to 7 m
Standing: ....none

A personal note: Serve this sauce with fresh fruit instead of cream or over cake or fruit cobblers.

Ingredients:

2 cups (500 mL) milk

1/3 cup (80 mL) sugar

1 tbsp (15 mL) cornstarch

1/4 tsp (1 mL) salt

3 eggs

1 tsp (5 mL) vanilla or almond extract

Method:

• Measure milk in a 4-cup (1 L) glass measuring cup.

• Add sugar, cornstarch, salt and eggs. Beat with a rotary beater until smooth.

• Microwave at MEDIUM-HIGH 4 to 5 minutes, or until mixture begins to bubble, stirring twice during the last half of the cooking time.

• Microwave another minute or two at MEDIUM, if necessary.

• Stir in vanilla or almond extract.

• Beat until smooth with rotary beater.

• Serve warm or cold.

Butterscotch Sauce

Preparation : . . . .**10 m**
Cooking : . . . .**from 5 to 7 m**
Standing : . . . .**none**

• This old-fashioned recipe remains famous for its flavor and its finesse.

A personal note : This sauce may be kept from 12 to 15 days in the refrigerator. It is easy to reheat the required quantity 1 to 2 minutes at HIGH, as needed.

Ingredients :

3 tbsp (50 mL) all-purpose flour

1/2 cup (125 mL) dark or light brown sugar

A pinch of salt

1 cup (250 mL) cold water or light cream

2 or 3 tbsp (30 or 50 mL) butter

1 tsp (5 mL) vanilla extract

1/4 tsp (1 mL) almond extract

Method :

• Place the flour, brown sugar and salt in a microwave-safe bowl.

• Mix well. Add the water or cream. Stir well.

• Microwave 3 minutes at HIGH, stir.

• Microwave 2 minutes more at HIGH, stir.

• The sauce is cooked when it is smooth and creamy. If the ingredients were very cold, you may to have to microwave 2 more minutes at MEDIUM to finish the sauce.

• Add the butter, the vanilla and almond extracts and stir until the butter melts.

• Serve hot or at room temperature.

Chocolate Chip Sauce

Preparation:	.....................**5 m**
Cooking:	..............**from 3 to 4 m**
Standing:	.......................**none**

A personal note: This sauce is flavored with cinnamon, but an equal quantity of nutmeg or ground cardamom or allspice will vary the sauce without spoiling its quality. Serve warm over ice cream.

Ingredients:

1 6-oz (175 g) package of chocolate chips*

3 tbsp (50 mL) each water and milk

1 tsp (5 mL) vanilla extract

1/2 tsp (2 mL) allspice or cinnamon

* Use milk or dark chocolate chips.

Method:

• Place in a microwave-safe bowl the chocolate chips, water and milk. Microwave 3 minutes at MEDIUM, stir well. If some of the chips are not melted, microwave another minute.

• Add the vanilla and the allspice or cinnamon. Stir until well mixed.

Rum Chocolate Sauce

Preparation:	...................**10 m**
Cooking:	..............**from 6 to 7 m**
Standing:	.......................**none**

A personal note: You can make this sauce a few days ahead of time, if you wish. Store it in a glass dish or jam jar. When ready to serve, microwave, uncovered, 3 minutes at HIGH.

Ingredients:

2 1-oz (28 g) squares unsweetened chocolate

1/2 cup (125 mL) water

3/4 cup (200 mL) sugar

1/4 cup (60 mL) butter

1/4 tsp (1 mL) salt

2 tbsp (30 mL) rum *or*
  1 tsp (5 mL) vanilla

Method:

• Place chocolate and water in a 4-cup (1 L) glass measuring cup or bowl. Microwave, uncovered, 3 minutes at HIGH.

• If chocolate has not melted completely, microwave another minute.

• Add sugar, stir until well mixed with the chocolate. Microwave 2 to 3 minutes at MEDIUM.

• Add butter, salt, rum or vanilla. Stir and use.

Hot Chocolate Sauce

Preparation: .5 m
Cooking: . . . . .from 3 to 5 m
Standing: . . . . .none

A personal note: Dutch cocoa is the very best of all, but nowadays cocoa is expensive, so choose the one you wish. But do not use sweetened cocoa for this super sauce.

Ingredients:

1/2 cup (125 mL) pure unsweetened cocoa

1/2 cup (125 mL) sugar

1/4 tsp (1 mL) salt

1 tbsp (15 mL) cornstarch

1/4 cup (60 mL) corn syrup

1/4 cup (60 mL) heavy or light cream

1/4 tsp (1 mL) vanilla extract

1/4 tsp (1 mL) almond extract

Method:

• Combine cocoa, sugar, salt and cornstarch in a microwave-safe bowl.

• Stir in the corn syrup and the cream.

• Microwave 3 to 5 minutes* at MEDIUM, stirring twice. The sauce will become glossy and creamy.

• When tepid, add vanilla and almond extract. Stir.

• Serve or let stand until cooled.**

• If the sauce has been refrigerated and it is too thick, place at room temperature for 2 hours or warm up at MEDIUM 30 to 40 seconds.

The time is difficult to determine exactly, as it depends on how cool the ingredients are.
*** Sauce thickens quite a bit as it cools.*

Best Hot Fudge Sauce

Preparation: .5 m
Cooking: . . . . .8 m
Standing: . . . . .none

A personal note: This is a super "not economical" fudge sauce — one of the best sauces, yet, and to my surprise even better when made by the microwave method. Serve hot or tepid.

Ingredients:

1/2 cup (125 mL) rich cream

3 tbsp (50 mL) butter (unsalted, when possible)

1/3 cup (80 mL) each white and brown sugar

A good pinch of salt

1/2 cup (125 mL) cocoa

Method:

• Place the cream and the butter in a microwave-safe bowl, microwave 4 minutes at MEDIUM.

• Stir in the remaining ingredients and stir until well mixed. Microwave 4 minutes at MEDIUM, stirring after 2 minutes of cooking. Serve hot or at room temperature.

• It will keep 3 to 4 weeks refrigerated and well covered.

• Warm what you require 1 to 2 minutes at MEDIUM.

Melba Sauce

Preparation: . . . . .10 m
Cooking: . . . . .10 m
Standing: . . . . .none

A personal note: One of the tastiest dessert sauces, Melba Sauce will keep for 2 weeks covered in the refrigerator.

Ingredients:

1 10-oz (300 g) package frozen raspberries*

1/2 cup (125 mL) sugar

1 tbsp (15 mL) cornstarch

1/2 cup (125 mL) currant or apple jelly

1 tsp (5 mL) lemon juice

1 tbsp (15 mL) brandy

* 2 to 3 cups (500 to 750 mL) fresh raspberries can replace the frozen raspberries. This does not vary the cooking period.

Method:

• Unwrap frozen raspberries, place in a 4-cup (1 L) microwave-safe dish. Microwave, uncovered, 4 minutes at HIGH.

• Move the raspberries around, stir, break up and turn over. Microwave another 2 minutes at HIGH.

• Blend the sugar and cornstarch. Stir into the raspberries with the currant or apple jelly, lemon juice and brandy.

• Microwave at HIGH 4 minutes, stirring twice.

• When creamy, pour into a sieve, strain well to remove raspberry seeds. Pour into an elegant serving dish.

• Serve hot or cold. To serve hot, reheat 1 minute at HIGH.

Marshmallow Sauce

Preparation:	**10 m**
Cooking:	**4 m**
Standing:	**none**

A personal note: This light sauce can be flavored according to your taste. It's excellent over ice cream, sponge cake and creamy pudding.

Ingredients:

1/4 cup (60 mL) water or cranberry juice

1/2 cup (125 mL) sugar

1/2 cup (125 mL) miniature marshmallows

1 egg white

1/2 tsp (2 mL) vanilla extract *or*
   1/4 tsp (1 mL) almond extract

Method:

• Place in a microwave-safe bowl the water or cranberry juice and the sugar. Microwave 2 minutes at HIGH.

• Stir until sugar is completely dissolved, then microwave 2 minutes at HIGH. The mixture will turn to a thin syrup.

• Add marshmallows and stir until they are melted. Set aside to cool.

• Beat egg white until foamy. Gradually add to cooled mixture, stirring constantly.

• Flavor with the extract of your choice.

• This sauce will keep 4 to 6 days refrigerated.

• If it separates, simply give it a good stir before serving. It will regain its creamy consistency.

Helpful hint: A Dried Apricot Mousse. Place apricots in a bowl, cover with orange juice. Microwave 6 minutes at MEDIUM, let stand 5 minutes. Purée in a blender. Beat 2 egg whites and fold into purée. Refrigerate.

Maple Pecan Sauce

Preparation:	**5 m**
Cooking:	**3 m**
Standing:	**none**

A personal note: This is a super sauce to serve over ice cream all year round, over bread pudding in the winter and over fresh strawberries in the summer.

Ingredients:

2 tbsp (30 mL) butter

1/4 cup (60 mL) water

3 tbsp (50 mL) maple syrup

3/4 cup (200 mL) brown sugar

1/4 cup (60 mL) cream

1/4 cup (60 mL) pecans or walnuts

Method:

• Place the butter in a microwave-safe bowl and melt 2 minutes at HIGH. Add the water, maple syrup and brown sugar. Stir well. Microwave 3 minutes at HIGH. Add slowly, while beating, the cream and the pecans or walnuts.

• When I serve this sauce over fresh strawberries, I omit the nuts and place a jug of cream on the table for everyone to use to taste.

• The sauce replaces the sugar on the berries.

Orange Sauce

Preparation: . . . . .5 m
Cooking: . . . . .2 m
Standing: . . . . .none

A personal note: You can use either rum or rose water in this sauce — or omit them both. Rose water is more exotic than rum; it is also more difficult to find. Personally, I like to have a bottle of rose water on my flavorings shelf at all times. If you prefer to omit the rum or rose water, the sauce is very well flavored with the orange rind and juice and the cloves.

Ingredients:

1 tbsp (15 mL) butter

1 tbsp (15 mL) flour

3 whole cloves

Grated rind and juice of 2 oranges

2 tbsp (30 mL) rum *or*
   1 tsp (5 mL) rose water

Method:

• Place the butter in a microwave-safe bowl and melt 1 minute at HIGH

• Add the flour and stir.

• Add the remaining ingredients, stir and microwave 2 minutes at HIGH.

• Pour hot over peeled oranges, thinly sliced. Refrigerate

Tart Lemon Sauce

Preparation: 8m
Cooking: . . . . .from 4 to 5 m
Standing: . . . . .none

A personal note: My favorite sauce for plum pudding and other types of steamed pudding.

Ingredients:

1/2 cup (125 mL) butter or margarine

1 cup (250 mL) sugar

1/4 cup (60 mL) fresh lemon juice

Grated rind of 1/2 a lemon

Grated rind of 1 orange

1 tbsp (15 mL) water

1 egg

Method:

• Place the butter or margarine in a microwave-safe bowl, microwave 1 minute at HIGH.

• Beat in the sugar, lemon juice, lemon and orange rind.

• Add the water and the egg, stir until well blended.

• Microwave 3 minutes at HIGH, stirring every minute.

• Cover, cool. As the sauce cools, it thickens.

• Serve cool or hot.

• To serve hot, reheat 1 to 2 minutes at MEDIUM.

Superb Tangy Rhubarb Sauce

Preparation:	15 m
Cooking:	from 8 to 9 m
Standing:	none

A personal note: Serve this sauce cold with creamy dessert or ice cream, or fold in **1 cup (250 mL) sliced fresh strawberries** in the sauce while hot.

Ingredients:

4 cups (1 L) rhubarb, diced

3 tsp (15 mL) cornstarch

1 tsp (5 mL) orange rind, grated

1/4 tsp (1 mL) nutmeg

1 cup (250 mL) sugar

1/2 cup (125 mL) fresh orange juice

Method:

• Combine all the ingredients in a large glass mixing bowl. Stir thoroughly.

• Microwave at HIGH 8 to 9 minutes, or until mixture boils and thickens, stirring once or twice.

• Cool, then refrigerate.

Hot Blueberry Sauce

Preparation:	10 m
Cooking:	7 m
Standing:	none

A personal note: This sauce is super hot over sponge cake, cold over ice cream! Add two peeled and thinly sliced apples, cook in the same manner and you will have a delicious purple applesauce.

Ingredients:

2 cups (500 mL) fresh blueberries

1/2 cup (125 mL) sugar

Grated rind of 1/2 a lemon

1 tbsp (15 mL) lemon juice

1/2 cup (125 mL) water

1 tsp (5 mL) cornstarch

2 tbsp (30 mL) apple or orange juice

Method:

• Place in a microwave-safe bowl the blueberries, sugar, lemon juice, grated lemon rind and water. Stir until well mixed. Microwave 4 minutes at HIGH, stir.

• Add the cornstarch mixed with the apple or orange juice, stir. Microwave 3 minutes at MEDIUM-HIGH, stir after 2 minutes of cooking. The sauce is ready when it is creamy and glossy.

ALPHABETICAL INDEX

913

INDEX

EGGS

GENERALITIES

RECIPES

FISH AND SEAFOOD

MEATS

BEEF

GENERALITIES

RECIPES

LAMB

GENERALITIES

RECIPES

PORK

GENERALITIES

RECIPES

VEAL

GENERALITIES

RECIPES

PASTAS

GENERALITIES

RECIPES

POULTRY AND GAME

GENERALITIES

RECIPES
CHICKEN
DUCK
GOOSE
PARTRIDGE
PHEASANT

QUAIL
RABBIT
TURKEY

RICE

GENERALITIES

RECIPES

SAUCES

GENERALITIES

RECIPES

SOUPS, BROTHS, CHOWDERS, CON-SOMMÉ, POTAGE

BROTHS

CHOWDERS

CONSOMMÉ

CREAM

GARNISHINGS

POTAGE

SOUPS

VEGETABLES

HELPFUL HINTS INDEX